"This is three books in one. Rael Meyerowitz surveys how key figures in psychoanalysis—Freud, Ferenczi, Klein, Loewald, Green and others—have thought about loss and mourning. He sets these in historical relation to each other, showing how each one's ideas built on what had gone before. And he discusses these texts as works of literature, drawing fascinating connections with poetry and fiction beyond the psychoanalytic field. All this in eight very readable chapters—an impressive achievement. Academically stimulating, deeply informed psychoanalytically, and warm and personal at the same time, this is a splendid book."
Michael Parsons, *British Psychoanalytical Society and French Psychoanalytic Association, author of* The Dove that Returns, The Dove that Vanishes *(2000) and* Living Psychoanalysis *(2014)*

"Rael Meyerowitz approaches central psychoanalytic concepts with a refreshingly open, thorough, and independent mind, a mind informed not only by close reading of classic and other texts but also by his earlier training in, and ongoing passion for, literature and literary criticism. This is a thought-provoking book, for students, practitioners, and others alike."
Mike Brearley, *British Psychoanalytical Society, author of* The Art of Captaincy *(1985) and* On Form *(2017)*

"I have had the pleasure of working with Dr. Meyerowitz for several years, in the Fitzjohn's Unit of the Tavistock Clinic, trying to address the needs of patients with severe mental health problems, and I have always felt these patients to be in the best of hands. Now I can see that Rael's clinical sure-footedness is buttressed by impressively deep learning and imagination in the theory of psychoanalysis. I therefore recommend this book without hesitation to clinicians and theoreticians alike."
Francis Grier, *editor-in-chief*, International Journal of Psychoanalysis

MOURNING AND METABOLIZATION

By bringing together perspectives from psychoanalysis and literary study and considering the reciprocal relation between ideas about mourning and our internal worlds, this book provides a guide to thinking theoretically about loss and how we deal with it.

Rael Meyerowitz conceptualizes the work of psychic internalization required by loss in terms of bodily digestion and metabolization. In this way, successful mourning can be likened to the proper processing of physical sustenance, while failed mourning is akin to indigestion, as expressed in various forms of melancholia, mania, depression, and anxiety. Borrowing from the methodology of literary criticism, the book conducts a detailed treatment of these themes by drawing on a series of psychoanalytic works, including those of Freud, Ferenczi, Karl Abraham, Klein, Loewald, Torok, Nicolas Abraham, and Green, while paying close critical attention to a selection of literary works such as those by William Faulkner, Wallace Stevens, and Sylvia Plath.

Aimed at clinicians as well as readers with a more academic interest in psychoanalytic theory and language, the close-reading format offered by this book will also enable students in psychoanalytic and psychotherapy courses to engage deeply with some central texts and key concepts in psychoanalysis.

Rael Meyerowitz is a psychoanalyst and psychotherapist in London. With a background in literature and philosophy, he teaches extensively on psychoanalytic topics and their intersection with other disciplines. He is the co-editor of *Turning the Tide* (2018), on the work of the Tavistock and Portman NHS Foundation Trust's Fitzjohn's Unit.

Tavistock Clinic Series
Margot Waddell, Jocelyn Catty, & Kate Stratton (Series Editors)

Recent titles in the Tavistock Clinic Series
Addictive States of Mind, *edited by Marion Bower, Rob Hale, & Heather Wood*
A for Adoption: An Exploration of the Adoption Experience for Families and Professionals, *by Alison Roy*
Assessment in Child Psychotherapy, *edited by Margaret Rustin & Emanuela Quagliata* Childhood Depression: A Place for Psychotherapy, *edited by Judith Trowell, with Gillian Miles*
Child Psychoanalytic Psychotherapy in Primary Schools: Tavistock Approaches, *edited by Katie Argent*
Complex Trauma: The Tavistock Model, *edited by Joanne Stubley & Linda Young*
Conjunctions: Social Work, Psychoanalysis, and Society, *by Andrew Cooper*
Consultations in Psychoanalytic Psychotherapy, *edited by R. Peter Hobson*
Contemporary Developments in Adult and Young Adult Therapy. The Work of the Tavistock and Portman Clinics, Vol. 1, *edited by Alessandra Lemma*
Couple Dynamics: Psychoanalytic Perspectives in Work with the Individual, the Couple, and the Group, *edited by Aleksandra Novakovic*
Doing Things Differently: The Influence of Donald Meltzer on Psychoanalytic Theory and Practice, *edited by Margaret Cohen & Alberto Hahn*
Group Relations and Other Meditations: Psychoanalytic Explorations on the Uncertainties of Experiential Learning, *by Carlos Sapochnik*
Inside Lives: Psychoanalysis and the Growth of the Personality, *by Margot Waddell*
Internal Landscapes and Foreign Bodies: Eating Disorders and Other Pathologies, *by Gianna Williams*
Living on the Border: Psychotic Processes in the Individual, the Couple, and the Group, *edited by David Bell & Aleksandra Novakovic*
Making Room for Madness in Mental Health: The Psychoanalytic Understanding of Psychotic Communication, *by Marcus Evans*
Melanie Klein Revisited: Pioneer and Revolutionary in the Psychoanalysis of Young Children, *by Susan Sherwin-White*
New Discoveries in Child Psychotherapy: Findings from Qualitative Research, *edited by Margaret Rustin & Michael Rustin*
Oedipus and the Couple, *edited by Francis Grier*
On Adolescence, *by Margot Waddell*
Organization in the Mind: Psychoanalysis, Group Relations, and Organizational Consultancy, *by David Armstrong, edited by Robert French*
Psychoanalysis and Culture: A Kleinian Perspective, *edited by David Bell*
Researching the Unconscious: Principles of Psychoanalytic Method, *by Michael Rustin*
Reason and Passion: A Celebration of the Work of Hanna Segal, *edited by David Bell*
Sexuality and Gender Now: Moving Beyond Heteronormativity, *edited by Leezah Hertzmann & Juliet Newbigin*
Short-Term Psychoanalytic Psychotherapy for Adolescents with Depression: A Treatment Manual, *edited by Jocelyn Catty*
Sibling Matters: A Psychoanalytic, Developmental, and Systemic Approach, *edited by Debbie Hindle & Susan Sherwin-White*
Social Defences against Anxiety: Explorations in a Paradigm, *edited by David Armstrong & Michael Rustin*
Surviving Space: Papers on Infant Observation, *edited by Andrew Briggs*
Sustaining Depth and Meaning in School Leadership: Keeping Your Head, *edited by Emil Jackson & Andrea Berkeley*
Talking Cure: Mind and Method of the Tavistock Clinic, *edited by David Taylor*
The Anorexic Mind, *by Marilyn Lawrence*
The Groups Book. Psychoanalytic Group Therapy: Principles and Practice, *edited by Caroline Garland*
Therapeutic Care for Refugees: No Place Like Home, *edited by Renos Papadopoulos*
Therapeutic Interventions with Babies and Young Children in Care: Observation and Attention, *by Jenifer Wakelyn*
Thinking Space: Promoting Thinking about Race, Culture, and Diversity in Psychotherapy and Beyond, *edited by Frank Lowe*
Towards Belonging: Negotiating New Relationships for Adopted Children and Those in Care, *edited by Andrew Briggs*
Turning the Tide: A Psychoanalytic Approach to Mental Illness. The Work of the Fitzjohn's Unit, *edited by Rael Meyerowitz & David Bell*
Understanding Trauma: A Psychoanalytic Approach, *edited by Caroline Garland*
Waiting to Be Found: Papers on Children in Care, *edited by Andrew Briggs*
"What Can the Matter Be?": Therapeutic Interventions with Parents, Infants, and Young Children, *edited by Louise Emanuel & Elizabeth Bradley*
Young Child Observation: A Development in the Theory and Method of Infant Observation, *edited by Simonetta M. G. Adamo & Margaret Rustin*

MOURNING AND METABOLIZATION
Close Readings in the Psychoanalytic Literature of Loss

Rael Meyerowitz

Routledge
Taylor & Francis Group
LONDON AND NEW YORK

Cover image: "Internal World" (2021), by Natasha Keqin He

First published 2023
by Routledge
4 Park Square, Milton Park, Abingdon, Oxon OX14 4RN

and by Routledge
605 Third Avenue, New York, NY 10158

Routledge is an imprint of the Taylor & Francis Group, an informa business

© 2023 Rael Meyerowitz and The Tavistock and Portman NHS Foundation Trust

The right of Rael Meyerowitz to be identified as author of this work has been asserted in accordance with sections 77 and 78 of the Copyright, Designs and Patents Act 1988.

All rights reserved. No part of this book may be reprinted or reproduced or utilised in any form or by any electronic, mechanical, or other means, now known or hereafter invented, including photocopying and recording, or in any information storage or retrieval system, without permission in writing from the publishers.

Trademark notice: Product or corporate names may be trademarks or registered trademarks, and are used only for identification and explanation without intent to infringe.

British Library Cataloguing-in-Publication Data
A catalogue record for this book is available from the British Library

Library of Congress Cataloging-in-Publication Data
Names: Meyerowitz, Rael, 1953– author.
Title: Mourning and metabolization : close readings in the psychoanalytic literature of loss / Rael Meyerowitz.
Description: Abingdon, Oxon ; New York, NY : Routledge, 2023. | Includes bibliographical references and index.
Identifiers: LCCN 2022021953 (print) | LCCN 2022021954 (ebook) | ISBN 9781032210780 (hbk) | ISBN 9781032210797 (pbk) | ISBN 9781003266631 (ebk)
Subjects: LCSH: Loss (Psychology) | Psychoanalysis. | Bereavement—Psychological aspects
Classification: LCC BF575.D35 M48 2023 (print) | LCC BF575.D35 (ebook) | DDC 155.9/3—dc23/eng/20220824
LC record available at https://lccn.loc.gov/2022021953
LC ebook record available at https://lccn.loc.gov/2022021954

Every effort has been made to contact copyright-holders. Please advise the publisher of any errors or omissions, and these will be corrected in subsequent editions.

ISBN: 978-1-032-21078-0 (hbk)
ISBN: 978-1-032-21079-7 (pbk)
ISBN: 978-1-003-26663-1 (ebk)

DOI: 10.4324/9781003266631

Typeset in Palatino
by Apex CoVantage, LLC

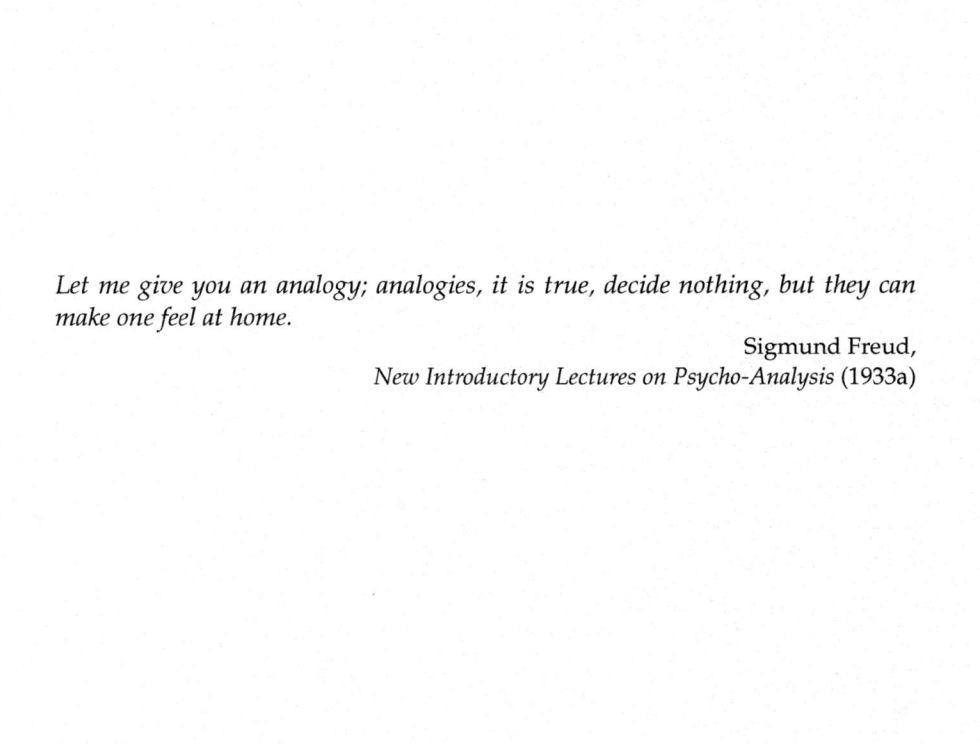

Let me give you an analogy; analogies, it is true, decide nothing, but they can make one feel at home.

Sigmund Freud,
New Introductory Lectures on Psycho-Analysis (1933a)

CONTENTS

SERIES EDITORS' PREFACE   xi

ACKNOWLEDGEMENTS   xiv

**Introduction:
mourning and the internal world
in psychoanalysis and literature**   1

1   Sigmund Freud: early explorations—
mapping the territory of the mind   28

2   Sigmund Freud: later models—
identification, internal structure, and the ubiquity of loss   58

3   Sándor Ferenczi: inventing introjection;
Karl Abraham: phenomenologist of depression   96

4   Melanie Klein: positioning the object
and rebuilding the internal world   152

5   Hans Loewald: turning ghosts into ancestors—
internalization and emancipation   209

6   Nicolas Abraham and Maria Torok:
    rescuing introjection from the crypts of incorporation   258

7   André Green: fading and framing—
    the metaphorical mother lost and restored   312

Conclusion:
meaning, mourning, and mortality in Freud and Auden   368

REFERENCES   403
INDEX   412

SERIES EDITORS' PREFACE

Since it was founded in 1920, the Tavistock Clinic—now the Tavistock and Portman NHS Foundation Trust—has developed a wide range of developmental approaches to mental health which have been strongly influenced by the ideas of psychoanalysis. It has also adopted systemic family therapy as a theoretical model and a clinical approach to family problems. The Tavistock is now one of the largest mental health training institutions in Britain. It teaches up to 600 students a year on postgraduate, doctoral, and qualifying courses in social work, systemic psychotherapy, psychology, psychiatry, nursing, and child, adolescent, and adult psychotherapy, along with 2,000 multidisciplinary clinicians, social workers, and teachers attending Continuing Professional Development courses and conferences on psychoanalytic observation, psychoanalytic thinking, and management and leadership in a range of clinical and community settings.

The Tavistock's philosophy aims at promoting therapeutic methods in mental health. Its work is based on the clinical expertise that is also the basis of its consultancy and research activities. The aim of this Series is to make available to the reading public the clinical, theoretical, and research work that is most influential at the Tavistock. The Series sets out new approaches in the understanding and treatment of psychological disturbance in children, adolescents, and adults, both as individuals and in families.

In *Mourning and Metabolization: Close Readings in the Psychoanalytic Literature of Loss*, Rael Meyerowitz draws on his extensive clinical experience in and teaching of psychoanalytic psychotherapy and psychoanalysis, along with his prior training as a literary critic, to offer close readings of key psychoanalytic texts, from Freud to Green. Through this "close reading", drawn in technique from the literary critical tradition, he succeeds in offering an account of the development of psychoanalytic thinking about loss and its corollary, the development of an account of the internal world: the two, he argues, are intrinsically linked. In so doing he advocates attending to the internal world on two levels: psychoanalytic understanding of the inner psychological processes of the individual; and psychoanalysis itself "as a body of knowledge and endeavour . . . [with] a shifting, metatheoretical inner life of its own".

The effect of Meyerowitz's technique of close reading is to carry the reader through detailed examinations of key literary and psychoanalytic texts until one reaches an overview, as it were: an account of the development of this culturally and therapeutically significant body of work that reaches across professional boundaries. Interdisciplinary in his commitment to use literary texts in a "quasi-clinical way", Meyerowitz also attends to different psychoanalytic approaches, recognizing that psychoanalysis frequently fails to be "the field of common and cooperative endeavour that we need it to be". Acknowledging his debt both to secondary literature and his own clinical experience in private practice and in the Tavistock's Fitzjohn's Unit, he eschews literature reviews or clinical vignettes, preferring to forge "my own path, . . . through these frequently thorny theoretical thickets". His stated intention in avoiding secondary commentaries is to "preserve, as far as possible, the sense that these are my own thoughts about and responses to the text". Implicitly, however, he also offers us his own process in writing the book as a true metabolization of his clinical, theoretical, and literary experience.

The strength of the book's theoretical range—it spans Sigmund Freud to André Green, with chapters on Sándor Ferenczi and Karl Abraham, Melanie Klein, Hans Loewald, and Nicolas Abraham and Maria Torok—is that it allows Meyerowitz to compare and contrast some of the subtler points of difference between these writers' positions. Quoting from the Wallace Stevens poem "Auroras of Autumn", for instance, in which the poet bids farewell to the idea of the mother, Meyerowitz contrasts a Kleinian reading—"a poetic account of how a good internal version of the mother is established and retained"—to interpretations in the light of Green or Loewald, in which the mother "step[s] back from personal prominence to provide a frame or structure inside which further development can occur".

In taking up metabolization as the central metaphor in the understanding he offers of internal processes of mourning, Meyerowitz interrogates the question of "why metaphor—and especially these body-based metaphors—should have come to constitute a kind of privileged class or domain in the language of psychoanalysis". In noting the ambivalence towards metaphor in psychoanalytic writing, perhaps derived from the increasing influence of "evidenced-based" ways of thinking, he advocates for the centrality of metaphor and analogy in furthering the understanding of the mind's interiority.

Meyerowitz is not afraid to criticize—or, more properly, critique—thinkers whose work has been central to the history of the Tavistock. In particular, he points out the limitations of Melanie Klein's work in supplying a satisfying metatheoretical position on mourning. He asks, "is it enough to think of the internal world as consisting, rather concretely, of 'homuncular' representatives of external objects, which must be rendered good, whole, and real and need continual re-establishing in the mind? Does the work of mourning—at least under less problematic circumstances—not offer a more comprehensive and permanent attainment, a more thoroughly digested, metabolized, and thus durable result?" He argues, further, that "we might regard a proper or more complete internalizing process as going beyond the dynamics and problematics of the internal world as representation, towards a more thoroughly achieved digestion and metabolization within the psyche".

Meyerowitz's account of the central role of loss and mourning in psychoanalytic literature is, as he acknowledges, a revisiting of issues that have been central to the psychoanalytic movement. Indeed, he asks whether he might risk "doing little other than going over old ground, re-stating the bleeding obvious", and warns that he will only succeed "if I can traverse this psychoanalytic ground again as evocatively, usefully, and creatively as possible". Readers of this certainly creative and evocative book, whether students or teachers, clinicians or theoreticians, will be grateful that he has taken such a risk.

ACKNOWLEDGEMENTS

It will soon become clear to readers that this book has been incubating for half a lifetime, that its preoccupations have been with me in one form or another for several decades. However, it originated more immediately from a course on depression and the internal world devised and taught over recent years in several different contexts: on the Tavistock's adult psychotherapy course (M1), the British Psychoanalytic Association and British Psychotherapy Foundation clinical trainings, as well as on University College London's psychoanalytic studies programme. I want to thank all the students who participated in those courses for the fecund responses, creative ideas, and cogent links that they brought to these topics; I hope I have taken in and metabolized them all well enough in this final product to do justice to their contributions. In fairness, given the literary aspects of the book, thanks are no less due to my teachers, colleagues, and students from earlier academic times, at universities and colleges in South Africa, Israel, and the United States, from and with whom I discovered the pleasures of getting close to texts and doing them justice.

The last 20 years have been spent in London, working as a psychoanalyst and psychotherapist, gathering and internalizing invaluable data in the process. Over an even longer period, I was myself the patient of several therapists and analysts, in different countries and at varying frequencies of treatment, culminating in two lengthy analyses in succession. Though the book makes no explicit reference to any of this experience, gleaned from both sides of the clinical dyad, there is no doubt that everything I say in this book is thoroughly informed by and could not have been written without what accrued to me in those contexts. The processes of psychic digestion and metabolization seem even more miraculous and mysterious, perhaps, when they go to work on gains and losses in those contexts than on the more cognitive or intellectual acquisitions acknowledged above. My gratitude is therefore due both to all my patients and to all the clinicians who helped me when I was a patient.

Grateful thanks are due to those who encouraged me in this project even when it was not always clear why I was pursuing it and whether it was worth while. Having already shepherded me through a difficult time editing a previous book for the Tavistock Series, Margot Waddell, more than anyone, played that role. She read almost every word in the earlier stages of the process and was unstinting with her support and praise. I cannot thank her enough for her belief in me and this book. I wish also to thank Jocelyn Catty and Kate Stratton at the Tavistock Series for all their faithful encouragement, appreciation, and assistance. Unfortunately, the publication process was significantly delayed and became most frustrating, as the effects of the Covid pandemic seemed to render endless the already vexed matter of applying for permissions from several sources for the unavoidable use of extensive quoted textual material in this close-reading project. I am indebted to Georgina Clutterbuck at Routledge who stepped in belatedly and worked tirelessly to correct previous errors and expedite these tedious tasks. I also want to thank Eric and Klara King at Communication Crafts for their swift, gimlet-eyed editing and their kindness and support.

In truth, not all that many people have read early versions of these chapters. However, I was able to share some of the book's content by way of invitations to present my work in a few different forums in the months before lockdown. I wish to thank the Tavistock Scientific Meetings Committee, Joan Raphael-Leff who runs the Anna Freud Centre's Academic Forum, and the 1952 Club for opportunities to air my thoughts, participate in fruitful discussion, and receive helpful feedback.

In terms of both his detailed, assiduous comments on the entire manuscript—courtesy of his own impressive close-reading skills—and what must have been countless hours of technical and administrative assistance with thankless and often fruitless tasks, no one has worked harder to bring this book into being than Era Trieman. I could not have wished for a more dedicated, hard-working, and faithful stand-by-me right-hand man. Modest to a fault, he also makes it difficult to thank and reward him accordingly, but I will keep trying to find ways to express my enormous gratitude to him.

Finally, there is my family: my adolescent son and daughter—Seth and Hannah—who have had their own recent lives cruelly disrupted by the mess that Covid made of their final years at school; they have had to suffer prolonged periods of time closeted at home, not least with an at-times irascible father who would insist on trying to write a book at this most inopportune time. I thank them both, but perhaps it is better to just say, "Sorry, guys!" Apologies are also due to my wife, Tracey, who bears the brunt of so much in our household but who also happens to be an outstanding reader and editor; she is the person in the world who keeps me most honest, not merely in life at large but, more crucially, where my writing style is concerned. To the extent that this book is free of prolixity, obfuscation, and unnecessary rhetorical flourishes, and if it has some cogency of argument and textual clarity, she is responsible. There is no possibility of repaying my debts to her, but she deserves—and has—my eternal gratitude.

Credits List

The author also gratefully acknowledges the permission provided to reprint the following materials:

- Abraham, N. & Torok. M. ([1972] 1994). 'Mourning or melancholia: introjection versus incorporation' and Torok. M. 'The illness of mourning and the fantasy of the exquisite corpse' (1994). In: *The Shell and the Kernel: Renewals of Psychoanalysis: Volume I*, translated & edited by N. Rand (pp. 125–138; pp. 107–124). © University of Chicago Press. Reproduced with permission of the Licensor through the Copyright Clearance Center.
- "In Memory of W B. Yeats," "September 1, 1939," and "In Memory of Sigmund Freud," copyright 1940 and © renewed 1968 by W. H. Auden; from COLLECTED POEMS by W. H. Auden, edited by Edward Mendelson, Used by permission of Random House, an imprint and division of Penguin Random House LLC. All rights reserved.
- "In Memory of W B. Yeats," "September 1, 1939," and "In Memory of Sigmund Freud," copyright © 1940, 1939, 1940 by W.H. Auden, renewed. Reprinted by permission of Curtis Brown, Ltd. All rights reserved.
- "A Rose for Emily," copyright 1930 and © renewed 1958 by William Faulkner; from COLLECTED STORIES OF WILLIAM FAULKNER by William Faulkner. Used by permission of Random House, an imprint and division of Penguin Random House LLC. All rights reserved.

- "The Dead Mother" from *Life Narcissism Death Narcissism*, by André Green, translated by Andrew Weller. Used by permission of Free Association Books. All rights reserved.
- Klein, M. (1935) A contribution to the psychogenesis of manic-depressive states, 16:145–174, *The International Journal of Psychoanalysis*, copyright © Institute of Psychoanalysis, reprinted by permission of Taylor & Francis Ltd, on behalf of Institute of Psychoanalysis http://www.theijp.org/
- Klein, M. (1940) Mourning and its relation to manic-depressive states, 21:125–153, *The International Journal of Psychoanalysis*, copyright © Institute of Psychoanalysis, reprinted by permission of Taylor & Francis Ltd, on behalf of Institute of Psychoanalysis http://www.theijp.org/
- "On Internalization" and "Internalization, Separation, Mourning, and the Superego", from Papers on Psychoanalysis by Hans Loewald © Yale Representation Limited. Reproduced with permission of the Licensor through PLSclear.
- Excerpts from "Daddy" and "Morning Song" from The Collected Poems, Sylvia Plath. Copyright © 1960, 1965, 1971, 1981 by the Estate of Sylvia Plath. Editorial material copyright ©1981 by Ted Hughes. Used by permission of HarperCollins Publishers.
- Excerpts from "Daddy" and "Morning Song" from The Collected Poems, Sylvia Plath. Reprinted by permission of Faber and Faber Ltd.
- "The Auroras of Autumn," copyright 1948 by Wallace Stevens; from THE COLLECTED POEMS OF WALLACE STEVENS by Wallace Stevens. Used by permission of Alfred A. Knopf, an imprint of the Knopf Doubleday Publishing Group, a division of Penguin Random House LLC. All rights reserved.
- Excerpts from "The Auroras of Autumn" copyright 1948 by Wallace Stevens; from THE COLLECTED POEMS OF WALLACE STEVENS by Wallace Stevens. Reprinted by permission of Faber and Faber Ltd.
- Excerpts from "Sunday Morning" copyright 1948 by Wallace Stevens; from THE COLLECTED POEMS OF WALLACE STEVENS by Wallace Stevens. Reprinted by permission of Faber and Faber Ltd.
- Excerpts from "The Woman That Had More Babies Than That" copyright 1957 by Wallace Stevens; from OPUS POSTHUMOUS by Wallace Stevens. Reprinted by permission of Faber and Faber Ltd.

Introduction:
mourning and the internal world in psychoanalysis and literature

Psychoanalysis, perhaps more than any other discipline, discourse, or scientific endeavour, has taken upon itself the task of exploring systematically the very notion of an internal world, how it arises or is constructed. It has also provided some of the most profound, sophisticated perspectives on the complexities of loss in human life. However, it has also suffered from a great deal of theoretical obfuscation and muddle—a confusion of tongues, to use Sándor Ferenczi's phrase—around these very issues. I am hardly the first to notice this; these matters have been investigated repeatedly, if not exhaustively, throughout the annals of psychoanalytic writing. By trying once more to address the centrality of mourning in psychoanalysis and the concomitant or consequential significance of internal psychic processes, might I be doing little other than going over old ground, re-stating the bleeding obvious?

Freud, on at least two occasions towards the end of his career (in chapter VI of *Civilization and Its Discontents*, 1930a, and in his unfinished paper on the "Splitting of the Ego in the Process of Defence", 1940e), introduced what for him were newer perspectives on crucially important topics by admitting that he might be wasting ink and paper, half-convinced that what he was about to adumbrate was nothing but common knowledge. I remind my reader and myself of these moments of Freudian self-doubt because of similar concerns about the project that I am undertaking here.

Commonplace or old hat as these themes may be, reviving them here will succeed only if I can traverse this psychoanalytic ground again as evocatively, usefully, and creatively as possible: that will surely depend on the freshness of my approach—on whether there is anything novel in the substance of what I am offering. Where I do feel that I am on solid ground is in my conviction that the theoretical—and terminological—muddles and confusions associated with these topics are to a significant extent due to our tendencies, as Freud's scattered children and heirs, not to listen to one another across the divides between and even within our respective psychoanalytic cultures and, indeed, not to attend to such divisions within ourselves. We tend to weaken our discipline—which has in any case almost always had to defend itself strenuously against attacks from without—by using it as an arena for parochial internal one-upmanship and (un)civil strife, failing to treat it as the field of common and cooperative endeavour that we need it to be, perhaps now more than ever.

The wish to resist and remedy such small-difference self-centredness has prompted me to bring together and look closely at several views on this subject area—both from certain moments in the early history of psychoanalysis and from the diverse traditions that arose after it began to migrate from Central Europe to other parts of the world—in the hope that we might arrive at a deeper, more sophisticated, and complementary understanding of these matters via respectful comparison and contrast.

As I suggested, uncovering "internality" itself, in its manifold guises, has been a primary mission of psychoanalysis, one of its major contributions to the systematic or scientific study of the human mind. It has offered several, if not multiple, different ways of considering this internal landscape, various angles from which to approach it: to try to address them all exhaustively would be to set oneself a truly hubristic task. One might nevertheless begin by considering the psychoanalytic internal world from at least two perspectives or on two levels. In the first place, of course, there is the specific clinical and conceptual attention that psychoanalysis, whenever and wherever it is practised, pays to the psychic processes occurring internally within any given human subject. Second, taken as a body of knowledge and endeavour, psychoanalysis may be said to have a shifting, metatheoretical inner life of its own—what we could even call its immanent or intra-disciplinary self-image. I will necessarily be tracking some of the changes in the self-conception of the discipline as new developments unfold in different locations and over the course of the twentieth century.

Freud's earliest dynamic, systemic, and topographical accounts of unconsciousness—or the Unconscious—already presuppose that such phenomena are internal, in the sense that they exist, metaphorically speaking, "further within" the human psyche, "deeper down" relative to the conscious and preconscious parts of his first topography of the mind. Freud's second topography or structural model, moreover, is predicated on the idea that the unconsciousness is not a unitary or singular entity or phenomenon, but that each of the three provinces or agencies of the mind—id, ego, and superego—possesses a certain measure, and its own specific version, of the discrepancy or tension between external unawareness and internal knowledge. Though always taken as read, these fundamental and definitive contributions that Freud's theories of unconsciousness have made to a mental or psychological internal world are not my theme here.

Since Freud, there have been many periodic attempts in the course of psychoanalytic history to provide theoretical understandings of the internal world and to redefine its terms. Again, while I cannot hope to address comprehensively the relations between all those efforts and my own, I will briefly acknowledge just two such attempts, if only with the aim of differentiating and indicating the specificity of my view. Considering these issues from an ego-psychological and developmental perspective, and based on the empiricist dictum that we cannot, even in the first instance, know or gain access to external reality except by having it pictured or represented internally, Joseph Sandler and his colleagues (Sandler, 1993; Sandler & Rosenblatt, 1962) provided an account of the building up of self- and other-representations within a "representational world".

More recently—and emerging from a quite different European philosophical tradition and thus employing a different language—the French analysts César and Sara Botella (2004) addressed the issue of how experience is registered or "figured" phenomenologically in the internal landscape, taking their cue from Freud's distinction between *Darstellung* and *Vorstellung* (or word- and thing-representations, in James Strachey's often problematic translations). A psychoanalytic perspective on the internal world can hardly ignore these complex and significant accounts of how things are pictured, presented, registered, or figured psychically—or sometimes fail to be, in the cases of highly disturbed patients. Though such perspectives provide important structural substrates and carry thematic implications for my interests, my approach takes a different tack.

This book is loosely based on a course about mourning, depression, and the internal world that I taught for several years and in different formats on the psychoanalytic psychotherapy training programme at the Tavistock (M1) and in several other psychoanalytic contexts in London. While harking back to my own previous career as a literary academic, it also takes considerable recent inspiration from the way that Thomas

Ogden reads psychoanalytic texts. His book *Creative Readings* (2012) is a collection of close textual encounters with psychoanalytic writings, beginning with "Mourning and Melancholia" (1917e) and featuring papers by Susan Isaacs, W. R. D. Fairbairn, Donald Winnicott, Wilfred Bion, Hans Loewald, and Harold Searles. Besides being theoretically important, Ogden finds these papers eminently *readable*, and he impressively emphasizes and savours the experiential—the almost *textural*—quality of getting to grips with and immersing himself in them. There are, of course, many other analysts who read and work in similarly literary, close-encountering ways; in contemporary British psychoanalysis, the names of Michael Parsons (2000) and Ron Britton (1998) spring immediately to mind.

My project also begins with a chapter that has "Mourning and Melancholia" as its central focus and then embarks on equally intense textual engagements with—or exegetical journeys through—a series of psychoanalytic writings that pertain to and branch off from the topics introduced in that seminal paper. These include other works by Freud himself and papers by Sándor Ferenczi, Karl Abraham, Melanie Klein, Hans Loewald, Nicolas Abraham, Maria Torok, and André Green. Though the book is effectively a history of certain psychoanalytic ideas and tackles these texts in an ostensibly orderly, chronological fashion, it is also a personal—not to say idiosyncratic—guide through this cross-cultural terrain. My selection may seem limited, or even biased, but I make no claim to providing a comprehensive survey of the reference area. This is essentially a chronicle and map of my own path, forged through these frequently thorny theoretical thickets, and will have to stand scrutiny accordingly. I have thus refrained, for the most part, from providing literature reviews or referring to other readings of these papers, familiar though most of them may be.

While teaching the original course and attempting to view both loss and psychic internalization with fresh eyes, I found myself repeatedly drawn to what is again by no means a new idea, but one with consequences or ramifications that may not have been sufficiently appreciated, thought through, or utilized in psychoanalysis. This perspective leans on an analogy or metaphor, whereby the psychic processes involved in coping with loss are viewed as the figurative equivalent of a kind of metabolic or digestive process. Since the earliest psychoanalytic writings on these topics, we have been familiar with the idea that some form of internal representation or figuration follows or accompanies loss, as the necessary internal aspect or dimension of the mourning process.

It began to occur to me, however, that this did not go far enough: that, optimally, taking in a representation of the lost object, or creating an internal version of it, might be only a waystation on a path towards the more thoroughgoing assimilation and further integration of the someone or something being mourned. I am suggesting, in other words, that we might regard a proper or more complete internalizing process as going beyond the dynamics and problematics of the internal world as representation, towards a more thoroughly achieved digestion and metabolization within the psyche.

In saying this, one realizes that all human experience—not only loss *per se*—can and perhaps needs to be dealt with in this way. Doubling back on that thought, however, I then wonder whether this might be precisely because all human experience is predicated on loss—in the first place, as it were. These are some of the central thoughts animating this book, to be pursued and investigated at length. I trust that it is already evident that they might carry significant implications for how we work as clinicians, how we think about our analytic or therapeutic encounters, and, indeed, how we conceive of bringing these to completion.

While psychoanalysis has always paid close quasi-anatomical attention to the oral and anal orifices at either end of the alimentary system, where there is exchange or an interface with the external world, it has been significantly less concerned with the interim operations and activities that go on internally, on the journey between the two. Alimentary perspectives have nevertheless been with us implicitly since at least as far back as the *Three Essays on the Theory of Sexuality* (1905d), where Freud could not even introduce sexuality or the libido—the topic for which he would become most renowned—except by way of "the analogy of the instinct of nutrition, that is of hunger". Later in the same text he elaborates on the nature of the earliest oral desires, saying that the "satisfaction of the erotogenic zone is associated, in the first instance, with the satisfaction of the need for nourishment". This is then generalized to the far-reaching claim that the entire realm of sexuality "attaches itself to functions serving the purpose of self-preservation". For Freud, the satiated baby at the breast thus become the "prototype of the expression of sexual satisfaction in later life" and the basis upon which later, non-incestuous objects can eventually be (re)discovered (1905d, pp. 135, 181–182, 222).

Obviously, Freud's analogies here are not just between the nutritional and the sexual but, more generally—or at another conceptual level— between the physical and the mental. This way of thinking, whereby the psyche is seen to operate in ways that lean or are propped upon certain fundamental physical or physiological processes, has been familiar in psychoanalysis since the start: indeed, this metaphorical dimension or substrate in psychoanalytic thinking may even lay claim to being its primary conceptual *modus vivendi*. This was certainly the basis of the sophisticated reading and theorizing of Jean Laplanche (1970), who elaborated brilliantly upon this relationship in Freud between the register of need and that of desire; I will later be discussing how Wilfred Bion (1962) became one of the few major psychoanalytic theorists to adopt and utilize the analogy of digestion to describe the workings of psychic inner world.

However, this does not mean it is universally acknowledged or considered desirable within psychoanalytic discourse to lean too heavily or exclusively on figurative language; there are many who would view this sceptically and regard it as contentious. Despite the ubiquity of figures or tropes within psychoanalytic writing, there is also an equal and opposite tendency to curb their use or to take them only so far and no further, perhaps because of a scepticism about taking "mere" metaphors or analogies too seriously.

It is surely legitimate to ask why metaphor—and especially these body-based metaphors—should have come to constitute a kind of privileged class or domain in the language of psychoanalysis. Is this perhaps a consequence of Freud's famous dictum from *The Ego and the Id* (1923b) that "the ego is first and foremost a bodily ego"? Many who cite those words either mistakenly misquote "bodily" (that is, body-*like*) as "body" and miss the simile or metaphor implied. Moreover, they often neglect to quote the whole sentence, conveniently eliding Freud's addendum that the ego "is not merely a surface entity, but is itself a projection of a surface" (p. 26)—a statement that also purports to keep matters more firmly rooted in the psychic realm which is Freud's intention, both here and elsewhere in his oeuvre. These, of course, are complex issues that can only be touched on or glanced at here.

What I want to register is my appreciation that there may be much at stake in this decision to rely on this thematic metaphor as the main organizing principle of my book. However, I would stand by the claim that applying an extended alimentary conceit or trope (to resort to terms that are even more decidedly literary) as my central guide is not merely acceptable or tolerable, but exemplifies a sanctioned, legitimate approach within psychoanalytic discourse. I am prepared, in any case, not only to risk taking the analogy seriously, but also to push it to the limits of its usefulness, which also means that I intend to treat it elastically and to play with it as much as it will allow.

Like a meal, a loss must be swallowed, digested, and metabolized— and some of it evacuated: after all, one hears such things loosely expressed in ordinary language and in clinical contexts all the time. In my view, the aptness of this idea emerges logically from the equally common idea that no real grieving can occur *without* some form of internal processing—that is, the psychic equivalent of a physical "taking in"—taking place. The language of psychoanalysis has responded or followed suit by bringing forth a confusing plethora of words denoting such processes: *internalization, identification, introjection, incorporation*, to name the most prominent of them. It will be part of my task to try to establish some useful distinctions or differentiations among this babel/babble of terms and to explore their intimate relations with each other, with the intention and hope of bringing a semblance of order to bear upon them.

It may be important at this juncture to put forward a general statement of conviction about psychoanalysis that might provide the underpinning of an endeavour of this kind. As I see it, the essence of psychoanalysis—and its beauty—lies in it being a therapeutic practice and theoretical discipline in which conceptual antinomies can be thought about in ongoing tension with one another, held up for contemplation in the mind without the pressurizing requirement of a quick either/or choice or answer. Body and mind, conscious and unconscious, object/ive and subject/ive, external and internal, literal and symbolic, concrete and metaphorical, scientific and hermeneutic—these and other manifestly opposed terms and concepts are often considered together, in mutually implicating pairs: this makes it possible for them to be explored or interrogated openly, leaving them open to a more thorough investigation of the nature of their opposition.

In consequence, psychoanalytic terms that ostensibly appear to confront and eschew each other can metamorphose into a more complex, intimately obverse relation; or an absolute and diametric ideational division can ease and resolve itself into a continuum displaying points of only relative difference. How often do we find Freud and later analysts introducing psychic phenomena or concepts that begin their metatheoretical lives in defensive opposition to a preferred procedure and to therapeutic progress—repetition in the transference rather than the imperative to remember is a prime example—only to turn into essential and enabling tools of the trade?

Conversely, some ideas or terms might start out as inextricably close neighbours, hard to tell apart, but develop into structurally crucial polarities: like self-preservative needs (instincts?) versus libidinal wishes (drives?); Eros versus the death drive; drive-discharging versus object-seeking; discrete objects versus ambient environments; the nurture of environment versus the nature of endowment; loving others (having them sexually) versus identifying with (being like) them; and mourning a loss versus succumbing to depression—the last two pairs being those with which this book is most concerned. Even in an age when prevailing views of science and evidence-based research seem to militate against this approach, demanding clear resolutions and proven certainties, psychoanalytic thinking at its best preserves and uses all such differentials and tensions without trying reductively to resolve, reconcile, or simplify them. I hope that my own work here will be seen to exemplify these aims and intentions.

* * *

Earlier intellectual and theoretical interests notwithstanding, I do not think I could or should have tried to write this book without the clinical experience that I have accrued over the last two decades. I now spend most of my time working privately as a psychoanalyst and psychotherapist, where many if not most of my patients would be considered—and, indeed, might well see themselves as—suffering from depression or melancholia.

Perhaps the therapeutic lessons most relevant to this book, however, have been learned at the Tavistock, where I was first taken on as an honorary psychotherapist during the early years of my analytic training. My clinical work there has primarily been in the Fitzjohn's Unit, a specialist service for patients with complex and enduring mental health difficulties, those often designated by such derogatory tags as "borderline" or "personality disorder". Putting aside questions about whether such diagnostic categories are apt or useful, what is clear is that these patients tend also, almost without exception, to have experienced terrible, often traumatic loss, and thus to be severely damaged internally as a result. They are, therefore, depressed, regardless of whether they bear an additional diagnosis of bipolar affective disorder or major depression, which many of them in fact do. The work of the Fitzjohn's Unit was the subject of a book featuring clinical papers by my colleagues, also published in the Tavistock Series (Meyerowitz & Bell, 2018).

The current book, by contrast, is essentially a theoretical project, dealing primarily with psychoanalytic ideas and concepts, and I have decided to refrain from providing any exemplification of those ideas from my own clinical experience. My approach might also be characterized as literary, and in more ways than one. It is primarily so in the sense that I propose to interpret psychoanalytic texts in a close-reading manner that would be more familiar to students of literature than to those of psychology or the social sciences. Of course, the fine-tuned, keen-eyed attention to detail, the entertaining of multiple, overdetermined meanings that characterize those practices, will also be familiar from Freud's dream interpretations and case histories. This is a tendency that now affects—some might say, *in*fects—the entire history of psychoanalytic writing.

Many of those interested in Freud's Jewish roots, including myself (Meyerowitz, 1995), claim that these habits originate in the Talmudic and Midrashic exegesis and argumentation practised for centuries by Jewish scholars in relation to Biblical holy writ. In the literature departments of the modern academy, however, remarkably similar practices have come to constitute the standard approach to the novels, stories, poems, and plays that are the objects of study. Whether I am drawing here on my own phylogenetic Jewish origins or my more ontogenetic university experience as a student and teacher of literature—or both—matters not. I will in any case be applying such zealous scrutiny to the eminently close-readable psychoanalytic papers that I have chosen to interrogate, perhaps in the expectation of finding angels as well as devils in their detail.

The other sense in which my project is literary is that—perhaps in lieu of case material and in a quasi-clinical way—I will from time to time be exemplifying and expanding upon the implications of the concepts and theories I am investigating by introducing other kinds of texts, by referring to, citing and reading closely a range of literary works along the way. No less than case material from clinical work with patients, these texts provide valuable evidence and constitute wise and insightful examples of the experience and understanding of life and loss; I feel that my recourse to them is true to the spirit of the whole enterprise. It is also a tribute to the rich stores of literary history that—long before the advent of psychoanalysis—have always provided us with a repository of accounts of human loss, separation, mourning, and how we cope internally with these facts of life. Certain literary texts can, I believe, be seen not only as addressing such themes generically, but as anticipating, emulating, or embellishing an at least proto-psychoanalytic approach to these predicaments. The book's subtitle is meant to suggest that *all* the texts read and explored under its aegis—even the literary, ostensibly non-psychoanalytic ones—might be considered as contributions to the specifically psychoanalytic literature of loss.

I have even selected a primary literary text for the purpose—one that can serve as exemplar-in-chief. This is "A Rose for Emily", a short story written by William Faulkner in 1930, one of the finest examples of its genre. Though it is a staple—at least in the United States—of introductory literature courses, it may not be quite so well known in the British Isles. So, to whet the appetite (and perhaps encourage the digestive process), I will briefly introduce and summarize the story here, pre-emptively registering a "spoiler alert", particularly regarding its ending. I would suggest that, instead of relying on my summary, it would be far better for readers unfamiliar with it to now devote a few minutes to making personal acquaintance with the tale. It is readily available in many editions and collections, is easily accessible on the internet, and will not take at all long to read.

Like most of Faulkner's fiction, the story is set in the American South, in the extended aftermath of the Civil War. It concerns the strange life and times of Miss Emily Grierson, daughter of a famous Confederate general, in the fictional town of Jefferson. Intricately plotted, and with a shocking and ingeniously delayed denouement (that the narrative might be said only to *pretend* to hold back), the story starts and ends with Miss Emily's death. In the intervening pages, episodes from her life are rendered in a seemingly scrambled manner, as though via the scatty composite mind of several generations of ordinary townspeople who have both interacted with her over the years and closely watched the events that unfolded around her. An object of awe-struck fascination, her story is therefore told haphazardly, its episodes recalled as if in random fashion. Despite coming across as gossipy, nosey, and petty, the townspeople also function like the chorus in a Greek tragedy, pity and terror being very pertinent to what the story eventually reveals; this effect is heightened by the unusual third-person-plural narrative voice.

On closer examination, it becomes clear that the apparent confusion and matter-of-factness of the narrative are authorial devices, calculated to lull the reader into semi-forgetful complacency or carelessness, to induce a repetition of the elision of a crucial occurrence that the townspeople supposedly failed to infer during Miss Emily's history. Once the sequence of events is laid out in linear order, the plot is revealed to be intricately constructed, extremely precise, not confused in the least. It is replete with all manner of clues and subtle information about the ordering and even dating of events and therefore about the final "reveal" that has been hiding in plain sight.

Miss Emily has been raised by and lives alone with her father; no mother is mentioned. There is a highly stratified class- and status-related hierarchy in the town, with the social consequence that the ex-general will not permit his daughter to be courted by the local young men, none of whom is deemed good enough. These aristocratic conditions are reinforced with the threat of violence, represented in the form of a tableau (or screen memory) of the father, armed with a horsewhip, forbidding access to the house and his charge. But she does not appear to protest; she apparently dotes on and is devoted to this father. His death is a crucial event, revealing the first signs of strangeness—not to say pathology—in Miss

Emily. She refuses to allow the removal of the body for burial; the townspeople must force the issue. A prolonged seclusion ensues, with the hint that Miss Emily has suffered a breakdown of some kind. When she reappears on the streets, she seems changed and is seen before long in the company of a day-labourer from the Yankee North: his very name, Homer Barron, hints at the post-Civil War sacking of the South by unscrupulous northerners, popularly known as carpetbaggers or robber barons. It soon looks as if he and she are a courting couple. This is considered scandalous by the community, and well beneath Miss Emily's dignity; there is an attempt to call in some of her relatives, to have them prevail upon her to behave appropriately, but to no avail.

Then there are various mysteries: Barron disappears, returns, then disappears again for good; in the interim, Miss Emily has gone out and purchased a man's toilet set (a wedding gift?) but also some rat poison. Later, from the vicinity of the Grierson house, a bad smell emanates but eventually dissipates. Time passes; Miss Emily is seen more rarely, hardly leaves the house, grows imperiously older, greyer; she refuses to accept the installation of post-boxes or to modernize in any other way. With no means of support, she becomes the embodiment of genteel poverty, and a succession of the town's mayors and councillors concoct elaborate schemes to rescind her taxes and help her in other ways, disguising the implicit and transparent charity that she would never have stooped to accept.

During all this time, Miss Emily has lived with only a black servant for company. The town occasionally sends local officials around to try to persuade her to comply with a new regulation: she either refuses to see them or sends them packing with withering, silent stares. The upper floor of the decaying house has fallen into disuse; there is the constant sense that the townspeople are craning and straining, trying desperately to get a glimpse of what is going on within. Eventually Miss Emily dies, in a downstairs room. The serving man lets the townspeople in, then walks out through the back door, never to be seen again. After the funeral is held, with requisite respect and ceremony, befitting the family's status, it is finally time to invade the now empty house and satisfy all the accumulated prurient curiosity. The door must be broken down to gain access to the upstairs bedroom, where the skeletal remains of Homer Barron are discovered in the bed; on the indented pillow next to him lies a long strand of grey hair.

This simultaneously thrilling and horrifying tale will provide a handy recourse throughout the book, a ubiquitous ubiquitously prominent—and conveniently schematic—fictional companion piece, serving as both instance of and commentary on the various theories of mourning I examine. I refer to, quote from, and make interpretations of it regularly throughout the book, but I hope it is already evident that it offers a fitting example—a macabre and chilling, disturbed and disturbing account—of a mourning process gone badly awry, or, if you will, an exemplification of the concreteness of failed mourning or melancholia, of what can happen when the tragic inability to properly internalize or metabolize loss supervenes.

My specific way of responding to such stories—and to all good writing, whether psychoanalytic or literary—can no doubt be traced to some extent to the fads and fashions of literary criticism that prevailed during my time as an academic, an era dominated by deconstruction and reader-response theory. Under these theoretical dispensations, there were assumptions of a kind of pervasive textuality and of the multiplicity, uncertainty, and subjectivity of interpretation. This was accompanied by the phenomenological reversal of traditional literary critical vectors, a shift in emphasis from how in-control readers can interpretively manipulate a text or bend it to their critical will, to the much less controllable power that a text can wield, the reactions it can induce in susceptible readers. These approaches would, in a manner of speaking, challenge amateur readers' or professional critics' claims to being active and confident readers *of* literary works and regard them, instead, as nervously and passively at the mercy of being read *by* them. The literary scholar was thus encouraged to be more mindful of the text—and respectful of it in a new way—not merely as the venerable recipient of critical attention or object of interpretation, but as a subject in the exchange, playing an equal or even dominant part in the relationship.

One of the most important books of this reader-response era was Norman Holland's *5 Readers Reading* (1975), an account of a literary critical experiment in which the author recorded, in some detail, the personal and psychological responses of five of his students to their engagements with a literary text: none other than the story, "A Rose for Emily". Though this was not what consciously led me to make such extensive use of the story here, it is surely no accident that it has assumed such a prominent place in this book. A critic deeply interested in psychoanalysis, Holland demonstrated the story's admittedly provocative, prurient power to stimulate each of the students profoundly as well as differently, even idiosyncratically, generating desires, anxieties, fantasies, and counter-responsive narratives that exemplified the psychic particularity or valency of the reader.

Quite apart from such theories of literary engagement, serious readers—professional or otherwise—know full well that one can at times feel quite invaded or pervaded by a certain story or poem, as if that text were capable of "knowing" its reader and thus indelibly affecting her- or himself through the encounter. A resonant and popular rendition of this phenomenon is Charles Fox and Norman Gimbel's song *Killing Me Softly*, which became a hit in 1973 when sung by Roberta Flack: she listens to another performer's song through the medium of which she feels he is playing and singing her very life, has somehow gained access to her most intimate feelings, knows her inside out. My own most prolonged and thoroughgoing literary encounter of this kind—personal as well as critical—was with the American modernist poet Wallace Stevens, subject of my masters and doctoral dissertations, and someone who also features in this book. Setting out to wrestle intently and intensively with Stevens's writings entailed that they, and he, would come to pervade and affect me deeply, at times seeming to read my mind no less completely and comprehensively than I was attempting to penetrate his.

I am convinced that such literary encounters contributed greatly to my later decision to train as a psychoanalyst. If anything, the ensuing clinical experiences have reinforced such challenges to orthodox or conventional approaches to reading and interpretation. To put it in the form of a question: when one considers reader and text and, in parallel, analyst and patient, who reads whom? Which of the pair in each case is subject and which object? Which provides the interpretation, and which receives it? The standard or straightforward perspective would have it that the reader reads (or analyses) the text in the same way that the analyst analyses (or reads) the patient; but perhaps it has always been known—if not necessarily acknowledged—that the situation is never that simple, in either sphere.

In keeping with the ever-growing importance of countertransference in psychoanalytic clinical work, it is now clearer than it was before that no such encounter is ever unidirectional. Not only must the contemporary analyst recognize and be aware of the extent to which he or she is affected—and, indeed, often quite accurately "read"—by the patient, but this awareness has progressively come to be regarded as one of the most valuable sources of information about the state of the analysis or therapy at any given moment. Such thinking has become commonplace in recent decades—a development that may, for a change, have brought more unity than division to the relations between the different psychoanalytic schools. Going one step further than most of their British counterparts, however, proponents of American intersubjective or relational psychoanalysis even regard it as part of the analyst's responsibility not merely to acknowledge, tacitly and to themselves, but to explicitly convey, disclose, or make plain to the patient that something like this is happening between them—perhaps with the intention of democratizing the analytic process.

* * *

Returning to the book's literary intentions and qualities, I wish to emphasize the importance of poetry in this context. In addition to using the Faulkner story extensively and referring occasionally to other literary works, I break off from time to time from my readings of psychoanalytic texts to look closely at certain relevant poems by Wordsworth, Shelley, Yeats, Stevens, Plath, and Auden. There is another nod here to Thomas Ogden, who, in *Conversations at the Frontier of Dreaming* (2002) and elsewhere, has also tried his hand—and succeeded brilliantly—at reading literary and poetic texts by the likes of Jorge Louis Borges, Robert Frost, Seamus Heaney, and, indeed, Wallace Stevens. It is perhaps redundant to say that the entire realm of poetry is always already elegiac, suffused by melancholia and mourning, and not only by virtue of boasting a major sub-genre bearing the name of elegy. The ex-literature student and teacher in me fears, therefore, that if one undertakes, in a book like this, to include *some* exemplary poems, it potentially opens the floodgates to the entire age-old force of lyric literature that might threaten to overwhelm, with its sheer volume and historical depth and reach, a modest century's worth of psychoanalytic thinking on these topics.

Though this book is emphatically not itself a work of literary criticism, I am nevertheless pleased to be able to draw for my purposes on the wealth of wisdom inherent in both the poetic contemplation of human loss as well as the critical appreciation and understanding of that quest and tradition. I am indebted to two helpful volumes of actual literary criticism, very much worth mentioning in this context: *The English Elegy: Studies in the Genre from Spenser to Yeats* by Peter Sacks (1985) and Jahan Ramazani's *Poetry of Mourning: The Modern Elegy from Hardy to Heaney* (1994). Not only do they provide excellent readings of the poets in question, but they manifest an almost unquestioned urge or duty to peruse them with Freud's "Mourning and Melancholia" clearly in mind and within a more broadly psychoanalytic frame of reference. They both seem fully aware that no contemporary attempt to get to grips with poetic mourning can hope to do so adequately without it.

Though agreeing on that score, the two books also differ in interesting ways regarding their attitudes towards mourning and the function of elegy. This is partly because of the different (if slightly overlapping) periods that they focus on, with Sacks covering the tradition of English elegy in its near entirety and Ramazani focusing on mourning in English and American poetry in the twentieth century. Loosely speaking, one might see Sacks as taking a more traditional stance: while recognizing that elegy has had to move with the times and that elegiac poetry has become progressively more critical of its own generic traditions, he still rather venerates its original function, including its meliorative capacities and even therapeutic pretensions. Consequently, Sacks also seems to respect and support Freud's attempt to distinguish between mourning and melancholia and will, at times, bemoan the modern elegy's more melancholic strains—its resistance to cure or consolation—as something of a loss for the poems, poets, and readers concerned.

Taking issue with Sacks, Ramazani adopts an explicitly more radical position. For him, the comforting, ameliorating conventions of elegy were sorely in need of the subversive and ironic rendering that they received in the last century, and if this also meant issuing a challenge to the "orthodoxy" of distinguishing too clearly between mourning and melancholia, then so be it. As his title suggests, Ramazani will not cede the term "mourning", even when he seems to be advocating a melancholic revolution. He suggests that the solace of a so-called proper mourning process, and any poetry that might abet it, is neither possible nor even desirable in certain existential or literary circumstances. Modern versions of the genres of poetic grief ought not, he suggests, to reconcile or conciliate too readily, not least when overwhelmingly tragic and traumatic events are their subject matter. Perhaps accordingly, where Sacks for the most part sticks with Freud and reads him accurately and approvingly, Ramazani extends his psychoanalytic reach beyond Freud, to the work of disciples and challengers like Karl Abraham, Melanie Klein, Jacques Lacan, and Julia Kristeva.

Another helpful and stimulating critical account of the poetry of loss—albeit one dealing with a different literary and linguistic tradition—is Richard Stamelman's *Lost Beyond Telling: Representations of Death and Absence in Modern French Poetry* (1990). Though an American academic, Stamelman is clearly steeped in French intellectual culture and, as his title suggests, he takes for granted that poetry, criticism, theory—indeed, any writing whatsoever—knows self-consciously that its attempts to recoup human loss and the consolations it offers are essentially illusory. All losses, it would appear, are "lost beyond telling", though this knowledge does not deter writers from trying, time and again, to tell them, to find a route or ruse to carry them to this impossible goal.

Stamelman draws on an entire French (and Francophile) textual legacy that is insistently and self-consciously aware that life itself is characterized and shot through by loss and its cognates, like absence, death, and lack. At one moment, he tries to list as many of the synonyms of loss as he can come up with, specifying more than 30 terms, including those that probably feature most frequently in this book: mourning, melancholy, grief, and separation. That every word is itself an elegy or monument to the absence that it signifies; the fact that words might kill their referents in their futile attempts to resurrect fleeting moments of presence; that these can only be signalled belatedly or in retrospect—such ideas provide a taste of the French cuisine of the negative that Stamelman serves up. His book encompasses poets from Charles Baudelaire to Edmond Jabès and engages with prose writers and critics like Michel de Montaigne, Marcel Proust, Maurice Blanchot, and Roland Barthes. Though there are also references to Freud, and to Lacan and other French analysts, one gets the impression that by the time psychoanalysis and its theories of mourning were taken up in France—somewhat belatedly and only gradually at first—it served to reinforce cultural familiarity with a ubiquitous topic that its literature already takes for granted.

Given that my book includes two chapters representing French psychoanalysis, it may be of interest to consider how this cultural perspective on the necessity and relentlessness of loss relates to the *raison d'être* of psychoanalysis. For most analyst practitioners, loss readily becomes a clinical matter that requires treating when its pains and pathologies become evident. By contrast, it is perhaps no accident that Lacan, the doyen of French psychoanalysis, appears to eschew the treatment of symptoms and even the amelioration of suffering—not to mention any aim to cure—in favour of a purist, clear-sighted (if also impossible), existential injunction that bids us face, as squarely as we dare, the all-encompassing truths of loss and lack. As my late chapters attest, not all French psychoanalysis takes things to quite such an extreme. Any attempt to put words to loss—whether they are spoken out loud in the consulting room or written down as text—is not dissimilar to the psychic task of internalizing or introjecting a loss. Indeed, it is one method of doing so. What must be admitted, however, is that even if solace or compensation is sought in this form, it always incurs the cost of recognizing that such procedures can only mark or point to the place of the empty tomb and are themselves indicative of the immutability or permanence of loss itself. There is a much longer debate to be had on these matters, and I try to entertain it further as the book proceeds.

Having mentioned earlier the confusion that surrounds words designating internalization in psychoanalysis, it might be opportune to draw some pre-emptive support from one final critical text from my academic past that has been enormously helpful for the theoretical and metapsychological substrate of this book. *Identification Papers* by Diana Fuss (1995), an American professor of literature and of feminist and gay and lesbian cultural studies, provides an invaluable guide to the richness and confusion of internal-world-speak in psychoanalysis.

Unencumbered by clinical considerations and with an astute eye for paradox and contradiction, Fuss produces a probing account of how Freud both wrestles with and manipulates this difficult notion of identification. While she sees him as doing so for his own relatively conservative ideological purposes, she also recognizes that these are inherently slippery and elusive machinations, likely to take possession of those who would control them. Radical as Fuss's critical and socio-political agenda may be, she sees Freud's conceptual "slip-ups" as both transparent and instructive enough for his continuing importance and relevance to be ensured. Indeed, the respect Fuss accords him is aptly captured by the cover design of her book, featuring passport photographs of a very elderly Freud, set against the backdrop of what appear to be his own identity or identification papers, presumably required for his final departure from Nazi-occupied Vienna in 1938.

Reading Fuss, one recognizes the intimate connection between identification and metaphor. When identifying with someone (and, indeed, when transferring to them), one, as it were, "carries oneself over" to the other, or grants access and invites them into a new relation with oneself. Metaphor, of course, behaves in a similar way: it renews the perspective on one reference area by transferring itself to another. Fuss notes the metaphorical or figurative nature of the psychoanalytic project at large:

> Freud's concept of self-other relations fundamentally presupposes the possibility of metaphoricity—of iterability, redoubling, translation and transposition. The Greek *metaphora*, meaning transport, immediately implicates the transferential act of identification in the rhetorical process of figuration. [pp. 5–6]

Referring to psychoanalysis as "a mixed metaphor system", Fuss, intriguingly, sees Freud as elaborating "his theory of identification through three principal figures: gravity, ingestion, and infection" (p. 13). While she produces persuasive interpretive evidence regarding all three tropes, the metaphors of ingestion appear to predominate in her discourse, corroborating my own intuitions about their significance.

Pre-empting my own examination of the tricky conceptual relations of internality as they are extended to the cognates or synonyms of identification (internalization, introjection, incorporation), Fuss also visits these adjacent or overlapping terms, while paying specific attention to the significance of loss and mourning to this entire terrain. Although I now find myself disagreeing, on clinical grounds, with some of her pronouncements, she articulates fundamental truths that are very worthy of citing. Freud, she says, "gives us a much clearer picture of the vital role mourning plays in the act of identification. All identification begins in an experience of traumatic loss and in the subject's tentative attempts to manage this loss". She adds: "identification works as a form of elegy, remembering and commemorating the lost object by ritualistically incorporating its serial replacements."

With specific reference to the oral-alimentary dimension of these matters, Fuss names and situates prominently the all-important but oft-forgotten object that any account of loss must address:

> Like the return of the living dead, the repressed maternal resurfaces to remind us that, when we mourn, it is the impossible return of the lost maternal object that we lament. For Freud, mourning is always a maternal bequest, an inheritance from the mother. [p. 38]

As we know, Freud's entrenched paternalism led him to often abjure, ignore, and repress his own best insights—not least about the "maternal bequests" of psychoanalysis—and this is just one of the blind spots that Fuss seeks to illuminate in her book, one that is also taken up and highlighted in mine.

Fuss takes on a series of diverse texts exemplifying her political preoccupations with the injustices and intellectual incoherencies of prejudice, but her introduction and opening chapter provide the theoretical basis that makes her book so relevant to my rather different concerns. Identification, she tells us, is bound to be unreliable and unstable, not least because of its inextricable closeness to the terms that it is defined against—namely, identity, on the one hand, and desire or object love, on the other. Though identity may strive to embody something external, stable, and unitary, the simple difference between "public identity" and "private identification" cannot be sustained for long: this is because "Identification inhabits, organizes, instantiates identity. It operates as a mark of self-difference, opening up a space for the self, to relate to itself as a self, a self that is perpetually other" (p. 2).

As far as the second opposition is concerned, Freud's distinguishing of "identification (the wish to be the other) from sexual object choice (the wish to have the other)" is vulnerable to the following binary-busting questions: "What is identification, if not a way to assume the desires of the other? And what is desire, if not a means of becoming the other whom one wishes to have" (pp. 11–12)? This propensity for posing difficult questions is again exemplified when Fuss later notes the conceptual tension inherent in Freud seeing identification both as the earliest way of connecting with an object and as the later way of recouping the loss of an object: "If identification *is* an abandoned object-relation, then how can it simultaneously be the *precondition* for an object-relation" (p. 47)?

There is a great deal in Fuss's study that can be seen to anticipate—and, indeed, set an agenda—for my own. To mention one final thing about her work: she does not neglect to draw attention to the limits of identification and, therefore, to the un-assimilability or indigestibility of certain losses. Under the dark shadow of the Holocaust, she reminds us, "Theories of identification survive in modernism and postmodernism, but only as painful and poignant meditations on the possibility of identification's own impossibility." Those of us who work as clinicians cannot, perhaps, afford to accede completely to the logical starkness of a formulation like this. That is because, whether we are working with individual survivors of genocide and other large-scale atrocities or of private catastrophes like parental abuse and neglect—and the transgenerational sequelae of both—we are often required to be the repositories of hope and possibility for patients for whom such prospects are well-nigh gone.

Nevertheless, Fuss's invaluable perspective—and she cites the highly relevant loss-work of Jacques Derrida, Dori Laub, and Cathy Caruth—must be borne in mind for many of our cases:

> Not all losses, it seems, can be recuperated. Trauma, defined as the withdrawal of the Other, marks the limit case of a loss that cannot be assimilated. To the extent that identification is always also about what cannot be taken inside, what resists incorporation, identification is only possible traumatically. [pp. 39–40]

Whereas, again, we clinicians cannot afford to regard all trauma so bleakly, Fuss gives us—through the linguistic logic of the limit case that she employs so effectively—something to hold up before our eyes when our therapeutic zeal and ambition threaten to outstrip what is possible.

* * *

I turn now to the body of this book and how it is organized. The first two chapters are devoted to charting the evolution of Freud's thinking about loss and the internal world via close analyses of the texts most relevant to these themes. Remarkably enough, these topics did not preoccupy Freud in the earliest years of psychoanalysis. Indeed, in the context of his work at the time, "Mourning and Melancholia" (1917e), favourite text of so many of Freud's followers, seems rather to burst onto the scene, apparently out of the blue. However, before treating this celebrated and seminal paper as the focal point of Freud's newer concerns and urtext of my entire close-reading project in chapter one, I remind readers of some important developments that did pre-empt its arrival.

Freud's intellectual horizons had begun to expand during the preceding years, via his speculative foray into anthropology in *Totem and Taboo* (1912–13) and a new set of clinical and theoretical interests, first explored in his book on Leonardo da Vinci (1910c) before finding fuller expression in "On Narcissism: An Introduction" (1914c). These texts provide different but essential starting points insofar as they begin to give credence and attention to phylogenetic as well as ontogenetic developments internal to the psyche: Freud posits that the subject is capable of complex relationships with both its precursory, not-personally experienced prehistory and its own past, current, and future self. With long historical hindsight, moreover, we realize that it is not coincidental that these concerns irrupt into—and interrupt—Freud's mind just as the First World War erupts in Europe, providing many reasons for mourning and the failure to do so.

The distinctions that Freud draws in "Mourning and Melancholia" are about contrasting responses to loss. A not always noticed feature of his account is that it is only in relation to melancholia that he sees fit to outline a set of dynamic internal consequences of the loss—conflictual, problematic, pathological ones, at that. He describes a split or rift in the melancholic mind, whereby a moralistic, judgemental part of the ego—the precursor of what he will later call the superego—attacks the part that has established an identification with an ambivalently regarded object. Hence the famous, resonant, if also enigmatic line: "Thus the shadow of the object fell upon the ego."

By contrast, in the case of so-called normal or ordinary mourning (though Freud seems also to discover, somewhat to his chagrin, that no mourning process is ever straightforward), it is purportedly possible for the loss to be dealt with as an external matter, through reality testing, albeit in a painful, piecemeal, prolonged manner. The mourner gradually comes to terms with the absence of the actual lost object and eventually withdraws libidinal or psychic investment from it. The analogy with digestion and metabolization, though already implicit in this text, is not yet as prominent as it will later become.

My second chapter begins with a glance at *Beyond the Pleasure Principle* (1920g), Freud's post-war foray into the dynamics of trauma—or unassimilable loss—and the resulting introduction of the death drive. It goes on to explore Freud's expanding view of the mind's internal landscape, where he gradually comes to recognize that all loss results in dynamic, internal, or constitutional change. As I would phrase it, some digestive or metabolic process—successful or otherwise—is always already occurring in these psychic situations. Having explored identification more closely in *Group Psychology and the Analysis of the Ego* (1921c), Freud introduces his structural model of the mind in *The Ego and the Id* (1923b). He asserts there that the process of identification with parental figures required in the vexed negotiations of the Oedipus complex brings the superego in its wake and determines its nature. However, just prior to introducing the superego, Freud also suggests—almost in passing—that the ego itself is established in analogous ways: through some form of giving up and taking in, contingent upon loss. What is insinuated here is that there can be no internal development, no structuring of the human psyche, without some experience of bereavement.

Shortly thereafter, in *Inhibitions, Symptoms and Anxiety* (1926d), Freud revises his whole theory of anxiety, that familiar companion to depression in psychiatric diagnostics and treatment. Where he had previously considered it a kind of quantitative emotional residue, a waste-product of sexual frustration, Freud now views anxiety more expansively. He recognizes that it is linked in complex ways with experiences of dependency and loss from birth onwards, including separation from the breast, the mother, and later the superego itself. No longer focused quite as doggedly on either lacking or losing the penis as such, anxiety has become a less libidinal matter and now has far more to do with self-preservation or survival. If depression is the consequence of losses that have already occurred, then anxiety arises when threats, dangers, losses, or separations are pending—a simple point that nevertheless carries nuanced implications about the relations between these two mental states.

Familiar as this historical survey of Freud's thinking may sound, he clearly did not arrive at these ideas all at once. In this opening pair of chapters, I trace carefully how he progressively gets to grips with the perennial, ubiquitous nature of loss and separation, the vicissitudes of mourning and anxiety; and how he is concomitantly driven to posit an internal world and to develop an account of the psychic processes required for its construction.

During the same years, Freud's most important contemporaneous disciples and colleagues, Sándor Ferenczi and Karl Abraham, were making their own, at times quite independent, contributions to the same set of issues. I discuss these in chapter three. In one of his earliest psychoanalytic papers, "On Introjection and Transference" (1909), Ferenczi detected a need for—and therefore coined—the central concept of introjection. Shortly thereafter, in "On the Definition of Introjection" (1912), he was already at pains to correct what he saw as gross misunderstandings and misuses of the term. Though not writing explicitly about loss or mourning in these papers, Ferenczi was adamant that introjection be understood not in some defensively reduced or limited way, but as a virtual *modus vivendi* or operating system, armed with which the ego extends its interests and goes out to meet, embrace, and encompass the outside world—essentially by absorbing it into an inner space. Having introduced this key theoretical concept several years before "Mourning and Melancholia" was written, Ferenczi seems to anticipate the problematic confusion that would ensue among the various terms denoting processes of internalization within psychoanalytic discourse.

For his part, Abraham had accrued considerably more experience than Freud of working with depressed, melancholic, and what we now call bipolar patients. Stealing a march on Freud's famous metapychological paper, he had already begun to write quite eloquently about these cases in "Notes on the Psycho-Analytical Investigation and Treatment of Manic-Depressive Insanity and Allied Conditions" (1911). Later, having thoroughly digested not only "Mourning and Melancholia" itself but also Freud's more recent works, Abraham produced his longer and more ambitious monograph on such conditions, "A Short Study of the Development of the Libido, Viewed in the Light of Mental Disorders" (1924). In this invaluable paper, he creatively extended Freud's theory of the psycho-sexual stages and, with frequent recourse to terms like introjection and incorporation (using them interchangeably), he simultaneously conceived an internal landscape, rich in clinical material, to account for what goes on psychically when people are struggling to come to terms with their losses.

By the time Melanie Klein (analysand of both Ferenczi and Abraham) comes to write about these issues in two classic papers, "A Contribution to the Psychogenesis of Manic-Depressive States" (1935) and "Mourning and Its Relation to Manic-Depressive States" (1940), the idea that all loss must have internal consequences seems to be taken for granted. In chapter four, I outline how Klein introduced and developed the notion of internal objects: psychic representatives of significant external figures dwelling within the inner, phantasy regions of the subjective world. These internal versions are not mere copies or precise inscriptions of their external equivalents, and they are always in need of checking against the latter. The relative proximity of the phantasmatic to the real thus becomes a marker of the relative psychic health of the individual. Because they are linked with early losses, these internal objects can only be established precariously, and they are therefore threatened with extinction or contamination every time a newer loss is sustained. They need continual reinstatement, along with the internal version of any more recently lost object.

One conceptual consequence of this influential notion of internal objects is an implicit challenge to Freud's original attempt to distinguish clearly between a successful mourning process and less successful, pathological states of depression and melancholia (including mania). A close reading of Klein gives the impression that she prefers these distinctions not to be too clear, at least not theoretically. Her view is that, in our hapless attempts to deal with the losses assailing us from the beginning (including birth itself and weaning) and throughout life, we are all prone to becoming psychologically ill in some measure and are susceptible to a range of ailments to which the diagnostic language of mental illness might be applied. Klein not only coined a psychiatric name—"paranoid-schizoid"—for the chronologically earlier and more pathological of her two positions, but she also referred to the somewhat more sober, painful, if realistic later state as not the "mourning" but the "depressive" position. Though Klein would sometimes speak of overcoming that position, perhaps we now count ourselves lucky if we manage merely to sustain and suffer this depressive attitude, given the perennial risk of slipping back into paranoid-schizoid functioning and the mad splitting, projection, and denial that characterize it.

While some of Klein's ideas have been inordinately helpful, providing crucial insights into the human psyche, not least where the psychopathology of loss is concerned, I make no secret of my sense that there is something unsatisfying about her metapsychological accounts of how things are processed in the internal world. Gifted, imaginative, and clinically astute as she so obviously was, Klein seems to stop short of reaching for a more dynamic and comprehensive theory of such processes. To put it more bluntly and interrogatively: is it enough to think of the internal world as consisting, rather concretely, of "homuncular" representatives of external objects, which must be rendered good, whole, and real and need continual re-establishing in the mind? Does the work of mourning—at least under less problematic circumstances—not offer a more comprehensive and permanent attainment, a more thoroughly digested, metabolized, and thus durable result?

The remainder of the book might be thought of as an attempt to describe, support, and reinforce more thoroughgoing theoretical accounts of what happens internally when human loss—and perhaps human experience more generally—is transmuted, transformed, or translated into intrapsychic terms. Towards the end of the Klein chapter, I discuss Bion's way of taking her legacy forward via his theory of containment, where he advances an explicitly digestive way of thinking about or imagining internalizing processes. The familiar metaphor frequently used to exemplify his theory—that of the mother bird taking in and pre-digesting in her crop what is otherwise unpalatable and indigestible for her fledgling—has obvious resonances with my themes. Equally crucial is Bion's idea that what is being offered to the neophyte baby or patient by the more experienced mother or analyst is not just the physical food or psychic sustenance itself, but also a capacity: the wherewithal to eventually accomplish one's own independent digestive process.

One of the most impressive psychoanalytic theorists of negotiating and crossing the divide between the external and the internal realms is the European-born American analyst, Hans Loewald, whom I discuss in chapter five. Anchored in a firm focus on Freud's original contributions (even as he reads them in his own inimical, at times quite maverick fashion), Loewald built up a powerful, detailed picture of human psychic structure in a series of brilliant papers, written in his quiet, almost self-effacing style. Two of these papers have a very direct bearing on the topics at hand: "Internalization, Separation, Mourning, and the Superego" (1962) and "On Internalization" (1973), where he takes a serious and sophisticated look at the metapsychological implications of the psychoanalytic conception of an internal world.

Loewald seems to believe that for each external, interpersonal event or interaction in our lives (including, but not limited to, experiences of loss), there is an internal, intra-psychic consequence: he refers to the process governing the transition from the former to the latter as internalization. For Loewald, this does not necessitate the setting up of some internal version of that external phenomenon—or even of the relationship with it. What he posits instead is that gradual, mutative, structural changes ensue, contributing to the development and enrichment of the ego and the superego, affecting the nature of the relationship between these two agencies (as well, no doubt, as their respective relationships with the id and the external world) and therefore determining the shape of the self.

These changes are referred to and described by Loewald in a variety of evocative ways: he speaks of the psychic equivalents of both "destructive anabolic" and "constructive catabolic" processes, terms that exemplify and make a link with my theme of metabolization. He describes the internal gains that can result from and compensate for external losses as "a ripening of the personality in adult life". With such an optimistic and individualistic view of the possibilities of internal human progress or growth, Loewald may at times sound too American (or ego-psychological) for British tastes, but what his perspective provides is an account of what an optimal and optative mourning process might look like, against which one might measure the various forms of failed mourning that we so often encounter in our clinical work.

Moving back across the Atlantic to France for chapters six and seven, the language changes in more senses than one. I first explore the work of two French psychoanalysts with Ferenczian–Hungarian roots, Nicolas Abraham and Maria Torok, who wrote both separately and as a couple for many years on an interconnected range of clinically inspired and theoretically far-reaching topics. Again, I focus on two papers that have important bearing on my theme: Torok's "The Illness of Mourning and the Fantasy of the Exquisite Corpse" (1968) and a paper co-written by both authors, entitled, "Mourning *or* Melancholia: Introjection *versus* Incorporation" (Abraham & Torok, 1972).

Where Loewald elaborates upon the term "internalization" (and goes on to discuss the similarities and differences between this term and "identification"), Abraham and Torok seem to avoid or eschew these terms. They use a somewhat different psychoanalytic lexicon while exemplifying a typically French emphasis on language itself. True to their origins, they prefer to pick up from Ferenczi's frustrations with the misuse of and confusion about his own term, "introjection". They are at pains to emphasize the difference between this metaphorical—and more properly psychic—term as it was originally intended by Ferenczi, on the one hand, and a more concrete, literalistic concept like incorporation, on the other; the latter is much more bound to acts of actual ingesting, swallowing, and its roots in physical orality *per se*.

There are some clear resonances here with the Kleinian distinction between the depressive capacity for symbolic functioning and the use of what Hanna Segal (1954) calls "symbolic equation" more characteristic of psychotic or paranoid-schizoid states of mind. Abraham and Torok suggest that the more capable someone is of such symbolic, metaphorical, or introjective work, the more likely they are to deal adequately with loss and achieve the proper transformations of mourning. The alternative melancholic outcome is powerfully invoked in the idea that a loss not processed in this more psychic-figurative way can result in a reinforcement of the concrete fantasy that one has really swallowed and incorporated the lost object. The lost person or entity then ends up "encrypted" within the subject's internal psyche-soma, not amenable to any form of working-through, walled off from the digestive "juices" that might eventually dissolve it and bring mourning to a close. If this invokes macabre and ghoulish scenes from the genres of horror in literature and film, this is because ghosts, zombies, and their ilk are quite precise, if also rather concrete, representations of the failure to mourn. Exemplifying psychic indigestion, such "unlaid" or "undead" objects return to wreak revenge, turning the tables to feed off the living.

Remaining in France for my penultimate chapter, I devote it to André Green's hugely influential paper, "The Dead Mother" (1980). Typically for a French analyst, Green favours a philosophical, linguistic, and literary approach to psychoanalytic thinking, and his paper constitutes an important attempt to forge some essential cross-cultural and metatheoretical connections within psychoanalysis. The fact that he filters his concerns through a perspective on the difficulties of mourning makes this a fitting final theoretical text with which to engage. Importantly, this is mourning in relation to an object that has not actually died: the dead mother complex concerns mothers who are dead only in the sense of being chronically distracted, depressed, dead-in-life, rather than deceased as such.

Green took the theoretical needs of psychoanalysis very seriously indeed. Though he loved an intellectual argument and would gladly foment one, he was also one of the great unifiers of psychoanalysis and a pioneer of attempts to reconcile—via his considerable erudition—the hermeneutic–philosophical psychoanalysis of Europe, with the scientific–empirical psychoanalysis of Anglophone object relations. His paper is animated by an ambitious attempt to extend a structural(ist) psychoanalytic metapsychology from the realm of the father where it originated and has traditionally resided (in the work of Freud, Lacan, and others), to that of the mother, traditionally the province of more developmentalist forms of psychoanalysis whose hegemony over this maternal territory he wishes to dispute.

By addressing himself to the phenomenon of the dead mother, Green tries to provide the same symbolic/metaphorical perspective on the maternal breast as that which traditional psychoanalysis has applied to the paternal penis. In a sustained challenge to Freud and especially Lacan, Green identifies not one but two types of loss and, therefore, of anxiety. He distinguishes the blood-red losses of the paternal kind (associated with wounding, castration, having a precious body part violently removed) from the monochromatic, black and/or white losses of the maternal kind (associated with separation from the breast or the mother's love). It is to this latter type of loss that Green devoted much of his energy and working life, dealing extensively with absence, blankness, and what he calls the work of the negative.

The conclusion of the book features a reading of one of Freud's own most literary pieces of writing, "On Transience" (1916a). This brief essay was written near the start of the First World War and commissioned for a volume of literary pieces by well-known German writers. It is intimately concerned with attitudes towards grief, the very issue that Freud was then beginning to address in "Mourning and Melancholia". A lyrical and emotionally touching piece of writing, it features a poet much-troubled by loss. Quite poem-like in its own right, the essay seems to invoke, in the mind of this reader, other kindred poets and poems. If returning to Freud's essay in the company of such poets is a fitting way of ending the book, it is even more apt to do so alongside the closer exploration of a poem about the death and loss of Freud himself by one of the most important English poets of the last century. W. H. Auden's celebrated elegy, "In Memory of Sigmund Freud" (1939a), was written shortly after Freud's death and the outbreak of the Second World War, both events occurring in September 1939.

Therefore, these final readings hark back to the beginnings or brinks of both catastrophic world wars of the last century. Brief though it is and written a quarter-century before Freud's own death, "On Transience" can be seen to stand both retrospectively and pre-emptively for all its author's efforts on behalf of individual sufferers from psychological distress as well as civilization at large. I hope that treating it as a coda to my own textual endeavours extends the reach of this little text well beyond its own temporal moment. Among other things, Auden's poem makes much of what Freud left behind as a cultural inheritance. It helps us to see that psychoanalysis, having arisen in an era that featured not just one but two wars to end all wars, was bequeathed at a juncture in time when it could not have been needed more urgently. Many years on, however, and now in a new millennium, the start of which has hardly been short on universal trials and atrocities, we continue in our struggle to earn and be worthy of this legacy: we still strive to take it in, to metabolize it, to allow it to do its work for us.

CHAPTER ONE

Sigmund Freud: early explorations— mapping the territory of the mind

When precisely does the notion of a "psycho-active" internal world—featuring inner events and *dramatis personae* and thus not limited just to the fact of the mind's dynamic unconsciousness—first take hold of Freud's imagination? And when does its intimate association with loss and mourning begin? As I said in the Introduction, this set of interests is not prominently present at the beginning of the psychoanalytic enterprise. Excepting two passages in Freud's correspondence with Fliess (Freud, 1950 [1892–1899], Drafts G and N), noted by Strachey (1957b) in his introduction to "Mourning and Melancholia", references to such issues are few and far between in the first fifteen years of Freud's psychoanalytic trajectory. During this period, his primary preoccupations were with the taxonomy of the transference neuroses and the importance of sex and sexuality to their aetiology.

There was, of course, a strong clinical focus and a preponderance of case histories in Freud's early oeuvre, set going by *Studies on Hysteria* (1895d). By 1910, Freud had already published three of his five major case histories, exemplifying each of the neuroses in turn: conversion hysteria ("Dora", 1905e), anxiety hysteria ("Little Hans", 1909b), and obsessional neurosis ("Rat Man", 1909d). A fourth case history, focusing on psychosis or schizophrenia, emerged shortly after ("Schreber", 1911c), but it served rather more as a counterexample. This was, after all, the case that was not a case, in the sense that Freud did not clinically analyse the man himself but produced instead a psycho-literary reading or analysis of his autobiography. Publishing such a text also indicated that while psychoanalysis might have the wherewithal to understand these more serious—and less transferential—ailments, it did not regard them as treatable by its methods. Even the major theoretical works of this early period—*The Interpretation of Dreams* (1900a) and *Three Essays on the Theory of Sexuality* (1905d)—can be read as accompanying Freud's aims and ambition of establishing specifically, if not quite exclusively, the psychoanalytic treatment model for the psychoneurotic illnesses.

In the second decade of the century, Freud's clinical zeal began to wane, and something different—a theoretical turn—came progressively to dominate his preoccupations. The change was not abrupt: Freud spent some time during the early years of the new decade writing and compiling the clinically focused "Papers on Technique". Significantly, his four-year analysis of the Wolf Man also took place during this same period before the First World War. One can easily forget when this analysis had taken place because, having quickly written it up in 1914, Freud only published this last of his major case histories several years later (1918b). On a recent rereading for the occasion of teaching the case, I was struck anew by how anxious a text it is, as exemplified by Freud's perhaps over-zealous arguments and interpretations, the urgency with which he elaborates his complex libidinal themes and time frames (regarding sexual aetiology, the relevance of the psychosexual stages, and the primal scene in particular). There is the sense that he was cramming virtually all his psychoanalytic experience and knowledge into the case, not least by seeming to find elements of all three psychoneuroses in this unfortunate patient's pathological state.

Aside from Freud's well-known need to defend himself vigorously at the time against the apostasy of Jung and Adler, might these signs be read as an indication that Freud was, in any case, approaching a kind of crossroads in his career, a change of focus? Was Freud pulling out all the stops and packing so much into this case history as a kind of farewell to his absolute commitment to earlier clinical convictions and theoretical beliefs? These are big questions that perhaps cannot be properly explored, let alone answered, here.

The theoretical tone of the new period had in any case already been set and heralded by the brief but metapsychologically crucial "Formulations on the Two Principles of Mental Functioning" (1911b). Freud's interest in the clinical facts and effects of narcissism—first in *Leonardo da Vinci and a Memory of His Childhood* (1910c) and later more systematically in "On Narcissism: An Introduction" (1914c) itself—played a major role in characterizing this new era. Freud's more theoretical shift was firmly consolidated during the traumatic years of the war, when his clinical work all but dried up and he had time on his hands for more abstruse endeavours. The culmination of these developments was the important series of texts that came collectively to be called the "Papers on Metapsychology". The last of these, "Mourning and Melancholia" (1917e), would in time gain a reputation as one of Freud's most central and seminal texts.

Viewed from the perspective of this general historical development, however, Freud appears to plunge quite sharply and suddenly—both clinically and theoretically—into the themes of this paper, producing the effect that it burst onto the scene rather unexpectedly. The other papers in the series are about such familiar topics as the instincts, repression, the unconscious, and dreams. Strachey (1957a, p. 106) tells us, moreover, that five of the seven "missing" metapsychological papers that Freud infamously—and perhaps impulsively—destroyed were on "Consciousness, Anxiety, Conversion Hysteria, Obsessional Neurosis and the Transference Neuroses in General", with the two remaining ones likely to have been on "Sublimation and Projection (or Paranoia)".

In other words, virtually all the other metapsychological papers were on frequently discussed topics that had been prominent in Freud's thinking from the beginning of the psychoanalytic enterprise. With hindsight, it might therefore appear curious that he should decide to include an account of depression and loss among these papers, given the apparent rarity and relative absence of his interest in those matters up to that point.

On the other hand, to take the view that mourning and melancholia were entirely unexpected or anomalous issues for Freud, somehow not in keeping with the rest of his work, would be the consequence of not attending closely enough to the path of his intellectual evolution. Strachey and many later commentators seem mainly to accommodate and explain the advent of "Mourning and Melancholia" by remarking on the significance of "On Narcissism" (Freud, 1914c)—and I will also be tracing the connections between these two texts. (We might also wonder, in passing, why *that* paper—also on the relatively new psychoanalytic concept of narcissism—was *not* included in his metapsychological series.) There is evidently considerable puzzlement and even mystery surrounding these matters—and not only in relation to why Freud destroyed those other, no doubt invaluable, papers. What comes into focus, however, are other, sometimes less noticed contexts and backdrops for the appearance of "Mourning and Melancholia", which I outline here.

Mourning an original crime

There exists, in my view, an occupational hazard in the teaching of Freud on psychoanalytic training programmes: it is a tendency to leave out and neglect—in the interests of having a more easily managed, clinically relevant, and thus reduced version of Freud at one's disposal—what some would regard as his more wayward interests and less central writings. A recent decision to buck that trend and to re-read and include *Totem and Taboo* (1912–13) in a comprehensive year-long Freud course that I teach regularly, reminded me that Strachey does in fact mention the precursory importance of that text to "Mourning and Melancholia", particularly in relation to "the whole question of the nature of identification" (1957b, p. 241), a central concept in both texts. One rediscovers in the reading how crucial the issue of mourning is to *Totem and Taboo*, especially in the climactic final pages, where Freud clinches his carefully constructed case about the original murder and ingestion of the primal father by his horde of frustrated sons. This surely helps to establish and to crystallize why the topics of both mourning and internalization were on Freud's mind in the period just prior to "Mourning and Melancholia".

It is highly likely that Freud's foray into the anthropological ur-myths and collective or phylogenetic mental possessions of humankind that are the preoccupations of *Totem and Taboo* were stimulated by his short-lived "romance" with Jung, then at its height. However, the nature of his engagement with these materials remained true to his own approach, not least to the recognition that conflict and ambivalence lie at the heart of the matter. In the slow build-up to the revelation of his own myth of origins, Freud constructs elaborate arguments—based on his own clinical cases and those of Ferenczi, in which animals feature prominently—to the effect that, in their ancient totemic roles, these wild as well as domestic fellow creatures were already transference figures—substitutes for ancestors or parents, particularly fathers.

He also becomes especially interested in the importance of totem meals: the killing and eating of the sacred totem animal is itself taboo at all other times, but on special festival occasions these actions are not only permitted, but required. Moreover, says Freud, "When the deed is done, the slaughtered animal is lamented and bewailed. The mourning is obligatory, imposed by dread of a threatened retribution." He then asks: "What are we to make, though, of the prelude to this festive joy—the mourning over the death of the animal?" If the members of the tribe or clan "rejoice over the killing of the totem . . ., why do they mourn over it as well?" The answer seems precisely to turn on the complex issues of identity and identification: "the clansmen acquire sanctity by consuming the totem: they reinforce their identification with it and with one another". Their subsequent joy "might well be explained by the fact that they have taken into themselves the sacred life of which the substance of the totem is the vehicle".

It is shortly hereafter that Freud first reveals, in a footnote, what he calls the "hypothesis, which has such a monstrous air", about the ousted sons who together manage to overthrow their thwarting father, thus sealing their fraternal bond:

> Cannibal savages as they were, it goes without saying that they devoured their victim as well as killing him. The violent primal father had doubtless been the feared and envied model of each one of the company of brothers: and in the act of devouring him they accomplished their identification with him, and each one of them acquired a portion of his strength. The totem meal, which is perhaps mankind's earliest festival, would thus be a repetition and a commemoration of this memorable and criminal deed, which was the beginning of so many things—of social organization, of moral restrictions and of religion. [1912–13, pp. 140–142]

After his painstaking, many-pages-long attempt to master and digest an entire anthropological field pertinent to his subject, Freud's thinking and writing ascends to a glorious, and frankly manic, crescendo. When he puts on these seven-league boots and gets into his stride, he traverses huge expanses of cultural and intellectual territory—and in an extremely compelling manner, at that.

So utterly convinced is he of the verities of this ur-myth of the unconscious and its phylogenetic relevance for the development of the human psyche, that he wields it as a powerful, all-purpose intellectual weapon, using it to account for some of humanity's most significant and sacrosanct historical and cultural possessions. Leaning heavily on ideas about the inevitable return of even the earliest repressed events and urges, his analysis rampages through comparative religion, outlining how pagan beliefs, with their animistic totems and precariously held taboos, give way to the only apparently more sophisticated monotheistic faiths—first of the Judaic father, then of the Christian son—which nevertheless retain visible remnants of their incestuous, murderous, and guilty origins.

The trajectory of Greek tragic drama—even as it builds its *dramatis personae* gradually, one actor at a time, to arrive at its eventual tripartite or oedipal form—is also reinterpreted in terms of the structuring dialogical tension between the hero-as-father and the filial chorus. For Freud, this is in effect yet another creative, but also circularly repetitive, re-scripting of an original tale of ancient tyranny, primordial envy, and parricide, followed forever by waves of irrepressible remorse, regret, and revenge. As he goes on to suggest, the endless reiteration evident at the heart of these phylogenetic cultural phenomena seems to manifest, on the grandest scale, not a grieving process brought to a successful, reconciled conclusion but, rather, humanity's melancholic failure to mourn deeply enough to learn from previous sins or crimes.

Totem and Taboo perhaps suffered the twin fates not only of being largely eschewed by clinical psychoanalysis, but also of being intellectually side-lined, discredited as unscientific and fanciful on anthropological and evolutionary grounds, not least for its Lamarckian assumptions about heritability. These critiques are themselves now subject to biological dispute, but I have no intention of contending with them, nor can I discuss what has been called Freud's "phylogenetic fantasy" in any greater detail here. However, I am interested in the intellectual journey that brought him to the topics at hand. In Freud's phantasmatic excursion into this adjacent but unfamiliar field, we have happily discovered him converting the actualities of ingestion and incorporation into the psychic tropes of identification and internalization. He discusses in the process, and on the largest scale, humanity's ongoing psychic need to mourn and come to terms with the perpetration of primordial acts of violence that may lie at the source of our most fundamental, originating, pre-personal losses.

Narcissistic pre-emptions

Most readers of Freud are far readier to regard Freud's foray into the intricacies of narcissism as a proper and legitimate "prequel" to "Mourning and Melancholia". Preceding the latter by just a year, "On Narcissism: An Introduction" (1914c) provides the axis of—and access to—the kind of internal world that I am investigating here. This three-part paper is replete with various explorations of narcissistic structure and functioning, which remain compelling and fascinating to this day. They include the crucial recognition that it is the narcissistic withdrawal of libidinal cathexis away from objects that is central to psychotic functioning and renders such patients relatively immune to psychoanalytic intervention. It is also where Freud introduces an inner landscape, featuring an active "ego ideal", and begins to consider the internal relations between the different parts of the mind that he will later term "agencies".

Freud makes his fullest characterization here of the libido as a kind of energy or "quantity" with a certain "investment" potential. Subject to "cathexis" and "allocation", it is therefore a force that can be directed towards objects as well as withdrawn from them, back upon the ego where it originates, serving as "the libidinal complement to the instinct of self-preservation" (1914c, pp. 73–74). In his deliberations, Freud suggests that the state of the ego at any given moment is crucially determined by the distribution of libido, by way of its virtually "hydraulic" action. The ego is depleted of self-worth if the ego libido is in low supply relative to object libido—for example, when one is in love, a dangerous state as far as one's narcissistic supplies are concerned. Alternatively, it can be possessed of an ample store of self-love or self-esteem when the balance tips in the other direction, though here too, excess is dangerous and may render the ego isolated, unable to love others, and dangerously out of touch with reality. He later makes it clear that the libido, whether in its object-oriented or self-directed guise, can over-accumulate or become dammed up, and that both conditions create pathological effects—neurotic and psychotic, respectively.

Further along, at the beginning of the second part of the paper, Freud predicts that psychotic illnesses "will give us an insight into the psychology of the ego" (p. 82). Indeed, this new concept of narcissism, and the attendant idea that there might be all manner of psychic activity going on, even in a mind that has apparently withdrawn interest or cathexis from the outside world, necessarily suggests a busy, active internal world. When Freud tries to tell us why patients suffering from narcissistic ailments might not be treatable psychoanalytically, he does so in terms of what is happening "on the inside" of such patients. A neurotic patient may have "given up his relation to reality"—or to real objects in external reality—but we discover in analysis that "he has by no means broken off his erotic relations to people and things. He still retains them in phantasy." By contrast, the psychotic (or "paraphrenic") patient "seems really to have withdrawn his libido from people and things in the external world, without replacing them by others in phantasy" (p. 74).

The significance of this difference will be of immeasurable importance for psychoanalysis. What exactly it means to retain an object "in phantasy" is of interest when we examine, in chapter four, the work of Melanie Klein, especially in relation to her idea of there being internal equivalents in the mind to the external objects of the outside world. What Freud seems to be saying, in the meantime, is that there is a form of withdrawal from—or loss of—an object in external reality that may *not* result in, or be accompanied by, an internalized or phantasy form of such an object. The blankness of psychosis—as André Green would put it—may be due precisely to its attempt to bring about a complete retreat from reality, its wish to escape troubling objects in all their incarnations. It is thus a wish to return to an imagined state of pure, utter objectless-ness. As Freud says, "This leads us to look upon the narcissism which arises through the drawing in of object-cathexes as a secondary one, superimposed upon a primary narcissism" (p. 75).

Freud engages in some complex and ambitious taxonomic speculations in this text about the various psychotic and neurotic ailments and how they might be categorized in relation to the quantities of libido that accumulate in either the ego or the object. (The important question of where melancholia fits into this taxonomy is addressed only in later texts, after this ailment has been introduced and its characteristics adumbrated.) There are also some entertaining, if contentious, opinions about creatures who, in Freud's estimation, tend to be more narcissistic (cats, children, and women), *vis-à-vis* their more object-related counterparts (presumably, dogs, adults, and men)!

A person's object choice, which can be either "anaclitic" or narcissistic, is seen to be based upon where he or she is placed on the continuum between these two poles, and this can, in turn, influence—if not determine—the gender of one's sexual partner. Freud seems almost to imply that the most stable kind of relationship—if not the most egalitarian—is that between a narcissistically self-loving person and an anaclitic other whose overvaluing "other-love" is devoted in equal measure to the former. On the other hand, even the most object-seeking individual may find some lost narcissism miraculously restored to them via their intimate associations with more narcissistic beings, especially children, on whose behalf or for whose sake all manner of crimes and misdemeanours might be tolerated: "Parental love, which is so moving and at bottom so childish, is nothing but the parents' narcissism born again, which, transformed into object love, unmistakably reveals its former nature" (p. 91). What is perhaps most interesting, even startling, for my purposes, is the fact that Freud does not use the concept of identification to describe these relations—indeed, the actual term does not appear in the text at all.

It is the third part of "On Narcissism" that is perhaps of greatest interest to us, because it is there that Freud begins to elaborate upon the human capacity to internalize, to take something into the psyche, in such a way that an entity of sorts becomes established within. It is this "something" that Freud will eventually name the superego. After Freud tries to dispense with several of Adler's ideas at the beginning of this section, he asks a vital question about what happens to the ego-libido of the normal adult, supposing that it is not possible "that the whole of it has passed into object-cathexes". Connecting, for the first time, his new thesis of narcissism with a considerably refined version of the theory of repression, he speaks of how "the subject's cultural and ethical ideas", those that motivate repression, are never experienced in merely intellectual fashion. On the contrary, the subject "recognizes them as a standard for himself and submits to the claims they make on him". Repression, Freud goes on to say more precisely, "proceeds from the self-respect of the ego" (p. 93). This is tantamount to the ego establishing an ideal for itself, something against which it is to be measured, and which will therefore bring the censoring part of the ego, or conscience, into play. Thus, the ego-ideal simultaneously makes repression possible and—in the form of an internal object of sorts—serves as a substitute or compensation for the lost narcissism of childhood.

Typically, Freud's metapsychological mind pauses to make subtle distinctions between idealization and sublimation (the former being a vicissitude of the object of the drive, whereas the latter has to do with its aim), but he then goes on to say yet more about this "special psychical agency which performs the task of seeing that narcissistic satisfaction from the ego ideal is ensured" (p. 95), by keeping a careful watch over the ego and measuring it according to an ideal standard. He does not have to invent or discover such an agency, because it is readily recognized by us, bearing the name "conscience". Freud then discusses the self-watching, potentially persecutory activities of this internal phenomenon—its connections with paranoia—as well as our tendencies to object to and rebel against its strictures, to project and re-externalize these, rather than accept the admonitions coming from within.

As we shall see, by the time Freud writes *The Ego and the Id* (1923b), it is to a more complex and composite internal entity—made up of the ego ideal itself plus this more conscientious, moral(istic), judging part—that he will give the name, "super-ego", the agency that admonishes not only our actions but our wishes, too. Though the last pages of "On Narcissism" are replete with intriguingly related variations and corollaries, as Strachey (1957c) says, it is "over-compressed . . . its framework bursting from the quantity of material it contains" (p. 70), so perhaps it is best to take leave of it now and proceed directly to its successor and sequel.

The mysteries of melancholia

Many consider "Mourning and Melancholia" (1917e) to be one of Freud's finest papers. It is elegantly written and pleasing in its form; it succeeds, in my view, because it is structured primarily by an intriguing and ground-breaking argument that he pursues with careful precision through the text. One can, I believe, claim this without necessarily disagreeing with Thomas Ogden's brilliant reading of the paper, where he rightly notes that Freud is one of those authors who "think what they write" (rather than vice versa)—that is, he discovers what he thinks in the process of writing and does not disguise his "false starts, his uncertainties, his reversals of thinking", even his "shelving of compelling ideas" when he has insufficient clinical evidence to back them up (2012, p. 11). Ogden's view may prevail without contradicting the fact that a powerful line of thinking runs through the paper, giving it a complex coherence. Here I first try to follow the fundamental organizing logic of the text—that is, Freud's attempts to account in turn for both melancholia and mania—before going back over it for a second time, advancing my own "take" on it and thereby establishing the thesis and setting the tone for the rest of the book.

"Mourning and Melancholia" was the last published of Freud's five surviving "Papers on Metapsychology". With a glance back at the previous paper, in which he revisits dreams (1917d), Freud begins by saying that he "will now try to throw some light on the nature of melancholia by comparing it with the normal affect of mourning". He immediately warns that any conclusions he might reach will be tentative in the extreme and will lay no claim to "general validity". He alerts his readers to the fact that melancholia is both a fluctuating, ununified diagnosis within psychiatry and one that seems to point to "somatic" as well as "psychogenic" causation (an early version of the contemporary psychiatric distinction between "endogenous" and "reactive" forms of depression). He does, however, claim to know enough about the so-called normal condition of mourning—stating, indeed, that mourning is something we all know about and accept as a painful but necessary part of ordinary life—to be able to use it as the basis for an understanding of the more disturbed condition of melancholia.

Aside from noting that this seems to reverse Freud's usual practice of extrapolating from psychopathology to the normal functioning of the mind, it is worth pausing to wonder how and why Freud came to consider these two states of mind as comparable and contrastable in the first place. Was he unique in noticing their commensurability so astutely? Of course, as Freud famously acknowledged and as this book attests, poets and writers had previously arrived at or approximated such truths or insights, but perhaps no other scientist of the mind had synthesized these in such a clearly stated and coherent way before. Freud does not explain his juxtaposition at any length, saying only that their "correlation ... seems justified by the general picture of the two conditions". He then declares that what links them is the key issue of *loss*. Whether it is "the loss of a loved person" due to death, or of "some abstraction... such as one's country, liberty, an ideal" (1917e, p. 243), Freud is evidently convinced that what both joins and separates mourning and melancholia is the fact that they constitute different ways of dealing with loss.

I often ask students of this text, especially if they are already working as clinicians, whether they think that melancholia—or depression—is invariably about, or caused by, loss. If Freud himself readily grants that these are not always "psychogenic affections" or due to what he also refers to as "environmental influences", might we also have to be hesitant about tying all depressive states to the losses, traumas, and other tribulations that people suffer, whether literal, symbolic, or phantasmatic? Perhaps we do need to be cautious in this respect; and yet for a psychoanalyst it is compelling to think that we may be able to make distinctions—existentially, clinically, and even diagnostically—between successful and unsuccessful negotiations of loss, given that as humans we are always having to negotiate losses of one kind or another, from the very moment of birth onward, if not sooner. Is there ever a patient who walks into a consulting room for whom loss of some kind is not an issue, if not *the* issue?

Freud proceeds, in orderly fashion, to outline the symptomatic similarities and differences between mourning and melancholia. He says that the two conditions have several features in common—namely, "a profoundly painful dejection, cessation of interest in the outside world, loss of the capacity to love, inhibition of all activity". The sufferings of both the mourner and the melancholic are typified by these experiences of emotional pain, existential indifference, and psychic inertia.

However, there is one feature of melancholia that seems absent from mourning, and Freud describes it, in language both precise and elegant, as "a lowering of the self-regarding feelings to a degree that finds utterance in self-reproaches and self-revilings, and culminates in a delusional expectation of punishment". Freud does not elaborate any further on this crucially distinguishing, shibboleth-like state of mind at this point in the text, though he will be returning to it later. He speaks instead of the painstaking nature of a proper process of mourning, emphasizing how much hard work it requires. No sooner has he done so, however, than he finds himself telling us why mourning falters or fails, reminding us that even when reality confronts them with an undeniable loss and even if a substitute object is ready to hand, "people never willingly abandon a libidinal position". Indeed, such opposition to the dictates of reality testing can sometimes take an extreme form, "a clinging to the object through the medium of a hallucinatory wishful psychosis" (p. 244).

This might be the moment at which to return to "A Rose for Emily" by William Faulkner (1930). The eponymous character's "clinging" to a lost object features twice in the story, once after her father dies, when she refuses to allow the removal of his body, and again when she contrives to keep—and continues to sleep with—the body of her murdered lover in their marriage bed. The two events are, of course, intimately linked by the strong presence of an incestuous oedipal constellation. A Southern belle like Miss Emily, even when fallen from grace along with the rest of the Confederate aristocracy after the American Civil War, must remain a girl whose father no other man can compete with or match.

A screen-memory image diligently reinforces and frames this situation:

> We had long thought of them as a tableau, Miss Emily a slender figure in the background, her father a spraddled silhouette, his back to her and clutching a horsewhip, the two of them framed by the back-flung front door. [1930, p. 123]

The revenge that Emily later takes upon this life-thwarting father is over-determined, inevitable, and ambivalent. On the one hand, she defies him, albeit after his death, by "stepping out" with Homer Barron—a wholly unsuitable working-class Northerner—and then even marrying him. On the other hand, lest he desert her (as her father had done—if only by dying), and as a way of keeping faith with her father's standards and prohibitions, Homer can be allowed neither to leave nor to live. It would be difficult to imagine a better—or more horrifying—exemplification of the denial of loss by what Freud calls "a hallucinatory wishful psychosis", than this fictional account of Miss Emily's hanging on endlessly to her object, for dear life and beyond death.

Returning to "Mourning and Melancholia", Freud now embarks on a vivid description of the painstaking work of detachment that is required in a successful mourning process. Similarly to the way that Freud and Breuer's original cathartic method was supposed to free the hysteric from her symptoms one by one, so must the ego eventually free itself from the clutches of the lost object: "Each single one of the memories and expectations in which the libido is bound to the object is brought up and hyper-cathected" before its grip on the ego can be loosened or prised off—one finger at a time, as it were. This is a "psychically prolonged" process, and Freud admits here that he is frankly puzzled by the fact it should be so very lengthy and painful—it does not seem to make sense in terms of the psychic economics of the situation and his assumptions about humans as pleasure-seeking (and pain-averse) creatures. We see here that Freud is in fact quite perplexed by certain features of mourning itself, let alone those of melancholia. In my view—and in keeping with Ogden's—it was Freud's capacity to be wrong, to expose himself creatively to his own puzzlement, to question what he did not know, that allows the paper to rise to levels of greatness and to result in a lasting and fundamental contribution to the understanding of human responses to loss.

Having tried thus to account for the work of mourning, Freud goes on to wonder whether there is a similar—or different—kind of work that goes on in melancholia. When he considers how depressed or melancholic people deal with loss, there tends to be even less clarity, more confusion. Firstly, the loss suffered may be of a somewhat different order, for example, that of a jilting or betraying object—as in the case of Miss Emily or, indeed, Miss Havisham in Dickens's *Great Expectations* (1860), abandoned on her wedding day; or, even if there has been an actual death, it is not quite clear either what it is about the object that has been lost or where the loss inheres or resides. This provides a first hint of the fact that in melancholia, the experience of the loss is happening elsewhere, beyond consciousness or at unconscious levels, with the consequence that even if work of some kind—analogous to that of mourning—is going on somewhere, it is difficult to get a sense of how it is proceeding (p. 245).

Now Freud describes again the main symptom that differentiates the melancholic from the mourner, namely, the abject state of the former—the "diminution in his self-regard", the "impoverishment" of his ego—and goes on to link this with something quite typical of the depressed person, namely, an anorexic "refusal to take nourishment". He also reminds us that such forms of self-abasement and self-deprivation—the depletion not only of physic nourishment, but of the stores of self-esteem—can lead on to acts of self-harm and even, ultimately, to suicide. These are dangers to which he had already alluded in his paper on narcissism, and he will be returning to these in due course, to describe precisely how—or by dint of what metapsychological means—such eventualities might ensue. What Freud does say at this point, without going into detail, is that whereas losing the object impoverishes the mourner's world, for the melancholic, it is the ego or self that is rendered poor and empty.

The next step in Freud's account of the dynamics of melancholia is nothing short of brilliant. He says, counterintuitively, that in a sense the melancholic is quite right to demean himself in this way. Indeed, it is perhaps only a depressive sensibility that can perceive so truly, and experience so personally, the human capacity for pettiness, egoism, dishonesty, and the myriad other self-serving sins of which humans are capable and culpable. In a footnote, Freud cites *Hamlet*—aptly enough, given that Freud's criteria would surely identify this Shakespearean character as the quintessential haunted melancholic—on how nobody would escape a whipping were they to be accorded the treatment they justly deserve.

However, as Freud then astutely observes, the accuracy of such self-accusations is beside the point; their truth notwithstanding, most narcissistically self-protective—and thus "sane"—people cannot afford to think such ugly thoughts about themselves. Anyone as self-tormenting, as persuaded of his own wretchedness as this, must be considered ill, virtually by definition. Freud goes on to remark, ironically, that the more conscientious a person is, the more likely he or she is to be self-demeaning in this fashion—far more so than someone less worthy would be. Indeed, the impression given is not one of shame about this abased, denigrated state, but of a kind of masochistic pride in it. As Freud says, "there is the presence in him of an almost opposite trait of insistent communicativeness which finds satisfaction in self-exposure". In melancholia, Freud now repeats, the loss suffered is in relation not to an object—as in the case of mourning—but to the ego, or, more precisely, to the latter's "self-respect" (pp. 246–247).

These melancholic dynamics seem to provide Freud with an excellent segue to a new consideration of the role of "the agency commonly called 'conscience'", last discussed in the paper on narcissism, where the ego-ideal was introduced. In this version of the genesis of what will later become the superego, Freud again takes note of how a critical part of the ego splits off and can, as he puts it, "become diseased on its own account", presumably by way of an increase in its harsh, persecutory judgement of the remainder of the ego. Putting it succinctly, Freud says: "In melancholia, dissatisfaction with the ego on moral grounds is the most outstanding feature."

With this insight at the ready, Freud returns to his central argument and reveals the most pertinent clue in his quest to solve the mystery of the paradoxical nature of the melancholic's self-hatred: the depressive, it turns out, is covertly and unconsciously complaining not about himself, but about someone else. Here, says Freud, is "the key to the clinical picture: we perceive that the self-reproaches are reproaches against a loved object which have been shifted away from it and on to the patient's own ego". Although at some level there are angry accusations and quasi-litigious grievances being levelled against this significant but disappointing other, they have, "by a certain process, passed over into the crushed state of melancholia" (pp. 247–248).

This process, says Freud, is in fact not difficult to explain: he goes on to speak of the shattering of what had already been a brittle and fragile—albeit intense and adhesive—attachment of the melancholic to the object in question. In a typically self-protective, narcissistic move, the patient disinvests precious libido from this wounding object, bringing it back into the ego. Crucially in this instance, however, the ego-libido does not merely return unaccompanied, so to speak: the aim in this situation, it appears, is not just a temporary withdrawal from both the lost object and the world, with the eventual intention of re-attaching the libidinal investment to a different object at some later moment (as might be expected in mourning), but "to establish an identification of the ego with the abandoned object". The famous and enigmatic phrase follows: "Thus the shadow of the object fell upon the ego", Freud's pithy metaphorical attempt to render what happens when the loss of a relationship with an object gives way to, and is replaced by, an identification with it. He adds: "In this way an object-loss was transformed into an ego-loss and the conflict between the ego and the loved person into a cleavage between the critical activity of the ego and the ego as altered by identification" (p. 249).

Thus, the attempt to understand the nature of melancholia seems to have led Freud to this important concept of identification, one that will grow in significance and prove crucial and essential to the unfolding of Freud's thinking and to psychoanalytic theorizing at large. It must be remembered, however, that hitherto he had made only limited use of this term and given it little conceptual attention. Significantly, however, it is in "Instincts and Their Vicissitudes" (1915c, pp. 129, 132)—the first of his metapsychological papers—that the term begins to feature more prominently. There Freud revisits some important implications of narcissism as he adumbrates these vicissitudes, such defensive features of instincts as their capacity to reverse their aim and change their object.

It is interesting that when he is concerned, later in that text, to explain the complexities of love or, rather, *loving* and its various opposites (indifference, hating, and being loved), he also resorts briefly to the cognates of identification—incorporation and introjection—as well as to the equal-and-opposite mechanism of projection. Using the register of orality, Freud is here trying to account for the very primary, concrete manner whereby we try to bring and keep close what is loved—to the point of taking it in and having it inside ourselves—while distancing ourselves from or expelling unwanted objects. It is noteworthy that Freud uses the term "introjection" for the very first time in "Instincts and Their Vicissitudes" (p. 136) and justly credits Ferenczi with its coinage. I examine Ferenczi's contributions to these developments in chapter three.

One struggles to see how Freud had previously managed without recourse to these internalizing terms and might feel that they were a long time coming. However, it is perhaps also obvious enough, with hindsight, why such concepts as identification and internalization, as well as introjection and incorporation, were not initially as central to Freud as they would later become. Even if these terms began to be more familiar during the war years, when Freud drew his ideas together in this series of metapsychological papers, they would not come fully into their own until the vicissitudes of object relations—and thus the need for a more detailed, elaborated account of an internal world—became a prominent feature of Freud's theorizing.

Furthermore, one also realizes—perhaps with something of a retrospective shock—that in "Mourning and Melancholia" Freud is not yet saying that *all* loss requires or is accompanied by some such process of internalization or identification. At this point in time, it is not mourning but only melancholia, with its failure to process losses externally and realistically, that seems to call for an internal(izing) solution to—or compensation for—its struggle with the loss of the object. In melancholia, therefore, the afflicted ego—with the tainting penumbra of the ambivalently loved object shading it—can now permit itself to be roundly criticized and bullied by the special agency that Freud is still at this stage referring to as conscience, later to be known as the superego.

Turning now to other features of his theory of narcissism, Freud explains the processes at work in cases where there is "a strong fixation to the love object", but where "the object-cathexis has little power of resistance". The evidence suggests that, for such a person, the choice of an object has been made not on an anaclitic, but on a narcissistic basis. If an object is chosen on these grounds and if loss and disappointment subsequently ensue, the way is clear for a regression to narcissism proper and what can now be called a "narcissistic identification with the object". Instead of acknowledging—and experiencing—the actual loss of the object, the subject replaces an erotic bond with a narcissistic joining or identification, with the result that, "in spite of the conflict with the loved person the love-relation need not be given up". Here Freud refers us to his claim that, in its earliest forms, "identification is a preliminary stage of object-choice" and reminds us of the ambivalent nature of what happens in the "oral or cannibalistic" libidinal phase, where the only way to love or identify with an object is via an incorporative devouring of it. Thus, what a regression to this stage enables the melancholic to do, at least in fantasy, is to maintain a finely poised love–hate connection with the eaten-up object, whereby it is simultaneously both kept and killed.

Freud again mentions the depressive symptom of refusing nourishment, which is clearly relevant to this oral context, citing his colleague, Karl Abraham, who was the first to speak of the cannibalistic aspects of the oral phase and to write about the connection between melancholia and anorexia. As we shall see later, Abraham has a great deal to contribute to these deliberations about melancholia and manic-depressive illness. Freud's own clinical experience with melancholic patients is, as he readily admits, not extensive, and therefore the empirical basis of his deliberations is limited. Though he now tries, in successive paragraphs, to establish links and distinctions between melancholia and the transference neuroses that he knows more about, perhaps we need not dwell here on these sections of the text.

The central argument of "Mourning and Melancholia" has by now become clear enough. Freud summarizes it at this juncture by specifying that the dynamics of melancholia lie somewhere between mourning and narcissism, partaking partially of each. He then usefully proceeds to describe, at greater length, the extent and ingenuity of the hateful, hostile, vengeful attacks that can be perpetrated upon the object by the melancholic—but secretly, as it were, without these feelings ever being openly expressed. Beneath the disguise of a self-satisfied form of self-hatred, an internalized sadomasochistic dynamic operates between the critical conscience and the part of the ego under the shadow of the object. As Freud puts it, "the hate comes into operation on this substitutive object, abusing it, debasing it, making it suffer and deriving sadistic satisfaction from its suffering".

He goes on to spell out how the melancholic might takes things yet further: he might end up committing suicide by attempting to kill the object that has taken up residence inside him. In Freud's own words: "The analysis of melancholia now shows that the ego can kill itself only if, owing to the return of the object cathexis, it can treat itself as an object." In the long run, however, the object itself emerges victorious: "the object has, it is true, been got rid of, but it has nevertheless proved more powerful than the ego itself" (pp. 251–252). Freud reminds us that the only other circumstance in which such an abjection of the ego occurs with comparable intensity—when it is so overwhelmed by the object—is in the perhaps equal-and-opposite condition of being in love.

As one might already detect here, Freud is preparing to embark on an exploration of what is, for him, perhaps the most difficult feature of melancholia to grasp or understand: that of mania. Before doing so, however, he identifies several other problems with melancholia that he continues to ponder but that remain un(re)solved. Just how analogous is its trajectory to that of mourning? Does it come to an end in the same way or for the same sorts of reasons? Is there similar work being done in relation to reality testing in both cases? Resorting to a resonant image that he will return to again right at the end of the paper, he speaks of melancholia in terms of "an open wound" that draws a rush of "cathectic energies" or "anticathexes" to the site of the breach, "emptying the ego until it is totally impoverished", leaving it in a dangerously over-anxious state that can result, for example, in the well-known depressive symptom of insomnia.

Finally, and immediately before a break in the text that seems to forewarn the reader (by representing, perhaps, the large intake of breath needed to tackle the vexed issue of mania), Freud asks whether "a loss in the ego irrespectively of the object—a purely narcissistic blow to the ego—may not suffice to produce the picture of melancholia" (pp. 252–253). This seems like a rather odd query. Must there not always be an object involved at some stage of the proceedings, and has Freud not already said as much? Moreover, given that he has already established that melancholia is an at least partially narcissistic condition, is it not highly likely that the ego will experience any significant narcissistic blow in a melancholic manner? Its strangeness notwithstanding, the question prompts me to think that, for the sake of full understanding, we must treat the dynamics and problematics of loss no less broadly than Freud treats sexuality in the earlier part of his career. Only if loss is seen as an expanded, extensive, and ubiquitous phenomenon will we be able to examine our different methods of dealing with it thoroughly and properly, as the rest of this book will try to do.

The machinations of mania

Melancholia is a no-win situation, a disorder, one could say, where nobody is a winner and in which both subject and object lose and are lost. However, it is also a sure and insidious sign of a manic-depressive dynamic when the focus on winning and losing becomes too prominent in the clinical picture. We might introduce Freud's deliberations on mania by reiterating his own realization that in situations where a loss is not being mourned and in which a melancholic "solution" prevails, the manifest picture is not always that of a victorious object dominating an abject, abased, and apathetic ego. In the inter- and intra-personal conflict typifying depression, the embattled ego may discover a powerful desire—and at times an ability—to win the contest by avenging itself upon the tormenting object.

In the internal, identificatory, and persecutory dynamics of melancholia that Freud has already laid out, this is most evident in instances where the ego does not necessarily seek the final solution of suicide—that is, the ultimate demise or destruction of the object (and hence of the self). Perhaps, rather, it is in the vengeful nature of depressive sadism (or sadomasochism, more precisely) to spare the object, to keep it alive (or in that in-between state where it is neither alive nor dead) with the intention of continuing to punish it and witness its suffering—while the ego also goes on suffering unconsciously, of course.

The existence of an internal world entails that these dynamics can occur even once the object has already died—and we again need look no further than the eponymous Emily for an example of such an outcome. Though she will later end up killing Homer, her second "love" object, the townspeople reveal their astuteness about her condition far earlier, when she tries to prevent them from removing her father's dead body. They comment:

> We did not say she was crazy then. We believed she had to do that. We remembered all the young men her father had driven away, and we knew that with nothing left, she would have to cling to that which had robbed her, as people will. [Faulkner, 1930, p. 124]

This also makes sense of her subsequent necrophiliac need to keep a body in her bed, where the composite phantasmatic object that is made up of her lover and her father can be cherished and punished, simultaneously and eternally.

It is in such situations that one can witness the explicit retaliatory cruelty of the melancholically afflicted subject towards its object. At other times, perhaps just as cruelly, the subject affects a kind of indifference, and goes about its business pretending not to care at all about the object. These are just some of the equal-and-opposite mental states of mind typifying the counterpart of melancholia known as mania. One senses that Freud is rather tentative and even reluctant to proceed in the endeavour of clarifying this odd juxtaposition.

Clearly, he finds the manic change-around fascinating, calling it a "remarkable characteristic of melancholia", while noting that it is not a necessary or ubiquitous feature of depressive constellations. When it does appear, it is evidence for "the hypothesis of a circular insanity", that is, manic-depressive illness, or what is nowadays called bipolar affective disorder. Freud indicates in advance that he does not expect to be able to answer all the questions that this rather strange state poses, and he again openly expresses his puzzlement: what is this frequently but not inevitably present, obverse condition of melancholia all about?

In his initial attempt at an answer, Freud seems not to venture far beyond rather obvious and banal descriptive juxtapositions, to the effect that mania and depression are both intimately related and yet in stark contrast and opposition to one another. Indeed, he feels that he has not much to go upon, other than "a psycho-analytic impression" and "general economic experience". The former suggests (and here other unnamed "investigators" are credited) "that both disorders are wrestling with the same 'complex', but that probably in melancholia the ego has succumbed to the complex whereas in mania it has mastered it or pushed it aside".

The economic perspective allows him to see that the "joy, exultation or triumph" of mania are akin to any other sudden release and relief from a condition of abstemious self-control, from "some oppressive compulsion, some false position" suddenly shrugged off, producing states of mind characterized by "high spirits, by the signs of discharge of joyful emotion and by increased readiness for all kinds of action . . . in complete contrast to the depression and inhibition of melancholia". Asserting that "mania is nothing other than a triumph of this sort", Freud reminds us that, as with the losses of melancholia, "what the ego has surmounted and what it is triumphing over remain hidden from it" (pp. 253–254).

Summarizing these interim thoughts on mania, Freud says—again rather vaguely—that "the ego must have got over the loss of the object (or its mourning over the loss, or perhaps the object itself)"; there is a release of "the whole quota of anticathexis" that had been needed and utilized to bind the wounds of the melancholic phase, thus suddenly freeing the ego from its bond to the object. He is, however, dissatisfied and impatient with this account, saying that it poses more questions than it answers, and reiterates that he has little hope of understanding or clarifying these matters very much further. In my view, Freud runs into even more trouble when, reaching for too precise an analogy, he again makes a direct but futile appeal to the situation in "normal mourning". There too, he says, the loss of the object is finally overcome, having previously absorbed all the ego's energy—but why then, he asks, "is there no hint in its case of the economic condition for a phase of triumph" (p. 255)?

One only rarely sees Freud as baffled as he seems to be here. While this may not be the only reason why he is so flummoxed, one has a sense—particularly with the hindsight that Melanie Klein's later work on mania provides—that he does not fully appreciate the import of what is perhaps the most significant aspect of mania. One might wish to assume that Freud is well aware of the triumphant nature of mania: the word "triumph" certainly features prominently enough, and mania is even clearly referred to above as "a phase of triumph".

However, what Freud seems not quite to grasp—as Klein (1935, 1940) will do in the two memorable papers on manic-depressive conditions that we will later explore—is that mania's defensive triumph is in fact over the lost object itself. What Klein makes clear is that the very wish to vanquish and eclipse the object, to adopt a superior, omnipotent position in relation to it, is the most significant and addictive attraction of the manic state. It is important to bear in mind here that, at this point in his career, Freud had not yet discovered or come to appreciate the dark, destructive power of the death drive.

Returning to his quest for economic parallels, Freud conjectures that in mourning there is no extra energy left over for manic "expenditure" because the "work of severance is so slow and gradual" that the ego exhausts itself in dealing with and finally accepting "the verdict of reality" regarding the loss of the object. But he still resists the implication that melancholia might not have as much in common with mourning as his theory would prefer. Freud's insistence that comparable economic situations pertain in both is also predicated on the assumption that an object with too little significance for the ego would not require a prolonged and agonized leave-taking of any kind. What he may not yet be fully cognisant of, however, is the difference between a process of long duration—as in the relatively linear trajectory of mourning, where there is at least the possibility of an ending—and one that is structurally set up to be endless—that is, when manic-depressive circularity ensues.

The further complication with melancholia—what Freud calls "something more than mourning"—has to do with the ambivalence to which the melancholic ego is prone, either constitutionally or because of environmental circumstances in which "the threat of losing the object" featured prominently. This is also why the manifestation of melancholia often has causes other than the actual death of the object. Unlike in mourning, the "countless separate struggles" in melancholia are characterized by an evenly matched battle between love and hate, with the former trying to hold on libidinally to the object while the latter attempts to detach libido from it (pp. 255–256).

Continuing to claim that there is work being done in melancholia too, Freud reverts to a different metapsychological perspective and tries to account for these differences topographically. The work of melancholia may indeed be proceeding, albeit in the unconscious regions of the psyche, where it is the currency of things, rather than words, that pertains. Freud is appealing to an important distinction between "thing-" and "word-presentations", recently adumbrated in Section VII of his paper on "The Unconscious" (1915e).

In mourning, where the object is given up slowly, one aspect at a time, the situation is nevertheless eased and abetted by the capacity to represent loss in language. In melancholia, the object must be surrendered without this benefit, thus prolonging the process and, indeed, accounting for its excessive lamentation and monotony. While the work of mourning also happens—or at least begins—in the realms or at the level of thing-memory, the relative absence of ambivalence allows for a more normal bringing-to-consciousness, via the word-presentations provided by the preconscious system. As Freud says, "This path is blocked for the work of melancholia." Thus, the ambivalence of the melancholic relationship—where "traumatic experiences in connection with the object may have activated other repressed material"—is what keeps those dynamics "withdrawn from consciousness" and from the solace of putting things into words.

Freud claims that the "outcome characteristic of melancholia" sets in once the libidinal cathexis manages to abandon the object at last and draws back into the ego. He seems to indicate that it is only at this stage that we have melancholia proper, with its quality of potential endlessness. What he leaves implicit and neglects to repeat in this iteration of the story is the crucial fact that the libido is bringing back with it an unwelcome guest (or ghost), an internalized version of the object that sets in motion an identificatory colonization of a part of the ego. Though "love escapes extinction" in this manner, the internal persecution of that part of the ego by the "critical agency" of conscience can now proceed apace (pp. 256–257).

There may be a tacit assumption here that these proceedings can now occur at least somewhat more consciously, but one sees that Freud has yet to appreciate the extent to which even the most persecutory predations of this (proto-)superego can remain unconscious, inducing such strange but clinically proven possibilities as an unconscious sense of guilt, a phenomenon that he will elaborate upon more fully once the superego proper comes into being.

Soon enough, however, Freud does acknowledge that consciousness has little say in what happens in melancholia and therefore cannot really aid in ending its torment. The ego still "debases itself and rages against itself", and he seems not to understand very much about this predicament, why it is so, and how it will ever ease or cease. While he claims that "it is not difficult to perceive an essential analogy between the work of melancholia and of mourning", there is perhaps more hope than conviction here, as well as in the statement that there must be a precise equivalent to what happens when "mourning impels the ego to give up the object by declaring the object to be dead and offering the ego the inducement of continuing to live".

As unconscious and ambivalent as the struggles of melancholia are, Freud still insists that they must eventually yield a result comparable to that of mourning, releasing "the fixation of the libido to the object by disparaging it, denigrating it and even as it were killing it". He thinks the ego can explicitly or consciously "enjoy in this the satisfaction of knowing itself as the better of the two, as superior to the object" (p. 257). At the very least, this appears to bring Freud closer to seeing what Klein will see so much more clearly—namely, the ego's compelling need to triumph over the object.

The fact is, however, that Freud is still unhappy with his own two-minded speculations and their contribution, particularly, to the understanding of mania. Nearing the end of his text, he says that he had expected that the psychic economics of mania would be explained by the ambivalence dominating melancholia. He now adduces a comparative fact that might thwart such expectations: two of the three preconditions of melancholia (the loss of the object and ambivalence) are also to be found in "the obsessional self-reproaches arising after a death has occurred"; in other words, there can be ambivalence in at least some situations where an actual mourning process is underway. And yet, there is still no manic phase to be found after such instances of mourning, even when they appear to involve the persistent self-blame that can bespeak ambivalence.

Freud is thus compelled to concede that the main differentiating phenomenon in melancholia's relations with the lost object is not so much ambivalence as the "regression of libido into the ego", the narcissistic trapping or binding of libido which, when released or reversed, "becomes free and makes mania possible". Repeating this sentiment for a third time, Freud says that the "struggle over the object" characteristic of mourning, is replaced in melancholia by the "conflict within the ego". Freud also reiterates his earlier simile, saying that this is "like a painful wound", requiring significant anticathectic resources to cope with it.

But here, having brought pain back to mind, Freud—abruptly, virtually in mid-paragraph—brings proceedings to a close, saying, "it will be well to call a halt and to postpone any further explanation of mania until we have gained some insight into the economic nature, first, of physical pain, and then of the mental pain which is analogous to it". Unsatisfactory though this may be, he justifies his sudden ending by saying that "the interdependence of the complicated problems of the mind" (p. 258) forces such premature closures, postponing matters until the results of other inquiries might come along to rescue him from these vexed deliberations.

"It's alimentary, my dear Sigmund!"

It is my conviction that no exegetical treatment of a text is ever a merely disinterested attempt at elucidation for its own sake. It is now time to come clean with my own conception of the central feature underlying the dynamics of mourning and melancholia: as I see it, Freud's seminal paper is adumbrating and pointing the way, albeit only subliminally, to the analogy of mental or psychological digestion. That is, the issues it explores can be interpreted according to the model of a digestive or metabolic system, thus accounting for the fact that some people succeed, while others fail, to process their losses internally and psychically. Putting it simply, therefore, one might say that where so-called successful mourning requires a thoroughgoing capacity to work over or digest a loss, melancholia, mania, and other depressive conditions might usefully be understood as various forms of psychic *in*digestion.

Let it be clear that I am by no means suggesting that Freud had any such analogy or metaphor consciously in mind. Still, insofar as he explicitly saw the oral psycho-sexual stage as playing a significant part in the paper's concerns, it is easy enough to start by tethering my approach to these textual moments. I hope, however, to take things considerably further than that. I will try to develop my thesis by making my way back over "Mourning and Melancholia", pausing at certain passages where digestive or alimentary terms either make an actual appearance, or may be alluded to, and can be explicated accordingly.

It is when Freud starts to use the language of work to describe what happens in mourning that we get a first clue to the usefulness of digestive metaphors. The kind of work involved in mourning, Freud tells us, can only be done slowly, "bit by bit, at great expense of time and cathectic energy". As I suggested earlier, it is significant that Freud acknowledges a struggle to understand what it is about this process that makes it so prolonged and so difficult: "Why this compromise by which the command of reality is carried out piecemeal should be so extraordinarily painful is not at all easy to explain in terms of economics" (p. 245). Clearly, such difficulties do not sit well with Freud's tendency to see us as fundamentally hedonistic creatures, adherents of the pleasure principle.

Perhaps it might have been easier for him to comprehend the longevities of loss-work had the metaphor of a digestive process been more explicitly in his mind—though perhaps it is already hinted at, unconsciously or subliminally, in that word, "piecemeal". Of course, it is not Freud but his translator who has chosen this English word for its German equivalent, but nonetheless Strachey may himself have been tuned in to how useful a word it is, denoting a process that happens one grain at a time, while also hinting at the other meaning of "meal", namely, an aggregation of food items eaten together.

Freud's rigorous description of the process of mourning, and the ensuing theoretical frustrations, puts me associatively in mind of what parents say to children on the beach or at the pool, about not going into the water right after lunch because the meal is still being digested, making it dangerous to venture forth while that process (which takes so excruciatingly long) is underway. Similarly, Freud knows—even if not quite explicitly—that such digestive work is of vital importance and simply cannot be rushed or evaded. By contrast, it is the potential endlessness of the melancholic predicament, its circularity and stasis, that makes me doubt whether Freud is accurate or right in wishing to apply the idea of work to its proceedings, too: the implication for me is that—because of a dearth of digestive work—the melancholic may never get to go swimming again!

I would also suggest that, as Freud's descriptions of the self-immolating agonies of the melancholic are developed in these pages, we begin to get a picture of someone who is gnawing at himself, eating himself up in an anguished and self-torturing fashion—this in contrast with the mourner, the person who supposedly knows whom or what he has lost and thus actually has something *other* than himself to chew on! This might again be giving the impression of a rather macabre—and indeed distasteful—theory of depression, and I hasten to say that this is neither incidental nor gratuitous.

I would by no means be the first to suggest that the entire genre of horror in film and literature is informed—possessed, even—by the dynamics of melancholia and constitutes a creative attempt to come to terms with the difficult issues of loss and mourning. This is particularly true of zombies—the so-called "living dead"—for are these not, after all, concrete or literal embodiments of improperly buried, un-mourned, undigested melancholic objects who are no longer alive but refuse to die, and who rise from their graves to devour and feed off the living?

I think that Freud himself comes closer to an explicit acknowledgment of an oral-alimentary perspective on these issues when, while trying to explain the simultaneously terrible and "enjoyable" (that is, masochistic) self-accusations of the melancholic and their justification, he describes these as the effect of "the internal work which is *consuming* his ego" (p. 246, emphasis added). This comes shortly before Freud explicitly outlines the crucial difference between the mourner's "loss in regard to an object" as distinct from the depressive's "loss in regard to his ego". The predicament of depression affords us the following view of a division in the internal psychic landscape: "We see how in him one part of the ego sets itself over against the other, judges it critically, and, as it were, takes it as its object" (p. 247).

This, as we have seen, is an early formulation of the genesis of what Freud will later call the superego. The critical, judgmental part of the ego can behave very cruelly towards the other part, and this is nowhere to be seen more clearly than in people suffering from melancholia or depression. Thus, it is as if this bullying, moralistic conscience takes the other part of the ego as a denigrated object, with whom it has a kind of permanent and particularly bitter bone to pick. And this begins to make more sense when Freud provides the crucial insight that the excessive persecutory blame that the depressive appears to heap upon himself is in fact (also) directed at someone else with whom there is a powerfully ambivalent identification.

We recall that, in explaining this further, Freud needs to give an account of the process of identification, summed up in his famous phrase about the shadow of the object falling upon the ego. For, as soon as one part of the ego identifies with a lost object towards whom the subject experiences negative emotions and even hatred, the other persecutory and moralistic part can begin to feast. Again, I do not resort to this last word lightly. In the very next paragraph, while further explaining the mechanism of identification, Freud speaks of it as an early way of relating, "a preliminary stage of object-choice" by means of which "the ego picks out an object". He goes on to say that "the ego wants to incorporate this object into itself, and, in accordance with the oral or cannibalistic phase of libidinal development in which it is, it wants to do so by devouring it" (pp. 249–250).

Clearly, the literal acts of eating and ingesting—I would also add of digesting and metabolizing—are intimately involved in these earliest, most concrete forms of identification. So, when the ego picks out an object, it also picks *on* it, by taking ownership of it in bullying fashion, and even *at* it, as one might do with one's food. And, again, it is surely no accident that it is here that Freud goes on to cite his colleague and disciple, Karl Abraham, on the prominence of anorexia in melancholic patients who, one assumes, must be unconsciously aware of their cannibalistic inclinations and therefore horrified at the nature of their own appetites.

Though Freud goes on to suggest that there are different forms of identification, some more primitive or pathological than others, it must also be the case that every person who dies or is lost is subject to a modicum of negative feelings and therefore is inevitably taken in with at least some ambivalence. We might expect that even when the most beloved objects are lost, they must—just by dint of dying and thus abandoning the subject—come in for at least some of the treatment typically meted out in melancholia, prolonging the digestive, metabolic work of mourning. This might be seen to carry the implication that the two states of mourning and melancholia need not be wholly or diametrically opposed, but can be located as points on a continuum, and that the distinction between them is one of degree, rather than kind.

As this book goes on to show, there are interesting and useful distinctions to be made between theorists who prefer to think of these conditions as utterly separable and distinct, and those who see them as continuous and difficult to tell apart. Though Freud seems here to be focused, perhaps unwittingly, on their similarities and, as we have witnessed, often appeals to their analogical relations in his quest to understand them better, he is still primarily in the business of wanting to distinguish them as best he can, placing them on either side of a dividing line between the normal and the pathological.

While trying to account for mania (which might be regarded as the obverse of melancholia, as distinct from its opposite, namely, mourning), Freud ends up describing the essentially sadomasochistic nature of the manic-depressive ego's relations with its object. To put this in oral-digestive terms, the object—far from being digested slowly and metabolized "respectfully"—is first devoured savagely or just swallowed whole, then revived or regurgitated, only to be sadistically chewed up (or choked down) all over again. Freud says here that the "complex of melancholia behaves like an open wound" (p. 253), an image he returns to at the very end of the essay.

I may perhaps be accused not only of morbidity but also of stretching a point when I associate this image with that of a bloodied mouth. Again, though this may not be Freud's consciously intended idea, one may at least speculate that the melancholic condition invites such an image because of the predominance of primitive oral identification and the resulting undifferentiated enmeshment of subject and object. This enables the bipolar patient to pick or gnaw at himself via the object—and at the object via himself—in cruel, sadomasochistic fashion. And, once again, such perverse dynamics are what make it difficult for the wounds of mourning to heal.

Kleinian analysts, who would go further than Freud in recognizing the triumphalism inherent in mania, place great emphasis on projective mechanisms and highlight the destructive power of various forms of evacuation in psychic life. Abraham, one of Klein's analysts, was aware of the anal-sadistic as well as oral-cannibalistic fixation points of melancholia and provides the early source for this perspective. If we follow this tendency momentarily, alongside my guiding metaphor, we might ask the question: what form of psychic indigestion does mania exhibit?

Well, in oral-alimentary terms, the primary intent of mania might be thought of as a kind of psychic up-chuck—that is, a violently repudiating reaction to the problematic presence in the system of an indigestible object, heretofore lodged stubbornly inside the psychic alimentary tract of the melancholic. Mania effectively adopts the radical, phantasmatic, and concrete solution of vomiting the object up and out (evacuation can take place, after all, *per os* as well as *per anum*). After claiming that "in mania, the ego must have got over the loss of the object" (only temporarily, we might add, given the cyclical or bipolar nature of manic-depressive illness), Freud again corroborates the importance of the digestive tract when he describes the manic person as going forth to seek replacements for the expelled object "like a ravenously hungry man" (p. 255).

As we will recall, when Freud asks why it is that there is no equivalent to mania in the normal mourning process, he conjectures that the work of mourning is so painstaking and strength-sapping that there is simply no energy left at the end for manic flourish or frenzy. (We shall see in later chapters that both Karl Abraham and Maria Torok dispute this claim.) Again, one might put it slightly differently by saying that if the loss of the object is properly worked on, worked over, and worked through, its psychic digestion can be successfully completed without leaving an indigestible residue or remainder. What complicates matters for the depressed or bipolar patient, as Freud realized, is not only the degree of ambivalence towards the lost object, but the fact that the vicissitudes of the condition are played out largely unconsciously, "in the region of the memory trace of *things* (as contrasted with *word*-cathexes)" (pp. 256–257). The phantasmatic evacuative strategies of manic-depressive illness may thrive in the more corporeal, unconscious realm of things, but, ironically, they can gain no purchase, or traction, in the conscious or preconscious world of words or symbols.

In chapter six I explore how Nicolas Abraham and Maria Torok reinforce this distinction by emphasizing the differences between *incorporation* and *introjection*. Though both terms refer to the internalization of something or someone and are related to identification, incorporation is seen as the melancholic's all-too literal or concrete version, whereas introjection, by contrast, is the more metaphoric or symbolic form of internalization necessary for the proper process of mourning. The melancholic patient—having swallowed his object whole, as it were—treats it as if it were quite literally stuck in his craw or digestive tract, neither alive any longer nor yet fully dead. Alternatively, when in a manic phase the patient may behave as if this same object can be magically expelled or concretely evacuated by simply getting rid of it in a projective way—via one orifice or another. One realizes, in fact, that these are all literalistic phantasies that prevent any actual digestive transition from taking place, rather than pieces of what one might call real psychic work: as I have suggested, Freud, in his zeal to find something akin to work taking place in both mourning and melancholia, could not quite conceive of this significant difference.

So, contrary to Freud's interim and possibly premature conclusion that the "characteristic of detaching the libido bit by bit is, therefore, to be ascribed alike to mourning and melancholia" and "is probably supported by the same economic situation" (p. 256), one might instead surmise that the manic-melancholic way of dealing with loss is not merely a prolonged version of mourning. It is more than likely to partake of a kind of "eternal return", to become a viciously circular enterprise, precisely because of the reliance on concrete fantasies that take the devouring and/or expelling of the object literally, in a magical or even psychotic fashion.

Ogden tells us that the melancholic internal world "is powerfully shaped by the wish to hold captive the object in the form of the imaginary substitute for it—the ego-identified-with-the-object"; thus, "the internalisation of the object renders the object forever captive to the melancholic and at the same time renders the melancholic endlessly captive to it" (2012, p. 20). Such a situation, then, is bound to render impossible the more metaphorical, psychic digestive process of mourning, which, though it may take time, can happen, and does indeed *work*.

Contrastingly, when Freud goes on to describe how the melancholic ego finally rids itself of the ambivalently loved and hated object, the implication is that such an object must virtually, or almost literally, be (b)eaten to death! Hence, he adds: "It is possible for a process in the *Ucs.* to come to an end either after the fury has spent itself or after the object has been abandoned as valueless" (p. 257). Or, as we might conjecture in the parlance of this book, the undigested object might finally be relinquished and dispensed with once the melancholic self or subject has finally become convinced that this is an object whose psychic nutritional value is nil; only then can there be a release from its clutches.

As we have already noted, by the time Freud arrives at the last paragraph of "Mourning and Melancholia", there is a very palpable tone of frustration and dissatisfaction. He clearly feels that he has not really gotten to the bottom of his topic, not least because he has only limited experience of treating such patients. He says, tellingly, that he needs to know a great deal more about pain of all kinds before going any further. Thus, he does not really conclude his deliberations here; he simply breaks off, putting these themes aside. To provide a final, oral-digestive gloss on his last thoughts, Freud seems sated, to have had his fill, and to be heartily sick of gnawing away at this contentious bone.

By way of ending his own essay on "Mourning and Melancholia", Ogden provides a wry gloss on Freud's ending:

> The solipsistic world of a psychoanalytic theorist who is not fully grounded in the reality of his lived experience with patients is very similar to the self-imprisoned melancholic who survives in a timeless, deathless (and yet deadened and deadening) internal object world. [2012, p. 32]

One might perhaps note, in concluding this first chapter on Freud, that it is not only the clinical experience of pain and loss that had been relatively absent from Freud's life heretofore. Unbeknownst to him, such experiences in his private life were in fact queuing up to assail him in the few short years ahead. As will become evident near the end of this book, when we explore his short paper "On Transience" (1916a), written at the same moment as "Mourning and Melancholia", the pain of the First World War (when Freud's sons were sent to endanger their lives at the front) had not yet had its full impact; moreover, the tragic losses of a daughter and a grandson, as well as the advent of his own painful and disfiguring cancer, were still waiting in the wings.

CHAPTER TWO

Sigmund Freud: later models—identification, internal structure, and the ubiquity of loss

Truth and self-protection

Freud's theoretical zeal did not abate with the end of the war. Indeed, if the 1910s were the years in which he aggregated and summarized his theories and put them in order, then the 1920s was to be the decade of their massive revision and renovation. Freud was particularly discontented with his instinct or drive theory, regarding it as one of the most necessary and yet most vexed, obscure parts of his metapsychological picture of the mind. In *Beyond the Pleasure Principle* (1920g), he embarked on nothing less than a complete overhaul of that theory, culminating in his introduction of the death drive and the bringing together of the previously juxtaposed libidinal and self-preservative instincts under the aegis of Eros.

This work might also be regarded as Freud's response to the horrors and losses of a war that he only just managed to survive intact, but also as his preparation for the personal, political, and psycho-social troubles and losses that still lay ahead. We witness, in this fascinating and enigmatic text, Freud's versatile mind stretched very widely indeed, between allowing his speculative metaphorical imagination to soar to its outer limits, on the one hand, and trying desperately to stay grounded by anchoring his enterprise in the minutiae of microbiology, on the other.

Though I cannot devote very much time and space to *Beyond the Pleasure Principle*, I do want to at least describe the developments in one key section, particularly because of the theory of trauma adumbrated there and the necessity of considering its relevance to the themes of this book. An anxious atmosphere pervades the entire text, and much that Freud advocates in it is offered tentatively, pre-empting those later moments in his career when he will claim not to know whether he is about to waste paper and ink or his readers' time. Thus, Section IV begins with him saying that "What follows is speculation, often far-fetched speculation, which the reader will consider or dismiss according to his individual predilection" (1920g, p. 24).

What Freud goes on to offer is the important idea that—as human entities in an assailing environment—we need an apparatus to protect ourselves against overwhelming quantities of stimulation coming from without (and from within), arguably even more than we require the wherewithal to receive stimuli and information from those sources. In describing the mind's outermost *Pcpt.–Cs.* system—nucleus of the entity that he will soon begin designating more definitively as the ego—the metaphors he employs are suggestive of castle battlements or a skull-like structure. Insofar as its primary purpose is self-protective, this system at least tries to withstand the predations of external reality by presenting hard, stony, or bony surfaces to it—though, of course, internal attacks cannot be defended against in this fashion.

Because it is too dangerous to be exposed to the full brunt of what's out there, the receptive sense organs can afford only to take samples of it, by peeping out from apertures in this defensive, wall-like structure. Alert to the threat of being flooded or overwhelmed, our sensorium dares not take in more; we make do with and extrapolate from relatively limited bits of information to try to understand our world. One of my favourite movie moments illustrates this situation very well: when, in *A Few Good Men*, the zealous, fresh-faced rookie (Tom Cruise) demands the truth from gnarled, hard-bitten veteran (Jack Nicholson), the wise, if cynical, reply barked back at him is that he lacks what it takes to deal with the truth!

The importance to my metabolic theory of mourning of what Freud says here regarding human processing capacities is that there are limits on what we can take (in) and cope with. Clearly, there are certain events—devastating, catastrophic losses—that we are incapable of digesting and metabolizing. Trauma is, by definition, a massive, tsunami-like occurrence that floods entire systems, a brutal event that tramples and rides roughshod over the barriers that attempt to contain it. To that extent, it cannot be meaningfully registered or experienced by an ego as such. When it comes, specifically, to the cruelty visited by humans upon one another, these can be world-shattering moments, whether they happen on a mass public scale or in secret domestic spaces. The consequences are such that the victims simply cannot absorb, come to terms with, or recover from them.

Speaking of such situations in terms of melancholia or a failure to mourn may seem inappropriate, disproportionate, and wide—or perhaps short—of the mark. Freud, of course, assumed that certain urges or wishes that arise in the interior of the layered mind can also operate with enormous traumatic effect, with the result that we are forced, by means of our projective defensive capacities, to treat them as if they came from without. Again, if something needs to be projected, it is because it is too much to keep in mind; there must be—virtually by definition—a dearth or absence of any introjecting, processing, digesting, or metabolizing going on within.

The only other passage in *Beyond the Pleasure Principle* that I will glance at takes us back to Freud's ideas about psychoanalytic writing and, indeed, the very nature of his entire enterprise. If ever there was a text in which he felt torn asunder by the tensions between figurative and scientific thinking—or perhaps between the literary and the literal—this would seem to be it. And yet, in the penultimate section of this work, Freud produces a conciliatory moment that reinforces his uniqueness and maintains his contemporary relevance. He bids us "not feel greatly disturbed in judging our speculation upon the life and death instincts by the fact that so many bewildering and obscure processes occur in it". This, he says, "is merely due to our being obliged to operate with scientific terms, that is to say with the figurative language, peculiar to psychology".

This wrong-footing, deconstructive way in which the scientific and the figurative are not contrasted but aligned more closely and made almost synonymous, bequeaths a renewed conviction about why one has chosen to be part of the psychoanalytic project. Freud clinches it brilliantly by adding, "We could not otherwise describe the processes in question at all, and indeed we could not have become aware of them." Though he goes on to express his familiar wish for the elucidating certainties that future developments in either chemistry or biology might bring, Freud does not neglect to say, of all such scientific concepts, that "they too are only part of a figurative language; but it is one with which we have long been familiar and which is perhaps a simpler one as well" (p. 60).

Intricacies of identification

If we turn our attention back now to the psychoanalytic interest in an internal world and how it is constituted, *Group Psychology and the Analysis of the Ego* (1921c) represents an important developmental moment. Strachey (1955) tells us in his Editor's note that Freud had begun work on it in the spring of 1919, at almost the same moment that he started writing *Beyond the Pleasure Principle*. However, as Strachey rightly says, the two works have little in common. Representing another of the frequent detours and byways pursued by Freud during his career—and no doubt compelled by what he had witnessed about mass behaviour during the war and the Russian Revolution—this book finds him attempting to explore and explain psychologically what humans are capable of when acting as a collective or mass, in gangs or in groups.

For my purposes, it is the second rather than the first part of his title that is significant, because "the analysis of the ego" had already become for Freud an ongoing enterprise, one that would soon culminate in *The Ego and the Id* (1923b). As a concept that is key to both concerns—groups as well as the ego—it is identification that literally takes centre stage in this work. Chapter seven, bearing the name "Identification", begins at almost the precise mid-point of the book and is the only piece of sustained writing in Freud's oeuvre devoted specifically to this psychic phenomenon.

Having spent almost half of the book describing various aspects of group functioning via the theories of other scholars, in the sixth chapter he arrives at what his own science might contribute to these deliberations: he wishes to consider the affective bonds that bring people together (while not neglecting the aversive ones that keep them apart), beginning, of course, with sex and love. He expects that these will help him discover the "conditions which can be transferred to the ties that exist in groups". The last sentences of that chapter read as follows:

> But we should also like to know whether this kind of object-cathexis, as we know it in sexual life, represents the only manner of emotional tie with other people, or whether we must take other mechanisms of the sort into account. As a matter of fact we learn from psycho-analysis that there do exist other mechanisms for emotional ties, the so-called *identifications*, insufficiently known processes and hard to describe, the investigation of which will for some time keep us away from the subject of group psychology. [1921c, pp. 103–104]

Freud thus presages this foray into identification by again alerting us to the differences between libidinal object relations and these strange psychic phenomena that are "insufficiently known" and "hard to describe". To take a good look at them will itself require quite a lengthy excursus, a digression from his main pursuit.

So, having alerted us to the fact that identification is a different kind of bond with an object from a sexual or loving one, he begins the ensuing chapter by saying that identification is also "the earliest expression of an emotional tie with another person", presumably preceding any other such tie. It is perhaps unclear why Freud does not consider early identifications to be an initial form of the expression of love itself, rather than a qualitatively different kind of emotional tie. Surely both the earliest forms of love and those that later tend to become the basis of long-term relationships require the glue of identification, whatever else they may be based on.

But Freud is still building his argument here, and, typically, his first example is that of a little boy's "special interest in his father", considered as a prelude to his later oedipal trajectory. At this stage, the boy would like to be or become like his dad, to emulate him, though the way Freud puts it suggests that there is already more to it than this: the boy, he adds, also wants to "take his place everywhere" (p. 105). One might at this point question Freud's view and wonder whether he is not allowing the later, more clearly conflictual oedipal relations to colour retroactively the picture of these earliest identifications. Are early identifications like these always incipiently tainted by conflict, or does conflict ensue only from the tricky triangulations of desire and competition that are yet to come?

Of course, Freud has only recently posited the death drive as an inherent or innate phenomenon. While Klein, one of its strongest advocates, will declare that aggressive oedipal feelings are present from the beginning, one way that Freud tackles this quandary is to attribute these early ontogenetic identifications at least partially to phylogenetic pre-history. This involves, as we have seen, his own tale of origins, expressed in *Totem and Taboo* and elsewhere, involving the ancient and heritable conflict between a primordial father and his disgruntled sons, as a collective or communal complement to every individual's discrete oedipal struggles.

Freud's story continues, however, in familiar fashion, with the little (heterosexual?) boy then developing what Freud calls a "true" or "straightforward sexual object-cathexis" to his mother, with the consequence that he "notices that his father stands in his way with his mother. His father-identification then takes on a hostile colouring and becomes identical with the wish to replace his father". Thus, the ambivalence of identification is now fully acknowledged, as present "from the very first", capable of turning as easily "into an expression of tenderness" as "into a wish for someone's removal".

Here it is not phylogenesis that Freud appeals to for an explanation; instead, he tells us that identification in its earliest form is "a derivative of the *oral* phase", which is by its very nature ambivalent because the desired object is "assimilated by eating and is in that way annihilated as such". Freud refers to the fact that even the actual cannibal's "devouring affection" applies only to people with whom there is an intimate involvement, those that he cares about, even if these feelings are also admixed with enmity and hatred. In other words, ambivalence is inherent in the very nature of the oral tie with the object, which must, as it were, be eaten up and possessed inside and therefore cannot survive as a separate entity.

Freud does then try to account for the equivalent situation in the little girl's development, though still with the primary focus on the father as object. It is only in later texts that he, and others after him, will realize that the neglected, underestimated place of the mother in these developments and constellations can result in even more complex outcomes. At this moment, though, the intention is not to give a comprehensive account of the Oedipus complex, but to clarify the mechanism of identification and—perhaps rather desperately—to establish a clear distinction between it and other human ties or bonds.

What we now get is the following classical, oft-cited definition of this essential difference:

> It is easy to state in a formula the distinction between an identification with the father and the choice of the father as an object. In the first case one's father is what one would like to *be*, and in the second he is what one would like to *have*. The distinction, that is, depends upon whether the tie attaches to the subject or to the object of the ego. The former kind of tie is therefore already possible before any sexual object choice has been made. It is much more difficult to give a clear metapsychological representation of the distinction. We can only see that identification endeavours to mould a person's own ego after the fashion of the one that has been taken as a model. [p. 106]

One sees here how Freud is grappling to hang onto this distinction, struggling to keep it from collapsing into itself—something that Diana Fuss's *Identification Papers* (1995) points to so astutely, as discussed in my Introduction. Though his subject-versus-object point is useful, explaining why it is that we can have identification from very early on, Freud concedes that the metapsychological level presents significant difficulties.

These might perhaps be expressed by philosophical and linguistic questions: what *is* the difference—in the complex exchanges constituting any significant relationship—between being and having the other person? Can these really be kept meaningfully separate? I cannot be sure, of course, whether these questions reflect what was troubling Freud, but the banality of the last sentence in the above quotation betrays his struggle and confusion; it clings to and re-states what is obvious, fundamental, and incontrovertible, but it is neither profound nor illuminating.

Freud now wants to "disentangle identification" in neurotic symptoms: if a young (heterosexual?) girl develops a cough like her mother's, this identification might express her rivalrous oedipal wish to take her mother's place in her father's affections. If the cough resembles her father's (as in the case of Dora), it exemplifies the way in which the object love for her oedipally forbidden father has regressed to (the earlier tie of) an identification with him. Thus, symptomatic identification can take the form of either a subjective/narcissistic link with an object (mother, in this instance) or an objective/anaclitic connection with an object (father). Either way, as Freud says, "where there is repression and where the mechanisms of the unconscious are dominant, object choice is turned back into identification—the ego assumes the characteristics of the object". Perhaps what is most obfuscating in Freud's musings here is the way that human emotional bonds seem both to begin with, and to end up as, identifications.

If this is a *"dis*entangling", one wonders how much more complex things might get when *all* the oedipal possibilities and permutations come into play. Freud notes that "in these identifications the ego sometimes copies the person who is not loved and sometimes the one who is loved". This somehow strikes one as reductive and unsatisfactory: surely, in the above example, the girl might go on loving her mother while emulating her and might also be hating (or not necessarily loving) her father even as she imitates him. Does one need to resort to the sometimes used but rather clumsy formulation "dis-identification" to make more sense of these dynamics?

There is a good example in "A Rose for Emily", where the mother is conspicuous by her complete absence from the tale, but Emily seems to identify in a very concrete and bodily way with her father. After Homer Barron has apparently disappeared for good and Emily is not seen on the streets of Jefferson for many months, the townspeople declare their accurate, if only partial, understanding: "Then we knew this was to be expected too; as if that quality of her father which had thwarted her woman's life so many times had been too virulent and furious to die." As the very next paragraph describes it, by the time she is seen again, Emily has changed and aged: she is fatter (as if she has incorporated or is incubating something?) and her hair has gone grey. We are also told that, until the end of her life, it remained "that vigorous iron-gray, like the hair of an active man" (Faulkner, 1930, p. 127). In chapter three I explore the implications of this detail more fully; suffice it to say here that it illustrates that identifications emerge from feelings of resentment and hatred, no less than from those of reverence and love.

Rather oddly, I think, Freud now wants to propose a third type of neurotic symptom, where, as he claims, "identification leaves entirely out of account any object-relation to the person who is being copied". His example is hysterical contagion of the kind that can affect whole groups of teenage girls in matters of love, where emotions run high and include frustrations, repressions, jealousies, and guilt. Once again, I find myself wondering why Freud thinks there are no object relations at play here, though perhaps what he means is that the emotional resonances among such individuals are somewhat less intimate than those that pertain, say, between parents and children.

Of course, these are precisely the kinds of identification—where there is perhaps not much of a personal object relation to begin with—that operate in the formation of larger groups of people and serve to connect them with a charismatic leader. In this context, Freud goes on to mention briefly, but not to pursue very far, "the process which psychology calls 'empathy' and which plays the largest part in our understanding of what is inherently foreign to our ego in other people". He opts instead to stay for now with what he calls "the immediate emotional effects of identification" (pp. 107–108).

Freud adduces two more examples from psychoanalytic experience, each of which brings us back, and progressively closer, to the link between identification and loss (though perhaps that link has in any case been implicit all along). The first is Freud's understanding of what happens in instances of male homosexuality, where a boy's intense oedipal link with mother might culminate in an identification with her that does not require him to (fully) abandon her as an object. One might say that he identifies not with the *object* of her desire, but subjectively with the *desire itself* (for him) or, as Freud puts it, "he transforms himself into her and now looks about for objects which can replace his ego for him, and on which he can bestow such love and care as he has experienced from his mother".

Strachey's footnote (p. 108) reminds us that Freud had put forward this idea in his book on Leonardo (1910c), and it is sometimes thought (wrongly) to be his sole way of accounting for a so-called homosexual outcome in men. Perhaps the importance of the argument for our purposes is his dawning realization that any and perhaps all kinds of object loss will bring identification (back) into play. He expresses this broadening of his perspective as follows: "Identification with an object that is renounced or lost, as a substitute for that object—introjection of it into the ego—is indeed no longer a novelty to us" (pp. 108–109).

Putting it thus, not least by resorting to Ferenczi's term "introjection"—about which much more will be said further on—Freud reminds us that loss itself happens in a variety of ways, few of which are under the subject's control in any meaningful sense. This is the reason that the recourse to internalizing strategies is so important: our fragile egos would simply not cope without the compensatory possibilities that they provide. Having put forward a new, more extensive view of identification/introjection and its ubiquity, in Freud's second example he revisits the text—and the affliction—in which he first noted its power and necessity as a response to loss:

> Another such instance of introjection of the object has been provided by the analysis of melancholia, an affection that counts amongst the most notable of its exciting causes the real or emotional loss of a loved object. A leading characteristic of these cases is a cruel self-depreciation of the ego combined with relentless self-criticism and bitter self-reproaches. Analyses have shown that this disparagement and these reproaches apply at bottom to the object and represent the ego's revenge upon it. The shadow of the object has fallen upon the ego, as I have said elsewhere. The introjection of the object is here unmistakably clear. [p. 109]

Clear though it might be, what feels just as important is Freud's implicit recognition that this is by no means the *only* instance of the taking of an object into the ego—indeed, this is not even his first example of it here. The other instances are, perhaps, less starkly pathological than melancholia and they do not necessarily entail the internal sadomasochism implicit in this picture of the melancholic ego, as "divided, fallen apart into two pieces, one of which rages against the second".

Freud first refers to the part or piece of the ego that "has been altered by introjection and which contains the lost object", but he is becoming better acquainted with the other piece, too. He ends the chapter by characterizing this "critical agency" in some detail, perhaps in anticipation of what he will say in *The Ego and the Id* (1923b), where he will also rebrand it as the superego. Still calling it the "ego ideal" here, Freud enumerates its functions of "self-observation, the moral conscience, the censorship of dreams, and the chief influence in repression", and notes its origins in our childish narcissism, as an entity that offers us an image of what we might strive to be, by way of compensation for what we once were and have now lost.

What Freud is not yet saying—but will make abundantly clear in *The Ego and the Id*—is that this agency is itself the product of identificatory and internalizing processes: this ego ideal/superego is tantamount, at least initially, to the internal version of the parents' moral order, deriving from the vexed negotiations of the Oedipus complex. But what this means, in effect, is that both the ego and the superego are not just "altered by introjection" and do not only contain, or harbour, internalized external phenomena, but are constructed out of them, in the first place, as it were. But of this, more later.

It is worth spending a bit of time on the eighth chapter of *Group Psychology*, "Being in Love and Hypnosis" (particularly the love part), if only because of the way it further complicates the whole picture of an internal world. As I alluded to earlier, Freud now goes into the differences, degrees, and vicissitudes of loving feelings, which requires him also to explore the interactions between identification and idealization in mental life. His earlier emphasis on hedonistic, selfish, sexual love seems to have given way to an appreciation of love's manifold complexities and an even deeper recognition of the extent to which love can in fact leave one at the mercy of the object.

As Freud reminds us, he had already taken note (in his paper on narcissism) of the fact "that when we are in love a considerable amount of narcissistic libido overflows onto the object" and that in such circumstances, "the object serves as a substitute for some unattained ego ideal of our own". He elaborates the matter further, noting that the loving idealization of the object can, ironically, gradually diminish the desire for and satisfactions of sex itself. The object becomes, in a sense, too special to spoil or touch, which eventually leaves the subject or ego in a downright dangerous state whereby it

> becomes more and more unassuming and modest, and the object more and more sublime and precious, until at last it gets possession of the entire self-love of the ego, whose self-sacrifice thus follows as a natural consequence. The object has, so to speak, *consumed* the ego. [1921c, pp. 112–113, emphasis added]

My reasons for repeatedly emphasizing the word "consumed" will by now, I hope, be obvious. I would wish my reader to be reminded immediately of Freud's use of this word to describe the predations of depression in "Mourning and Melancholia" and of my claim that it reinforces what I call the alimentary or digestive substrate of these matters.

Moreover, echoing what was noted in my reading of that text, we are now re-encountering the surprising metapsychological similarities between being depressed and being in love. Freud sums up the dangers of the situation with a short, italicized sentence: "*The object has been put in the place of the ego ideal.*" Again, we must bear in mind that Freud's main concern here is to outline the preconditions—and, indeed, the dangers—of situations in which the falling in love is not with a partner but with a charismatic leader, such as Hitler (or Trump or Putin), and where this also occurs not individually but *en masse*. One might even suggest that such psychopathically seductive personae are at their most attractive to a populace that finds itself in states of both psychic and economic depression.

Freud comes to realize that the ins and outs of identification are enormously intricate, and he sometimes ties himself in knots in his attempt to clarify them. Ironically, the next paragraph begins with an apparently confident claim that at least one clear distinction is possible:

> It is now easy to define the difference between identification and such extreme developments of being in love as may be described as "fascination" or "bondage". In the former case the ego has enriched itself with the properties of the object, it has "introjected" the object into itself, as Ferenczi (1909) expresses it. In the second case it is impoverished, it has surrendered itself to the object, it has substituted the object for its own most important constituent. [p. 113]

Here the term "introjection" is not only properly credited to Ferenczi but is even used accurately and according to his specifications, which are soon to be outlined in my next chapter.

What Freud is trying to define here does not reduce neatly to the earlier foundational one between identifying with (or being) the object, on the one hand, and loving (or having) it, on the other. Clearly, what he has been trying to outline in the foregoing paragraphs is that there are in fact certain states of being in love that are closer to being possessed *by* the object than to having it in any real or meaningful sense. If anything, when one is in thrall to an object in such ways, it may be said to have—or, indeed, to consume—you. What he is trying valiantly to establish is the crucial distinction between a more benign form of internalization and the more predatory, potentially malignant, hostile take-over that other forms of internalization seem to perpetrate.

Might it have been helpful and clarifying if Freud had now explicitly considered the possibility that identification and introjection may not be coterminous, and acknowledged the role that *projection* plays in—or as—identification? As we shall see, Klein and her followers would later pursue this course of action by ramping up the idea that one might psychically send or disperse parts of oneself *into* others (and thus become poorer through losing them), as described and defined by the notion of projective identification. We will later debate whether this term makes these matters any clearer or muddies the theoretical waters.

There is also another future theory of mourning and melancholia, offered by Nicolas Abraham and Maria Torok, that will cleave to and insist upon the distinction between different kinds of internalization. Their attempts to maintain and consolidate such differences turn on retaining the name *introjection* for positive or normal processes, and using *incorporation* to characterize more concrete, negative, or pathological manifestations. This would also correspond with my own claim that mourning entails the possibility of the absorption, dissolution, and digestion of the object, whereas melancholia always finds these processes difficult, impossible, or undesirable, and amounts to nothing less than a perpetual state of psychic indigestion.

In the meantime, back here in *Group Psychology*, Freud is wrestling uncomfortably with the economic contingencies and vicissitudes surrounding identification, with how the ego can emerge from these machinations either enriched or impoverished. He offers an alternative formulation:

> In the case of identification the object has been lost or given up; it is then set up again inside the ego, and the ego makes a partial alteration of itself after the model of the lost object. In the other case the object is retained, and there is a hypercathexis of it by the ego and at the ego's expense. [p. 114]

The word "identification", therefore, does not appear to apply to the latter outcome, but has Freud now said anything substantially or materially different? Is the important opposition not still between a salutary, advantageous form of taking in and an unwelcome, disadvantageous one?

It is surely crucial to know the difference between something taken in ego-syntonically that the subject is happy to accommodate and a toxic taking-in that colonizes and takes over the ego. One might also need to specify what it means to say that, in the latter situation, the object is "retained". As the example of Miss Emily suggests, the retaliatory retention of the object in melancholia or other failures to mourn is often of a constipated kind or partakes of the perverse need to cling to it, be it alive or dead—or, indeed, "pickled" in some encrypted, purgatorial place between the two.

In such vexed moods, nothing seems to satisfy Freud's need to get things right, for he now raises a different difficulty—about the status of the external object, or the ego's hold on it, in such situations—in the form of two questions: "Is it quite certain that identification presupposes that object-cathexis has been given up? Can there be no identification while the object is retained?" Thus, again, Freud challenges the very oppositions on which his own argument seems to depend.

As I said earlier, we might well admire such moments in which we see his courageous self-criticism on display. On the other hand, this does play havoc with his need to be—and our wish that he be—clear. But, instead of tackling his own questions here, he changes tack again and claims that something else "embraces the real essence of the matter, namely, *whether the object is put in the place of the ego or the ego ideal*" (p. 114). This is indeed crucial, and a version of this question will occupy our attention later, but we should keep in mind that in this text Freud is still trying to work out something quite particular about group behaviour. The following two chapters of *Group Psychology* are firmly focused on the herd or horde, where we can perhaps leave him to it without accompanying him any further.

However, in his eleventh and penultimate chapter, entitled "A Differentiating Grade in the Ego", Freud's attention does return—inexorably, it would seem—to what is happening in the internal world of the individual. He tells us that his forays into the libidinal dynamics of groups have led him back to a further exploration of the intrapsychic relationship—and distinction—between the ego ideal and the ego from which it has emerged, "to the double kind of tie which makes this possible—identification and putting the object in place of the ego ideal". He wants to consolidate—and, indeed, justify—the existence of the latter entity to the world of psychology at large, and usefully puts these more recent, internal developments into the context of earlier, outwardly directed preoccupations:

> Let us reflect that the ego now enters into the relation of an object to the ego ideal which has been developed out of it, and that all the interplay between an external object and the ego as a whole, with which our study of the neuroses has made us acquainted, may possibly be repeated upon this new scene within the ego. [p. 130]

Freud is gearing up for the momentous shifts in his model of the mind that will be rolled out in *The Ego and the Id*: these will include a new way of conceiving a psychic world in which the different personified parts or agencies that together constitute the subject or self conduct their dramatic, conflictual relations with each other on an internal stage.

He is in fact already warning that too much divisiveness among our "mental differentiations", as he terms them, can destabilize the personality and may lead to breakdown. He first mentions some other possible disturbances to inner equilibrium: there can be threats to our narcissistic self-sufficiency and integrity from the world of external objects, from whom we therefore need to retreat periodically; and we can also be destabilized by the fundamental inner division between conscious and unconscious experience, familiar from our dreams and neuroses, which we may try to cope with by means of comedy and laughter. However, his focus is on the division at hand: "It is quite conceivable that the separation of the ego ideal from the ego cannot be borne for long either, and has to be temporarily undone" (pp. 130–131).

In other words, what we might call the moral pressure that the ego ideal exerts on the ego to better itself must also occasionally find a release valve of some sort. And Freud goes on to mention the importance of lawful, socially sanctioned temporary "transgression", the blowing-off of steam, provided by the "institution of festivals", the "excesses" and "debaucheries" exemplified by the "Saturnalia of the Romans and our modern carnival". These may be crucial for society's very fabric, if the latter is not to be permanently rent or ripped to shreds by the more constant, desperate, and frustrated forms of acting out to which people might resort if they never feel good enough—in moral terms—to satisfy their ego ideals. In a rather ingenious move, Freud notes that these moments of release entail a transient kind of triumph of the ego over the ego ideal, the shrugging off of an ethical burden, akin precisely, of course, to what happens when the depressive phase in a bipolar illness suddenly gives way to the manic one.

Freud becomes momentarily, and rather oddly, embroiled in the old question of whether or not manic-depressive conditions *per se* are "psychogenic"—whether they have "external precipitating causes". He does try, however, in his own words to "keep to what is clear" and manages finally to arrive at an eloquent metapsychological description of what we might term the "inter-agential (object-)relations" pertaining in such cyclical or bipolar pathology:

> On the basis of our analysis of the ego it cannot be doubted that in cases of mania the ego and the ego ideal have fused together, so that the person, in a mood of triumph and self-satisfaction, disturbed by no self-criticism, can enjoy the abolition of his ambitions, his feelings of consideration of others, and his self-reproaches. It is not so obvious, but nevertheless very probable, that the misery of the melancholic is the expression of a sharp conflict between the two agencies of his ego, a conflict in which the ideal, in an excess of sensitiveness, relentlessly exhibits its condemnation of the ego in delusions of inferiority and in self-depreciation. [p. 132]

It is really on the above note—with this revisiting of some familiar themes from "Mourning and Melancholia"—that the substance of Freud's *Group Psychology* is effectively brought to its conclusion (though there is also a

"Postscript", consisting primarily of brief forays along various side alleys that Freud was not able to traverse in the main body of the text).

Perhaps Freud has done little more here than go over old ground, but he is also beginning to re-formulate those earlier ideas in terms of a still-incipient conceptual schema that is almost but not quite in his grasp, not yet fully at his disposal. Thus, the scene is set for the even newer terms and more inventive structures that he will confidently introduce in *The Ego and the Id*, and it is to this text that we now turn our attention.

Constructing the agencies of the mind

What I want to suggest here is that *The Ego and The Id* (1923b) harbours certain crucial developments in Freud's thinking that go somewhat unnoticed, or at least unremarked, amidst the plethora of other significant conceptual additions and modifications—not least his new structural model of the mind—for which the book is justly famous. The third chapter in Freud's game-changing text, "The Ego and the Super-Ego (Ego Ideal)", is of particular importance, as it not only introduces a second new term to the psychoanalytic lexicon (to accompany the id, named earlier) but also gives an account of its genesis, involving complex processes of internalization and identification. The superego—now decisively named as such by Freud (after a decade of using precursor cognates like "conscience", "ideal ego", or "ego ideal")—is seen to be the product of a momentous process whereby the parental figures are simultaneously or successively given up as incestuous objects and their legacies permanently installed in the structure of the developing mind.

In the first chapter of this work, Freud reviews his ideas about conscious and unconscious aspects of mental functioning for the sake of justifying and explaining the need for a new arrangement that does not rely, as the previous model did, on a single unwieldy category in which to house the multiplicity of unconscious meanings and contents uncovered during the quarter-century or so of psychoanalytic experience and research.

In his second chapter he draws on several of his earlier metapsychological texts to arrive at a more refined and circumscribed notion of what precisely the ego is. The path having been paved by *Beyond the Pleasure Principle*, the ego is now spoken of as an agency that originates at the perceptual interface with the outside world, on the outskirts or superficies of the mental apparatus.

Freud goes on to complicate this account, gradually attributing more complexity to the ego, not only by acknowledging its multiple functions and psychically unconscious defensive aspects, but by recognizing its very ontology as more figurative, metaphorical, or phenomenological than previously. This is captured by one of the text's most famous sentences, one that is often not cited in full: "The ego is first and foremost a bodily ego; it is not merely a surface entity, but is itself the projection of a surface" (1923b, p. 26). The word "bodily" does not quite equate to "body" here, and we are thus reminded, lest we lose sight of it, that the ego is a mental not a physical phenomenon: indeed, it is brought into being by a form of projection, a psychic process or action.

The id has also just been named for the first time—courtesy of Georg Groddeck and his just-published *Book of the It* (1923)—and Freud has attempted to map his new structural model of the mind onto the older one, even resorting to a diagram for the purpose. With *Genesis*-like authority, Freud declares, "We shall now look upon an individual as a psychical id, unknown and unconscious, upon whose surface rests the ego.... The ego is not sharply separated from the id; its lower portion merges into it" (pp. 23–24).

Freud begins his third chapter by saying that if the above situation—involving just an id and an ego—constituted the whole picture of the mind, "we should have a simple state of things to deal with". The superego is introduced as a "further complication", almost as if it is a metapsychological misfortune that there is a need to acknowledge it. But we *do* in fact have "to assume the existence of a grade in the ego, a differentiation within the ego", as he had also described it several times before, including in "On Narcissism" and *Group Psychology*. He says that we must now "widen our range a little" because a certain unconscious quality of this third mental agency "is the novelty which calls for explanation".

It is this widening of Freud's range over the next few pages—even before he ties the coming into being of the superego more specifically to the negotiations of the Oedipus complex—that interests me, because it is here that he again becomes embroiled in the problematics of identification. I need to follow carefully in his footsteps at this point, because where he treads will greatly determine the direction of my own journey in this book.

He begins by looking back at what he had said in "Mourning and Melancholia":

> We succeeded in explaining the painful disorder of melancholia by supposing that an object which was lost has been set up again inside the ego—that is that an object-cathexis has been replaced by an identification. At that time, however, we did not appreciate the full significance of this process and did not know how common and how typical it is. Since then we have come to understand that this kind of

> substitution has a great share in determining the form taken by the ego and that it makes an essential contribution towards building up what is called its "character". [p. 28]

In these pages, therefore, Freud seems preoccupied not only with how the superego comes into being, but also with how initially the ego *itself* comes to be constituted.

There may be something essentially odd, absurd, or even incoherent about trying to get behind, before, or underneath the existence of the ego—the very entity, after all, that does our thinking—to ask whether and how it comes into being. Such paradoxicality is perhaps captured earlier in the text by one passing but remarkable description resorted to by Freud in his first attempt to characterize the ego and list its tasks: the ego, he says, "is the mental agency that supervises all its own constitutive processes" (p. 17). This reminds me of a terrible anecdote, told to me by someone who worked in child protection, of a very young child so neglected that she had to learn to change her own nappy.

It may not be entirely clear whether Freud is already, in the longer quotation above, thinking about the ego as a conceptually separate entity from the "grade" or "differentiation" that would emerge from within it. But I believe it is fair to assume that it is the early ego—before it gives rise to the superego—that is being spoken about here. Freud's text leaves it somewhat ambiguous as to whether there is indeed a two-stage process discernible here, whereby first the ego and later the superego are constituted by different internalizing moments or forms of identification; Hans Loewald will later make this more explicit, as chapter five attests.

What is already emerging, however, is that this process called "identification" is a much more fundamental building block of psychic development than Freud has hitherto granted or realized. By linking his thoughts here with "Mourning and Melancholia", he suggests, at least implicitly, that when *any* object cathexis or relationship is either lost or undergoes a significant change, some form of setting-up inside the ego is to be expected. As Freud says, such outcomes are crucial because they contribute to the eventual "form" or "character" of the incipient ego, and clearly this does not happen only when there is a manifestly melancholic outcome, which, we recall, is particularly typified by rather persecutory, sadomasochistic dynamics.

Recalling the pronouncements of *Genesis* once again, Freud speaks of the state of things, at "the very beginning, in the individual's primitive oral phase", where, he speculates, "object-cathexis and identification are no doubt indistinguishable from one another". Thus, it is only at a later moment—when there is both more object-relationality and greater psychic separation between having someone else and being (like) them—that substitution of the former by the latter is even possible. Because of the oral nature of our first encounters, we "relate" (if this word can even be said to have meaning so early on) by appropriating, devouring, and incorporating the object, by treating it as already ours—to have and to hold, as it were. Whether this "ownership" is nothing other than a subjective illusion or fantasy is immaterial—after all, at this early stage the so-called real world, with all its strictures and frustrations, has in a sense not even come into being yet.

It is only once a first differentiation, between the id and the ego, has occurred—after this initial internal emergence and separation begins to crystallize and a division of labour or function is established—that a concomitant external separating out of subject and object can also happen: only then, one supposes, can the very experiences of having and losing be felt, if not yet thought. With the assumption that such developmental moments have already occurred, Freud can return to the more familiar account of the compensatory and defensive dynamics that any kind of loss or separation brings in its wake:

> When it happens that a person has to give up a sexual object, there *quite often* ensues an alteration of his ego which can only be described as the setting up of the object inside the ego, as it occurs in melancholia". [p. 29, emphasis added]

So, now identification can take the form of a compensatory mechanism or defensive dynamic that can be used to render any and every loss more bearable.

However, there is that curious qualification, "quite often". On the one hand, Freud is clearly re-thinking his earlier presumption—namely, that this internal "setting up" occurs only in melancholia—but perhaps he is still reluctant to say that it happens on all occasions, whenever there is any loss whatsoever. To do that would be to recognize that there are indeed several different forms of internalization and identification, variations on this theme. As we are about to see, he is rapidly approaching just such a recognition.

The last-quoted sentence is completed with the words, "the exact nature of this substitution is as yet unknown to us". This apparently refers to the kind of substitution, or "alteration of the ego", that provides compensatory solace of some kind but is not melancholic in nature. And it is here that Freud pens three important sentences—and makes use of the same synonym or cognate of identification as in *Group Psychology*—expressing the idea that there can be a different form of taking-in and setting-up within the ego:

> It may be that by this *introjection*, which is a kind of regression to the mechanism of the oral phase, the ego makes it easier for the object to be given up or renders that process possible. It may be that this identification is the sole condition under which the id can give up its objects. At any rate the process, especially in the early phases of development, is a very frequent one, and it makes it possible to suppose that the character of the ego is a precipitate of abandoned object-cathexes and that it contains the history of those object-choices. [p. 29, emphasis added]

Later chapters will make more of the term "introjection", invented and first used by Freud's colleague, Ferenczi, as far back as 1909. Both he and his French–Hungarian heirs, Abraham and Torok, were concerned that the word be used accurately and not be confused with similar or adjacent concepts.

As we shall see, these analysts question the relative proximity of introjection to the concretely oral or zonal meanings referred to here by Freud. Reserving the term "incorporation" for these more regressive dynamics, they try to distinguish as clearly as possible between the two terms. Suffice it for now to note that Freud appears to reach for introjection—albeit for a possibly inaccurate understanding of it—just as important new ideas about the ubiquity of internalizing processes and their ego-formative powers are occurring to him. When he speaks here of the ego as "a precipitate of abandoned object-cathexes", containing and preserving these "object-choices" inside itself—as a kind of "history" or autobiographical genealogy—there is a strong implicit suggestion that these phenomena have metaphorically undergone a *digestive* process: they have been *metabolized* or integrated within the ego, thus contributing to its "character".

There is a significant footnote on this same page of *The Ego and the Id*, where Freud mentions the beliefs of so-called "primitive peoples" (an epithet and a way of referencing other or past cultures that we might now find jarring and problematic). He speaks of how, in those cultures, "the attributes of animals which are incorporated as nourishment persist as part of the character of those who eat them" (p. 29), and he goes on to make links with cannibalism, totem meals, and holy communion. Strachey (p. 29) also directs our attention at this point to the relevant parts of Freud's *Totem and Taboo*, reinforcing the connections discussed in chapter one. As we saw there, oral-alimentary issues involving ingestion, digestion, and identification and its synonyms play a significant part in those deliberations or speculations.

Having re-opened this whole area of interest—also revisited by him not long before in *Group Psychology*—Freud's astute, imaginative mind offers a few complex corollaries: that a more mature ego might develop "a capacity for resistance" to deeper levels of identification, perhaps for the purpose of fending off psychic invasion and preserving an already established identity; that there are situations in which an identificatory process might begin even before the object cathexis is surrendered, where the character change happens pre-emptively, as a way of forestalling loss.

There is a definite sense here that Freud is beginning to enjoy playing with his new psychic terms. Now that he has "characterized" and can anthropomorphize these new agencies—id and ego—he ingeniously animates them, treating them as personae engaged in dramatic, complex, often difficult relationships with each other. The ego, he tells us, can take advantage of its capacity to alter itself through identification with the erotic object by trying, in this fashion, to attract and thereby gain traction and control over the unruly (and bereaved) id:

> When the ego assumes the features of the object, it is forcing itself, so to speak, upon the id as a love-object and is trying to make good the id's loss by saying: "Look, you can love me too—I am so much like the object". [pp. 29–30]

Another paragraph follows in which Freud considers the narcissistic transformation, desexualization, and sublimation of overtly libidinal relations when the action or drama turns inward or goes indoors, as it were. He then also considers the pathological possibilities of too many identifications, where the consequence might be an ego that disintegrates or fragments into multiple, mutually conflictual bits.

But these are, frankly, just asides. For Freud is about to embark upon the central intention of the chapter, namely, to describe the process whereby the workings of identification and internalization culminate in their perhaps most momentous product, the creation of the superego. Before doing so, via an account of "the triangular character of the Oedipus situation and the constitutional bisexuality of each individual", Freud tells us that "the effects of the first identifications made in earliest childhood will be general and lasting". He suggests that these have *pre*historic or phylogenetic roots and are "not in the first instance the consequence or outcome of an object-cathexis": later and more specific identifications that are the products of loss "thus reinforce the primary one" (p. 31).

My reasons for the careful laying out of Freud's thinking in the opening pages of this chapter are, I hope, becoming clear. What Freud comes very close to saying here is that there are early forms of these psychic processes which we might be tempted to name as *"primary* identification". We might be similarly tempted to posit something called, "primary *mourning"*, but there is something highly incongruous about prefacing these states of mind or mental strategies—that seem so linked to secondary phenomena and are usually thought to arise as the consequence of something else—with a word denoting firstness. The point is that the necessity both to mourn and to identify with what is lost runs so deep in the psyche that it is virtually impossible to imagine a stage of life, either individual or collective, when neither of these human requirements or capacities would be operative. Perhaps only the religions so discredited by Freud—with their phantasmatic narratives of both firstness and lastness, about where we come from and are going to—have dared to make it their business to imagine and embellish such times or places.

Freud—unlike Klein, as we shall see—regarded the emergence of the superego as a relatively late development, firmly linked with the oedipal, and genital, moment. However, what he alludes to in the third chapter of *The Ego and the Id* is that the ego itself—well before the extrusion (or is it *in*trusion?) of a superego—is also constituted or shaped out of identificatory consolations for losses both little and large, phylogenetic as well as ontogenetic, suffered by the subject (or is it only by its id?) at the very earliest times. The idea that we are always already mourning something, and hence needing solace or compensation, is thus tacitly, if not explicitly, acknowledged here by Freud. Later in this book, I will also explore how Hans Loewald and André Green—each in his different way—regard such dynamics as the virtual centre point and *raison d'être* of the psychoanalytic enterprise.

It seems wrong to simply take my leave right in the middle of this important Freudian chapter, before the substance of its task is accomplished. There is and will be so much more to say and ask about the superego: do we consider it to be the first "internal object", for example, or is it, perhaps strangely, the ego itself that should claim this status? Freud continues, moreover, to wrestle with—and is at times unclear and quite self-contradictory about—the psychic trajectory and relevance of identification in this chapter. Does it always presuppose the introduction of the object into the ego or are there identifications that stop shy of this move? And how does our constitutional bisexuality intersect with our early object choices and identifications? Which of these factors is, in the long run, more responsible for our eventual sexual identities?

There is a sense that Freud rather fudges these difficult questions, and then struggles to sort out the respective contributions of the mother- and father-identifications to the outcome. When he proffers his italicized conclusions, they sound too vague and unspecific to be entirely satisfactory:

> *The broad general outcome of the sexual phase dominated by the Oedipus complex may, therefore, be taken to be the forming of a precipitate in the ego, consisting of these two identifications in some way united with each other. This modification of the ego retains its special position; it confronts the other contents of the ego as an ego-ideal or super-ego.* [p. 34]

There are one or two moments, later in *The Ego and the Id*, that merit further attention in this context. In chapter four, Freud reminds us that just a year or two earlier, in *Beyond the Pleasure Principle*, he had undertaken another great reform of his conceptual apparatus—of his drive or instinct theory—via the introduction of Eros and the death instinct. He makes a first attempt here to integrate these two new developments—renovated instinct theory and structural model of the mind—into a more comprehensive metapsychological picture.

But it is the fifth and last chapter, "The Dependent Relationships of the Ego", where Freud seems both to plumb greater depths in his engagement with all these matters and to offer some insights that are relevant to my own enterprise. Writing with greater clarity than he could muster earlier in his text, Freud gives this account of the relations between the ego and a superego that is beginning now to emerge more clearly into its own and to achieve a certain degree of independence from its parent entity:

> Thus we have said repeatedly that the ego is formed to a great extent out of identifications which take the place of abandoned cathexes by the id; that the first of these identifications always behave as a special agency in the ego and stand apart from the ego in the form of a super-ego, while later on, as it grows stronger, the ego may become more resistant to the influences of such identifications. The super-ego owes its special position in the ego, or in relation to the ego, to a factor that must be considered from two sides: on the one hand it was the first identification and one which took place while the ego was still feeble, and on the other hand it is the heir to the Oedipus complex and has introduced the most momentous objects into the ego.... Although it is accessible to all later influences, it nevertheless preserves throughout life the character given to it by its derivation from the father-complex—namely, the capacity to stand apart from the ego and to master it. It is a memorial of the former weakness and dependence of the ego, and the mature ego remains subject to its domination. As the child was once under the compulsion to obey its parents, so the ego submits to the categorical imperative of its super-ego. [p. 48]

Freud's writing admirably captures the paradoxes and ironies inherent in these mental developments and can virtually serve as an explanation of why the internal landscapes of our minds are so complex—and why our struggles with those superegoic "bullies", conscience, guilt, remorse, and self-punishment, can be so profound and debilitating.

I introduced this long quotation by suggesting that it is the ego that is, in a certain sense, the parent—indeed, the mother—of the superego, insofar as it gives rise to it, gives figurative birth to it, out of itself. By contrast, Freud emphasizes that it is the superego that holds onto, and is permanently marked by, its paternal/parental characteristics—because of the identifications with the parent figures that make up its substance—and, therefore, it always or often takes the ego to task. So, we may ask of this internal relationship between ego and superego: who parents—and, thus, who obeys—whom? This question is not just of theoretical interest; it is almost always one of the most vital questions in any clinical situation, certainly those involving work with depressed or melancholic patients, where it is invariably the superego that is asserting its authority most cruelly.

This is related, one might suggest, to Freud's ambivalence—evident in the quotation, where it is unclear whether the superego is to be located "in the ego, or in relation to the ego"—about whether to grant the superego full independence or to continue to see it as a part of the ego. Freud seems to recognize how predatory and persecutory a superego can become if set free from the ego's guidance and capacity to mitigate its harshness. He will soon go on to explain that part of the superego's negative potency is also due to its deep-structural connections with the id. These two agencies may be diametrically opposed in their intentions, but they nevertheless share unconscious, irrational bonds which allow them, under certain circumstances, to join forces and make common cause against the ego. In chapter five, on Loewald, I explore these inter-agency relationships again, especially those between the ego and the superego, in the context of thinking about just how far one might take the metaphor of psychic metabolization.

In the meantime, Freud explores the superego's capacity to influence and sabotage the progress of analytic work—by imposing "a moral factor, the sense of guilt" and a kind of masochistic refusal to relinquish "the punishment of suffering"—to the point that the patient might turn against the analyst and the very prospect of getting better, a phenomenon that would become known as "negative therapeutic reaction". When these emotions remain largely unconscious—when, as Freud says, they are "dumb"—the patient "does not feel guilty, he feels ill".

As Freud tries to gain more understanding of such feelings, he turns to a familiar juxtaposition of "two very familiar maladies", obsessional neurosis and melancholia, this time in terms of how they stack up against each other where guilt is concerned. He claims not to know why guilt plays such an important part, why it is so powerful in these illnesses, but notes its significant contributions to both. The difference, it would seem, turns on how much the ego both knows about—or can afford to resist— the guilt that the superego brings to bear on the situation.

In the obsessional case, Freud says, "the sense of guilt is over-noisy but cannot justify itself to the ego" which then desperately seeks some form of absolution from the analyst. Freud advises against providing it and advocates sticking to the psychoanalytic task of discovering the repressed impulses that are causing the guilt. Using his new anthropomorphizing style, he adds that "in this case the super-ego knew more than the ego about the unconscious id". In melancholia, the superego's "hold upon consciousness" is even more powerful, but here "the ego ventures no objections; it admits its guilt and submits to the punishment".

This fresh formulation reinforces—and allows Freud to reiterate—an earlier judgement:

> We understand the difference. In obsessional neurosis what were in question were objectionable impulses which remained outside the ego, while in melancholia the object to which the super-ego's wrath applies has been taken into the ego through identification. [p. 51]

Freud now makes a short detour through hysteria and allied states where, he tells us, guilt tends to remain entirely unconscious "because the origin of conscience is intimately connected with the Oedipus complex, which belongs to the unconscious". However, he soon returns to his main intention of establishing the differences between obsessional and melancholic conditions.

He sets about this task with the tools of his new mental schema at his disposal, featuring the triumvirate id, ego, and superego; he waxes lyrical in this account of how and why, in melancholia, superegoic guilt is so very severe and virulent:

> If we turn to melancholia first, we find that the excessively strong super-ego which has obtained a hold upon consciousness rages against the ego with merciless violence, as if it has taken possession of the whole of the sadism available in the person concerned. Following our view of sadism, we should say that the destructive component had entrenched itself in the super-ego and turned against the ego. What is now holding sway in the super-ego is, as it were, a pure culture of the

death instinct, and in fact it often enough succeeds in driving the ego into death, if the latter does not fend off its tyrant in time by the change round into mania. [pp. 52–53]

By contrast, Freud notes, in obsessional neurosis—though the suffering can be "as distressing and tormenting"—the patient "never in fact takes the step of self-destruction"; this seems to be because the ego remains consciously aware of its rage is against an external object which has been retained as such and has not been invited into—and hidden within—the internal world. While the obsessional ego may therefore try to refuse the guilt imputed to it, by fending it off "with reaction formations and precautionary measures", it ends up feeling attacked on two fronts. Though the brutal extremes of each may be blunted, the ego still "defends itself vainly, alike against the instigations of the murderous id and against the reproaches of the punishing conscience" (p. 53).

In short, one might say that relative to the melancholic, the obsessional patient is both less advantaged by the privileges and less privy to the problems of identification and internalization. Whereas the obsessional patient rigorously attempts to control and censor external reality, the melancholic tries to exert these constraints internally. However, there is something particularly chilling about the idea that what has entered, "entrenched itself", and is "holding sway" in the melancholic superego is something very deadly indeed: "a pure culture of the death instinct".

As he approaches the conclusion of this breakthrough book, and perhaps in identification with the trials and tribulations of an embattled ego, it is understandable that Freud should try to assess the real potency of the latter, by making an inventory of its strengths and weaknesses. Though the strengths are numerous, there is a definite inclination towards specifying the weaknesses. At one point, an unflattering comparison is made between the ego's powers and those of "a constitutional monarch, without whose sanction no law can be passed but who hesitates long before imposing his veto on any measure put forward by Parliament" (p. 55).

Then, in a brilliant paragraph, insult is heaped upon injury as Freud famously speaks of "this same ego as a poor creature owing service to three masters and consequently menaced by three dangers: from the external world, from the libido of the id, and from the severity of the super-ego". Here we again witness an anthropomorphizing Freud adding flesh to the bones of this description in a distinctly literary style, as if outlining the plot of a melodrama or farce; the three agencies are clearly characters on his inner stage and he has not neglected to include the "external world", as the extra villain in the piece.

The insults intensify, as Freud has his ego lose all dignity and rush about in a flat panic—in truly unauthoritative, un-parental fashion—trying to keep everyone happy. He thoroughly skewers the ego's role, perhaps beginning with a sly dig at himself, *qua* analyst, and all the rest of us analysts, as follows:

> In point of fact it behaves like the physician during an analytic treatment: it offers itself, with the attention it pays to the real world, as a libidinal object to the id, and aims at attaching the id's libido to itself. It is not only a helper to the id; it is also a submissive slave who courts his master's love. Whenever possible, it tries to remain on good terms with the id; it clothes the id's *Ucs.* commands with its *Pcs.* rationalizations; it pretends that the id is showing obedience to the admonitions of reality, even when it is in fact remaining obstinate and unyielding; it disguises the id's conflicts with reality and, if possible, its conflicts with the super-ego too. In its position midway between the id and reality, it only too often yields to the temptation to become sycophantic, opportunist and lying, like a politician who sees the truth but wants to keep its place in popular favour. [p. 56]

As if he is anticipating an important direction that his interests will take in the next few years, this portrait is of a thoroughly inadequate and rather anxious ego, scrambling to fulfil unenviable tasks and to fend off trouble coming at it from all angles.

In fact, the last pages of Freud's text are rather preoccupied with *anxiety* and the different forms it can take. I will not go into these important matters now because they will soon be taking centre stage in the pages that follow. But it is perhaps worth glancing at and briefly considering what Freud has to say about death itself as he nears the end of this text:

> It presents a difficult problem to psychoanalysis, for death is an abstract concept with a negative content for which no unconscious correlative can be found. It would seem that the mechanism of the fear of death can only be that the ego relinquishes its narcissistic libidinal cathexis in a very large measure—that is, that it gives itself up, just as it gives up some *external* object in other cases in which it feels anxiety. I believe that the fear of death is something that occurs between the ego and the super-ego. [p. 58]

Seeming first to want to claim that we do not really have a mental or conceptual category for death itself, what Freud goes on to say recalls *Beyond the Pleasure Principle*, where he suggests that all we want to do is die in our own fashion and that death can even be thought of as a coping mechanism of sorts. The implication seems to be that when the going gets very tough, the ego might get going: if the losses and worries become too much to bear, or the superego too persecuting, an ego might be wise enough to treat itself as it would a bad object, one no longer worth having. It might then be the time to say enough is enough, to rid oneself of oneself, to bow out and depart life's stage.

Some structural implications

Before proceeding to the matter of anxiety that will before long become Freud's major preoccupation, it is worth pausing briefly for a glance at one or two of the papers that followed hot on the heels of *The Ego and the Id*. Freud seems rather to revel in the discoveries gleaned in that pivotal text, eager to play with the new set of conceptual or metapsychological toys he has uncovered there. Among the other clarifications offered by his new model of the mind, Freud thinks it can be used to consolidate his diagnostic or taxonomic understanding of mental illness.

In "Neurosis and Psychosis" (1924b) he offers the perhaps overly simple thesis that, if neurosis is to be regarded in terms of a conflict between the ego and the id, then psychosis must be one that pertains between the ego and reality or the outside world. Though in a slightly later paper—"The Loss of Reality in Neurosis and Psychosis" (1924e)—he feels forced to issue a retraction of these too-neat divisions, what he does *not* retract is the following:

> We may provisionally assume that there must also be illnesses which are based on a conflict between the ego and the super-ego. Analysis gives us a right to suppose that melancholia is a typical example of this group; and we would set aside the name of "narcissistic psychoneuroses" for disorders of that kind. [1924b, p. 152]

This is to see melancholia not only as lying somewhere between neurosis and psychosis, but also as the consequence—like the fear of death itself in the last quotation from *The Ego and the Id*—of "something that occurs" in the internal relationship between the ego and the superego. Though this aetiology is paramount and had already been implicit in "Mourning and Melancholia", it is nevertheless important to have it corroborated in this more categorical way and re-formulated in the terms of Freud's new theoretical schema.

In "Negation" (1925h), moreover, there is a first-principle or philosophical endeavour to understand the function of naysaying in psychoanalysis, from which Freud then extrapolates what he calls, more generally, "the function of intellectual judgement". The relevance to my purposes of this brief but far-reaching exploration lies again in how he expresses these ideas. According to him, this function has two fundamental tasks: "It affirms or disaffirms the possession by a thing of a particular attribute; and it asserts or disputes that a presentation has an existence in reality". These are two different kinds of judgement, under the aegis of the "pleasure-ego" and the "reality-ego", respectively. The first of these is described as follows:

> Expressed in the language of the oldest—the oral—instinctual impulses, the judgement is: "I should like to eat this", or "I should like to spit it out"; and, put more generally, "I should like to take this into myself and to keep that out". That is to say: "It shall be inside me" or "It shall be outside me". As I have shown elsewhere, the original pleasure-ego wants to introject into itself everything that is good and to eject from itself everything that is bad. [pp. 236–237]

Apart from the fact that we find here an important precursory moment where Freud anticipates Klein's descriptions of splitting, projection, and paranoid-schizoid functioning more generally, this is yet another clear corroboration of the importance of oral-alimentary imagery in the explanation of such dynamics, one that also exemplifies Freud's attempt to appropriate introjection, Ferenczi's specific coinage, in the process.

Freud also explicates "the other sort of decision made by the function of judgement—as to the real existence of something of which there is a presentation (reality testing)", which one can again see as pre-empting an important aspect of Klein's depressive position. Here he adds a profound and paradoxical sentence reinforcing the importance of loss—and thus mourning and melancholia—to crucial mental capacities such as these: "But it is evident that a precondition for the setting up of reality testing is that objects shall have been lost which once brought real satisfaction" (pp. 237–238). The entire psychoanalytic world would surely agree that without such experiences and the capacity to face and bear losses like these, living and functioning in the complex, compromised, real world is rendered very difficult indeed.

Anxiety and loss

Although I do not intend to traverse the entire history of Freud's ideas and theories about anxiety, it is worth paying some attention to where that trajectory concludes, in *Inhibitions, Symptoms and Anxiety* (1926d), arguably his last major theoretical work. There Freud consolidates a significant shift in his views on the matter, and this has the effective consequence of placing loss—or separation, as he sometimes prefers to call it here—at the root cause of virtually all states of anxiety. This implicitly elevates the issue of how we deal with losses or separations—that is, whether we mourn them or become melancholically stuck with them—to the potentially most determining variable in psychic life.

Freud arrives, by degrees, at the important realization that anxiety can take the form of either a salutary early-warning system or a devastating and overwhelming flash flood. Thus, what is of crucial importance is our psychic preparedness for the various testing losses that will threaten and assail us throughout our lives. Strachey (1959) lists and specifies these in his introduction to the text as follows: "birth, loss of the mother as an object, loss of the penis, loss of the object's love, loss of the super-ego's love" (p. 82), though of course there are many other losses that could be added.

Strachey also remarks that *Inhibitions, Symptoms and Anxiety* was prompted and provoked by Otto Rank's *The Trauma of Birth* (1924), a publication that Freud really had to grapple with and that became the bane of his life around this period. He seemed unable to decide whether Rank had brought something valuable to psychoanalysis or had produced nothing but a contentious and perhaps rather foolish distraction. Freud's own book is one of those "large, loose, baggy monsters"—to quote Henry James's (1921) famous comment on certain nineteenth-century Russian novels—and Strachey says that "Freud found an unusual difficulty in unifying the work" (p. 78). This is betrayed by a title that cannot quite make up its mind on a single central theme and by the need for a "tidying-up" final section, entitled "Addenda", to which some of the most illuminating and clarifying insights in the work are consigned. I limit myself here to those sections where Freud's ideas about anxiety, depression, and loss are seen to intersect and impact significantly on each other.

When proceeding through this unwieldy text, one gets the sense that Freud feels caught between wanting to utterly repudiate his earlier theory of anxiety—seeming quite ashamed of it at times—and wishing to defend it or even to find reason to somehow maintain it, as a kind of keepsake or harmless subsidiary clause in a new contract. The earlier hypothesis proposed that anxiety is nothing other than some sort of by-product of libidinal frustration or repression, produced rather concretely by the siphoning-off of a certain amount of undischarged libido and transforming or transmuting it into a quantity of anxious affect.

Strachey lists several different places in Freud's work where this view is expressed, including in a footnote in the 1920 edition of *Three Essays on the Theory of Sexuality*, where Freud, with his reliable penchant for the apt metaphor, declares that libido is related to anxiety "in the same kind of way as vinegar is to wine" (1905d, p. 79). Though there is some evidence that Freud had some doubts about this idea from quite early on, he also espoused it for many years and even struggled to relinquish it completely in the current work, where it is at times almost comical to witness him trying to reserve a little place for it somewhere within his new theory.

The fact of the matter, however, is that Freud had—whether he fully accepted this or not—moved on from those earlier, more concrete, virtually "hydraulic" theories of the libido, if not from the libido itself. Another way to characterize these new ideas about anxiety is to say that with them Freud returns to the other pole of an old distinction, to the somewhat neglected notion of self-preservation. We may remember that hunger is the first and most obvious manifestation of the need for self-preservation, a force that Freud placed in opposition to libido (even though the latter is also inferred from and propped upon the former) in his first instinct theory. In his determination to trace anxiety to the right sources this time around, Freud seems to want to go back to basics, to return first and foremost to a biological perspective, while simultaneously making use of his recently formulated structural model of the mind.

These combinations allow him to declare—stating what now seems obvious—that anxiety is always a response to a danger of some kind, to a threat to self-preservation. He extrapolates from this supposition to say that most, if not all, dangers refer or relate to losing or being separated from something or someone. Freud goes on to describe these experiences in terms of the conflicts and struggles for ascendancy among his new internal characters, id, ego and, superego (as well as the fourth element in the equation, external reality, or the outside world). Summing up Freud's intentions in such an orderly way somewhat conceals the convoluted, stop-start, meandering process by which he gradually arrives at these insights in this book.

The above ideas begin to fall into place near the end of the seventh chapter. Freud has been revisiting the complex ways in which castration anxiety generates the animal phobias featured in the Little Hans and Wolf Man cases, including in this picture the active part that he can now attribute to the superego. However, he is now ready to start drawing some more general conclusions: "Anxiety is a reaction to a situation of *danger*. It is obviated by the ego's doing something to avoid the situation or to withdraw from it." He later adds, via his consideration of the traumatic neuroses, that "it would seem highly improbable that a neurosis could come into being merely because of the objective presence of danger, without any participation of the deeper levels of the mental apparatus" (1926d, pp. 128–129).

Though thus far it is still castration anxiety that dominates Freud's conception of the problem, and though he again insists that there is no category in the unconscious mind that would allow us to fear death itself or "give any content to the annihilation of life", he is now edging closer to a broader perspective. Trying also to keep in mind the recently re-invoked traumatic anxiety, where, as he had said in *Beyond the Pleasure Principle*, "the protective shield against external stimuli is broken through and excessive amounts of excitation impinge upon the mental apparatus", Freud now produces an impressive set of links:

> The statement I have just made, to the effect that the ego has been prepared to expect castration by having constantly undergone object-losses, places the question of anxiety in a new light. We have hitherto regarded it as an affective signal of danger; but now, since the danger is so often one of castration, it appears to us as *a reaction to loss, a separation*. . . . The first experience of anxiety that an individual goes through (in the case of human beings, at all events), is birth, and, objectively speaking, birth is a separation from the mother. It could be compared to a castration of the mother (by equating the child with a penis). Now it would be very satisfactory if anxiety as a symbol of a separation, were to be repeated on every subsequent occasion on which a separation took place. [p. 130, emphasis added]

There is, one might say, a lot wrong with this statement. Many of us no longer agree with the "castratizing" of loss in this fashion—that is, Freud's insistence on treating all losses or separations as metaphorical or symbolic castrations, whether or not they really are akin to (and regardless of whether they temporally precede or succeed) the fear of castration proper.

Nevertheless, there is a potentially welcome corollary lurking in such thinking, namely, that castration could itself be regarded as just one loss among many, and that the universal issue could turn out to be loss or separation as such. In fact, Freud becomes progressively less concerned with extending the dynamics of castration anxiety and more interested in "the affective reactions to a separation", which, he notes, are usually seen as "pain and mourning, not anxiety". He closes the chapter with a reminder of "Mourning and Melancholia" and the still unsolved problem of why mourning "should be such a painful thing" (pp. 130–131).

Having tentatively made this connection between anxiety and mourning, Freud becomes more curious about it. He begins the next chapter by launching an inquiry into "what anxiety really is", and he now decides that it is "something that is felt", an unpleasant affect, and therefore comparable to other such affects, like "tension, pain or mourning". What are the nuances and differences, he now wants to know, that both link and separate these feeling states? It is noteworthy that we now find Freud beginning to be more interested than ever before in the nuanced, qualitative distinctions between different emotional states, rather than seeing them in primarily quantitative terms, and he will return to these somewhat vexed and puzzling issues right at the end of the book.

Given that Freud seems to have been driven back into biological and early-life perspectives in his search for the "first principles" of anxiety, the event of birth keeps cropping up in his deliberations, compelling him to cross swords with Rank. Freud clearly wants to make room for birth in his own account of anxiety, but it is no less important that he find a place for it that does not fall into the excesses, exaggerations, and absurdities that he finds in Rank's recent book.

As we track these movements in the text, we can see a subtle shift in Freud's entire view, not only of anxiety, but of what he prioritizes in mental life. These are, in fact, break-through moments in Freud's development, and they are accompanied by a renewed capacity to see the world from an infant's point of view. Contemplating such fears as being left alone or in the dark or with a stranger, Freud identifies these as situations "of missing someone who is loved and longed for" and thus brings the figure of the mother firmly into focus.

He will now have another go at trying to formulate a more unified view of anxiety—this time one that does not rely on castration as its primary trope. With the mother in mind, Freud is now writing resonantly as well as presciently, sounding far more like the legitimate precursor of all later object-relations perspectives:

> The child's mnemic image of the person longed for is no doubt intensely cathected, probably in a hallucinatory way at first. But this has no effect; and now it seems as though the longing turns into anxiety. This anxiety has all the appearance of being the expression of the child feeling at its wits' end, as though in its still very undeveloped state it did not know how better to cope with its cathexis of longing. Here anxiety appears as a reaction to the felt loss of the object; and we are at once reminded of the fact that castration anxiety, too, is a fear of being separated from a highly valued object, and that the earliest anxiety of all—the "primal anxiety" of birth—is brought about on the occasion of a separation from the mother. [p. 137]

Yes, both castration and birth are referenced here, included in the catalogue of potential losses or separations and the concomitant states of anxiety that ramify from what Freud refers to as the "cathexis of longing".

However, neither is now being put forward as having psychic priority, as the *fons et origo* of anxiety *per se*.

He does not hesitate to take this one step further. It is not even the "loss of object" itself that lies at the existential source of the feeling: the mother, he says, is desperately missed and summoned vocally by the infant, "because it already knows by experience that she satisfies all its needs without delay". Thus, the actual danger against which protection is sought—and in response to which there is such an anguished outcry—"is that of non-satisfaction, of a *growing tension due to need*, against which it is helpless" (p. 137). Despite having arrived at a fresh appreciation of this needy, helpless infantile state and the dependency on maternal provision that it invokes, Freud still stays shy of the full implications of object-relatedness. The object's usefulness is what determines its significance, and this falls well short of Fairbairn's (1952) later radical and uncompromising claim that the ego is not primarily expedient, not satisfaction-, but object-seeking.

Nevertheless, there has already been a significant shift in Freud's view, one that is easily missed if one fails to remember the crucial distinctions of his earlier instinct theory or regards it as having been completely superseded by the more recent version. Here is a passage in which Freud's object-relations credentials are, I think, firmly clinched and consolidated:

> When the infant has found out by experience that an external, perceptible object can put an end to the dangerous situation that is reminiscent of birth, the content of the danger it fears is displaced from the economic situation onto the condition which determined that situation, viz., the loss of object. It is the absence of the mother that is now the danger; and as soon as that danger arises the infant gives the signal of anxiety, before the dreaded economic situation has set in. This change constitutes *a first great step forward in the provision made by the infant for its self-preservation*, and at the same time represents a transition from the automatic and involuntary fresh appearance of anxiety to the intentional reproduction of anxiety as a signal of danger. [pp. 137–138, emphasis added]

As the last sentence suggests, anxiety should, can, and does change from a quantum to a sign. And as the italicized phrase suggests, it is in the service of self-preservation, rather than at the behest of the libido, that signal anxiety is seen to operate here.

One source of overwhelming traumatic anxiety can, of course, be the libidinal and aggressive urges welling up in the id, and it is therefore up to the ego to muster a defensive early-warning system against them. But this system must also mobilize against certain needs stemming from dangers that appear to come from without and to threaten its very existence when the external object safeguarding survival is absent. Perhaps words like "satisfaction" or "gratification" can be applied ambiguously enough to mask the fact that relative libidinal *desires* and absolute self-preservative *needs* represent different urges or states of mind. Winnicott (1960a) will later make good use of this distinction, encouraging us, as clinicians, to know the difference well enough to frustrate the former but gratify the latter.

Here, Freud seems to have subtly turned his attention away from desire and towards need as he tries to broaden the base for his understanding of anxiety and reaches for a more general and encompassing account of it. However, it is also advantageous to Freud at this moment to blur such distinctions. In so doing, he can have his cake and eat it, by distinguishing different forms of anxiety while also identifying family resemblances among them and keeping them all under the same rubric.

He does so in the next few pages of the text by describing a linked series of developmental, age- or stage-appropriate responses to successive kinds of danger:

> The progress which the child makes in its development—its growing independence, the sharper division of its mental apparatus into several agencies, the advent of new needs—cannot fail to exert an influence upon the content of the danger-situation. We have already traced the change of that content from loss of the mother as an object to castration. The next change is caused by the power of the super-ego. With the depersonalization of the parental agency from which castration was feared, the danger becomes less defined. Castration anxiety develops into moral anxiety—social anxiety—and it is not so easy now to know what the anxiety is about. [p. 139]

As with so much else in Freud's conception of development, while it is optimal for a person to move seamlessly from each one of these anxiety states to the next, there is always the propensity to get stuck or fixated along the way, which can result in the developmental passage being only partial at best. This then poses the question: how does one move on from one kind of anxiety to another without being burdened by the residue of its previous forms, which would exacerbate each new situation, creating a perhaps generally anxious personality?

Freud seems to combine an attempt to address such a question with another, similar catalogue of the typical succession of anxious trials that humans are subject to:

> This study of the determinants of anxiety has, as it were, shown the defensive behaviour of the ego transfigured in a rational light. Each

> situation of danger corresponds to a particular period of life or a particular developmental phase of the mental apparatus and appears to be justifiable for it. In early infancy the individual is really not equipped to master psychically the large sums of excitation that reach him whether from without or within. Again, at a certain period of life his most important interest really is that the people he is dependent on should not withdraw their loving care of him. Later on in his boyhood, when he feels that his father is a powerful rival in regard to his mother and becomes aware of his own aggressive inclinations towards him and of his sexual intentions towards his mother, he really is justified in being afraid of his father; and his fear of being punished by him can find expression through phylogenetic reinforcement in the fear of being castrated. Finally, as he enters into social relationships, it really is necessary for him to be afraid of his super-ego, to have a conscience; and the absence of that factor would give rise to severe conflicts, dangers and so on. [pp. 146–147]

As clear, straightforward, and realistic (note the repetition of the word "really") as this sounds—as "transfigured in a rational light" as it may appear—it is perhaps more descriptive than explanatory.

What Freud does not really offer is any account of how these fears or anxieties are overcome or worked through, though it is implicit and obvious that the nature of the caregiving received by the individual will be—or will have been—crucial from the start. Moreover, not all that much overcoming or working-through may be required if, as he suggests, each of these fear or anxiety responses is appropriate and necessary only in its respective moment, making them easier to cope with one at a time, as development proceeds.

Skipping forward now to the "Addenda" chapter, I will mention just one or two passages where similar clarity is reached: for example, in relation to the two main categories of anxiety that his new theory has identified:

> Thus we attributed two modes of origin to anxiety in later life. One was involuntary, automatic and always justified on economic grounds, and arose whenever a danger-situation analogous to birth had established itself. The other was produced by the ego as soon as a situation of this kind merely threatened to occur, in order to call for its avoidance. In the second case the ego subjects itself to *anxiety as a sort of inoculation*, submitting to a slight attack of the illness in order to escape its full strength. It vividly imagines the danger situation, as it were, with the unmistakable purpose of restricting that distressing experience to a mere indication, a signal. [p. 162, emphasis added]

Following this very useful distinction (and the particularly apt metaphor of inoculation), a few pages later Freud says, more pithily, "Anxiety is therefore on the one hand an expectation of a trauma, and on the other a repetition of it in a mitigated form" and adds that the expectation of anxiety "belongs to the danger-situation, whereas its indefiniteness and lack of object belong to the traumatic situation of helplessness" (p. 166).

The whole point of working through Freud's thoughts about anxiety in this text—and I am aware that this part of the exegetical journey might have felt a little prolonged and arduous—was to accompany him to the brink of a moment rather similar to the one he faced earlier in his career, in "Mourning and Melancholia". There, in tackling depression, he addressed how we deal with loss, our relative successes or failures in this regard. Is it not ironic—and fascinating—that we now, more than a decade on, arrive with him at the self-same question in relation to anxiety, which, it turns out, is also something that is intimately bound up with loss and separation?

Freud himself did not miss this irony: indeed, he virtually concludes *Inhibitions, Symptoms and Anxiety* by taking note of it in the final section of the final chapter. The latter is entitled "Anxiety, Pain and Mourning", and it thus repeats and mimics the tripartite structure of the title of the book, as well, perhaps, as the juxtaposing way that it explores these themes:

> The problem before us arises out of the conclusion we have reached that anxiety comes to be a reaction to the danger of a loss of an object. Now we already know one reaction to the loss of an object, and that is mourning. The question therefore is, when does that loss lead to anxiety and when to mourning? [p. 169]

It is as much as Freud can do to pose such a question; he is certainly not ready to answer it. And yet, it is evident that his explorations into the nature of mourning (and melancholia) have provided the stimulus for these later enquiries about how anxiety is to be considered and dealt with.

Here he finally addresses, if perhaps in a rather rudimentary way, the question of how depression and anxiety interact in the mind and come into meaningful clinical relation with one another. Yet he was perhaps never confident that he knew enough about these conditions, what distinguishes them, or, indeed, how they are related. It is important to note—and we will soon be exploring this in detail—that many of Freud's deliberations on these matters were dialogical responses to Karl Abraham who, given his greater experience with patients suffering from these ailments, was often intuitively there ahead of him. Abraham recognized that many patients present with the symptoms of both depression and anxiety;

he proffered the idea that whereas the former is linked with grief about a painful past, the latter represents the fear of a similarly troubled future.

It is interesting that, even down to our day, these two "illnesses" (or are they more like "meta-states" characterizing, accompanying, or contributing to various more discrete or defined psychopathologies?) continue frequently, if not invariably, to be mentioned together in descriptive or diagnostic accounts. The recognition of their proximity has latterly been reinforced within psychiatry via the psychotropic claim that certain newer types of antidepressant medication will ease the symptoms of both conditions simultaneously.

From the psychoanalytic vantage point of later and current generations, the thoughts of Freud and Abraham still sound and feel theoretically important and clinically resonant, though they also leave us with a residue of puzzling and frustrating questions. As clinicians, we surely try to help our patients to work through their anxious states—no less, say, than their depressive ones. But are we meant to do the same kinds of things with anxiety? How precisely are we meant to help patients to process it, to release its fixated aspects, to at least ease the passage from one developmental type to another, to escape traumatic incursions of it while embracing its signal form? Are there more and less effective ways of doing all of this, and is there more to know, conceptually, about the treatment of anxiety as such?

Might it be worth while, for instance, to posit a parallel of sorts by suggesting that mourning is to melancholia what signal anxiety is to traumatic anxiety? Indeed, could some light be shed on these puzzles and dilemmas by bringing the metaphors of digestion to bear on anxiety, too? Would it be possible to consider anxiety-as-warning as a more thoroughly internalized, introjected, or integrated form of the all-too-concrete, ego-destructive predations of anxiety-as-trauma? Can the latter be converted into the former? Do we dare encourage and try to help even deeply traumatized patients to gradually tolerate, take in, and metabolize quantities of anxiety—to turn extraordinary, unbearable losses into more ordinary, bearable ones—in the hope and belief that we can sufficiently shore up their ego-systems to cope with, rather than succumb to, invasion and devastation?

I can myself offer little more at this stage than the plethora of questions and speculations that has burst out above. In addition to standing before them, however, what we have also run squarely into, once again, are the limits of internalization. It is the very existence of anxiety—particularly in its traumatic, overwhelming, unbound, uncontainable forms—that poses vital questions about the procedures that such terms as binding, containing, processing, assimilating, digesting, metabolizing (and many others) refer to. We must surely concede that there exist experiences of loss and separation so severe that no signalling system, mourning process, or internalizing capacity would be equal to or able to handle.

It is almost time to proceed beyond Freud himself, first to consider the contributions of his two most important disciples and contemporaries, Ferenczi and Abraham, and thence to what post-Freudians like Klein, Loewald, Abraham and Torok, and Green have to offer. So, I will conclude my textual explorations of Freud by suggesting that, at the very least, his altered and revised ideas about anxiety can—and perhaps must—be read as an extension of the problems of mourning and melancholia.

As many others have noted, Freud's own psychoanalytic emphases underwent significant changes in the latter part of his career. To consider these changes in the light of how he extended his reach beyond the transference neuroses and brought depression and a new conception of anxiety under the aegis of his therapeutic and theoretical gaze is as important a perspective as any. It serves to consolidate the seismic shift in the entire focus of psychoanalysis—even during Freud's own lifetime—from the id-based realms of wish and desire to the ego-states of lack and loss. This is a shift captured by the immortal words of the 1969 song by The Rolling Stones, "You can't always get what you want". Though they repeatedly intone this universal and tragic truth and refrain, the lyrics also suggest that—with some (therapeutic?) effort and perhaps a bit of luck—you might find what you *need*.

CHAPTER THREE

Sándor Ferenczi:
inventing introjection;
Karl Abraham:
phenomenologist of depression

By the end of the first decade of the century, psychoanalysis was no longer just a one-man show. Well before Freud had begun to make some of the conceptual and theoretical shifts concerning mourning and the internal world laid out in chapter one, he was no longer operating primarily in a vacuum or flying solo; nor, indeed, was he still working with or confiding both his dreams and his doubts to just one single trusted companion at a time—a Josef Breuer or a Wilhelm Fliess. He had begun to gather around him an "inner circle", a small band of enthusiastic and (at least initially) faithful fellow travellers, whose mission it would become to co-create the new science, as well as to preserve and protect it against detractors and enemies. This more communal expansion of psychoanalysis was presaged earlier, just after the turn of the century—following Freud's break with Fliess—by the formation in Vienna of the Wednesday Psychological Society, a group of mostly Jewish physicians and intellectuals (already including the likes of Alfred Adler and Wilhelm Stekel) who met regularly to discuss some of the embryonic ideas of psychoanalysis.

The transformation of this quite casual and local social gathering into the much more urgently required, international, Camelot-like round table of knights-errant that would become known as the Secret Committee was a reaction to the turbulent rise and fall of Freud's romance with Carl Jung during these years. This is a tale told entertainingly—if somewhat melodramatically and salaciously—in *The Secret Ring* by Phyllis Grosskurth (1991), who was also one of the biographers of Melanie Klein (Grosskurth, 1986).

Freud was surprised and flattered by the interest of Jung, who visited him for the first time in 1907 from the Burghölzli Clinic in Zurich, perhaps the foremost psychiatric hospital of its time. Freud was soon setting much store by this "great white hope", the young "Aryan prince" who, it was believed, would rescue psychoanalysis—the "Jewish science"—from this designation and take it forward into a less parochial future. Things, as we know, did not work out that way. Having already seen off rebellions from Adler and Stekel, Freud bitterly parted company with Jung in 1913 in much the same way, regarding their differences from him as apostasy, just as he would continue to do with allies or acolytes who would sooner or later disappoint him.

In 1905, Freud had met a precocious young Viennese intellectual called Otto Rank and kept him close by conscripting him as secretary, first of the informal Wednesday group, and later of the Viennese Psychoanalytic Society. Then, during the same period in which Jung came on the scene, he became acquainted in quick succession with the Russian Max Eitingon, the Welshman Ernest Jones, Karl Abraham from Germany, and Sándor Ferenczi from Hungary. Freud's biographer, Peter Gay (1988), would designate these four as "the foreigners". Along with Hanns Sachs, another member of the Wednesday group in Vienna, these men would later make up the trusted, six-strong inner circle that Jones (the only non-Jew in it) instigated and encouraged Freud to create in the wake of the loss of Jung and his other early supporters.

It must be remembered that these men were all, like Jung, some 15 to 25 years younger than Freud. He gave each of them a ring symbolizing—and perhaps enforcing—their apostolic commitment to him. A famous photograph, taken in 1922, depicts the seven together. Eitingon was a wealthy man and provided much-needed funds for the fledgling psychoanalytic community. Jones was the organizational mastermind behind many of the group's pragmatic activities, and he would continue in this role on behalf of the wider psychoanalytic movement during the decades ahead. Much later, in 1938, he was responsible, with the help of Marie Bonaparte, for rescuing Freud and his daughter Anna from the Nazis.

However, there can be no doubt that it was to Abraham and Ferenczi that Freud looked for both intellectual and personal succour. Having met the two men less than a couple of months apart between late 1907 and early 1908, each would become a constant, invaluable companion as Freud took his therapeutic and theoretical endeavours forward in fresh directions and as they pioneered psychoanalysis in Berlin and Budapest, respectively. They would both predecease him: favourite sons dying tragically before their father, thus imposing on him more occasions for mourning. It is by no means a matter of chance that a collection of essays entitled *Psychoanalytic Pioneers* (Alexander, Eisenstein, & Grotjahn, 1966), penned by later analysts about their major early predecessors, opens with chapters on "Karl Abraham: The First German Psychoanalyst" and "Sandor Ferenczi: Pioneer of Pioneers".

Though one may speak of them in the same breath or include them in the same sentences (and here within a single chapter), the differences between the two men in spirit and personality, and in their respective relationships with Freud, were large and defining. Where Abraham was the stable and faithful scion, loath to challenge Freud even over real theoretical disagreements and despite his experience exceeding Freud's own in important clinical areas, Ferenczi was the more challenging and erratic, if also charming and disarming child who never stopped pestering Freud with his personal insecurities and demands for attention. It is easy, of course, to exaggerate, polarize, and parody these differences, but they are illuminating nonetheless, highlighting the internal tension and ambivalence in what Freud himself desired and sought from his disciples.

The importance of Ferenczi and Abraham for my specific purposes is that each made, in his own different way, extremely important textual contributions towards the changing trajectory of Freud's thinking, as characterized in chapters one and two. Of course, Abraham and Ferenczi made these contributions relatively early in the history of psychoanalysis: throughout their curtailed careers, they remained committed to a Freudian psychoanalytic model that revolved around the centrality of sexuality and repression.

However, it is also true to say that they were instrumental, even during those years dominated by Freud, in nudging psychoanalysis forward from its one-person emphasis on the transference neuroses and their sexual aetiology, towards a more object-related and internal-world focus on loss and the narcissistic neuroses of melancholia and depression. As we shall see, where Ferenczi's role was to provide, with quirky brilliance, a crucial conceptual tool for the creating and theorizing of an internal world, Abraham's was to render, with clarity and acumen, the relevant clinical and phenomenological experience to enrich the psychoanalytic perspective on depressive illness.

Sándor Ferenczi

"On Introjection and Transference" (1909)

Time and again over the course of his career, Ferenczi would make importunate, if usually deferential, demands of a perplexed Freud, who would respond by urging this insecure and volatile younger man—who was also, for perhaps too short a time, his analysand—to take a breath and be a little more circumspect. These tensions characterized the professional and personal relationship between the two men throughout a close though ambivalent 25-year association that almost ended in schism but was instead cut abruptly short by Ferenczi's premature death in 1933. One of Freud's last papers, "Analysis Terminable and Interminable" (1937c), can be read in part as an elegy to his mercurial disciple, colleague, and friend. Their respective temperaments and approaches to psychoanalytic work would also go forth to create quite different legacies and leave distinguishing marks on later incarnations of their enterprise.

It all began when Ferenczi, working as a young doctor in Budapest in the early years of the century, found himself deeply dissatisfied and at odds with the positivistic trends prevailing in orthodox psychiatry at the time. Though he had already been drawn to psychoanalysis and had begun to use a version of the psychoanalytic method in his clinical work, he must surely have experienced a year like no other after his first meeting with Freud. They began, almost at once, an enthusiastic therapeutic and theoretical collaboration. So meteoric was his rise to prominence that Ferenczi was invited in 1909 to accompany Freud and Jung on their momentous trip to the United States, where Freud delivered his first public lectures on psychoanalysis at Clark University.

Published in the same year, "On Introjection and Transference" was Ferenczi's first important piece of psychoanalytic writing. Not only providing a detailed commentary on the concept of transference, one that would have a hand in extending the relevance of the term and making it the very touchstone of psychoanalytic practice and thought, the paper also introduced the brand-new concept of introjection, in the hope of providing further understanding of the neurotic—as well as the normal—mind.

What we learn about Ferenczi from this early paper will remain characteristic of his career as a whole: that he cared deeply and passionately for his patients and wanted to provide them with nothing less than a cure; and that, with this end in view, he was also determined to get both his clinical technique and his metapsychological thinking straight. It is already evident, moreover, that these vocational desires and professional ambitions could manifest themselves somewhat fervently and anxiously, perhaps in emulation or identification with the very patients he was so keen to help. As he discusses the sufferings of neurotic patients and the difficulties experienced by the doctors who try to treat them, one notes the contrast between Ferenczi's zealous, hyperbolic, uneven style, punctuated by moments of rhetorical brilliance, and the calmer, more considered (if no less brilliant) tones of Freud's writing.

Turning now to the paper itself, though introjection is named first in the title, Ferenczi does not introduce it until several pages have elapsed. Perhaps it is apt, given his position as the young acolyte and relative newcomer, that he unveils his own coinage and contribution as a supplementary metapsychological supporting act to the main event, namely, Freud's notion of transference. It is the latter that occupies pride of place, provides the overall context, and takes up most of Ferenczi's attention in the paper, and he perhaps wishes to impress his senior colleague with the extent of his own investment in the concept. He begins by citing, without preamble, the now famous Freudian passage in which "transferences" are described as "new editions or facsimiles of the impulses and fantasies" experienced towards the original object who is replaced "by the person of the physician". This quotation is from the Dora case (Freud, 1905e) where Freud, by his own admission, failed to pay sufficient heed to this phenomenon and therefore achieved only limited success in her treatment.

Though he does not go into this failure, it is more than likely that Ferenczi's wish both to explore the transference and to bring a new term to bear on the proceedings were very much affected by his own struggles to treat neurotic patients fully and successfully (not to mention a tendency to become sexually embroiled with some of them). Ferenczi does not mention and may or may not have had in mind Freud's earlier attempt to explain and define transference in the very last pages of *Studies on Hysteria*, co-authored with Breuer (1895d). Though it manifested only belatedly in the treatment with the latter, the neurotic susceptibility and recourse to the erotic transference of the first patient of psychoanalysis, Anna O, emerged so suddenly and with such force that the physician promptly fled the fancies and fantasies that she directed towards him.

I adduce these well-known historical facts at least partially to remind us of the extent to which the early psychoanalysts were preoccupied with—and perhaps bedevilled by—the problematics of what would become known as the "transference neuroses", a category that Ferenczi's paper would also help to create. The second part of this two-part paper now reads as if it belongs to psychoanalytic pre-history; it goes to great lengths (by providing copious clinical examples) and is at pains to prove, contra the French hypno-psychiatrists Charcot and Bernheim and their followers, that transference, with its deep roots in the earliest parental/oedipal complexes, explains virtually all of what goes on in hypnosis and suggestion.

Though the latter methods were initially important to Freud, Ferenczi claims that those who continue to use and advocate them—while maintaining a wilful failure to appreciate the facts and workings of transference—can easily be led astray and end up hoist by their own petard. Male physicians with female patients are particularly liable to develop the narcissistic delusion that they have somehow been transformed from ordinary doctors into irresistible lotharios or gurus with special powers, but they can then get themselves into hot water—as Breuer's experience with Anna O and Freud's with Dora attest.

My focus, however, will be primarily on the first, shorter part of Ferenczi's paper, which lays the groundwork and bears the subtitle "Introjection in the Neurosis". Here, before heralding his new concept, Ferenczi launches a virtual advertising campaign for transference, becoming a vociferous spokesperson for its centrality in psychoanalytic work with neurotic patients. According to him, the neurotic has an intense need to transfer, to find in the environment someone upon whom to work out ancient childhood emotions associated with their original significant objects:

> With increasing experience one becomes convinced that the apparently motiveless extravagance of affect, the excessive hate, love and sympathy of neurotics, are also nothing else but transferences, by means of which long forgotten psychical experiences are (in the unconscious phantasy) brought into connection with the current occasion, and the current reaction exaggerated by the affect of unconscious ideational complexes. [1909, p. 36]

Though he is later at pains also to insist that this tendency to transfer is not all that extraordinary—merely an intensified and perhaps more desperate version of what we are always doing in our relationships with others—it is still striking just how much emphasis Ferenczi places on transference as the neurotic phenomenon *par excellence*.

Various other typical traits—including "the inclination of psychoneurotics to *imitation*, and the 'psychical infection' so frequent among hysterics", as well as their "impressionability" and "capacity to feel in the most intense way for the experiences of others"—are then linked to transference by means of another significant term: "The patient copies the symptoms or character traits of a person when . . . he *identifies* himself in his unconscious with him" (p. 37). Here is more evidence, in Ferenczi's writing no less than in Freud's, that certain interrelated concepts—the various cognates, synonyms, or subsets of internalization—are coming to the fore and growing in significance at or around this period in the development of psychoanalytic thought. However, in this early paper Ferenczi is still concentrating on the neurotic illnesses on which psychoanalysis is founded and does not appear to have anything approaching mourning and its pathologies on his mind.

It is therefore interesting that he now proceeds to write about what he sees as another set of typically neurotic tendencies, connected with the concrete takings-in of ingestion and digestion. He gets there by way of the claim that neurotics, with their typical aversion to things explicitly sexual or violent, transfer these interests from certain bodily regions or acts to others that they find less offensive or not as difficult to contemplate consciously:

> An example of this is the unconscious identification of grossly sexual genital functions with those of the oral organs (eating, kissing), as was first established by Freud. In a number of analyses I have been able to prove that the partiality of hysterics for dainty feeding, their inclination to eat indigestible material (chalk, unripe fruit, etc.), their peculiar search for exotic dishes, their preference or idiosyncrasy in regard to food of a particular form or consistency, that all this was concerned with the displacement of interest from repressed erotic (genital or coprophilic) inclinations, and was an indication of a lack of sexual satisfaction. [p. 38]

It is noteworthy here that Ferenczi's catalogue of oral-alimentary behaviours and ailments pertains not only to the mouth and the oesophagus but to the gut and the rest of the alimentary apparatus as well. His faithfulness to Freud and the essentially sexual aetiology of all such oral freakery might sound a little reductive to the contemporary psychoanalytic ear, but, at least for my purposes, what it signifies is the way that various forms of "taking in"—whether physical, mental, or both—are becoming more current in the psychoanalytic thinking of the time.

Though we have yet to arrive at Ferenczi's new coinage, we can already see how, either consciously or otherwise, he is building his case for the necessity of a concept like introjection. In the meantime, such mental acts as transferring, displacing, and identifying are all emerging as pertinent variations on the theme of repression, the neurotic defence against facing incestuous desires and the aversions, anxieties, and conflicts that they engender. Ferenczi is mindful that the common defensive tasks of these terms might cause them to lose their specificity and bleed into each other—and many a student of psychoanalysis, down to our own day, has struggled to keep them separate in his or her mind. Psychoanalysis itself was still young enough in 1909 for these mental mechanisms to be regarded primarily as defensive manoeuvres, directed against the discomfits of sexuality; they were yet to be regarded as usefully constructive developmental and formative measures in themselves.

The later careers of both Freud and Ferenczi, and the psychoanalytic dispensations that followed, would also eventually bring into prominence the fact that there are other kinds of need—associated more, perhaps, with self-preservation and self-worth, as well as loss and separation, than with libidinal desire—that can also be consigned to the unconscious underworld. As they make their return to consciousness from being repressed or disavowed, these states of mind are no less unpleasant and difficult to acknowledge and can therefore call forth a whole range of different defensive measures.

Having noted the general inclination of neurotics to transfer to all and sundry, Ferenczi begins at this juncture to describe the actual workings of the transference in the clinical, and specifically psychoanalytic, context. In anticipation of Hans Loewald's evocative way of describing the invitation or summons that analysis issues to the ghosts of the patient's unconscious (discussed in chapter five), Ferenczi notes that "A course of psycho-analytic treatment offers the most favourable conditions for the occurrence of such a transference" (p. 39).

He then employs a resonant metaphor from the realms of chemistry, as he appears to offer an early account of what, following Bion, we might today describe as psychoanalytic containment:

> The impulses that have been repressed, and are gradually becoming conscious, first meet *"in statu nascendi"* the person of the physician, and seek to link their unsatisfied valences to his personality. If we pursued this comparison taken from chemistry we might conceive of psychoanalysis, so far as the transference is concerned, as a kind of *catalysis*. The person of the physician has here the effect of a catalytic ferment that temporarily attracts to itself the affects split off by the dissection. In a technically correct psycho-analysis, however, the bond thus formed is only a loose one, the interest of the patient being led back as soon as possible to its original covered-over sources and brought into permanent connection with them. [pp. 39–40]

While struggling with the somewhat obscure writing—or translation—of Ferenczi's text here, one might also quibble, from a contemporary perspective, about whether the analyst *can* in fact retain the position of unaffected catalyst in this clearly very affecting relationship; or about when precisely the task of returning our patients to a focus on "covered-over sources" or original objects should be undertaken. What is far more pertinent, however, is the fact that Ferenczi now proceeds to lay out, with the help of clinical examples, the reasons and conditions that make the psychoanalytic physician the best conduit or container for the drawing forth and working through of the neurotic patient's positive and negative transferences.

He reminds us once more that the analyst is in fact only capitalizing on what he calls "the general neurotic *passion for transference*", the consequence of the patient's quest to quiet the excess of emotion that cannot be entirely disposed of, even by the most fully achieved repressive withdrawal of libido from original complexes:

> He manages also to neutralise a greater or less part by the way of conversion (hysteria) or of substitution (obsessional neurosis). It seems, however, as if this bond were scarcely ever an absolute one, so that a variable amount of free-floating and complex-escaping excitation remains over, which seeks satisfaction from external objects. The idea of this excitation could be used to explain the neurotic passion for transference, and be made responsible for the "manias" of the neurotic. [p. 46]

Just prior to this paragraph, Ferenczi had also attempted to place these thoughts about neurotic functioning within the context of Freud's first theory of anxiety which, as we have seen, was later to be retracted and revised. We should not be surprised that these "residual" feelings are anxious ones, regardless of whether we accept the idea that they are the provenance of the non-satisfaction or strenuous evasion of forbidden sexual desires.

The stage is now set and the time finally right for Ferenczi to bring on his new concept. The immediate context that he provides is the contrast, as he sees it, between neurotic and psychotic mechanisms. Here Ferenczi seems to distinguish two levels of psychotic psychopathology: the more severely ill patient, "suffering from dementia praecox... detaches his interest from the outer world and becomes auto-erotic", while the (merely) paranoid patient does not quite manage this degree of detachment and "so projects on to the outer world the interest that has become a burden to him" (p. 47).

Having introduced the psychotic/paranoid side of things, as well as the mechanism of projection that is one of its ploys, Ferenczi now puts the case for the other major category of mental illness and its characteristic coping method:

> The neurosis stands in this respect in a diametrical contrast to paranoia. Whereas the paranoiac expels from his ego the impulses that have become unpleasant, the neurotic helps himself by taking into the ego as large as possible a part of the outer world, making it the object of unconscious phantasies. This is a kind of diluting process, by means of which he tries to mitigate the poignancy of free-floating, unsatisfied, and unsatisfiable, unconscious wish-impulses. One might give to this process, in contrast to projection, the name of *Introjection*. [p. 47]

Ferenczi now draws together this new formulation and the terms that preoccupied him earlier, as follows: "The neurotic is constantly seeking for objects with whom he can *identify* himself, to whom he can *transfer* feelings, whom he can thus draw into his circle of interests, i.e. *introject*" (pp. 47–48, emphasis added). While the paranoiac, too, can be said to search out objects, it is for the equal and opposite purpose of seeking a target for the externalization, expulsion, or evacuation of his unwanted libido.

Ferenczi further characterizes these differences by both specifying and generalizing them, accordingly:

> So finally there appear the opposite characters of the large-hearted, impressionable, excitable neurotic, easily flaming up with love of all the world or provoked to hate of all the world, and that of the narrow-souled, suspicious paranoiac, who thinks he is being observed, persecuted, or loved by the whole world. The psychoneurotic suffers from a widening, the paranoiac from a shrinking of his ego. [p. 48]

When Ferenczi goes on to extend these processes beyond psychopathology, suggesting that his deliberations might be regarded as nothing less than the revision of "the ontogenesis of ego-consciousness", the non-defensive or non-pathological aspects of introjection (and its opposite, projection) come into focus.

The neurotic and paranoid versions are, Ferenczi claims, "merely extreme cases of psychical processes the primary forms of which are to be demonstrated in every normal being" (p. 48). He then provides a developmental account of how "primal" or "primordial" versions of these processes create the earliest distinction between self and world (after an initial stage of undifferentiated "monism") and thus give rise to the very possibility of object relations. They also leave procedural and structural legacies, furnishing the ego with capacities to deal with all future occasions involving difficult affects; the ego now has the wherewithal—and the "choice"—either to expel unpleasant emotions by projecting them, or to tolerate and make a home for them by introjecting them.

I can only note in passing—though it is again tempting to explore this further now—how these passages presage later psychoanalytic developments. In Britain, for example, Ferenczi's ideas give rise to quite contrasting traditions. Here, on the one hand, are the germs of fellow Hungarian and British Independent School pioneer, Michael Balint's ideas about "primary love", as well as his idiosyncratic distinction—regarding the relative proximity of objects to the ego and the magnetic attractions and repulsions felt towards such objects—between "ocnophils" and "philobats" (Balint, 1952, 1959, 1968).

On the other hand, one sees no less clearly Ferenczi's influence on the Kleinian distinctions between "paranoid-schizoid" and "depressive" functioning, where the former is dominated mostly by primitive forms of evacuative projection (as well as concrete incorporation), and the latter may extend the ego's welcoming inclusion of objects via the capacity for psychic introjection, while enabling projection to be used in the service of communication. Both Balint and Klein were Ferenczi's analysands, and it is fascinating to bear witness to both how much and how differently he influenced each of them. Then there is also Ferenczi's legacy in France, where—as we see in chapter six—Nicolas Abraham and Maria Torok take his notion of introjection forward in quite different ways.

We return to Ferenczi's text as we are nearing the end of this first part of the paper, and here we find him reverting to his primary intentions, namely, to promote the vital significance of transference and to forge even more links with introjection, particularly where the treating of neurosis is concerned. Via more examples of how the two operate in tandem in clinical work with such patients—and a link with Jung's "stimulus-word" association experiments—Ferenczi seems now to be preparing for the second, polemical part of the paper. Raising and countering potential objections from practitioners who are sceptical of psychoanalysis, most of Ferenczi's criticism are reserved for those (ab)users of hypnosis and suggestion who stumble into the transference unwittingly and fall foul of it. If such therapists fail to realize that the neurotic patient is already out there searching compulsively for a cure via transference and introjection, or if they insist on remaining oblivious to the psychoanalytic understanding of these urges, they will find themselves just as much at the mercy of these processes as the patients themselves.

A few paragraphs before the conclusion of this section, there is a particularly strong, if clumsy, piece of writing (again, this might well indicate a significant translation problem) that is worth reproducing because it exemplifies Ferenczi's clinical ambition and zeal. He has already insisted several times in the paper that before and until neurotic patients discover psychoanalysis—and even if they never do—they have a "natural" inclination to heal themselves via relations that can be accounted for, in theoretical terms, by the internal dynamics of transference and introjection. This self-help method, however, is invariably misguided and cannot suffice as a cure; as Ferenczi puts it, "It would be very wrong to want to imitate Nature slavishly and to follow her along a road where . . . she has shown her incapacity" (p. 56).

Instead, Ferenczi suggests, we need to go one better, beyond natural tendencies, to apply the stringent "artificial" methods of psychoanalysis if we wish to bring proper healing to the individual neurotic sufferer:

> Psycho-analysis wishes to individualize, while Nature disdains this; analysis aims at making capable for life and action persons who have been ruined by the summary repression-procedure of that Nature who does not concern herself with the weakly individual being. It is not enough here to displace the repressed complexes a little further by the help of transference to the physician, to discharge a little of their affective tension, and so to achieve a temporary improvement. If one wants seriously to help the patient one must lead him by means of analysis to overcome—opposing the unpleasantness-principle—the *resistances* (Freud) that hinder him from gazing at his own naked mental physiognomy. [pp. 56–57]

This, for me, captures the essential value of our therapeutic practice and could stand as a mission statement or Hippocratic Oath for psychoanalysis. It represents a fierce ethical retort to anyone wishing to subjugate its focus on the worth and welfare of the single patient to the general ethical principle of the greatest good for the greatest number, or to an evolutionary perspective that focuses only on the species and the survival of the fittest; nor will it sacrifice the demanding goals of comprehensive and thoroughgoing treatment and settle for irresponsible therapeutic half-measures.

To conclude this discussion and bring the focus firmly back to the profound significance of Ferenczi's invention of introjection, I refer to just one more passage, this time from the second part of the paper. Ferenczi makes a simple but resonant statement: "That children should willingly and indeed cheerfully obey their parents is really not at all obvious". He bids us recognize that "so long as the child knows only auto-erotic satisfactions", the child is neither keen nor likely to be obedient, for this is when parental strictures might well be experienced as "an external compulsion, and as something unpleasant" (p. 77).

Evidently, Ferenczi does not regard object relations proper, requiring the separateness of self and other, as extant or possible from the start of life. However, "with the beginning of 'object-love' it becomes different. The loved objects are introjected, taken into the ego. The child loves his parents, ... he identifies with them in thought" (p. 77). Surely, with this focus on how love and obedience come about—what we might call the ethical dimension of the relationship between parents and children—Ferenczi is anticipating the moment in *The Ego and the Id* when Freud adumbrates the genesis of the superego. We have already examined those developments, but here it is Ferenczi who seems well ahead of his time, heralding—via his term "introjection" and the related concept of "identification"—these complex ways of conceiving an internal world.

To be more explicit about the paradoxes and complexities of these developments: they reside in the fact that for humans to get along, even minimally (let alone to love each other), for there to be any kind of respect for each other's separate existence (for us not to literally eat or incorporate our children, or they us), some form of fellow-feeling must needs arise. Ferenczi reminds us that only under such conditions can we bear—and find some consolation and compensation for—the loss (of the illusion) of an initially all-powerful narcissistic solipsism, of being the one who matters most. We can manage this task, that is, only if we can learn to encompass, accommodate, and somehow make the metaphorical room or psychic space in our minds for the infuriating but also necessary other who insists on inhabiting our external worlds and standing in our way.

"On the Definition of Introjection" (1912)

Though it might be quite clear to us in retrospect that Ferenczi had already added something important to psychoanalytic thinking with his new term, there were to be some interesting, if not very welcome, developments in its early intra-disciplinary reception. Barely three years after publishing "On Introjection and Transference", Ferenczi felt compelled to pen a short addendum essay, "On the Definition of Introjection", because he had run into a difficulty—one that would repeat and become a virtual occupational hazard in the future development of psychoanalytic theorizing.

A certain Dr Maeder, Ferenczi tells us, had conflated introjection with something that he called "exteriorization", and this prompted Ferenczi to attempt to correct what he regarded as a serious misunderstanding of his new term.

Ferenczi does not, in the first instance, go into an explanation of why he thinks Maeder has misunderstood. He first offers a reiterated definition of his coinage, seeming to want to show that it referred to the very opposite of an exteriorizing process. He writes:

> I described introjection as an extension to the external world of the original autoerotic interests, by including its objects in the ego. I put the emphasis on this "including" and wanted to show thereby that I considered *every sort of object love* (or *transference*) both in normal and in neurotic people (and of course also in paranoiacs as far as they are capable of loving) as an extension of the ego, that is, as introjection. [1912, p. 316]

Perhaps even here, phrases like "an extension to the external world" and "an extension of the ego" might appear to suggest an *ex*ternalizing or *ex*teriorizing of such interests, but Ferenczi clearly wants to place his emphasis on the "including" or inclusive action of introjection.

The next paragraph begins with a sentence in which he seems determined to render his perspective on this *internalizing* process yet clearer, as if he wants to make it even less subject to any chance of misapprehension or misappropriation: "In principle, man can love only himself; if he loves an object he takes it into his ego" (p. 316). This Ferenczian view of how the ego first encounters its world is clearly predicated philosophically upon a primary narcissistic or "one-person" psychological position, as exemplified in my concluding thoughts about the earlier paper. There would no doubt have been the expectation on Ferenczi's part of Freud's full agreement on this issue: indeed, this would receive explicit metapsychological corroboration from the soon to be published paper, "On Narcissism" (Freud, 1914c).

A statement like Ferenczi's, however, especially the part before the semicolon, would be really jarring to many contemporary post-object-relational psychoanalytic sensibilities. Who now would say, with such apparent impunity, that—"in principle"—a person, subject, or ego can only love her-, him-, or itself? Neither Ferenczi nor Freud, however, would have needed to defend this position; they appear to have taken it thoroughly for granted.

The real value of Ferenczi's thought process here, and that of his newly invented notion, may lie not so much in how closely he keeps pace with and even anticipates Freud's thinking, but in his prescience concerning many later psychoanalytic developments. His conceptual creativity, like his later clinical challenges to psychoanalytic orthodoxy, are problematizing—but in the best, most enabling sense of the term. He poses useful, if complicating queries for us about subjectivity, the creation of selves, and about how to regard the entire distinction between internalizing and externalizing;

we might be tempted to question whether these terms even mean the same things for us nowadays as they then meant for him.

Leaving that to the side for the moment, another thing that might be said about Ferenczi's manifesto is that introjection—as he defines it—does not appear to require any specific loss to begin its operations. In the context of this book, this is an important realization. Introjection is seen here not merely, or primarily, as a mental mechanism responding strategically or defensively to loss or separation, but as a virtual operating system for the mind and as the very way for the human ego to have any object relations whatsoever. And yet, does this not beg the very question as to whether any such capacity would have been necessary in a being that was not already so susceptible to the predations of loss from the very beginning?

Returning to his text, we find Ferenczi resorting to an amusing example from the realms of fable in his attempt to explain introjection:

> Just like the poor fisherman's wife in the fairy tale, on to whose nose a curse made a sausage grow and who then felt any contact with the sausage as if it were her own skin, and had to protest violently against any suggestion of cutting off the unpleasant growth: so we feel all suffering caused to our loved object as our own. [p. 316]

Though this is not his ostensible topic, it is also as if Ferenczi is approaching the kind of insight that Freud would grope towards two years hence in "Mourning and Melancholia", about how loss is dealt with in depression. The point seems to be that, in certain cases, an extremely adhesive bond of a certain kind is established with the object, and even where it might be in the interests of the subject to sever that bond and free itself, efforts to do so are resisted for dear life or, indeed, unto death.

At the risk of sounding entirely too literal or concrete, one is tempted to inquire whether this parable of the sausage might be misleading: does it provide Ferenczi with what he needs here? Would it not be a better, metaphorically more apt example or image of introjection if the sausage were actually to be eaten, taken into the alimentary canal—via ingestion, digestion, and metabolization? In that case, a sausage *not* taken in, one that merely grows *onto* a nose, might be seen to exemplify only the more literalistic, adhesive bonds that we might wish to attribute to incorporation! But Ferenczi is not explicitly concerned with this distinction here; if anything, he might well be wanting to keep the psychic meanings of introjection as far away as possible from the zonal incorporations of the oral stage that are precisely too tainted by association with the concrete, physical actualities of eating and ingestion.

Such complex distinctions will, I hope, become more serious and more lucid—indeed, more relevant—in later chapters, particularly when discussing Abraham and Torok, who precisely *do* attend to both the differences and similarities between introjection and incorporation, in the context of distinguishing between mourning and melancholia. In the meantime, Ferenczi must be allowed to make his more general or extensive case:

> I used the term introjection for all such growing on to, all such including of the loved object in, the ego. As already stated, I conceive the mechanism of *all transference on to an object*, that is to say *all kinds of object love*, as *introjection*, as *extension of the ego*. [pp. 316–317]

These two sentences are intended to establish as clearly as possible, once and for all, how Ferenczi would like his new concept to be utilized and understood: as the means or mechanism whereby the ego might be enriched by attaching more of the world to itself or having desired objects inside itself.

Ferenczi wishes also to reiterate the following clinically significant distinctions: a neurotic is more prone to an excessive or addictive use of introjection (and hence transference). A paranoiac, by contrast, is enslaved by projective tendencies, the need to get rid of objects—or even to dispense with love and emotional attachment altogether: "The true paranoiac could think of part of his own nose (his own personality) as a sausage and then cut it off and throw it away; but nothing could induce him to tolerate something foreign growing onto it." Ferenczi again also insists that these are not just clinical differences, because "the same mechanisms occur in normal people" (p. 317).

At this point in the text there is an interesting footnote, expanding these categories and applying them more widely to intellectual life at large:

> One could, for instance, classify the metaphysical systems of philosophy as systems of projection and introjection. The materialism which dissolves the ego completely into the external world marks the climax of projection; solipsism, which includes the whole external world in the ego, the maximum of introjection.

Thus does Ferenczi wish to establish, as clearly, firmly, and deeply as possible, vital distinctions between acquiring and disposing, gathering up and getting rid, keeping and evacuating; these are fundamental ways to distinguish generally and typically between people and their pursuits, as well as clinically between neurotic and psychotic functioning: "In any case projection in paranoia and introjection in neurosis play so much more important a role than all the other mechanisms that we can regard them as characteristics of these clinical entities" (p. 317). As already noted, these examples of Ferenczian thinking would go on to significantly influence the respective traditions of both Melanie Klein and Michael Balint.

Despite Ferenczi's wish to clarify the differences between projection and introjection, however, the way in which the prefixes in-, pro-, and ex- are bandied about in this paper, suggests more than a little interchangeability and perhaps considerable confusion. Many questions might be raised here. Perhaps the most familiar one is whether or not we are object-relating creatures from the very start—and we might expect Ferenczi (along with, say, Winnicott) to give the opposite answer from that of Fairbairn and Balint (as well as Klein) in this regard.

But there are other, logically prior, more fundamental questions, too, including: How precisely does one go about establishing *any* form of contact, primary relation, or identification with an external object? Putting it biblically, does one go forth actively, or send out emissaries or an entourage, to meet and greet the other at the well, so to speak? Or does one just fling open one's tent and oneself in hospitable, albeit passive, invitation and await the other's arrival? And are there real or substantive differences here, or is there nothing more to them than a matter of manners or etiquette?

Perhaps the whole business of "out" versus "in" can turn completely upon itself, refusing to remain as neat, discretely separable categories. If we also consider and factor in the meanings of identification, things can become even more complicated. What happens when we practice what is apparently the negative of identifying with or relating to an object—that is, when we repudiate, dissociate ourselves from, or aversively rid ourselves of someone or something? Is the negative of identification itself a species of identification, or its very obverse or opposite? And is it this kind of confusion that spawns or necessitates an oxymoronic concept like "projective identification"?

Anticipating the later chapter on Klein, this last question points to the perennial difficulties with this coinage, its internal self-divisions and the unclarity and inconsistency of attempts to define or explain it. While Freud was already using the term and concept "projection" well before the turn of the century, it was Ferenczi's belated coining of its opposite and the brave attempt to maintain some control over its use that seem to have stimulated these significant metapsychological consequences. My guess is that, notwithstanding his influential analysand's later introduction of the composite concept of projective identification, and her followers' elevation of this term to prominence in their paradigm, Ferenczi would probably have considered it a misnomer and a contradiction in terms.

He was nevertheless capable of pre-empting or accounting in advance in this paper for some of the later clinical consequences and theoretical thinking that would develop under the aegis of both projection and projective identification, as follows:

> In a really successful paranoid projection (for instance, in a delusion of persecution) one part of the mental personality itself . . . is deprived of its connexion with the ego, deprived, so to speak, of its civic rights, and as it cannot be so simply removed from the world, it is treated as something objective, something alien. Such a transformation of the purely subjective into something objective may be referred to as projection. [p. 318]

Moreover, while Ferenczi's quite convoluted explanatory attempts in the latter part of the paper blur the bifurcations of his earlier statements, he at least concludes with this attempted clarification:

> Anyhow, Maeder's exteriorization must be considered not as projection, but as a special kind of introjection which incidentally occurs also in normal people, and I propose to stick in the future to the notion of introjection which well describes all our past experiences. [p. 318)

Risking banality and bathos, perhaps all we can say at this juncture is that are these intricate, vexed matters that we may be relieved to be leaving behind. However, we will not be permitted to put them aside for good: they will be with us again later in this book, even if we are now bidding farewell to Ferenczi's engagement with them and our personal engagement with him.

It seems a bit odd that, with someone as prominent in the annals of psychoanalysis as Ferenczi, we should be limiting our interest to two papers written in just the first handful of years of his involvement in the field. His reputation was not, after all, established solely on this basis and would not rest primarily on this early conceptual ingenuity. It would be enhanced exponentially over the next two decades by his dedication, especially, to advances in technique, clinical innovation, and a general devotion to the welfare of patients, even at the expense of orthodox therapeutic rules or protocols.

However, as the reading of these papers suggests, Ferenczi was acutely attuned, from the first, to the way the theoretical winds were blowing and should thus also be remembered for his contributions to the prevailing intellectual climate of psychoanalysis. It is no surprise that these formative metapsychological thoughts would still retain their significance and bear revisiting many years on and after many turns of the psychoanalytic seasons.

Karl Abraham

"Notes on the Psycho-Analytical Investigation and Treatment of Manic-Depressive Insanity and Allied Conditions" (1911)

The importance of Karl Abraham's contributions to psychoanalytic thinking about melancholia and manic-depressive illness cannot be overstated. As a psychiatrist, with considerably more experience of patients with depressive illnesses than Freud, Abraham ventured to write this paper as early as 1911. (He evidently had a propensity for long titles, and his analysand, Melanie Klein, also adopted the habit, at least when writing about similar topics.) It therefore preceded "Mourning and Melancholia" by a good three years and may well have provided Freud with the spur or inducement to write his own seminal paper.

As with Ferenczi's "Introjection and Transference", this paper was arguably Abraham's first significant piece of psychoanalytic writing. Though always the faithful disciple, more willing or likely than Ferenczi to defer and concede priority, yet here was Abraham venturing to broach the complexities of bipolar illness well before Freud had really got near them. Even if some of Abraham's closely descriptive and explanatory accounts in the paper might now seem theoretically inchoate, they preempt the many subsequent attempts to tackle serious depression and prefigure several yet to be named or adumbrated psychoanalytic concepts that will prove crucial in its understanding.

The first page or two of the paper seem particularly important. Abraham begins by noting both how relevant "depressive states" are to psychopathology and yet how neglected they are in the psychoanalytic literature, relative to the attention given to "states of morbid anxiety". Referring to both as "affects", he is observant and ahead of his time (psychiatrically as well as psychoanalytically) when he comments that these two are in fact "often present together or successively in one individual; so that a patient suffering from an anxiety-neurosis will be subject to states of mental depression, and a melancholic will complain of having anxiety".

He goes on to append a rather simple, but refreshing and enlightening formula, namely, "Anxiety and depression are related to each other in the same way as are fear and grief. We fear a coming evil; we grieve over one that has occurred." This also carries the corollary that what fear and grief have in common is that they are the more ordinary or normal responses to future and past losses, respectively; what anxiety and depression share, by contrast, is that they are the more problematic or pathological reactions to these losses.

Abraham's text is peppered with such comments, noteworthy and striking in their simple profundity. Another example seems to anticipate the importance of a concept like the death drive: "Every neurotic state of depression, just like every anxiety-state, to which it is closely related, contains a tendency to deny life." In fact, by this point in the paper, Abraham had already noted the difference between "sadness or grief and neurotic depression, the latter being unconsciously motivated and a consequence of repression" (1911, pp. 137–138).

This is an astutely pre-emptive—if still incipient—recognition of the essential distinction that Freud would develop between the ordinary if difficult feelings associated with grief and mourning, and the morbidities of melancholia, which can at times take the guise of a resistance to—or failure of—all feeling whatsoever. However, one cannot but be struck by the fact that after this early reference, we hear nothing more of "grief" in the rest of Abraham's paper, and "mourning" never once appears by name. What this might betoken is not clear, though perhaps in this respect he is like many other psychiatrists—in our day no less than his—whose daily work with bipolar disorder and the serious or psychotic end of depression might obscure or inure them to the obvious. But it still seems incomprehensible that Abraham should be even the least bit out of touch with the commensurability or proximity to each other of mourning and melancholia and the issue of loss that links them. Perhaps, at the very least, this serves to make even more remarkable Freud's synthetic yoking together of these two states of mind a few short years later, his capacity to see as clearly as he did the psychic relevance of their similarities as well as their differences.

One also notes that—like Ferenczi and probably most of Freud's adherents at the time—Abraham seemed fully persuaded of the sexual aetiology of most if not all mental or psychiatric conditions. He is perhaps all too ready to attribute depression to repression and the frustrations of libidinal gratification, as Freud had erroneously done with anxiety. As alluded to previously, Abraham's theorizing may not always keep pace, but there are many perceptive descriptions and incipient insights in this paper. It constitutes an important precursor to his later, longer paper that we will review below, where Abraham would go on to make invaluable contributions to psychoanalytic thinking about the illnesses of mourning and would enable Freud himself to eventually conceive a whole new category for them, namely, the "narcissistic psycho-neuroses" (Freud, 1924b).

It is soon evident that Abraham is primarily interested in the more severe depressive illnesses, especially those that "run a 'cyclical' course in which there is an alternation between melancholic and manic states".

He is clearly keen to establish his specific credentials where such patients are concerned: he enumerates and briefly describes six recent cases of this kind. He notes, like Freud, the similarities between such states of "depressive psychosis" (p. 138) and obsessional neurosis; and he provides, in the central part of his paper, a single, exemplary case history of one of his latest patients, occupying several pages and providing a plethora of illuminating symptomatic detail.

In this patient's depressed periods, he suffered from apathy, inhibition, suicidal inclinations, and self-punitive wishes. A hypomanic phase was late arriving, but when it did it was characterized by enormous bursts of activity, euphoria, great enterprise, good humour, volatility of thought, flights of ideas, and quick, forceful behaviour; but, while manic, he could also be irritable, impulsively violent, aggressive, and beset by powerful sexual urges. Abraham also gives information about this patient's family background, connecting these biographical details with what will become a central strand of his understanding of what ails patients suffering from these conditions. As he sees it, their libidinal development is compromised and interfered with mostly by ambivalence—an inability to reconcile loving and hating feelings—and by the predominance of hatred and the triumph of sadism.

Using the example of Shakespeare's defective, vengeful, treacherous king, Richard III, whose ruthlessness was matched only by his ambition, Abraham seems to anticipate—again, before such developments had received their full Freudian treatment under the banners of narcissism, melancholia, the death drive, or the superego—the significance of "morbid states, such as feelings of guilt", resulting "from the suppression of these frequent impulses of hatred and revenge" (p. 146). It is this turning inward of aggressive, sadistic, envious, and destructive impulses—taking the form of massive guilt feelings as well as masochism—that is so characteristic of what we witness in the predatory self-persecutions of our depressed or melancholic patients.

What is most impressive about Abraham's paper is his ability to capture phenomenologically—and sympathetically—what it is like to encounter these patients. In this respect, the piece looks forward specifically, in its precise and evocative descriptions—and in its form as well as content—to Joan Riviere's later (1936) paper about patients who suffer from negative therapeutic reactions. It is not difficult to see, moreover, how an entire Kleinian tradition, especially its contributions to the treatment of depression, emerges from Abraham's modest early paper. Abraham's accounts are, if anything, more illuminating when he is describing the manic phase of bipolar conditions than the melancholic, and in this, too, he anticipates—and no doubt influenced—Melanie Klein's clinical astuteness about the defensive power of mania.

Abraham devotes the last several pages of his paper to the "therapeutic effects" of treating manic-depressive illness by means of psychoanalysis, and one is impressed by his humility—indeed, by his sense of surprise that he has been able to help such patients at all. He at one point admits that, in one of his cases, he "had begun treating it precisely at that period when the melancholia was passing off, and that it would have been cured without my doing anything" (p. 155). On the other hand, his faith in the efficacy of the psychoanalytic method was vastly strengthened by his ability to treat these serious illnesses in this manner.

As we know, Freud was himself sceptical for most of his career about whether patients verging on the psychotic side of the diagnostic spectrum could be treated psychoanalytically at all. Yet, Abraham was already making confident claims for his therapeutic craft based on his work with these hard-to-reach patients:

> By the help of a psycho-analytical interpretation of certain facts and connections I succeeded in attaining a greater psychic *rapport* with the patients than I had ever previously achieved. It is usually extraordinarily difficult to establish a transference in these patients who have turned away from all the world in their depression. Psycho-analysis, which has hitherto enabled us to overcome this obstacle, seems to me for this reason to be the only rational therapy to apply to the manic-depressive psychoses. [pp. 153–154]

He finishes the paper on a similarly strong and confident note, first acknowledging the incompleteness of what psychoanalysis can claim to know, but also claiming that it alone "will reveal the hidden structure of this large group of illnesses" (p. 156).

It is in Abraham's final sentence that he really throws down the gauntlet at the feet of the psychiatric establishment:

> And moreover, its first therapeutic results in this sphere justify us in the expectation that it may be reserved for psycho-analysis to lead psychiatry out of the *impasse* of therapeutic nihilism. [p. 156]

As we have seen, what is so striking about this early paper is the extent to which it was possible for Abraham to discuss his depressive and melancholic patients in such detail from a psychoanalytic point of view, not just without recourse to later Freudian theories, but with scarcely any reference to the language of object loss and separation or, indeed, to internalizing mechanisms like identification, introjection (only recently named by Ferenczi), or incorporation.

Of course, this is merely to register the fact, once again, that psychoanalytic metapsychology was only just beginning to discover and offer such internalizing perspectives. And it gives me an opportunity to reiterate that it is no accident that the attention to mourning, melancholia, and object loss started to occur at roughly the same time as the elaboration of an internal world began to take centre stage in psychoanalysis. As we are seeing, Freud's two most significant and faithful disciples during his lifetime aided the recognition of these conjunctions in the years preceding and leading up to "Mourning and Melancholia" by dividing the field between them, each assisting the founder and their science in his own fashion.

"A Short Study of the Development of the Libido, Viewed in the Light of Mental Disorders" (1924)

One has only to read the "Introduction" to "Part I" of this later paper—which is anything but short—to realize that the years elapsed, and the knowledge gained, since Abraham's earlier paper have greatly increased his technical and theoretical expertise. In this Introduction, he notes that it is Freud's theory of the pre-genital stages of the libido, and how it intersects with the central concept of regression that has allowed Abraham to factor in both the sadistic-anal and oral-cannibalistic dimensions of melancholia, which the paper exemplifies in detail.

Though he may himself have had a hand in inspiring it, the advent of Freud's "Mourning and Melancholia" made an enormous impact on Abraham's thinking; he first credits it with the confirmation of his own view "that melancholia stood in the same relation to normal mourning for a loss as did morbid anxiety to ordinary fear" (Abraham, 1924, pp. 418–419). Though this is quite close to what Abraham had said at the start of his own earlier paper, it also recalls the relative dearth of references to mourning or loss in that paper. More importantly, one is made aware of the extent to which these psychoanalytic ideas were co-created by the work of both Abraham and Freud, no doubt as much via their correspondence and conversations as their published works, and so much so that it is difficult in retrospect to disentangle and specify the precise contributions of each.

Abraham goes on to say that Freud "approached the problem of melancholia from another angle, and he made the first step towards the discovery of the mechanism of that illness", rightly emphasizing perhaps the most crucial idea in "Mourning and Melancholia": "He showed that the patient, after having lost his love-object, regains it once more by a process of introjection (so that, for instance, the self-reproaches of a melancholic are really directed toward his lost object)." Abraham's own intention is to establish a firm connection between the libidinal-stage perspective (to which he will also add considerable detail, rendering a more complex version of it than Freud's) and the internalization of loss; he states that "the introjection of the love-object is an incorporation of it, in keeping with the regression of the libido to the cannibalistic level" (pp. 419–420).

Abraham seems to communicate here that he has now more thoroughly understood—indeed, digested—the connection between the internal dynamics of melancholia and the mechanisms creating an internal world. We might wonder, however, whether fellow Freud disciple Ferenczi might have had something to say about his using these two terms denoting internalization—introjection and incorporation—as more or less interchangeable or synonymous. As I have said, there will be questions raised about this conflating tendency wherever it appears, even when it may seem somewhat pedantic or premature on my part to ask them.

In fairness, there would be no quarrel with Abraham's formulation here were it certain that it is melancholia—as opposed to mourning—that he is addressing or describing; for it is precisely in the former condition that one *does* find precisely the kind of psychic confusion whereby introjection regresses to, or collapses into, incorporation. Conceptually, as well as clinically, however, the differences between the two terms will prove very significant; if this was only alluded to by Ferenczi, it is clarified further as this book progresses.

Though both men pre-deceased Freud, Abraham's death—at the age of just 48—came sooner and was even more sudden and tragic than Ferenczi's eight years later. This long paper (more like a monograph or short book, in fact) was completed just a year before his demise and would probably rate as his most important contribution to the evolution of psychoanalytic thought. It provides a comprehensively fleshed-out and more fully exemplified account of depressive and manic-depressive functioning than either his own earlier paper had managed, or Freud ever attempted. Again, Abraham's ongoing work with greater numbers of patients of this kind enabled him to make more explicit the implications of Freud's somewhat more speculative or metapsychological approach to melancholia and its vicissitudes.

Abraham's opening pages also credit Freud with having finally nailed down what one might call the object-relational differences between melancholic and obsessional states, saying that, in the former cases, "the event of underlying importance is the loss of the object which precedes the outbreak of the illness, and that this does not happen in obsessional cases" (p. 420). By 1924, as this suggests, Abraham had himself begun to recognize more fully the nature and centrality of these object relations, and thus to probe the following questions: What happens to the object—what form or status does it assume—when it is not present or when there is the threat of it absenting itself externally? If there is such a loss or separation, does it gain representation as an internal entity or phenomenon? How do psychiatric illnesses and their symptoms express the different ways of dealing, not only with the loss of libidinal satisfaction, but with the loss of the object itself? These are the kinds of issues that have begun to intrude into the psychoanalytic landscape and will gain in prominence in subsequent decades—and Abraham's seminal paper makes some important inroads into this territory.

The lengthy first part of the paper is headed, "Part I: Manic-Depressive States and the Pregenital Level of the Libido". Following the introduction, it is subdivided into seven numbered and named sections, each dealing with an aspect of melancholia and manic-depressive illness. The second part, "Part II: Origins and Growth of Object-Love", is far shorter and does not require subdivision; it is here that Abraham establishes and sets out comprehensively his schema for the psychosexual stages. Having produced a more complex rendition of these developmental waystations than the one that Freud introduces in his *Three Essays on the Theory of Sexuality* (1905d), Abraham's version comes replete with a tabulated summary.

Under the heading "Stages of Libidinal Organization", Abraham has subdivided the oral, anal, and genital stages into two sub-stages each; there is also a parallel column, detailing the corresponding "Stages of Object-Love". Though I am jumping ahead here, it might nevertheless be helpful to briefly summarize these stages:

1. the earliest is the oral-sucking stage, in parallel with objectless "auto-erotism", and designated "pre-ambivalent" by Abraham;
2. then comes the oral-cannibalistic stage, corresponding to "narcissism (total incorporation of object)", the first of four successive "ambivalent" stages;
3. the earlier anal-sadistic stage is next, characterized by "partial love with incorporation";
4. this is followed by a later anal-sadistic stage (somewhat less sadistic, as we shall see, and more to do with retention than destruction), featuring "partial love";

5. the still-ambivalent earlier genital or phallic stage is when—as Abraham rather oddly phrases it—we get "object-love with exclusion of genitals";

6. finally, there is the genital stage proper with at least the potential for complete "object-love" in a "post-ambivalent" relationship (p. 496).

Abraham's schema can in fact be regarded as the precursor of Anna Freud's (1965) later and even more elaborate work on parallel lines of development in childhood. It is probably familiar territory and an integral part of psychoanalytic education and knowledge for all analysts. What is significant for me, however, is the way that Abraham's melancholic or manic-depressive patients seem to provide him with the specific clinical key, or missing link, in this elaborate parallel chronology of developments. They might be said to occupy a literally central place in the schema, hovering or vacillating somewhere between (in both psychosexual and alimentary terms) late oral and early anal stages and between narcissism and object love, clearly exemplifying ambivalence towards their objects. It is the first part of the paper, with its abundance of clinical material, that lays the groundwork for this perspective, and that is where I concentrate my close-reading focus and try to trace Abraham's arguments in the pages ahead.

Returning to Part I, the first subsection is entitled "Melancholia and Obsessional Neurosis: Two Stages of the Sadistic-Anal Phase of the Libido", where Abraham connects aspects of both controlling and losing the object to various anal acts and their figurative descriptions. He adduces some impressive clinical and etymological evidence, mentioning, for instance, that in certain languages, including German and English, the words for "dropping" something—or, indeed, animal "droppings"—and those denoting "loss" or "losing" are closely associated.

Having reiterated that patients with these two conditions show remarkably similar characteristics, Abraham clinches the argument about their differences in ingenious, if also schematic, fashion by specifying the psycho-sexual "loci" or fixation points of obsessional neurosis and melancholia in relation to the two chronological levels of the anal stage:

> On the later level the conserving tendencies of retaining and controlling the object predominate, whereas on the earlier level those hostile to their object—those of destroying and losing it—come to the fore. The obsessional neurotic regresses to the later of these two levels, and so he is able to maintain contact with his object. [p. 432]

This "placing" of the obsessional neurotic in the later of the two anal substages moves such a patient developmentally closer to a mature capacity for love and the more comprehensive, consistent, and fully achieved whole-object relations of the genital stage. It is on these grounds that the obsessional's tendency to preserve or hold onto his object—that is, to anally retain it—can usefully be distinguished from the less-than-fully object-relational, bipolar patient's predisposition to throw out the baby with the bathwater, to be rid of the problem along with the person causing it.

Abraham places great store by this distinction, and his description pre-figures Melanie Klein's manner of separating paranoid-schizoid from depressive functioning in relation to the object:

> This differentiation of the anal-sadistic stage into a primitive and a later phase seems to be of radical importance. For at the dividing line between these two phases there takes place a decisive change in the attitude of the individual to the external world. Indeed, we may say that this dividing line is where "object-love" in the narrower sense begins, for it is at this point that the tendency to preserve begins to predominate. [p. 432]

Abraham has already conceded that in quiescent intervals, "during the period when his symptoms are absent the manic-depressive patient can transform his instincts in the same way as the obsessional neurotic" (p. 432). When such a patient is ill, however, the earlier anal sub-stage—where the urge is to expel, evacuate, and destroy the object—holds sway in the mind. Surely this is what leads us to regard as more serious the mental illnesses of melancholia and depression, given this leaning towards the ditching and destruction of the object—and, indeed, of the self.

Before concluding this subsection of the paper, Abraham also sets the scene for discussing the pertinence of the oral-cannibalistic stage to these same illnesses. He claims that traversing the crucial object-relational watershed that he has identified between obsessional and narcissistic neurosis leads to further consequences:

> We shall see later that the process of regression in melancholia does not stop at the earlier level of the anal-sadistic stage, but goes steadily back towards still more primitive organizations of the libido. It thus appears as though when once the dividing line between the two anal-sadistic phases has been crossed in a regressive direction the effects are especially unfavourable. Once the libido has relinquished its object-relations it seems to glide rapidly downwards from one level to the next. [pp. 432–433]

Abraham's warning has a bearing on what will later become known—in psychoanalytic circles and beyond—as the capacity for object constancy or object permanence: the ability to hang on to one's (conception of the) object in the face of its absence.

Abraham's appreciation of the significance of this issue predates and pre-empts the emphasis it would receive from object-relations theories that would later surge to prominence. He knows that if this capacity of the ego or subject is compromised—if the temptation to jettison the object is strong (perhaps because of an original object having been disappointing, or worse)—it faces psycho-sexual regression as a veritable slippery slope. This fate, and the associated mood, again recall a popular song: Paul Simon's *Slip Slidin' Away*, from 1977, is about melancholic, homeless-sounding men and women who cannot seem to get—or at least to stay—where they need to be; thus, they find themselves either remaining in no-hope places and unpropitious situations or drifting off in yet further wasteful and undesirable directions.

Instead of, or before, proceeding immediately "backwards" to the relevance of the oral stage in melancholia, however, Abraham interrupts himself—or, rather, embarks upon a necessary diversion. He devotes the second subsection of his paper ("Object-Loss and Introjection in Normal Mourning and in Abnormal States of Mind") to an attempt to assess the implications for his own thinking of Freud's "Mourning and Melancholia". This amounts to an inquiry into the most vital discovery made in that text, "into the event which ushers in the actual melancholic illness—that event which Freud has called the 'loss of object'—and into the process, so closely allied to it, of the introjection of the lost love-object" (p. 433).

This may well be the most significant part of Abraham's paper for my purposes, and for more than one reason. It includes a rather remarkable autobiographical passage that speaks volumes about the nature of his personal relationship with both Freud himself and the process of mourning; it also exemplifies how insightful Abraham's views on these issues were, while simultaneously providing an object lesson in how the lack of clarity about the differences and similarities between the terms denoting internalization can compromise such insights.

Abraham's criticism of and oedipal struggle with Freud were always far better tempered and disguised than Ferenczi's, but they show themselves more clearly in these few pages than perhaps anywhere else in his writings. He manages both to praise his psychoanalytic father for his genius, while also calling his bluff on the limits of his understanding of what happens psychically in mourning, let alone melancholia. Abraham first provides an instructive example, from the work of another analyst, of how internalization can turn loss into melancholic self-accusation. This is the case of a depressed woman who took upon herself the crimes of her father "with whom she lived, and to whom she clung with all an unmarried daughter's love" (p. 434). This may remind us right away of Faulkner's "A Rose for Emily" and the kind of relationship that the title character had with her father, and I will say more about this below.

However, having praised and corroborated Freud's idea "that the self-reproaches of melancholia are in reality reproaches directed against the loved person", Abraham also appears to disparage this summary statement as somehow too easy and superficial, and as insufficiently explanatory. Perhaps alluding to and subtly insisting on his own more extensive experience of treating depressed patients, Abraham writes:

> It is only by means of a regular psychoanalysis that we are able to perceive that there is a relationship between object-loss and tendencies, based on the earlier phase of the anal-sadistic stage, to lose and destroy things; and that the process of introjection has the character of a physical incorporation by way of the mouth. Furthermore, a superficial view of this sort misses the whole of the ambivalence conflict that is inherent in melancholia. [pp. 434–435]

Though he does not seem at first to be aiming these admonishments directly at Freud, Abraham says that "our knowledge of what takes place in normal mourning is equally superficial; for psycho-analysis has thrown no light on that mental state in healthy people and in cases of transference-neuroses". Without quite making this explicit either, Abraham might be expressing his puzzlement at how little psychoanalytic attention had yet been paid to the problems of mourning and to the possibility that these might have something other than genital sexuality at their source.

Once Freud is mentioned by name, however, there seems to be little doubt that Abraham is concurring with the master's own self-critical caveats, where he admits that what he knows of this whole clinical area is quite sparse and partial. Again, Abraham expresses this with both deference and ambivalence:

> True, Freud has made the very significant observation that the serious conflict of ambivalent feelings from which the melancholic suffers is absent in the normal person. But how exactly the process of mourning is effected in the normal mind we do not at present know. [p. 435]

Abraham will go on to demonstrate that his own experience and theoretical skills can enhance and take further the psychoanalytic understanding of such states.

Abraham begins his quest to do so by introducing a patient of his own, a man who lost both his wife and his infant in childbirth while undergoing his analysis. Abraham asserts confidently that the case will demonstrate "that in the normal process of mourning, too, the person reacts to a real object-loss by effecting a temporary introjection of the loved person" (p. 435). Even before laying out the details of the case and describing how this man dealt with his terrible double bereavement, Abraham claims that it is "quite evident that he had reacted to his painful loss with an act of introjection of an oral-cannibalistic character".

He tells us that the grieving man—in a manner "reminiscent of the refusal to take nourishment met with in melancholiacs"—had virtually stopped eating for several weeks. However, after eating his first good meal for a long time, he brought a dream "that he was at the *post-mortem* of his late wife" (p. 436). It features two scenes: in the first, the dismembered parts of his wife's body are reunited, and she is joyfully restored to him; in the second, the dissecting room is transformed into a butchery with dead animals.

Abraham's interpretations emphasize the paradoxical or ambivalent juxtaposition of the loving/nurturing and destructive/cannibalistic elements in the dream and make links between the oral imagery and the patient having recovered sufficiently from his grief to begin eating again. Abraham then tries to extrapolate from the clinical situation to what is happening on an intrapsychic and metapsychological level:

> Consuming the flesh of the dead wife is made equivalent to restoring her to life. Now Freud has shown that by introjecting the lost object the melancholiac does indeed recall it to life: he sets it up in his ego. In the present case the widowed man had abandoned himself to his grief for a certain period of time as though there were no escape possible from it. His disinclination for food was in part a playing with his own death; it seemed to imply that now that the object of his love was dead life had no more attraction for him. He then began to work off the traumatic effect of his loss by means of an unconscious process of introjection of the loved object. While this was going on he was once more able to take nourishment, and at the same time his dream announced the fact that the work of mourning had succeeded. The process of mourning thus brings with it the consolation: "My loved object is not gone, for now I carry it within myself and can never lose it". [pp. 436–437]

I have quoted Abraham at length here to demonstrate both his acumen and his error, but I want to mitigate the latter immediately by saying that anybody "playing with" with such metaphors and imagery is bound to court similar difficulties.

The question at stake, once again, is about the crucial clinical difference between a "proper" mourning process and one that ends in a melancholic impasse—though perhaps it must be borne in mind that at that moment in time and in psychoanalytic conceptualizing, the finer points of such distinctions may not yet have been appreciated or even perceived. The very idea that one may set up an object within the ego is still a relatively novel one. Thus, to know the differences, and the gradations of difference, between doing so for the pathological purpose of persecuting an ambivalently loved and too-concretely incorporated object, versus doing so to both preserve a connection with and enhance the mourning for a lost object via a more metabolic introjection of it—these are subtle matters indeed, both clinically and theoretically.

We must bear in mind that in "Mourning and Melancholia" Freud was just as concerned with the metapsychological similarities between melancholia and mourning as with their differences. On the other hand, he also seemed to suggest that internalizing processes are required or set in train *only* by melancholic narcissism and ambivalence, that they are not usually a feature of normal mourning. It is unsurprising, therefore, that—like many analysts to come—Abraham may be confused and might therefore blur these distinctions, at least in theoretical terms. Here he seems convinced—or perhaps simply assumes—that he is presenting a patient going through a "normal process of mourning", who thus provides a good example of what happens in the internal landscape of an ordinary mourner's mind. But this is certainly not proven beyond any doubt by his account. To properly assess these convictions, one might want to know why the patient was in treatment in the first place: was he one of Abraham's depressed patients, and therefore of a more melancholic disposition—even when grieving or *in* mourning—than his analyst realizes or wishes to believe?

Such challenges to Abraham may, to some extent, be beside the point. The far more important implication of Abraham's perspective is his recognition that *some* form of taking in—what he is in this instance referring to, accurately or otherwise, as "a temporary introjection"—occurs not only in cases of melancholia, but in mourning situations, too. As I tried to show in chapter two, Freud himself had only just come to a similar realization in the recently published *The Ego and the Id*. As Abraham tells us in a later footnote (p. 461), he was in fact reading and trying to absorb this landmark Freudian text while in the very midst of writing his own.

This almost simultaneous dawning on both Freud and Abraham of such ideas, namely, that many if not all experiences of loss—and not just the ones with pathological outcomes—are accompanied by internalizing processes of one kind or another, will have significant repercussions for psychoanalytic theorizing. It will encourage the future burgeoning of psychoanalytic descriptions and accounts of such psychic events; many, however, will struggle to distinguish among the terms and forms of internalization and to sustain a clear enough conceptual sense of the differences between more and less successful ways of mourning the loss of an object.

We are, of course, constantly mindful that such comparisons and contrasts—between successful and failed mourning—are in any case only ever relative and equivocal. Nevertheless, Abraham's work is worth dissecting in this fashion precisely because his enthusiasm for—and perhaps naivety about—a whole new province of psychoanalytic thinking allows us to see why this area of discourse remains so vexing, even now, a century on.

When Abraham summarizes his deliberations about his patient's grieving with the statement that "This psychological process is, we see, identical with what occurs in melancholia" (p. 437), I again feel compelled to quibble: does he really mean, "identical"? And it is frankly a relief that he then rescues himself in the very next sentence, saying, "I shall try to make it clear later on that melancholia is an archaic form of mourning." As if catching his own overstatement and standing corrected, he acknowledges that they are not quite identical, but perhaps one is an older, more primitive version of the other. When he also adds that his clinical example "leads us to the conclusion that the work of mourning in the healthy individual also assumes an archaic form in the lower strata of his mind", we appreciate that Abraham is trying to figure out—in *his* mind, in the moment, and in the very act of writing these words—how, exactly, such mentally stratified processes are related to one another.

We also get an inkling here of how Melanie Klein, his patient and protégé, will develop her ideas about more and less archaic or primitive levels of functioning (paranoid-schizoid versus depressive). She, too, will be less likely than others to maintain a clear-cut or rigid distinction between the normal and the pathological where mourning and melancholia are concerned. Perhaps both Klein and her analyst-mentor were more aware than most of how fine such margins can be and how easily an apparently healthy individual might slip-slide into serious mental illness.

I find it intriguing that, at just this point in the text, Abraham turns to an example of dealing with loss and grief from his own personal history: the death of his own father. That it also involves his ambivalence towards Freud's "Mourning and Melancholia"—and, perhaps less consciously, also towards *The Ego and Id*, which had only recently appeared—makes it interesting on several levels, as we shall see.

Abraham leads off with an example from the work of Georg Groddeck, the maverick doctor–philosopher who had just featured in Freud's latest text by providing him with the name for *"das Es"*—the id. Abraham cites Groddeck's account of a patient whose hair turned grey when his father died and his claim that this was "an unconscious tendency on the part of the patient to become like his father, and thus to absorb him in himself and to take his place with his mother". Abraham then makes a startling confession:

> When Freud published his "Mourning and Melancholia", so often quoted in these pages, I noticed that I felt a quite unaccustomed difficulty in following his train of thought. I was aware of an inclination to reject the idea of an introjection of the loved object. I combated this feeling in myself, thinking that the fact that the genius of Freud had made a discovery in a field of interest so much my own had called forth in me an affective "no". [p. 437]

It is to his analytic credit that Abraham is so aware of his oedipal rivalry with Freud and is courageous enough to commit his admission to paper, to readily reveal his "affective 'no'". We register, moreover, how much it matters to him that this "field of interest"—to do with the vicissitudes of depression and loss—be seen as his own domain, the psychoanalytic arena in which his contributions will really count. This long 1924 paper is surely an attempt to consolidate this claim and, indeed, to reclaim something from Freud's earlier "coup".

It is noteworthy, of course, that Abraham should attempt to take issue with Freud precisely on the matter of the internalization of the lost object. Aside from anything else, Abraham is struggling to take in *his* object at this very moment: that is, to swallow the bitter pill of "Mourning and Melancholia", not least because what Freud seemed to have discovered there was precisely the right theoretical medicine! Abraham, the psychoanalytic son, must absorb the loss of seeing Freud, the father, eclipsing or getting ahead of him yet again.

The way that Abraham comes to terms with this loss or disappointment is by linking it to another pertinent loss—namely, the death of his actual father. As he discloses, this event had occurred during the year before his envious encounter with "Mourning and Melancholia" and at that time *his* hair, too, "rapidly turned very grey and then went black again in a few months' time" (an example, again, of what he had previously called a *temporary* introjection). While he had already "attributed this to the emotional crisis" of losing his father, whose greyness he had consciously noticed when he last saw him alive, only now is he ready to accept what he calls "the deeper connection" (p. 437) that both Groddeck and Freud had adduced.

Abraham's last words on the subject are, again, telling: "It thus appears that my principal motive in being averse to Freud's theory of the pathological process of melancholia at first was my own tendency to employ the same mechanism during mourning" (p. 438). Thus, Abraham would perhaps rather not face the full brunt of his jealousy and envy of Freud and displaces these uncomfortable emotions, first onto a more personal, and then onto a more intellectual or theoretical plane. But he is also bravely communicating the uncomfortable thought that he might himself have fallen prey to melancholic identification in his own dealings with loss.

It seems that Abraham is helped to get over both personal and professional ignominies by the very discovery that such internal processes do in fact occur in ordinary mourning as well. In the following paragraph, he provides his most refined and coherent account yet of how these forms of internalization are both alike and distinct:

> Nevertheless, although introjection occurs in mourning in the healthy person and in the neurotic no less than in the melancholiac, we must not overlook the important differences between the process in the one and in the other. In the normal person it is set in motion by real loss (death); and its main purpose is to preserve the person's relations to the dead object, or—what comes to the same thing—to compensate for his loss. Furthermore, his conscious knowledge of his loss will never leave the normal person, as it does the melancholiac. The process of introjection in the melancholiac, moreover, is based on a radical disturbance of his libidinal relations to his object. It rests on a severe conflict of ambivalent feelings, from which he can only escape by turning against himself the hostility he originally felt towards his object. [p. 438]

The clarity of this passage is exemplary, and it is also no accident that Abraham—having worked through some of these issues—is now able to draw more extensively on "Mourning and Melancholia" and to make ample use of Freud's distinguishing criteria. One might wish that he had, in addition, heeded Ferenczi's call for precision about how "introjection" is to be understood. To resort to my own idle fantasies, had he also been privy to what his namesake, Nicolas Abraham (and Maria Torok), would say half-a-century hence, he might have ring-fenced that term for use in relation to mourning and chosen another, more appropriate internalizing term like "incorporation" for more melancholic cases.

This is a good moment to turn again to our literary companion piece, "A Rose for Emily", and pay it some sustained attention. I have already hinted at similarities between how one of Abraham's patients guiltily incorporated and identified with her father's criminality and Emily's more hyperbolic, murderous, vengeful embodiment and enactment of her father's cruelties towards her. Additionally, Abraham's interest in the psychosomatic manifestation of such identifications with dead fathers, in the form of greying hair, is serendipitously echoed in Faulkner's tale.

The narrating townspeople—their essential bafflement, ignorance, and failure to put two and two together notwithstanding—are sufficiently nosey and enthralled by Emily to pay close, constant, and at times perceptive attention to her over the years and thus throughout the story. In the penultimate section, after Homer Barron's disappearance and Emily's period of self-seclusion, we get this description:

> When we next saw Miss Emily, she had grown fat and her hair was turning gray. During the next few years it grew grayer and grayer until it attained an even pepper-and-salt iron-gray when it ceased turning. Up to the day of her death at seventy-four it was still that vigorous iron-gray, like the hair of an active man. [Faulkner, 1930, pp. 127–128]

This not only announces, as I have suggested, Emily's melancholic (over-) identification with her cruelly thwarting father, but also sets up the horrifying discoveries that bring the story to a close.

Having broken into the sealed bedroom to find the skeleton of Barron in the bed, the narrators' last observations in the story's final sentences are redolent with necrophiliac implications:

> Then we noticed that in the second pillow was the indentation of a head. One of us lifted something from it, and leaning forward, that faint and invisible dust dry and acrid in the nostrils, we saw a long strand of iron-grey hair. [p. 130]

The point of using the macabre extremes of this story as exemplary, is to emphasize just how concrete identification is, or can be, at its most primary level. It is Abraham who provides a thorough exploration of these oral-cannibalistic, alimentary dimensions and spells out their implications. From his perspective, as well as mine, Miss Emily's powerfully ambivalent feelings towards her father, unconsciously dominated by revenge and hatred, can result only in an incorporative, virtually reptilian ingestion of the object.

Her wish is to hold fast, first to her father's body and then, even more literally, to that of the utterly inappropriate man whose literally corporeal presence in her life, house, and bed is intended both to replace and to torment her oedipal object. The father is kept sadistically present—in body as well as mind, so to speak—to be taunted by her transgressive defiance. Barron's skeletally final, "profound and fleshless grin"—also referred to as his "grimace of love"—reinforces these meanings. Moreover, when the description continues, "What was left of him, rotted beneath what was left of the nightshirt, had become inextricable from the bed in which he lay" (p. 130), this seems the very image of his comeuppance: as if he had been offered up as a sacrificial meal upon an altar and had become one with it. Indeed, one might see this marital and death bed as itself a giant, flesh-eating maw that had closed on him, swallowing him whole and uniting him permanently with the woman he had seduced but then threatened to betray and abandon.

It was Faulkner's stroke of psychic genius to convey the identification between this daughter and her father so comprehensively, as virtually complete. One imagines that Abraham might have admired this portrayal, capturing as it does the essence of the melancholic state and expressing the full range of its psycho-sexual pathology. When we first meet Miss Emily as an elderly woman in the opening section of the story, her crimes have already been committed. This is not yet known by either the reader or the delegation of aldermen who have come to confront her, but she is described as follows:

> They rose when she entered—a small, fat woman in black, with a thin gold chain descending to her waist and vanishing into her belt, leaning on an ebony cane with a tarnished gold head. Her skeleton was small and spare; perhaps that was why what would have been merely plumpness in another was obesity in her. She looked bloated, like a body long submerged in motionless water, and of that pallid hue. Her eyes, lost in the fatty ridges of her face, looked like two small pieces of coal pressed into a lump of dough as they moved from one face to another as her visitors stated their errand . . . Then they could hear the invisible watch ticking at the end of the gold chain. [p. 121]

As many an undergraduate has either seen spontaneously or been helped to see, this is a brilliant if ghastly depiction of stasis, stagnancy, inertia, and—frankly—constipation or anal retention.

The reader goes on to discover the details of how Emily will allow nothing to pass (through her) or to develop (in her), will permit nothing to be either taken (from her) or given (to her)—as if she even has the power to rob language of its own prepositions! She has contrived—indeed, killed—to keep things just as they are, or as she wants them to be, denying both life and death in the process. She haughtily stares down and defies the newer generations, whether they arrive as tax-collectors or as purveyors of post-boxes, representing modernity and change. And she tries to bury time itself, to secrete it below her waist, and, of course, to keep it still and static in the bedroom above.

However, this first portrait of Emily also evokes truths about her situation that she cannot afford to acknowledge: after all, the head of her aristocratic cane is indeed "tarnished", and, whether she likes it or not, time *can* be detected, ticking away inexorably "at the end of the gold chain", also representing the end of her pretentious Southern lineage. In a later metaphorical image she is seen silhouetted in a window, "like the carven torso of an idol in a niche": she is a vestige, a historical curiosity, a figure standing stubbornly for an utterly outmoded faith or system. There is another sentence that captures her in resonant epithets, denoting both the lingering potency of her surface serenity and immovability and—noting the diagnostically apt last adjective—how disturbed and disturbing she is: "Thus she passed from generation to generation—dear, inescapable, impervious, tranquil, and perverse" (p. 128).

Returning to Abraham after this interlude, we follow as he continues to explore the permutations of grief and depression and to make interchangeable use of both introjection and incorporation, though showing a preference for the former. His next example concerns a patient with a painful history of premature losses and a complicated, ambivalent relationship with his mother. His confusion about grief came fully to the fore when his mother died—again, while the patient was still in treatment with Abraham. When he returned from the funeral, we are told, his mood "was by no means that of a sorrowing son; he felt, on the contrary, elated and blissful. He described to me how he was filled with the feeling that now he carried his mother safely in himself, his own forever" (p. 441). One is again tempted to ask: is this an instance of mourning or of melancholia?

What clinches it in favour of the latter, apart from the presence of suspiciously manic emotions, is the extent to which the patient is disturbed by the presence of the mother's dead body in the house and the prospect of having to bury her, which is again reminiscent of Emily's feelings about her father's body in the Faulkner story. Clearly, these are subtle matters, and we require the context of the entire analysis to be at all sure, but there is something crucial about how the external reality of loss, its literality, tends to be dealt with by the manic-depressive patient.

In the case of Emily—and potentially with Abraham's patient, too—the fact that an actual death has happened and that there is a body that needs interring is an idea that is too real and traumatic to be borne. The actual funereal requirements and arrangements are then transposed or transferred—in their very concreteness—to the bereaved subject's impossible, phantasmatic, and macabre conviction that, while a certain kind of burial may be needed, the object's resting place must not be in the earth, but inside their own bed, body, or mind, where a more appropriate crypt has been made ready.

Abraham, however, remains persuaded that he is discussing a patient who is now—at least in relation to his recently deceased mother, and thus in the most ordinary sense—a mourner. There has been an actual death, after all, and one might therefore understand Abraham's assumption. And yet, even to go along with such matter-of-factness is perhaps to fall prey to a certain literality and to neglect the most important differences between mourning and melancholia. In my own view, at least, the implication of Freud's initial distinction is that it turns primarily not on what kind of loss has been incurred, but on how it is processed. Thus, even if Miss Emily is technically a mourner when she loses her father, what she goes on to exemplify so powerfully is a melancholic and manic failure to mourn, of the most extreme kind.

Of course, Abraham's patient is not a fictional character, and we can extrapolate only so far from what we are told about him, given the analyst's need to protect his anonymity. Abraham tells us that if he were able to say more, he "could make this process of *incorporating* the mother still more evident". A few sentences later, he says that this man "strove against this heaviest loss that could befall him by employing the mechanism of *introjection*" (p. 441, emphasis added). Again, I want to problematize this interchangeable use of the two terms and, though I am aware of asking too much of Abraham here, I think that he provides a useful confusion, pointing us towards a clearer understanding of the differences between "true" mourners and melancholics as far as the construction and capacities of their respective internal worlds are concerned.

This is clinched for me in the following paragraph, where Abraham at first finds it "astonishing" that this man should come away from his loss with such feelings of happiness; however, he then appears to resist his own doubts about the meaning of the patient's high spirits and chooses to regard the latter as evidence of an ordinary mourning process. And he does so via a highly questionable adaptation of one of Freud's famous and familiar phrases:

> But our surprise is lessened when we recollect Freud's explanation of the mechanism of melancholia. We have only to reverse his statement that "the shadow of the lost love-object falls upon the ego" and say that in this case it was not the shadow but the bright radiance of his loved mother which was shed upon her son. In the normal person, too, feelings of affection easily oust the hostile ones in regard to an object he has (in reality) lost. [p. 442]

One problem here is with the word "easily", not least because we have seen repeatedly just how much Freud struggled with, but finally acknowledged, the fact that mourning is anything but easy. Moreover, that feelings of grief can turn into elation and bliss so quickly makes us suspect that, far from having made a real recovery from mourning, the patient may be resorting here to the fantasies of mania—what Klein will call a manic defence.

This patient appears to palliate himself with the promise that his mother need *never* be lost or given up because she is permanently inside him, but in a concrete or incorporative way. If anything, Abraham seems to join the patient in his mania, with his hyperbolic and idealized replacement of Freud's infamous "shadow" with the image of the mother's "bright radiance". As this section ends, we suspect that Abraham has himself been somewhat seduced—taken in, so to say—by the patient's manic conviction. We come away less persuaded than he was that the case at hand "was not one of melancholia" and that "the loss *in reality* of the object was the primary event" (p. 442).

In the third subsection of the paper, "The Process of Introjection in Melancholia: Two Stages of the Oral Phase of the Libido", Abraham treats this earlier psycho-sexual moment in parallel fashion to the two-stage anal phase that had been the focus of the first subsection. He introduces this via the "slippage" he had spoken of earlier from anal to oral symptomatology in a melancholic patient whose loss of his mother and other women in his life first led him to develop anal-retentive symptoms, including a "compulsion to contract his *sphincter ani*". Abraham sees the latter as indicating an "over-determined" identification with his lost objects, doing double duty by defending against both the losses themselves (by trying to hold these female objects within) and the ensuing "passive homosexual attitude towards his father". A new symptom then developed as this man began to experience "a compulsive fantasy of eating the excrements that were lying about . . . the expression of a desire to take back into his body the love-object which he had expelled from it" (pp. 443–444).

This patient provides Abraham with a clear and persuasive account of a regressive process, a descent from an upper-level anal wish to hold on to his object to a lower-level anal wish to expel or kill it, and thence to an even more primary, guilty, and manic wish to re-incorporate orally this discarded and destroyed object. Abraham then links the two adjacent psycho-sexual stages—the anal-sadistic and the oral-cannibalistic:

These are the impulses of expelling (in an anal sense) and of destroying (murdering). The product of such a murder—the dead body—becomes identified with the product of expulsion—with excrement. We can now understand that the patient's desire to eat excrement is a cannibalistic impulse to devour the love object which he has killed. [p. 444]

He goes on to connect these tendencies, via the work of anthropologist–psychoanalyst Géza Róheim, to cannibalistic practices proper and the likelihood that "in their archaic form mourning rites consisted in the eating of the dead person" (p. 444).

Freud, of course, explored similar ideas in *Totem and Taboo,* and we can also draw a connection with the story of Miss Emily, who might be said to carry out the metaphorical equivalent of "eating shit", cannibalism, or necrophagia via the act—which is both vengeful and self-punitive—of keeping the body of the murdered Homer Barron in her bed and sleeping with it for many years, thereby living off it and sustaining herself on it.

Abraham uses the rest of this section to further establish and shore up—via clinical examples as well as in theoretical terms—the oral dynamics that begin to emerge from behind or beneath the anal ones. Particularly when characterizing the cannibalistic phase, he gives us yet another glimpse of how some of his ideas "fathered" those of Melanie Klein. Having first mentioned the "strong perverse cravings" (p. 447) in melancholic patients, which can be partly satisfied by oral sex, he continues:

> But they chiefly used to indulge in very vivid phantasies based on cannibalistic impulses. They used to phantasy about biting into every possible part of the body of their love-object—breast, penis, arm, buttocks, and so on. In their free associations they would very frequently have the idea of devouring the loved person or of biting off pieces of his body; or they would occupy themselves with necrophagic images. They sometimes produced these various phantasies in an uninhibited and infantile way, sometimes concealed them behind feelings of disgust or terror. They also often exhibited a violent resistance against using their teeth. One of them spoke of a "chewing laziness" as one of the phenomena of his melancholic depression.... I showed some years ago (in 1917), in cases of melancholia where the patient absolutely declines to take nourishment, that his refusal represents a self-punishment for his cannibalistic impulses. [p. 448]

The Kleinian development of this violently devouring dimension of childhood and adult psychopathology is well known, and I examine it in chapter four. The preoccupation with teeth is, moreover, a topic followed up in chapter six on the work of Maria Torok.

A little further on in this section, however, Abraham offers yet another clinical example, where this time the patient evidences the existence of another, earlier aspect of orality. He begins with what might be thought an odd distinction, one that he does not elaborate on:

> A young man suffering from depression—though not a melancholic one—used to feel himself almost miraculously soothed by drinking a glass of milk which his mother handed to him. The milk gave him a sensation of something warm, soft, and sweet, and reminded him of something he had known long ago. In this instance the patient's longing for the breast was unmistakable. [p. 450]

Ignoring this presumed but unexplained difference between a melancholic depression and some other kind, we find Abraham declaring that while voracious "oral-sadistic impulses" might dominate the manifest clinical presentation, underlying such impulses—below, prior to, or deeper than these—"there lurks the desire for a pleasurable, sucking activity".

This then allows him to elaborate more fully the metapsychological duality of the oral stage:

> We are thus obliged to assume that there is a differentiation within the oral phase of the libido, just as there is within the anal-sadistic phase. On the primary level of that phase the libido of the infant is attached to the act of sucking. This act is one of incorporation, but one that does not put an end to the existence of the object. The child is not yet able to distinguish between its own self and the external object. Ego and object are concepts which are incompatible with that level of development. There is as yet no differentiation made between the sucking child and the suckling breast. Moreover, the child has as yet neither feelings of hatred nor of love. Its mental state is consequently free from all manifestations of ambivalence in this stage. [p. 450]

Abraham clearly assumes and believes, therefore, that there is such an earlier, toothless oral sub-phase, where there is a pre-ambivalent mix-up of subject and object and what amounts to an initial, age-appropriate experience of incorporative merger of the child with its mother.

As we saw above, Ferenczi also appears to accept the existence of such a phase, as does Freud himself, for example, in his theory of primary narcissism and—despite his lack of emotional resonance with it—in his analysis of Romain Rolland's notion of an "oceanic feeling" in the opening chapter of *Civilization and Its Discontents* (1930a). Moreover, Winnicott, Balint, and the entire Independent tradition in Britain take the existence of such a stage as a virtual *raison d'être* of their psychoanalytic approach. However, in spite of the views of both of her venerable analysts, Klein does not lend this moment any developmental credence, seeming either to repudiate or ignore it. Most post-Kleinians also appear to work, or certainly write, as if they recognize no such stage in human life.

These disputes—if, indeed, this is what they are—tend to take us beyond clinical and even theoretical considerations and into the realm of first principles and even matters of belief or faith. Are these primary moments in human development subject to anything like proof or evidence, or do they turn—simply but fatefully—on how one happens to posit or assume the configuration of our origins, one way or the other? So, do we see ourselves as governed by some secular psychic version of original sin, perhaps inhabited by the death drive, subject to innate conflict and mutual enmity from the very start? Or might some of us at least be fortunate enough come into the world "trailing clouds of glory", in the words of Wordsworth (1807, p. 193), via a blissful, benign, not-yet-individuated beginning and abetted by generous dollops of unstinting maternal solicitude and preoccupation?

Inevitably, I cannot pursue these issues any further here: it would take us very far afield indeed. Suffice it to say that Abraham's elaborate six-stage temporal map of psychosexual development gives rise to many interesting avenues of exploration. For now, however, we must turn our attention back to the specific machinations of depression and melancholia, where two of the most ambivalent moments in his developmental schema—the second, cannibalistic oral phase and the first, sadistic anal phase—pertain and prevail.

The fourth part of Abraham's essay is entitled "Notes on the Psychogenesis of Melancholia", and he seems here to want to flesh out certain aspects of what Freud said in "Mourning and Melancholia" regarding the paradoxical mixture of self-effacing abjectness and overweening grandiosity that we find in such patients. Clearly, this is also connected to the structural complexity of the relations between the ego and the incorporated object, which is loved and hated, admired as well as denigrated; the patient can display a confusing—as well as ingenious—unconscious capacity to obfuscate the roles of victim and persecutor in the psychic situation, and thus to play both parts.

Of course, whether at any given moment these internal dynamics are more depressed or more manic will contribute crucially to the clinical picture. "Patients like these", Abraham reminds us, "are especially fond of displaying a superior scepticism about the discoveries of psychoanalysis" (p. 455). In addition to what Abraham terms "the introjected reproach aimed at the love-object", such a patient will also proudly present himself as "guilty of every sin committed since the beginning of the world" and "a monster of wickedness" (p. 456). Abraham provides the following succinct summary of the situation:

> Thus melancholia presents a picture in which there stand in immediate juxtaposition yet absolutely opposed to one another self-love and self-hatred, an overestimation of the ego and an underestimation of it—the manifestations, that is, of *a positive and a negative narcissism*. [p. 456]

As we are witnessing, Abraham's paper is nothing if not thorough, and he seems to want to provide a veritable psychoanalytic users' guide to depressive illness.

He now takes it upon himself to list "a number of aetiological factors in this disease" and mentions the following necessary but not separately sufficient preconditions:

1. "A constitutional factor", where melancholic psychopathology seems to run in the family and oral issues are preponderant;
2. "A special fixation of the libido on the oral level", featuring powerful, insatiable urges to use the mouth for various kinds of gratification;
3. "A severe injury to infantile narcissism brought about by successive disappointments in love", represented by early and then further serial losses of this kind;
4. "The occurrence of the first important disappointment in love before the Oedipus-wishes have been overcome", which can leave the subject's ego forever weakened, exposed, and traumatized;
5. "The repetition of the primary disappointment in later life", likely to bring on—or be the proximal cause of—the actual melancholia (pp. 457–459).

These factors seem to lose their discrete specificity and merge into each other somewhat, but Abraham has nevertheless provided a handy taxonomy of relevant features. There is an interesting moment, not long after he completes his list, when Abraham seems to want to say, quite explicitly and categorically, that in melancholia—as opposed to the other neuroses—the focus is on the problematics of the relationship with the mother rather than the father (p. 460). He then appears to catch himself in one of those anxious moments where he suspects he may have said something critical of the Freudian paradigm and backtracks somewhat, making sure to give priority to the Oedipus complex and therefore to an emphasis on the roles of both parents. However, this bit of political kowtowing perhaps allows him to come forth more strongly again: "What I have just said does not invalidate my previous statement that in melancholia the whole psychological process centres *in the main* round the mother" (p. 461).

What is also of interest, as I mentioned before, is Abraham's perhaps premature but determined attempt to take in, even as he is composing his own text, the recently published *The Ego and the Id*, mentioned in a footnote at this juncture. He seems to have grasped intuitively one of the most striking and significant features of the Freudian internal world that he finds adumbrated in this new work: namely, that introjection (or identification) is responsible for the formation of the newly named superego, in the wake of the resolution of the Oedipus complex.

Abraham's own formulations are particularly pertinent to melancholic "self-criticisms and self-reproaches—especially those of a delusional nature" and seem initially to cleave to what Freud had said earlier, in "Mourning and Melancholia". He speaks of the melancholic patient instituting a double introjection: he takes in the "original love-object upon which he had built his ego ideal" *and* the persecutory conscience by means of which he both berates himself and inflicts the "merciless criticism of the introjected object". Each of these introjects (or are they incorporations?) assumes its respective place within the depressed psyche via a different internalizing or identificatory process and in relation to the original parental objects.

Abraham's telling example features a patient in whom the twofold process expressed itself in "an unfavourable judgement passed by his introjected mother on his introjected father". Moreover, this patient's psychotic delusions about infestations of lice could also be analysed in terms of his fury towards the composite parental couple for filling the house with vermin-like younger siblings who displaced him and deprived him of his mother's affection (pp. 461–462).

A little further on, we then find Abraham exploring, via another clinical example, the more destructive aspects of melancholic object relations, specifically where a patient's mother is concerned. She is imagined as a dangerous crocodile with cruel, emasculating jaws, inevitably evoking the very kinds of retaliatory phantasies of oral and anal aggression that Klein would later write about so graphically. Abraham emphasizes once more the ambivalence of such phantasies: "They involve on the one hand a total or partial incorporation of the mother, that is, an act of positive desire; and on the other, her castration or death, that is, a negative desire tending to her destruction".

He goes on to describe melancholic aetiology as a dramatic three-phase process within the patient that ensues when there has been "unbearable disappointment from their love-object". The first act or urge is "to expel that object as though it were faeces and to destroy it"; second is "the act of introjecting and devouring it—an act which is a specifically melancholic form of narcissistic identification"; finally, in act three, with the object lodged and imprisoned within, the "sadistic thirst for vengeance now finds its satisfaction in tormenting the ego"—and, one might add, the typical dynamics of the melancholic internal world can now unfold in earnest (pp. 463–464).

Like Freud, however, Abraham would also like to believe that there can be an eventual end to such melancholic machinations, perhaps via a "gradual appeasement of sadistic desires"; the object might then risk emergence from hiding and the ego might agree to "restore it to its place in the outer world". No sooner has this rather hopeful scenario been suggested, however, than Abraham becomes aware of the likelihood that "in his unconscious the melancholiac regards this liberation from his object as once more an act of evacuation". He gives the relevant example of a patient who, on beginning to emerge from his depression, dreamt that "he expelled with the greatest sensation of relief a stopper that was sticking in his anus" (p.464).

In other words, what Abraham is not quite—or yet—saying is that what is heralded here may not be a recovery from, but a repudiation of, the melancholia, via manic triumph over the object that caused it. He will go on to discuss the topic of mania, but he now concludes this section with some rather evocative sentences:

> This act of expulsion concludes the process of that archaic form of mourning which we must consider melancholia to be. We may truly say that in the course of an attack of melancholia the love-object goes through a process of psychological *metabolism* within the patient. [p. 464, emphasis added]

I trust that by now there is no need for me to explain why I might find these sentences important and in need of both pausing over and parsing. The idea here of a certain internal "process" or passage reminds one that the alimentary canal is itself a continuous internal tunnel, beginning at the mouth and ending at the anus. One assumes a necessary connectedness and mutual implication among all the diverse dynamics along the way.

Once again, it is my general or overarching theme in this book that all human experience of object loss, separation, and mourning requires and implies an internal process. Thus, linguistic-conceptual tropes involving metabolization are not just useful or apt: they seem virtually required or summoned, as we try to think, talk, or write about such processes. I have also tried to make clear, as a corollary, that it then becomes just as imperative to conceive of failed mourning—that is, depressive or melancholic conditions—in terms of various failures to metabolize, as forms of psychic indigestion, some of which can be catastrophic, even life-threatening.

Abraham appears to corroborate these perspectives by noting that in melancholia the lost object does indeed undergo a journey of sorts through the psychic alimentary canal. But he does not seem to take his own idea—that melancholia is "an archaic form of mourning"—seriously enough. Whereas he posits that melancholia can wind towards an eventual end, it is apparent that this passage of successive internal stages often does not come to a spontaneously satisfactory digestive-metabolic conclusion. On the contrary, it seems to be "on repeat", returning eternally, in circular or bipolar fashion, to the same manic-depressive—or evacuative–incorporative—moments with which it began. It is only when there is genuine, fully achieved, more-or-less linear mourning—as opposed to the melancholic parody of it—that one might hope for, or even expect, more complete anabolic and catabolic conclusions, whereby the loss can be acknowledged fully while the self also ends up suitably, and structurally, enriched by its proper processing.

Extrapolating more specifically and less critically from Abraham's brave theoretical speculations and clinical applications regarding the psychosexual stages, one is reminded that our alimentary orifices seem capable of *both* incorporating or taking in *and* evacuating or expelling a variety of objects, real as well as phantasmatic. Despite the purists or puritans among us who might prefer that each "end" should mind only its own limited, circumscribed, and functional business, mouths can also expel things aggressively and violently, and anuses can take things in pleasurably and lovingly. Technically, I have sometimes chosen to consider an un-metabolized evacuation as an "up-chuck" or vomit, rather than a "bowel movement", where there might be the confusing implication that a "proper" digestive process might indeed have taken place. But perhaps one must be extremely wary of putting too much pressure on the vehicle of the metaphor—of treating it in ways that are too pedantic, concrete, literal, or graphic—such that the tenor is relegated or ignored, and the essential meaning missed or sacrificed.

Though I will not go into any detail about it, the following, fifth subsection of Abraham's text, "The Infantile Prototype of Melancholic Depression", consists of a single case history outlining the traumatic childhood antecedents of a melancholic illness and featuring hellish, Little Hans-style dreamscapes with horses, carts, and tortured men "who could neither go on living nor die" (p. 466). Near the end of this clinical example, Abraham resorts to a rather technical-sounding term to describe or diagnose the mental state of the patient at five-years old, namely, a "primal parathymia"; that is, he suffered from some fundamental confusion of affect and mood in relation to his oedipal objects.

According to Abraham, the patient ended up carrying a hopeless ambivalence into all subsequent attempts to find love, "and every failure to do so brought with it a state of mind that was an exact replica of his primal parathymia. It is this state of mind that we call melancholia" (p. 469). The idea that there might be a very early version, a prototype of depression—indeed, that we might all be melancholic in some very essential or primal way—will be of significance when we explore, in chapter four, the way Klein takes some of these ideas forward.

"Mania" is the succinct title of the sixth subsection of Abraham's paper, and I want now to turn attention to what he has to say on the topic. He is aware of wishing to avoid tackling this phenomenon, reminding us that Freud, too, seemed to hesitate to take it on. Though Abraham says that mania would have remained even more of a mystery were it not for the psychoanalytic investigation of melancholia, he nevertheless notes that Freud "has penetrated so much more deeply into the nature of the depressive states than into that of the manic ones" and predicts that he himself will add to this knowledge "only in a very slight degree and in but few respects" (p. 470).

Is this just another example of Abraham's obsequious modesty in relation to Freud? It is perhaps interesting that, instead of now returning to "Mourning and Melancholia" (where we have seen that Freud may not be at his best on the topic of mania), Abraham opts to discuss Freud's more recent contributions, mentioning *Group Psychology* in a footnote and availing himself of the term "superego", newly minted in *The Ego and the Id*. He states the perhaps obvious point that, whereas in melancholia the superego manifests its "function of criticism with excessive severity", in mania "we see it use no such harsh criticism of the ego". Consequently, when the mood switch occurs, the patient will have exchanged "those feelings and delusions of inferiority" for "a sense of self-importance and power" (p. 471).

Abraham speculates about what happens metapsychologically in this transition, suggesting that, with the manic patient having "thrown off the yoke of his super-ego", the latter "has become merged" in the ego, such that the "difference between ego and super-ego has now disappeared", albeit temporarily. If this is his view of the intrapsychic situation in mania, Abraham also appears very clear-sighted about the object-relational dimension of it. Attributing this insight to Freud (despite the impression that Freud was not, in fact, quite so clear about it), he writes that "in the manic condition the patient is celebrating a triumph over the object he once loved and then gave up and introjected" (p. 471).

He follows this up by saying, astutely enough, that in mania the "'shadow of the object' which had fallen on the ego has passed away". As we saw earlier, Abraham gives a positive inflection to this moment: of the sun breaking through radiantly and penetrating the gloom and glumness of the depressive phase. There is the vague impression that he is not just describing this situation but, disconcertingly, identifying with the manic patient's sense of liberation—as if their experience might amount to more than a mere illusion of liberty. As he goes on to say, such a patient "gives himself up to his sense of regained freedom with a kind of frenzy" because "the withdrawal of his super-ego allows his narcissism to enter upon a positive, pleasurable phase" (pp. 471–472).

It may be that Abraham's capacity to write evocatively about such patients is not only due to his vast psychiatric experience with them, but also because he has a way of putting himself inside their experience, as any good psychoanalyst must. When he proceeds to highlight the oral dimension of mania, we are reminded not only that Freud had himself spoken of the ravenous hunger with which the manic individual pursues new experiences, but also why he had found Abraham so helpful on the eating issues associated with manic-depressive illness:

> Now that his ego is no longer being consumed by the introjected object, the individual turns his libido to the outer world with an excess of eagerness. This change of attitude gives rise to many symptoms, all of them based on an increase in the patient's oral desires. A patient of mine once called it a "gobbling mania". This appetite is not confined to the taking of nourishment alone. The patient "devours" everything that comes his way. We are all familiar with the strength of the erotic cravings of the manic patient. But he shows the same greed in seizing on new impressions from which, in his melancholic state, he had cut himself off. Whereas in his depressive phase he had felt that he was dispossessed and cast out from the world of external objects, in his manic phase he as it were proclaims his power of assimilating all his objects into himself. [p. 472]

Abraham is only mid-way through this long paragraph but I feel compelled to interrupt him so as to comment on some of these very valuable oral-assimilative thoughts about mania, not least because they bespeak a view of mania that is slightly different from the one that I have been advancing.

As far as Abraham is concerned, mania is not only about voiding something or getting rid of a troublesome presence that has been squatting on the patient's life during the melancholic period. At least ostensibly, mania is also fun: an outbreak of exuberance, not only freedom from constraint or restriction, but freedom to act out and embrace all and sundry. When he is no longer being consumed by a succubus-like object, the manic patient becomes a voraciously greedy, appetitive perpetrator. Experiencing an incorporative yearning of vast, grandiose proportions, he would no doubt want to claim, along with American poet Walt Whitman, "I am large . . . I contain multitudes" (1855, p. 63). Abraham implicitly reminds us here of what our bipolar patients often tell us while mired in melancholia: how much they miss the ebullience and elation, the good old days, of their mania.

To his credit, however, Abraham is no less *au fait* with that other dimension of mania, the one linked more closely with up-chuck or evacuation. Abraham's long paragraph resumes and concludes as follows:

> But it is characteristic that this pleasurable act of taking in new impressions is correlated to an equally pleasurable act of ejecting them almost as soon as they have been received. Anyone who has listened to the associations of a manic patient will recognize that his flight of ideas, expressed in a stream of words, represents a swift and agitated process of receiving and expelling fresh impressions. In melancholia we saw that there was some particular introjected object which was treated as a piece of food that had been incorporated and which was eventually got rid of. In mania, *all* objects are regarded as material to be passed through the patient's "psychosexual metabolism" at a rapid rate. And it is not difficult to see from the associations of the manic patient that he identifies his uttered thoughts with excrement. [p. 472]

This idea, that it is possible for objects to pass through what Abraham gratifyingly calls the patient's "psychosexual metabolism", or psychic alimentary canal, without touching sides or being absorbed, reminds me of the work of colleagues at the Tavistock.

Julian Stern is a psychiatrist and psychotherapist who has investigated so-called unexplained medical conditions, specializing in gastrointestinal or alimentary ailments, which he has written about extensively (1999, 2003, 2010, 2013). Typically, these patients end up seeking psychological help only after long periods engaged with physical medicine in the vain hope of curing chronic conditions (like Crohn's disease or even extreme forms of anorexia), sometimes via drastic, unnecessary, and irreversible surgical procedures. Clearly, such patients' initial preference for physical prognosis and intervention over any psychological explanation or treatment would indicate that they find the more psychic forms of digestion and metabolization just as threatening as their physiological equivalents and that they therefore try strenuously—and unconsciously—to "bypass" them. Stern's work reminds us that to think *only* metaphorically about ingestive, digestive, metabolic, and evacuative difficulties might misrepresent the phenomenological experience of these patients and therefore the aetiological and diagnostic confusion surrounding this kind of suffering.

In a personal communication, Stern described a group of patients who were literally, physiologically, unable to assimilate or absorb very much from what they ate, regardless of the quantities they ingested. Though manifestly neither anorexic nor bulimic, these patients seemed psychically to allow or compel whatever sustenance they took in to pass through their digestive systems virtually unprocessed. We might speculate that they either felt undeserving, unworthy of the food they were consuming—as a melancholic patient might—or did not regard the nutrition as worthy of them—as might befit the kind of manic patient described here by Abraham. In the latter case, the food or object is thus utterly devalued, seen as something not good enough for their alimentary or metabolic attention. Thus, the manic fun resides in the imperious dismissal of all kinds of sustenance, need, or help as unnecessary and beneath contempt. Of course, both attitudes must apply because, as we already appreciate, such equivocal, ambivalent, and circular sets of feelings, about the ego as well as the object, typify the manic-depressive picture.

Abraham seems now to be intent on solving Freud's problem of finding an analogy "in the normal mind" of the "reversal from melancholia to mania" (p. 472). When discussing Freud earlier, I tried to suggest that there might have been something a bit misguided about this quest, given the clarity with which Freud managed, in the first place, to distinguish mourning from melancholia. Should we really or necessarily have to expect a phase equivalent to that of mania when mourning is at an end?

Abraham sought this parallel in apparently ordinary recovery processes, saying that "when the mourning person has gradually detached his libido from his dead object by means of the 'work of mourning' he is aware of an increase in his sexual desires" (p. 473), as well as in his more sublimated social and intellectual activities. Resorting once again to Róheim's anthropological work for corroboration, he instances ancient mourning rituals in which sudden outbreaks of libidinal wishes and acts after mourning could compel another symbolic killing and eating of the mourned object.

Is Abraham's suggestion that the revival of sexual feeling, which "shows like a faint replica of archaic mourning customs" (p. 473), persuasive enough to really clinch the argument about there being parallel manic, or even quasi-manic, events that occur in the wake of mourning? We will later explore how Maria Torok takes up this issue; she explicitly cites Abraham's claim and addresses the intrusive irruption or sudden emergence of unwanted sexual feelings in the body and mind of the mourning subject—not just after, but during and in the very midst of periods of grief.

What we might also glean from this material is a preview of Klein's convictions about the mourner's need to revive and repeat—via a re-internalizing and re-establishing of the original lost object in the internal world—earlier psychic processes that somehow come undone each time a new loss is incurred. This suggests that, according to some analysts, there is no such thing as a fully achieved, complete, or successful mourning process; that even under optimal circumstances, the ambivalent dynamics of melancholia are not, and can never be, entirely absent.

As usual, it is when he turns to clinical examples of manic behaviour and dynamics *per se* that Abraham seems to come into his own. One patient gave way to an intense wish to eat great quantities of meat, pursuing this goal in a relentless orgiastic frenzy until utterly stuffed. Abraham emphasizes the archaic cannibalistic roots of such urges and how they corroborate "Freud's view that in mania the ego is celebrating the festival of its liberation", taking the phantasmatic form "of a wild excess in eating flesh" (p. 474). For me this evokes *Where the Wild Things Are* (1963), Maurice Sendak's wonderful children's tale that is suffused with tropes of angry, manic orality.

The book features a naughty boy called Max who dresses in a wolf suit and runs riot at home; when his mother reprimands him, he threatens to devour her and is promptly and punitively sent to bed without supper. In his subsequent dream or imaginative foray, however, Max enacts thinly-disguised cannibalistic revenge. As his room turns into a forest, he sets sail for a savage land where he uses magical powers to turn the tables on the fearful, giant, sharp-toothed, doubtless carnivorous inhabitants, and then spends pages carousing wordlessly with them. Having been crowned their king, he lords it over them, sends *them* to bed without supper!

However, delicious subliminal smells start seeping into this fantasy world and seem to persuade him to give up this raw existence for the promise of a cooked meal. So, notwithstanding fierce, violent protestations from the wild things, who are so fond of him that they threaten to eat him up in an incorporating, annihilating way, he sails home again. And, though she had banished him hungry to his room at the start, he finds that his mother has left him a forgiving, sustaining hot supper at the end.

Interestingly, near the end of the current section of his paper Abraham might be seen both to concur with Sendak's maternal focus in the story and to anticipate his analysand Klein's accounts of the infant's violent wishes to attack the mother. He questions Freud's paternal ur-story about "man's 'primal crime'" being the killing and eating of the primal father by a band of brothers, as adumbrated in *Totem and Taboo* and elsewhere; Abraham feels compelled to point out that, in his own experience, "the criminal phantasies of the manic patient are for the most part directed against his mother".

He cites the example of a patient who identified with the emperor Nero's killing of his actual mother and burning of her symbol, the city of Rome. One wonders, however, whether a warning might have registered in Abraham's mind a moment later, concerning Freud's own complex attachment to that city. Because, having issued his challenge, he almost immediately retracts or compromises it, saying that "those emotions directed at the mother are of a secondary kind; they were in the first instance aimed towards the father" (p. 474). Evidently, Abraham's own patricidal wishes and tendencies fill him with such guilt and anxiety that he cannot entertain them consciously for very long; thus, he ends up confessing them unconsciously, betraying his allegiance to the mother in the process!

The seventh and final subsection, entitled "The Psycho-Analytic Therapy of Manic-Depressive States", sees Abraham both setting out the aims of such treatments and evaluating his own efforts for the cause. He expresses high hopes, but warns against "a premature optimism as regards psycho-analysis", no less than against "the traditional attitude of nihilism" that he had previously identified and decried among his psychiatric colleagues. He speaks of heeding Freud's advice about the right moment at which to take on such a patient: during a "free interval" between manic and depressive periods, when there is at least the possibility of a meaningful transference being established. He also states his ambitious intentions of going further than mere symptom relief, "to do away with the regressive libidinal impulses of the individual and to effect a progression of his libido until it reaches the stage of genital organization and complete object-love" (p. 476).

However, Abraham evaluates his own interim successes with manic-depressive patients with his usual modesty and realism, tentatively listing them while claiming that the cases should all be regarded as works in progress. Having documented certain observable or objective changes, moreover, he speaks near the end of this final subsection of "the subjective value which psycho-analytic treatment has for depressive patients". Quite apart from later, longer-term benefits, these hard-to-reach patients also have the phenomenological experience of more immediate "mental relief" during the process of analytic therapy. Abraham can thus claim, with the appropriate reservations but also with cautious confidence, that "we cannot deny that psycho-analysis does exercise an effect on patients suffering from the circular insanities" (p. 479). Notwithstanding that they were written almost a century ago, one wishes that contemporary psychiatric guidelines for the treatment of such patients and the mental health community at large would take heed of Abraham's words and pay attention to his claims.

This is not, of course, where Abraham's long monograph ends. Though far shorter, Part II, entitled "Origins and Growth of Object-Love", is an attempt not only to fill in the gaps in his complex psychosexual schema, but to complete the concomitant object-relational picture to which the depressive oral and anal dynamics laid out in Part I have contributed so richly. As always, there are several inviting topics to explore in this part of the text, but mentioning or sign-posting just a few of them will have to suffice.

First, it is interesting—but how significant is it?—that where virtually all the patients exemplifying his ideas about melancholia in Part I are men, the significant examples in Part II come from his work with two female patients who, as he suggests, were more neurotic than melancholic. Second, on the way to including "full" genitality and object love in his developmental model, Abraham speaks at some length about partly completed introjections which he refers to as *"partial incorporation* of the object" (p. 487) and thereby seems again to be preparing the ground for the later efflorescence of Melanie Klein's ideas and theories concerning part-objects. Third, Abraham makes a valiant attempt to situate not only neurotic but also psychotic—or at least paranoid—patients, as well as those with perversions, on his sexual-stage continuum, and to ascertain thereby how fully they are able to relate to or take in an object (pp. 489–491).

As he had done in concluding Part I, Abraham again provides a brief description of what the final phase and optimal outcome of a psychosexual and object-relational teleology should look like. Apparently keeping faith until the end with Freud's insistent central focus on the presence or absence of the penis, he writes:

> We must not forget, too, that the genitals are more intensely cathected by narcissistic love than any other part of the subject's own body. Thus everything else in the object can be loved sooner than the

genitals. On the level of the "phallic" organization of the libido, as Freud calls it, the last great step in its development has obviously not yet been made. It is not made until the highest level of the libido—that which alone should be called the genital level—is attained. Thus we see that the attainment of the highest level of the organization of the libido goes hand in hand with the final step in the evolution of object-love. [p. 495]

Certainly, at that moment in psychoanalytic history—and in keeping with Abraham's fully elaborated six-stage psychosexual schema (p. 496)—this formulation of a developmental outcome would have sufficed and gained the approval of many if not all working analysts.

However, to what extent do contemporary analysts still think of psychic development as a linear evolution culminating in "full genitality"? Does Abraham's six-step schema have as much relevance or pertinence for analysts today as it had in his day? Do we still think that it is in such terms that we would best describe and assess the prospective end point of a developmental process or an analytic recovery?

It might be interesting to consider the implications for the depressed patients who have, after all, been the primary focus of Abraham's paper. Despite all the attention he has paid to matters both oral and anal in the course of this work, Abraham now appears to be shifting attention away from the alimentary tract altogether. Is it an expression of his need to keep the faith or return to the fold when he speaks of genital attainment as the final measure of psychoanalytic healing and success? Is this the only way to evaluate it?

The thrust of my book suggests, perhaps, that there is another way to outline what a completed or optimal treatment for such a patient might look like. We might choose to characterize the task by staying with oral-alimentary terms rather than adopting a different bodily register: can we not be seen as helping to achieve a thorough digestion or metabolization of lost objects, perhaps incestuous ones first and foremost, leaving the patient free once again to introject or have their fill of new objects?

I may again be guilty here of taxing Abraham unnecessarily with fanciful speculations and expectations from the psychoanalytic future. And yet it is fascinating that he chooses to spend the last few pages of the paper drawing on his medical knowledge to consider and explain the parallels between early embryonic biology and what happens in later psychic development: "We have long since learned to apply the biogenetic principle of organic life to the mental (psycho-sexual) development of man" (p. 498). The post-birth, psychic version of this unfolding must necessarily lag temporally behind anatomical and physiological processes occurring primarily in utero. Abraham elaborates upon this gap as follows:

> The biological model upon which the developmental processes discussed in this paper are based takes place in the earliest embryonic period of the individual, whereas the psychosexual processes extend over a number of years of his extra-uterine life, namely from his first year to his period of puberty. [p. 499]

In his account of these staggered but analogical developments, Abraham emphasizes the extent to which—both biologically and psychically—"the intestinal canal, and especially the apertures at either end" (p. 499) dominate the early picture, and he goes into some considerable biological detail to describe this primacy.

What Abraham seems at pains to emphasize is the fact that there are enormously intricate dynamics at work in these alimentary regions, long before the genital body and mind arrive on the scene. Staying with what he calls "the correlate in biological ontogenesis"—the tenor of the metaphor—he waxes lyrical in his description of the

> intestinal mechanisms for retaining what has been taken into the body. These consist in constrictions and enlargements, annular contractures, branching passages, divagations ending blindly, manifold convolutions, and finally the voluntary and involuntary sphincter muscles of the anus itself. At the time that this complicated arrangement for the retention of objects is being formed there is as yet no sign of the appearance of the uro-genital apparatus. [p. 501]

I would read Abraham to be subtly alluding here to the fact that these complex and fundamental (using this word both literally and figuratively) digestive, oral/alimentary/anal dimensions of human development had not yet been given their full due; heretofore, psychoanalysis had been dominated by Freud's obsession, not so much with sexuality *per se*, as with the sexual apparatus and a focus on the psychosexual significance of the penis or phallus.

For Abraham to have said this much already constituted a brave and risky act. To have issued his challenge any more loudly or explicitly than by way of these suggestive hints that bring his seminal paper to a close would have been to risk the wrath of a master who never tolerated disagreement or insurrection from his acolytes easily or with equanimity. Abraham was one of the few of Freud's followers who managed to live and die without incurring too much of Freud's familiar displeasure at any hint of filial infidelity. As their correspondence testifies, however, Freud sensed these late differences and became quite unkind, even to this most faithful of disciples, near the end of his curtailed life (Freud & Abraham, 1966).

Whether one regards it as an unbridgeable gulf or a mere stream that is easily forded, Abraham remains located on the former side of a gap between earlier psycho-libidinal and later object-relational forms of psychoanalysis. Nevertheless, insofar as his main and major task in this paper was to bring into prominence how alimentary processes and thinking inform and contribute to the understanding of depression and the internal worlds of patients who suffer from it, he at times appears to be gazing longingly over to the farther shore. At least for some, that would be the Promised Land, where a deeper, broader, and less single-minded version of our therapeutic and theoretical endeavours might prevail. It is thus apt that this book's next chapter should be about Melanie Klein, analysand of both analysts discussed in this chapter.

If, as I have argued elsewhere (Meyerowitz, 1995), Freud is akin to the biblical Joseph insofar as he, too, was a famous interpreter of dreams who made a name for himself in exile, perhaps Ferenczi and Abraham may be regarded as the Moses and Aaron figures, tasked with leading the people out of Egypt. But then we are bidden to think that it is Klein's innovative and boldly original object relations approach that places her in the role of Joshua, representing the new generation that would carry psychoanalysis across the Jordan and into Canaan.

CHAPTER FOUR

Melanie Klein: positioning the object and rebuilding the internal world

"A Contribution to the Psychogenesis of Manic-Depressive States" (1935)

When one ventures to read almost any paper by Melanie Klein, there is the sense of beginning *in medias res*, as great epic poetry is meant to do. The experience is something like opening the *Iliad* to find its disgruntled hero already threatening violence and retribution for slights and insults that had taken place before we came on the scene. There is, in other words, a powerful, immediate, and rather frightening sense, when reading Klein, that one has been plunged into a world in which there has been plenty of "previous", and for which one is therefore not quite prepared.

This famous and essential first paper on manic-depressive states is no exception, and perhaps one of its most important features is Klein's account of how earlier, primary anxieties, belonging to what will be named in a later paper as the *paranoid-schizoid* position, interfere with and compromise the *depressive* position, which is named here for the first time. Klein's reader comes away not just with vivid descriptions of unsettled states pertaining to our earliest negotiations of loss, but with some actual experience of the confusion, apprehension, and anxiety that abiding in such unsteady spaces entails.

Briefly mentioning her earlier work but without much further ado, Klein starts with an "account of a phase of sadism at its zenith". Even in the first months, the human infant's earliest aggressive urges are directed at—and indeed into—the mother's body and are dominated by "scooping", "devouring", and "destroying" impulses (of which, it is somehow the "scooping" that sounds most violent). She also mentions right away that the infant—already acutely attuned, as it must be, to good and bad experiences in relation to a breast that both feeds and frustrates—has at its disposal primitive capacities, "the mechanisms of introjection and projection", whereby it can either take in or get rid of such experiences.

Included in this packed first paragraph is also the perhaps controversial idea that it is not only externally caused frustration, but the baby's own inherent aggression projected onto or into the breast, that can render the latter bad. Klein then proceeds to introduce her trademark idea about the internal representatives of external phenomena or objects, as follows: "These imagos, which are a phantastically distorted picture of the real objects on which they are based, become installed not only in the outside world but, by the process of incorporation, also within the ego." The paragraph finally draws to a close with a sentence in which Klein claims that the primitive "anxiety-situations" and concomitant "defence-mechanisms" characterizing this earliest era add up to a phenomenology "comparable to that of the psychoses of adults" (1935, p. 145).

That Klein uses two different terms to denote "taking in" provides a first point of interest here. When she says that the creation of these imagos—or what will come to be called internal objects—is the product of incorporation, is this mechanism to be considered the same as or different from introjection, which she had introduced earlier in the paragraph? It seems that Klein, like Karl Abraham (but unlike Ferenczi and, as we shall see, Nicolas Abraham and Maria Torok), does not really distinguish between these two terms but uses them interchangeably. As I will argue, this has either intentional or inadvertent consequences for her theories of loss and mourning and, perhaps, for her more general metapsychological position in the psychoanalytic landscape.

There is the implication that the differences between successful and unsuccessful negotiations of loss—between mourning, on the one hand, and melancholia or depressive illnesses, on the other, and between psychic health and illness at large—are very much a matter of degree for Klein and may easily disappear altogether, conceptually if not clinically. This allows or accompanies such statements as the one with which her first paragraph ends: the suggestion that there is, at the very least, a strong analogy—if not something much stronger than analogy—linking the experiences of early childhood and the mental illnesses of adults.

Before plunging any more deeply into Klein's text, I want to note that she herself lived a life that was thoroughly suffused with loss. Her views were obviously informed by the events of her life—as is the case for us all—even if we must, of course, be wary of attributing her ideas solely to personal experience. Klein, as her biographers (Grosskurth, 1986; Kristeva, 2000; Likierman, 2001) tell us, was virtually born into loss and went on to suffer numerous bereavements and abandonments. Her older sister became ill and died at a young age, which had the effect of turning her mother into a domineering and thwarting presence (external as well as internal) for her surviving daughter, despite the latter's struggles to accommodate and keep faith with this overbearing maternal object. When Klein was a young woman, she lost both her father and her beloved brother in the same year; her marriage, that followed apace, was not a success and led to estrangement and eventual separation from her husband. Later, a man with whom she had become deeply involved moved to Palestine just when the relationship might have flourished.

During the very period when she was writing these two famous papers on manic-depressive states, she suffered the death of one of her two sons, possibly by suicide. There were also serious conflicts with her daughter, whose professional apostasy was experienced as a public betrayal within the psychoanalytic community, leaving Klein hurt and humiliated. And then there were all the losses associated with the starts and stops of her career: financial circumstances prevented her from studying medicine, precipitating her subsequent migrations through the cities of Central Europe, from Vienna through Budapest to Berlin—these being, of course, the early centres of psychoanalysis. Having departed Ferenczi's couch in her move from Hungary to Germany, her next analyst, Abraham, died suddenly only a year after he had taken her under his wing. In the nick of time, one might say, she was invited to make one further move: to London, where despite continuing trials and traumas, she felt welcome, was able to settle down, and went on to have an illustrious career and create a psychoanalytic dynasty.

After such a catalogue of personal losses, separations, and itinerant wanderings (albeit with a good ending), we return to the impersonal text with a little more context. And it is the first few paragraphs and pages of the paper that are crucial to an appreciation of the distinctive angle from which Klein approaches her subject. She continues with a summary of her ideas about the earlier—indeed, the very earliest—anxieties that her extensive work with children had uncovered and that she had been devoted to describing from the start of her clinical career. She now introduces the "earliest methods of defence against the dread of persecutors". The latter seem to come from all sides, from without and within, but there is a great initial reluctance on the part of the ego to acknowledge them. Opting for a phrase that had little currency yet in psychoanalysis, Klein speaks of this defence as "scotomization, the *denial of psychic reality*" (p. 145).

Characteristically, Klein compresses these ideas into dense sentences with multiple clauses in which one feels that there is far too much going on for comfort. We are first bidden to believe that we start out in life as creatures who feel hounded and targeted, but that we find this too disturbing to accept and thus wipe out the very perception of danger. We might recall that Freud—in "Neurosis and Psychosis" (1924b)—grappled with the term "scotomization", coined by the pioneering French psychiatrist and psychoanalyst, René Laforgue. It denotes an action that is far more obliterating than mere repression or even disavowal: not a consigning of something to unconsciousness so much as a rendering of it never to have happened. Furthermore, the abysmal thing that Klein says is being denied in this fashion is something called "psychic reality"—and we do not know yet quite what this betokens. What we are made aware of is that, for Klein, an internal world—something real in a psychic rather than a physical sense, replete with a population of inner versions of external objects—is present from (near enough) the very beginning.

Clearly, Klein is attempting to cover quickly ground that she has more painstakingly laid out in earlier texts, but it is still extraordinary that at this point we are still only on the first page of her paper. What seems to happen next in her account is that other protective or defensive measures, temporarily restricted by the power of primary denial, start to kick in, and the persecutors are now subject to relieving "expulsion and projection". Her argument continues: if the very primitive defence of denial "forms the basis of the most severe psychoses", then overuse of the phantasmatic actions of projection carries with it the occupational hazard of paranoia. She says that "infantile psychotic anxiety" can be "bound and modified by obsessional mechanisms", which—like so much else in the Kleinian universe—are said to make an early appearance.

It is only at this point—two dense paragraphs in—that Klein pauses to make her intentions in the paper plain: she proposes "to deal with depressive states in their relation to paranoia on the one hand and to mania on the other" (pp. 145–146), basing her views on a wide range of clinical experience with both disturbed and normal children and with adults.

At this moment, Klein rather hurriedly introduces, and condenses into a few brief sentences, what she sees Freud and Abraham to have said about the significance of object loss in melancholia: "The real loss of a real object, or some similar situation having the same significance, results in the object being installed within the ego. Owing, however, to an excess of cannibalistic impulses in the subject, this introjection miscarries and the consequence is illness" (p. 146).

This clipped description conceals rather more than it reveals. As we have seen, the nature of these internalizing processes was hardly arrived at all at once by either Freud or Abraham. As their heir, Klein is, of course, at liberty to take some of their work as read and to start from where they left off. However, there is a suspicion that in her zeal to put forward her own view of the internal world she might be by-passing, reducing, or obfuscating some of the external complexities inherent in object loss, as discussed by her predecessors.

We shall later see that Klein begins her 1940 paper on mourning and manic-depressive states with an exploration of reality testing, suggesting that events in the outside world are important for her perspective, that what happens internally would be contingent upon "the real loss of a real object". However, in the current paper, at least, environmental factors—including the external actualities of loss—do not feature prominently in her account. We must, of course, do Klein the courtesy of reading her on her own terms and accept that where the loss of the loved object is concerned, her focus is primarily on the internal process; the elaborate machinations of her populous internal world can therefore be seen to follow accordingly.

Indeed, for Klein, it is precisely this determination—to stick with what is happening internally and not to be too distracted by external events—that is used to justify the claim that she be regarded as the true daughter and rightful heir of the psychoanalytic approach. Even if one would rather eschew such monarchical metaphors, preferring that our field should have no truck with thrones and accessions (or, indeed, futile rivalries that discussions, controversial or otherwise, seem unable to fully resolve or metabolize), it is surely this internal world focus that has made Klein's contribution to psychoanalysis so unique.

Klein's next question—and how she answers it—is quite instructive in this regard: "Now, why is it that the process of introjection is so specific for melancholia?" The initial answer—prefaced by a statement of belief—has a wrong-footing effect: she believes "that the main difference between incorporation in paranoia and in melancholia is connected with changes in the relation of the subject to the object, though it is also a question of a change in the constitution of the introjecting ego". Apart from my perennial question about the synonymizing interchangeability of incorporation and introjection, it is also not clear to me how this serves as an answer to the question about the specificity of introjection in or for melancholia when it seems that in paranoia, too, some form of introjection (or incorporation) takes place.

Is this nothing more than pedantry on my part, or an unforgiving attitude towards Klein's writing style, which has never been renowned for its elegance or even clarity? Things do become a little clearer when Klein cites Glover's picture of the early ego: it is like a federation or (dis)array of predominantly oral and anal "ego-nuclei". She then uses this description to convey the severe limitations in the ego's capacity to identify with objects: with sadistic oral and anal dynamics in the ascendancy, this fragmentary ego can at best take in only "partial objects" (p.146).

I am prompted here to ask yet another question: what, for Klein, is the difference between introjecting, incorporating, or internalizing an object and *identifying* with it? It seems that, though this may not be the case for other theorists, she sees identification as a secondary event, occurring at a subsequent developmental moment. It is as if there are two stages: one might initially take in an object, but only identify with it later. When Klein comes to discuss the nascent depressive position, she will specify one its central goals as *full* identification with the object, with the implication that this goal is achievable only by a more mature and integrated ego, and with a whole and not just a part-object.

While it is the illness of manic depression—and how it both differs from and is intimately connected with paranoid illness—that is occupying Klein's attention, she is trying, at the same time, to glean or distil out a more general phenomenon, called a "position": that is, something more ubiquitous or pervasive than the malaise providing its name. As was mentioned before, perhaps the most striking and encompassing theme of this paper is how earlier paranoid anxieties persistently and endlessly interfere with later depressive tasks. One implication of this seems to be that even under extreme aggressive/defensive paranoid conditions, a first step in the process of taking in the object can still be accomplished. However, one may then only have it inside oneself in a dismembered or distorted state. There is clearly much work still to be done in the second step—namely, to render the object whole, real, and good—before the ego can identify with it, regard it with compassion and sympathy, and show concern for the suffering inflicted upon it.

Though Klein will only actually name the depressive position later in this paper (and will not name the paranoid-schizoid position for another decade), her ideas about both positions are already unfolding in these opening pages, and she now ventures to describe some crucial differences between them:

> In paranoia the characteristic defences are chiefly aimed at annihilating the "persecutors", while anxiety on the ego's account occupies a prominent place in the picture. As the ego becomes more fully organized, the internalized imagos will approximate more closely to reality and the ego will identify itself more fully with "good" objects. The dread of persecution, which was at first felt on the ego's account, now relates to the good object as well and from now on preservation of the good object is regarded as synonymous with the survival of the ego. [pp. 146–147]

Assessed in the light of what we have explored thus far in the work of Freud, Ferenczi, and Abraham, this now more clearly recognizable Kleinian "position statement" makes interesting reading. While traversing the history of these ideas in the company of their authors, I mostly try to proceed as if, like them, I am not yet privy to later psychoanalytic developments. This allows me to see that the advent of Klein and what she made of the work of her forebears is more remarkable for her departures from than for her allegiance to them.

So, what are these newer features, unique to Klein? In the depressive position—which is itself a brand-new idea, after all—the internal object must become not only more whole, but also more real and more good (so to speak); one might think that there are enough contradictory tensions among these attributes to make the attaining of all three goals together rather difficult. Furthermore, though they might be more achievable when persecutory dynamics relent a little and the ego's personal safety feels less acutely precarious, a new and unexpectedly onerous set of duties seems to accompany the depressive dispensation: it is now the safety of the *object* that takes centre stage. Full identification suggests not only more responsibility for the object's care, but the recognition that the ego's own fate and welfare is now thoroughly contingent upon and tied up with that of the object.

One of the most challenging features for me of Klein's approach to these internal dynamics is their moralizing—or even moralistic—dimension. In earliest infanthood, the ego cannot yet be faulted for "looking after number one" in its defensive struggle to survive its phantasmatic persecutors, via the mechanisms of denial, splitting, and projection. Very soon, however, the onus shifts decisively onto the ego's own ethical responsibilities, not least in relation to the earlier damage inflicted, albeit also in phantasy, on the object during that original flight/fight or paranoid mode of existence.

Despite knowing that no one adheres more keenly than Klein to Freud's claim that our destructive urges—no less than our libidinal inclinations—are bred in the bone, present in us from the start, it is still not easy to understand her rush to heap retroactive responsibility, not to say blame, on this still-inchoate, fledgling ego. Neither Freud nor Abraham by any means ignores morality in their theories—after all, the superego itself will result or emerge from such internal dramas—but it is given far more weight and temporal priority by Klein, especially where the subject's role of perpetrator and/or repairer of damage to the object is concerned. And, as we know, Klein applies these moral or ethical categories of goodness and badness and dates the advent of the superego—or at least an incipient, embryonic version of it—to a much earlier developmental moment than do her predecessors.

Returning to Klein's text, her reasoning becomes perhaps partially clearer when she returns to the issue of loss—our primary topic here, after all. It is when the object becomes less split and thus more integrated that the ego's "ruthlessness"—to intrude, perhaps cheekily, Winnicott's (1958b) term—must be tempered, its claws retracted. For it is now the entire object, not just a piece or part of it, that can be lost; or, as Klein phrases it: "Through this step the ego arrives at a new position, which forms the foundation of the situation called the loss of the loved object. Not until the object is loved *as a whole* can its loss be felt as a whole" (p. 147).

It must be remembered, however, that even if it is love that is now at stake, the need to be better behaved towards the object is still being fuelled by somewhat expedient or narcissistic motives, insofar as the ego or subject is now more aware of how much it depends on the presence of this object and its love. Here we get a dizzying account of the many anxieties that beset an ego at this transitional point in its development, stemming from both paranoid threats *from* the object and depressive dangers *to* the object. The former state or position has by no means surrendered its hold, such that the objects taken in by the ego—in incorporative, cannibalistic, and hence destructive ways—must themselves be suspected as having turned toxic and dangerous within. This can easily lead to an anorexic dynamic, whereby the very act of eating feels like a downright dangerous practice.

If appetite nevertheless increases, by virtue of a fuller and more depressive identification with a good object, a terrible repetitious ambivalence may ensue, whereby the ego vacillates between a greedy—if also loving—wish to have and devour the object and persecutory guilt about the destruction that is perpetrated in the process. For Klein, the only way out of this impasse is onwards and upwards, towards Eros in its more humane, caring, and perhaps sophisticated guise: "In this stage the ego is more than ever driven both by love and by need to introject the object" (p.147).

We begin to understand that for Klein the introjection of the good object is an urgent necessity precisely because bad objects, or bits of objects, are still at large: they have not been—and perhaps can never be—gathered up and rendered completely neutral or harmless, even if they are no longer quite as dangerous as they were when paranoia was at its height. This entails that the capacities and achievements of the depressive position are themselves transient and contingent, and that the primitive predations of the paranoid position—and the defences it summons—are never far off, always threatening to return.

It is for such reasons, as Klein's later paper will attest, that the internal good object is never established once and for all but needs reinstating every time a new loss is incurred. This seems to imply that despite Ferenczi's high hopes for its efficacy, introjection is itself a capacity with significant limitations. Yes, Klein admits, it enables "the phantasy that the loved object may be preserved in safety inside oneself"; and yet, when

> consideration for the object increases, and a better acknowledgement of psychic reality sets in, the anxiety lest the object should be destroyed in the process of introjecting it leads—as Abraham described—to various disturbances of the function of introjection. [pp. 147–148]

Having given Ferenczi's work some attention in chapter three, I cannot help indulging my theoretical fancy for a moment and asking: what if Klein had kept more consciously in mind here not just Abraham, but her earlier analyst, and understood his own definition of the term that he coined a bit more thoroughly?

What, indeed, if Klein had developed—even pioneered—a proper differentiation between incorporation and introjection and utilized it as one of the bases of her distinction between paranoid and depressive functioning? Would this not have given her an effective linguistic or metaphorical tool, enabling her to better describe situations in which the prevalence of paranoid phantasy was playing psychic havoc within the internal world, or causing the internalizing function to miscarry? She might then have been able to portray these paranoid processes as precisely too concrete, literalistic, or incorporative, in contrast with depressive capacities that might enable a more successful, stable, psychically effective, or introjective—and, dare I say, digestive or metabolic—outcome.

But these are precisely not Klein's metaphors or metapsychological perspectives: one is left having to accept that, for her, hard-won depressive scenarios are never fully consolidated as permanent attainments—not even conceptually or in theory. Paranoia is too potent a force and will inevitably be back to challenge even the most well-established depressive internalizations. This is plentifully evident as Klein writes about the various prospects in store for the object that undergoes an internalizing process, beginning with the wishful "phantasy that the loved object may be preserved in safety inside oneself" (p.148).

Unfortunately, what Klein calls "a better acknowledgement of psychic reality" brings with it the realization that one's insides might not, in fact, be a safe place for either the object or the ego, as she outlines in the following paragraph:

> In my experience there is, furthermore, a deep anxiety as to the dangers which await the object inside the ego. It could not be safely maintained there, as the inside is felt to be a dangerous and poisonous place in which the loved object would perish. Here ... the ego becomes fully identified with its good, internalized objects, and at the same time becomes aware of its own incapacity to protect and preserve them against the internalized, persecuting objects and the id. This anxiety is psychologically justified. [p. 148]

One wonders perhaps whether that redundant, possibly defensive, final sentence might be read as subtly betraying Klein's own doubts about what she is saying here. Ostensibly, however, even the subject's own id is regarded as an enemy, and her apprehension about the paranoid position and its primitive power is paramount: she fears its capacity to undermine and overwhelm more salutary, object-protective, depressive inclinations and any possibility that the internal world might become, and remain, a refuge or safe space.

Klein backs up this rather pessimistic conviction by citing Abraham on the prevalence in melancholia of anal-sadistic dynamics, where the urge to expel and destroy the object prevails. Because, for Klein, the dynamics of this psychosexual phase or stage also "initiate the depressive mechanism", this mechanism itself remains vulnerable to destructive, regressive tendencies and predations:

> If this be so, it confirms my notion of the genetic connection between paranoia and melancholia. In my opinion, the paranoiac mechanism of destroying the objects (whether inside the body or in the outside world) by every means by which oral, urethral and anal sadism can command, persists, but in a lesser degree and with a certain modification due to the change in the subject's relation to his objects. [p. 148]

It appears, however, that the threats posed by destructive anal inclinations at this developmental moment can have opposite effects, both filling the ego with dreadful self-doubt and leading to more positive outcomes. Introjection may fail to protect the good object from internal attacks, but perhaps something worse would happen if over-zealous projective action led to this benign object being cast out into the ether, along with its bad counterpart. This anxious concern leads, Klein claims, not only to "greater use of introjection of the *good* object as a mechanism of defence", but also "causes the mechanisms of expulsion and projection to lose value".

Here Klein introduces a crucial defensive weapon in her war against destructiveness and the death drive, namely, "that of making reparation to the object". The ego experiences an impulsion "to make restitution for all the sadistic attacks that it has launched on that object", but, as always, there is a caveat. The ego can be confident neither of the "authenticity" of its own reparative wishes or capacities, nor that the good object is genuinely benign. When Klein enumerates the pitfalls that may lie in wait for this ambivalent, self-suspecting ego's best intentions, her account ascends to a crescendo of aggressive, destructive possibilities:

> Some of its objects—an indefinite number—are persecutors to it, ready to devour and do violence to it. In all sorts of ways they endanger both the ego and the good object. Every injury inflicted in phantasy by the child upon its parents (primarily from hate and secondarily in self-defence), every act of violence committed by one object upon another (in particular the destructive, sadistic coitus of the parents, which the child regards as yet another result of its own sadistic wishes)—all this is played out, both in the outside world and, since the ego is constantly absorbing into itself the whole external world, within the ego as well. [pp. 148–149]

Towards the end of the long final sentence, there does seem to be an allusion to Ferenczi and his idea that the ego is always trying to take the outside world into itself. This, we might remember, is Ferenczi's very definition of introjection; for him it is a modus vivendi, not merely a defensive manoeuvre.

The way that Klein takes these matters up, however, with her relentless focus on attack and defence, creates a rather different atmosphere. Reading such passages makes one think that if the Oedipus story—of heinous original acts committed unwittingly and discovered belatedly—is the guiding spirit of Freud's opus, then for Klein it is Hamlet's more knowing version of the tale, replete with agonizing self-doubt, prolonged paralysis, and a lurking explosion of pent-up, vengeful violence. She goes on to describe not an integration of good and bad objects, but a confusion between them: both may be "menaced by the id" (which, in Klein's hands, appears so suffused with and compromised by aggression and violence that it has lost all connection with pleasure and appetite). Therefore, because of oral sadism, "it is not only the vehemence of the subject's uncontrollable hatred but that of his love too which imperils the object" (p. 149).

Perhaps it is precisely because introjection is seen only, or primarily, as a defence that there can be neither a lasting, reliable feeling of safety nor anywhere to hide from these myriad anxieties, for both the internal object and the ego. Klein gives no balancing account here of how ordinary development might occur at the metapsychological level. As powerful as they are, her tales of the plight of the embattled ego are "heads I win, tails you lose" scenarios. Though Klein is talking about a quite particular and precarious developmental moment for the ego, in which a vital crossing is being negotiated, its agonies still seem quite hard to imagine or bear, nor do they seem redeemable:

> It now becomes plain why, at this phase of development, the ego feels itself constantly menaced in its possession of internalized good objects. It is full of anxiety lest such objects should die. Both in children and adults suffering from depression, I have discovered the dread of harbouring dying or dead objects (especially the parents) inside one and an identification of the ego with the objects in this condition. [pp. 149–150]

It seems incongruous to hear Klein talking about the "anxiety *lest* such objects should die", because by now we have become familiar with the idea that death—or loss or separation—is a precondition for acquiring a compensating inner object in the first place.

However, at least in this paper, Klein is mainly describing depressed patients and is not (yet) interested in mourning as such or any possible differentiation of it from melancholia. Is this the reason why no sense of an internal working-through or breaking-down—nothing resembling a digestive or metabolic process—is mooted in her language? At this stage, she might argue, the depressive concern is for the plight and preservation of the internal object. The task is to keep it alive at any cost, and therefore it should precisely *not* be subjected to such processes.

One gets the sense from Klein's writing that objects are not internalized only, or even primarily, because they have been externally lost; it would appear that, prior to any loss, we always already carry an internal version inside us of any external object. As she says, "From the very beginning of psychic development there is a constant correlation of real objects with those installed within the ego" (p. 150). Again, she appears to be drawing on Ferenczi's notion that introjection is a primary mental operating system, the only way for an ego to connect with the external world, and must not be thought of—at least not in the first instance—as the product of loss or as a defence.

The irony or paradox here is that insofar as Klein's internal objects inhabit their own psychic realm, they do not have to be *rendered* real because, in at least in one sense, they simply *are* real, no less so than their external equivalents. They are, that is, quasi-independent ontological part-entities or -selves, each with its own experiences, desires, agendas, and defences—homunculi, in a word. For Klein, they do not appear to be symbolic or even metaphorical phenomena as such; though they may reside in a different psychic dimension, these internal inhabitants seem to "exist", are alive (if imperilled), and capable of being no less dangerous and predatory, or vulnerable and susceptible, than their outer versions or their host, the ego.

Here, perhaps, is another reason why, for Klein, any idea of a permanently—or perhaps even temporarily—safe and secure internal haven is an illusion. This may also account for why John Steiner (1993), one of her ardent followers, will later describe psychic retreats as wholly defensive phenomena, avoidant hiding or squatting places with little or no habitational legitimacy, thus very *un*like Winnicott's (1951) transitional spaces, which Steiner erroneously attempts to reframe in terms of such retreats.

Klein continues to present the tricky double-bind-like anxieties that the ego faces at this juncture in its development. What she calls "a child's exaggerated fixation to its mother" is not only due to ordinary dependence on her, but to all manner of anxious and guilty feelings about the state that she may be in as a result of his murderous phantasies. These are compounded by further anxieties about the vengeful retaliations that he feels she might perpetrate against him, "either because of her *death* or because of her return in the form of a *'bad'* mother". To make things worse, dreading the loss of the internal good-object mother stimulates concerns that the real, external mother might die—and, of course, vice versa. Attempting to be more precise about these psychodynamic situations, Klein says:

> The processes which subsequently become defined as the "loss of the loved object" are determined by the subject's sense of failure (during weaning and in the periods which precede and follow it) to secure his *good, internalized* object, i.e. to possess himself of it. One reason for his failure is that he has been unable to overcome his paranoid dread of internalized persecutors. [p. 150]

Claiming support from some of her contemporary English colleagues, Klein advances with more clarity to her theoretical conviction that "the influence of the early processes of introjection upon both normal and pathological development" is "very much more momentous" than, and different from, what her psychoanalytic antecedents had thought.

But why and whence, then, so much fear and dread? Why is early life, for Klein, so fraught with terror and trauma? It is here that she reintroduces and explains her radical notion that the superego is formed much earlier than Freud and others supposed. Though, as we saw in *The Ego and the Id*, Freud would have wholly agreed that "even the earliest incorporated objects *form the basis* of the superego and enter into its structure" (my emphasis), for him these objects only come to play *that* role at a later moment, after the Oedipus complex has been worked through, and, indeed, after already having contributed to the formation of the ego itself.

For Klein, however, the question of how the ego comes into being and develops—the metapsychological process via which this occurs—seems of little interest as a theoretical matter. Given all the other uncertainties of her internal world, she nevertheless seems confident of the ego's ubiquitous "there-ness": it is one of the few constants in the shifting sands of her psychic landscapes. However, by positing an early and menacing superego, Klein's account puts the ever-present but initially inchoate and vulnerable ego under enormous, anxious pressure from virtually the start of life. Her clinical experience helped her, she claims, to "arrive at a more complete understanding of the earliest phases of psychic development, of the structure of the super-ego and of the genesis of psychotic diseases" (pp. 150–151).

If we accept this early advent of the superego, says Klein, "its relentless severity in the case of melancholia becomes more intelligible". The moralistic persecution that characterizes this illness leaves the ego "prey to contradictory and impossible claims from within". She usefully refers, in oral-alimentary terms, to the "gnawing of conscience", parsing this as the vicious, predatory, primitive superego "devouring of its victim", the ego, just as Freud had described it in "Mourning and Melancholia" and *The Ego and the Id*.

However, Klein thinks she has taken things even further here:

> It is this part of the picture only—namely, the cruelty of the "good", i.e. loved, objects within—which has been recognized by general analytic opinion, namely, in the relentless severity of the super-ego in the melancholic. But in my view it is only by looking at the whole relation of the ego to its phantastically bad objects as well as to its good objects, only by looking at the whole picture of the internal situation

> which I have tried to outline in this paper, that we can understand the slavery to which the ego submits when complying with the extremely cruel demands and admonitions of its loved object which has become installed within the ego. [pp. 151–152]

Klein's urgent, insistent tones can sometimes sound convincing without necessarily persuading through cogent argumentation. There is certainly some obscurity and potential contradiction here. Is the "loved object which has been installed within" a good object, or is it precisely a combined, ambiguously good-and-bad object that would better explain the difficulty and complexity of "the whole picture" that she sees herself as portraying here for the first time? Moreover, it is certainly not clear that Freud or "general analytic opinion" would have regarded the internalized object in melancholia as an entirely "good" one in the first place: indeed, it must have been at least somewhat "bad" for the ambivalence typical of the condition to pertain.

In Klein's version, the early need to separate goodness and badness through splitting increases the intensity of both, resulting in "a conception of extremely bad and *extremely perfect* objects" (p. 152). The latter, under the guise of what Freud had previously termed the ideal ego, can become moralistically excessive and exacting, making impossible demands on the embattled ego. Klein seems to have worked back around again to the ways in which paranoid (and schizoid) anxieties continue to bleed into the difficult-enough anxieties of the depressive position.

However, she does also want to be conceptually clear, and thus rather insistently outlines the differences between these positions:

> But they can be distinguished one from the other if, as a criterion of differentiation, one considers whether the persecution-anxiety is mainly related to the preservation of the ego—in which case it is paranoiac—or to the preservation of the good internalized objects with whom the ego is identified as a whole. In the latter case—which is the case of the depressive—the anxiety and feelings of suffering are of a much more complex nature. [pp. 152–153]

Klein seems occasionally to resort in this fashion to relatively simpler, more polarized accounts of these complicated dynamics, producing passages where there is sudden clarity, and this is often what the many purveyors of reductive summaries of Klein's complex and at times confusing ideas tend to offer. Here she tells us again that, when paranoid anxieties and functioning prevail, the ego experiences itself, passively and unambiguously, as the one in the dyad being devoured or endangered by the object; once a more depressive dispensation has developed, it is the ego recognizing its own active destructiveness and endeavouring to counter and make up for such urges and acts.

Klein reiterates her central ideas several times in the course of the paper, and one discerns a cyclical pattern whereby a conceptually unambiguous picture is succeeded by a murkier one, which ensures that the complexity and confusion that can prevail at the divide between the paranoid and depressive positions is not forgotten. This is exemplified when she lists some of the many anxieties that the depressive ego—in the wake of having identified more fully with a fragmented and abject object—may experience in relation to its own "crimes" and the enormity of the reparative tasks:

> how to put the bits together in the right way and at the right time; how to pick out the good bits and do away with the bad ones; how to bring the object to life when it has been put together; and there is the anxiety of being interfered with in this task by bad objects and by one's own hatred, etc. [p. 153]

Evidently, what interferes with the essentially depressive duties that Klein is specifying are fears and worries that are both paranoid and depressive in nature.

Returning to the theme of not just the good but the perfect object, Klein now writes astutely about how reparation and restoration—depressive position tasks *par excellence*—are compromised by the over-ambitious need to return a once-perfect mother to her pure, beautiful, unblemished state. The idea, in other words, that one has not only ravaged and ruined such a being but is now powerless to make up fully for her destruction, is a fateful one. Any attempts by the object to atone, pay one's debts, and do better "are coupled with despair, since the ego doubts its capacity to achieve this restoration", and this will affect, in turn, "all sublimations and the whole of ego-development".

The demands of proper depressive love are great indeed: "the ego comes to a realization of its love for a good object, a whole object and in addition a real object, together with an overwhelming feeling of guilt towards it." By identifying fully with such an object, one takes on regret and remorse for what one has already done to it, as well as all manner of anxieties about any menace to its future preservation or safety, not least from the dastardly designs of one's own id; finally, one experiences sadness about the anticipated loss of this object which, all the ego's efforts notwithstanding, it cannot preserve alive forever.

For Klein, moreover, the id's intentions are utterly untrustworthy: there is high anxiety about the danger of the ego "being carried away by the id and so destroying the loved object". Providing a rare mention in this paper of the emotions of mourning, she says that this is precisely what promotes "the sorrow, feelings of guilt and despair that underlie grief" (pp. 153–154). One registers, with some surprise, the implication that for Klein it is more important for the ego to reconcile or make good its connections with the internal object than with its own id!

This represents a significant and striking departure from Freud, who was never as "down on" the id as Klein appears to be. We get a glimpse here into just how different—and differently constituted—Klein's internal universe is from that of Freud. Or, to put it in other words, when the internal landscape is occupied not only by an id, an ego, and a superego, but must also make room for myriad internal versions of external objects, it is no wonder that all parties might struggle to get along in this crowded space.

Klein spends the next page or two reiterating and explaining once again how depressive injunctions, fuelled by love, are made so much more difficult by incursions of hatred and self-doubt. She further details the effect of paranoid mistrust and instability on the ego's depressive efforts to achieve a modicum of equilibrium and to get on with its expiatory endeavours in relation to the object. Klein stipulates diagnostically that once the ego has reached the depressive position, "the liability to depression is always there", but, because the ego can also easily slide back into the paranoid position, "we frequently meet depression along with severe paranoia" (p. 155). We are again made aware that psychopathology—actual illness of one kind or another—is never far from Klein's thoughts, even when she is apparently outlining psychic situations that are part and parcel of the normal mind.

Having satisfied herself that she has covered the differences between paranoid and depressive ways of relating to the loved object, Klein now looks at this divide in terms of attitudes toward food, as an ostensibly separate topic. Viewed in the light of this book's concerns, what she says is both instructive and contentious:

> The anxiety of absorbing dangerous substances destructive to one's inside will thus be paranoiac, while the anxiety of destroying the external good objects by biting or chewing, or of endangering the internal good object by introducing bad substances from outside into it, will be depressive. Again, the anxiety of leading an external good object into danger within oneself by incorporating it is a depressive one. On the other hand, in cases with strong paranoiac features I have met phantasies of luring an external object into one's inside, which was regarded as a cave full of dangerous monsters, etc. Here we see the paranoiac

reasons for an intensification of the introjection-mechanism, while the depressive employs this mechanism so characteristically, as we know, for the purpose of incorporating a *good* object. [p. 156]

The taking in of edible "substances"—that is, food—quickly becomes about the fate of the internal object. This is, of course, precisely Klein's point: her immediate concern is with the phantasmatic idea of what is happening in the object-relational mind of the eater or consumer.

To that extent, one might say, there is no such thing as an ordinary meal: one way or another, there is always already an object for the subject to be anxious about. Either the object is endangered in the process of its internalization by the violent actions of eating, or the already internalized object is affected by the ingestion of other noxious substances—and the outcome then turns on the subtle difference between deliberately "luring" or inadvertently "leading" the object to its fate. And, in that final sentence, there is again the sense that incorporation and introjection are at best confused or may even have had their meanings reversed.

Naturally, these ideas are of significant oral-alimentary interest, but Klein's treatment of these matters seems to bifurcate and lie either side of my own. Either the phantasies she reflects on are all-too-concrete, the dangers all-too-literal, the anxieties all-too-real—hardly figurative or metaphorical at all—or they sound too imaginary and unreal, beggaring the belief of the reader who is left wondering about their status in any mind, however disturbed or unconscious. Unlike my assumption that the work of internal processing (particularly of loss) can and should be something like digestion, with the accompanying distinction between more and less successful versions of it, Klein's view seems to be that these processes are vexed and problematic *per se*, fraught from the start and forever, for everyone.

Via the introduction of hypochondriacal symptoms and their different meanings in paranoid versus depressive circumstances, Klein brings us the benefit of her clinical acumen by discussing, at some length, a patient who presented with powerful, greed-induced phantasies about tapeworms and cancer devouring him from within, as well as other psychosomatic alimentary symptoms. Both in this case and in clinical material introduced later in the paper, she traces a trajectory leading from paranoid to depressive anxieties and imaginings: these individuals gradually work towards the discovery of compassion and concern for the objects that had taken up residence inside them.

At one point, Klein says of the former patient, "that at about ten years of age he had definitely felt that he had a little man inside his stomach who controlled him and gave him orders, which he, the patient, had to execute, although they were always perverse and wrong" (p. 157). Though this is, of course, the very concrete phantasy of a child, and one who would later become a disturbed adult, one cannot help thinking that Klein's own ideas about internal objects are quite well represented by it. These often give the impression of being rather established, immovable, indissoluble "homuncular" entities, not subject to change, except insofar as the ego's attitude changes, from fear *of* them, to fear *for* them.

It is always a relief to come across the clinical sections in Klein's papers; with their strong focus on the transference, they serve not only to exemplify her at times excessive-sounding ideas but to render them much more believable. In this instance, they embolden her to describe in more detail depressive states and their intertwined relations with the paranoid ones from which they derive. There is also an explanation, in a footnote, of her overall preference for the term "position", rather than "phase" or "state": her term has the merit of indicating the possibility of a rapid switch or "change-over" from one set of characteristic features to another (p. 159).

Klein now provides a definitive statement of the composition of this novel conception that she is hereby introducing to the psychoanalytic community:

> In my view, wherever a state of depression exists, be it in the normal, the neurotic, in manic-depressives or in mixed cases, there is always in it this specific grouping of anxieties, distressed feelings and different varieties of these defences, which I have here described and called the depressive position. [p. 160]

This heralds Klein's brief foray into arguably the most important clinical consideration when it comes to depressed patients: namely, their potential suicidality. Mentioning Abraham and Glover (and she might well have included Freud here), Klein grants the received view that suicide is an act "directed against the introjected object". However, she puts forward a more complex perspective, claiming, paradoxically, that the suicidal ego "also always aims at saving its loved objects, internal or external" (p. 160).

Effectively, this can only work under the conditions of a split, whereby good internal objects and the part of the ego identified with them might protect themselves by attempting to be rid of the part that is identified with bad internal objects and the hateful id. In other situations, suicidal urges can have an outward-directed purpose: the subject wants to liberate the objects in "good" external reality from his "bad", burdensome presence, and "we perceive in such a step his reaction to his own sadistic attacks on his mother's body, which is . . . the first representative of the outside world" (pp. 160–161). As we have seen so often in this paper, what distinguishes Klein from her psychoanalytic colleagues is that this depressive emphasis is far less on the ego's victimhood or what it has suffered than on what it has meted out or perpetrated.

After much anticipation, we finally arrive at what Klein has to say about the condition of mania. She begins with a glance at what Freud had said: that while "mania has for its basis the same contents as melancholia", it is also a way of escaping the latter. Klein immediately adds that mania's "way of escape"—or "refuge"—is not only from the trials of melancholia or depression, but also from the tribulations of paranoia. The ego is trapped by a complex situation consisting of both "torturing and perilous dependence on its loved objects", on one hand, and "dread of bad objects and of the id", on the other.

Wishing desperately to evade all these binding ties, the ego will resort to a variety of "mutually incompatible" measures. Klein then specifies that mania is essentially characterized by the *"sense of omnipotence"* and "based on the mechanism of *denial*" (p. 161). In relation to the latter, she again both cites and takes issue with the views of a psychoanalytic colleague—this time Helene Deutsch, who regards denial as linked with castration and thus as a feature of the phallic phase—and traces its defensive origins to the very earliest internal persecutory anxieties, reiterating that if psychic reality can be denied, then so can many another thing in the external world.

Perhaps another aside is in order here. One realizes, with some surprise, that there are times when Klein seems to write as if psychic reality might almost precede, or exist independently of, its external equivalent. This prompts fundamental metapsychological questions about how this psychic reality—that which denial denies, so to say—comes about in the first place if it is not already the result of the frustrations or impingements imposed by the actual environment. Is it the product, as seemed implicit earlier, of a capacity for a kind of primary Ferenczian introjection? Or are we meant to accept that an internal psychic reality is with us in some innate way, from the beginning?

There is also the related question of how, in the apparent absence of any theory of the ego's origins, Klein can account coherently for the process whereby the ego matures or is progressively strengthened over time. We might need to recognize—and content ourselves with the fact—that Klein has little interest in what she might regard as speculative, unobservable metaphysical theories about how these entities originate. If adumbrating her clinically derived perspective requires that she make some basic assumptions or take certain psychological situations as given, then a pre-existing ego with in-built psychic interiority perhaps fits the bill.

Returning to Klein's view of mania, we find her trying to account for the futility of manic overactivity—perhaps like that of an engine revving noisily in neutral—by referring to the invidious, ambivalent bind that the ego faces in such situations. As she tells us, it is "unwilling and unable to renounce its good internal objects and yet endeavours to escape from the perils of dependence on them". This can only be turned into some sort of "compromise" if the ego is temporarily capable of "*denying the importance of its good objects and also of the dangers with which it is menaced from its bad objects and the id*". It can then use its hyperactive mode, "to *master and control* all its objects". Of course, these capacities of the manic ego are based wholly on phantasy and depend on what Klein calls "*the utilization of the sense of omnipotence*" (p. 161).

Referring to it in terms of a "manic defence" (she will later also speak of a manic position), Klein goes on to characterize this state of mind by listing its boasts in one of her long, packed paragraphs. Under the sway of mania, the ego can deny the fear of the parental objects, make unrealistic reparation to them, prevent them from causing internal harm to itself or to other objects, and stop them from either copulating dangerously or dying within. In the meantime, however, while these internal objects are being controlled and manipulated in omnipotent phantasy, "the existence of this internal world is being depreciated and denied". Klein also briefly compares obsessional neurosis and mania, declaring the latter's controlling methods the more violent—but also the more magically reversible—of the two: "That is to say, the objects were killed but, since the subject was omnipotent, he supposed he could immediately call them to life again." One of Klein's patients "spoke of this process as 'keeping them in suspended animation'" (p. 162).

Klein associates the killing of the object with the paranoid position and the reviving of it with the depressive position. Recalling Freud's description of the ravenous hunger and feasting of manic patients (we also remember Abraham's phrase, "gobbling mania"), Klein understands the voracious attitude—both literal and figurative—displayed in mania partly in terms of the desperate attempt to maintain a depressive capacity for the introjection of good experiences and objects. Thus, there is a denial that such wholesale introjection can lead to bad, dangerous consequences, too—as if in mania, the ego tries to persuade itself that the id's urges are not so destructive after all and that the good objects are in no real danger.

While some of Klein's ideas about the internal world, as we shall see, resonate with those of Nicolas Abraham and Maria Torok, the inflection given to them here is quite different. In Klein's version, there is the implication that when the ego's all-controlling manic phantasies are ascendant, it can be utterly cavalier with objects in the internal world, manipulating and toying with them, doing what it pleases with them. For Abraham and Torok, the object is also "in suspended animation", but for them this is an encrypted state, whereby the object lodges or sticks in the ego's craw: to that extent the ego is less controlling than controlled, a situation apparently more melancholic than it is manic. In my parlance, the object is felt to be indigestible, and therefore the most likely manic solution to such a problem would come in the form of an evacuative up-chuck.

Interestingly, despite her later gravitation towards and emphasis on projective and expulsive mechanisms (discussed at the end of this chapter), Klein's view of mania is not wholly, or even primarily, focused on this or any other way of getting rid of the object. What she would have us see is that there are plenty of cruel and torturous things that can be done—with a kind of insouciant impunity—by the manic ego to the internal object, of which simply casting it out or throwing it away is by no means the only one.

As we have seen, Klein sets great store by the mechanism of manic denial, without which this kind of impunity—in an ego usually so prone to being hounded by its precocious superego—would be impossible and unthinkable. Citing Freud, she now explains—in oral-alimentary terms—how mania amounts to a kind of psychopathic merger of the ego with the ego-ideal:

> The ego incorporates the object in a cannibalistic way (the "feast" as Freud calls it in his account of mania) but denies that it feels any concern for it. "Surely," argues the ego, "it is not a matter of such great importance if this particular object is destroyed. There are so many others to be incorporated." This *disparagement of the object's importance and the contempt for it* is, I think, a specific characteristic of mania and enables the ego to effect that partial detachment which we observe side by side with its hunger for objects. [p. 163]

Here is the evidence of how well Klein understands mania: she really gets inside and elucidates the ego's manic triumph over the object, here referred to as the "disparagement" of and "contempt" for it. Under these manic conditions, it would seem, her usual emphasis on the dangers of introjection to both ego and objects can be suspended.

Interestingly, Klein can even speak quite positively of manic "detachment" as "an advance, a fortifying of the ego in relation to its objects", compromised as this may be by some of the more primitive methods that it employs. Though her discussions of internalization are themselves at times frustratingly un-nuanced, Klein's account of mania is nevertheless useful and congruent with ideas about depression and digestion. In the quotation above, it is effectively the contempt towards the object's nutritional value that the manic subject is expressing when Klein has it say, in effect, that there are many fish in the sea.

This resonates with the attendant notion explored in the previous chapter, that under certain psychic conditions, objects may be taken in, but they pass through the system completely unmetabolized and without affecting it in any way. That is, if it is only some form of incorporation (and not introjection, in Ferenczi's sense) that is manifesting itself in mania, then its cannibalism and gobbling greed need not entail any internal processing at all; however much this may be at the expense of the object, the manic ego can thus claim to remain unaffected, neither fed and enriched nor starved and damaged.

Klein now promises to "make a few suggestions about the part which paranoid, depressive, and manic positions play in normal development" but wants first to exemplify—by way of two of patient C's rather mad-sounding dreams—her ideas about what she terms "the psychotic positions" (p. 163). (This sudden proliferation of "positions" will not, of course, stand the test of time: Klein will eventually settle on just two of them.) What follows is the clinical centrepiece of the paper, five dense pages of sustained detailed analysis, reminiscent of how Freud would inundate the manifest content of dreams with his interpretations, proliferating latent meanings in his zeal to reveal their overdetermined dynamics.

As always in Klein's clinical accounts, the writing rises to the occasion and the ideas are rendered far more compelling than they would have been without clinical corroboration. There is, however, something quite overwhelming—not to say manic—about this performance, which seems again to exemplify and emphasize just how difficult it is to "graduate" to depressive functioning from more primitive and paranoid beginnings.

The first dream features the patient trying to manage his aged, bedbound parents on a train journey. He urinates into an elaborate receptacle as they watch, concerned that the sight of his large penis will humiliate his father. There are associations to bowls, gas-mantles, and hence to flames, burning, and poisoning. In the second dream, his mother is frying a live creature in a pan and seems oblivious or indifferent to her cruelty; he associates to various methods of torture—especially by burning—and to the phantasy that, as his analyst lights her cigarettes, matchheads are flying dangerously towards him on the couch. I will not attempt to list Klein's interpretations, but they describe a plethora of hellish, primarily paranoid-schizoid wishes and phantasies, followed by trepidatious depressive concerns about the damage these have wrought and the patient's desperate attempts to undo and repair it.

The harbouring of objects that are both actively harmful and dead or dying is again powerfully exemplified, and a dreadful, convoluted double-bind is outlined as follows:

> At any time the parents may have dangerous intercourse, burn and eat each other and, since his ego has become the place where all these danger-situations are acted out, destroy him as well. Thus he has at the same time to bear great anxiety both for them and for himself. He is full of sorrow about the impending death of the internalized parents, but at the same time he dare not bring them back to full life . . . since intercourse would be implied in their coming fully to life, and this would then result in their death and his. [pp. 167–168]

A little further on, Klein consigns to a footnote a relevant comment that would be more than worthy of inclusion in the body of the paper. She says that "the paranoiac conception of a dead object within is one of a secret and uncanny persecutor", which can resurface guilefully precisely because it is not quite dead: it vengefully awaits its chance to get its own back "because the subject tried to do away with him by killing him (the concept of a dangerous ghost)" (p. 168). As we have already seen in this book—and it will be discussed again emphatically in the following chapter on Hans Loewald (chapter five)—ghosts, zombies, and other forms of the living dead are familiar guests of the troubled internal world.

In a paragraph summarizing what she had hoped to show in these dream-led clinical passages, Klein again highlights the very earliest uses of internalization and how they inevitably predispose the ego to reality-distorting psychotic and paranoid difficulties. The object relations of this early period are necessarily precarious, unstable, and war-like; attacks and counterattacks predominate, accompanied by "sorrow and distress about the impending death of the incorporated objects" as well as terrible "hypochondriacal anxieties" about the state of the ego itself.

The intention to make reparation does, of course, resurface but even this can be problematic if it takes the form of "an attempt to master in an omnipotent manic way the unbearable sufferings within which are imposed on the ego". It is only in the final sentence of the paragraph that Klein strikes a slightly more hopeful note: "We also see how the masterful and sadistic control of the internalized parents becomes modified as the tendencies to restoration increase" (p. 169).

After her resonant and harrowing clinical example and some of the psychotic disturbances that Klein has just described, normal development feels like something of an afterthought. Given what appears to be her rather pessimistic perspective on all these dynamics, perhaps it is not so surprising that she devotes only limited space and scope to discussing how the so-called normal child works through them, saying that she will confine herself to just "a few remarks of a general nature" (p. 170).

Klein first recaps some of the discoveries made in her original work with often quite disturbed children: she outlines the split, divided, part-object world of the paranoid-schizoid infant in the first months of life, before proceeding to the coming together that will herald the subsequent depressive moment. She also speaks, virtually for the first time in the paper, of how an actual mother in the external world might mitigate the worst excesses of paranoid anxiety for her baby.

Klein is known for ignoring or downplaying these external-world actualities, preferring to concentrate on the presumed phantasmatic dynamics in the infant's mind. Even while acknowledging here that the child's early life-experiences with mother are important, she claims unapologetically that "only since we know more about the nature and contents of its early anxieties, and the continuous interplay between its actual experiences and its phantasy life, can we fully understand *why* the external factor is so important". For Klein, as she spells out, a more reliable relation to objects can begin to happen only once the early divisions between what is real and imagined, good and bad, increasingly "intermingle and colour each other". Only then can this newly named depressive position arise and ensue, "when the child comes to know its mother as a whole person and becomes identified with her as a whole, real and loved person" (pp. 170–171).

Klein certainly needs no convincing that loss is at the heart of the matter. Indeed, it is Klein who has taught us most about the ordinary but formative losses and frustrations that we all experience as infants when mother and her breast keep coming and going, time after time. As she says, "this loss reaches its climax at weaning". But she explicitly disagrees with the views of Rado, and implicitly with Freud, about the onset of guilt in the still suckling infant. Where Rado emphasizes the safety and comfort of the early fusion of the baby with its mother, Klein seems to assume that a degree of separation already exists, along with some inchoate capacity to perceive difference.

She effectively says that—stemming from its early introjections—the infant at the breast is already beset by persecutory anxieties and the conflict between love and hate. These resemble and prefigure, albeit more mildly, the states of a disturbed adult melancholic patient (and, of course, a paranoid one). She confidently insists that "these sufferings, conflicts, and feelings of remorse and guilt, resulting from the relation of the ego to its internalized object, are already active in the baby" (p. 172).

Klein's language now conveys the rather uncomfortable sense that—regardless of whether there is necessarily any external good object on which to base this—the onus in fact falls primarily on the child to accomplish the following task:

> If the infant at this period of life fails to establish its loved object within—if the introjection of the "good" object miscarries—then the situation of the "loss of the loved object" arises already in the same sense that it is found in the adult melancholic. [p. 172]

Success or failure in this regard might, she suggests, have a significant determining effect on later mental health. There is, of course, constant interference from paranoid and manic inclinations, and the task can sometimes feel insurmountable.

Though Klein again mentions the possibility that a "happy relationship to its real mother" might enable the child "to overcome the depressive position" (p. 172), it is not at all clear what such an overcoming might look like. At times it seems as if Klein can say little more about how psychic transitions and achievements—and the overcoming of paranoid anxiety, sadism, and ambivalence—become possible, other than via the sheer accumulation of multiple, repetitive, trial-and-error attempts to achieve wholeness, goodness, and reality where the object is concerned. This is precisely where a digestive component might have enhanced Klein's conception of the depressive position: it would have provided an account with more focus on just how the infant avails itself of a loving breast, not only by taking in this good object, but also owning and utilizing it via a properly metabolic psychic process. To my mind, this feels sorely and conspicuously absent from Klein's account.

Her paper is fast approaching its conclusion, and there is a sense that Klein must now reiterate certain milestones that she sees as crucial to the ego's future capacities to thrive—or even just survive. The moment at which the introjecting of whole (as opposed to part-) objects becomes possible constitutes "a crossroads from which the ways determining the whole mental make-up radiate in different directions". In the next paragraph she says that "failure to maintain the identification with both internalized and real loved objects may result in psychotic disorders, such as depressive states, mania, or paranoia" (p. 173).

One wonders: Does she see all such states as psychotic? Or is it that Klein is only interested in the hard end of these conditions, where they do verge on the psychotic? She also takes the opportunity to cite her daughter

Melitta Schmideberg's (1930) work on the ego's defensive tendency to take flight to the good object, a habit that carries the dangers of either "slavish dependence" on external objects or psychotic over-valuation of internal incarnations of such objects.

As I come to the end of what is a rather long close reading of the paper, other realizations and questions abound. Klein not only makes no attempt to distinguish here between mourning and melancholia (or between introjection and incorporation), but she does not even seem to differentiate clearly between object love (or libidinal cathexis) and identification. Is this because, as Freud says, they are indistinguishable at the beginning of life, and Klein's own focus is so clearly on these earliest dynamics?

Perhaps what is more to the point is that, given her suspicions of the id, Klein has moved so much further away from sex and sexuality than we saw Freud to be doing as his career progressed. Might she prefer to think of the positive dimension of human relations more in terms of our need and capacity for sympathetic identification with one another than as the manifestation of what we want, wish, or desire from each other?

Either way—and however she might define such achievements—Klein does attempt, at this late juncture, to speak to the "normal development of the child and its capacity for love". For this to be achieved and ensured, not only must the "central" or "nodal" depressive position be reached, but, as she states several times, it can and should itself be overcome or worked through. However, we are left with little clarity, still struggling to envisage what this overcoming of the depressive position might mean or look like.

Even in the final sentence of her paper, however, Klein is still introducing nuances in her thought: she repeats that so much depends on "the modification undergone by the earliest mechanisms (which remain at work in the normal also) in accordance with the changes in the ego's relations to objects" but adds that success in these endeavours might also require judicious use of or "successful interplay between the depressive, the manic and obsessional positions and mechanisms" (pp. 173–174). This suggestive idea leaves the reader mildly puzzled and wanting further explication. Perhaps we can only wait and see whether clarifications are to be had from the equally important paper, on similar topics, that Klein would write just half a decade later.

"Mourning and Its Relation to Manic-Depressive States" (1940)

With "mourning" featuring as the first word in its title, Klein seems intent on tackling this topic, perhaps by way of making up for its virtual absence from her earlier paper. Freud's "Mourning and Melancholia" is, moreover, referenced from the very beginning and is never far from Klein's thoughts throughout—not least, perhaps, because it is her aim to challenge some of its ideas and establish her own more confidently and forcefully. One is struck right away by the specificity of Klein's angle of approach to Freud's text: given her preoccupation in the previous paper with the relations between internal and external objects, she seems interested mainly in the way he grapples with "the testing of reality" (1940, p. 125) in mourning and cites, in her own opening paragraph, three separate passages where this is his topic.

We recall that Freud does indeed struggle to understand why the mourner must work so long and hard to acknowledge fully that an object in the real world has been lost. Klein, it would appear, thinks she can provide an answer to this puzzle and offers these two sentences introducing her own approach:

> In my view there is a close connection between the testing of reality in normal mourning and early processes of the mind. My contention is that the child goes through states of mind comparable to the mourning of the adult, or rather, that this early mourning is revived whenever grief is experienced in later life. [p. 126]

It is particularly the last clause of the quotation that reads like something new. Klein seems to say that subsequent occasions for mourning have the retroactive effect of triggering primary, original experiences of loss, and she will both repeat and develop this idea extensively.

However, she first spends some time re-introducing the central idea of her earlier paper, namely, "the conception of the *infantile depressive position*". She tells us that whereas the 1935 paper had tried to connect this position to "manic-depressive states" (the phrase shared by the two titles), she now intends to complete the triangle by bringing in the relations of each to so-called "normal mourning". She immediately insists, however, that the baby's earliest experiences of loss, "just before, during and after weaning", are not to be considered normal but as akin to psychopathological states. After all, she had named this not the mourning but the depressive position, referring to it as "a melancholia in *statu nascendi*".

Klein, it seems, wants to persuade us that early life, suffused as it is with inevitable frustrations and separations, is not only pathological but tragic; it is a predicament, moreover, that it would not be too fanciful to compare with paradise lost and original sin:

> The object which is being mourned is the mother's breast and all that the milk and the breast have come to stand for in the infant's mind:

namely, love, goodness and security. All these are felt by the baby to be lost, and lost as a result of his own uncontrollable greedy and destructive phantasies and impulses against the mother's breasts. [p. 126]

We might wish to recall what Freud makes of the baby's experience at the breast in *Three Essays on the Theory of Sexuality* (1905d, pp. 181–182)—how much it differs from and contrasts with Klein's conception here. His emphasis is on that scene as the epitome of fullness and fulfilment, the blissful precursor of all our future moments of sexual pleasure and consummation.

Insofar as Klein's focus is positive at all, it is already quite different from Freud's by being fixed firmly on "love, goodness and security", values perhaps less firmly associated with the libido and more tilted toward self-preservation. More significantly, however, Klein's emphasis is primarily negative: on how quickly we contrive to lose what we have had through an inability to curb our voracious, aggressive urges. For her, therefore, these early experiences seem to author all future encounters with sorrow and regret and are the heralds of absence, emptiness, and lack. This is something that Lacan appreciated about Klein's approach, much as he also was scornful of her aversion to and fear of desire itself.

More difficulties follow apace, according to Klein, in the form of her early version of the Oedipus situation; no matter how vague and incipient their external existence for the infant, third-party objects—father and siblings—are already subject to murderously competitive feelings. The attendant aggression against these rivals gives rise to "feelings of guilt and loss", as well as "sorrow and concern about the feared loss of the 'good' objects". Along with all this emotional turmoil in relation to external objects, says Klein,

> go those processes of internalization on which I have laid so much stress in my work. The baby, having incorporated his parents, feels them to be live people inside his body in the concrete way in which deep unconscious phantasies are experienced—they are, in his mind, "internal" or "inner" objects, as I have termed them. [p. 127]

This internal world is created and constructed out of the child's actual real-world encounters, but it is also distorted, "altered by his own phantasies and impulses". In a brief, hopeful statement, Klein adds that if the external world is populated by "people predominantly at peace with each other and with the ego, inner harmony, security and integration ensue" (p. 127).

One is left with the sense, nevertheless, that in Klein's world pacific outward conditions never prevail for long, and thus there is often a dearth of such inward calm and unity. Indeed, Klein goes on immediately to outline, in a long paragraph about the mother, just how difficult it is to achieve a clear or accurate—that is, a properly reality-tested—perception of what the maternal object is like. There are different, vying internal versions of her, partially based on perception, but also on negative phantasy and paranoia. If the resulting "doubts, uncertainties and anxieties" are to be resolved, the child must keep trying to observe and measure the similarities and differences: "The visible mother thus provides continuous proofs of what the 'internal' mother is like, whether she is loving or angry, helpful or vengeful" (p. 128).

Mental health or illness, then, will be contingent upon the extent to which external realities are able to dispel internal concerns. In a rather convoluted sentence, Klein again makes the effort to speak up for the optimistic possibilities inherent in these trying tasks:

> On the other hand, a certain amount even of unpleasant experiences is of value in this testing of reality by the child if, through overcoming them, he feels that he can retain his objects as well as their love for him and his love for them, and thus preserve or re-establish internal life and harmony in face of dangers. [p. 128]

The idea here seems to be—paraphrasing Nietzsche—that what does not destroy, makes stronger; that is, the capacity to emerge from and survive negative external events reinforces the inner core.

It becomes progressively and paradoxically clearer that, for Klein, what occurs in the outside world at large (with her concomitant focus on reality testing) is significant less in its own right than as a template for testing or assessing the state of the internal world. An accumulation of actual "enjoyments" and "happy experiences", she tells us, will "increase love and trust" and "help the baby step by step to overcome his depression and feeling of loss (mourning)". They "enable him to test his inner reality by means of outer reality" and, ultimately, to strengthen "his hope that his 'good' objects and his ego can be saved and preserved". Experiences of an opposite, unpleasant kind with loved external objects will, by contrast, "increase ambivalence, diminish trust and hope and confirm anxieties about inner annihilation and external persecution" (p. 128).

Klein brings these thoughts together as follows:

> In the process of acquiring knowledge, every new piece of experience has to be fitted into the patterns provided by the psychic reality which prevails at the time; whilst the psychic reality of the child is gradually influenced by every step in his progressive knowledge of external reality. Every such step goes along with his more and more firmly

> establishing his inner "good" objects and is used by the ego as a means of overcoming the depressive position. [p. 129]

Making links with earlier work, Klein now wishes to fit these newer contributions into her rather pathogenic picture of the inner lives of ordinary children. The upshot is that, according to Klein, every normal child must struggle not only with "anxieties which are psychotic in content" and an "infantile neurosis" but must contend with an "infantile depressive position", to boot. Klein tries to garner support for her claims by footnoting a passage from Freud to the effect that neurosis may be more the rule than the exception in children.

Whether or not we agree with Klein that children undergo early versions of all these psychiatric illnesses (or, indeed, with her early dating of the superego), she does reprise, reinforce, and take significantly further Freud's relatively late recognition of the temporal and structural centrality of depressive dynamics to the developing mind:

> This conclusion I can now state more precisely, as a result of my work on the infantile depressive position, which has led me to believe that it is the central position in the child's development. In the infantile neurosis the early depressive position finds expression, is worked through and gradually overcome; and this is an important part of the process of organization and integration which, together with the sexual development, characterizes the first years of life. Normally, the child ... arrives step by step at a good relation to people and to reality. I hold that this satisfactory relation to people depends upon his having succeeded in his struggles against the chaos inside him (the depressive position) and having securely established his "good" internal objects. [pp. 129–130]

Klein's next goal in this paper will be the establishment of an even clearer conceptual distinction between her two main psychic positions than she had provided previously.

We are by now thoroughly aware that whereas in the earlier, primary, paranoid position the ego is in the grip of a terror of persecution by dangerous, predatory part-objects, the later, secondary, depressive position is characterized by concern for the safety of the whole object and sorrow for the damage that the ego has inflicted upon it. If, in the previous paper, Klein seemed more intent on demonstrating how the former anxieties pervade and affect the latter, here their differences seem of greater moment: "There are thus two sets of fears, feelings and defences, which, however varied in themselves and however intimately linked together, can, in my view, for purposes of theoretical clearness, be isolated from each other."

She also sees fit to provide a word denoting the depressive equivalent for "persecution"—her term for what the ego characteristically feels in the paranoid position—and settles on "a simple word derived from everyday language—namely the 'pining' for the lost object". With its slightly old-fashioned ring, this word captures rather aptly the sorrowful mood of mourning, as well as its long-suffering—indeed, insufferable—and unbearable quality. Recognizing the tendency to react against such feelings allows Klein to re-introduce into the equation the "*manic defences*, or the *manic position*" (p. 130).

Klein now states that "fluctuations between the depressive and the manic position are an essential part of normal development". If the paranoid defences and position are the old enemy, so to speak, their manic equivalents represent a newer, more contemporary adversary. Conceptually neat and clear as this may sound, however, the depressive position's moralistic stipulations can at times be so imperious and render the subject so anxious about its self-worth that they provoke an extreme manic push-back, including recourse to primitive mechanisms previously used in battles with the forces of paranoia.

In a long footnote, Klein again refers to the balancing function of extreme versions of internal objects: polarized "phantastically 'bad' persecutors" on the one hand, and idealized, unrealistically good objects on the other, virtually necessitate or entail each other in the infant's mind. She cites, in corroboration, both an early paper of her own and, once again, her daughter's work on "the connections between idealization and distrust of the object" (p. 131). Primary defences end up having to combat both paranoid and depressive demands:

> Omnipotence, denial and idealization, closely bound up with ambivalence, enable the early ego to assert itself to a certain degree against its internal persecutors and against a slavish and perilous dependence upon its loved objects, and thus to make further advances in development. [pp. 131–132]

Immediately hereafter Klein sees fit to quote at length (well-nigh a whole page) from her earlier paper on manic-depressive states, detailing the necessary, if rather uneasy, back-and-forth, trial-and-error fashion in which paranoid mistrust and splitting eventually give way to depressive tolerance and unification.

Klein sees the ego as employing manic methods—as well as obsessional ones—to buy it time in its long struggle to achieve secure depressive-position ascendancy over the obstinate, conspiracy-dominated concerns of the paranoid position. Klein refers to this array of interim measures in language that denotes organized positions as well as discrete defences. Mania and obsession operate in tandem, with each giving way to the other, like a wrestling tag-team:

> The young child, who cannot sufficiently trust his reparative or constructive feelings, as we have seen, resorts to manic omnipotence. For this reason, in an early stage of development the ego has not adequate means at its disposal to deal efficiently with guilt and anxiety. All this leads to a need in the child . . . to repeat certain actions obsessionally (this, in my view, is part of the repetition compulsion); or—the contrasting method—omnipotence or denial are resorted to. When defences of a manic nature fail, defences in which dangers from various sources are in an omnipotent way denied or minimized, the ego is driven alternately or simultaneously to combat the fears of deterioration and disintegration by attempted reparations carried out in obsessional ways. [pp. 132–133]

Significantly, it is while dealing with the interactions between mania and the other psychic constellations adumbrated here that the complex matter of manic triumph is given its fullest and clearest treatment.

Klein seems to again equivocate about the desirability or usefulness of this central aspect of mania. While the intentions of both mania and obsession are at least partially reparative, they easily become excessive, tend towards frenzy, take things too far. Klein issues a particular warning about triumph in this regard:

> The desire to control the object, the sadistic gratification of overcoming and humiliating it, of getting the better of it, the *triumph* over it, may enter so strongly into the act of reparation (carried out by thoughts, activities or sublimations) that the benign circle started by this act becomes broken. [p. 133]

Such situations lead inevitably to a retreat from the prospects of reparation and a return to even more defensive inclinations, whether of a paranoid, obsessional, or manic type.

Klein considers what happens in "normal development", where a better established psychic balance or "equilibrium" and less internal strain or ambivalence might give rise to a more positive version of triumph (though one wonders whether she might have employed some other term akin to it, like "ambition" or "the wish to succeed"). Though they are "closely bound up with contempt and omnipotence" and "the child's burning desire" to defeat and eclipse the parents, Klein seems prompted to acknowledge a more salutary aspect of these strivings:

> In addition to rivalry, his wish, mingled with fears, to "grow out" of his deficiencies (ultimately to overcome his destructiveness and his

bad inner objects and to be able to control them) is an incentive to achievements of all kinds. In my experience, the desire to reverse the child-parent relation, to get power over the parents and to triumph over them, is always to some extent associated with desires directed to the attainment of success. [pp. 133–134]

However—by contrast, say, with Heinz Kohut's (1971, 1977) self-psychology perspective on such matters and his more encouraging and forgiving views of narcissism—it is no surprise that Klein does not dwell on this positive perspective for long; the pendulum immediately swings back the other way, with something of a vengeance.

She now makes fully explicit how (self-)destructively narcissistic such emotions can be. The wish to tower omnipotently over old, infirm parents or weaker siblings brings in its wake lashings of guilt and remorse about what these objects are being subjected to, thwarting the very successes desired in the first place. Excess triumph (or any significant degree of it, perhaps) "often cripples endeavours of all kinds", leaving those who experience it "obliged to remain unsuccessful, because success always implies to them the humiliation or even the damage of somebody else". Moreover, the "subject's triumph over his objects necessarily implies to him their wish to triumph over him, and therefore leads to distrust and feelings of persecution" (p. 134).

What results is either depression or an intensification of manic and other defensive measures, and thus, having begun on an upbeat note, this page-long paragraph now ends on a distinctly less hopeful one:

> The triumph over his internal objects which the young child's ego controls, humiliates and tortures, is a part of the destructive aspect of the manic position which disturbs the reparation and re-creating of his inner world and of internal peace and harmony; and thus triumph impedes the work of early mourning. [p. 134]

There follows a reiteration of some of the more general features of hypomanic behaviour, with an emphasis on how people in the grip of it think or act on a grand scale and tend to ignore the precise and finer details of their behaviour—the very details that obsessional types take so seriously.

Klein again reminds us that it is basically denial that animates the sweeping, contemptuous gestures of the hypomanic mood, the fervent wish to be oblivious to the damage caused and to obliterate the debts incurred. But Klein is still prompted to try to rescue our "upward mobilities"— our ordinary inclinations towards achievement and success—for the side of the good, that is, for their contributions to depressive-position development and psychic health: "The child's growing skills, gifts and arts increase his belief in the psychic reality of his constructive tendencies, in his capacity to master and control his hostile impulses as well as his 'bad' internal objects".

When this is accompanied by increased "belief and trust in his capacity to love, in his reparative powers and in the integration and security of his good inner world", the hyperbole of his defensive phantasies can recede: "manic omnipotence decreases and the obsessional nature of the impulses towards reparation diminishes, which means in general that the infantile neurosis has passed" (p. 135). Perhaps it is worth reiterating—and intruding—here that, at their heights, manic thrashings and obsessive pedantry are not the conditions under which the calmer proceedings of psychic digestion and metabolization can comfortably occur.

By this point—and we have already advanced some way into the paper—there seems to have been enough preamble or reinforcement of previously established perspectives. Klein is now ready to proceed to this paper's main task, namely, "to connect the infantile depressive position with normal mourning". Having previously only hinted at—or given little foretastes of—her ideas about mourning, she begins to make her case in earnest and at greater length. Still responding to the original question that plagued Freud about why mourning is so painful and prolonged, Klein seems surprised that he should have thought it could be otherwise. What she suggests is that, even under the most optimal or normal circumstances, no mourning process is over once and for all, and this is because the original objects can never be fully or securely mourned in the first place. Clearly, this carries the implication that, for Klein, the differences between mourning and melancholia are at best relative in theory and often irrelevant in clinical practice.

This view of things turns on the fact that for Klein there is always a struggle for ascendancy between two internal versions of every significant object, and thus their fates rarely coincide and are not easy to reconcile:

> The poignancy of the actual loss of a loved person is, in my view, greatly increased by the mourner's unconscious phantasies of having lost his *internal* "good" objects as well. He then feels that his internal "bad" objects predominate and his inner world is in danger of disruption. We know that the loss of a loved person leads to an impulse in the mourner to reinstate the lost loved object in the ego (Freud and Abraham). In my view, however, he not only takes into himself (reincorporates) the person whom he has just lost, but also reinstates his internalized good objects (ultimately his loved parents), who became part of his inner world from the earliest stages of his development onwards. These too are felt to have gone under, to be destroyed, whenever the loss of a loved object is experienced. [pp. 135–136]

One might imagine, on Klein's behalf, how this predicament is experienced existentially by the mourner—in the first-person, so to speak: If this beloved object in the outside world can die and abandon me, then surely the good objects inside me can do the same. And then I could be left with only the bad ones in charge of my inner world.

Here, in any case, is a first clear and explicit statement of Klein's ideas about what is going on in the mind when there is a later occasion of actual loss or death and, thus, for mourning. Apparently no specific, contemporary, external bereavement can be suffered without it affecting the state of the internal world—indeed, without causing upheaval and alarm in its midst. But this is also where certain philosophical questions start to proliferate about the premises of these proceedings: what has been the ontological status of those internal objects up to now? What is their link with loss, and to what extent are they its products? Is an internal version of an external object—whether good or bad—ever lost, as such? Is it only lost in phantasy—and what precisely does this mean?

Returning to the quotation above, there is something confusing about Klein attributing the *re*instating of the lost loved object in the ego to Freud and Abraham, when for them, it could be argued, loss occasions the need to "instate" it there in the first place. Of course, Klein's presumption allows her to maintain an important kinship with these two forebears, but there are essential, if subtle, differences here. Klein's repeated use of that prefix, "re-" (including "reincorporates") is far from trivial: it is an indication that, for her, the establishing of an internal version of the object is not—to start with, or necessarily, or absolutely—contingent upon the kind of loss that requires a mourning process.

One might say that the establishment of these internal objects happens anyway (via primary introjection) or perhaps because of the need to cope with all the inevitable little losses of earliest life, attendant upon the comings and goings of the primary object. But are these not to be classed as minor, if myriad, occasions for mourning? What else might they be? Klein assiduously draws our attention to these early losses, and to the importance of weaning—arguably the first major loss of a lifetime (after, that is, the "loss" of birth). And, one may wonder, how does all this relate to Freud's idea that the baby staves off such early losses by hallucinating the absent breast? Should we regard an hallucination as an internal object—or might it be the other way round?

There are far too many puzzles and queries here, but that is surely because Klein's internal world is quite a different place from the one sketched in the earlier chapters, courtesy of Freud, Ferenczi, and Abraham. As specified before, and as Klein clearly states here, no once-and-for-all or even relative security is on offer in her world. Even though her early ego may already have the capacity to establish internal versions of external objects, these are always either good or bad, and the former are never *so* securely ensconced as to be completely reliable or unassailable. These good objects are always subject to attack by their bad counterparts, the id, or events in the outside world and are easily destabilized by new losses.

Klein's subtle and resonant metaphor concerning the consequence of a new loss is telling: she speaks of the mourner's sense that the original (parental) good internal objects have also "gone under". She thereby invokes the sinking or floundering feelings associated with mourning; it is as though what the ego experiences in times of grief and despair is a kind of swamping or drowning, feelings of being dragged down both by the sheer weight of current and past lost objects—and perhaps by the burdensome duty of having to dive down into the depths to raise them up and revive them. For Klein this is tantamount to a reactivation of the "early depressive position" and thus of all the attendant feelings "derived from the breast situation, the Oedipus situation and from all other sources", including paranoid persecutory fears about what the "dreaded parents" (p. 136) might do by way of revenge.

To exemplify it all, Klein invokes the situation of a woman who has lost her child. When one arrives at this moment in her paper—about ten pages in, and as the first hint in it of clinical material as such—it is with a sense of shock that this worst-case scenario of grief should be the one that comes so readily to her mind as an example of mourning. It is by now well established, however, that she was consulting her own tragic experience here—indeed, that this woman (whom she will go on to call Mrs A) is in fact herself. In the pages that follow, she emphasizes that this mourning subject feels punished by an internal mother who is retaliating for original thieving and murderous attacks perpetrated upon the maternal object. The dominance of such hateful, suspicious, ambivalent, mistrustful feelings in her internal world makes any help or comfort that she might drive hard to come by or accept.

In a poignant passage, Klein expounds upon and extrapolates from her plight:

> The pain experienced in the slow process of testing reality in the work of mourning thus seems to be partly due to the necessity, not only to renew links to the external world and thus continuously to re-experience the loss, but at the same time and by means of this to rebuild with anguish the internal world, which is felt to be in danger of deteriorating and collapsing. Just as the young child passing through the depressive position is struggling, in his unconscious mind, with the

task of establishing and integrating his inner world, so the mourner goes through the pain of re-establishing and re-integrating it. [p. 136]

We again find the prefix "re-" in frequent use here, with its indication that there is little in human development that can be permanently secured and established. The poetic phrase, "to rebuild with anguish the inner world" might stand as an elegiac title or epigraph for the ongoing, never-completed task, not only of every mourning process, but of every human life, from beginning to end, as it suffers and tries to survive its multiple, frequent losses, large and small. However, while it is hard to disagree with this view of the human condition, it also seems unduly harsh to be living with the constant, perennial, or imminent threat that one's internal world "is in danger of deteriorating and collapsing".

The language surrounding her metaphor of rebuilding carries implications that lie at the heart of the seeming impossibility of Klein's quest. Far from permitting the anabolic and catabolic processes whereby the internal world might absorb a lost object and utilize its sustenance to strengthen the structure of the self or the ego, she seems to require, as a psychic duty, that we somehow keep trying to re-establish or reconstruct—as a kind of concrete memorial—an internal version of the object itself. But this alternative metaphor itself collapses if the attempted memorial is always being built with unreliable materials and on foundations so precarious that it is in constant danger of crumbling. This is surely a melancholic version of mourning and, if the digestive metaphor can be retained at all, then it is perhaps in bovine form, whereby the cud of loss must be regurgitated, re-chewed, and re-swallowed again and again, perhaps endlessly. It in any case contrasts starkly with the moment in Ogden's reading of "Mourning and Melancholia", where he insists that proper grieving requires the object to be thoroughly killed, that "one must do the psychological work of allowing the object to be irrevocably dead, both in one's own mind and in the external world" (Ogden, 2012, p. 31).

If we accept Klein's account, how are we to distinguish—in her terms—between the "real" pathology represented, for example, by Miss Emily's inability to keep her dead father down or to prevent his tomb from disintegrating, on the one hand, and a more successful mourning process, on the other? The fact that the cadaver of Homer Barron ends up in her bed is surely evidence of how badly digested and shallowly buried her father is in her internal world. Barron, the later lost object, is so incestuously associated with this father in the first place that, when he dares to walk abroad with an insouciant swagger in the town of Jefferson, he will need to be killed and put where Emily can keep close watch over him; she thus makes sure that no significant object of hers will ever go wandering off again! Does Klein's theory struggle to offer us any account of death and mourning that does not necessarily invoke the undead in this way, even if we might all agree that "A Rose for Emily" presents an especially macabre and extreme version of melancholia?

Given Freud's own frequent recourse to archaeological analogies, it would be an interesting exercise to compare his clinical and theoretical uses of construction and reconstruction with those of Klein. Perhaps it is unsurprising and no accident that such metaphors should feature, implicitly or explicitly, in the discourse of two (Jewish) analysts whose destinies were forged during the first half of a century and on a continent that generated and hosted two of the most devastating, decimating, obliterating wars of all time. Klein's sentiments above both echo and challenge the hopeful but frankly desperate last sentence of Freud's lyrical essay, "On Transience", written near the beginning of the First World War: "We shall build up again what the war has destroyed, and perhaps on firmer ground and more lastingly than before" (Freud, 1916a, p. 307). I examine this essay in detail at the end of the book, but it is perhaps important to bear in mind that Klein is writing her second paper on mourning and manic-depressive states in the year after Freud's death, and at the start of the second of those wars.

Ironically, however, at this moment in Klein's text, when the psychopathology of loss is at stake, she seems more at odds with Freud than ever. Where he says quite explicitly, at the beginning of "Mourning and Melancholia", that mourning is not itself an illness, she says that normal mourning reactivates "early psychotic anxieties"; she then adds: "The mourner is in fact ill, but because this state of mind is common and seems so natural to us, we do not call mourning an illness." The next statement is therefore hardly unexpected: "I should say that in mourning the subject goes through a modified and transitory manic-depressive state and overcomes it" (pp. 136–137). To put it succinctly, for Klein it is not mourning that provides the model for melancholia—if anything, it is the other way around.

In the paragraphs that follow, where Klein is rightly concerned with the dangers that manic triumph poses to the mourning process, her disagreements with Freud are made even more explicit. She again outlines how triumphalism is an expression of ambivalence and hatred—as if, under its aegis, just continuing to live might be experienced as a sadistic victory over the lost object—and can only bring further, exacerbating guilt in its wake. She cites Freud's statement about the "phase of triumph" being absent from normal mourning and his attempt to keep mania theoretically separate by consigning it to manic-depressive pathology. She has no qualms about contradicting him and seems persuaded that it is the very presence of mania in ordinary mourning that makes it so prolonged and painful.

Klein drives home her point of view as follows:

When hatred of the loved object in its various manifestations gets the upper hand in the mourner, this not only turns the loved lost person into a persecutor, but shakes the mourner's belief in his good inner objects as well. The shaken belief in the good objects disturbs most painfully the process of idealization, which is an essential intermediate step in mental development. With the young child, the idealized mother is the safeguard against a retaliating or a dead mother and against all bad objects, and therefore represents security and life itself. [pp. 137–138]

Klein's return to ideas about idealization is an interesting development. In the rest of this and the next paragraph, she justifies and rationalizes the—albeit temporary—need to hold onto "the feeling of possessing the perfect loved object (idealized) inside".

Because of powerful hatreds—both historical and contemporary—the mourner needs this image of an ultra-good object to stave off prospects like punishment, retaliation, and deprivation at the hands of the ultra-bad objects that might return to haunt him or her. (As an "ideal" and unregenerate example of paranoid-schizoid functioning, Miss Emily is, of course, virtually defined by precisely such split idealizations and denigrations of her lost objects.) While for Klein the mourner might begin the process while in the grip of paranoid (and schizoid) dynamics, as the work of mourning progresses a more depressive capacity can hopefully come about. This might allow an internal gap or split to close and make for greater trust in both external objects and the "intentions" of the internal good object. Only then can he or she "bear to realize that this object was not perfect, and yet not lose trust or love for him, nor fear his revenge" (p. 138).

It is just at this moment that Klein begins to speak of Mrs A by name. Though this woman has suffered "the shattering loss of her young son, who had died suddenly while at school" (p. 138), Klein is at pains to distinguish her as a normal mourner, not a melancholic. Her experience is introduced as an "instance"—not as a clinical example—and there is nothing in the text to suggest that Klein is Mrs A's analyst, therefore providing another clue as to who this person might really be. Later, by contrast, there is a briefer and more conventional presentation of an actual clinical case, that of D, a middle-aged man who—already quite a disturbed patient to start with—suffers the death of his mother while in treatment with Klein. As in the earlier paper, Klein makes extensive use of the dreams of these two individuals, but perhaps the significant difference here is the emphasis on the trajectories of their efforts to recover from loss.

Klein gives us a vivid and detailed account of Mrs A's mourning process. She is first pictured as a shocked and traumatized woman, numbed by the experience of grief, unable to find relief in tears, caught up in paranoid-schizoid divisions and divisiveness. In her dreams and phantasies there are complex struggles of identification with her vengeful mother and ambivalent relations with an older brother, both of whom have already died. Manic denial and triumph predominate initially, but soon, via another dream, the beginnings of sorrow and guilt become evident, along with Mrs A's own wish to remain in life rather than follow her son into death.

Klein interrupts her account to quote a slightly longer version of one of the "reality testing" passages from "Mourning and Melancholia" with which she began her paper. She then interprets Freud's description of the mourner's decision to cut ties with the dead object because of the "narcissistic satisfactions" of being alive as demonstrating "in a milder way the element of triumph which Freud seemed to think does not enter into normal mourning" (p. 141).

Mrs A's mourning now embarks upon a phase of greater reconciliation with her internal objects. She reclaims an appreciation of good things through an interest in beautiful houses, thereby suggesting a wish to placate these figures by re-accommodating them more comfortably in her inner world. She also now cries more sorrowfully, achieving greater relief: as Klein puts it, in unusually ordinary-sounding terms, "the mourner is able to surrender fully to his feelings, and to cry out his sorrow about the actual loss". Klein suggests that this release of emotion is "held up in certain stages of grief by an extensive manic control" and is thus enabled by a relaxing of these strictures upon them. Then "the processes of ejecting and projecting" are freer to perform their evacuative tasks; bad feelings are "equated to excrement", and they can now be expelled more easily, as tears.

This liberation seems to extend even to the emotional states of the internal objects themselves. Mrs A seems to feel that her internal objects—perhaps particularly the maternal one—are no longer angry, dangerous, or persecutory, and are now able to mourn along with the subject, to share her grief, to be sorry for her loss: "The tears which she shed are also to some extent the tears which her internal parents shed, and she also wanted to comfort them as they—in her phantasy—comforted her" (p. 142–143).

Though this too is resonant, suggestive of poetic, elegiac sentiments, it is also one of the places where Klein's "homuncular", concrete-sounding rendition of internal objects jars and seems to take things a bit too far. What is not clear when Klein attributes to these internal figures the ability to respond with real emotions is just how metaphorical such attributions are intended—or can be taken—to be. Klein's literalistic way of phrasing things—somewhat like her propensity for "body-part-object-speak" which later fell out of favour even among her own followers—may beggar the reader's belief, compromising the inclination or wish to regard these textual moments more figuratively. And it has prompted, at least in me, the need to find more sophisticated ways of theorizing and formulating the work of psychic introjection and the creation of an internal world.

In the meantime, Klein evocatively lists and describes the successive stages of coming to terms with and recovering from loss. Persecution gradually gives way to pining, and hate, to love; a new kind of usable, non-destructive dependence comes about. And, while the full force of psychic pain and grief can now be experienced, this too is felt to be on the side of life. Creative sublimations become possible again; wisdom and an appreciation of others can accrue. Klein extends her reach beyond mourning (a word that she appears to reserve for death *per se*) to the suffering of other experiences of disappointment, loss, and pain. She extols the virtues and benefits of a proper process of working-through and again links it with the infantile depressive position—the arriving at but also the overcoming of it, something that continues to be an at least implicit possibility.

Such processes, however, are rarely linear or straightforward. Klein intersperses her general accounts with more particular references to the ebbing and flowing of Mrs A's personal mourning process. Though she is indeed dreaming and seeing friends again, she suddenly finds being out and about terribly disorienting and alienating and is compelled to retreat to the safe base of home. Klein returns repeatedly to the view that the external world will be found threatening, rather than consoling, if the internal world remains in a dubious or chaotic state.

Klein now claims that "every advance in the process of mourning results in a *deepening* in the individual's relation to his internal objects"; repeating the key word later in the paragraph, she adds, perhaps paradoxically, that "a *deepening* in internal relationships" can lead to "greater independence from external as well as internal objects" (p. 144, my emphases). I am prompted to ask how precisely she understands this to happen, what form she sees such deepening to take. As far as one can tell, she surely cannot mean a more thoroughgoing consolidation or secure ensconcing of such objects, or a confidence about really possessing them inside. One assumes that they continue to be precariously held, cannot be relied upon as permanent or durable acquisitions, and will come under threat again when the next loss occurs.

So, would it not be preferable if Klein's meanings could be reframed, if not necessarily in the language of digestion or metabolization, then—following her own language—in terms of submitting these internal objects to a kind of transformative submersion? Prompted by her own word "deepening", reminiscent of her earlier metaphor of "going under"—and with Freud's title, "The Dissolution of the Oedipus Complex" (1924d) in mind—I would rephrase this interrogatively as follows: might we wish to regard Klein's internal objects as *soluble*, at least to some extent? If so, in what medium might that process be possible and, indeed, what would the resulting *solution* be like?

There is now a rather confusing paragraph in which Klein ostensibly attempts to lay out "the differences between the early depressive position and normal mourning". She first says that the baby's experiences of grief—at the loss of "breast or bottle", representing the good object inside him—usually occur when the mother herself is still around. By contrast, in grown-up grief—involving "the actual loss of an actual person"—the mourner's help must come from the good object which he has "established" internally in his formative years. However, she then seems to say that it is precisely in those years that the young child will struggle with the fear of loss and, thus, to establish his good internal object securely, hence his need for and dependence on the mother's continued presence. This is said to resemble the adult mourner's reliance on family and friends, with whose real, external support "the restoration of the harmony of his inner world is promoted, and his fears and distress are more quickly reduced" (p. 145).

Though this makes a kind of overall sense, I find these frequent changes in the subject-position—from infant to grown-up to young child and back to adult—a bit incoherent and obscure; the argument seems circular and there is some indecision about whether it is contrast or comparison that Klein is reaching for here. It is difficult to ascertain whether it is the external or internal objects that are of most use in these difficult negotiations with loss. While it may be easy and true to conclude that both are crucial and mutually reinforcing, this also seems theoretically rather evasive.

In the meantime, Klein continues her theoretical tussles with Freud and, to a lesser extent, Abraham. As previously, her rather pithy and reductive summaries of others' work can leave something to be desired. She grants Freud priority for "discoveries about the nature of the archaic processes at work in melancholia", but only Abraham is credited for the insight that "such processes also operate in the work of normal mourning". It will be remembered that Freud also made a substantial contribution to that insight, albeit several years after "Mourning and Melancholia" (in *Group Psychology* and *The Ego and the Id*), but certainly before Abraham published his crucial paper on the development of the libido in 1924.

When Klein then goes on to attribute to Abraham the idea that the mourner "succeeds in establishing the lost loved object within the ego, while the melancholic has failed to do so", this does not quite ring true and sounds like something of a misrepresentation on her part. For Abraham (as well as Freud), the melancholic *does* manage to install the object in the ego (via identification with it), for it is only by doing so that he may then proceed to persecute that object, as well as himself, internally. Despite what she herself has said or implied elsewhere, Klein seems almost to have forgotten here that some form of internalizing is always already proceeding, in any and every situation in which an object is lost. One would not expect to have to remind her that there are such things as ambivalent or bad internal objects, too, and that these might indeed achieve a certain form of installation or internalization, even if the psychic consequence is then something more nefarious than the salutary form of taking in that establishes a good, or even idealized, object inside the ego.

I do not think that this is merely pedantic nit-picking on my part. It is this kind of conceptual predicament that makes it imperative that we distinguish more clearly among different kinds of internalizing moves or processes. The distinction between mourning and melancholia, or more generally between successful and unsuccessful ways of dealing with loss, does not necessarily turn on *whether* an internalization of the object has taken place; it has much more to do with *how* it happens—or, more specifically, on how the object gets treated once admitted to the internal world. It is also the concreteness or otherwise of the process that seems crucial to me, this being the reason why it is important to know, and even to insist upon, the differences between introjection and incorporation.

Staying with Klein's contributions to these dynamics: while she agrees that setting up the lost object internally is "the characteristic feature of normal mourning", she adds the now-familiar corollary that this also requires the "reinstating" and "recovering" of all the previously internalized loved objects that the current loss has somehow dislodged or released from psychic safekeeping. One might surmise that, for Klein, a new loss in some sense unhinges the ego, and this implies something like a gate swinging open, leaving a gap or aperture through which all the previously well-corralled internal creatures can make their escape; and this will now necessitate the arduous work of rounding them up again. Explaining the early installation of these internal figures, she seems now to appreciate belatedly—albeit parenthetically—Freud's contributions to these matters: "(It was the understanding of the processes of introjection in melancholia and normal mourning which, as we know, led Freud to recognize the existence of the super-ego in normal development)" (p. 145).

This concession, however, is only a prelude to Klein again outlining her differences from Freud and it occasions a more detailed account of her own ideas about these internalizing processes and the provenance of the superego:

> As I have often pointed out, the processes of introjection and projection from the beginning of life lead to the institution inside ourselves of loved and hated objects, who are felt to be "good" and "bad", and who are interrelated with each other and with the self: that is to say they constitute an inner world. This assembly of internalized objects becomes organized, together with the organization of the ego, and in the higher strata of the mind it becomes discernible as the super-ego. [p. 146]

Whereas for Freud the superego emerges from and after the ego—having been a "grade" within it, as he says—for Klein it appears to have its own parallel, separate, and contemporaneous organizational development.

Klein is yet more explicit about these differences when she says that Freud recognizes only the relatively more external and abstract contributions of "the voices and the influence of the actual parents" to these proceedings, while her own findings reveal the presence of "a complex object-world, which is felt by the individual, in deep layers of the unconscious, to be concretely inside himself". Though circumscribed by the notion that it is "felt by the individual", and is therefore presumably the product of phantasy, I trust that by now there can be no doubt about the literality or, to adopt her word, concreteness of Klein's internal world.

This is further brought home by words like "innumerable" and "multitude" to describe its inhabitants. When she adds that "all these objects are in the inner world in an infinitely complex relation both with each other and with the self" (p. 146), she vividly conjures up a crowded, chaotic extended internal family, or even an inner village, beset by petty conflicts and rivalries and perhaps by scandalous, quasi-incestuous relationships. We might imagine here precisely the kind of small town that Miss Emily inhabits; serendipitously, "A Rose for Emily" is the opening story of a subsection of Faulkner's *Collected Stories* (1977) entitled "The Village".

By specifying her differences from Freud in respect of the superego and the internal landscape of the mind, Klein thinks she has thereby explained or accounted for her ideas about mourning, too. To my mind, a crucial aspect is left unexplained, namely, her conviction that any new loss will necessarily or inevitably destroy or at least destabilize this internal landscape, such that a wholesale "rebuilding"—and re-populating—is required, and that this is what "characterizes the successful work of mourning". She also claims that understanding the internal world in this way "enables the analyst to find and resolve a variety of early anxiety-situations which were formerly unknown, and is therefore theoretically and therapeutically of an importance so great that it cannot yet be fully estimated"—a large claim, to say the least.

We are asked to accept that Klein's analytic perspective on the machinations of mourning would help us inestimably with plumbing the mysterious depths of early anxiety; but also vice versa: "the problem of mourning can only be more fully understood by taking account of these early anxiety situations" (p. 146). Perhaps this helpfully describes the mutuality of two different therapeutic or developmental moments but, from a theoretical point of view, it also sounds logically circular and thus rather suspect.

Klein now turns her attention to patient D for a clinical illustration of one of these anxiety situations which she regards as highly significant in manic-depressive illness, namely, "the anxiety about the internalized parents in destructive sexual intercourse". In D, "a man in his early forties, with strong paranoid and depressive traits", these "fears and phantasies" emerged with force when his mother died after a long illness. Klein gives a quite detailed account of two successive sessions, the first of which features the following: accusations and complaints about his mother; a dream in which she is menaced by a dangerous farmyard bull while he makes his guilty escape; associations to blackbirds singing; the killing (and preservation) of American buffaloes; and other stories about the threatening behaviour of bulls, including on his father's farm where he had spent part of his childhood.

We are told that D learns of his mother's death in the gap between the two sessions, but he does not report this to Klein at the start of the second session. She takes up his manifest hostility and hatred towards her in the transference, suggesting that she stands not only for each individual parent, but for the composite parental couple that they comprise. These parents are rendered more threatening by virtue of being internalized and therefore active inside him in sexually destructive ways. Klein interprets that the raging bulls and noisy blackbirds represented the dangerous sexual intercourse of his parents, which was so unendurable on this particular morning because of his guilt about the bull dream, and owing to an acute state of anxiety about his dying mother. Thus his mother's death meant her destruction by the bull inside him, since—the work of mourning already having started—he had internalized her in this most dangerous situation. (pp. 147–148).

It is only after Klein had also pointed out some of the more positive, hopeful, or reparative aspects of this material—including the sexually procreative meanings inherent in it—that D both tells her of his mother's passing and appears to accept her interpretations of these internal dynamics. This is followed by his experience of some welcome sadness and relief. However, in the ensuing sessions, both before and after his mother's funeral, D continues to dream about destructive events, often involving two figures, and Klein continues to interpret these in terms of destructive intercourse—actual and symbolic, external as well as internal—between all the possible pairings: the parental couple, one or other of the parents and D himself, the analyst and a parent, or D and the analyst.

As Klein goes on to claim, "Through the analysis of these emotions referring to the actual parents in sexual intercourse, and particularly through the analysis of these internalized situations, the patient became able to experience real mourning for his mother." The implication, of course, is clear: that without Klein imputing to him and then analysing these destructive, id-led phantasies of what was being perpetrated within himself, there could be no release of the more benign feelings that were intertwined with and entrapped by them. She says that D "had repressed and denied from his early days onward" many more positive and loving emotions in relation to his parents, but by "going through this mourning with sorrow and despair, his deeply buried love for his mother came more and more into the open, and his relation to both parents altered" (p. 151).

Klein is bringing her deliberations to a close, which signals a need to repeat yet again all her central ideas about the depressive position, manic-depressive illness, and mourning as they have been developed and explicated over the course of both papers. As befits this paper, she does attempt to keep the focus on mourning *per se* and the consequences of a failure to mourn. She rehearses all the defensive methods used by the ego to evade the work and suffering necessary either to "overcome successfully the infantile depressive position" or to mourn in earnest any later loss. The outcome of the latter will be contingent upon the former and upon the state of the internal object world. She tells us that people who cannot mourn will end up being dominated by hatred and strong tendencies towards paranoid-schizoid functioning; at the very least, they will be condemned to a stunted, circumscribed existence. Thus, even if they manage somehow to avoid serious psychopathology, this might come at the price of "a severe restriction of their emotional life which impoverishes their whole personality" (p. 152).

There is, however, a new idea in these last paragraphs, to do with what might be called substitutive or alternative ways of dealing with the losses of those who are not that easy to love or mourn. Klein suggests that people possess the "capacity to keep alive in other directions some of the love which they deny to their lost objects". This might occur if an interest in or devotion to other objects or activities—which "do not in their minds come too close to the lost object"—are readily available or can be discovered. Though such ploys—or what Klein calls "relations and sublimations"—could be seen as defensive or avoidant, "they may nevertheless offer some reassurance and relief from guilt, for through them the lost loved object which has been rejected and thus again destroyed is to some extent restored and retained in the unconscious mind" (pp. 152–153).

When I came across these sentiments, I could not help recalling Nicholas Wright's play *Mrs Klein* (1988) which seemed to me to apply this premise to Klein herself, to her own ways of dealing with loss. The play suggests that Klein—in the very period during which these papers were written—sought solace for both the death of her son and the apostasy of her analyst-daughter in an even deeper commitment to psychoanalytic work and, more particularly, via her "adoption" of an enthusiastic psychoanalytic acolyte, in the person of Paula Heimann, as her surrogate child or object-in-need (though Heimann, too, would eventually leave the Kleinian fold). Though some might see this play as a hostile attack on her character, I disagree and think that there is something touchingly human in this portrayal of Klein, in that its central idea (which is, after all, one of Klein's own) represents some relenting on the otherwise rather strict-seeming demands that her theory of mourning places on the subject or ego.

There is a powerful sense, after all, that Klein sees mourning as an extremely arduous task; it is one made more difficult by the requirement that, in addition to the immediate grieving over a current loss, one must also put one's internal house in order by reinstating the disrupted "good standing" of the original significant objects. One then wants to ask (perhaps a bit concretely) whether she necessarily means the mourner's internal parents themselves? Must they be rendered good in the mind regardless of whether they were benign or malign in external reality? Klein's own tendency to sound very concrete or literal persuades one that she does tend to insist on this criterion for a fully achieved mourning process. And yet here she is, just before the end of this very influential paper, saying that the goodness we try to take in and establish inside as we attempt to recover from loss and return to life—the meaningful person or purpose via which we do so—is sometimes not a version of the lost object itself, whether current or historical, but a substitute someone or something else in its place.

This, of course, is precisely what psychoanalysis tries to offer by way of the transference and, in the next paragraph, Klein suggests that if we as analysts can reduce the destructive, persecutory, and hateful anxieties in our patients, we enable them "to revise their relation to their parents— whether they be dead or alive—and to rehabilitate them to some extent even if they have grounds for actual grievances". Klein has seemingly returned to a focus on what patients make internally of their external relations with parents—and how a later remaking might be achieved in analysis—but there is both a conciliatory tone in the qualifying phrase "to some extent" and an important concession in her acknowledgement that "actual grievances" against real parents might indeed be legitimate. When she also says that "greater tolerance" allows the possibility "to set up 'good' parent-figures more securely in their minds", is there a hint that this might not be required all over again from scratch every time a new loss occurs?

Perhaps what I am reaching for here and trying to secure is my own good-internal-object version of Klein herself, one that is a little less demanding and a bit more compassionate and forgiving. At these moments, at least, that version is not far off, insofar as Klein seems distinctly to be putting second chances on offer: as she says, it is the purpose of our therapeutic work to help our patients "to experience emotions— sorrow, guilt and grief, as well as love and trust—to go through mourning, but to overcome it, and ultimately to overcome the infantile depressive position, which they have failed to do in childhood" (p. 153).

In the remaining two paragraphs, we witness Klein returning to a somewhat more strongly stated version of the central ideas with which we are now so familiar. Mourning and manic-depressive states are compared as well as contrasted. She assumes that both start out from—and hark back to—the infantile depressive position, with its implication of childhoods beset by early, if "transitory", bouts of both deep grief and mental illness. Perhaps uncharacteristically, however, she draws a firm dividing line between normal mourners and those who either mourn in "abnormal" ways or fail to mourn. The latter group "have been unable in early childhood to establish their internal 'good' objects and to feel secure in their inner world. They have never really overcome the infantile depressive position."

As tragic as this predicament sounds, even ordinary mourning is no easy undertaking. Though the early depressive position might originally have been better negotiated in such cases, it is nonetheless "revived by the loss of the loved object" and must again be "overcome by the methods similar to those used by the ego in childhood" (p. 153). As if granting the rewards for such hard work, Klein's final sentence has an incantatory, liturgical, almost prayer-like rhythm:

> It is by reinstating inside himself the "good" parents as well as the recently lost person, and by rebuilding his inner world, which was disintegrated and in danger, that he overcomes his grief, regains security, and achieves true harmony and peace. [p. 153]

Postscript: Later Klein and Bion

I am aware of the arbitrariness of focusing solely, even if closely, on Klein's papers on manic-depressive states in attempting to account for her contributions to the issues I am investigating in this book. Though these two papers are possibly the apotheosis of Klein's achievement, a culmination represented by the invaluable concept of the depressive position, there were several more important papers to come, at least two of which have clear relevance here: "Notes on Some Schizoid Mechanisms" (1946) and "On Identification" (1955). Moreover, as far as the specific themes of digestion and metabolization are concerned, it would be remiss and irresponsible to say nothing about that perhaps most important of post-Kleinian theorists, Wilfred Bion, who addresses such issues directly and explicitly in his enigmatic but influential book, *Learning from Experience* (1962).

By 1940, Klein had yet to arrive at a complete crystallization and definition of—or even an established name for—the psychic position that temporally precedes the depressive one. However, with the publication of her 1946 paper, the paranoid-schizoid position is finally named as such, its dynamics are thoroughly explicated, and the two positions are again helpfully juxtaposed.

The other major event in the evolution of Klein's thinking, heralded in this paper, is the advent of projective identification, the defence mechanism that she now sees as predominating in paranoid-schizoid and psychotic functioning. This original notion would progressively gain traction in Klein's thinking and eventually take centre stage in the work of many of her followers. It is also evident that as investment and involvement in these more expulsive, outwardly directed processes increased, interest in the equivalent introjective or internalizing forms of identification seemed to wane somewhat and become less prominent.

This is certainly borne out in the later paper entitled "On Identification". Klein begins this paper by again paying tribute to the work of both

Freud and Abraham, saying that since their discoveries, "introjection and identification have played a central role in psycho-analytic thought and research" (1955, p. 141). Despite her ready recourse to the former internalizing term invented by Ferenczi, his name remains conspicuously absent from her discourse. Indeed, as she introduces her own contributions to these themes—and illustrates them, via the detailed reading of a story by the French writer Julian Green—it becomes quite clear that her own discourse has shifted significantly, away from introjection (and incorporation) and towards the externalizing, projective version—or aspect—of identification.

As I suggested, this shift towards projective identification would have momentous Kleinian consequences: the more ordinary and generally less pathogenic introjective forms of identification and their psychic consequences would gradually receive less attention. This would expose a conspicuous and widening gap—perhaps a fault-line—in the constitution and theorizing of the internal world according to Klein and her followers.

Having said that, if we return to "Notes on Some Schizoid Mechanisms", we discover some interesting if less characteristic moments, where Klein appears to renew and rethink her focus on what is happening inside the psyche. There are now some hints at, or gestures towards, seeing internal objects as subject to *some* form of processing—akin, perhaps, to digestion or metabolization—when she begins to speak of the "assimilation" of internal objects. One of the paper's major themes is the splitting that leads to fragmentation of both ego and object, and it is in a section on "Splitting in Connection with Projection and Introjection" that she introduces this idea of internal assimilation.

This is discussed in relation to the idealization of the internal good object and the subsequent clinging or fleeing to it. Having perhaps always been a somewhat ambivalent or contentious notion for Klein, here idealization is viewed as a defensive manoeuvre on the part of the ego, one that can have some dire psychic consequences:

> From this mechanism various serious disturbances may result: when persecutory fear is too strong, the flight to the idealized good object becomes excessive, and this severely hampers ego development and disturbs object relations. As a result the ego may be felt to be entirely subservient to and dependent on the internal object—only a shell for it. With an unassimilated idealized object there goes a feeling that the ego has no life. [1946, p. 9]

Suddenly, and perhaps rather belatedly, Klein seems now to be considering the consequences of a failure to assimilate a relatively benign internal object, where such an object then comes to loom too large in the internal world, taking up space, crowding the ego, squeezing the life out of it.

It is noteworthy that where Klein had previously referred—in both papers on manic-depressive states—to the work of her actual daughter, Melitta Schmideberg (1930), when addressing the idealization of the object at this juncture, she turns to a paper by her "surrogate" daughter, Paula Heimann (1942). Klein refers in a footnote to Heimann's description of "a condition in which the internal objects act as foreign bodies embedded in the self" and credits her with introducing "the concept of the assimilation of internal objects", seen to be "essential for the successful exercise of ego-functions and for the achievement of independence" (pp. 9–10). A little further on in her paper, Klein repeats that a negative consequence of "the weakening and impoverishing of the ego resulting from excessive splitting and projective identification" is that such an ego becomes "incapable of assimilating its internal objects, and this leads to the feeling that it is ruled by them" (p. 11).

What could this word "assimilation", as used first by Heimann and then by Klein, possibly betoken other than some method of accommodation, absorption, or integration—or a psychically metabolic or digestive process? How else might an ego come to curb an internal object's formidable power as a tyrannizing force of occupation? These are, for me, crucial questions, linking my lengthy close readings of Klein's work to the overall themes of this book and particularly to its subsequent chapters.

We see, in chapter five, how Hans Loewald describes situations where insufficiently internalized objects are seen to haunt the psyche like unlaid ghosts. Similarly, in chapter six, we find Abraham and Torok writing about the way that improperly mourned and introjected figures become immured or encrypted internally, entrapping the egos in which they reside. And again, in chapter seven, on Green, we can witness how—having been installed by loss in her child's mental space—the melancholic "undead" mother refuses to either live or die. Each of these analytic theorists might be said to be grappling with the problematics of mourning in the internal world, and specifically with what might be called the dynamics of assimilation or digestion.

The transitional language that Klein is perhaps just beginning to employ here, courtesy of Paula Heimann, is applied to overly idealized objects but might equally be applied to other objects causing internal trouble or in need of processing. Couched in more positive terms, my claim is that some such assimilatory procedure is precisely what does—or should—pertain as far as any significant internalized figure is concerned (and thus in relation to any mourned object), so that the ego might eventually both strengthen and free itself as it develops. This is why to designate or denote such internal psychic processes by means of words like integration, absorption, dissolution, or, indeed, assimilation (others, including sublimation, might even apply)—and to speak of them metaphorically in alimentary, digestive, or metabolic terms—seems so apt in these contexts.

However, as I have suggested throughout this reading of Klein, there is very little by way of follow-up on such hints and a relative absence of ideas about what the assimilation of an internal object—were it to be successful—might look like or result in. (This seems closely related to the fact that we also never get an account from Klein of what *overcoming* the depressive position might mean for her, even if she seems to offer it as at least a theoretical possibility.) Klein never really developed a working theory of how—or even whether—the thoroughgoing assimilation of an object, or a more comprehensive and stable introjection of it, might occur. For the most part, the fate of the objects in Klein's internal world does not seem to involve their metabolic breakdown or psychic absorption and assimilation into the substance of the ego. For her, it would seem, internal objects—good and bad—tend to retain an unbudgingly stubborn, concrete, and ever-present existence.

Wilfred Bion

In addition to his being a highly original psychoanalytic thinker in his own right, Wilfred Bion was arguably also Klein's chief, most distinguished, and most creative heir. One is therefore tempted to think that some of Bion's most important contributions to psychoanalytic theorizing—which *do* hinge precisely on the possibilities of psychic digestion—were developed for the very purpose of making up for certain blind spots or lacunae in Klein's thinking. His theory of containment is based on the idea that it is a mother's initial task to assimilate and partially metabolize experience on behalf of her as-yet compromised or incapable infant, and then to then feed it back in a semi-digested—and thus more palatable and psychically available—form.

For Bion, these early exchanges are contingent upon the use of projective identification in a more communicative, rather than a purely evacuative or destructive way; but they must also presume at least some incipient ability on the part of the infant-receiver to take something in. It seems that the infant can perform its projections quite effectively from the start, getting rid of what Bion refers to as "beta-elements" by depositing them in the mother—for her attention, so to speak. What it cannot yet do as efficiently is the work of psychic introjection and digestion that mother's "alpha-function" provides.

Ultimately, however, it is this metabolic capability itself that will also be offered, taught, exemplified, and bequeathed by the mother (and internalized by the infant), such that the internal processing—of life and loss—might eventually become a proper ego capacity of the recipient, too. One might say that Bion is supplementing Kleinian thought by considering both projection and introjection, as well as their interactions, in the light of primary interpersonal relationships and in terms of his theory of container and contained. There is an excellent paper by Ignês Sodré (2004) in which she outlines in considerable clinical detail how the forms of projective and introjective identification must be seen as mutually implicating and inextricably intertwined, in both normal and pathological circumstances.

Bion lays the foundations for these ideas in *Learning from Experience* (1962)—with its strange and somewhat obsessional philosophical orderliness, featuring numbered paragraphs—where he is intent on devising a highly abstract, symbolic, notational, quasi-mathematical calculus for such processes. Terse and prolix by turns, Bion's style invites and is worthy of plenty of close attention, but I will content myself with looking at just two passages in which digestion is mentioned by name and dealt with explicitly.

In chapter 3, while attempting to distinguish between two fundamental concepts in his idiosyncratic terminology, Bion writes: "Beta-elements are stored but differ from alpha-elements in that they are not so much memories as undigested facts, whereas the alpha-elements have been digested by alpha-function and thus made available for thought." On the previous page he had already said that "beta-elements are not felt to be phenomena, but things in themselves" (1962, pp. 6–7).

Clearly, this is a perspective that recognizes a vital philosophical distinction between phenomena and noumena, as derived from Kant, or what Lacan might see as the difference between the symbolic and the real. It is also claiming, relatedly, that for material reality to be converted into psychic food-for-thought, a certain kind of internal processing is necessary.

Almost in passing, Bion brilliantly connects these ideas with some of the essentials of psychoanalysis, referring to how dreaming provides the vital sanity-preserving divide between waking and sleeping, and between conscious and unconscious experience, the absence of which is tantamount to madness:

> Freud showed that one of the functions of a dream is to preserve sleep. Failure of alpha-function means the patient cannot dream and therefore cannot sleep. As alpha-function makes the sense impressions of

the emotional experience available for conscious and dream-thought the patient who cannot dream cannot go to sleep and cannot wake up. Hence the peculiar condition seen clinically when the psychotic patient behaves as if he were in precisely this state. [p. 7]

Bion then refers us to a later moment in his book, when his "use of the terms 'digested' and 'undigested' will be investigated". This takes us to chapter 12, where, after a discussion of Klein's notion of projective identification, he specifies the necessity of also attending to equal-and-opposite processes: "But projective identification cannot exist without its reciprocal, namely an introjective activity intended to lead to an accumulation of good internal objects" (p. 32).

While one might question whether it is such an "accumulation" that is its aim, I completely support and concur with Bion's balancing mention of introjection here. He goes on to outline, perhaps in needlessly explicit detail, the analogical parallels between the physical supplying of milk to the infant and the supplying of the simultaneous and no less necessary "sensations of security, warmth, well-being, love" to its psyche:

Thus we may say that milk is a material substance and is related to alimentation and is presumably dealt with by the digestive tract. Love on the other hand we may regard as immaterial though comparable with milk for the mental welfare of the child. [p. 33]

Bion also provides an endnote, one sentence from which is worth citing: "The term 'welfare' itself suggests that mental development like physical development depends on the efficient working of a mental alimentary system" (pp. 101–102).

Given how clear, explicit, and even pedantic Bion is about these matters, perhaps I am spared having to elaborate on why this sentence sates my own conceptual appetite so thoroughly. What does merit a mention, however, is the fact that Bion—similarly to Ferenczi when he introduced introjection—is not exploring this theory of mental digestion in the context of loss, mourning, or melancholia, but describing the operations of the mind at large, in an early object-relational context. In the next paragraph, he puts this succinctly and pragmatically as follows: "It may be useful to suppose that there exists in reality a psycho-somatic breast and an infantile psycho-somatic alimentary canal corresponding to the breast" (p. 34).

While discussing good and bad breasts (both actual and metaphorical or psychic) and the limitations of the baby's capacities to comprehend, receive, or take in, he makes the connection to his famous notion of maternal "reverie" in a complex sentence that really turns up the volume on these parallel processes:

> We may deduce from reverie, as the psychological source of supply of the infant's needs for love and understanding, what kind of psychological receptor organ is required if the infant is to be able to profit from reverie as it is able, thanks to the digestive capacities of the alimentary canal, to profit from the breast and the milk it supplies. [p. 36]

Bion then asks: "what are the *factors* of this function that relate directly to the mother's capacity for reverie?" As he understands full well, unless mother brings a certain quality of receptivity, care, love, and attention as an accompaniment to a physical feed, the infant's psychic meal will be lacking in substance and sustenance.

Of course, some mothers have more and others less of a capacity for reverie and alpha-function, and certain babies can assimilate what they are offered, or tolerate frustration, better than their peers; the relational results of their pairings will always vary accordingly. Though loss or deprivation are clearly not Bion's primary themes, we infer that psychically dissatisfied babies, children, and adults will be prone to depression, a familiar symptom of which is a fixation on concrete, bodily alimentation: that is, they may end up either eating voraciously and insatiably or starving themselves—and, in either case, failing to thrive.

I will cite just one more sentence from this Bion chapter—the penultimate one, in fact—where, in the wake of his deliberations, he states that "We have thus approached a mental life unmapped by the theories elaborated for the understanding of neurosis" (p. 37). Concise though it is, this statement says a great deal. Bion does not pursue its implications any further, but by doing so briefly, perhaps I can bring this chapter to an appropriate close.

The sentence might belong comfortably enough in the manifesto of any object-relational movement wishing to plant its psychoanalytic flag either alongside or in the place of the banner of drive theory. I choose, however, to also read it as a nuanced allusion to the importance within psychoanalysis of mourning and the internal world. The significance of the sexual life of human beings, with all its physical and mental vicissitudes and discontents, was established early on in our psychoanalytic history by Freud's original concerns with neurotic illness. Without jettisoning its close connection with sexuality, the shift to alimentary matters and the concomitant focus on maladies of loss and separation—both during Freud's own development and thereafter via the efforts of other theorists in the annals of our discipline—represents something different. It is a venture into new territory that necessitates, as Bion suggests, a new map. I hope that my endeavours here will be appreciated as an attempt to lay out both the history and the geography of this venture.

Having tried to give an account of the British Kleinian perspective in this chapter, I now continue the narrative and extend the scope of this close-reading project by crossing an ocean and turning my attention to a North American approach to these matters, that of Hans Loewald.

CHAPTER FIVE

Hans Loewald: turning ghosts into ancestors—internalization and emancipation

If one is to venture into the intricacies of Hans Loewald's psychoanalytic thought, it is perhaps apt to begin with a passage from the paper for which he is best known, "On the Therapeutic Action of Psycho-Analysis" (1960). Well into that paper, Loewald is deeply engaged in what is, for him, a familiarly intense dialogue with Freud—this time about no less a subject than transference—in the sober intellectual and even technical language he habitually employs for the purpose. Suddenly, however, he breaks off to embark upon a rather unusual foray into the realms of epic poetry and the supernatural.

Drawing on Freud's reference, in *The Interpretation of Dreams*, to a line from the *Odyssey* in which ghosts are awakened to life by the tasting of blood, Loewald makes a declaration of his own view of the workings of transference:

> The transference neurosis, in the technical sense of the establishment and resolution of it in the analytic process, is due to the blood of recognition, which the patient's unconscious is given to taste so that the old ghosts may reawaken to life. Those who know ghosts tell us that they long to be released from their ghost life and led to rest as ancestors. As ancestors they live forth in the present generation, while as ghosts they are compelled to haunt the present generation with their shadow life. Transference is pathological insofar as the unconscious is a crowd of ghosts, and this is the beginning of the transference neurosis in

DOI: 10.4324/9781003266631-6

analysis: ghosts of the unconscious, imprisoned by defences but haunting the patient in the dark of his defences and symptoms, are allowed to taste blood, are let loose. In the daylight of analysis the ghosts of the unconscious are laid and led to rest as ancestors whose power is taken over and transformed into the newer intensity of present life, of the secondary process and contemporary objects. [1960, pp. 248–249]

As Loewald's paragraph winds down, returning from the underworld of figurative language to the more reassuringly familiar formal terminology of psychoanalysis by its end, one has the sense that he might almost have alarmed himself with this extraordinary analogy and needs to recover his saner, more familiar textual style as soon as possible.

I am by no means the first to marvel at this passage: indeed, some very eminent American analytical scholars—including Stephen Mitchell (Mitchell & Black, 1995, Epigraph and p. 191) and Jonathan Lear (2003, pp. 205–206)—have given special attention to it. Loewald's ghosts provide a resonant, stark, and slightly alarming metaphor that—perhaps like all particularly effective figurative language—seems to accomplish so much more than a "mere" metaphor or analogy usually can. Its suggestion is that psychoanalysis, and the transference it engenders, is a mad, risky enterprise, which starts out with nothing less than the deliberate coaxing or luring of ghosts from their unconscious graves or lairs out into the open—that is, into the arena of the psychoanalytic setting—to be fed "the blood of recognition" (a phrase with biblical as well as Greek mythological resonances).

One might even imagine these ghouls riotously dancing and cavorting in that transitional analytic arena, much like the beastly creatures in Maurice Sendak's children's classic, *Where the Wild Things Are* (1963), mentioned in chapter four. We remember Max, who has been behaving so badly that his mother has sent him to his room with no supper. But he sails away in his mind to an island inhabited by dangerous, apparently frightening monsters. Far from being afraid, Max takes charge and rules over them while they all romp around wordlessly, in carnivalesque style, with Max leading the way, giving all the instructions. After finally subduing the creatures and wearing them (and himself) out, Max begins to feel lonely, to miss his own creature comforts, and—no doubt—his mother, too. So, he bids his importunate minions goodbye and sails home again, to a hot supper and a warm bed.

As in Sendak's book, Loewald's ghosts, these unruly emanations of the unconscious, may at first run amok, but they are eventually "laid and led to rest", tamed and brought to rule by some process of working-through.

They are thereby transformed into helpfully metabolized and contained ancestral aspects of the personality, "living forth" in the patient's internal world, as opposed to what they had been previously: haunting, thwarting, un-mourned, indigestible demi-presences. "Those who know ghosts" best—and only too well, we might say—are precisely those melancholic and depressed souls who wander among us, more permanently laden with their cargo of otherworldly internal objects, unable to either lay down their burden or lay themselves down to rest.

I will briefly introduce and contextualize Hans Loewald, who may still not be known as well as he deserves to be, at least outside American psychoanalysis. He was born in Germany and educated there and in Italy before fleeing Nazi Europe. Most of his fellow émigrés—not least the triumvirate of Heinz Hartmann, Ernst Kris, and Rudolph Loewenstein, pioneers of ego psychology, the dominant force in American psychoanalysis for several decades—were already psychiatrists as well as practising psychoanalysts before coming to America. Belonging to a slightly later generation, Loewald was more akin to the inventor of self-psychology, Heinz Kohut, insofar as both men were already psychiatrists when they arrived in the United States but trained as analysts in their adoptive country. As in the case of Kohut, this blend of European and American education allowed Loewald to produce and theorize a unique psychoanalytic perspective, maintaining a dialogue with, but not belonging to, the hegemonic ego-psychology framework.

Unlike all the abovementioned colleagues, Loewald did not go on to become the founder of a psychoanalytic school. Even within American circles, he seemed to prefer to work independently and to occupy a quieter, more liminal role. His career and theoretical contributions tended to remain firmly within the psychoanalytic fold, though he nevertheless managed to become one of the most important figures in post-war American psychoanalysis. With a background in philosophy—having studied, and then fallen out with, no less a figure than Martin Heidegger—he was able to produce an enormously flexible and synthetic understanding of psychoanalytic terms and concepts, repeatedly infusing these with—or drawing maieutically from them—subtle nuances of meaning, the import of which may still be awaiting fuller understanding and appreciation.

Despite the reverence accorded him by many American psychoanalysts, past and present, Loewald seems deserving of more recognition and close attention than he has received, certainly on this side of the Atlantic. His intense, complex, yet elegant and articulate writings still appear to hold the potential to mend theoretical rifts among the diverse, if unnecessarily rigid and competitive, schools of thought and practice within psychoanalysis.

Perhaps unlike his ego-psychology contemporaries, who focused their attention on developing and adapting the implications of Freud's later structural model along certain quite circumscribed lines, Loewald was interested in the whole of the founder's oeuvre and tried constantly to enhance and update his influence and relevance. But he also paid close attention to new developments in the psychoanalytic world of his own time, not least in the schools and schisms of the British object-relational scene.

There may nevertheless be some objections to my championing of Loewald's version of internal world dynamics, on the grounds that it appears to return psychoanalytic thinking to the "bad old days" of one-person psychology, and to risk foregoing the gains of the object-relations revolution. But this would be to read Loewald narrowly and superficially, as well as to miss the mark of what I am attempting in this book, which is to try to put theorizing about loss and mourning back on a firmer metapsychological footing. Few analysts would be better qualified to help with this task than Loewald, who troubled himself to submit the discoveries and claims of Freud and others to the kind of rigorous scrutiny befitting a genuine scholar of both philosophy and psychoanalytic theory.

In fact, many of Loewald's most significant insights are concerned with a kind of concomitance between intrapsychic and interpersonal shifts in the developments and regressions of the individual. For him, each new stage manifesting itself outwardly as a change in external object relations—indeed, every outward, intersubjective event—is reflected in and mutually affected by an internal or intra-subjective change in the structure of the self. He almost always bases his quietly radical revisions and subtle re-appropriations of classical theory on an adherence to Freud's own terminology.

Both in the paper on therapeutic action and in a book called *Psychoanalysis and the History of the Individual* (1978b), Loewald reminds us that transference, though apparently an object-relations term *par excellence*, has several meanings in Freud's texts, including an important intrapsychic one. He goes back to some of Freud's early uses of the term, where the internal movement of psychic energy through different levels in the mind is also referred to as transference. Loewald is emphasizing that there are internal crossings or transitions across the vertical divides between conscious, preconscious, and unconscious experience, as well as in the dynamic mental intercourse among id, ego, and superego. It is the relative ease with which these moves are made—and not just in one developmental direction but back and forth—that is for him the hallmark of real psychic freedom and, hence, health.

Elsewhere, Loewald (1978a) points out that language itself passes over or traverses the divide between primary- and secondary-process levels of organization and sophistication in the mind, thus passing from more literal or concrete to more abstract or figurative meanings and registers—and back again. This invaluable insight has helped to consolidate my own speculations about psychic digestion and metabolization, and the differences and similarities among the terms denoting internalization in the psychoanalytic lexicon—themes that Loewald has in fact tackled explicitly in the two papers I examine in detail here.

In these papers, Loewald can be seen to elaborate on the processes of internalization that bring about the most favourable psychic consequences for psychoanalytic patients and, indeed, for all of us. Though the necessities of actual mourning provide perhaps the best examples of how such processes either are accomplished or fail, what Loewald attempts is nothing less than a laying out or making explicit of how the human mind works, how a self comes to be constituted.

To my own mind, because loss seems so central to such efforts, there is the implication that our lives must be subject to a kind of *primary mourning*. But this phrase is no sooner on the page than one feels the urge to retract it, or to remove the word "primary" from it. After all, if the necessities of mourning are at the source of the human mind's self-constitution, then this is precisely because, paradoxically, such processes always and necessarily take place after, or come in the wake of, loss. To this extent, it is difficult to see them as primary. Perhaps it is simpler to say that all human progress is predicated upon loss and that loss is our lot from (almost) the very beginning. And, as I have often said in this book, none of this is new in psychoanalytic thinking; we have known this all along. But let us now see what Loewald has to say on such matters.

"Internalization, Separation, Mourning, and the Superego" (1962)

This paper, with its title listing four important psychoanalytic concepts, is presented in very orderly fashion. It consists of three numbered parts, with a three-paragraph introduction and a slightly longer concluding summary. The first paragraph—which requires no explicating here—reads like an abstract of the paper in which Loewald specifies and lays out his plans and intentions with exceptional clarity.

In the second paragraph, there is a timely reminder that in Part 3 of *The Ego and the Id*, where the superego is named and introduced, Freud seems to suggest that this superego is not the first or only psychic entity to be constituted by internalizing processes. In the first place, as it were, and before the superego is formed by the relinquishing of oedipal objects and the acquiring of moral agency by identification with them, the ego itself is structured in analogous ways. Or, as Loewald puts it, "Introjections and identifications preceding the oedipal phase and preparing the way for its development go into the formation of the ego proper" (1962, p. 257).

In my own perusal of these very pages of Freud's text, I have noted that he is far from clear on these matters. Indeed, the provenance of the ego itself is, perhaps unsurprisingly, a puzzling topic in psychoanalysis at large. Is it to be posited as present and taken for granted from the start (dispensing with the need to explain how it arises), as Klein seems to prefer, or must one try to account for its advent, as Loewald appears to do here, via early processes of internalization and identification?

According to Freud's account, there are early or primary identifications that are not the result of object loss. We have encountered these claims before, but it is perhaps still difficult to know exactly what they mean. As I suggested above, there may be something incoherent about the idea of primary mourning and therefore also of a primary identification with objects that have yet to be lost. And yet, the implicit conviction that there can be no individual internal development—whether of ego or superego—without the accompanying fact of loss in human existence remains compelling, not least because of the very paradoxes surrounding these issues.

Returning to the text, one admires how careful Loewald is with such distinctions, as if he really wants to draw out the subtleties in Freud's rather pithy and confusing account of these early, almost pre-historic moments of self-constitution. He says that while the "origins of the superego are to be found also . . . in those early identifications", it is not until there is "a relinquishment of oedipal objects . . . as external objects, even as fantasy objects" that such objects become germane or pertinent to the formation of the superego. The requisite conditions seem to be that they must already have been "set up in the ego by which process they become internal objects cathected by the id". This is called a "narcissistic cathexis" involving "a process of desexualization in which an internal relationship is substituted for an external one" (pp. 257–258).

The upshot here is that the substitutive internal relationship that Loewald is talking about is the inter-agency relationship between id and ego, although the latter is always being modified by internalization and identification. These complex internal relations will later also include and involve the superego, once the latter has differentiated out from the ego and become its own internal entity, via processes that Loewald is explicating here. What we do not find here or elsewhere in Loewald is the solidifying or hypostasizing of the internal version of the object or an account of a direct relationship between the ego and an internal (or "fantasy") object that represents or stands in the place of the external object.

To translate this into my own terminology (to which Loewald has of course made a major contribution), the so-called internal object is always already being metabolized and converted into the substance of the ego. Thus, we are already seeing the extent to which Loewald's internal world is both an elaboration of Freud's and a quite different one from Klein's.

Perhaps noting their complexity and wanting to be sure that he is being clear enough, Loewald seems to want to recap these ideas in the third and last paragraph of his introduction (though Loewald seldom recaps anything without adding another nuance or wrinkle of meaning). He speaks of "two types or stages of identification: those that precede, and are the basis for, object cathexes and those that are the outcome of object cathexes formed in the oedipal phase". While the latter are what make up the superego, the former are its "forerunners" or "origins" but are also, "considered in themselves, constituent elements of the ego proper". Loewald then adds something extra, telling us that the early ego-forming identifications occur at a time "when inside and outside—ego and objects—are not clearly differentiated". The later superego-forming identifications, by contrast, happen in relation to objects that have *already* separated out and are therefore capable of cathecting and being cathected, both libidinally and aggressively; here, identification presupposes or is contingent upon the giving up or "relinquishment" of such objects (p. 258).

As I argued in previous chapters, these ideas or protocols are crucial both in the context of the development of the ego and as far as loss and mourning are concerned. There are positions or questions at stake here that are philosophically foundational for psychoanalysis and can therefore create fierce intra-analytic rifts and disputes: do we consider the ego an entity that requires building up or constructing, or is it somehow there, at least minimally, from the start? And if it can be made (and modified) in the manner suggested by Loewald, precisely what manner of building block is primary identification if it does not require a loss or separation to bring it about?

His explanatory caveat might simplify this matter somewhat: if at first there is no separation (yet) between self and other, then there can also be no difference (yet) between relating to and identifying with an object. However, we know that there is at least one psychoanalytic approach that is not amenable to the implicit notion of some initial subject/environment merger—or baby/mother mix-up—out of which discrete identity must emerge. To put it bluntly, while Winnicottians may like this idea, Kleinians certainly do not. But perhaps we must now proceed to the body of Loewald's text, to put more flesh on these rather abstract bones.

In Part I of the paper, Loewald advances directly into the realm of mourning and speaks mainly about how loss is dealt with in the specific and "artificial" context of psychoanalytic endings. He says that "the end phase of an analysis may be described as a long-drawn-out leave taking—too long, it often seems, from the point of view of ordinary life". In daily life, he thinks, we tend to say our goodbyes more quickly, perhaps to spare ourselves "the embarrassment, the ambiguity, and pain" of finding ourselves "torn between the grief of separation and the eager anticipation of the future awaiting us" (p. 258).

Perhaps these sentiments, especially the last part of this sentence, already give us a foretaste of a certain attitude towards loss that we might rather lazily or reductively want to label as "American". We shall become more acquainted with a central idea in Loewald's work—namely, that losses are also for "moving on" from, that they can be considered in terms of what good may come of them, that they can be utilized for the improvement of our independent futures. I am reminded of the Western movie musical *Paint Your Wagon* and Lee Marvin's tuneless refrain, "I was born under a wandrin' star": one of the song's verses ironically captures one American way of dealing with transience and loss in the picaresque claim that while home is ostensibly a beloved original place to which one longs to return, there is a secret hope that one will never get there!

We need, of course, to guard against stereotypes and generalizations. Nevertheless, what we are about to rediscover is a certain forward-looking, meliorating attitude with which British and European analysts may find themselves less familiar and perhaps at odds. One may even say that Loewald is hereby reviving and taking more seriously Freud's puzzled question about why we do not get over our losses more swiftly or treat them more hedonistically, according to the dictates of the pleasure principle.

Following Freud, Loewald acknowledges that some people do rather prolong their farewells, but he puts a fine point upon the fact that it is not the farewell itself but the continued presence of the loved object that they are trying to extend. In any case, he says, "an attempt is made to deny loss": the denial may be directed either at the emotional relevance of the loved person, or at the necessity of having to take leave of them and "venture out on our own". This, says Loewald, is tantamount to denying either the past or the future. Sounding quite matter of fact, he then claims that, notwithstanding such stalling ploys, "In true mourning, the loss of the beloved person is perhaps temporarily denied but gradually is accepted and worked out by way of a complex inner process" (pp. 258–259).

As we have begun to suspect, however, the notion of "true mourning" may be nothing more than a convenient fiction, and the very existence of psychoanalysis may testify to this. The way analysis works, Loewald now suggests, is that it encourages, fosters, and enacts an exaggerated version of these procedures under its aegis or on its dramatic stage. An important difference "is that experiences purposefully and often painfully made explicit in analysis usually remain implicit in ordinary life". In the heightened atmosphere or "hypercathected mode" of the transference, endings are prolonged and thus worked through thoroughly, as if with the intention of re-training the patient in matters of mourning.

In keeping with Freud's formulations in "Mourning and Melancholia", where the painstaking and time-consuming nature of mourning is emphasized, patients—especially those beset by melancholia or depression—might need reminding, to be shown how to do this again. In a well-conducted analytic ending, "neither the existence of the person from whom we part nor the anticipated life without him can be denied". Whether we like it or not, in this more "explicit experience of parting, the person from whom we take leave is becoming part of the past, and at the same time we move into the future, which is to be without him" (p. 259).

Loewald then explains how the analyst's representative roles, his "having stood at times for mother, father, and other loved and hated figures", have the catalytic effect of temporarily drawing these figures out of from within the subject's inner structure, and thus these "internal relationships . . . have become partially external again during analysis". The word "partially" is crucial here and might allow us to appreciate the differences in tone or nuance between this perspective and what we saw Klein, in chapter four, to be saying. This word is repeated when Loewald goes on to elaborate, as follows:

> The internalizations by which the patient's character structure became established in earlier years have been partially undone in the analytic process and have been replaced by relationships with an external object—the analyst standing for various objects at different times. In other words, internalizations have been to a degree reversed; internal relationships constituting elements of the ego structure have been re-externalized. [pp. 259–260]

If we compare this with the rather dire and drastic sense created by Klein around what happens to earlier internal objects when new losses occur,

Loewald's view seems to posit or assume that a rather more securely established internalization of these original objects was at least possible and may have occurred in the first place.

Though Loewald acknowledges, along with Klein, that later instances of mourning will unsettle internal affairs within the ego to some extent, he appears to welcome this consequence and expresses no anxiety about it. The difference seems to turn on the question of just how much stability has already been achieved in the internal world and, therefore, how much destabilizing it is prone to. Insofar as Loewald sees these as relative or partial processes that need only occur "to a degree", they do not necessarily cause upheaval or crisis, but can stir things up in a limited and useable way, in the service of a better outcome (especially, of course, when this happens within the controlled environment of an analysis). Again, one wonders whether Loewald's thinking is enabled by operating within a more optimistic cultural context that encourages and allows him to proffer a best-case scenario. This is not to say that worse or worst cases are not possible or even likely at times.

When Loewald says that psychoanalysis creates the conditions—indeed, the opportunity—for such re-externalizations, this is surely a more considered, or less dramatic, way of talking about how the "ghosts of the unconscious . . . are allowed to taste blood" by being set free in the transference. As that passage suggested, the final aim of the procedure is a more thoroughgoing and properly achieved re-internalization, as befits a successful mourning process, whereby the rabidly disturbing ghosts are finally "led to rest as ancestors".

In the present paper, Loewald says that the analyst, too, like all the earlier objects, must eventually be lost and internalized, a process that is enhanced by the exaggerated emphasis on the ending of the analysis—and, we might add, by the interpreting of weekend and holiday breaks and other gaps during the treatment. As the end approaches, "The pressure of the impending separation helps to accelerate this renewed internalization although the process of internalization will continue and come to relative completion only after termination of the analysis" (p. 260).

Beginning with a perhaps deceptively simple formula or declaration, Loewald now turns his attention to how these phenomena feature in life at large: "The death of a love object, or the more or less permanent separation from a love object, is the occasion for mourning and for internalization." He then adds that it is the threat or awareness of one's personal demise or mortality that will both affect and effect this human tendency to internalize.

There is a tantalizingly brief aside at this point in the essay when Christianity is described as "initiating the greatest intensification of internalization in Western civilization". Christ is seen as "the ultimate love object, which the believer loses as an external object and regains by identification with Him as an ego ideal" (p. 260). Loewald's way of using of the latter Freudian term—one that fell into relative disuse after the superego became established as the term of choice—suggests that one might see the ego ideal as positioned transitionally somewhere between the ego and the superego, as a concept that allows traffic across what can sometimes seem an unbridgeable divide. In Loewald's short excursus, Christ becomes the great exemplar of a fully accomplished psychic internalization, identification, and sublimation. He is the lost object *par excellence* who can be thoroughly communed with by being taken in and metabolized, body and soul, assimilated as a psychic possession by his Christian mourners, and absorbed into their structures, systems, and very being.

Loewald resumes his more matter-of-fact manner in the next paragraph by reminding us that loss does not always result in mourning and internalization, suggesting once again that "either the existence or the loss of the object may be denied" and that this constitutes "the opposite of mourning". He tells us that "external substitutions may be sought" instead and proceeds to provide a few brief clinical vignettes (which tend to be rare in his writings) of how these attempted solutions reveal the presence of deep melancholia or depression. They allow him to describe in these patients the absence of "firmly established internalizations" and the consequences of such failures of mourning: newer relationships cannot be formed; sublimation and a productive working life cannot be achieved; a stable superego is not properly secured.

In one of these examples, Loewald speaks of a man who had denied the earlier death of his brother and thus clung to his son with "all the force of this never-relinquished attachment". The son, unsurprisingly, "had great difficulty *emancipating* himself from his father because of the guilt involved in severing this tie" (p. 261, emphasis added). I highlight the word "emancipating" here because, as we shall see, it will become something of a touchstone term for Loewald, who regards the achievement of psychic freedom as a major developmental and analytic aim.

Now he can return to making a clear statement about the parallels between a successful mourning process and the resolution of the analytic transference neurosis, of how the latter might enhance the former. Though, of course, the analyst is offered to the patient as a substitute object, the eventual "goal" of the treatment "is to resolve the transference neurosis". Loewald also links this to the resolution of—or failure to resolve—the Oedipus complex. In negotiations of all three "intimately related" situations (the Oedipus complex, mourning, and the transference neurosis), success must be measured in terms of internal consequences.

What issues from Loewald's faithfulness to Freud—as well as his partial leaning towards ego psychology—is an account of internalization as restructuring, "by which relationships with external objects are set up in the ego system as internal relationships in a process of further ego differentiation"; what is achieved thereby is further separation, self-definition, and emancipation. The "incestuous love object"—whether the original parental figure or its analytical substitute—needs finally to be relinquished and the external relationship transformed "into an internal relationship within the ego-superego system" (p.262).

This is entirely unlike Klein's account of such processes, where success in the depressive position and in mourning is determined by the (re-)establishing of good "representative" internal objects in the mind. Though she is not mentioned here by name, she might well have been in Loewald's thoughts when, in this section's final sentence, he insists on a "sharp distinction . . . between a relationship to fantasy objects and an internal relationship that is constituent of ego structure" (p. 262).

For Klein, what happens to the actual lost object—its fate, as it were—is to be transported to the inside and transmuted into an internal (and hopefully good) object. It then needs to be watched over and appeased lest it be antagonized and retaliate, maintained as a substantial, live presence lest it be damaged, destroyed, or lost (again, as it were). For Loewald, the mourning and internalization of the lost object will allow it to dissipate, dissolve, or fade—to be absorbed, digested, and metabolized—with the passage of time.

Wallace Stevens, "Sunday Morning"

I want to consider these differences via a detour through the work of the American poet Wallace Stevens, who, over the course of his career, was quite preoccupied with the persona of the mother in his poetry. I look at two poems by Stevens, composed more than three decades apart: both are long poems, with multiple stanzas or cantos, a form for which Stevens is renowned.

The first, called "Sunday Morning", dates from 1915, when Stevens, albeit no longer that young a man, was still inexperienced in poetic terms: the poem is from his first collection, *Harmonium*. (Stevens, it might be mentioned, had an exacting day job as an insurance executive;

extraordinarily, he wrote his poetry on the side and in secret.) Insofar as the poem can be said to have a narrative, it concerns a young woman relaxing—in very secular fashion—on a Sunday morning. As things unfold, however, she will also use the occasion to think about her relationships with faith, mortality, and the afterlife. We are not made aware of her historical church-going affiliations or beliefs; she is happy enough with her present-day worldly pleasures and they appear, at first, to forestall any lingering, guilt-inducing religious sentiments. When she dozes off and dreams, however, something disturbing intrudes into her sun-filled, secular scene; she feels the shadowy "Encroachment of that old catastrophe" (Stevens, 1915, p. 67).

There are, in fact, two voices in the poem, the second belonging to the poet himself—or, rather, to a narrator of sorts—who conducts an intra-poetic dialogue with the female persona. Both the woman's own attitudes and the entire poem seem to vacillate on the question of whether the world as we know it might suffice, or whether some belief in a life after death is necessary. In beautiful lines in the second stanza, she appears to embrace the sequential immanence and impermanence of human feelings, including those of loss and mourning:

> Passions of rain, or moods in falling snow;
> Grievings in loneliness, or unsubdued
> Elations when the forest blooms; gusty
> Emotions on wet roads on autumn nights.
> [p. 67]

But, after the back-and-forth of further debate, the fifth stanza begins rather differently, with her saying that, though she is pleased enough with her secularity, there is still a nagging need for something more durable and less subject to decay.

And it is here, in response to these sentiments, that the voice of the narrator seems to boom forth and declare:

> Death is the mother of beauty; hence from her,
> Alone, shall come fulfilment to our dreams
> And our desires.
> [pp. 68–69]

As will become clear later, in the Conclusion, when I look at Freud's literary essay, "On Transience", the idea of death as the mother of beauty resonates powerfully with *his* attitudes towards loss and mourning. On the one hand, the whole of Stevens's above-quoted sentence seems to suggest that death is a terminus and that nothing more awaits us at the end of the journey. On the other hand, however, because of its maternal guise here, death can be conceived of as the welcoming embrace of a long-lost but re-found object and, to that extent, as the culmination or apotheosis of all that we might ever have wanted. The other meaning inherent in these lines—very much in keeping with Freud's view in "On Transience"—is that without mortality, the taste or tinge of temporality and temporariness that it lends to everything we are and do, no creative urge or appreciation of beauty would be either necessary or possible.

If, as we are told, this mother-who-is-death represents and points the way to oblivion and finality, then she also stokes or provokes appetite and romance, enabling the entire gamut of our emotions and passions. In the following stanza, sounding a bit like Keats in "Ode on a Grecian Urn" (1819, p. 134), Stevens pokes fun at the idea of heaven as a changeless universe that resembles ours but is static, frozen in time, and therefore not only soulless but pointless. The stanza concludes with a verbatim repetition of his earlier metaphor, adding further explications of its meaning:

> Death is the mother of beauty, mystical,
> Within whose burning bosom we devise
> Our earthly mothers waiting, sleeplessly.
> [p. 69]

Again, though death is the only end, we might imagine or devise it as an anxiously anticipating, faithful mother who will not betake herself to bed until her child, her charge, is home safe. Why she is mystical and why her bosom burns (with love? with anxiety?) are perhaps less clear, but there is something very substantial about this mother and this conception of death: she waits and abides as an actual, immanent mother might.

Freud again comes to mind: concluding his essay on "The Theme of the Three Caskets" (1913f), he proposes a similar idea, as follows: "of the three inevitable relations that a man has with a woman—the woman who bears him, the woman who is his mate and the woman who destroys him"—it is this latter, final "Mother Earth who receives him once more"; resembling the original, earthly mother and repeating her embrace, it is "the silent Goddess of Death, that will take him into her arms" (1913f, p. 301).

After all the debating and soul-searching, both "Sunday Morning" and its protagonist seem to throw in their lot with the natural and secular world. The final stanza resolves and reiterates that, for better or worse, we live under the illumination of a natural sun, not the personified gaze of a supernatural god, and are thus dependent on the successions of daily, seasonal, and mortal change. But, as such, we live liberated, unshackled lives: we are free, that is, from both the transcendental consolations and the superegoic duties of religion. The poem draws to a close with another simple, beautiful description of ordinary but sustaining scenes from American landscapes. It then culminates with a magnificent final image, which seems to suggest a way of claiming a modicum of choice, control, and compromise in the face of mortality:

> And, in the isolation of the sky,
> At evening, casual flocks of pigeons
> Make ambiguous undulations as they sink,
> Downward to darkness, on extended wings.
> [p. 70]

Like these birds at dusk, we might opt to drift and descend willingly into death, relatively reconciled, and in our own fashion.

Wallace Stevens, "The Auroras of Autumn"

Stevens' later poem, "The Auroras of Autumn", was written in 1947, when he was in his late sixties, eight years before he died. It can be read as a long meditation—using the sinuous, shifting, multi-faceted Northern Lights as an extended, meaning-changing trope or objective correlative—on the approach of death. It is longer and far more complex than "Sunday Morning", comprising 12 cantos, each made up of eight three-line stanzas. I will make no attempt to account for the trajectory of the whole poem but will concentrate particularly on one canto (III), where the mother again appears—and disappears.

This happens in the second of three consecutive cantos, each beginning with an identical phrase ("Farewell to an idea...") denoting a scenic and conceptual ending or goodbye. The first of these recalls many other Stevensian moments: there is a solipsistic setting, an isolated cabin on a deserted beach, where a man—a self—stands alone and faces his fate, this time in the form of the spectral, spectacular aurora borealis in all its myriad shades and motions. The third canto addresses the father, portrayed as a complex, ambiguously composite figure—part powerful god (Jehovah or Jove), part manic prankster, part controlling theatre director or movie mogul, part buffoon: the poet seems caught between admiration and contempt, not quite knowing how to accommodate him.

However, it is the second, middle farewell that concerns us here, the one featuring the mother. There have been other, interim mothers in Stevens's poetry, but I would suggest that this constitutes the return of the mother of "Sunday Morning"—her reincarnation, one might say, were that not to suggest a very concrete, meaty mother, who she precisely is not. Perhaps it is rather late in the day and redundant to point out how psychologically attuned Stevens's poetry is, but when he says that

> The mother's face,
> The purpose of the poem, fills the room.
> [Stevens, 1947, p. 413]

one (again) hears many psychoanalytic echoes and is struck by this poet's almost matter-of-fact acceptance of the truths of sublimation!

What follows is the very quintessence of lyricism where, as in the earlier poem, Stevens describes and conveys a deeply comforting sense of returning to a physically and psychically well-heated home and being reunited with a maternal presence who has been waiting for you all along. The eager expectancy of dreams, we are told, with their wish-fulfilling orientation, are no longer required, because everything that one has ever desired is now here, present.

And yet, what is the nature of this presence or possession or provision—what has it become? There is a setting, a house, but it is not solid; it is only demi-present, its atmosphere vague or flimsy, as if it is undergoing a gradual fading, a ceding of substance. Though unquestionably *there*, the mother herself is also on the way to dissolution, *en route* to a different state of existence; we are told (twice) that she now offers something trans*parent*, perhaps denoting that it is obvious, see-through—perhaps no longer enigmatic or mysterious—while also suggesting a kind of crossing over, perhaps from one manner of *parent*ing or mothering to another. Her main gifts, we discover, are now abstract qualities, like peace and gentleness; interestingly, however, and again with psychological astuteness, Stevens tells us that her wish to render these qualities may be limited and constrained by the child's inherent capacity to have them, take them in, embrace and embody them.

There is a series of indications about the mother's own ontological status or state of being:

> And yet she too is dissolved, she is destroyed.
> She gives transparence. But she has grown old.
> The necklace is a carving not a kiss.
> The soft hands are a motion not a touch.
> [p. 413]

Though there is a suggestion here that ageing includes a kind of ossifying, atrophying, petrifying process, the primary direction seems to be towards a kind of gradual—and, indeed, gentle—disappearance (perhaps like that of the Cheshire cat in *Alice in Wonderland*). It is as if the mother herself is slowly becoming an abstract entity; or, in the words of Loewald, turning into an internalized ancestor rather than remaining, paradoxically, an all-too-solid ghost or zombie (an incorporated internal object); or, in my parlance, as if she is being steadily digested and metabolized.

It has perhaps taken more than half a lifetime for this slow metabolizing of the mother to take place. Stevens's actual mother is long gone, but at this late moment in his psychic and literary existence, a few short years away from his own demise, he can now conceive of her in such terms. As is evident, however, this does not mean that death is all—or always—about a gentle, gradual, sublime, ethereal descent: some of the canto's later imagery has an ominous, matter-of-fact brutality about it, as if the poet is not fool enough to think that human violence (and the death instinct) is completely absent.

Written, as it was, just two years after the end of the Second World War, possibilities like crumbling houses, burning books, and threats of rifle-wielding thuggery—and therefore deaths of a traumatically overwhelming kind—can scarcely be, and are not, ignored in this poem. Still, the emphasis here is on protection, tenderness, and unity:

> They are at ease in the shelter of the mind
> And the house is of the mind and they and time,
> Together, all together . . .
> [p. 413]

The image of the auroras casting their frosty light over proceedings, from without and on high, reinforces the primary atmosphere of the canto: the idea of death as a falling asleep, saying good night, or—to cite the title of another Stevens poem—"Waving Adieu, Adieu, Adieu".

This mother makes one final appearance, in a later canto of the poem. Stevens asserts there—echoing the sentiments of "Sunday Morning"—that the remarkable auroras are not to be taken as a religious or supernatural symbol. Indeed, sounding virtually Kleinian, he seems to suggest that like (or as) the mother, these lights are real, true, and good; no less so for being abstract, intangible, unspecific, almost impersonal—or what might even be called *internal*—objects.

Though the paradoxes proliferate here, Stevens has conjured for us, and we clearly discern, a benign but ethereal mother of both light and sound—though she is not thereby an unreal, mystical, or phantasmatic one. Translated into alternative psychoanalytic language, she might be seen as the environment mother; her ambient and containing music flows sensuously into us, to be translated and digested by the mind, creating not just ego and superego, but the very categories of psychic existence:

> As if, awake, we lay in the quiet of sleep,
> As if the innocent mother sang in the dark
> Of the room and on an accordion, half-heard,
> Created the time and place in which we breathed . . .
> [pp. 418–419]

* * *

Having bathed in this mother's dissolving song, we return to Loewald just as he begins the second part of his paper, where he gets down to a close consideration of the vicissitudes and cognates of "internalization". This term, he says, "covers" several other psychoanalytic concepts denoting "certain processes of transformation by which relationships and interactions between the individual psychic apparatus and its environment are changed into inner relationships and interactions within the psychic apparatus". And here Loewald specifies, among others, "such 'mechanisms' as incorporation, introjection, and identification or those referred to by the terms 'internal object' and 'internalized object'", hinting at the considerable confusion inherent in the similarities and differences among them.

His concise working definitions of some of these terms are clarifying and useful: "The word 'incorporation' most often seems to emphasize zonal, particularly oral, aspects of internalization processes. 'Introjection' ordinarily is used for ego aspects of the same processes." As I have suggested in earlier chapters, this distinction—though not always noticed or made because it is subtle and far from absolute—is crucial to the differences between less and more successful methods of dealing internally with loss: the more concretely incorporative or "zonal" (to use Loewald's word) the process, the less psychically effective it is. When he turns his attention to identification, Loewald rightly says that it "probably is the term that is the most ambiguous": here, "internalization per se is only one element" in its workings, not least because—as Klein and her followers have drawn to our attention—"projection plays an important part in them" (pp. 262–263).

Accounting, as he now tries to do, for the terms in his title, Loewald states that "the significance of separation has been of concern to psychoanalysis since its beginnings, and in many different contexts and ramifications". He goes on to give an impressively long, though not exhaustive, list of relevantly related concepts, ranging from "separation anxiety, castration fear, loss of the love object", through "mourning, depression, ego boundaries", to "superego origins, oral aggression, frustration, and others beside". He then provides a clear statement of how we try to cope with this ubiquitous existential problem:

> If one asks how human beings deal with the anxieties and frustrations of separation and loss, the answer may be: either by external action designed to reduce or abolish the sense of separation or loss, or by an internal process meant to achieve the same end.

For Loewald, however, separations and losses are not only to be bemoaned or regretted; there are also psychic gains to be made from such experiences.

While Klein and her followers would surely number such achievements as making reparation, rebuilding the internal world, and enhancing symbolic functioning among the psychic advantages that arrive in the wake of loss and separation, Loewald is also thinking about gains of a more immediate kind. As he writes: "separation may be experienced not as deprivation and loss but as liberation and a sign of mastery". One also seeks "emancipation" from the "love–hate object", something that may or may not be facilitated or abetted by the objects themselves. Paradoxically, failure to (be helped to) separate may itself "be experienced as deprivation". As we know, parents or analysts who provide too much or go on providing for too long, who fear to frustrate their charges, to deal with negative emotions, or to end things in a timely way, can do more harm than good.

Speaking with exemplary wisdom, Loewald outlines the possible alternatives in such scenarios:

> However, it seems that emancipation as a process of separation from external objects—to be distinguished from rebellion, which maintains the external relationship—goes hand in hand with the work of internalization, which reduces or abolishes the sense of external deprivation and loss. Whether separation from a love object is experienced as deprivation and loss or as emancipation and mastery will depend, in part, on the achievement of the work of internalization. [p. 263]

Perhaps it is in his advocacy of such values as emancipation and individuation that this European-born psychoanalyst celebrates the mores of his adoptive home in the United States, and, to this extent at least, he resembles many of his fellow refugee and émigré analysts who, between them, primarily under the aegis of ego psychology, redrafted the psychoanalytic constitution of the United States in the post-war era. Consequently, though such American psychoanalytic products as ego psychology, self-psychology, intersubjectivity, relational analysis, as well as Loewald's less-easily definable approach, may differ widely from one another, all appear to share a respect for personal psychic freedom and to advocate the ethos and eventual aim of emancipation for—and from—the analytic relationship.

Turning for a moment to "A Rose for Emily"—a very American tale, after all, albeit one set in the particularly retrograde environment of the post-Civil-War South—we see that Emily's actual relationship with her father during his lifetime, and how she later internalizes it in an all-too concrete manner after his death, scuppers her chances of achieving psychic freedom. On the one hand, Loewald warns, when there is "aggression and overwhelming intrusion and invasion from the outside, the need for separation may become imperative". Equally, however, "under such circumstances the need for union may become imperative (identification with the aggressor); through such union aggression is removed by different means" (pp. 263–264). In effect, someone like Emily is trapped in an oscillation between these equally untenable positions.

Her behaviour after her father's death, the public flaunting of a relationship with the Northern day labourer Homer Barron that her bullwhip-wielding father would have forbidden in the most extreme and violent manner, indicates the extent to which she has longed for freedom from his oppressive, incestuous paternal yoke. Apart, perhaps, from becoming sexually intimate with a black man (and she is in fact very deeply involved with her black servant, the only other person who knows, quite literally, where the bodies are buried), one could not imagine this daughter choosing a less suitable suitor, given that no other man whatsoever was considered good enough for her while her father was alive.

On the other hand, as the townspeople-narrators of the story astutely tell us when they interpret her refusal to relinquish her father's body, "she had to cling to that which had robbed her, as people will" (Faulkner, 1930, p. 124). These twin, obverse, inseparable attitudes of both a violent casting away of the object and a desperate clinging to it are then expressed for a second time, when Emily effectively repeats the dynamic with her father but also takes more control of it: she first "removes" Barron, does away with him by killing him, but then manifests the appropriative, incorporative wish to be united with her lover/persecutor by keeping his body close, ensconced forever in her bed and in her deeply disturbed mind.

Loewald speaks of the exploration of "various modes of separation and union" and concludes from them that there are, in fact, no unambivalent human relations, if only because they are all rooted in this "polarity inherent in individual existence of individuation and 'primary narcissistic' union". He also regards this as the essential reason for Freud's insistence on dualistic, conflict-based models of human functioning. However, and perhaps paradoxically, Loewald thinks that this fundamental ambivalence between separateness and togetherness can also account for Heinz Hartmann's 1939 concept of the secondary autonomy of the ego, insofar as the latter can be seen as a positive, individuating, and emancipating consequence of the painful, anxious relinquishments of loss—what Loewald calls "a necessary evil . . . that is turned into a virtue" (p. 264).

Questioning and wishing to refine his own descriptions, Loewald spends the next few paragraphs in metapsychological consolidation of his ideas. Following Freud closely, he again refers to and distinguishes between the later, loss-based "oedipal identifications" that constitute the superego and earlier identifications that effectively belong to the realm of "primary narcissism". Along with "primary aggression", which is masochistic in nature, these initial states are then succeeded by "some process of externalization", because of which all subsequent secondary "reinternalization" will carry the mark of object cathexis, of having been "qualified and differentiated by externalization".

Having now encountered objects, these foundational human drives will never be the same again, so to speak, and this is what Freud means when he talks of the shadow of the object falling on the ego. As Loewald goes on to put it:

> Figuratively speaking, in the process of internalization the drives take aspects of the object with them into the ego. Neither drive nor object is the same as before, and the ego itself becomes further differentiated in the process. Internalization is structure building. [pp. 264–265]

The ego was, in other words, originally formed and continues to be constructed and characterized—to become, in a word, itself—by encountering the object world and internalizing those experiences.

Loewald continues to flesh out his earlier claims by taking us "one step further" in a philosophical or metapsychological conception of these phenomena, saying that

> we have to understand the stage of primary narcissism and primary aggression not as a stage where libido and aggression are still cathected in a primitive ego rather than in objects, but as a stage where inside and outside, an ego and an object world, are not yet distinguishable from one another. [p. 265]

To this extent, these early moments and movements are category- or boundary-creating and cannot yet be "sequentialized". It does not make sense, therefore, to ask whether internal precedes external (or vice versa) because these very differences—and categories of difference—are in the process of forming or coming into being. Moreover, only after the establishing or constituting of this more differentiated ontology does it also become possible to consider projection and introjection as defensive mechanisms or manoeuvres.

This perspective is, as we shall see, crucial to Loewald's view of what happens at later developmental moments, when the giving up and taking in of objects become familiar procedures and, indeed, inevitable mental requirements. He seems to consider psychic development as a kind of rhythmic oscillation between identification and individuation, at successively higher levels of self-organization. One can easily see in this a perspective similar to that of post-Kleinian analysts—who suggest that development happens in progressively spiralling alternations between paranoid-schizoid and depressive positions—albeit expressed in remarkably different terminology and tone:

> Ego, objects, and boundaries of and between them—at first non-existent, later still indistinct and fluid—gradually become more distinct and fixed, although by no means in an absolute or definitive fashion. Side by side with object relations, processes of identification persist and re-enter the picture in new transformations representing resumptions of boundary-setting, differentiating processes, notwithstanding their prominent aspects as defences against loss of love objects. [p. 266]

Linking these ideas to mourning—and to "the end phase of an analysis" as its "replica"—Loewald sees the secondary internalizations that follow and replace object cathexes as liberating the individual and building internal structure.

With a glance back at Freud's initial ideas about mourning, when his focus was perhaps mainly on the external task, Loewald reminds us that

> Mourning involves not only the gradual, piecemeal relinquishment of the lost object, but also the internalization, the appropriation of aspects of this object—or rather, of aspects of the relationship with the lost object which are 'set up in the ego' and become a relationship within the ego system. [p. 266]

He goes on to make specific reference to the "relinquishment of the oedipal objects that leads to the formation of the superego" (p. 266), where the significant difference from mourning is that—under the most propitious circumstances—the external objects are not lost as such but remain present and are active in assisting the child with internalizations and differentiations.

Speaking quite technically, Loewald then spells out what is required at this developmental moment: the parents must

> change their attitude; they promote a partial detachment, a decathexis of libidinal-aggressive drives from themselves as external objects so that an amount of such drive energy is freed for narcissistic recathexis. Moreover, some drive energy becomes available for eventual recathexis in non-incestuous external relationships: parents promote emancipation. [p. 267]

Akin in its pithily conclusive tone to the earlier "Internalization is structure building", the nicely alliterative last phrase—"parents promote emancipation"—captures the essence of this rather difficult role.

I can never read this description—or injunction—without thinking that it is far more easily said than done. Loewald reminds us—again wisely—that such partial stepping aside or into the background to enable the child's narcissistic acquisitions and non-incestuous future relations is also undertaken for the parents' own sakes. Abetting the conversion of the original relationships with their children into internal self-structures and effecting the re-constitution of these relationships on a newer non-incestuous basis also allows the parents to free themselves and enhance their own psychic development.

This resolution—or "dissolution", Freud's term—of the Oedipus complex thus becomes the prototype of all future mourning, and Loewald emphasizes that adequate parental provision for this early task will help the subject "to mourn external objects in later life without the object's interacting help". One hears echoes here both of Bion's ideas about the container teaching the contained how to contain and of Winnicott's (1958a) notion that being alone in the presence of the mother teaches the child how to be truly alone.

A successful analysis with a suitable ending, moreover, will have the effect of leading retroactively "to a healthier resolution of the Oedipus complex than the patient had been able to achieve before, and to a more stable superego". Loewald compares the emancipation from the analyst *qua* external object after termination to the experience of adolescent emancipation from the parents, which, he says, "repeats the oedipal struggle on a higher level" (pp. 267–268). Both are later negotiations of separateness, congruent with different developmental stages.

One notes again both the similarities and the differences in the relations among earlier and later experiences of loss in Loewald and Klein. The primary difference is that the latter does not appear to have anything like as much optimistic conviction as the former; she might require more persuasion to believe that repeated experiences of mourning would necessarily achieve or accrue the progressively firmer establishment of settled or benign conditions in the internal world.

Having previously introduced the narcissistic dimension of these structural developments, Loewald begins the third part of the paper by revisiting Freud's essay "On Narcissism", where the rudiments or prototypes of what will later become the superego are discussed for the first time. Once more exhibiting a finely tuned attention to detail in his reading of Freud, he usefully distinguishes between the "ideal ego" and the "ego ideal". The ideal ego is said to represent a perhaps nostalgic and past-oriented identification with the parents as ideal(ized) figures: a "recapturing of the original, primary narcissistic, omnipotent perfection of the child himself" or "an attempt to return to the early infantile feeling of narcissistic self-sufficiency".

One is reminded here—equally and oppositely—of both Kohut's (1971, 1977) treatment of narcissism by means of compensatory mirroring, idealizing, and twinship transferences and Lacan's (1949) scornful, derisory account of the ego's hallucinatory delusions about its reflected integrity and specialness in the mirror stage. After all, Loewald says and implies, the ideal ego arises as a defensive response to helplessness and impotence and the wish to recapture the state of primary narcissism: "the child reaches out to take back from the environment what has been removed from him in an ever-increasing degree since his birth: identification that attempts to re-establish an original identity with the environment" (p. 268).

By contrast with this attempt to "take back" or reclaim something from the past, Loewald tells us, "the term 'ego ideal' indicates more clearly that this state of narcissistic perfection is something to be reached for, wished for in the future". He says that there must be in this quest "an element of projection", where the latter term carries within it—at least in this instance—something of an orientation towards what is to come. The philosopher Stanley Cavell (1990, 1992), in his writings about the forward-looking strivings of American Transcendentalist writers like Emerson and Thoreau, refers to something quite similar, his preferred term for which is "perfectionism". Once again, Loewald stresses here the developmental importance of the parents' contributions and guidance, their projections, idealizations, expectations, fantasies, and illusions (he uses all these words) about both themselves and their children: there are mutual wishes here "about the other's state of perfection, or at least about the other's perfectibility".

Unlike Lacan, Loewald urges that we "not scoff at such fantasies". Provided that "expectations are allowed to be continuously shaped and tempered by an increasing realistic appraisal of the stage of maturity and of the potentialities of the object", such projective fantasies arising between parents and children—as well as their gradual "disillusionment"—are "essential for the development and maintenance of a sound superego". One hears echoes here of both Winnicott and Kohut, and there is something touching and generous in Loewald's recognition that such wishes are "based on old longings in all concerned" (p. 269).

Turning now to the superego itself, Loewald reminds us that Freud saw it as "the heir of the Oedipus complex", and, on those grounds, it must be distinguished from its precursory terms, "ideal ego" and "ego ideal". The term "superego" only applies once certain psychic boundaries, borders, and limits are more firmly established. These include the consolidation of dividing lines between ego and objects and hetero- and homosexual objects, as well as between external and internal versions of ideals, demands, judgements, and authorities. Loewald signals his essential agreement with Freud in this regard by citing one of his well-known phrases, stating that "The superego is constituted of those authorities that are clearly internal and have become a 'differentiating grade in the ego,' thus being clearly differentiated from external love-hate authorities and ideal images." Referring to clinical findings in serious mental illness, he goes on to talk in some detail about shifting structural relations among the agencies of the mind that can alter because of "a mobility of so-called introjected objects within the ego system, suggesting shifting degrees of internalization and externalization which bring the introjects more or less close to the ego core" (p. 270).

There is a great deal of psychic activity going on here, and Loewald's theorizations are at quite a heady and even abstruse level: one needs to pay heed simultaneously to the dynamic motility of these object relations, the different depths of their inclusion or extrusion, and the internal effects of these moves. This attention to detailed changes that can occur in the constitution of and relations among the different structural agencies—that is, id, ego, and superego—is not a perspective that most recent British analysts adopt or find familiar. Mindful, perhaps, of the fact that—at least for Freud—the superego originally emerges from the ego just as the ego emerges from the id, Loewald sees these internal inter-agency relations themselves as being subject to varying degrees of sameness and difference, or merger and separateness. And this is due, in the first place, to the fact "that the modification of external material for introjection, brought about by internalization, varies with the degree of internalization" (p. 271).

We are here witness to the subtlety of Loewald's distinctions: something external may be internalized or taken in at different levels and to different degrees. And it is here that he makes the nearest approach yet to the language of digestion or metabolization to make his point: "A comparison with physiological assimilation is suggested whereby organic compounds are ingested and subjected to catabolic and anabolic changes in the course of assimilation into the body substance" (p. 271). We recall that even Klein resorts to the word assimilation in "Notes on Some Schizoid Mechanisms" (1946), but Loewald's leanings on and readings of Freud seem to bring him more easily to the use of such metaphors to describe his own image of the internal world and its dynamics: effectively, it is when a more thoroughgoing introjection or assimilation into the psychic substance is possible that less persecutory internal relations can ensue.

Essentially, the idea is that the superego can either differentiate itself from the ego (almost) entirely and therefore be utterly at odds with it (producing a very persecutory or punitive dynamic), or join with it (again) and become indistinguishable from it (with such varied consequences as unconstrained hedonism or even psychopathy). There are, of course, many gradations between these two polar possibilities. The more porous or permeable this boundary is, the more closely the superego approaches a re-integration with the ego (to the point of virtual merger with it), the more ego-syntonic and less moralistic does it become.

Loewald uses Ferenczi's example of what happens to "sphincter morality" when the ego and superego can develop side by side and achieve a more peaceable relationship with one another. Having begun as a consciously experienced and perhaps excruciating superego demand, the more that sphincter control is internalized as a capacity—that is, the more "automatic" it becomes—the less it comes under the superego's aegis; it can transform instead into "a rather primitive ego function". Loewald reminds us that this process is also subject to temporary reversal in traumatic, threatening, or stressful circumstances, when this apparently well-established capacity to control one's bowels "regains the quality of a demand" (p. 271) that cannot always be met. Moreover, the original parental trainings, attitudes, and expectations will have an inevitable and significant effect upon these internalizing trajectories, for better or for worse.

Loewald's second example is much more to the point for our purposes, because he turns now to the internal dynamics of mourning itself. Here, he says, there may initially be "something like a new intake of objects into the superego structure insofar as elements of the lost object, through the mourning process, become introjected in the form of ego-ideal elements and inner demands and punishments". But this may only be the first phase of a prolonged, "progressive" (and metabolic) mourning process, which may take years in adults, "so that eventually what was an ego-ideal or superego element becomes an element of the ego proper and is realized as an ego trait rather than an internal demand" (p. 271).

Once again, it may well be possible to translate what Loewald is saying into more Kleinian or British School language: is he not effectively talking about the journey from paranoid-schizoid to depressive position functioning, the process of establishing a good object in the internal world? Perhaps there are similarities, but the differences are not just linguistic or terminological, or between an ego-psychological approach versus an object-relational one. Loewald's perspective seems to offer a more sophisticated and thoroughgoing—as well as optimal—account of how our losses contribute to the creation and development of the internal structure of the mind: in his own terms, what he is talking about here is precisely the turning of ghosts into ancestors.

Loewald offers the simple example of a son coming to resemble his father more after the latter dies, saying that "only then can he appropriate into his ego core given elements of his father's character". Saying that they would lead him too far afield, Loewald refrains from providing other examples, particularly "from psychotic conditions". We may recall two comparable examples from earlier in this book—one in relation to the aging of Miss Emily and the other a personal anecdote told by Karl Abraham—where, in each case, a bereaved child's hair turns grey in identification with a dead father.

It is perhaps crucial to discern and maintain the difference between Emily's totalizing, incorporative, melancholic—and psychotic—identification with her damaging parental figure, and the apparently only temporary introjection effected by Abraham while mourning and identifying with his far more benign father. Loewald's father–son resemblance is more in keeping with Abraham's example but perhaps even more benign, bespeaking a more permanent inheritance that the son may eventually acquire—or "appropriate"—via a successful, metabolic internalization.

There is again the link to "a conception of the superego as a structure", but one that is itself subject to structural change. As indicated above, in optimal circumstances, some superego features "may become elements of the ego proper"; but, under more pathological or borderline conditions, involving regressive "ego disorganization and reorganization", such elements may again separate out and "return, as it were, into the superego and be further externalized" (p. 272). One might say, indeed, that in so doing they again crystallize and solidify, becoming or approximating to concrete, internal-object-like entities.

Stretching Loewald's theorizing a bit further, it appears that, precisely because they are rigidly walled off from more benign ego influence, those internalizations that are incorporated within a too-moralistic superego and remain concrete and indigestible end up rendering this agency predatory and persecutory. These are like the ideas developed, but in quite different language, by Fairbairn (1952), in whose conception internal objects only come about or become necessary as by-products of certain pathological psychic developments.

Crucially, Loewald does not neglect to remind us that the trajectory of these processes is, even under the most favourable conditions, not linear or unidirectional, but complex and dialectical. "During periods of psychic growth", he tells us, "the change of superego elements into ego elements is a continuing process", but the superego is itself always being further enriched "through interactions with the object world"—that is, by way of new external relationships, followed by their later internalization, and so on. He speaks of a spiralling movement whereby a return "to the type of identifications characterized as ego or primary identifications—the person thereby regaining a measure of narcissistic wholeness" can then be succeeded by "giving up such self-sufficiency by further involvement with others" (p. 272).

Loewald may be seen here as paying tribute to an expansive, truly Ferenczian version of introjection as he gives eloquent voice to these processes, beginning with a particularly resonant opening phrase:

> The ripening of the personality in adult life, whether through analysis or other significant life experiences, is based on the widening and deepening of relations that the enriched and more differentiated ego entertains with external reality, understood and penetrated in new dimensions. [p. 272]

Mustering hopeful and forward-looking perspectives on the superego—though not without acknowledging psychic risks and pitfalls—Loewald continues to write passionately, almost lyrically, about these possibilities.

Successes and failures, he again says, depend on the mutual capacities and timings of what the parents can provide and what the child is ready to receive. The superego, he claims, "inasmuch as it is the internal representative of parental and cultural standards, expectations, fears, and hopes, is the intrapsychic representative of the future". Loewald speaks on behalf of a superego that is perhaps mostly ego ideal—and a far cry from the persecutory and predatory agency that British psychoanalysis perhaps specializes in and understands so well. He declares: "Only insofar as we are ahead of ourselves . . . can we be said to have a conscience", adding that "the voice of conscience speaks to us as the mouthpiece of the superego from the point of view of the inner future which we envision". What this amounts to, in fact, is a challenge to the introjective capacities of the ego: is it "capable or incapable of encompassing the superego as the inner future toward which to move" (p. 273)?

In Loewald's dream of the future, as we might put it, of a superego that "merges" with the ego and is "no longer differentiated from it", the torturous psychic phenomenon of guilt—which amounts to nothing other than "a form of tension between ego and superego"—might disappear entirely. Idealistic, optative, or plain wishful as this thought may be, by allowing his mind such oneiric freedom, Loewald is perhaps not just theorizing, but exemplifying these ideas. He concludes this third section of his paper by saying that his meditations on internal psychic structures and their "modes of organization" are best understood not only in spatial or quasi-anatomical terms, but also as a kind of temporal mapping. Echoing but also adapting Freud's meta-psychological musings at the end of *An Outline of Psycho-Analysis* (1940a), Loewald generalizes the project intriguingly to all three agencies of the structural model, suggesting that

> It might well be useful to explore further not only the superego in its relations to the temporal mode future, but also the time dimensions of id and ego and their relations to the temporal modes past and present. [pp. 273–274]

However fascinating, this rather sudden shift in focus opens horizons that cannot be fully explored in the space—or time—that he has left himself in the current paper.

Loewald concludes with a brief but resonant summary. As mentioned previously, he has the knack of saying something new in every iteration of an idea. He makes the clear and succinct statement that: "The work of mourning is not confined to a gradual relinquishment of the lost object, but also encompasses processes of internalizing elements of the relationship with the object to be relinquished." Nowadays there would be little disagreement with that view—namely, that the content of what is internalized is often, perhaps always, a relationship with an object rather than just the object itself. This is followed, however, by something with a more characteristic Loewaldian emphasis: though separations from loved ones, he says, "may be experienced as deprivation", we must also bear in mind that "separation, in certain crucial events in human life, also has the significance of emancipation and lack of separation may be experienced as deprivation" (p. 274).

Loewald reiterates the twofold quality of these emancipatory benefits: there is the initial gain of "an internal substitution for an externally severed object relationship", but this is also followed by the "resumption of early boundary-setting processes by which a further differentiation and integration of the ego and of the object world on higher levels of development takes place". He repeats his important insight that human development itself is ambiguous, consisting of a rhythmic dialectical oscillation between two opposed sets of wishes, or what he calls "the duality or polarity of individuation and primary narcissistic identity with the environment" (p. 275).

These are Loewald's psychoanalytic translations of frankly Emersonian—that is, quintessentially American—ideas: humans want to be either entirely separate, self-sufficient entities (on the one hand), or wholly, oceanically, united with the universe (on the other). Perhaps at their extreme edges, these apparently contradictory desires come full circle and approach each other again: what they have in common is the wish to know nothing about, to be blissfully unaware of difference, whether internal or external, and thus to be utterly (at) one.

This meta-psychological duality is inscribed in the vicissitudes of the superego, "whose elements may change and move either in the direction of the ego core or in an outer direction toward object representation". As we have seen, Loewald seems to agree with Fairbairn—and to disagree with Klein—about such "object representation"; internal objects are, for him, not ubiquitous or necessary features of the inner landscape, but epiphenomena or perhaps the by-products of a certain superegoic state. It is with a final glance at his own belatedly introduced, provisional, and tentative ideas about the "temporal structuralization" (pp. 275–276) of the three mental agencies mapping id, ego, and superego onto past, present, and future—that Loewald brings his paper to a close.

"On Internalization" (1973)

During the following decade, Loewald continued to contemplate the issues that we have witnessed him engaging with above, and "On Internalization" represents, if anything, a more sophisticated intensification of those interests. The intellectual scale of his ambitions is evident as he begins by offering his readers a short, sharp series of juxtaposed and relative "viewpoints" or "standpoints" from which to peruse human "psychic life".

Though Loewald himself refrains from doing this, one immediately wonders whether these can be categorized according to the various schools of psychoanalysis that were fine-tuning and consolidating themselves at the time. The first is a recognizably Freudian perspective, namely, "the standpoint of the sexual and aggressive drives, of id psychology", where what matters is only the direct and immediate gratification of needs; anything less constitutes "at best a detour, at worst a failure" and earns humankind the epithet, "the sick animal" (1973, p. 69). This strikes one as a rather harsh and foreclosing characterization, quite a departure from Loewald's usual, more considered style.

The reductive and negative tones are sustained when, still in his opening paragraph, he describes the second "viewpoint of object relations as the manifestation of these needs". This, we are told, introduces such mental effects as "narcissism, psychic structure formation, internalization"—that is, the very themes and processes that Loewald dealt with in his earlier paper and that are, indeed, of special interest to me in this book. This might be a viewpoint attributable to a slightly later Freud (alongside his close associates, Ferenczi and Abraham)—more characteristic, as I have argued, of the theoretical interests that began to develop in psychoanalysis from around 1910 onwards. Here, however, these internal consequences and developments are viewed collectively—and dismissively—as "a second-best born of frustration, disappointment and fear, a defensive flight from reality or adaptational devices of dubious merit" (p. 69).

When Loewald advances a third vantage position, "the standpoint of the inner life of man", it is again described so critically that one struggles to take it seriously. What he now suggests is that this internal world perspective, posited as a way coping with or adapting to external loss, can itself become so prominent that it paradoxically renders outer reality unreal; the actual lost objects can "seem themselves like substitutes, fleeting, ephemeral, insubstantial in comparison with the enduring inner reality" (p. 69). Perhaps something close to this was mooted in my discussion of Klein in chapter four; her focus on an inner world, populated by its compelling internal objects, can sometimes appear to eclipse the importance of the real world, or minimize the role of external objects. So, is it the Kleinian dispensation that is the object of Loewald's third unflattering description?

Perhaps it is time to put aside these attempts to identify and specify Loewald's targets here because, as one reads on, one begins to realize that Loewald's intentions are quite deliberately rhetorical: these three exaggerated, parodied, limited, and limiting accounts are straw men, set up in this fashion to prove a point. And this is because there is, for him, yet another, more positive angle from which to approach the life of the mind—albeit one that may be a variation on, or subset of, "the standpoint of the inner life of man"—and this is what he calls "the point of view of psychic structure" (pp. 69–70).

According to this perspective—the one that Loewald appears to favour—we might see "the instinctual drives as elements, rudiments, as primitive manifestations of man's psychic life", and not as mere by-products of biology that have degraded "to defensive and unhealthy forms of life". Similarly, "early object ties may be viewed then as necessary antecedents, as foreshadowings and portents of intrapsychic relations and structures" that make precursory contributions to the process whereby individual humans become or develop into themselves by interacting "with the world of external reality" (p. 70).

What Loewald acknowledges, in any case or more generally, is that "the secret of success in understanding more about the conflicted and ambiguous creatures that we are" lies precisely in the "oscillation" among all these different viewpoints, "in their juxtaposition and combination"; this also creates and sustains what, in another memorable phrase, he refers to as the "richness and imprecision of psychoanalytic psychology".

Moreover, he appreciates the fact that psychoanalysis "does not view the psychic life of the individual in isolation, but in its manifold relations and intertwining with other spheres and aspects of life, such as social-cultural life and the somatic-biological sphere". All these considerations notwithstanding, says Loewald, "the ultimate commitment of psychoanalysis as a science is to human psychic structure and functioning and their development and vicissitudes". Thus, if the physical sciences have "physical nature" as their topic and the biological sciences take the "nature of life" as theirs, then "it is the nature of the individual psyche that is the topic of psychoanalysis" (p. 70), even if it thereby constitutes only a subset of the psychological sciences at large.

When Loewald thinks and theorizes in this manner, his breadth and scope of vision allows one to see psychoanalysis simultaneously as both a unified broad church that can contain many internal differences under its rubric, and a discipline with a quite defined and specific remit or reference area. One also sees here how Loewald defines his own approach, both in relation and in opposition to the prevailing American ego-psychological trends of his day. Though this may be overstating it somewhat, one might look back and see ego psychology as engaged in a perpetual struggle not to preside over—or, indeed, not to cause—the swallowing up of psychoanalysis by either the social sciences (anthropology, sociology, and other branches of psychology), on the one hand, or the biological or medical sciences, on the other. Loewald's multi- and meta-perspectival approach ensures that psychoanalysis can both stake a claim to its own particularity and define the realms of its legitimacy as clearly as possible.

Now he turns his attention to the term that provides the title of his paper: "The concept of internalization allows us to approach the question of how psychic structure and psychic functioning come about and how they are maintained." His intention here is not to explore the particular "functions and purposes" of the psychic structures that we call ego and superego, or what these agencies do once they are up and running, so to speak; instead—and in keeping with the intentions of his previous paper—he wishes to consider "by virtue of what genetic and dynamic principles" they come into being and then manage to persist and develop. And he pre-empts what he will say with a statement defining his conception of internalization, as "the basic way of functioning of the psyche, not as one of its functions" (pp. 70–71). This is very reminiscent of how Ferenczi sees introjection: not primarily as a discrete defence mechanism or psychic manoeuvre, but as the *modus operandi* of the psyche itself.

Here, as in his previous paper, Loewald names and briefly examines several of the linguistic cognates that cluster around his central concept: "*internalization, internalize, inner world,* and *internal world*". Yielding, perhaps, to the influence of his philosophical background, he first devotes a long paragraph to Nietzsche's use and understanding of internalization, within a moral or ethical context. This philosopher, he tells us, did not see it as a response to external pressures or internal stimuli, but as a kind of intrapsychic conversion or transfiguration of mainly aggressive urges into "the formation of a soul, of a 'psychic apparatus'". Nietzsche's deliberations demonstrate what Loewald calls "an abrupt and conscious change of viewpoint", whereby "the unhappy fate of an animal whose instincts become unhinged" metamorphoses into "the novel and fascinating 'spectacle' of the genesis of a soul, of man as human" (pp. 71–72).

Turning to Freud (who, he says, was more influenced by Nietzsche than is generally acknowledged) and having said that he "rarely uses the word 'internalization'", Loewald nevertheless enumerates several texts where the concept does appear (including some of those examined in this book's earlier chapters), and he comments that Freud speaks of an inner or internal world when referring to "thought processes (ideational representation) as well as to identification" (p. 72).

In a brief review of the psychoanalytic literature of "internality" (which I will not try to reproduce in any detail), Loewald dips into the work of several of his contemporaries—all central figures associated with ego psychology: Hartmann, Loewenstein, Schur, Rapaport, Sandler, Schafer. He does so primarily to make a crucial distinction, one that I also tried to address in the Introduction to this book. What Loewald will *not* be referring to in his conception of internalization is the building or mapping of any item-for-item version in the mind of the phenomena in outer reality—along the analogical lines, one might suggest, of model villages in miniature scale. As he puts it:

> My own use of internalization refers to the processes involved in the creation of such an internal world and to its structural resultants, and not to the construction of inner models, schemata, or maps, which are representations of the external world of objects and of their relations. [p. 73]

Despite a rare mention of Klein by name, while hinting at the similarity or parallel between the modes of representation just listed and "the Kleinian concept of internalization and internal objects", Loewald—rather disappointingly—says that he will not be discussing these either (p. 73).

After this protracted preamble, the body of "On Internalization" consists of two named sections, the first and longer of which is entitled "Internalization and Repression-Defence". Loewald introduces it by saying that he will initially "subsume under the term 'internalization' a variety of differently named processes". As in the previous paper, he provides a short list of these (though this time without defining them): "psychic incorporation, introjection, identification, and an instinct's turning round upon one's own person" (p. 73). Then he revisits the Freudian theory of repression in its broadest conception, but as seen through the lens introduced at the beginning of the paper, namely, that of different standpoints or viewpoints.

This capacity to view things from different, shifting angles is something that we might now begin to refer to as Loewald's theory of psychic relativity: when we observe mental phenomena, everything is contingent upon where we are standing. If, as he posits, one adopts the point of view of the constancy principle (which Freud initially saw as governing all instincts or drives), then any urges or processes that enhance and promote living—or life itself—must appear defensive in nature and intention. They are, after all, "deviations, detours on the road to a state of rest, and must ultimately be understood as defences against influences that disturb the original state of rest". Such defensiveness, then, might be regarded as fundamental, as "the essential function and purpose of psychic processes" at every developmental level (pp. 73–74).

However, Loewald observes, when repression—that *primus inter pares* of Freudian defence mechanisms—fails or "misfires in what is called the return of the repressed", something ironic, paradoxical, and certainly interesting occurs. The ego—the very seat of the defences—that had previously been working so hard to exclude these repressed contents, might now be tempted to admit them into its own substance, so to speak: "Instead of defending against the troublesome material by repressing it, the ego, especially in analysis, may accept and include the material in its own organization."

Loewald queries what has happened here: has the ego suddenly relinquished one of its central roles and duties, that of defending against disturbing and disruptive influences? He does not answer this question directly but indicates—in his newly noted guise as theorist of psychoanalytic relativity—that "our standpoint has shifted" from that of the "constancy or Nirvana principle" to that of the ego itself. Seen from this perspective, "defense has been replaced by acceptance, the ego has been enriched . . . by a gain in its organization and functioning" (p. 74).

Seeing things from such different points of view is not only the organizing principle of this paper but is clearly one of the hallmarks of Loewaldian thinking more generally. It is a development and refinement, perhaps, of Freud's own enhanced capacity—after the renovations of his structural model in 1923—to regard psychic functioning from the alternative and competing viewpoints of id, ego, and superego. Here, Loewald is effectively saying that, because it has only the best intentions of leading us to a quiescence in the quickest way possible, "repression, to the extent that it is successful, deadens and restricts psychic life". By contrast, when the ego manifests its more inclusive inclinations and the wish to achieve a higher level of organization, "far from getting closer to a state of rest, there is more life" (p. 74).

As the title of this section of his paper suggests, therefore, Loewald is intent on exploring the complex relationship between two psychic needs or urges: namely, repression (or defence more generally) and internalization. As previously, Loewald refers to an important moment in Freud's work—one that I too have examined carefully—where the constitution or coming into being of both the ego and the superego is discussed in terms of processes of internalization, identification, and introjection. He suggests that the ego is further enabled to continue to develop and flourish throughout life—sometimes via the interventions of psychoanalysis—not only by the overcoming of repression, but by the encouraging of such concomitant inner processes.

This is made explicit in the next paragraph, where Loewald spells out that, as psychoanalytic clinicians, we know full well that some defences must fail for the psyche to succeed—and that, ultimately, it is internal change or success that we seek:

> Internalization, in the sense of identification as used by Freud most explicitly in the third chapter of *The Ego and the Id*, is a process radically different from repression as a defense mechanism of the ego by which the ego protects its own current organization. In internalization, in contrast, the ego opens itself up, loosens its current organization to allow for its own further growth. [p. 75]

It will by now be evident that Loewald is implicitly outlining a theoretical way of distinguishing between normal and pathological outcomes where psychic development and the structures of the internal world are concerned. When discussing the superego in this context, he says that its formation need not be the product of a defensive process because, under optimal conditions, the Oedipus complex itself does not necessarily have to be dealt with or resolved by means of repression.

While acknowledging that Freud did not clarify this matter thoroughly enough, Loewald reminds us that Freud's "The Dissolution of the Oedipus Complex" (1924d) puts forward a rather different procedure from repression, one that Loewald seizes on and embellishes in his own fashion:

> The impulses involved in the Oedipus complex are not repressed, to the extent to which a genuine superego structure is formed, but, as Freud puts it, the complex is destroyed, dissolved. In its stead and out of its elements psychic structure is formed by the process I call internalization. [p. 75]

The specific implication here is that the difference between a normal, benign—or "genuine"—kind of superego and a diseased, malignant, persecutory—and perhaps inauthentic—one will turn, precisely, on whether the trials of the Oedipus complex that give rise to it can be resolved by "dissolution" or require the services of repression instead.

After a final and crucial reminder that "internalization comprises much more than the formation of the superego; it is crucially involved in the formation of the ego itself", Loewald proceeds to explicate more thoroughly his own view of how such structure-building is achieved. He elaborates the link between what Freud calls the dissolution or destruction of the Oedipus complex and what he, Loewald, is calling internalization, emphasizing the ego's active "front foot" capacities, rather than its defensive ones:

> To the extent to which the complex is destroyed, the ego does not turn away from it, does not turn the complex away from itself, repress it,

but turns to it and "demolishes" it or assimilates it to itself. Such assimilation involves, using the analogy of biological metabolic processes, a destruction of relationships and structures into their elements and an internal restructuring of these elements within a different organizational setting, so that novel but in some ways related structures evolve. [pp. 75–76]

It is worth noting here that Loewald does not flinch from linking and mixing words like "dissolution" or "assimilation", denoting gradual or gentle procedures, with more violent-sounding terms like "destruction" or "demolition". The point seems to be that something is being thoroughly—not just temporarily—dealt with: a process is concluded or taken towards completion or closure.

At moments like these, one marvels at the breadth and depth of Loewald's theorizing. He first makes brilliant sense of Freud's counterintuitive claims about the Oedipus complex being thoroughly destructible or soluble, when elsewhere—for example, in the opening chapter of *Civilization and Its Discontents* (1930a) and in "Constructions in Analysis" (1937d)—Freud seems so insistent that nothing in the mind is ever destroyed, let alone this "core complex" of psychoanalysis. Moreover, like Winnicott (1949, 1969), he makes a virtue of the necessity of certain kinds of hateful and destructive feelings in human development. Indeed, it would not be at all difficult to bring Winnicott's ideas closer to those of Loewald, insofar as, for both, destructiveness tests the robustness and usefulness of the object—whether parent or analyst—and, if successful, promotes the enhancement and enrichment of the subject, qua child or analysand.

Of course, the fact that Loewald again turns to alimentary metaphors—"the analogy of biological metabolic processes"—to talk about these procedures is heartening and corroborating for me. He makes the point that ingesting, digesting, and metabolizing (Loewald will later reference the latter's destructive catabolic, as well as its constructive anabolic, aspects) are processes that break down the objects they act upon to extract what is needed by a psychosomatic system for the sake of surviving, thriving, and building new structural strength. Lest we miss the profound implications of what he is saying here, Loewald goes over them several times and at some length and, as always, adds nuance as he proceeds.

Aware, too, that he must go further "than Freud ever did" in making these distinctions between defensive and constructive processes in psychic life, he speaks a language similar to that of later Kleinians when they refer to total or whole-system effects in the mind:

> The libidinal-aggressive object cathexes of the Oedipus complex, by repression, are kept in a deficient mode of discharge processes with objects; they are not "destroyed" or assimilated by the coherent ego but are, instead, repressed, maintained in a state of lower psychic organization, and interactions with objects continue to take place on lower levels of psychic organization . . . on an infantile level. Internalization, on the other hand, is a process by which, in the example of superego formation, oedipal object relations are renounced as such, destroyed, and the resulting elements enter into the formation of higher psychic structure, leading in turn to the development of object relations of a higher order of organization. [p. 76]

Perhaps there is more than one way to parse or paraphrase Loewald's points here, but what I would emphasize is that under repression, things are kept concrete or—to repeat a previously used phrase—in a state of suspended animation.

As chapter six, on Abraham and Torok attests (in a different psychoanalytic language), repression tends to rule over an encrypted, melancholic internal world, one without much movement, in which few if any transformations are possible. Loewald is persuaded that the either/or he is laying out "depends . . . on environmental conditions, i.e., in the oedipal situation, on the parental figures", so that a Winnicottian destruction-followed-by-survival dynamic will prevail, and a benign "internal reconstruction in the form of the superego" will be possible only "where the oedipal relationships have been adequate, neither overwhelming nor excessively frustrating and prohibitory". In a typically resonant phrase, Loewald speaks of this positive internal outcome as a "transformation out of the ruins" (comparable with Klein's "to rebuild with anguish the internal world"), and, though this is not his primary focus here, he cites his previous paper, reminding us that the "process is akin to the work of mourning" (pp. 76–77).

Going yet further, Loewald takes on, as we might put it, the very idea of unconscious phantasy, saying that where this phenomenon is prominent, repression is prevalent. In such cases, even if detachment from the external oedipal objects is apparently achieved, the cathexes "persist in unconscious fantasies of such object relations" or "portrayals, as it were, of object relations". By contrast, "in genuine superego reconstructions", there is no need of such portrayals, representations, or internal versions of incestuous objects. He uses an analogy from what he calls "non-objective" forms of art (one thinks, for example, of abstract expressionism, the movement that put America at the cutting edge of the art world in the very post-war period during which Loewald is writing) where representational depictions are given up in favour of "new dimensions of reality organization" (p. 77).

Similarly, in Loewald's understanding of internalization, "a destruction of the object and of the ordinary relations with the object takes place, and a reconstruction, following new principles of structuring". Moreover, once the oedipal/superego moment is properly negotiated—and its dramatic pity and terror worked through—the actual relations with the parental objects can be resumed on a fresh footing, can attain "a new, more mature cast". With his by-now familiar forward-looking stance, Loewald claims that "For the child the reality of parents and other objects changes as he matures, he does not simply relate in a different way to fixed, given objects" (p. 77). As far as Loewald is concerned, in other words, both parties—parent as well as child, object no less than subject—are given opportunities to evolve.

As Loewald's earlier paper made clear, in certain circumstances the structuring accomplished by internalization "is reversible to some degree". Just as there can be a reversal of repression, allowing what was kept in abeyance under its effects to return to consciousness, so, too, might we expect a "loosening-up" of the superego structure and the concomitant re-externalizing of the relations that led to its formation, not least during an analytic process. Though—unfortunately, but as usual—Loewald does not provide any clinical examples, one imagines that what he has in mind are moments in the transference when the as-if quality of the analytic relationship gives way to something more concrete and hyper-real, and the analyst no longer represents but *becomes* the original object, particularly at fraught or emotionally heightened moments.

Loewald grants, moreover, that there is also a particular "lability of psychic structure in psychotic disorders", where such re-externalizations are therefore by no means uncommon; again, working with borderline patients familiarizes one with such outcomes. We might read this as something of a concession to Klein and her school, who are so closely attuned to psychotic processes—and therefore to the precarious instability of internal objects or structures—that they might be said to expect or anticipate these phenomena in many if not all clinical situations.

The relations and differences between internalization and repression are now rendered more complex by Loewald, who, in wishing "to be cautious", is willing to concede that repression itself might make *some* contribution to the formation of the superego and to internal-structure-building more generally; it cannot, however, do so on its own. Reminding us of Freud's change of reference from conflict between conscious and unconscious parts of the mind to that between the coherent ego and the repressed, Loewald points out that the ego's action of "turning away" repressed material leaves the latter split off and alienated, but thereby also substantially unmodified and intact: "it stays repressed and is not crushed" (p. 78).

When, by contrast, internalization—in Loewald's sense—is operating, there is an attempt by the ego not to eschew, but to absorb and accommodate, and thus to become structurally more "coherent" in the process. He repeats that the authentic superego "is not split off from the coherent ego but a further differentiation of it, a further organization of ego structure made possible by the dissolution of the Oedipus complex". Resorting to a nuanced analogy based on knowledge of how actual digestive and metabolic processes operate, Loewald writes: "We might say that such terms as desexualization and neutralization denote destructive catabolic phases of the process involved in internalization, while such terms as identification and sublimation indicate constructive anabolic phases of the process" (p. 78). Loewald's metaphor preserves the sense that the losses that must be endured in such processes run very deep within the system, both existentially and metapsychologically: no real anabolic change or gain can be made without paying a significant catabolic price.

While repression "could be a way-station on the road to internalization", it is also in its nature to defend the quiescent status quo against life-affirming disturbance. When active, repression is "characterized by the ego's defensive activity of protecting its current organization against disruptive influences": it tends to be "in opposition to internalization and prevents it, as much as it prevents or inhibits adequate interaction with the external world" (pp. 78–79). One might anticipate that the preservative encryption of the undigested and un-mourned dead—still to be discussed in the work of Abraham and Torok (chapter six)—must avail itself of repression as well as other defences—like incorporation—whose job it is to keep things as they are.

The melancholic example of Miss Emily, moreover, fits this profile perfectly: in the face of her catastrophic loss, nothing must be allowed to change. But as we know, including from elsewhere in Loewald's work, the repressed is always seeking to rise from its (shallow) grave, like any ghost or zombie; it cannot remain properly buried, or permitted to undergo the necessary organic and metabolic processes of decay and transformation, precisely because it is not amenable to and available for the psychic work of mourning, introjection, and internalization.

Interspersed throughout this paper, there are insightful and enlightening Loewaldian readings of Freudian developments that invite a fresh perspective on our most foundational concepts. Rehearsing Freud's final instinct theory and again casting it as "a change of viewpoint", Loewald reformulates the tension or opposition between Freud's two newly formulated drives in terms of an equally, if only implicitly, revised view of his principles of mental functioning: "The pleasure principle is newly defined as owing its reign to the power of Eros, while the old pleasure-unpleasure principle or Nirvana or constancy principle owes its power to Thanatos, the death instinct." This purported change is due, according to Loewald, to Freud finally accepting that, despite the constancy principle, "stimulus tension is, in and of itself, not necessarily unpleasurable" and therefore need not be avoided at all costs or removed forthwith. On the contrary, such unrequited or unresolved tension can be on the side of life; it has a binding, future-oriented function and "promotes higher or more complex organization of the psychic structures resulting from and promoting in their turn, psychic processes" (pp. 79–80).

Putting two and two together, as it were, Loewald sums up this part of his paper by saying, first, that "repression, insofar as it maintains psychic processes and structures on lower organizational levels, is under the sway of the death instinct or of the constancy-Nirvana principle". By contrast, "internalization, insofar as it leads to higher organization and an enriched psychic life, is under the sway of Eros or of the newly defined pleasure principle and its modification, the reality principle". Interestingly, the all-too-neat division that this suggests at first glance is not what Loewald is after here. Paradoxically, his formulation allows for a better acknowledgement that each process has "a share of the other" as they occupy the field between them.

This is in keeping with the Freudian idea that these drives had best remain closely intertwined, rather than become too defused or separate from each other. Loewald repeats the complex message that, though we dare not ignore or underestimate the protective value of repression, neither must we risk the overvaluing of internalization. If the latter operates "unchecked by the lure of objects external to the psyche's own structures", the result can be "inner sterility and diffusion" (p. 80). This is tantamount to saying that if we utterly eschew and defend against new sources of external stimulation and fresh interest from the outside world—that is, if we allow nothing more in, so to speak—we may become trapped in a narcissistic over-investment in our own internality. Thus, although internalization may already be under the sway of Eros, maintaining contact with the outside world remains a vitalizing and necessary activity.

In anticipation of the topic of the next section of the paper, Loewald introduces, in the final paragraph of this section, the "role of object ties and object relations". The developments that he has been tracing point inexorably to the fact that such objects are no longer to be regarded as merely expedient or just "for the achievement of satisfaction, that is, for discharge of stimulus tension". Insofar as these objects can also be identified with or introjected, they contribute to the building of the ego and the superego as internal structures or organizations. As we shall see, the comparisons and contrasts that preoccupy Loewald in the forthcoming part of the paper are those that pertain—as its title tells us—between "Internalization and identification" (p. 80).

Citing the earlier (1962) paper analysed above, Loewald tells us again that there are different levels of internalization, the earliest forms of which are involved in the primary establishment of subject and object, the initial differentiation of what is within from what is without. In the first instance, these boundaries "are only fleetingly present, fluid, blurred, so that at least no clear or constant distinction between self and object world, between inside and outside, is maintained". Object relations as such cannot really be conceived of until the Oedipus situation comes about; before this, "reality is pre-objective", as he puts it. Only with certain "first steps in ego organization" as a base can the later, post-object-relational superego be formed. Though he does not go into this in the paper, he pauses to take issue with Hartmann's notion of "primary ego autonomy", saying that, for him, it "raises metapsychological problems" (pp. 80–81).

Ironically, and despite their many psychoanalytic differences, Klein's tacit assumptions about the ego's origins are comparable to or compatible with Hartmann's, at least to the extent that she, too, seems to take for granted some pre-existing, relatively self-standing form of the ego at or near the beginning of psychic life (though she does not adopt this position either for the same purpose or with anything like the same ideological zeal and conviction). Insofar as Loewald regards the process of internalization as playing such a crucially formative part in ego—as well as superego—construction, he would clearly have to disagree with both Hartmann and Klein on this score: one imagines that he would find their assumptions of ego primacy ontologically untenable.

Perhaps Loewald's place on the psychoanalytic map is becoming clearer as we read his texts more closely: we might call him a self-styled Freudian radical, but one who is also abreast with and has leanings towards *some* more contemporaneous object-relational attitudes, if not others. Continuing very much in the vein of Winnicott, he suggests that it only makes sense to talk about objects in reference to pre-oedipal life if we posit, as it were, a "non-psychoanalytic observer" of the scene:

> The naïve observer sees a baby relate to his mother, one individual to another; but this is clearly not the psychological situation for the baby. Nor is it the psychological situation for the mother at all times, at any rate during early infancy. [p. 81]

This is surely an astute and accurate precis of the notion of primary maternal preoccupation, a re-statement—though not quite as pithy as Winnicott's (1956, 1960b) own—of the fact that there is no such thing as a baby. What is equally clear, however, is that it is being put forward not for its own sake, but because Loewald wants here to establish a certain baseline of human experience with the aim of making a wider point about future psycho-structural developments.

Loewald now reminds us that later experiences of ego-boundary porousness, or even self–other merger, can and often do occur, "in which the subject–object distinction tends to become blurred or temporarily to vanish, as for instance in a passionate love relationship and other 'ecstatic' states, which, while rare and exceptional, cannot be called pathological". Although at the beginning of *Civilization and Its Discontents* Freud struggles to accommodate or identify Romain Rolland's convictions about religious experience within his own mind, he does acknowledge the existence of such feelings, handily designated as "oceanic". Loewald concurs, saying of these "early levels of psychic development" that they "are not simply outgrown and left behind but continue to be active". He links them with his own earlier thoughts about "the reversibility of internalizations" (pp. 81–82).

The point seems to be that even the very earliest, most primary of internalizations that initially establish the differences between inside and outside can undergo a kind of reversal or regression: "a dedifferentiation may take place by which the two become re-merged and subsequently re-differentiate from one another in novel ways". In a manner once again reminiscent of Winnicott (1971), he considers this two-way directionality of psychic movement and structuration to be crucial for "the understanding of creative processes" (p. 82), as if this back-and-forth movement between merger and separation might be the way in which the requisite transitional space for such processes—a place betwixt and between—can come into being.

But Loewald has not yet reached the nub of his argument: he is still making his way towards it by steady and stealthy degrees. He goes on to suggest that we need not resort to extreme versions of subject–object confusion—that is, situations in which the ego's separate existence and integrity are at stake—to note that our everyday relations are suffused with such experiences:

> Any close, intimate object relationship has narcissistic features, identifications are involved. We become aware of this most acutely at a time of separation from such an object, or when we lose it. We may then feel that we have received a wound, as though a part of oneself has been torn off. [p. 82]

Of course, Loewald is now re-establishing the link with mourning (and melancholia), and he goes on to compare object losses with certain bodily-ego experiences, like sustaining a physical injury or even suffering damage to one's car. It is to this narcissistic dimension of loss that he seems intent on drawing to our attention, and we are again reminded of Freud's emphasis, in "Mourning and Melancholia", on the significance of narcissism to these dynamics and his characterization of the melancholic situation as resembling an open or painful wound.

Like Freud, Loewald is aware of the paradoxes operating here: object cathexis and identification eventually become virtual opposites, with the latter substituting for the former whenever a libidinal loss occurs; however, in our very earliest encounters, these two forms of connection with the object—having it versus being it—cannot (yet) be distinguished or separated. After drawing attention to this original conceptual/existential situation—the state of primary narcissism—he makes a statement about its consequences, namely, "that object relations contain elements of libidinal-aggressive cathexes as well as identification elements in varying proportions" (p. 82).

This, indeed, is the very legacy of our early experience with objects, that there will thenceforward always be some admixture, in any close relationship, between desire (and/or aversion) on the one hand, and identification (or what we might perhaps call "fellow-feeling") on the other. This is surely very close to what Ferenczi (1933) is talking about when he distinguishes in a late paper between the language of passion and that of tenderness.

One begins to realize that Loewald has been building all along towards specifying "the differences between identification and internalization" (two terms that are sometimes regarded as synonyms for each other, after all). His first gambit in this endeavour is to declare, somewhat surprisingly, that at least in his sense of the term, "Internalization involves a giving up of both, the libidinal-aggressive as well as the identification elements in object relations" (pp. 82–83). In what is effectively the climax of his deliberations, Loewald now explains the significance of these seemingly abstruse metatheoretical musings.

In the first section of the paper, repression was regarded both as an adversary of, and as playing a necessary but not sufficient part in, internalization. The parallel here—in the context of object relations—is that identification must be regarded as a process that to some degree *opposes* internalization, but also as an interim "way-station" on the road towards that end. The initial thrust of identification is towards "an identity of subject and object" and leads towards "merging or confusion of subject and object. Identification tends to erase a difference: subject becomes object and object becomes subject" (p. 83).

It becomes the task of internalization to take things further, beyond sameness or similarity, towards enhanced internal structure and the prospect of newer separations:

> When we speak of the internalization of object relations, such as in the resolution of the Oedipus complex and in the work of mourning, it is not, if the processes are brought to completion, a matter of maintaining identifications with the objects to be relinquished; the latter is the case in melancholia where the object and the identifications with the object cannot be given up. In internalization it is a matter of transforming these relations into an internal, intrapsychic, depersonified relationship, thus increasing and enriching psychic structure: the identity with the object is renounced. Internalization as a completed process implies an emancipation from the object. [p. 83]

This quotation may stand as a kind of apotheosis of Loewaldian thinking on such topics. These are, as it were, his colours nailed to the mast or his theses to the church door. The clear distinction between mourning and melancholia is back: if the process stalls at identification (or, indeed, repression)—what we may perhaps call only partial digestion—then melancholia prevails; if, and only if, further internalizing or metabolizing occurs, can we speak of a more successfully achieved mourning process.

Even if the optative personal freedom Loewald is proffering as an ultimate goal of these psychic procedures is granted as a conceptual possibility, would he stand accused of idealistic over-optimism about the human capacity for such fully achieved forms of internalization and introjection, digestion and metabolization? The very idea that all objects, internal no less than external, are destined for dissolution, destruction, assimilation, and absorption into the core structures of the individual mind—for the sake of what one might call personal psychic liberation and enrichment—may not be something that Klein, for one, would have found easy to countenance as either possible or desirable.

Would Loewald not also stand charged, not so much with ignoring, but with subordinating and even sacrificing the relational aspects of human life to the selfish goals of self-fulfilment or self-maximization? Is this, for want of a better way to put it, too individualistic and capitalistic—dare one say, too American—an advocation of the value of private psychic wealth? Where is the concern for and responsibility towards the other that is so prevalent, for example, in Klein's ideas about the contributions of reparation and gratitude to psychic health in the depressive position?

Lest this obvious point be missed, Loewald is clearly not recommending real-life selfishness or egocentrism, or even expressing moral opinions about how we should relate to our external objects; neither is he being so crass as to suggest that we should metabolize and absorb our forebears or ancestors so thoroughly that we thereby simply dispense with them and our memories of them, forgetting that they ever existed. His are theoretical, metaphorical, and metapsychological accounts of how he conceives of or imagines the workings of internal psychic processes. To that extent, it would be a serious category error to adjudge his theory better or worse—by ethical, ideological, or indeed superegoic standards—than those of Klein or anyone else.

Loewald does, however, go on to make plain what he sees as the real-world caveats and consequences of his conceptions:

> To the extent—always limited in the vicissitudes of human life—to which internalization comes to completion, the individual is enriched by the relationship he has had with the beloved object, not burdened by identification and fantasy relations with the object. [p. 83]

Evidently, he sees certain forms of pining, longing, and loss as burdensome, and it is the self-limiting nostalgic cleaving and melancholic clinging to the past that he is opposing here. However, he is also clearly aware of the dangers of an over-idealizing, too perfectionistic, wishful quality in his thinking about any given person's prospects of fully actualizing their psychic emancipation. From the perspective of "the development of the child's love attachments to his parents", the sacrificing and internal transformation of primary libidinal bonds will result in "freeing the individual for non-incestuous object relations". Hinting, perhaps, at Isaiah Berlin's famous distinction between positive and negative forms of liberty—and at his own distinction between ghosts and ancestors—Loewald adds that "This freedom is not simply freedom from old object ties that have been cast off, but an inner freedom that we call maturity, achieved by the internalization of old ties" (p. 83).

Playing with the verbal relations between identification and identity and citing Erik Erikson—another émigré European–American psychoanalytic contemporary who wrote extensively about these issues—Loewald again claims that the separate identities of both self and other are enabled and enhanced—"defined or redefined"—by internalization. "In this sense", he says, "identity does not mean identity between subject and object, but self-sameness, individuality"—what Erikson calls "ego identity". He also reiterates that our internal lives are in fact animated by a kind of bipolar back-and-forth between "internal identity, which makes object relations in the true sense possible, and identification that dissolves the difference between subject and object" (pp. 83–84).

It is suggested that the work of internalization gets done mostly at certain developmental moments, for example, during the latency period, after the *Sturm und Drang* of the Oedipus complex is (temporarily) over, or the early adult "moratorium" (so named by Erikson), by which time adolescent turbulence may have settled to some extent. It is interesting to consider that there is some dispute about the psychic status of such interim transitional periods: whether they existed in bygone eras or pertain similarly in other cultures or, indeed, are experienced at all by species that are close to humans in other respects. Putting such speculations aside, what is clearer is that we are not all capable of laying claim to the rest, recovery, and reconstruction that such periods promise. Are they luxuries that not everyone can afford?

Loewald does not engage in such debates but specifies one other period when the opportunities of internalization present themselves:

> Therapeutic analysis, of course, represents or should represent such an internalizing phase in life, the patient's need for which is so often brought about by upheavals of the nature of emotional disappointments, frustrations in work and love and of ambitions, calling for de-repressions, renunciations, and internal re-adjustments. Thus it is an inner necessity, not an arbitrary requirement for the sake of frustration *per se*, that an analysis, to be successful, be carried out in relative "abstinence," allowing for a period of respite from too much external involvement, to the extent to which this is possible in people's lives. [pp. 83–84]

Even—or perhaps especially—in his conception of analysis itself, Loewald's hopeful best-case-scenario attitudes cannot but shine through. He does seem to be aware, however, of his own tendency to overstate his distinctions, as well as his optimism about psychic outcomes.

After reneging slightly and re-stating the interim importance of identification in the building of internal structure, Loewald concludes his paper very aptly with lines from a famous poem—Andrew Marvell's "The Garden"—which, he says, "speaks of the metamorphosis on which I have tried to throw some light" (pp. 84–85). Marvell writes about "The mind, that ocean" as capable of plumbing its own greater depths, paradoxically "transcending" by way of *de*scending from the easy shallows of the quest for "resemblance" to the deeper fathoms of "Far other worlds and other seas"; this is achieved by acts that must destroy the known world to produce something creative and new:

> Annihilating all that's made
> To a green thought in a green shade.
> [1681, p. 50]

I want, by way of an answering echo to these ideas and images, to return to Wallace Stevens, who earlier provided us with some poetic/maternal respite.

Stevens once claimed, in one of his aphorisms or adages, that French and English are just different forms of a single language: perhaps he had the familiar French pun between *la mer* and *la mère* in mind when writing a poem entitled "The Woman That Had More Babies Than That". Conjuring a seascape of his own, he speaks there of how even the oldest and wisest of men can hear—as if, perhaps, by putting an ear to a shell—their mothers' lullabies echoing in their minds, and still feel—like an ocean breeze on the skin—the breath of these maternal songs. Stevens then offers this resonant image of aural self-fashioning:

> The self is a cloister full of remembered sounds
> And of sounds so far forgotten, like her voice,
> That they return unrecognized. The self
> Detects the sound of a voice that doubles its own,
> In the images of desire, the forms that speak,
> The ideas that come to it with a sense of speech.
> [1939, p. 82]

Stevens can be read here as saying that the self is created by a kind of developmental conversion or communion, whereby the mother's reverberating voice—whether still remembered or already forgotten—is taken into the plangent echo-chamber of the mind.

They are sounds that double and repeat the mother's songs, but these must be properly assimilated by her children, no matter their age; her images, forms, and ideas must be spoken anew and transposed into something that makes a different sense. For the sake of creating individual selves, the maternal voice must be thoroughly introjected and internalized, not merely incorporated in an amorphously universalizing way; thus may it be properly heard, heeded, and mourned, not suffered as an anguished, melancholy moan.

Yet other words echo here, recalling another, Shakespearean seascape:

> Full fathom five thy father lies;
> Of his bones are coral made;
> Those are pearls that were his eyes;
> Nothing of him that doth fade
> But doth suffer a sea-change
> Into something rich and strange.
> *The Tempest* (Act I: ii, 397–402)

So sings Ariel, albeit about fathers rather than mothers, but expressing similar sentiments: parents must drown, decay, and dissolve in the psychic depths, for the making of the filial mind.

It may be worth noting, even at this late moment in the chapter, that Stevens and Loewald in fact overlapped temporally and were near neighbours geographically: they plied their trades in mid-twentieth-century America, up or down the road from one another in the Connecticut cities of Hartford and New Haven, respectively. Stevens's sentiments resonate remarkably well with Loewald's conceptions: his lines capture the fluctuating tensions between forgetting and remembering in relation to a primary object, and can be read, in Loewaldian terms, as vacillating between a fully metabolized internalization, on the one hand, and the only partial (dis)solutions of both repression and identification, on the other. Where Stevens provides (along with Marvell and Shakespeare) the poetic sounds expressing such oceanic oscillations, Loewald is the psychoanalytic ancestor who bequeaths us an appropriate and serviceable theoretical language in which to discuss and debate their psychodynamic adumbrations.

CHAPTER SIX

Nicolas Abraham and Maria Torok: rescuing introjection from the crypts of incorporation

As the reader is aware, there has been a considerable amount of anticipatory allusion to the work of Abraham and Torok in earlier chapters: this is because it has been difficult to remain patient and not to refer, eagerly and pre-emptively, to the fecundity of their ideas and their contribution to this book's themes. Having emigrated from Hungary to France separately on either end of the Second World War, Nicolas Abraham and Maria Torok met, married, and trained as psychoanalysts in Paris. Writing both separately and together, they produced a novel and wide-ranging body of collaborative work that not only served to invigorate psychoanalytic thinking but extended pertinently to many other adjacent genres in the humanities, including literature, philosophy, history, and linguistics.

Nicolas Abraham, like his namesake Karl, died before his time (in 1975) and—along with his nephew, Nicholas Rand, a professor of French literature in the United States who became the pair's English translator—Torok continued and carried forward the legacy of their work.

The two books that Rand's translations have made available to the English-speaking world are *The Wolf Man's Magic Word: A Cryptonomy* (Abraham & Torok, 1986), which includes an introductory essay by Jacques Derrida, and a collection of papers entitled *The Shell and the Kernel: Renewals of Psychoanalysis, Vol. 1* (Abraham & Torok, 1994), which cover a rich and fascinating variety of interrelated topics.

My task in this chapter is to look closely at just two papers from this volume. Early in his Introduction to the latter, Rand also provides a detailed outline of an intended second volume of translated papers; unfortunately—and mysteriously—this second collection has never materialized. However, Rand's Introduction, as well as this section-by-section commentaries, are invaluable. His helpful categorizing of the clinical and theoretical preoccupations of Abraham and Torok reveals their perhaps typically French wish to renew or re-conceive Freud's intellectual legacy, as well as their interest in an array of interlinked topics, such as fantasy, sexuality, femininity, language, phantoms, grief, and trauma and its transgenerational transmission.

As Rand attests, the metapsychological centre of these concerns—faithful as the pair are to their Hungarian roots and allegiance to Ferenczi— is the concept of introjection, its ubiquitous and ordinary operations, its pathological blockages and failures, and the restoration of its functioning via psychoanalysis.

According to Rand, though Abraham and Torok do not provide a specific, dedicated, or systematic exposition of the concept, introjection is everywhere in their work, which is quite in keeping with the breadth and scope of the original Ferenczian meaning of the term itself. Rand makes several attempts to define the concept. Having first described it in rather broad terms as "a synthetic enlargement" of such Freudian processes as "abreaction, binding, working out, working through, and the work of mourning", he also refers to it as "a constant process of acquisition and assimilation, the active expansion of our potential to accommodate our own emerging desires and feelings as well as the events and influence of the external world". He calls introjection the "psychic counterpart" to our physical growth and development from infancy to adulthood (pp. 8–9).

I trust that I do not have to add too much here about how words like "enlargement", "acquisition", "assimilation", "expansion", and "accommodate" might all be heard to resonate with the metaphors of digestion and metabolization. Later, in *The Shell and the Kernel*, while introducing the section that houses the papers that I focus on, Rand also speaks of introjection in terms of the "enrichments and disturbances in the process of self-fashioning" and as "the principle of gradual self-transformation in the face of interior and exterior changes in the psychological, emotional, relational, political, professional landscape" (pp. 100–101). The task of introjection, in other words, is the very construction of a self. However, I will not attempt to explicate these descriptions any further here, in the hope that their meanings will become clearer as I explore the texts themselves.

It will be obvious that I am reading these two specific papers, the first written by Torok, the second a co-authored piece, because of their attention to mourning: how it might fail—or come to grief, so to speak—and give rise instead to what Torok's title refers to as "the illness of mourning". For these analysts—as the second paper's title ("Mourning *or* Melancholia: Introjection *versus* Incorporation") makes crystal clear—the failure of mourning and the failure of introjection are virtually synonymous, such that the presence of melancholia and the overuse of incorporation are the necessary indications of psychopathology in this area. Abraham and Torok seem to make these divisions between health and disease sound strict and single-minded; though they would no doubt stand by their dichotomies, things always become more interesting and more nuanced in the close reading, as I hope to show.

Maria Torok

"The Illness of Mourning and the Fantasy of the Exquisite Corpse" (1968)

Perhaps it is the macabre second phrase in this title that really catches the eye, and we will be encountering it as a theme soon enough. The paper consists of eight titled sections, each just a couple of pages long, except for the lengthier third one, which is subdivided into four parts (and where Torok tackles the theoretical origins of introjection). The opening section is called "A Revelatory Misunderstanding", where Torok reports a curious bit of psychoanalytic history that also provides an instructive parable on the nature of mourning. She does so by quoting at some length from a section of the extensive correspondence between Karl Abraham and Freud (Freud & Abraham, 1966), bringing to our attention an exchange from 1922 which she calls "astonishing".

In the opening letter, Abraham offers to "produce very nice material" from his clinical work, providing striking clinical illustrations of Freud's concept of "the incorporation of the love-object" while requesting, incidentally, that Freud send him a fresh reprint of "Mourning and Melancholia". He adds, perhaps as a comment on the perplexity about mania in that paper, that though Freud does not detect in normal mourning any "leap" comparable to that from melancholia to mania, he (Abraham) has found evidence of an arguably manic response operating in mourning, too. As we saw in his long paper, what Abraham is alluding to is the not-infrequent incidence of "heightened sexual need" or "an increase in libido some time after a period of mourning". He clearly hopes that Freud will also regard this as "a valid addition to the parallel between mourning and melancholia" (quoted in Torok, 1968, p. 107).

Freud responds two weeks later: having "reread" Abraham's letter, he presumably makes good on the request for a reprint which, he says, had initially escaped his attention. Then, after praising his colleague's abundant "scientific insight and intentions"—but without saying anything about his particular idea—Freud asks why Abraham does not consult his more recent writings about melancholia and mania in *Group Psychology and the Analysis of the Ego*, and he wonders whether that may have been his own unconscious motive for "forgetting" and not sending a copy of the older paper. He adds, "No absurdity is impossible for psychoanalysis" and wishes he could sit and discuss these matters with Abraham in person, as he finds it tiring to have to write about them of an evening.

Evidently somewhat flummoxed by Freud's letter, Abraham does not write back for more than a month. He then concurs that Freud's "oversight" about the reprint might well have been an unconscious message to himself not to neglect *Group Psychology*, but he reassures Freud that he is in fact well acquainted with that book. Indeed, he had only just been through it again, but still without discovering any reference to a reaction in mourning that might compare with mania. He then adds, sounding rather desperate, "I cannot see where I went wrong."

Suspecting himself of "blindness", Abraham nevertheless reiterates that he has so far not found anything in Freud's work that resembles or pre-empts his own view that an "increase of libido after mourning would be fully analogous to the 'feast' of the manic". In a very brief apologetic reply almost three weeks later, Freud again ignores the substance of Abraham's purported discovery, saying only that he had finally made sense of the misunderstandings and cross-purposes in their exchange: "You were looking for a normal example of the transition from melancholia to mania, and I was thinking of the explanation of the mechanism" (p. 108).

Torok does not comment in any detail on the exchange as a whole or, indeed, on Freud's unconvincing and possibly avoidant last word on the subject. But she does extrapolate from his apparently quite strenuous resistance to Abraham's important piece of clinical evidence, saying that "It demonstrates the reluctance we all feel when, in a sacrilegious move, we want to grasp the inmost nature of mourning." Though this statement may itself be somewhat opaque, it recalls to mind and reinforces—from Freud's side, so to speak—the honest evidence produced by Abraham in his 1924 paper that there were strong feelings of oedipal competition between the two men on the topics of melancholia and mourning.

As these letters attest, Freud was himself no less embroiled in these struggles for priority, though he perhaps affected to maintain a conscious unawareness of his own part in them. Torok concludes that Freud's reactions so discouraged Abraham from pursuing his own original angle—concerning the manic sexual feelings experienced by some mourners—that he did not expand on it sufficiently and thus evaded its fullest ramifications. Clearly, it is one of Torok's intentions in her own paper to take this matter up where he left off and to pursue "the theoretical and clinical consequences the problem most assuredly implies" (pp. 108–109).

In Torok's second section, bearing the title "'Normal Mania' and the Illness of Mourning", she provides a series of confessional statements by mourners—presumably from her own clinical practice—who were overcome by unwanted sexual sensations and feelings during a period of acute grief for a loved one. They all spoke "with shame, astonishment, hesitation, and in a whisper", mortified by the intrusion into their mourning minds of lusts and desires that felt unseemly, scandalous, and immoral. Claiming that these examples completely corroborate Abraham's insight, Torok intends to use them to shed light on the whole gamut of cases that come under the rubric of the "illness of mourning".

In particular, she wishes to know why such patients end up "overwhelmed with self-reproach and inhibitions, why they are subject to exhausting ruminations, physical diseases, constant depression, fatigue, and anxiety". They tend to show no interest in "objectal love", lose touch with creativity, and become mired in the nostalgia of "if only" (p.109). She also notes their disinclination to connect the original, morally aberrant, sexualized moment with these depressive symptoms, and it thus becomes the task of the analysis to do so.

After citing one or two more of the first-personal voices of such patients, exemplifying how they contrive to thwart recovery and undermine all possibilities of future love and happiness, Torok produces her own starkly italicized diagnostic statement on the matter:

The illness of mourning does not result, as might appear, from the affliction caused by the objectal loss itself, but rather from the feeling of an irreparable crime: the crime of having been overcome with desire, of having been surprised by an overflow of libido at the least appropriate moment, when it would behoove us to be grieved in despair. [p. 110]

Torok now lays out her agenda for the rest of the paper, claiming, first, that what Karl Abraham had intuited, and she has now made explicit, are "clinical facts": "A measure of libidinal increase upon the object's death seems to be a widespread, if not universal phenomenon." Not wanting to limit the clinical scope of these facts to mania alone, she thinks that "the untoward arrival of this kind of libidinal invasion" points to a "complex set of problems". She alludes to the importance of introjection and incorporation to these dynamics and undertakes to link the pathologies of mourning to a wider category of illness, which she intriguingly terms "neurosis of transition" (p, 110).

Without knowing in advance what precisely Torok means by it, this last phrase resonates very strongly with my own long-standing intellectual, linguistic, and (more recently) clinical interest in the tropes of passage in psychoanalysis: transference, transition, transience, transformation, and others in this extended family of terms (Meyerowitz, 1995, 2018). Of course, these concerns may also be regarded as germane to the current book: perhaps in emulation of the Styx-crossing journey between life and death, the mourner/survivor must experience the crossings of grief and the internal transitions attendant upon them. Torok makes plain here that to be preoccupied with mourning requires consideration of how the mourner—the one left behind, who has yet to make that final crossing—processes and moves on from the event, as well as how and why so many of us end up blocked or prevented from doing so.

William Wordsworth, "Surprised by Joy" (1812)

Before proceeding to Torok's own linguistic explorations and conceptual elaborations in the third section of her paper, I want again to intrude a poem into the proceedings, one that sprang to mind with Torok's word, "surprised", in the italicized quotation above. As she suggests, these mourners are utterly surprised—not to say shocked and appalled—by the intrusion of sex or desire into their grief.

Perhaps my association to the poem is similarly surprising, because, while Wordsworth's sonnet is clearly about grief, to locate it in this psychoanalytic context and bring sexuality to bear on it might seem just as scandalous as what happens to the minds and bodies of those grieving patients—the reader will soon see why. Here is the poem in full:

> Surprised by joy—impatient as the wind
> I turned to share the transport—Oh! With whom
> But Thee, deep buried in the silent tomb,
> That spot which no vicissitude can find?
> Love, faithful love, recalled thee to my mind –
> But how could I forget thee? Through what power,

> Even for the least division of an hour,
> Have I been so beguiled as to be blind
> To my most grievous loss?—That thought's return
> Was the worst pang that sorrow ever bore,
> Save one, one only, when I stood forlorn,
> Knowing my heart's treasure was no more;
> That neither present time, nor years unborn
> Could to my sight that heavenly face restore.
> [1812, p. 72]

It is well documented that the addressee in this poem is neither Wordsworth's wife, nor even his beloved sister, Dorothy, but his daughter, Catherine, who died at the age of three.

My association from Torok's ideas to this poem obviously turns on her patients' terrible guilt, though this is a word that she has not yet used in this context. This is clearly also what the poet feels at forgetting his grief for his lost daughter in a moment of pleasure or "joy" which, ironically, he spontaneously and impatiently wants to "share" with no one else but her. The other word for what he seeks to share is "transport", as if this moment of exceptional pleasure might lift him onto another plane, take him to a different world. This is yet another transitional word, after all, etymologically denoting motion, as well as conveyance (perhaps suggesting, even, how the father/poet might have carried his child in his arms while she was alive).

The paradoxes and complexities already abound as we begin to realize that though his joy removes him from his grief, it also takes him back towards Catherine, only for him to pull up short, remembering that she is no longer available but permanently away, "buried in the silent tomb". So, she cannot—indeed, *should* not—be turned towards in this manner. Perhaps the word "vicissitude"—which features significantly in psychoanalytic writing, as in "Instincts and their Vicissitudes"—is particularly apt, the contrast being between the constantly shifting, lively changes that it denotes and the stillness and stasis of the grave.

Am I in fact risking moral condemnation here by explicitly linking the poet's joy to a sexual feeling, even though this may seem implicit or at least plausible to me? In psychoanalysis, at least, we do not usually flinch from such connections or regard them as scandalous. We are not told what the joy was about, but, being Wordsworth, we can well imagine this poet transported into an ecstatic or blissful state—akin, even, to that of sexual excitement—by the sight of a field of daffodils. It hardly matters: what he has forgotten or been distracted from momentarily is that he is—or should be—in mourning ("grieved in despair", as Torok puts it) and ought not to be having any joyful experiences whatsoever.

Reaching desperately for some excuse, perhaps, the poet claims that it was no trivial emotion, but "Love, faithful love, recalled thee to my mind". But, again, this hardly helps: the very fact that he wants so much to turn to his daughter in joy and love, as if she were still alive, means that he has forgotten that she is dead and gone. Heaping extra blame upon himself, he asks "But how could I forget thee?"—that is, he accuses himself of forgetting not only the fact of her death, but of thereby forgetting Catherine herself. Under the aegis of his terrible persecutory conscience, a moment of joy seems to obliterate not just her death, but the very fact that she had ever lived or existed: it is as if, in other words, he has just killed her all over again.

In his third and final anguished question, the poet asks, "what power" could so have "beguiled" him as to leave him "blind", if only for the shortest interval of time, to his "grievous loss". If this is not to be taken as another unanswerable or rhetorical question, one might want to help him with a reply reminding him that Eros, the will to restore life and joy, is a force to be reckoned with. However, it is surely the equal-and-opposite, predatory power of the superego (also a word not yet used in relation to any of Torok's tormented mourners) that is prevailing and carrying the field in this poem. And here, surely, lies the essence of Torok's questions about such moments, too: why are the sexual or joyful feelings that enter these mourners' minds quite so terrible, why is this sin or crime so great, that their guilt and shame should potentially condemn them to endless, unremitting remorse?

Wordsworth goes on to do further penance by dedicating the sestet of the sonnet to abject remembrance of the only moment that was worse for him than the present one, namely, the day of his daughter's actual death or burial, when he had to face, forlornly, the finality of never seeing her again. But these lines seem themselves to descend in quality and to lose poetic force. The shocking, exciting, manic beginning of the poem yields to the rather staid, standard, conventionally elegiac, depressed final sentiments, with their stolid and predictable rhythms and rhymes. It is as though the price that Wordsworth must pay for his joyous, thoughtless, careless—dare one say, orgasmic—earlier moment is that of a sudden and serious lapse in his creative capacities, a failure to attain psychic sublimation via the poetic sublime. For a poet of his stature, this is surely a very apt melancholic self-punishment, one that suits the crime.

* * *

We return now to Torok's paper, in time for her to begin the metapsychological excursus of Section 3. The somewhat inelegant title provides a clear and vital clue to an essential difference: "Ferenczi's Concept of the Introjection of Drives Contrasted with the Concept of the Object's Incorporation". Its opening subsection—"Some Transformations of the Concept of Introjection"—recognizes the same messy terminological discrepancies that we have noted previously—what Ferenczi (1933) might have called a confusion of tongues—around these internalizing terms. As Torok notes, approaching "the problem of mourning and depression" requires one to "muddle through a conceptual terrain studded with obstacles" (p.110).

Her primary focus is, of course, on introjection, and she traces, as we have done, the fate of this term from its Ferenczian coining in 1909, through its (mis)uses by Freud, Karl Abraham, and Melanie Klein. Torok's exasperation is palpable: "the term 'introjection' has undergone so many variations in meaning that its mere mention is enough to arouse in me the suspicion of confused ideas, not to say verbiage". The only solution, she says, is to undertake the revival of the concept's "initial and rigorous meaning", which she has high hopes of utilizing "for clarifying the clinical facts noted above, as regards both their genesis and evolution", referring to the overflow of libido that she has noticed in her patients.

Torok also rather charmingly reminds us that the term "gives shape to the first great discovery Ferenczi made, being filled with wonder before the phenomenon of psychoanalysis" (pp. 110–111). Torok's celebration of her forebear's moment of discovery recalls another famous sonnet by an English Romantic poet: Keats's "On First Looking into Chapman's Homer". There, a readerly or textual experience is compared with the moment when the explorer Cortez and his bedazzled men encounter the Pacific for the first time and, in the poet's imagination,

> Looked at each other with wild surmise—
> Silent, upon a peak in Darien.
>   [1816, p. 9]

All wonderment aside, however, Torok is clearly critical of and in something of a snit with some of the big names of psychoanalysis for, on the one hand, crediting Ferenczi's fathering of the concept of introjection, but not bothering, on the other, to know or use it accurately enough.

She rightly says that the term was "travestied from the start" and that, despite its "pithiness" and apparent utility—and Ferenczi's second attempt to clarify it in 1912—it nevertheless became "muddled" and had "mutually exclusive meanings" attributed to it. Not only, says Torok, did introjection lose its original connection with transference for which it was at first intended as a synonym, but it began to be used wrongly, and ironically "to denote a mechanism characterized by the impossibility or the refusal to introject, at least in the sense originally intended by Ferenczi" (p. 111). In other words, as we shall see, the problem seems to inhere in the fact that introjection was likened to, and associated with, the literal act of incorporation, rather than the more psychic/figurative dynamic of the transference.

Though we have ourselves been over this ground, it is perhaps instructive to see just how exercised Torok gets by these lexical mishaps and misapprehensions. As I have done at length, she now rehearses more briefly the pertinent early work of Freud and Karl Abraham on these matters, including how the cognates of introjection—like identification and incorporation—came to be used more extensively in the context of object loss, mourning, and melancholia. We are told that, between 1913 and 1917, "Freud's views on identification—narcissistic forms of incorporation as opposed to incorporation in the neuroses—continued to gain in complexity and came to constitute the pivotal point in his economic understanding of the work of mourning". Torok adds that, for Freud, "the trauma of objectal loss leads to a response: incorporation of the object within the ego" (p. 111).

Using financial or fiscal metaphors (quite aptly, given the business and legal tender of such related terms as corporate and corporation), she says that the partial identification with the incorporated object "makes it possible both to wait while readjusting the internal economy and to redistribute one's investments". Continuing in this vein, she says that because "it is not possible to liquidate the dead", what happens is that "the bereaved become the dead . . . and take their time to work through, gradually and step by step, the effects of the separation". Specifying Karl Abraham's contributions, Torok credits him with establishing "that incorporation of the object and separation from it occur in the form of oral-cannibalistic and anal-evacuative processes" (p. 111).

It is possible that some of Torok's formulations sound slightly unfamiliar or obscure here—or at least they may not coincide precisely with my own reading of the history of these concepts. Given that both Freud and Abraham make extensive use of Ferenczi's term "introjection", Torok would have expected them at least to stay faithful to his conception of it and to differentiate it from the other terms; she clearly feels that this was far from being the case. Freud's later texts (particularly *Group Psychology* and *The Ego and the Id*) are roundly criticized for mistakenly equating introjection with identification, and for the mistaken assumption that introjection has to do with "the recovery of investments" from a lost object or an unattainable ego ideal—that is, with the processes necessary for the Oedipus complex to be overcome or dissolved. Her main or more general point seems to be that it is a gross mistake to see introjection as "compensating for a loss or lack": she will try to show "that completely different ideas inspired Ferenczi's concept" (p. 112).

It is perhaps useful to consider Torok's thinking in relation to Loewald's here—both their similarities and their differences. Though he is not at all in the business of resurrecting Ferenczi's legacy and therefore does not emphatically venerate the term "introjection", as Torok does, Loewald's preferred term, "internalization", appears to have a very similar meaning. This impression is reinforced when, like Torok with *her* Ferenczian word, he wishes to rescue his *own* favoured word from synonymity with identification and takes a complex view of their relations.

Interestingly, however, Loewald does not feel the need to keep loss of the object and mourning out of the picture; on the contrary, loss and separation are central to the ensuing psychic liberation and internal structure building towards which he sees the ego or subject to be striving. I had myself also noted earlier that Ferenczi did not coin introjection with specific reference to loss, and it appears that Torok takes this very seriously and follows suit.

In the following subsection, "Ferenczi's Text and Its Significance", she quotes substantially from Ferenczi's "On the Definition of Introjection" (1912), then summarizes it accurately, making no mention of loss:

> First and foremost, in the sense Ferenczi gave this concept, "introjection" is comprised of three points: (1) the extension of autoerotic interests, (2) the broadening of the ego through the removal of repression, (3) the including of the object in the ego and thereby "an extension to the external world of the [ego's] original autoerotic interests. [p. 112]

Torok now claims that this tripartite meaning of introjection was largely ignored by Ferenczi's peers and reduced "to a single superficial aspect: taking possession of the object through *incorporation*, that is, by putting it into the body or psyche".

As we shall see even more clearly in the next paper, both Torok and her partner, Nicolas Abraham, are determined to gainsay, eliminate, and remedy this synonymizing of introjection and incorporation. Here Torok repeats that Ferenczi's text carries the implication "that introjection cannot have as its cause the actual loss of an object of love". Instead, she thinks, it "operates like a genuine instinct", such that, in the manner of transference, its actions should be linked with the drives themselves and "the process of including the Unconscious in the ego through objectal contacts". Object loss, she appears to think, is something that interferes with or holds up such processes; it is, therefore, not something over which introjection presides and is none of its business, so to speak. Suddenly sounding very much like Loewald, Torok—perhaps with a glance at her earlier fiscal metaphors—says: "Introjection does not tend toward compensation but growth." It works to expand and extend the ego, rendering it more inclusive and capacious, and thus enabling it to invite, welcome, and contain "the unconscious, nameless, or repressed libido" (p. 113).

Let us not forget that these are the views of not only a Hungarian, but a French analyst, for whom Freud's earlier topographical model has by no means simply been superseded or improved upon by the later, structural one. To this extent, she remains a drive-oriented analyst, still convinced that what matters most in these intrapsychic dynamics is how the ego deals with unconscious wishes and demands. For Torok, therefore, objects are something of a means to an end: "it is not at all a matter of 'introjecting' the object, as is all too commonly stated, but of introjecting the sum total of the drives, and their vicissitudes as occasioned and mediated by the object" (p. 113).

Again, speaking in the name of Ferenczi, but sounding very French, Torok closes this subsection by elaborating on "the role of mediation", as conferred by introjection and played by the object—including the analyst, of course—in relation to the unconscious. By way of negotiating the back-and-forth between narcissism and object relations, "introjection transforms instinctual promptings into desires and fantasies of desire, making them fit to receive a name and the right to exist and to unfold in the objectal sphere" (p. 113).

Simply put, the purpose of introjection is, as far as Torok is concerned, the linking up of the innate, inherent wishes and wants of the intrapsychic libido with an external (and non-incestuous) object, towards whom desire may then be nominated, directed, and experienced. It goes without saying, of course, that Torok's emphases on both naming and desire point inexorably to the influence of Lacan and will inevitably put her at odds with—or at an oblique angle to—most of her Anglo–American psychoanalytic counterparts.

Thus, we detect both harmony and dissonance as resonating between the voices of Maria Torok and Hans Loewald at this moment. While both seem to be talking about libidinal liberation and intrapsychic shifts of one kind or another, where Torok chooses Ferenczian introjection as the means to these ends, Loewald opts for the more neutral-sounding internalization—perhaps precisely as a way of avoiding all the misprision that Ferenczi's concept has had to endure.

But how different are these two procedures from one another, other than in name? As I mentioned, Loewald, apparently unlike Torok and Ferenczi, does not seem to divide off the "compensatory" work of mourning one's object from the more salutary psychic actions that build internal capacities or structures. For him, the latter seem to constitute rewards resulting directly from the former. That is, if one negotiates and processes one's losses successfully (digests and metabolizes them thoroughly, perhaps), this entails the automatic earning or gaining of a richer, more complex, and more satisfactory internal world and external life. It would seem, in other words, that Loewald brings internalization into closer proximity with mourning, by contrast with isolating it from issues of loss, as Torok ostensibly does in the name of introjection and in keeping with Ferenczi's original stipulations.

But perhaps we need to remain patient, to wait and see how Torok takes these matters further forward. The following two subsections of this third section are both about incorporation: the first—"Incorporation: The Secret Magic Aimed at the Recovery of the Object of Pleasure"—is devoted to explaining not only how this concept differs from introjection, but also how the very properties that tend to be attributed erroneously to the latter, belong, in fact, to the former. Incorporation is referred to as a "fantasmic mechanism", one that "does suppose the loss of an object in order to take effect", a loss that has occurred "before the desires concerning the object might have been freed". This kind of loss, therefore, "acts as a prohibition and . . . constitutes an insurmountable obstacle to introjection"; a "prohibited object is settled in the ego to compensate for the lost pleasure and the failed introjection". This, says Torok, "is incorporation in the strict sense of the term" (p. 113).

One gets the impression that Torok is talking about a specific situation of grief (or grievance) here, and it immediately recalls "A Rose for Emily", Faulkner's brilliant portrayal of incestuous loss and its consequences. Surely this is just the kind of thing that Torok wishes to address as she characterizes incorporation: Miss Emily's father was never able to liberate his daughter libidinally, could not allow her release (or his own) from incestuous bonds; thus, when he dies, she is "bound" to try to keep or incorporate him—that is, she cannot but cling, quite literally, to his body—which the proper townspeople of Jefferson cannot permit. When she eventually appears to recover, emerges from her seclusion, and takes a lover, this is nothing but a sham or ruse. The only thing that Homer Barron can ever be for her is a like-for-like substitute for—a literal incarnation of—her father, certainly not a freely chosen love object. That is why his fate is sealed from the start. The previously disallowed corporeal incorporation of her father, as well her terrible revenge on him, can now be carried through as—simultaneously defiant and faithful—she takes this doubly forbidden object (Barron would have been disqualified both by the person of her father and by incestuous association with him) to her bed and kills him, preserving him there forevermore.

Continuing to specify the nature of incorporation, by contrast with introjection, Torok says that where the latter is "a gradual process", the former is "instantaneous and magical": it "obeys the pleasure principle" and functions in the same way as "hallucinatory fulfilments". Thus, it must also be a clandestine activity, one that hides its own workings, tries "to remain concealed". As if it is itself a shameful incestuous wish, "incorporation is born of a prohibition it sidesteps but does not actually transgress"; it does have the understandable intention, after all, of trying to recover "an object that, for one reason or another, evaded its own function: mediating the introjection of desires". However, as Torok reiterates, because it refuses "both reality's and the object's verdict, incorporation is an eminently illegal act", and, for this reason, "Secrecy is imperative for survival" (pp. 113–114).

Turning again to Faulkner's story: though the plot is shot through with subterfuge and turns on a deception, the narrative has only pretended to conceal its most horrifying or macabre moment—having provided many a pre-emptive clue along the way—until its very last line, featuring that "long strand of iron-gray hair" (Faulkner, 1930, p. 130). It emphasizes the extent to which Emily has herself been incorporated, swallowed up by and in these perverse machinations: such psychopathic secrets can ultimately only hide in plain sight and finally "will out".

In contradistinction, Torok presents introjection as an honest and transparent process that has no truck with secrets: it "works entirely in the open by dint of its privileged instrument, naming". She now juxtaposes the meanings of the two terms quite dichotomously:

> While the introjection of desires puts an end to objectal dependency, incorporation of the object creates or reinforces imaginal ties and hence dependency. Installed in place of the lost object, the incorporated object continues to recall the fact that something else was lost: the desires quelled by repression. Like a commemorative monument, the incorporated object betokens the place, the date, and the circumstances in which desires were banished from introjection: they stand like tombs in the life of the ego. [p. 114]

Lest this implication be missed, Torok's insistence that we adopt Ferenczi's introjection in its entirety entails the acknowledgement that it constitutes the ego's route to liberation from the object, providing a solution to, or even an evasion of, too great a dependence upon it.

This is, perhaps, why Klein and her followers might prefer to ignore or eschew these aspects of the term, to confuse it with incorporation, and thus to favour the installation of an internal object, in something like the manner of "a commemorative monument". Torok, by contrast, purports not to understand how anyone might confuse two mechanisms so at odds with each other, or "call these two movements—the introjection of drives and the incorporation of the object—by the same name" (pp. 114). And yet, it is evident that they do have a rather intimate relationship, albeit one of opposition or obversion: if anything, incorporation is the evil twin of introjection—a Mr Hyde (who "hides") to its Dr Jekyll—or the soiled and sordid underside of the same coin, as it were.

What is also striking here is how Torok is beginning to resort to the language of monuments and tombs, a set of tropes that will become central to—and the very signature of—her work with Nicolas Abraham. Miss Emily again provides the perfect example of a person-turned-monument or of someone entombed in her own life: she incorporates and embodies not only her father, but also the essentially stagnant, arrogant, non-budging recalcitrance of the post-Civil War Deep South, for which she thus becomes an emblem, "like the carven torso of an idol in a niche, looking or not looking at us, we could never tell which. Thus she passed from generation to generation—dear, inescapable, impervious, tranquil, perverse" (Faulkner, 1930, p. 128).

In the final subsection, "Incorporation: Its Origin, and Its Telling Nature", Torok—having worked so studiously at keeping them apart—can at last afford to explore, more explicitly and at its source, the relationship between introjection and incorporation. She speaks of an "archaic level on which the two mechanisms, though subsequently opposed, could still be fused", that is, at an early moment of the ego's functioning, which is of necessity entirely oral in nature:

> This type of process *signals* its meaning to itself by way of a *fantasy* of ingestion. Comprised exclusively of the oral libido's introjection, the ego consists at this stage in the use it makes of ingestion and its variants (salivation, hiccups, vomiting, etc.), in symbolic expressions, such as asking for or refusing food *regardless of the actual state of hunger* or, alternatively, fantasizing the consumption or refusal of food by means of the same mechanism but when the object is absent. The latter corresponds quite precisely to what is usually described as the mechanism of incorporation. [p. 114]

With this description as a base, she goes on to provide a brilliant account of how these dynamics can go wrong.

They become fixated or hypostasized, creating addictive personalities fobbed off with substances and the promise of concrete solutions to psychic difficulties, offered false incorporative compensations for their introjective losses:

> The fantasy of incorporation is the first lie, the effect of the first rudimentary form of language. It is also the first instrument of deception. Satisfying need by offering food does not sate the actual and persistently active hunger for introjection. The offer of food only serves to deceive it.... Thirsting for introjection despite an insurmountable internal obstacle, the ego tricks itself with a magical procedure in which "eating" (the feast) is paraded as the equivalent of an immediate but purely hallucinatory and illusory "introjection." Manic persons announce with fanfare to their unconscious that they are "eating" (an act signifying the process of introjection and satisfaction for the ego). Yet this is nothing but empty words and no introjection. When deprived of progressive libidinal nourishment, the ego regresses to this archaic level of magical attainment. [pp. 114–115]

I have quoted Torok at some length here because, of course, this attention to "ingestion and its variants" is of special interest to me.

Although she has yet to address depression explicitly, moreover, mania has now made an appearance, and her picture of an internal world is beginning to emerge. We may also start to anticipate how a psychic situation like André Green's "dead mother" (where the mother is not literally dead, but deeply depressed) might constitute just the kind of "insurmountable internal obstacle" that leads to symptomatology of the type that Torok is talking about. Her idea that—*qua* fantasy—incorporation "is merely a language *signalling* introjection, without actually accomplishing it", suggests intriguing linguistic ideas that are quite different from those of Lacan. (Incidentally, the latter might be seen by some as occupying a place that looms too large in French psychoanalysis, an inescapable, incestuous parent who will not let go and must be swallowed and incorporated if he cannot be properly digested or introjected.)

Along with other antinomies, Torok wants to posit that there are psychic languages that are calculated to deceive and obfuscate, that must be distinguished from those that point the way to truth and reality. She tells us that incorporation is a mendacious mechanism that establishes itself on the basis of a distortion of what introjection offers: to realize "that incorporation is a form of language, which merely *states* the desire to introject, marks an important step forward in psychoanalytic therapy". The lies of incorporation, in other words, always refer to the truths of introjection but require analytic translation or interpretation for the deceptive promises of the former to be uncovered. In one of the two brief examples that Torok provides, a man who has never masturbated dreams that his mother hands him a plate of asparagus and a fork. Torok renders its significance in the first-person voice of the son: "I wish she would relinquish her power over my penis and hand it over into my own hand, authorizing me to introject my desire for her" (p. 115).

Sounding briefly like the early Roland Barthes of *Mythologies* (1957), Torok considers the meaningful messages detectable in or beneath various cultural rituals and products: "Consider Popeye eating spinach; love potions; the fruit of knowledge whose ingestion by the first couple conferred on it genital sexuality; various cannibalistic rites; and the incorporative function of first communions, etc." As she brings the long third section of her paper to a close, Torok urges that these instances of incorporation, when viewed through the lens of psychoanalysis, be understood not as mere demands for gratification, but "as the disguised language of as yet unborn and unintrojected desires" (p. 115). Is Torok indicating and emphasizing that there are significant differences between oral appetite and genital desire, or warning against potential confusion between need and wish, self-preservation and libido?

It is perhaps worth restating at this point that this French psychoanalytic way of discussing desire, its frustrations, and the defences against it, remains somewhat unfamiliar to British School and perhaps also American psychoanalytic paradigms. It is as if the object-relations "revolution" (along, perhaps, with the different philosophical and cultural traditions underpinning and sustaining Anglo–American thought) has carried those versions of psychoanalysis too far afield, away from its sexual origins. Perhaps we need to recall here an important footnote in Freud's *Three Essays on the Theory of Sexuality* (1905d, p. 149), where he reminds us that it has not always been the case that the object—as opposed to the aim—of desire has been as venerated and as culturally extolled as it is in our times. Ideas around the expediency, even expendability, of the object, or regarding it as a means to an end, and the implication that what is introjected is not the object, nor even a relationship with it, but the desires themselves that the object is tasked with allowing, enabling, and actualizing in the subject: all of this can sound very foreign, not to say unpopular, to ears more used to the strains and refrains of English-language psychoanalysis.

If we listen attentively and sympathetically to Torok, however, we gain useful insights into how aberrant incorporative processes lie at the root of all manner of addictions, so many—if not all—of which are oral in origin. Indeed, we might even offer to define addiction in such terms, as a false incorporative compensation for a failed psychic introjection. Torok continues to elaborate this perspective in the next section of her paper ("Fixation and the Illness of Mourning"), seeking to link her careful teasing apart of incorporation from introjection with "Karl Abraham's idea of 'normal mania'", saying that "An increase in libido, leading at times to orgasm, is a reaction to a death." She believes that just such a metapsychological reconstruction of this shocking moment—along with its immediate repression—will lead us to "the core of the illness of mourning" (pp. 115–116).

What Torok goes on to describe, in vividly Gallic fashion, does nevertheless translate readily enough into Anglo–American terms. We are told that the (parental) object and the analyst are there to be used by the ego—perhaps similarly to the way that Winnicott (1969) speaks of the object being used—"to achieve its libidinal awakening and nourishment", or to arrive at what Loewald might call psychic emancipation.

For Torok, the object's introjective role here is that of "mediator" between the ego and the unconscious drives: it must, therefore, precisely *not* get in the way by presenting itself to the ego as an incorporative, substitutive, and incestuous "complement to instinctual satisfaction". It is only because the object "carries the promise of introjection" and holds the key to growth and development that the child (or patient) must make a prolonged and passionate investment in the parent (or analyst)—rather than for the latter's own sake, as it were. Once this job of libidinal liberation is done, the ego no longer needs to be beholden to the object; it can—and should—be released from its bond. Or, as Torok puts it, invoking the Lacanian imaginary: "When the process of introjection is complete, the object can descend from the imaginal pedestal where the ego's need for nourishment has placed it" (p. 116).

Torok now does bring death back into the picture, noting wisely that "the nature of the bereavement will be a function of the role the object played at the time of the loss". If by then there has been sufficient introjection of desires via or *vis-à-vis* the object, "no breakdown, no illness of mourning or melancholia should be feared", and, under such circumstances, Freud's rather matter-of-fact account of the mourning of the external object can be seen to pertain: in the course of time, the ego will, be able to reclaim its libidinal investment from the object "in order to fix itself on other objects that might be necessary for its libidinal economy". Though this work is painful, prolonged, and arduous enough, as Torok says, "the ego's integrity guarantees the outcome" (p. 116).

As we know, this is not always how things unfold. If, for one reason or another, introjection is left incomplete, then the death of a crucial object can produce a different outcome. Torok's language conjures up a rather stagnant, toxic, unpleasant, self-defeating internal picture as she explains the logic of such psychic developments:

> Because the unassimilated portion of the drives has congealed into an imago, forever reprojected onto some external object, the incomplete and dependent ego finds itself in a self-contradictory obligation. The ego needs to keep alive at all costs that which causes its greatest suffering. [p. 116]

If Torok had intentionally set out to interpret Faulkner's story, she could not have come closer to parsing its events. As the example of Miss Emily's attests, idolization and incest can take hold—and hold on—in perverse and ultimately deadly ways. It is then that something like a bad internal object—something emitting a bad smell—can crystallize and establish itself immovably within.

We recall that the often fooled and flummoxed townspeople are nevertheless wise enough to discern why Miss Emily must try to prevent the removal of her father's dead body. After all, she has unfinished business with him, and Torok again explains the perverse compulsion inherent in such situations: it is desperately believed, despite all the evidence to the contrary, that this external object and its hypostasized imago can still be "the repository of hope; the desires it forbade would be realized one day". Thus, because "the imago retains the valuable thing whose lack cripples the ego", it cannot under any circumstances be permitted to die and abandon its task. The irony is that this "objectal fixation is cemented"—precisely—by the fact that only "the warden of repression" can "authorize its removal", with the consequence that this ego will remain incarcerated in melancholia, "henceforth condemned to suffer the illness of mourning" (p. 116).

The following section announces itself as "An attempted reconstruction of the metapsychological moment of loss", which Torok prefaces with a further forthright statement of her convictions, saying that "The increase in libido is a desperate and final attempt at introjection, a sudden amorous fulfillment with the object." No matter how unexpected and surprising the "unbridled tidal wave" of desire that breaks over the astonished mourner, and despite an unwillingness to take either blame or responsibility for it, the event is by no means denied or repudiated.

With a sense of time running out, and because the ego has already been thwarted by both repression and an object that had endlessly prevented or denied the introjection of libidinal needs, death now hastens a panicky regression "to the archaic level of hallucinatory satisfaction". The ego's "long-contained hope is cornered in a desperate dilemma: deadly renunciation or fallacious triumph", so it plumps for the latter, resorting, as this last word suggests, to what is effectively a manic solution: "substituting fantasy for the real thing, magic and instantaneous incorporation for the introjective process". Defiantly repudiating renunciation, depression, and even death itself, the ego "exults in orgasm" (p. 117).

However, as is always the case with manic ploys, this comes with a price. The ego's defences bite back, return in force, and "this fleeting fulfillment is struck with explicit condemnation and immediate repression". Therefore, though the orgasmic moment itself may not always be wiped out by amnesia, "its link to a desire for the dying or dead object is always severely censored" and, as Torok says, it is "precisely the repression of this particular link", the failure to make the connection, that characterizes and maintains the illness of mourning.

Because of "the particularly intense resistance encountered in the analysis of such cases", one technical difficulty is the prospect of a too-sudden awakening from or undoing of the repression. If the patient is "Placed all too abruptly before their desire, without previously having had the chance to deconstruct their imago gradually", there is the risk of re-traumatization by the return of "the buried memory of an instant of illegitimate sexual delight" (pp. 117–118). This is what we might understand to be happening in Wordsworth's "Surprised by Joy". It also provides yet another corroboration of the importance of time in such matters, for the sake of gradual digestive processing rather than manic, counterproductive haste.

Returning to the macabre phrase in her paper's title, Torok invokes a kind of perverse fairy-tale atmosphere—reminiscent of the stories of the British feminist author Angela Carter (1979)—as she specifies that the psychic action of repression "not only separates, but also has to *preserve*" illicit desire in the concretely embodied form of "an 'exquisite corpse' lying somewhere inside it". Like the princely hero in *Sleeping Beauty*, the ego is therefore inexorably drawn to the task of searching for and then attempting to revive the interred imago that holds him in thrall. When such patients are in analysis, Torok suggests, they seem consciously oblivious of their quest; and yet, "Everything unfolds as though a mysterious compass led them to the tomb wherein the repressed problem lies" (p. 118).

In the last paragraph of this section, Torok brings a wonderfully apt and evocative literary example: the Gothic poem "Ulalume" by Edgar Allan Poe (1847, p. 39), in which a narrator wanders unwittingly (or unconsciously) through an ominously atmospheric landscape, ignoring the warnings of his Psyche, to enact—without memory, but with the fateful inevitability of desire—a horrifying, perhaps necrophiliac, anniversary return to the site of his beloved's grave. In keeping with her theme, Torok reads—indeed, diagnoses—this trajectory as "the revival of the unforgettable moment when the object's death permitted its magical conquest in the rapture of orgasm" (p. 118). It might be worth mentioning that Poe can be considered, both thematically and generically, as a prime literary precursor of both Faulkner and Carter.

Torok begins the next section ("A Clinical Example") with the view that the perception or diagnosis of this condition (which she continues to designate, perhaps a little oddly, as *the* illness of mourning, as if there are no other such illnesses) tends to come to the fore late on in analyses in which it arises. Her example is that of Thomas, a depressed young man—possibly the same one who had dreamt of the mother, the asparagus, and the fork—who eventually confesses to having been overcome by "carnal desires" as his mother lay dying, causing him to flee the deathbed scene. The previously secret, originating childhood moment—when the "incorporation of the imago, obstructing phallic and genital introjections, took place"—could then be remembered and revealed in the analysis.

Once, while bathing him, his mother had aggressively taken hold of his erect penis, telling him that this is how a woman might subdue a man who attacks her. Torok admirably captures the complex implications of this moment:

> The desire of the little boy and the mother met for an instant then, but for an instant only. The hardly reassuring idea suggested by the erection revealed at once the mother's desire and her superego's aggression toward the penis. This contradiction led to the boy's imaginal incorporation of both the desire and the mother's superego. Fixated on the imago, Thomas never stopped looking for this moment in order to overcome the prohibitive superego, hoping to carry off his mother's and his own desire in a common triumph. [p. 119]

In Torok's account of these confused and confusing symmetries of seduction and superegoic repudiation, there is also a crucial and equivalent transference moment that occurs just before the analyst's Christmas break, which is clearly being anticipated by the patient as a form of death. Thomas tells her that he is feeling "ruined" and then brings a dream in which it is not he but his mother who is having the carnal desires on her deathbed. Torok gives us his horrified reaction in the first person: "'her thighs are wide open. She is like an old prostitute.... And as I was watching her, I ruined, ruined, ruined. No! I urinated'" (p. 120).

We will later see how much both Nicolas Abraham and Torok make of these moments when a verbal slip or inversion, a piece of linguistic play, effects a psychic revelation: this, in fact, constitutes the very basis of their other book, *The Wolf Man's Magic Word* (1986). Here, it is the transposition of syllables—like the reversal of sexual roles—that reveals the truth: "Ever since his mother's death Thomas has been ruining himself for having 'urinated' that day" (where urinated really means ejaculated). Torok concludes her clinical example with a concise statement of its unfolding within the treatment setting:

> And now the repressed content revives in the transference: the analyst-mother is leaving and "dies." Thomas says to this old woman in the throes of death: I wish you could be a prostitute for me (and caress my penis in the tub) *since you desire it too*. Shaken after this session, Thomas can finally mourn for his mother and thereby somewhat lighten the load of his imaginal fixation. [p. 120]

Sylvia Plath, "Daddy" (1962)

As Torok's literary and linguistic sensibilities continue to resonate with my own, it is again a specific textual moment that stimulates an association to a highly pertinent poem. In this instance, when her patient compulsively repeats and scrambles the syllables of a key word with overdetermined meanings, I am reminded of the extensive use of stammering, stuttering repetition in Sylvia Plath's infamous and devastating poem about a thwarting, abusive parent: "Daddy" (1962, pp. 54–56).

Considered autobiographical or confessional, the poem was written just after Plath's acrimonious separation from Ted Hughes and only a few months before she killed herself; it can certainly be read in retrospect as an allusively diagnostic account of why these psychic disasters, now the stuff of literary legend, were almost destined to ensue. A much-interpreted poem, "Daddy" has been mined for "evidence" on both sides of a controversial para-forensic and litigious literary–critical blame-game that played out between supporters and detractors of these two major poet-personae during the decades after Plath's death in 1963. Indeed, it still rumbles on in the wake of Hughes' death a quarter of a century later. The journalist Janet Malcolm, who has also produced resonant and popular books about psychoanalysis (1981, 1984), wrote a detailed critical account of these exchanges (1994) but ended up inevitably being drawn into the fray herself.

These debates—or unseemly squabbles—notwithstanding, Plath's poem is very much worth considering in the context established here by

Torok's paper and as part of my own more general deliberations about mourning, melancholia, and internalization. Addressed to the long-since-deceased "Daddy" of the title, the poem consists of 16 five-line stanzas. Setting both tone and tempo from the outset, the very first line is a repeating, internally rhyming rejection or repudiation, asserting the father's unacceptability: "You do not do, you do not do".

Following this lead, the entire poem has a syncopated rhythm (at least to my musically untrained ear) and adopts a jazzy, ironic tone that manages somehow both to jar—given its weighty subject matter—and yet also to sound remarkably appropriate. While there is no consistent rhyme scheme, every stanza save one contains lines either ending in or rhyming with the poem's first word "you", including one occurrence of the word in German translation. Plath has effectively weaponized the second-person pronoun here, and the father stands accused and assailed by multiple post-mortem finger-pointing jabs or stab wounds, in an unrelentingly scathing personal attack that drips with poisonous contempt.

As in the fictional case of Faulkner's Miss Emily, and perhaps also Torok's clinical case above, the physical death of a parent might appear to offer ostensible or immediate freedom from tyranny, a momentary reprieve or release from incarceration. What is in doubt, however, is whether this alone can bring about genuine or lasting psychic liberation for the subject. As we shall see, the sheer manic defensiveness of Plath's poem—the vengeful vituperation and glee that she puts on display—suggest otherwise. It is perhaps only with hindsight, when we realize that he had died long before, that the father addressed in these scathing terms comes into view as an excessively bad, paranoid-schizoid internal object; therefore, she cannot be rid of him so easily.

In her early lines, with what is perhaps a glance at the cruelties of traditional Chinese foot-binding, the narrator imagines herself as a foot within her father's shoe, hinting at a trampled, suffocated existence, where she felt confined, constrained, stifled, and silenced for many years. The compulsive retaliatory urge to kill this abuser surfaces immediately, along with the paradoxical disappointment that his death had already intervened to prevent it. This is followed by the portrayal of a monstrous, monumental, deity-like figure, a gigantic, malign, beastly, and burdensome patriarchal presence; and yet, the speaker admits, she would never cease trying to regain his favour, indicating the tenacious power of ambivalence in such family relations.

Much to the outrage of certain critics, the fact that Plath's actual father was of German descent seems to enable or entitle her to adopt and systematically apply the tropes of Nazism and the Holocaust to this vividly imagined, brutally oppressive, sadomasochistic relationship between a father and his child. After the fourth stanza, this image of a jackbooted, German-speaking, quasi-Nazi father literally invades the language and imagery of the poem, rhythmically imitated and illustrated by the poem's marching, tramping repetitions. Alienated from his language, hating it, and finding it disgusting, Plath can neither communicate with this man nor read him accurately: she cannot bear to have his tongue in her mouth, so to speak, where it sticks like "a barb wire snare". But the father's reach is extensive, he seems ubiquitous; versions of him crop up everywhere, suggesting the transferential infectiousness of being possessed by a destructive internal object.

Though there is no Jewish ancestry in her family, Plath identifies with these quintessential victims, feels that she is beginning to talk like and metamorphose into a kind of part-object Jew, hounded down and sent on deportation trains to concentration camps. She also places herself in another category of person persecuted by the Nazis, seeing herself as a kind of fairground gipsy, with her mystical, fortune-telling tarot cards. No less stereotypical or satirical are the images of the father himself, though this somehow manages not to detract from, but in fact to enhance the horrifying effect. Claiming always to have feared this man, but also to desire him, Plath reaches a kind of perverse parodic climax with this self-skewering pastiche of female masochism:

> Every woman adores a Fascist,
> The boot in the face, the brute
> Brute heart of a brute like you.

Thus does Plath resort to a piling up of predictable and clichéd words and phrases, creating the most caustic, caricatured, typecast, war-film version of a Nazi imaginable.

Temporarily putting such imagery aside, Plath conjures up different roles for this father that are no less sordid and disturbing: from a picture she has of him, she describes a devilish schoolteacher, alluding slyly to what may be his paedophilic inclinations. Boldly—and perhaps offensively—exploiting dangerous racial stereotypes, Plath then has him morph into

> the black man who
> Bit my pretty red heart in two.

We then get a momentary biographical glimpse into what we assume might be Plath's actual past, as she juxtaposes the father's passing when she was just ten with her own first suicide attempt at twenty, which she now interprets as an attempt to join her father in death.

But she will have us believe that, even then, as the doctors were trying to put the bits of her back together again, she was hatching a plan full of revenge and repetition, one no less macabre than that of Miss Emily. Echoing arcane voodoo rituals, Plath vows to create her own version of the father, something—or someone—in his image. The implication is clear: she will set out to manufacture, or conjure, or find a man just like daddy, with a similar taste for torture, whom she might one day marry.

Plath had her fair share of therapy or analysis, and evidently possessed more than a modicum of self-knowledge about the oedipal sources of her attraction to the savage genius of Ted Hughes. The passion, turbulence, and violence of their relationship is well documented, and perhaps things could not but have ended badly between them.

Extrapolating perhaps too biographically from the poem, one is struck by both how well Plath seems to have understood her own psychic and existential predicament and how perversely she exploited it. Of course, no psychoanalyst would be fooled by the claim that she had everything so consciously planned and worked out in advance—this is surely the untenable retroactive manic ruse of a desperately depressed woman whose hope is almost extinguished.

And yet we might easily be persuaded that Plath was self-consciously quite aware of that, too. The vengeful speaker/persona of the poem purports to take control and replace her helpless victimhood with the assertion of full murderous responsibility for what she has done. She sees herself as having killed two men: if the first is her father, the second is her husband, though he is also credited (or debited) as the vampiric torturer who drained her lifeblood over the course of their marriage. It is as if Plath is taking the regressive opportunity here to inform her father of this ill-fated union, as if cruelly introducing him to the man who succeeded (and exceeded) him in sadism. But the two men are so completely identified with each other in her mind that they might as well be one and the same: a composite, incestuously illicit figure with an insatiable, devastating appetite for cruelty, who gradually steals the life of his victim and thus deserves to be put to death in turn.

As we have come to know about depression or melancholia since at least as far back as Freud and Abraham, when the ego identifies with the lost object, the latter may then be persecuted and killed off via the destruction of the self, and/or vice versa. Plath's poem draws to a close in a crescendo of other-directed, revenge-driven, horror-movie violence:

> Daddy, you can lie back now.
> There's a stake in your fat black heart
> And the villagers never liked you.
> They are dancing and stamping on you.
> They always knew it was you.

Her actual fate was, in fact, that of a lonely and tragic (and perhaps not fully intended) suicide. As Torok teaches and Plath's poem corroborates, such are the outcomes of the impossibility of introjection and mourning: they are attempts to substitute for these processes deadly, incorporative, bipolar parodies that flatter to deceive.

Plath's massive—and brilliant—poetic fantasy of retribution, the wish that she might exact and enact her revenge in the very medium that she and Hughes shared and cherished, perhaps does not, in the end, come off. Her last line effectively repeats what she had said ten lines earlier:

> Daddy, daddy, you bastard, I'm through.

The sentiment thus expressed can be read in more than one way. On the one hand, she is through with *him*, her object, in the colloquial American sense of having had it with him, taken as much as she can bear. But what she also conveys is that she is *herself* finished—has reached her limit or the end of her own tether. Having supped to the full at the animating feast of retaliation and provocation that has kept her poem and herself going, she is now exhausted, depressed, depleted of her manic poetic and existential energies; she is now close to the end, almost free at last—very nearly through, that is, to the other side.

* * *

We return to Torok's text in time to bear witness to her brief critical interpretation of Melanie Klein's approach to the vicissitudes of loss (in a section entitled "The Pain of Mourning and the Fantasy of the Exquisite Corpse"). Aptly, it is because of the "triumphant libidinal intrusion attendant upon object loss" that Klein is brought into the picture here: her profound understanding of the dynamics and dangers of triumph makes her contribution highly relevant at this juncture. In Torok's reading of Klein's answer to Freud's question about why mourning is so painful, the focus is less on reality testing than on the "manic sadistic triumph over the object" that Klein saw as integral.

Torok's emphasis, however, seems to differ slightly or subtly from Klein's own—or to constitute a nuance or corollary of it. For Torok, it is the feeling of triumph itself that is "badly tolerated" and hard to bear, and, for this reason, "the ego allegedly does everything in its power to turn a blind eye to this proof of its ambivalence". So, it is not so much the fact or presence of triumph as its "rejection or denial" that "blocks the work of mourning either temporarily or permanently. The remorse and the guilt felt on account of aggressive fantasies would then explain the pain of mourning" (p. 120).

Offering a more familiar summary, Torok then recalls that "according to Melanie Klein, every time a love object is lost, the original situation of objectal loss is revived". The accompanying depressive-position anxieties are thus about whether "the child's own sadism" might have caused the original loss of the good object, and it is this "specific anguish" that creates the despair "of ever being able to restore or reinstate the object permanently in order to guarantee the harmony and cohesion of the internal world". Having thus described "the Kleinian conception"—and seeming to want to accommodate it—Torok nevertheless regards it as providing only part of the solution to the pain of mourning. Neither aggression against, nor (the denial of) sadistic triumph over the good object holds the real key, which she thinks is better provided by the perhaps rather fine distinction "between an internal object and the imago" (pp. 120–121).

This differentiation is intended to stand as an alternative to Klein's distinction between metapsychologically equal-and-opposite good and bad objects, assumed to be simultaneously present in her internal worldview. Torok's distinction turns on there being two alternative internal situations, a more structural either-or: there will be a (good) internal object if it plays the role of "the fantasmic pole of the introjective process"; there will be a (bad) imago if it is constructed out of "all that resisted introjection and that the ego took possession of through other means, namely through the fantasy of incorporation" (p. 121).

Klein herself made occasional use of the term "imago", apparently as a general synonym for or precursor of the term "internal object": it tends to appear more frequently in her earlier work but only once in each of her two papers on manic-depressive states. (Imago is a term that seems progressively to have fallen out of favour in psychoanalytic discourse at large.) Klein could not herself have arrived at a distinction like Torok's because she either failed to make the distinction between introjection and incorporation or was simply uninterested in it. Given her abiding suspicion of the id, moreover, we would not have expected Klein to factor in anything resembling Torok's French insistence on the specifically sexual or libidinal function of introjection. Torok does seem to admire and salute Klein's clinical capacity to exemplify incorporation, to describe vividly cases where "this type of fixating imago exists". What Klein is seen as not appreciating, however, is the two-fold character of this kind of internal phenomenon: first, that "it was born of a failed introjective relation to an external object", and, second, that "its effect is always to prohibit sexual desire" (p.121).

Anticipating some of Green's ideas about the dead mother that I explore in chapter seven, Torok adds that such an imago tends to form "after a satisfaction was originally granted and then withdrawn". The imago is precisely a consequence and a sign of the fact "that a desire became retroactively reprehensible and unspeakable before it could be introjected". While granting the importance of the aggressive urges in this picture (which Klein is widely credited with highlighting), Torok reminds us that the early explorations of psychoanalysis established that "remorse and rumination arise at the libidinal spring of prohibited sexual desire". And here Torok can connect these quite theoretical considerations with the symptomatology of unrelenting, guilty self-torment characterizing the syndrome discussed in this paper: disturbingly for the grieving subject, the prohibitions of mourning notwithstanding, "desire concerning the object is both revived and satisfied" (p. 121).

With attention to almost literal, surgical detail, Torok specifies the significance of the "precise moment" to which such cases hark back: namely, when the object was dead or dying and "for an instant hallucinatory regression gratified desire". Even though denial and repression then immediately supervene, every subsequent revival of pleasure or "libidinal outburst" is experienced as a pain that "testifies to this moment as well as to the objectal fantasy which furnished its content". Because of its ambiguity, this pain is "genuinely 'exquisite'" and also "constitutes a valuable tool for analysis when it is understood in the medical sense of the term . . . because it points to the place where one needs to operate in order to unearth repression". Putting it in different and more macabre terms, Torok also says that the pain leads "to the tomb where desire lies buried": it is "a kind of 'here lies,' an inscription on which the name of the deceased long remains undecipherable". The patient's "self-torture is an invitation extended to the analyst to proceed with the exhumation" (p. 121), as well, perhaps, as a masochistic wish to be accused of a heinous crime.

In the remainder of this section as well as the next (and last), Torok offers some fascinating clinical material from cases exhibiting certain "special features". She says that these patients often bring dreams that are somehow both disturbing and relieving. One patient is recurrently accused in dreams of first eating someone and then burying them and must serve a life sentence for these crimes. Though the patient cannot yet "name their desire", the analyst in the transference is invited "to don the judge's robes" and hand down punishment for the double crime, the repression (burial), no less than the original deed (eating). The imprisonment, moreover, represents being "locked up in neurotic suffering as a result of repression". Acting also as a "morphologist", the analyst's tasks are "to reconstruct the event from a few scattered body fragments" and "to unmask the 'crime' of repression", but also "to identify the victim: the orgasmic moment experienced upon the object's death". These patients are virtually begging their analysts: "Help me find that moment so that I can come out of the impasse of my interminable mourning" (pp. 121–122).

A patient called Thérèse experiences sensual feelings whenever she has occasion to nurse somebody who is ill: she comes to both expect and dread this happening. She also realizes that she is "mysteriously attracted" to situations where this kind of caring might be required of her. Torok tells us that her analysis revealed "a massive repression of her father's death"—an inability to mourn that had lasted for more than a decade. In a "dream triptych" of a kind that Torok has come across in other grieving patients, Thérèse brings "marriage with an inaccessible man, an indictment for having eaten a corpse, a dentist predicting the exposure of her receding gumline, followed by the total loss of her teeth" (p. 122).

Torok concludes this section with a clear and astute clinical formulation:

> The much desired though deeply repressed union in love with her father was consummated hallucinatorily during the last rites. Therese's added repression of the moment of magical satisfaction directed her development toward an illness of mourning that endangered both her romantic relationships and her professional pursuits. [p. 123]

This also serves to introduce the final section of her paper, "The Vicissitudes of Transition and the Illness of Mourning", where Torok continues to explore the dental theme introduced above and to make quite far-reaching claims about it.

Near the beginning of this final section, Torok claims that "While dreams about 'eating and burying a corpse' characterize the illnesses of mourning, dreams about 'teeth' reach beyond this frame; they are found in nearly all analyses." It is "the language of 'teeth'" that enables Torok to make good on her earlier hint at the theme of psychic transition. Where Klein emphasized weaning as the first major or significant experience of loss, Torok puts her emphasis on this obviously contiguous or adjacent issue: "Teething marks the first great transition, hence its symbolic value in the evocation of transitions in general." She goes on to demonstrate how dreams or discourse featuring teeth can represent "the vicissitudes of libidinal reorganization" (a phrase that has distinct Loewaldian echoes), whether in relation to "the oedipal passage, adolescent growth, the attainment of adulthood or progress toward menopause" (p. 123). Of course, all such crossings, traversals, transformations, or transitions must necessarily involve losses and separations, too.

Torok gives another brief example, this time involving anorexia in an adolescent boy whose female teacher criticized him for being "too big". When this "biting" comment is transposed into a nightmare featuring rodents with frightening teeth and is interpreted accordingly, it uncovers oedipal anxieties about the size of his penis; thus, the dream "throws light on the conflict of adolescent transition and bears fruit in the psychoanalytic process". Anticipating some sceptical questioning, Torok claims that such dreams "authorize an answer" and again asserts that "The illness of mourning is a special case of a wider or more inclusive framework of disturbances that generally characterize periods of transition" (pp. 123–124).

Certainly, the new drive disturbances of adolescence call for further reconstructing introjections. These are precisely the times during which "irruptions" from the libido destabilize the ego, forcing it to "reorganize itself and its objectal relations". Torok writes with understanding and compassion for both the teenage subjects undergoing these changes and the (parental) objects trying to both permit and contain them. She reminds us that while the young person may be "mindful of the sweetness of its new drive", they may not yet be ready to "accommodate" it and thus may remain ambivalent towards it. However, says Torok (sounding very much like Loewald yet again),

> In cases where the object helps the child ever so slightly to introject the drive, giving it back to the child in objectalized forms, the transition need not degenerate into an insurmountable conflict. Introjection should proceed quite smoothly. [p. 124]

By contrast, things go awry when "the object is absent, lacking, or has performed a seduction": then "the introjection of new drives will be blocked and imaginal fixation will inevitably follow", along with "inhibitive developmental disturbances" in the subject.

In these final paragraphs, Torok rehearses some of her earlier claims and clinical examples. She asks, "How is the object who inhibits the ego's growth experienced?" and bids us think again of Thomas, the man whose mother had aggressively taken hold of his penis and yet was so clearly out of touch with her own desire. When she does fleetingly feel it, only to immediately repeal or reject it, the scene is set for the forms of psychopathology that Torok is concerned with here.

Perhaps her new point near the end—one that will be taken up again and further elaborated in the next paper, co-written with Nicolas Abraham—is that the child of such a parent is tacitly or unconsciously aware of the object's own struggle with incestuous desire and strongly suspects that such feelings are therefore reciprocated or mutual. This can only fuel "the child's unwavering hope that one day the object would once again be *what it was* in the privileged moment". This would entail nothing less than its overcoming of superegoic scruples, returning to the moment of incestuous seduction, becoming again "just like the child, an exclusive lover in its heart of hearts" (p. 124).

In her final paragraph, Torok tries to differentiate subtly between two situations or moments of loss. Earlier, a live parent has perpetrated a confusing, ambivalent seduction, leading to massive repression, metaphorical death, or "fixation—the loss of a moment of satisfaction and its being buried like a corpse"; later, when actual death or object loss occurs, an instance of the illness of mourning ensues. Presumably upon the death of the parent—which raises the stakes—the unanalysed former childhood circumstance returns and reveals itself as the cause of the adult malaise. Torok footnotes her colleague Michel de M'Uzan on the collaborative or convergent last gasp of desire that both the dying person and the survivor might try to muster between them right at the very end of life. We are told that this can have the consequence of "an anguished state of confused identity" (p. 124).

If the one who dies and the one who remains in life can either merge or reverse positions at such moments, then so, perhaps, can the tenor and vehicle of the central metaphor: if repression is like death, then surely death is also like repression. With Poe-like Gothic horror again supervening, Torok's last words read: "Paradoxically, the object who is dead because of real death revives momentarily the 'exquisite corpse' that together the dead and the survivors had both long before consigned to the tomb of repression" (p. 124).

Nicolas Abraham and Maria Torok

"Mourning or Melancholia: Introjection versus Incorporation" (1972)

The paper by Torok discussed above and this co-authored one are the first and second papers, respectively, that translator and editor of *The Shell and the Kernel*, Nicholas Rand, grouped together under the heading "New Perspectives in Metapsychology: Cryptic Mourning and Secret Love". There are three further co-written papers under this rubric, all of which would also have been worth explicating in detail.

We will content ourselves with "Mourning *or* Melancholia: Introjection *versus* Incorporation". Much like Torok's paper, it is also divided into short, titled sections, ten in all (some of them just a single dense paragraph long). The first, introductory section is given the heading "Metapsychological Reality and Fantasy", and it begins with a statement that is as bold and decisive as the title of the paper as a whole: "Incorporation denotes a fantasy, introjection a process" (1972, p. 125).

Abraham and Torok express some immediate appreciation of the fact that "Kleinian texts" clarified and brought this distinction into prominence, but they also take issue with Klein and her followers for prioritizing fantasy (or phantasy), in what they later call "a perilous reversal". They see fantasy as "a product of the ego", not as something that temporally precedes or takes conceptual precedence over it. Thus, we encounter once again an objection to and critique of Klein's metapsychology, particularly her view of the psychogenesis of the ego and/or the self.

Going further, Abraham and Torok wish to both limit and bring precision to the term "fantasy" (indeed, in *The Shell and the Kernel* the very first paper is devoted entirely to this task). In the context of the current paper's concerns, fantasy is seen as an essentially conservative, defensive, masking phenomenon, the aim of which is "preservation of the status quo", as against reality's dangerous demands for transition or change. One yet again hears resonances between these ideas and Loewald's views on repression as an essentially preservative force, by contrast with internalization which promotes emancipation and the renewing or restructuring of the inner world.

Winnicott, in *Playing and Reality* (1971), makes his distinction between fantasy or daydreaming, on the one hand, and dreaming proper, on the other, along similar lines. As important as the differences are purported to be, within British psychoanalysis, between this limited meaning of fantasy and the more ubiquitous Kleinian notion of phantasy, as elaborated by Susan Isaacs (1948), I doubt whether this would have persuaded Abraham and Torok to treat them that differently. Indeed, they suggestively go on to say that fantasies "refer to a *secretly perpetuated* topography" and that when we attempt to understand clinically a patient's particular fantasy, we do so in order to identify "the specific topographical change the given fantasy is called upon to resist" (p. 125).

Fantasy, in other words, may be read as a cry for help. Adopting the form of a wider rhetorical question, Abraham and Torok ask whether metapsychology does not have as its very intention "to explain how and why fantasy and its corollaries arise": it tries to "detect the transformation of the underlying process that is being opposed", moving the investigation "from the description of phenomena to their transphenomenal basis" (p. 126).

At the beginning of the following section, "Incorporation: The Fantasy of Nonintrojection", we are told that fantasy not only acts as an indicator of the resistance to psychic change, but also provides an intimate link with "the intrapsychic state of affairs it is supposed to protect". Bringing us closer to the specific task of the paper, Abraham and Torok introduce incorporation as a somewhat "lesser-known" fantasy (in comparison with "the arch-fantasies of the primal scene, castration, and seduction"):

> Introducing all or part of a love object into one's body, possessing, expelling or alternately acquiring, keeping, losing it—here are varieties of fantasy indicating, in the typical forms of possession or feigned dispossession, a basic intrapsychic situation: the situation created by the reality of a loss sustained by the psyche. If accepted and worked through, the loss would require major readjustment. But the fantasy of incorporation merely simulates profound psychic transformation through magic; it does so by implementing literally something that has only figurative meaning. [p. 126]

Perhaps there will be no more explicit or clear-cut rendering anywhere else in this book of the metatheoretical differences—which Abraham and Torok go on to outline brilliantly and at length—between mourning and melancholia and the concomitant ways in which lost objects are internalized in the case of each.

Moreover, my alimentary thesis finds clear linguistic corroboration in the very next sentence and the rest of this crucial paragraph: "So in order not to have to 'swallow' a loss, we fantasise swallowing (or having swallowed) that which has been lost, as if it were some kind of thing" (p. 126). This swallowing, or magical incorporation, exempts the bereaved subject from having to undergo the long, difficult internalizing processes of grief and mourning, from both admitting that there has been an external loss and having to metabolize that loss internally.

Turning to our exemplifying story, what Miss Emily could not do was to admit—that is, to allow in—the loss of her father (by at first literally refusing to admit the townspeople into her house to remove his body), and therefore could not permit the later loss of Homer Barron. In each case, she attempted to hold on to that which needed to be given up (that is, the corporeal object itself), to possess it "swallowed whole" inside her house, her bed, and her internal psychic system. Rather than undergo a process of change and reconstruction, she chooses literally to keep hold of a decomposing corpse. Hitchcock's 1960 film *Psycho* is a perhaps more famous but very similar example, albeit one featuring mother and son, rather than father and daughter.

Neither Emily nor Norman Bates could afford—did not have the psychic wherewithal—to undergo what Abraham and Torok describe as "the painful process of *reorganization*". As they say, when "in the form of imaginary or real nourishment, we ingest the love object we miss, this means that *we refuse to mourn* and that we shun the consequences of mourning". If we should eat—or even imagine ourselves eating—with the intention of either devouring the actual lost object or of fending off its loss, there can be no proper mourning; the latter requires the taking back of an investment or cathexis and implies that we "reclaim as our own the part of ourselves that we placed in what we have lost".

Far from being a mere synonym of introjection, incorporation—by refusing such fateful internal transformations—in effect declares its "refusal to introject loss" and reveals itself as what we might call a phantasmatic, literalistic, and problematic "embodiment" of that which should be a psychic process. What is here referred to as "the magic of incorporation" consists of two "moves": "*demetaphorization* (taking literally what is meant figuratively) and *objectivation* (pretending that the suffering is not an injury to the subject but instead a loss sustained by the object)." Whereas the former is well explicated in this section, the latter will be fully developed later in the paper. As Abraham and Torok say in summary, incorporation "reveals a gap within the psyche; it points to something that is missing just where introjection should have occurred" (pp. 126–127).

This perspective constitutes something of a return to Freud's original attempt, in "Mourning and Melancholia", to distinguish as clearly as possible between these two states or conditions, but without seeing them simply as split between external and internal (or, indeed, conscious and unconscious) processes. Drawing on Freud's fundamental ideas about libidinal cathexes and their narcissistic and anaclitic vicissitudes in "On Narcissism", Abraham and Torok seem to be saying that when a loss occurs and investments are drawn back to the bereaved subject from the lost object, there needs to be an accompanying re-adjustment (what Loewald sees as a potentially self-enriching restructuring) of the former's internal landscape. What had previously been left somewhat vague and implicit as regards the narcissistic consequences of loss, Abraham and Torok (like Loewald) attempt to investigate more thoroughly and explicitly. This allows these analysts to make finer and more accurate distinctions between successful mourning and states of depression than either Freud or Klein had been able to do.

Unsurprisingly—and in keeping with the Hungarian roots of these authors—Ferenczi now makes an important appearance, as he had done in the previous paper by Torok. In the third section, "Introjection Understood as the Communion of 'Empty Mouths'", they first pose a naïve question, perhaps on behalf of their potential critics: if introjecting literally means "casting inside", then "it is surely the same thing as incorporating, is it not?" It most certainly is *not*, of course! In much the same way as Loewald referred to "non-objective art" in the course of differentiating between internalization and repression, Abraham and Torok speak evocatively of the degree of distinction between introjection and incorporation as like that "between metaphoric and photographic images, between the acquisition of a language and buying a dictionary, between self-possession gained through psychoanalysis and the fantasy of 'incorporating' a 'penis'" (p. 127).

To dispel any lingering confusion, say Abraham and Torok, it is Ferenczi, "inventor of both the term and the concept", who should be allowed to determine what the term "introjection" means and how it is to be used. For him, introjection is "the process of broadening the ego", which is akin to or enhanced by "transferential love"—and we hear, in the latter phrase, echoes of "primary love", coined by the British Hungarian analyst Michael Balint (1952), though he is not mentioned by name. As Balint would no doubt concur, Abraham and Torok suggest that there is a primary form of such "love" or introjection at work "soon after birth" (p. 127).

Much as there is a wish to keep introjection and incorporation as distinct as possible, there is no avoiding the concrete centrality of the mouth itself in these early stages of development. However, it is what fills the mouth—or what it feels empty of—that will be crucial in this respect. Encroaching on the terrain of British object-relations theory—the territory of Klein, Fairbairn, Bion, Winnicott, as well as Balint—Abraham and Torok say that "the initial stages of introjection emerge in infancy when the mouth's emptiness is experienced alongside the mother's simultaneous presence" (p. 127).

Where the specifically French inflection of their ideas is retained is in relation to the place and function of language in the process, even at this earliest, supposedly pre-linguistic, moment:

> The emptiness is first experienced in the form of cries and sobs, delayed fullness, then as calling, ways of requesting presence, as language. Further experiences include filling the oral void by producing sound and by exploring the empty cavity with the tongue in response to sounds perceived from the outside. Finally, the early satisfactions of the mouth, as yet filled with the maternal object, are partially and gradually replaced by the novel satisfactions of a mouth now empty of that object but filled with words pertaining to the subject. The transition from a mouth filled with the breast to a mouth filled with words occurs by virtue of the intervening experiences of the empty mouth. [p. 127]

This filling of the empty mouth, first with the protolanguage of "cries and sobs" and later with words, is tantamount to a primary form of introjection.

And here, anticipating what André Green will say in "The Dead Mother" (1980), Abraham and Torok declare that "the mother's constancy is the guarantor of the meaning of words", comparing her assumed and essential presence in this regard to "the permanence of Descartes's God" (p. 128), insurer of all human knowledge. That these three French analysts specify the primary importance of the mother's role in relation to the acquisition of language should not be underestimated. They thereby offer an alternative to the Freudian/Lacanian insistence on absolute paternal priority, particularly where language is concerned (the "symbolic order" and "Law of the Father"). They were clearly not averse to linking their work with the mother-centric, object-relational developments that were taking place in Anglo–American or English-speaking psychoanalytic contexts at the time.

There is a more particular echo here of Winnicott's idea about being alone in the presence of the mother (1958a), where he specifies that enough of that kind of experience is what enables a later capacity for aloneness or solitude (as opposed to loneliness or abandonment). With their more linguistic inflection, Abraham and Torok say that only after her "guarantee" is established "can words replace the mother's presence and also give rise to fresh introjections. The absence of objects and the empty mouth are transformed into words; at last, even the experiences related to words are converted into other words" (p. 128). One might say, in other words, that if one has words, one is never alone.

Optimally, therefore, according to Abraham and Torok, what "replaces" the lost external object is not an internal version of it, nor even a discrete internal relationship with it. The way that they connect loss or separation with digestion or internalization is via the mediating, metabolic properties of language in its wider social function:

> So the wants of the original oral vacancy are remedied by being turned into verbal relationships with the speaking community at large. Introjecting a desire, a pain, a situation means channeling them through language into a communion of empty mouths. This is how the literal ingestion of foods becomes introjection when viewed figuratively. The passage from food to language in the mouth presupposes the successful replacement of the object's presence with the self's cognizance of its absence. Since language acts and makes up for absence by representing, by *giving figurative shape* to presence, it can only be *comprehended* or *shared* in a "community of empty mouths". [p. 128]

Of course, though rendered in quite another language, there is nothing here that is not either made explicit or at least implied in Hannah Segal's Kleinian theory of symbolization (1954). She, too, emphasizes the necessary capacity for tolerating external absence or separateness as that which enables, guarantees, or ensures the properly symbolic use of language and all other forms of signification. Again, it is when things are not optimal that we get to witness linguistic disturbances (the employment of "symbolic equations" instead of symbols) as well as the defensive use of fantasy.

Abraham and Torok begin the fourth section of their paper ("Incorporation: One Mouth-Work in Place of Another") with a question about this specific fantasy. If, for them, "all fantasies indicate the refusal to introject", why do only some fantasies take "the privileged form of introducing an object into the body?" They also put their question differently: "why are some fantasies directed at the very metaphor of introjection?" The answers are implicit in the questions: insofar as incorporation is a literal carrying out in action of the introjective metaphor, this can be seen to occur when there is a "reflexive treatment" of the latter, when it must become a more self-conscious rather than a spontaneous process. And this happens if introjection, in its inchoate form, "encounters a prohibitive obstacle", when the mouth "is unable to say certain words and unable to formulate certain sentences". Then, say Abraham and Torok, "we fantasize, for reasons yet to be determined, that we are actually taking into our mouth the unnameable, the object itself" (p. 128).

If these ideas—concerning what we might call fantasies of substitutive concreteness—are thought through thoroughly enough, they offer us a comprehensive theory not just of mourning and loss at large, but of ailments such as anorexia, bulimia, and other eating disorders, as well as an account of the way in which many forms of addiction and perversion operate. Abraham and Torok seem to have identified what lies at the source and heart of such conditions:

> As the empty mouth calls out in vain to be filled with introjective speech, it reverts to being the food-craving mouth it was prior to the acquisition of speech. Failing to feed itself on words to be exchanged with others, the mouth absorbs in fantasy all or part of a person... [p. 128]

In all these conditions, we effectively resort to satisfying the concrete body when the symbolic mind fails to encompass, contain, or introject adequately. Extrapolating from this basic idea, it is surely true that if the mouth can be filled up—as well as emptied out—in concrete, fantasy fashion, then so can the other orifices or secret places of the body and mind.

Of course, as we should not forget, the psychopathological states listed above can trigger both the desire to incorporate in this fashion and the equally literalistic aversion to or horror of doing so. This frankly manic *modus operandi* is a despairing, last-ditch strategy, but it attempts to persuade us that loss or lack can easily be dealt or dispensed with, need not be a problem at all:

> The desperate ploy of filling the mouth with illusory nourishment has the equally illusory effect of eradicating the idea of a void to be filled with words. We may conclude that, in the face of the urgency and the impossibility of performing one type of mouth-work—speaking to someone of what we have lost—another type of mouth-work is utilized, one that is imaginary and equipped to deny the very existence of the problem. Born of the verdict of impracticable introjection, the fantasy of incorporation appears at once as its reflexive and regressive substitute. This means of course that every incorporation has introjection as its nostalgic vocation. [p. 129]

One crucial implication of the metapsychological approach to these terms taken by Abraham and Torok is that although incorporation is a concrete version of introjection, this does *not* make it a more primary phenomenon. That is, even when there is a defensive regression to the imaginary fantasy of inserting objects into (or ejecting them from) the mouth and/or the rest of the alimentary system, this does not entail that our psychic lives once began with incorporations rather than introjections.

To put it simply, incorporative fantasies are not the same as or identical with the actualities of eating, ingesting, digesting, metabolizing (or, indeed, such "excorporating" acts as expelling, evacuating, vomiting, or defecating). To confuse such things is precisely to be in the concrete grip, or under the magical spell, of incorporation. As Abraham and Torok are careful to put it, incorporation is "the reflexive and regressive substitute" that has introjection "as its nostalgic vocation"—and not vice versa. It hopefully goes without saying that this does not carry the implication that introjection is itself more concrete because it starts to happen earlier—indeed, from the beginning of life: even so, it is always already a psychic or metaphorical process.

Starting a section called "False Incorporation", Abraham and Torok now ask the fundamental question, "Why are the words of introjection missing?" Again, the answer is already suggested in the question—and then rendered explicitly, and in italics: *"The abrupt loss of a narcissistically indispensable object of love has occurred, yet the loss is of a type that prohibits its being communicated. If this were not so, incorporation would have no reason for being"* (p. 129). Having said this so adamantly, the authors immediately provide a fascinating and moving example of a situation in which, appearances to the contrary notwithstanding, "reluctant mourning" did not beget incorporation as such.

They speak of a man who, after the death of his wife, would go to their favourite restaurant and—with the waiter's assistance and connivance—order two meals. He would then eat them both, playing both her part and his, as if she were still there with him. Though Abraham and Torok say that he was "clearly hallucinating the presence of a departed loved one", this does not entail that he was incorporating her. The "shared meal" is, they suggest, precisely what allowed him to keep her "outside his bodily limits": it meant that "even as he was filling his mouth's vacancy, he did not actually have to 'absorb' the deceased". This ritual is seen by Abraham and Torok as part of an—albeit bizarre—mourning process and not necessarily as a species of melancholia. The sheer spectacle of the man's actions, the fact that they were so open and public, ensures that it is not the latter: "Nothing of the sort would ever happen in cases of incorporation. Once an incorporation has occurred, no one at all should be apprized of it" (p. 129). As they go on to say, incorporation would have entailed a wholesale attempt to deny that any loss had happened at all, a situation with which we are by now fully familiar from Faulkner's melancholic tale.

Perhaps there are other forms of melancholia or depression, but Abraham and Torok seem intent on exacting considerable mileage from this form of it, while also keeping incorporation within quite particular limits by specifying what it is not. We are informed that many kinds of what we might call conspicuous consumption are precisely what prevent and protect against incorporation's insidious secrecy and the lure of its seductive, addictive promises. The funeral wake, for example is spoken of in such terms: when mourners or survivors break bread together, eat and drink in each other's company, their "communion here means: instead of the deceased we are absorbing our mutual presence in the form of digestible food. We will bury the deceased in the ground rather than in ourselves" (p. 129).

Extraordinarily, Abraham and Torok seem to think that even certain forms of cannibalism or "necrophagia"—when they are collective or group practices—are not to be thought of as incorporation. Though these practices are "born of fantasy", their communality transforms them into symbolic or dramatic acts, and thus "a form of language":

> By acting out the fantasy of incorporation, the actual eating of the corpse symbolizes both the impossibility of introjecting the loss and the fact that the loss has already occurred. Eating the corpse results in the exorcism of the survivors' potential tendency for psychic incorporation after a death. Necrophagia is therefore not at all a variety of incorporation but a preventive measure of *anti-incorporation*. [p. 130]

Just as Torok had done in her earlier paper, she and Abraham will now approach a clearer and fuller account of what the psychopathology of incorporation looks like in the following section of their paper.

Named "The Intrapsychic Tomb", this section begins with a summation of what the previous section had established: namely, that "Even when denied introjection, not every narcissistic loss is fated to incorporation". The latter supervenes, we are told, when there are *"losses that for some reason cannot be acknowledged as such"*. Under such special conditions, "the impossibility of introjection is so profound that even our refusal to mourn is prohibited from being given a language, that we are debarred from providing any indication whatsoever that we are inconsolable". This leads to a "radical denial" (p. 130) of any or all loss; one is forbidden to consult, speak to, commiserate with, or be consoled by anyone.

Ironically and paradoxically, in describing this languageless state, the writing of Abraham and Torok rises to new heights of eloquent explication:

> The words that cannot be uttered, the scenes that cannot be recalled, the tears that cannot be shed—everything will be swallowed along with the trauma that led to the loss. Swallowed and preserved. Inexpressible mourning erects a secret tomb inside the subject. Reconstituted from the memories of words, scenes and affects, the objectal correlative of the loss is buried alive in the crypt as a full-fledged person, complete with its own topography. The crypt also includes the actual

or supposed traumas that made introjection impracticable. A whole world of unconscious fantasy is created, one that leads its own separate and concealed existence. Sometimes in the dead of night, when libidinal fulfillments have their way, the ghost of the crypt comes back to haunt the cemetery guard, giving him strange and incomprehensible signals, making him perform bizarre acts, or subjecting him to unexpected sensations. [p. 130]

Cited here at length is a passage, also on the theme of ghosts and hauntings, to rival as well as stand in opposition to Loewald's vision of the ghosts of the unconscious.

In the previous chapter, we saw Loewald to be issuing a far more open, confident invitation to the denizens of the unconscious via the transference; they are courageously bidden to do their worst. This may be because Loewald is blessed with the new-world hope, or even conviction, that the internalizing, introjective work of mourning can prevail, and that the ghosts *will* eventually be tamed and led back to rest as ancestors. By contrast, what is represented by Abraham and Torok seems to carry the burden of a long history of melancholic, old-world failures to mourn. The insidious, indecipherable encryptions of incorporation are powerfully in the ascendancy; the ghosts are seen to take charge and become a law unto themselves.

To follow up the alimentary references: when everything is "swallowed and preserved", there can be no assimilation, digestion, or metabolization; when unuttered "words" and unrecalled "scenes" are accompanied only by unshed "tears", then where or what is the medium in which the necessary dissolution can take place? No processing or breaking down of anything is possible: on the contrary, a "full-fledged", hypostasized, internal fantasy object is built up, cobbled together out of fragmented and indigestible bits of "words, scenes, and affects", as well as "traumas", producing an aggrieved creature primed to run amok and cause intrapsychic chaos. The Golem of Jewish folklore as well as Frankenstein's monster might be regarded as apt externalized literary-cultural representations of such creatures.

A clinical example is provided: at the age of eight, a young boy had suffered the loss of a seductive older sister and had preserved her in the above manner. The secret was exposed via slips of the tongue (like giving his own age as the age she would have been had she lived) and kleptomania (he stole bras because she would have needed them at that age). As Abraham and Torok say,

> The boy's crypt sheltered the girl "alive" as he unconsciously followed her maturation. This example shows why the introjection

of the loss was impossible and why incorporation of the object became for the boy the only viable means of narcissistic reparation.[p. 131]

The shameful mark of seduction barred any open discussion or dialogue, so this was the only way left to him: effectively, the incorporation of, and the "subsequent identification" with, his sister.

One might say, recalling Loewald's view of this mechanism, that such complete or seamless identification—concrete and without remainder—is tantamount to a kind of enslavement to the object. And one is again struck by how different this version of identification sounds from that of Klein, for whom a full and complete identification with the whole object would seem to be the very goal of the depressive position.

Abraham and Torok go on to describe the boy's predicament as that of being "the carrier of a crypt", and they give this state the name of "*cryptophoria*". Perhaps this is only to state the obvious, but the aptness of the word crypt and its cognates is that they "carry", very precisely, the appropriate double or multiple meanings characterizing incorporation. After all, a crypt is a grave or a mausoleum, and to encrypt someone is thus to bury them. At the same time, to encrypt a message or text is to render it cryptic, unreadable, or indecipherable—that is, to hide it internally or place it in a crypt, inter it in an unmarked grave—one without a headstone or with an illegible one, so to say. Consolidating these meanings, the concluding sentence of this section reads: "To have a fantasy of incorporation is to have no other choice but to perpetuate a clandestine pleasure by transforming it, after it has been lost, into an *intrapsychic secret*" (p. 131).

As if further underlining its centrality to Abraham and Torok, they begin the next section with a sentence that reads: "The foregoing represents our hypothesis." This new section is entitled "Incorporation as Antimetaphor", and it is here, having declared their hypothesis, that the authors begin to unfold a metapsychological secret of their own, one that they have hinted at, but also held back—almost in emulation of the cryptic, clandestine machinations that they are writing about. The ego that resorts to incorporation is, they say, already "partitioned" or "split" by a shameful, usually sexual, secret.

Drawing on and alluding to the late Freudian themes of disavowal and the alteration and splitting of the ego, Abraham and Torok emphasize that the creation of an intrapsychic crypt depends upon pre-existing "dividing walls": "No crypt arises without a shared secret's having already split the subject's topography." Untellable though it may be, therefore, if the secret is sexual, then it is likely to have been shared with at least one other person. And here a crucial question is posed:

> In the realm of shame and secrecy, however, we need to determine *who* it is that ought to blush, *who* is to hide. Is it the subject for having been guilty of crimes, of shameful or unseemly acts? That supposition will not help lay the foundation for a single crypt. Crypts are constructed only when the shameful secret is the love object's doing and when that object also functions for the subject as an ego ideal. It is therefore the *object's* secret that needs to be kept, *his* shame covered up. [p. 131]

As we shall see, if the themes of this book often allude to the literary genres of horror and the supernatural, they are also suggestive of other categories of genre fiction, like the murder mystery or espionage novel.

Clever sleuths or spymasters that they are, Abraham and Torok have discovered, and are now able to reveal, the truth about the perpetrators and victims in this tale of cryptic incorporation. And—as in many such stories—once uncovered, the truth is retrospectively obvious, only one did not quite see it coming. Invariably, of course, it is the parental object who commits the incestuous sexual crime, who institutes the seduction, who carries out the abuse.

One is reminded of the important work of another French analyst, Jean Laplanche (1970, 1977), on the unavoidable seductions that are woven into the very fabric of early parent–child interactions, necessary for the awakening of desire and sexuality; this more ordinary situation, however, is clearly not—is the very opposite of—what Abraham and Torok have in mind here. Indeed, one might infer that what Laplanche is talking about—when it is occurring optimally—belongs squarely within the remit of introjection: incorporation, in contrast, provides evidence that an abusive, criminal act has been committed.

When the guilty party, who is also the love object, then dies (and, I would guess, even when they have not yet died but are lost in less final ways), "mourning does not proceed in the usual way with the help of words used figuratively". Somehow (and this is difficult to grasp), along with the loss of the object itself, there is also a loss of that which guarantees the very metaphoric—or perhaps symbolic, or even just mediating—qualities and properties of language. The significance of certain quite specific shameful words cannot be borne, and "The cryptophoric subject's solution, then, is to annul the humiliation by secretly or openly adopting the literal meaning of the words causing the humiliation" (p. 131).

This is precisely where introjective psychic processes are seen to regress to incorporative concrete fantasies of things being more literally inserted into the mouth. Interestingly, we are told that the "debased love object" (the veritable bad object in this case) thus inserted "will be 'fecalized,' that is, actually rendered excremental" and such melancholic incorporations (fantasies, to be blunt, of eating shit) are betrayed symptomatically by "unkempt outward appearance, filth, coprolalia, and the like". This, I hope, recalls to the reader's mind Karl Abraham's long paper where he connects the oral and anal dimensions of melancholia via images to do with droppings as well as coins that can also be picked up, ingested, and kept. For Nicolas Abraham and Maria Torok, however, the essence of these regressions *"is not their reference to a cannibalistic stage of development, but rather their annulment of figurative language"* (pp. 131–132).

To make this more explicit, the claim is that these victimized "cryptophores" are themselves so unconsciously ashamed of what their perpetrator-objects have done to them that they will go to great lengths to hide the crimes, or prevent them from being discovered as crimes, *per se*: "They neutralize, as it were, the material instruments of humiliation, the metaphors of dejection and excrement, by pretending that these disgraceful metaphors are edible, even appetizing" (p. 132).

Perhaps where others would speak of a trauma that has not been assimilated and cannot be symbolized, Abraham and Torok propose "a new figure of speech" to describe this fantasy action in linguistic terms. They call this "active destruction of representation" by the name *"antimetaphor"*, to be understood as "not simply a matter of reverting to the literal meaning of words, but of using them in such a way—whether in speech or deed—that their very capacity for figurative representation is destroyed". Instances of this kind of speech act "can be found in obscenities encouraging incest" (as, I would suppose, in "motherfucker"). However, say Abraham and Torok

> the most antimetaphorical of all is incorporation itself. *Incorporation entails the fantasmic destruction of the act by means of which metaphors become possible: the act of putting the original oral void into words, in fine, the act of introjection.* [p. 132]

This is exegesis at heady and perhaps abstruse intellectual levels, but its merit lies in providing a proper metapsychological, and even metalinguistic, basis for our psychoanalytic concepts and their clinical applications.

In the following section ("Fantasy versus Intrapsychic Reality"), it is repeated that this loss of the capacity for metaphor under the aegis of incorporation does not entail a return to some supposedly more primary moment when things were legitimately more concrete. Psychic regression does not, in other words, entail the literal opposite of developmental maturation or constitute a turning back of the clock, a regression merely in time. Incorporation may attempt to persuade us that such concrete solutions are available by resorting to powerful objectifying or hypostasizing defences—for example, what Abraham and Torok call "intrapsychic immurement", which entails "confinement, imprisonment, and (in extreme cases) entombment" (p. 132).

However, such ploys are far from unassailable: these attempts to exclude psychic reality by means of "a reassuring fantasy" do not prevail forever, and Abraham and Torok speak as if the disempowered words themselves clamour to force their way back into meaningfulness:

> The unspeakable words and sentences, linked as they are to memories of great libidinal and narcissistic value, cannot accept their exclusion. From their hideaway in the imaginary crypt—into which fantasy had thrust them to hibernate lifeless, anesthetized, and designified—the unspeakable words never cease their subversive action. [p. 132]

The defences introduced in this paper—demetaphorization, objectification or objectalization, and not excepting incorporation itself—all have the nefarious intention of making literal or concrete what should be metaphoric or psychic, not excluding language itself.

Clearly, Abraham and Torok suggest that there is nevertheless the possibility of a return from this quite peculiar form of repression and, by extension, from these other literalizing defences, a prospect of recovering the mind's capacity for figurative or introjective work. They briefly describe their own (1986) linguistic re-analysis of Freud's Wolf Man (Freud, 1918b), where they painstakingly uncovered "an untellable word" that somehow encapsulated all the incestuous psychopathology underlying the case and "condensed the Wolf Man's entire libidinal life as well as his sublimating activities". Everything appeared to turn on "the Russian verb *teret*, meaning 'to rub'" (denoting the fondling that occurred between the Wolf Man's father and sister). By transposing or inverting its letters (as in Torok's earlier example of "ruining" and "urinating"), it could be turned into the "magic word" *rtut*, meaning mercury, which the sister later drank as her means of killing herself. "It was the word", we are told, "the demetaphorized and objectified word, that had to be swallowed in a display of coprophagic bravado" (pp. 132–133).

Extrapolating from Freud's famous case, Abraham and Torok go on to say that it would be wrong to mistake this kind of incorporative defensive organization for "a hysterical type of repression", which it may superficially resemble, replete with the sexual content and the sense of something that returns. The all-important difference turns, indeed, on whose desire is being defended against or disguised. Given their prematurely sexualized history, no doubt both the Wolf Man and his sister experienced "hallucinatory wish-fulfillments" of their own. The important caveat, however, is that these "are not representative of the subjects experiencing them but of their incorporated object of love, here their father. Both the brother and sister identify with their father by means of the spurned word denoting him."

Though there are significant symptomatic differences between the siblings, their respective incorporative acts bespeak the fact that "the father is the one claiming the right to affirm his spurned desire"; in addition, through their identification with him, these "acts (sexual in the one case, and only apparently so in the other) have the narcissistic mission of bolstering the ego ideal". After all, in addition to being the victims of abuse, the subjects in such cases are trying to recover from the shame associated with the loss of the moral authority of a parent who is enslaved by his own disgraceful desires.

Somehow managing to sound both close to and distant from their Kleinian counterparts, Abraham and Torok conclude that "the primary aim of the fantasy life born of incorporation is to repair—in the realm of the imaginary, of course—the injury that really occurred and really affected the ideal object" (pp. 133–134). Their ideas about what imaginary incorporation is attempting to achieve are clearly akin to what Klein and her colleagues would call manic reparation, but the crucial difference here is that the damage that needs repairing has unquestionably been caused by the abusing object, rather than the abused subject. This subject will, however, also inevitably identify with the aggressor and therefore try to sort things out in potentially quite perverse and self-destructive ways, at least until such time as a psychoanalytic solution is attempted.

The penultimate section of the paper bears the title "Inclusion Topography", and Abraham and Torok want here to firmly situate their own ideas within the history of psychoanalytic attempts to arrive at a conceptual understanding of depressive illness. Following on from the potential danger of misreading the incorporative psychopathology of "cryptophores" as "hysterical or hysterophobic", they warn that such patients might end up having "*as if analyses*" (a phrase that appears in English in the original French text) that never manage to plumb the relevant depths or get to the most fundamental issues. Such misapprehensions need not be considered so unexpected, however, if we bear in mind that "incorporation is indeed a cryptic phenomenon, as regards both its genesis and its function". The clinical truth of the condition can conceal itself very effectively: it "hides behind 'normalcy,' takes flight in 'personality traits' and appears openly only in delirium, in the mental state Freud called narcissistic neurosis, that is, manic-depressive psychosis" (p. 134).

And yet Abraham and Torok think that the "inherently cryptic nature of incorporation" does not suffice to account for "the lack of recognition from which it has suffered". In a rather indicting statement, they claim that "Since Freud's essay on 'Mourning and Melancholia' nothing has emerged that would increase our understanding of the meaning of the fantasy life bound up with incorporation and so-called manic-depressive psychosis." They refer to Freud's correspondence with Karl Abraham, where the latter suggests that melancholia or the blocking of mourning might be the outcome of guilt in relation to destructive oral-cannibalistic and anal-sadistic desires. Freud, however, seemed to regard any appeal to such "instinctual factors" or to "the Oedipus complex or castration anxiety" as too general and suggested that his colleague seek assistance from the familiar triumvirate of "topographical, dynamic, and economic considerations", that is, from what he would himself refer to much later—and with considerably more ambivalence—as "the Witch Meta-psychology" (1937c, p. 225).

Pausing to intrude their own understanding of these instinctual factors as "composed primarily of fantasies", the authors regret that Karl Abraham was not encouraged to pursue some of his ideas further. Instead, a more retrograde trajectory was set in train, because his reluctance to adopt a properly metapsychological approach is seen to have influenced his analysand Melanie Klein to be similarly disinclined. The paragraph ends with a sentence that rather damns "Kleinian theory" with faint praise: it is described as "a rigorous, generous, and in some respects even grandiose theory, but one that proved unable to transcend a descriptive system of drives dependent on the universal centrality of fantasy" (pp. 134–135).

One may be tempted to criticize Abraham and Torok's sweeping historico-theoretical gestures as themselves rather "grandiose". Each of these forebears is seen to have faltered: Freud is tacitly accused of discouraging Karl Abraham's brave new ideas about depression; Abraham himself is criticized for being metapsychologically timid and causing Klein to be so, too; and Klein is taken to task for being too descriptive and making too much of fantasy.

Like many other French analysts, Abraham and Torok seem to prefer Freud's earlier metapsychology, particularly the so-called topographical model, and they return therefore to "Mourning and Melancholia"—but only for the purpose of establishing their own psychic mapping of the phenomena at hand. Though they admire "Freud's beautiful and difficult essay" and note that he attributed melancholia to an "ambivalent unconscious situation as regards the object", they respectfully disagree about the origins of the condition. What they are drawn to instead is "the recurrent image of an open wound", saying that in their view it is this that "the melancholic attempts to hide, wall in, and encrypt" (p.135).

Interestingly, Abraham and Torok do not think that either the wounding itself or the attempts to keep it secret happen in the unconscious: rather, these are events that occur in the preconscious-conscious system. They regard the whole process as recreating "in a single psychic area, system, or agency, the correlate of the entire topography, isolating the wound and separating it . . . from the rest of the psyche and especially from the memory of what had been torn from it". When they go on to say that such psychic machinations are "only justified when reality must be denied along with the narcissistic and libidinal import of the loss", we seem now to be in the late Freudian territory of the splitting of the ego, which Freud arrived at via his understanding of fetishism and where the defence mechanism of disavowal has an important role to play.

But Abraham and Torok make no reference to this; instead, they invent their own names for these procedures: "We propose to call this supplemental topography *inclusion* and one of us has earlier called its effect *preservative repression*. The derivatives of the fantasy of incorporation are related to the secret life of inclusion topography" (p. 135). The entrapping, enclosing, and perhaps foreclosing dynamic implicit in this phrase—connoting a kind of closing of ranks or circling of the wagons against external attack—is explored further in the following section.

This last, and longest, section of the paper is entitled "Melancholia: From 'Mourning' to Suicide". Abraham and Torok begin it by asking how their "hypothesis of incorporation" might affect the understanding of the place of ambivalence in melancholic loss. Where Freud posits some actual original disappointment in love, or mistreatment of the subject by the lost object, they "find it crucial to affirm the prior existence of a love totally free of ambivalence, to insist on the undisclosable character of this love, and finally to show that a real and therefore traumatic cause had put an end to it". The "counter-investments" that bring "hate, disappointment, and mistreatment" into play are therefore only secondary phenomena; any later "fantasized aggression" is seen as an extension of

> the genuine aggression the object actually suffered *earlier* in the form of death, disgrace, or removal—this being the involuntary cause of the separation. Inclusion does not occur unless the subject is convinced of the object's total innocence. [p. 136]

There seems to be a contradiction at the heart of this matter: on the one hand, something shameful has occurred, a crime perpetrated, or a sin committed; on the other, someone needs to be protected from prosecution and persecution. This is the tenor of these somewhat obscure injunctions, prohibitions, and pronouncements. But the word that would perhaps have helped most with our grasp of them is either deliberately or inadvertently made conspicuous by going unmentioned here, namely, incest. Surely this is the guilty and secret adult desire that Abraham and Torok reveal by concealing—allude to without naming—in their text?

By way of translating their abstract concepts into a narrative or quasi-clinical example, let us return once more to "A Rose for Emily". Here, too, there is no explicit mention of incest or sexual abuse; we are told, and only in passing, of the jealous guarding and closeting of a motherless daughter by a possessive paternal figure. In the light of Abraham and Torok's account, Emily's presumed fury and outrage should not be understood—at least not in the first place or from her conscious point of view—in terms of any seduction, maltreatment, or cruelty that her father might have perpetrated against her.

If these authors are to be believed, Emily's disappointment, hatred, anger, and aggression must be directed at the world for the way that it treated *him*, for its critique of him, and, ultimately, for taking him from her in death. As Abraham and Torok go on to elaborate in this final section, it is the presumed absolute and exclusive devotion of the object to the subject—of Emily's threshold-spraddling, whip-wielding father to his precious, virginal daughter—that is cherished by the latter; this occurs regardless of how the authorities, the townspeople, the arbiters of conventional morality, or, indeed, the harsh superego in her own mind might see and judge it.

It is perhaps far too hypothetical to ask whether Miss Emily, a fictional character, would have received a diagnosis of melancholia as such. By way of making a relevant distinction, Abraham and Torok propose that "when a narcissistic disappointment did originate with the object schizophrenia would set in, implying the destruction of both the object and the subject. It is not so with melancholics" (p. 136). Well, at least according to Freud, is this mutual destruction not precisely what can and does happen in melancholic suicide, when the ego takes in or identifies with the lost object and the superego then perpetrates terminal violence against both?

Moreover, if Emily's subsequent homicidal and necrophiliac actions in relation to Homer Barron are anything to go by, might she not have been adjudged schizophrenic, too? We need, however, to distinguish in Emily's case between two objects: where her father might have been the venerated and idealized original figure that Abraham and Torok are referring to here, his substitute, Barron, most certainly was not. Thus, we might say that if the death of her aristocratic, Confederate war-hero (albeit perhaps incest-desiring if not -committing) father rendered her melancholic, it was her threatened abandonment by the seductive, "easy-come, easy-go" Northern day labourer Barron who tipped her over into madness and murder.

Thus, if Abraham and Torok are to be given their due and allowed to impose their diagnostic criteria for melancholia, it must be in relation to the subject's primary object:

> Their undisclosable idyll was pure and devoid of aggression. It did not end because of infidelity but owing to hostile external forces. This is why melancholics cherish the memory as their most precious possession, even though it must be concealed by a crypt built with the bricks of hate and aggression. It should be remarked that as long as the crypt holds, there is no melancholia. It erupts when the walls are shaken, often as the result of the loss of some secondary love object who had buttressed them. Faced with the danger of seeing the crypt crumble, the whole of the ego becomes one with the crypt, showing the concealed object of love in its own guise. [p. 136]

So, we are to assume that it is only when Barron, the "secondary love object", appears—and threatens to disappear—that Miss Emily's original melancholia-preventing crypt is breached, and she is galvanized into mad and manic action.

Unbeknownst to the aldermen who are so reluctantly received near the start of the story, and even as the childish crayon portrait of her father on the "tarnished gilt easel" (Faulkner, 177, p. 120) presides over her blighted life in the parlour below-stairs, Miss Emily has also, in far more literal and perverse fashion, set up a secret new shrine in the bedroom above. Faulkner had already provided a suggestive, corroborating architectural description of the modernizing but still depressed Southern town of Jefferson, where these events take place:

> But garages and cotton gins had encroached and obliterated even the august names of that neighbourhood; only Miss Emily's house was left, lifting its stubborn and coquettish decay above the cotton wagons and gasoline pumps—an eyesore among eyesores. [p. 119]

Such subtle pre-emptive hints and oblique symbolic descriptions in the early pages of the story—referring to what is happening both inside and outside of Miss Emily's abode—serve to capture her desperate and degraded attempts to keep up appearances and shore up her crypt.

Abraham and Torok make a repeated point of emphasizing that for the subject in the grip of melancholic incorporation and defensive inclusion, it is always the object's fate that is under threat, rather than her own. Though from without it might appear that her inner world is beset by endless loss and depression, when so threatened, "the ego will fuse with the included object, imagining that the object is bereft of its partner". Then there begins what is only a "public display of an interminable process of mourning. The subject heralds the love-object's sadness, his gaping wound, his universal guilt—without ever revealing, of course, the unspeakable secret, well worth the entire universe" (p. 136).

Connecting this dynamic with Freud's surprise at the melancholic subject's lack of shame at the terrible things for which they stand accused and feel guilty, this can now be understood in terms of the *object's* readiness to commit crimes, break taboos, and suffer punishments for the sake of undying devotion to the subject. We might imagine Miss Emily speaking Abraham and Torok's next words in an internal soliloquy, with reference to both of her dead objects, her father as well as Homer Barron: "Being a melancholic, I stage and let everyone else see the full extent of my love object's grief over having lost me" (p. 136).

Continuing in this vein, Abraham and Torok further question whether those suffering from melancholia really do inflict pain upon themselves, even when from without this appears to be what they are doing. Though it was Freud who informed us that at some level there is always someone else, an object, involved in these internal dynamics, here the implicit relationship is framed more specifically: melancholic subjects, we are told, "lend their own flesh to their phantom object of love".

Another question is then posed: does the melancholic really love this object? For Abraham and Torok, this is an irrelevant or misleading question: "It matters very little since the phantom object is simply 'crazy' about the melancholic". The object having already endured ignominy, pain, and death, the melancholic will now gladly "embody" her hero, and they can thus join forces and direct their combined aggression "at the external world at large in the form of withdrawal and retreat from libidinal investments" (pp. 136–137). In Faulkner's story, of course, both fleshly embodiment and "mutual" withdrawal from the world (and from the passage of time and mortality itself) are represented in an appropriately ghastly manner. I find myself imagining Miss Emily addressing the dead father as follows: "Don't worry, daddy, the corpse in my bed means nothing to me. I still belong to you—I'm still your own little girl, as you've always wanted me to be."

Turning, in their long final paragraph, to clinical consequences and recommendations, Abraham and Torok speak of how such buried, encrypted objects "haunt the process of counter-transference" and endanger the entire therapeutic process. Underestimating the power of the original bond, the analyst may mistakenly see fit to "target the phantom object, not realizing that for the melancholic the phantom (the incorporated object) is the only partner". Treating this object as an aggressor or an abuser will be strenuously resisted by the melancholic patient who wants and expects the analyst to recognize, "behind all the disguise of hate and aggression", the object's underlying love for and devotion to herself. What she seeks from psychoanalysis, at least initially, is the analyst's "acceptance ultimately of the narcissistic bliss at having received the object's love despite dangerous transgressions" (p. 137).

What is clear is that Abraham and Torok would not be encouraging any early negative transference interpretations in analytic situations like these. They seem to think that the analyst must recognize—and, as it were, "indulge"—the subject's belief in an idealized relationship with the "included" object well before any exposure of it is attempted. In a lone sentence describing potentially positive outcomes, we are told that when and if such patients do "obtain this acknowledgement, the inclusion can gradually give way to genuine mourning and the fantasies of incorporation can be transferred into introjections". But if the analyst fails to offer this prerequisite or deal by provisionally accepting the fantasy, then "the original gaping wound will revive and will transform the analyst's comments on aggression into fresh narcissistic injuries" (p. 137).

The remainder of this paragraph—and of the paper—is devoted to the patient's manic response to this possible, not to say likely, outcome. She will react to any perceived negative analytic incursion by parading "the omnipotence of love", by singing a virtual aria to the object's fearless, dedicated allegiance to her, and by displaying "Triumph, scorn, fury, defiance in the face of shame"—emotions identified here as "some of the titles in the manic repertory". In something of an understatement, it is granted that "not much analytic progress is made under these circumstances, but at least the patient's life is safe".

The threat of suicide must nevertheless still loom large, even with manic retaliation operating with full force. Continuing to counterintuitively reverse the subject/object order, Abraham and Torok maintain the perspective—on behalf of the melancholic patient, as it were—that the real "loser" in the mourning stakes will always be the object (even when he is already dead). Thus, "the bereaved object is envisioned as having *not yet entirely lost* the partner for whom he is, as it were, mourning in anticipation" (pp. 137–138).

Convoluted as this may sound, there is a macabre logic here that certainly pays tribute to the desperate omnipotent fantasies behind these bipolar constructions. The authors appear to take very seriously—and to its logical conclusion—Freud's original idea that the melancholic ego can internalize and identify with the object so thoroughly that there is no clarity about who has lost and is mourning whom. It is precisely then, in this confused state of mind, that the risk of suicide may be greatest, and the subject might seek to kill herself as a way of killing—and thereby also saving—the object, or vice versa. We would do well to remember that it is Klein rather than Freud who anticipated and adumbrated such outcomes.

The final sentences of the paper read both ambiguously and rather ominously:

> So, when the subject learns from the analyst, in a repetition of the original trauma, that his secret lover *must* be attacked, he has no choice but to push his fantasy of mourning to its ultimate conclusion: "If my beloved is to lose me forever, he will not survive this loss." This certainty restores peace of mind to the subject, a picture of what recovery might look like. The cure will be complete the day when the "object" makes the supreme sacrifice. [pp. 138]

As was to some extent the case with Torok's earlier piece, this paper, too, ends on an enigmatic, ambiguous, and perhaps frustrating note. When writing alone, Torok at least made no bones about—and referred explicitly to—the actualities of parental seduction and incest. In the current paper, by contrast, there is perhaps both poetic and metapsychological licence for enacting in the text itself the toxic and consequential secrecy of these acts by not naming them; readers are thus kept guessing and get a taste of what the tortured internal worlds of such patients might feel like.

The conclusion of the paper takes things perhaps even further by being equivocal, offering mutually exclusive possibilities. It is quite unclear whether or not Abraham and Torok might be hinting here, in ironic fashion, at a final-solution-like suicide. Are such phrases as "ultimate conclusion", "peace of mind", and "supreme sacrifice" intended to suggest something like that? If so, it is very disturbing to consider that an analytic "error" or a mistimed interpretation might have such dire consequences, though no analyst can afford to ignore this possibility.

Is there, however, another possible and more positive meaning lurking in these last sentences? Are we perhaps genuinely being given "a picture of what recovery might look like"? Abraham and Torok might then be read as saying that, at the culmination of a successful analysis of such a patient, the "cure will be complete" when the *object* is finally persuaded to give up the ghost—that is, its bad internal imago-like presence—and to die a final and unselfish death; only then may the subject go free and in peace, without the requirement of a mutual melancholic suicide/homicide pact.

Perhaps the one thing that can be said with certainty is that, throughout the paper, Abraham and Torok stay as faithful to their central idea as the melancholic subject does to its encrypted object (and/or vice versa). As they see it, a patient suffering from this category of depressive illness—involving a chronic inability to introject or mourn, a melancholic taste for incorporation, and the overweening need to protect a precious if perverse object—might go to the ends of the earth and resort to the most extreme measures to preserve the *status quo*. The proper, arduous work of mourning, by contrast, requires the operational efficiency and effectiveness of introjection, appreciates the necessity—and virtue—of change via transition and translation, and thus makes use, for these purposes, of the metaphorical motions of psychic digestion and metabolization.

CHAPTER SEVEN

André Green: fading and framing— the metaphorical mother lost and restored

"The Dead Mother" (1980)

Over a long career, spanning half a century, André Green (who died in 2012) not only established himself as one of the most prominent and pre-eminent French analysts since Lacan, but was also a leading figure of his generation in the psychoanalytic world at large. Moreover, "The Dead Mother", his seminal and perhaps best-known paper, could also lay claim to being one of the most important psychoanalytic texts of recent times. It has received a great deal of critical attention since its publication, not only in France, but also from some of the highest-profile contemporary British and American analysts, notably in a collection of papers under the title *The Dead Mother: The Work of André Green* (Kohon, 1999).

As has been my wont in this book, I will not be referring to these or any other secondary commentaries on Green's paper. I refrain from doing so to preserve, as far as possible, the sense that these are my own thoughts about and responses to the text, but that should not suggest that I am uninfluenced by other voices and views, especially in relation to a paper as well-thumbed and pored over as this one. This is a dense and demanding piece of writing and can therefore benefit from considerable and repeated explication; historically, it is also the most recent of the papers tackled in this book, and its stature and topical importance makes it a fitting final theoretical text in my close-reading project.

Green's ambitions for the paper are quite clearly in evidence and certainly match the claims I am making for it. "The Dead Mother" can be read as a bold Franco–European bid to appropriate certain precious or sacrosanct parts of the Anglo–American psychoanalytic landscape, to effect nothing less than a hostile takeover of this territory. Green attempts to bring a typically French, philosophical, linguistic, and post-structuralist perspective to bear upon the empiricist and developmentalist inclinations of the pre-oedipal, maternally focused, object-relational approaches that have come to characterize psychoanalysis as practised on the farther shores of both the English Channel and the Atlantic. As I mentioned in my Introduction, Green was a formidable interlocutor who relished a feisty debate—hence, perhaps, my own rather combative language here. Viewed in slightly more tempered terms, Green had large-scale intellectual desires for a more unified psychoanalytic metapsychology, so he may also be regarded as someone who made strenuous efforts to reconcile different approaches to this terrain.

In keeping with these grand intentions, Green begins his paper with a sweeping statement: "If one had to choose a single characteristic to differentiate between present-day analyses and analyses as one imagines them to have been in the past, it would surely be found among the problems of mourning" (1980, p. 170). And this, surely, is what he also wants reflected in his pithy but dramatic title. Lest the latter be misunderstood, however, he tells us without further ado that he will not be discussing the psychological effects of the real deaths of mothers (and/or, perhaps, the deaths of real mothers), but would focus on children whose early lives were spent in the presence of a mother stricken with a certain form of depression.

In his opening paragraph, Green issues a stark warning about the long-term psychological consequences for such individuals and, opting for the word that Abraham and Torok also use to designate a (bad) internal object, speaks of how maternal melancholia can set up a dangerous "imago" in the mind,

> brutally transforming a living object, which was a source of vitality for the child, into a distant figure, toneless, practically inanimate, deeply impregnating the cathexes of certain patients whom we have in analysis, and weighing on the destiny of their object-libidinal and narcissistic future. Thus, the dead mother, contrary to what one might think, is a mother who remains alive but who is, so to speak, psychically dead in the eyes of the young child in her care. [p. 170]

Green seems intent on sustaining this very particular focus. He acknowledges that the actual death of a mother, especially by suicide, can cause profound harm to a surviving child, not least if there were already preceding difficulties in the maternal–filial relationship. Indeed, in that circumstance there can be catastrophic results that closely resemble the ones he wishes to expound upon in this paper.

Nevertheless, the stark reality of actual death, "its final and irrevocable nature, will have changed the former relationship in a decisive way", and he will therefore "not be referring to conflicts that relate to such a situation". In fact, the patients he is discussing will not, in the first instance, even have "sought help for a recognised depressive symptomatology" (p. 170). As will be borne out, Green's paradoxical quest here is to focus on this quite specific, nuanced instance of problematic mourning, but with the concomitant purpose of widening and extending the scope of our understanding of the general dynamics of mourning, thus energizing—as well as enabling—his ambitious metatheoretical agenda.

Though it would first become available to the English-speaking world in the collection *On Private Madness* (1986), Green wrote the paper in 1980 and situated it as the culminating chapter of his 1983 book, *Narcissisme de vie, narcissisme de mort* [*Life Narcissism, Death Narcissism*]. (It should be noted that I am referring to and quoting from this more recent and slightly more idiomatic English translation of the paper.) Green notes, accordingly, that when first encountering patients such as these, even if one is not immediately confronted by a depressed or melancholic state, one nonetheless becomes aware of "the narcissistic nature of the conflicts that are invoked, connected as they are with character neurosis and its consequences on the patient's love-life and professional activity" (1980, p. 171).

What I find interesting about this general characterization is how it might also apply to the malaise of patients who—increasingly around this same historical moment—were being identified diagnostically as "borderline" or as suffering from narcissistic or, indeed, other forms of "personality disorder". A few years previously, Green himself had written a ground-breaking paper called "The Borderline Concept: A Conceptual Framework for the Understanding of Borderline Patients" (1977) and began it in a fashion that bears a remarkable similarity to the start of the later paper that we are perusing here: "Just as the hysteric was the typical patient of Freud's time, the borderline is the problem patient of our time". More evocatively, he concludes the opening paragraph of the borderline paper by saying, "The mythical prototype of the patient of our time is no longer Oedipus but Hamlet" (1977, p. 61). This typically bold and stimulating pronouncement rings true; were we so tasked, we might well consider diagnosing Hamlet as both borderline and depressed!

What do we make of this connection? With 40-odd years of hindsight, we may now be feeling quite familiar with the diagnostic or phenomenological similarities between at least some patients suffering from that most commonplace, pervasive, and ubiquitous psychological condition of depression, and the more chronically disturbed and hard-to-treat patients who are distastefully and punitively labelled as being borderline or having personality disorders; nor, indeed, are we unaware that these are all maladies of "narcissism", another clinical term that perhaps also characterizes our times. Our knowledge is due in no small measure to Green himself, and it is surely greatly to his credit that he was, already back then, astute enough and so well-attuned to the *zeitgeist* as to notice and name accurately—in psychoanalytic terms—several of our era's chief existential, social, and diagnostic discontents.

Before taking his dead mother thesis any further, Green provides a psychoanalytic genealogy of his interests, saying that his own thoughts "owe much to authors who have laid the foundation of what we know about the problems of mourning". He first lists the names of Freud, Karl Abraham, and Klein and then refers to more specific texts by Winnicott, Kohut, Nicolas Abraham, Torok, and Rosolato. It is, of course, corroborating and gratifying that most of the author–analysts named are the very same ones (with a few differences) whom I have chosen to attend to in this book, reinforcing my decision to tussle textually with them.

Even if, in my view, Winnicott did not really offer a specific and detailed theory of mourning with which to engage in a book like this, his name is surely the one most conspicuously absent from my close readings, not least because his texts are so eminently literary and exegetically tempting. Moreover, his name cannot be considered as just one among others in Green's list: the impact and influence of Winnicott on Green was immense, and the latter seemed to become progressively more engaged with the former's ideas as his career progressed. Thus, to pay requisite attention to the rather special cross-cultural psychoanalytic relationship between these two figures—readily discernible in the paper at hand—may hopefully go some way towards making up for the absence from this book of a chapter on Winnicott himself.

Green now launches his own inquiry proper with a statement specifying the two precepts upon which, as he sees it, the "most widely shared psychoanalytic theory" of mourning and depression stands. The first of these may by now seem self-evident: "that of *object-loss* as a fundamental moment in the structuring of the human psyche, at which time a new relation to reality is introduced". Though it can be put thus simply or matter-of-factly, much of my own effort in this book has been devoted to re-establishing this idea, and it is surely worth re-stating from time to time, not least because non-psychoanalytic approaches to the clinical problems of depression often appear to ignore or bypass the issue of loss.

Perhaps it is a bit surprising that Green designates it as "a theoretical concept and not the result of observation, for this shows that a gradual evolution, rather than a mutative leap, has taken place" (p. 171). One sees perhaps what he means, insofar as depression characteristically announces or initially manifests itself without necessarily wearing the loss that is its cause on its sleeve. Still, it seems quite empirical enough—hardly all that theoretical—to acknowledge that loss and our negotiating of it lie at the root all human development, imposing upon us a stark existential difficulty, hard facts to keep before our eyes. Perhaps we should all prefer to forget or ignore this aspect of reality, but then, of course, it is likely to come back to bite or haunt us, with a vengeance.

Despite being "interpreted variously by different analysts", Green claims that the second fundamental and "generally accepted idea is that of a *depressive position*", which he sees as having more of a basis in observational or clinical practice. One may see this as Green's acknowledgement of the importance of Klein's, as well as Winnicott's (1954), contributions to these matters, not least their recognition that—like object loss itself—the depressive position is "an unavoidable event in the process of development". The implication is that nobody, even with the best maternal provision possible, is spared at least some depressive feelings and experiences—indeed, undergoing them "plays a formative role in the organization of his psyche". Perhaps not going quite as far as Klein herself, who seems to regard us all as beginning life in successive states of psychiatric distress, Green goes on to say that "a subject who never experiences any depression is probably more disturbed than someone who is occasionally depressed" (p. 171).

Concluding what is effectively his introduction to the paper, Green asks himself: what are the relations between, on the one hand, these two "general given facts"—object loss and the depressive position—and, on the other, the "singularity of the characteristics of this depressive configuration" identified by him—namely, the dead mother syndrome? Recalling our recent encounter with Abraham and Torok's ideas about the secret encryption of significant depressive-incorporative phenomena, Green, too, sees this dead mother scenario as "central, but often submerged among other symptoms which more or less camouflage it". Thus, it is his mission to explore the relevant processes and to discover—and uncover—what "constitutes this centre in psychic reality" (pp. 171–172).

"The Dead Father and the Dead Mother"

As with Abraham and Torok, the body of Green's text is divided into headed sections, six in all, but these are both longer and denser than those that organized the two papers by his compatriots. It is in the first section—entitled "The Dead Father and the Dead Mother"—that he makes his strong and persuasive case for the necessity of thinking in more structural, conceptual, and metapsychological ways about the maternal dimension of psychoanalysis. For Green, this is tantamount to bringing the maternal realm into line with what is already so well-established in psychoanalytic thought where the paternal–oedipal sphere is concerned, namely, its symbolic significance as adumbrated by Freud himself, elaborated by his line of "classical" followers, and—in Green's own French context—further enhanced under the influence of Lacan.

Psychoanalytic theory, we are told, "allots a major role to the concept of the dead father", particularly in relation to "the genesis of the superego". Here he refers explicitly to *Totem and Taboo*—and many other Freudian texts are implicated—where treating "the Oedipus complex as a structure, and not merely as a phase of libidinal development" also gives rise to a whole range of other concepts and an entire psychoanalytic conceptual system, including such Lacanian notions as "the Law and the Symbolic". These ideas, says Green, are "linked by the reference to castration and to sublimation as the fate of the drives" (p. 172).

Green then outlines the stark differences in the ways that psychoanalysis tends to treat the dead or absent maternal figure: "we never hear of the dead mother from a structural point of view" (though he concedes that some of Marie Bonaparte's work at least gestured in this direction). Despite Freud's later concessions to the versatility of the Oedipus complex, his cursory inclusions of its female and inverted forms, Green finds this of little help in tackling the problem and explaining the mother's structural "exclusion" or absence; he thinks "the answer lies elsewhere". It has to do with "a limitation imposed here by a purely realistic point of view", or the tendency towards and prevalence of what one might call a phasic, linear-time, or developmentalist perspective.

While the death of any specific father is configured psychoanalytically in relation to "the ancestor, to filiation, to genealogy, refers back to the primitive crime and the guilt which is its consequence", the dead mother is not viewed conceptually: it is as if the cultural, symbolic, or metaphorical dimension somehow does not apply or pertain to her. It surprises Green that there is "no articulation between these two concepts" (p. 172)—that is, between the psychoanalytic theory of mourning and the fundamental early losses associated with mother and breast—and he will now be seeking to remedy this glaring discrepancy or inequality.

Green recalls that despite eventually situating castration anxiety within a chronological series of other anxieties in *Inhibitions, Symptoms and Anxiety*, Freud nevertheless wants to preserve its conceptual priority, in much the same way that he retains the primary significance of repression in his metapsychological schema. Freud is credited with demonstrating an awareness of temporally earlier kinds of anxiety in relation to separation and loss, as he is with acknowledging that there are also more primitive defence mechanisms operating in psychic life. "However", says Green,

> in both cases, he specifically fixes castration anxiety and repression as a centre, in relation to which he places the other types of anxieties and different varieties of repression, whether they come before or after, which is proof of the structural or genetic character of Freudian thought. [p. 173]

This is an important statement, one that can be seen to mark definitively the differentiation of European hermeneutic–structuralist orientations and conceptions from empirical–developmentalist Anglo-American ones; the latter can be seen as more wedded to categorical spaciotemporal predictability and therefore to the clear unfolding of linear vectors.

Generally critical of this more scientific perspective and favouring the more (post-)structuralist or "constitutive conception of the psychical order" with its "symbolical organisation", Green appreciatively and approvingly claims that French psychoanalysis "has followed Freud on this point", where his heirs in other parts of the psychoanalytic world have not. As he soon makes clear, however, Green also decries and takes issue with the monolithic way in which paternally based symbols and images have come to dominate this approach to psychoanalysis in France, under the massive influence of Lacan.

Almost having to play devil's advocate in the process, Green holds the latter responsible for the reductive tendency to "'castratize'" all other varieties of anxiety and loss, and for the ubiquitous, all-encompassing quality of "the concept of lack in Lacanian theory". Aware that he might now be misconstrued as dissociating himself from the very point of view that he wants to espouse, Green claims that he is merely showing himself to be empirically and clinically wise enough to also see the pitfalls of this Lacanian approach, to recognize that one can end up "doing violence as much to experience as to theory to save the unity and generalisation of a concept" (p.173).

What Green then suggests is in fact a revolutionary alternative to both developmentalist and Lacanian conceptions:

> Thus, what I would propose, instead of conforming to the opinion of those who divide anxiety into different types according to the age at which it appears in the life of the subject, would be rather a structural conception which would be organized, not around one centre or one paradigm, but around at least two, in accordance with a distinctive characteristic, different from those which have been proposed to date. [p. 173]

Green proceeds, rather ingeniously, to distinguish and divide the field between castration (and the losses that resemble it) and losses or absences of another kind. The former is "evoked in the context of a bodily wound associated with a bloody act", with (fantasies of) the amputation or severing of a limb, an appendage, "linked by the 'little one detachable part of the body', whether it be penis, faeces or baby". By contrast with these forms of "'red' anxiety" that he has aggregated, Green states that there are anxieties that are not connected with physical violence or sundering as such: "whether referring to the concept of the loss of the breast, or of object-loss, and even of threats relative to the loss of the superego or its protection, and in a general manner, to all threats of abandonment, the context is never bloody" (pp. 173–174).

By no means denying the "destructiveness" that inheres in all anxiety states, Green indicates that this second category of anxiety is no less dire than the first.

While it may not be crimson-hued or sanguinary as such, there is also nothing particularly sanguine about it: "It bears the colours of mourning: black or white. Black as in severe depression, or blank as in states of emptiness to which one now pays justified attention." There is also an opportunity here for Green to stipulate what he sees as the pathological primacy of one monochromatic shade over the other: the empty, colourless depletions suffered at very fundamental, formative moments of deprivation lie at the root of the darker, outwardly directed feelings of bitterness, anger, and aggression that can subsequently typify the manifest picture.

For Green, "the sinister black of depression, which we can legitimately relate to the hatred we observe in the psychoanalysis of depressed subjects", is a secondary phenomenon, "a consequence rather than a cause, of a 'blank' anxiety which expresses a loss that has been experienced on a narcissistic level" (p. 174). It does not perhaps take much extrapolating or discerning to recognize here Green's tacit affinity—when confronted by a British choice—with a Winnicottian perspective over a Kleinian one.

However, Green has a way of taking up such issues and differences and creating out of them an approach that is uniquely and recognizably his own. The general trope of "blankness" and what he calls "the work of the negative" thoroughly characterize his brand of psychoanalysis. Though he says that he will not be rehearsing his earlier treatment of such negative phenomena, he does wish to "attach blank anxiety and blank mourning to this series". He goes on to contextualize these:

> The category of "blankness"—negative hallucination, blank psychosis, blank mourning, all connected to what one might call the problem of emptiness, or of the negative, in our clinical practice—is the result of one of the components of primary repression: massive decathexis, both radical and temporary, which leaves traces in the unconscious, in the form of "psychical holes". These will be filled in by re-cathexes, which are the expression of destructiveness which has thus been freed by the weakening of libidinal erotic cathexis. [p. 174]

Without mentioning her (yet) by name, Green then implies that Klein's preoccupations with "hatred", on the one hand, and "reparation", on the other, are somewhat misplaced and "secondary to this central decathexis of the maternal primary object".

Again, this sounds like something Winnicott would say, albeit with a French–Freudian inflection or accent. For Green, as well as Winnicott, these early dangers run very deep and pertain to the level at which total psychic obliteration can occur. (Green will also go on to link this with the crippling loss of a capacity for mental figuration.) If one targets only the hatred when treating such depressed patients, it "amounts to never approaching the primary core of this constellation" (p. 174).

Wishing to further flesh out his fundamental idea that "the fate of the human psyche is to have always *two* objects and never one alone", Green insists that the Oedipus complex should remain "the essential symbolic matrix" and central reference point, providing "an axiomatic triangulation" even where the clinical focus appears to be "pre-genital or preoedipal". Now referring explicitly to Klein, however, he does not consider it necessary to posit, as she does, some developmentally earlier, more primitive version of the Oedipus complex to sustain its centrality. In any case, he says,

> The father is there both in the mother and the child, from the beginning. More exactly, *between* the mother and child. From the mother's side this is expressed in her desire for the father, of which the child is the realisation. On the side of the child, everything which introduces the anticipation of a third person, each time that the mother is not wholly

present and her devotion to the child is neither total nor absolute (at least in the illusion he maintains in this regard, before it is pertinent to speak of object-loss), will be attributable retrospectively to the father. [pp. 174–175]

In fairness, many post-Kleinian analysts—like Ron Britton (1998), for example—understand and conceptualize the triangularity of the Oedipus complex in ways that resemble Green's "non-literalizing" account of these dynamics.

However, in the following paragraphs, Green both raises the stakes on the word "retrospectively" in his last sentence above, while also emphasizing the importance of maintaining a metaphorical perspective on these matters. Alluding to the idea of deferred action or *"après coup"*—much favoured in French psychoanalysis—Green is suggesting that all narrative, developmental, and even theoretical conceptions in psychoanalysis are, in fact, "after the fact" constructions. If the psychoanalytic father can be retrospectively "figured" and conceived by the child as the quintessence of "third-ness", then, from Green's point of view, mother-related psychoanalytic thinking needs somehow to follow suit:

> It is thus that one must account for the solidarity linking the metaphoric loss of the breast, the symbolic mutation of the relation between pleasure and reality—established retrospectively as principles—the prohibition of incest, and the double figuration of the images of mother and father, potentially reunited in the fantasy of a hypothetical primal scene which takes place outside the subject. It is from this scene that the subject *excludes himself* and constitutes himself in the absence of affective representation, which gives birth to fantasy, which is a production of the subject's "madness". [p. 175]

This is difficult, somewhat obscure prose but the gist of it seems clear enough: these fictional-figurative-theoretical accounts of self-fashioning—whether paternal or maternal in origin—become structures taken up and in by the subject himself, from the outside and always belatedly, as it were.

One might illuminate this by resorting analogically to a late Freudian distinction (though Green himself does not make this link): the phenomenological status of these narratives or discourses is established not in the realm of "material truth"—that of empirical, literal, or sequential fact—but amidst the retroactive tropes, hypotheses, and theories of "historical truth" (Freud, 1937d, 1939a). Green seems also to suggest that having been adopted (and, I would add, introjected and metabolized), these discourses will contribute to, or indeed, create, a separate psychic identity, via positive or negative fantasies that determine a sense of self, whether mad or sane.

Aware that his claims here are daring and might be received as both provocative and conceptually challenging, Green poses the question, "Why is this metaphorical?" He begins his answer by first restating that the "recourse to metaphor, which holds good for every essential element of psychoanalytic theory, is particularly necessary here". He refers to his borderline paper, where he had identified and outlined an originating distinction between "two Freudian versions of the loss of the breast". In "Negation" (1925h) Freud is said to treat it as a "theoretical and conceptual" moment, crucial to "the function of judgement", which is the theme of that text. But in *An Outline of Psycho-Analysis* (1940a) Freud "adopts a position which is less theoretical than descriptive"; there, says Green, "he accounts for the phenomenon, not theoretically, but in a 'narrative' form, if I may so describe it, where one understands that this loss is a process of progressive evolution which advances step by step" (p. 175).

Clearly critical of this latter approach, Green has a passing snipe at the in-vogue practice of infant observation that it has spawned. He will later engage in a famous public debate and confrontation over this matter with the American doyen of infant-observation research, Daniel Stern (Sandler, Sandler, & Davies, 2000). In Green's view, these two approaches are "mutually exclusive, rather as perception and memory exclude each other in theory", and he again specifies—perhaps a bit more transparently this time—his own staunch stance on the figurative, non-linear, and post-hoc way in which the psyche makes self-structuring sense out of primary loss:

> In the 'theory' that the subject elaborates about himself, the mutative interpretation is always retrospective. It is in the aftermath that this theory of the lost object is formed, and acquires its unique, instantaneous, decisive, irrevocable and basic characteristic. [p. 175]

Using a distinction borrowed from linguistics and used often in French literary–theoretical circles, Green says that not only the "diachronic", but also the "synchronic" dimension can be adduced in corroboration of his view.

With biting wit and irony, and with Klein and her followers in mind, he remarks that even the "fiercest partisans of the reference to the loss of the breast" have ended up "humbly watering down their wine" and admitting "that the breast is just a word to designate the mother". Clearly, Green's approach to the loss of the original maternal object is precisely not reliant on incorporative literality or the notion of a particularized, concrete, or "homuncular" internal object. As the reader will perhaps already have gathered, I would characterize Green's theory of internalization not only as structural or metaphoric, but also as introjective, digestive, and metabolic.

As he draws this metatheoretical section to a close, Green repeats his main point in the clearest possible terms: "One must retain the metaphor of the breast; for the breast, like the penis, can only be symbolic." Though the specific erogenicity of the suckling and succouring breast is itself undeniably compelling, the rest of the mother's body, as well as her actions and psychic presence, are no less relevant, both libidinally and otherwise, and cannot really be separated from the experience.

In a brief sentence, Green again resorts to the language of linguistics to describe how bodily contiguities are transformed into psychic representation: "The metonymical object has become metaphor for the object." Drawing analogically on the dangerous ease with which we ordinarily allow ourselves to speak too shallowly and reductively of the complexities "of loving sexual intercourse" as "the pairing 'penis–vagina'", Green intends to delve "more deeply into the problems relating to the dead mother" with a reiterated determination not to resort to concreteness, but to "refer to them as to a metaphor, independent of the bereavement of a real object" (pp. 175–176).

"The Dead Mother Complex"

In this second section of the paper Green tries to describe this phenomenon in language that has now descended from theoretical heights to a still general but relatively more clinical, "experience-near" level, as Kohut (1977) would put it. Green says that this complex "is a revelation of the transference", and, while it is repeated that the patient does not usually present with depressive symptoms, there are "more or less acute conflicts with objects who are close", again cementing the resemblance to borderline cases. While depression might be indicated, it is not manifest. Moreover, analysing the "classic neurotic symptoms" that are present seems beside the point. Making what was previously hinted at more explicit, Green continues:

> On the contrary, the problems pertaining to narcissism are in the foreground where the demands of the ego ideal are considerable, in synergy with or in opposition to the superego. The feeling of impotence is evident. An inability to withdraw from a conflictual situation, inability to love, to make the most of one's talents, to multiply one's assets, or, when this does take place, a profound dissatisfaction with the results. [p. 176]

Green's characterization of these hapless "dead mother" patients is so resonant and familiar that any psychoanalytic practitioner would recognize the description instantly and have no trouble identifying examples from clinical practice.

Once the treatment has properly taken hold, "the transference will reveal, sometimes quite rapidly, but more often after long years of analysis, a singular depression". Coining a useful new term, Green speaks of a "transference depression", by contrast with the transference neurosis: the patient may manage to shield this affective state from people in the outside world—what Green calls "the entourage"—but relationships with these figures continue to suffer in familiar fashion. At the risk of being too schematic, might one see Green to be suggesting here that where transference neurosis in psychoanalysis may traditionally be associated with the father, transference depression is more likely to pertain to the mother?

This clinical condition is, of course, "the repetition of an infantile depression" the specificity of which Green will now proceed to outline in some detail. As emphasized previously, this is not about a loss "in reality", an actual abandonment or separation: the maternal object can be—and most often is—still there. And yet, in another, more profound psychic sense, she is not:

> *The essential characteristic of this depression is that it takes place in the presence of the object, which is itself absorbed by a bereavement.* The mother, for one reason or another, is depressed. Here the variety of precipitating factors is very large. Of course, among the principal causes of this kind of maternal depression, one finds the loss of a person dear to her: child, parent, close friend, or any object strongly cathected by the mother. But it may also be a depression triggered by a deception which inflicts a narcissistic wound: a change of fortune in the nuclear family or the family of origin, a liaison of the father who neglects the mother, humiliation, and so on. In any event the mother's sorrow and lessening of interest in her infant are in the foreground. [p. 177]

Not only is this reminiscent of Freud's list of the types of loss that can set off a melancholic response, but one is again struck by the sense that Green is channelling Winnicott as he adumbrates the precipitating possibilities of a dead mother syndrome or complex.

What occurs "in this depression... that takes place in the presence of the object" is precisely *not* the kind of benign, attuned, and graduated maternal provision—following on from an initial period of primary attentiveness—that will eventually enable the subject's toleration of his or her own essential aloneness (Winnicott, 1958a). On the contrary, it is more like a blank psychic absence that leaves a gaping hole or void.

For any one of the variety of reasons listed by Green, mothers can become either depressed or defensively manic, and are therefore distraught and distracted, preoccupied and unavailable at the worst possible and most crucial moments, sealing the fate of the children in their charge. We might consider, as examples, the offspring of certain famous and tragic literary characters from nineteenth-century fiction, like Estella, adopted child of Miss Havisham in *Great Expectations* (Dickens, 1860), or Berthe, the daughter of Emma Bovary (Flaubert, 1856), or Sergei and Annie, the children of Anna Karenina (Tolstoy, 1877).

Green rightly notes that many would concur that "the most serious instance is the death of a child at an early age". Indeed, a dead mother's child is often regarded and treated—and no doubt resented—as either a replacement for another child lost before their birth or as the (un)fortunate survivor of a later loss. Frequently, the very existence of a ghostly, miscarried, or aborted child in the mother's history "remains totally hidden" or "rests on a secret" (p. 177) that, if detected and pieced together from subtle hints and indications during an analysis, can make some retrospective sense of the patient's malaise.

Green speaks now of "a brutal change of the maternal imago, which is truly mutative". The subject may have had an infantile pre-history characterized by "an authentic vitality", testifying that "a rich and happy relationship had been formed with the mother". But this suddenly seizes up, and Green speaks of how later photographs can capture powerfully, in contrast with earlier ones, the loss of this loving relationship, along with its enlivening potential. In other words, there can even have been a goodly provision of "primary maternal preoccupation" (Winnicott, 1956) and a relatively normal initial development of the mother–child relationship before this fateful, fatal moment. The important distinction between privation and deprivation is relevant here, and it is clearly an instance of the latter that Green is describing: something good had existed and now, in an instant, it is gone.

Green's metaphor for this disaster is powerfully reminiscent of "Ozymandias", Shelley's famous ironic sonnet about tyranny and the predations of time. Having skewered a long-dead autocratic king's arrogant words that had been carved on the plinth of his now utterly destroyed statue, and spoken truth to his power, the poem's last lines read:

> Nothing beside remains. Round the decay
> Of that colossal wreck, boundless and bare
> The lone and level sands stretch far away
> [1817, p. 100]

And here is Green:

> Everything seems to have ended rather like the disappearance of ancient civilizations, the cause of which is sought in vain by historians by making the hypothesis of an earthquake to explain the death and the destruction of palace, temple, edifices and dwellings, of which nothing is left but ruins. [p. 177]

The psychic equivalent of such catastrophic loss, Green suggests, is less readily visible: "the disaster is limited to a cold core" but it is one that will leave "an indelible mark on the erotic cathexes of the subjects in question" (p. 178).

Green expounds these consequences at some length, highlighting the traumatic abruptness of the moment when "the mother's sudden bereavement" impacts upon the child for whom, "without any warning signal, love has been lost at one blow". Further revealing his Winnicottian credentials, Green speaks of the "premature disillusionment" perpetrated by this event, with the consequence that there is "besides the loss of love, the loss of *meaning*; for the baby disposes of no explication to account for what has happened" (p. 178). As we know, Winnicott (1945) grants an initial period of illusion to the baby as a right and a privilege and speaks of the necessary disillusionment needing to be gradual, steadily titrated by the mother. When there is no such process but only an instantaneous tearing away of the veil, terrible damage is done.

The phrase "one fell swoop" comes to mind, with its Shakespearean origins. These words are first spoken in *Macbeth* by the protagonist's eventual nemesis, Macduff, in disbelieving despair on hearing about the slaughter of his wife and children:

> What, all my pretty chickens and their dam
> At one fell swoop?
> [Act IV: iii, 221–222]

Of course, Macbeth's anti-heroine wife is another female literary figure whose maternal credentials are critically contested and whose children would, in any case, have been better off unborn. Faced with a faltering husband, she infamously vows that she would pluck her nipple from her infant's mouth and dash its brains out to prove her brutal single-mindedness.

While the dead mother situation does not involve actual child murder, it is surely a kind of soul murder. This phrase that recalls Freud's Schreber case (1911c) to mind, provides the name of an important book by Leonard Shengold (1989), the full title of which is *Soul Murder: The Effects of Childhood Abuse and Neglect*. Riffing off the literary and psychoanalytic associations set going by this maddening syndrome, one may suggest that what the dead mother perpetrates—however unwittingly—is weaning with neither warning nor meaning.

What then tends to occur, according to Green, is that the child "interprets this deception as the consequence of his drives towards the object"; in other words, he cannot but blame himself and his desires for this outcome. If, at the same moment, the father-as-third should happen to come into prominence, then *he* is seen "as the reason for the mother's detachment". Green describes "a premature and unstable triangulation" whereby the father is either held responsible for the disaster or becomes the alternative object "of an early and particularly intense attachment" and source of potential salvation.

However, because the father may also be reeling from and preoccupied with the sudden descent into depression of his partner, he may not respond to his child's need to be rescued, picked up, and held, both literally and metaphorically. On the contrary, the child finds himself "caught between a dead mother and an inaccessible father", and, to make matters worse, if the latter cannot manage or intervene, he withdraws and "leaves the mother–child couple to cope with this situation alone" (p. 178).

What animates much of Green's account in this paper is the fact that this child is left not just with an awful loss to absorb, but with an enigmatic puzzle to solve. The child will try "in vain to repair the mother who is absorbed by her bereavement", and his failure to do so will make him "feel the measure of his helplessness". He will try to fend off anxiety about his own loss through "various active methods, amongst which agitation, insomnia and nocturnal terrors are indications", but will finally resort to "a variety of defences of a different kind". Initially, Green specifies, there is a "unique movement" that is two-fold: "*the decathexis of the maternal object and the unconscious identification with the dead mother*" (p.178).

The first of these two mo(ve)ments consists of an emotional disengagement and a representational disconnect from the mother herself—from the "live" version of her, as it were. Green speaks of this as "a psychical murder of the object, accomplished without hatred", making it sound rather more like compassionate euthanasia than violent matricide, though it is neither. He is at pains to emphasize its non-destructive, non-aggressive quality; it seems not to be a product of the death drive. What is implied is a kind of blanking or emptying-out that leaves what Green calls "a hole in the texture of the object relations with the mother which does not prevent the surrounding cathexes from being maintained": that is, ordinary life appears to continue as usual. Similarly, from the mother's side, she still loves and cares for her child—in a manner of speaking: "However, as one says, 'her heart is not in it'" (pp. 178–179).

The second consequence is an identification with the now blank or absent entity, with the empty space where the mother's psychic presence used to be—in effect, with her spectre or ghost. This kind of identification is a far cry from the internalizations or introjections discussed earlier in this book, whereby the subject is not only helped to cope with the loss of an object but also enabled to build inner structure and psychic freedom. Here, on the contrary, when what is taken in is effectively the emptiness of loss itself, the legacy is stultifying and non-productive, freezing the internal world and entrapping the ego, potentially forever. The analogy that comes to mind is an injection of air into an artery and the lethal cardiac damage that this can cause.

As Green says: "the other aspect of the decathexis is the primary mode of identification with the object", characterized in these cases by a kind of mirroring mimicry. After the subject's desperate and failed attempts to repair and enliven the deadened mother via such manic ploys as "artificial gaiety, agitation, and so on", it is as if a kind of "reactive symmetry is the only means by which to establish a reunion with the mother". The trouble is that this necessitates the wish to achieve complete sympathetic symbiosis, a need for seamless, unequivocal sameness with the object, "by becoming, not like it, but by becoming the object itself". It is as though a rather crude and futile deal is being struck in the mind: this ultimate identification provides "the condition for renouncing the object and at the same time retaining it in a cannibalistic manner" (p.179).

Resorting to language from previous chapters, one might say that Green is here describing the very opposite of an introjective internalization. This is more like an incorporative identification, resulting not in a proper mourning process, but some form of encrypted melancholic imprisonment. The subject and the (dead) object are shackled together, in the manner exemplified and illustrated by Miss Emily's style of attachment, notwithstanding the fact that the object at stake in her story is paternal and literally dead, rather than maternal and psychically so—though it would be easy to speculate about the relevance of the absent mother to that situation, too.

Green seems intent on distancing these defensive machinations from what one might think of as the Kleinian emphasis on primary aggression and hatred, attacks on the bad object emanating straight from the death drive, as it were. He notes the difference between the decathectic urge to be rid of the object in a retaliatory way that can later become unconscious, and this entrapping identification that "is unconscious from the start" and thus "comes about without the subject's ego being aware of it, and against his will". Pre-emptive detachment might then remain at the subject's disposal as a defence against any potentially abandoning or otherwise disappointing future object, but he will not know why he treats these later objects thus because "he will remain totally unconscious of his identification with the dead mother" (p. 179).

If Green sees decathexis and unconscious identification as making up a first pair of defences in the dead mother situation, the previously mentioned *"loss of meaning"* that it produces will call forth additional defensive manoeuvres. There has been an instantaneous and traumatizing event, leaving the subject with a huge unexplained void: "The 'construction' of the breast, of which pleasure is the cause, the aim and the guarantor, has collapsed all at once, without reason."

Playing devil's advocate, Green considers a tacit or hypothetical Kleinian-type "reversal" whereby the subject, "in a negative megalomania, would attribute the responsibility for the mutation to himself". However, he surmises, there would still be "a totally disproportional gap between the fault he could reproach himself for having committed and the intensity of the maternal reaction". Moreover, this type of self-blame would be the product not of a greedy or destructive id but of massive existential doubt: "At the most, he might imagine this fault to be linked with his manner of being rather than with some forbidden wish; in fact, being becomes forbidden for him" (p. 179).

Given "the vulnerability of his maternal image", this is a precarious predicament, one that "could induce the child to let himself die" if he cannot manage to divert these destructive castigations elsewhere, away from both himself and his depressed object. It "obliges him to find someone responsible for the mother's black mood". This calls forth, as Green had previously said, "an early triangular situation" or "a precocious Oedipus complex" made up of "child, mother, and the unknown object of the mother's bereavement". This leads to the blaming or scapegoating of an inchoate, condensed, composite figure, which might include the father. It is, I think, significant that for Green this early oedipal situation is not—again, as Klein would have it—a primary or universal phenomenon, but a consequence of this specific dead mother situation or syndrome.

After this short detour, Green now returns to the problem of meaninglessness and that "second front of defence", the second wave of countermeasures, which seems to be as complex and multifaceted as the first. Here Green identifies three different defensive tactics—as if he is of a mind to provide one each for Kleinian, Freudian, and Winnicottian tastes, respectively, and in that order.

Again emphasizing that this is "neither primary nor fundamental", he first specifies *"the releasing of secondary hatred"*, characterized by "regressive wishes of incorporation, but also anal features which are coloured with manic sadism where it is a matter of dominating, soiling, taking vengeance upon the object, and so on". Secondly, there is *"auto-erotic excitation"*, whereby the subject might relentlessly seek out loveless, purely sensual, erogenous satisfaction—"organ pleasure at the limit"—where body and psyche are dissociated, and the sharing of enjoyment or true object-relating are completely eschewed. Green also says that this splitting of love and pleasure "is the foundation for hysterical identifications to come".

The last of the three is clearly of greatest interest to Green; here, *"the quest for lost meaning structures the early development of the fantasmatic and the intellectual capacities of the ego"*. If this third consequence appears to owe most to Winnicott (in fact, the other two are also influenced by him), it is because Green makes more obvious use here of certain tropes and terms. The features of this defence include "a frantic need for play which does not come about as in the freedom for playing" but as a manifestation of the *"compulsion to imagine"*; a parallel *"compulsion to think"* will also come to dominate the patient's intellectual life. The entire defensive organization that is mobilized against the dead mother disaster is eloquently summarized:

> Performance and auto-reparation go hand in hand to coincide with the same goal: the preservation of a capacity to surmount the dismay over the loss of the breast, by the creation of a *patched* breast, a piece of cognitive fabric which is destined to mask the hole left by the decathexis, while secondary hatred and erotic excitation are teeming on the edge of an abyss of emptiness. [p. 180]

In addition to his use of "play" itself, Green seems also to be playing with Winnicott's (1951, 1971) notion of the transitional object here.

However, as is the case with the pseudo-play of these anxiously compelled patients, the bits of cloth, imagination, or intellectual work that they deploy cannot operate in truly transitional fashion: the function of such objects is too bound up with or circumscribed by the necessity of patching a gaping hole or covering a bleeding wound. Green's language surely indicates that he also has in mind *both* Freud's figurative description of the psychotic ego's belated attempt to recover a modicum of sanity after breakdown as the application of a patch over the terrifying black hole that has opened in the texture of reality, *and* his twice-repeated metaphorical use of the image of an open wound in "Mourning and Melancholia".

Green's analysis of the "overcathected intellectual capacity" of such patients is taken further as he describes the projective aspect of this mechanism. Another consequence of the unbearable subjective internal state that is mother's "death" is a transference "to the outside scene—the scene of the object". This is now a puzzle for the patient to solve, a mystery to be investigated: "Henceforth he devotes his efforts to guessing or anticipating." However, it is this "compromised", wounded, and weakened ego—"which has a hole in it from now on"—that will predominate in all future artistic or intellectual proceedings, "either on the level of fantasy . . . or on the level of knowledge". Green suggests that it is not uncommon for "highly productive intellectualization" to originate there and to achieve success in another displaced sphere or "theatre of operations", but insofar as it is still being used "to master the traumatic situation . . . this attempt is doomed to fail".

Having in mind, no doubt, many creative, academic—or even psychoanalytic—personae, Green acknowledges that ostensible and real-enough professional success can be built on such "precociously idealised sublimations", though it is also often the case that high achievers such as these find themselves unable to be nurtured and sustained by their own achievements. The price, in any case, will be paid somewhere else. These sublimations "reveal their incapacity to play a stabilizing role in the psychic economy, because the subject remains vulnerable on a particular point, which is his love life" (pp. 180–181).

Green is nothing if not quite brilliant here; his anatomizing of these afflictions is particularly insightful and affecting. Any new wound suffered by the subject on love's ground, he tells us, "will awaken a psychical pain and one will witness a resurrection of the dead mother", who, at least while she is thus ascendant again, temporarily "dissolves all the subject's sublimatory acquisitions". These painstakingly accumulated achievements themselves, along with any attempted relationship with a new partner, may put up some resistance, combining forces to try to revive one another. Green, however, holds out little hope: "soon the destructiveness overwhelms the possibilities of the subject who does not dispose of the necessary cathexes to establish a lasting object-relation and to commit himself progressively to a deeper personal involvement which implies concern for the other" (p. 181).

This sense of failure—of not having what it takes, lacking emotional stamina for proper commitment to anyone or anything—is itself devastating, as Green will go on to show. In a powerful passage, worth quoting in full, he describes the predicament of being in the very throes of abject depressive hopelessness, caught in the relentless clutches of an entrapping internal object:

> The patient has the feeling that a malediction weighs upon him, that there is no end to the dead mother's dying, and that it holds him prisoner. Pain, a narcissistic feeling, surfaces again. It is a hurt which is situated on the edge of the wound, colouring all the cathexes, filling in the effects of hatred, of erotic excitement, the loss of the breast. In a state of psychical pain, it is as impossible to hate as to love, impossible to find enjoyment, even masochistically, and impossible to think. There is simply a feeling of being held captive which dispossesses the ego of itself and alienates it to an unrepresentable figure. [p. 181]

A subtle move takes place here, from an emotionally arid existential situation to the dimension of failed representation. Green effectively leads us to the psychic fact that there is no end to the dead mother's dying precisely because, by being all-too-concretely ensconced, she cannot undergo any form of metaphorical transformation, translation, or transition to a different medium.

This mother cannot, in other words, be figured, processed, assimilated, digested, or metabolized. And because she occupies the whole field in such a stolid manner, she will remain, quite literally, irreplaceable, an obstacle in the way of any other person to whom (or pursuit to which) the subject may wish to grant intimate psychic access. Using Ferenczi's term with the kind of accuracy that would have impressed its inventor, Green speaks of a subjective "trajectory" characterized by "a hunt in quest of an unintrojectable object, without the possibility of renouncing it or losing it, and indeed the possibility of accepting its introjection into the ego". All the other objects of such a subject are destined to remain peripheral, in orbit, "at the limit of the ego, not wholly within, and not quite without. And with good reason, for the place is occupied, in its centre, by the dead mother" (p. 181).

The analyses of such patients will inevitably proceed for some time along normal-neurotic lines, with what Green calls "the examination of the classic conflicts". Even where there is some apparent progress, however, the analyst is unpersuaded of any substantive success, not least because "all this psychoanalytic work remains subject to spectacular collapses, where everything again seems to be as on the first day". Though initially keen to feel that the analysis is helping, the analysand eventually comes to acknowledge "the insufficiency of the transferential object, that is, the analyst" who unwittingly ends up colluding with the patient's wish to avoid "approaching the central core of the conflict" (p. 182).

Green admits to his own analytic "insufficiency", to having blind spots in his work with these patients; he expresses this, however, in relation to a different sense organ, saying that he "had remained deaf to a certain discourse" with them. Having "guessed the defensive value" of their myriad grievances against the mother and sensing that what lay beneath was a powerful kind of attraction to her, he remained puzzled as to "why this situation continued", presumably even after thorough and extensive analytic work had been dedicated to it.

When Green reveals the nature of his blindness or deafness, one is reminded of how Abraham and Torok spoke of both the hidden, encrypted aspects of their cases and the need—if an analyst is to have any chance of uncovering the secret topography in such instances—to keep the focus firmly on the object rather than the subject. Green writes: "*My deafness related to the fact that, behind the complaints concerning the mother's doings, her actions, loomed the shadow of her absence.*" Despite the clear structural similarities, we also see here how subtly different Green's dead mother object is from Abraham and Torok's more actively perpetrating one. Indeed, where Green's patients' ostensible or conscious complaints are about the mother's doings and actions, what really lies behind this—and what the analyst has been deaf to—is the terrible black hole of her lack of presence. Her psychically and emotionally available self, her positive existence, has departed; instead, she is, in Green's evocative words, "absorbed, either with herself or with something else, unreachable without echo, but always sad. A silent mother, even if talkative" (p. 182).

Green tries to capture the phenomenological effects of the dead mother's departure: it is as if, by "leaving" in this way, she has absconded with all the love that had been invested in her by the child who is thus left bereft of "her look, the tone of her voice, her smell, the memory of her caress". Virtually quoting Abraham and Torok, Green writes, "She had been buried alive, but her tomb itself had disappeared"; the empty hole she has left behind "made solitude dreadful, as though the subject ran the risk of being sunk in it, body and possessions."

In relation to this sinking feeling, Winnicott is now invoked by name, but for the purpose of expressing a rare disagreement with him. Green now thinks that "the concept of *holding*" and its failures do not sufficiently account for the sense of "vertiginous falling" experienced by some dead mother patients. When Winnicott (1974) speaks of a baby's or patient's experience as "falling forever", there is necessarily the sense of someone being dropped. What Green offers is an alternative description—indeed, a different set of metaphors—spelling-out what he sees as happening in such instances of "psychical collapse" (p. 182).

He first likens this to "what fainting is to the physical body", then resorts to his trademark, technical-sounding terms:

> The object has been encapsulated and its trace has been lost through decathexis; there has been a primary identification with the dead mother, transforming positive identification into negative identification, that is, identification with the hole left by the decathexis (and not identification with the object), and with this emptiness, which is filled in and suddenly manifests itself through an affective hallucination of the dead mother, as soon as a new object is periodically chosen to occupy this space. [pp. 182–183]

Even where it falls aesthetically short of Winnicott's quirky everyday lyricism, Green's language is expressing very potent metapsychological ideas. Elaborating the implications of all things negative became Green's psychoanalytic mission, and here he shows us that a cathected absence is a far trickier and more tenacious adversary than any actual (bad) object.

Just when the coast seems clear, when the subject, tempted by a potential new partner and the prospect of a real relationship, mistakenly thinks that there is a psychic vacuum to be filled, what Green calls the dead mother's "affective hallucination"—what I take to be something like her ghost—comes forth and shows itself in frightening and forbidding fashion. Though much of what happens at the centre of the complex stays hidden or unseen, Green sees fit to name and explicate the more manifest psychic needs of the subject as they circle or cluster "around this nucleus", surrounding its core of emptiness. There appear to be three main organizing aims: "to keep the ego alive" (requiring a subjective mixture of hatred, sensory excitement, and some form of meaning); "to reanimate the dead mother" (through any means that might stimulate the object's emotions or attention); and "to rival with the object of her bereavement" (attempting to banish any third party who is luring her away) (p. 183).

As he nears the end of this section of the paper, Green pre-empts "the serious technical problems" that these patients pose, but he will do no more at this juncture than offer a few clinical hints. Referring to an earlier paper of his own, he advises against the use of the analytic "rule of silence", claiming that it "only perpetuates the transference of blank mourning for the mother"—presumably onto the analyst, who is then also rendered dead, so to speak. He also eschews the application of "the

Kleinian technique of the systematic interpretation of destructiveness" in such cases. On the other hand, while he does think that Winnicott's (1969) approach to destructiveness in his paper on the use of an object is indeed useful and apposite, he critiques his otherwise esteemed English colleague in typical French fashion: Winnicott, we are told, "somewhat underestimated the sexual fantasies, especially the primal scene" (p. 183)—and Green thereby anticipates the main topics of the next part of his paper.

"Frozen Love and Its Vicissitudes: The Breast, the Oedipus Complex, the Primal Scene"

Green begins this third section with a timely reminder of the importance of ambivalence in all forms of depression. He feels, however, that he has not yet sufficiently described "the affective and representative decathexis" providing the context for ambivalence in the dead mother complex. There, he now claims, "the inability to love only derives from ambivalence, and hence from an overload of hatred, in the measure that what comes first is *love frozen* by the decathexis". This cryogenic halting—and Green resorts to some other, related metaphors: "The object is in hibernation, as it were, conserved by the cold"—are intended to convey the sudden stalling of any lively flow, both of feeling and of time, by a catastrophic withdrawal of psychic investment. He is, yet again, keen to insist on the non-primacy of hatred and refers to Freud's theory of the fusion of the life and death instincts to explain this: "Repressed hatred is the result of instinctual defusion, any unbinding weakening the erotic-libidinal cathexis, which, as a consequence, frees the destructive cathexes" (pp. 183–184).

More pertinently, however, Green delineates the self-delusion of the subject who, naively, thinks positive cathexes can simply be reclaimed from the dead mother and put at the disposal of new loving relationships. Such a person may consciously consider "his reserve of love to be intact"; he "declares himself ready to become attached to another object"; he believes that "the primary object no longer counts for him". However, he does not realize that what he has left behind is love itself, "which has fallen into the *oubliettes* of primary repression". It is not so much ambivalence that prevents him from loving, but the fact that "his love is still mortgaged to the dead mother"; he may in a sense still be potentially wealthy in love, "but he can give nothing in spite of his generosity, for he does not reap enjoyment from it" (p. 184).

As the transference begins to take hold in such analyses, the confidence and bravado of the subject's "defensive sexualisation which had occurred hitherto" is eroded. Having been erected, Green suggests, on the flimsy and precocious basis of "intensive pregenital satisfactions and remarkable sexual performance", the patient's erotic life falters and ebbs away. Suddenly, there is neither anyone worthy of desire nor anyone who desires him (or her). As Green puts it, "A profuse, dispersed, multiple, fleeting sexual life no longer brings any satisfaction." In such conditions, "subjects who are under the empire of the dead mother can only aspire to autonomy".

Previously "avoided" or "shunned", solitude now becomes the only recourse, and the subject "nestles into it", imagining that he is now truly alone. "He thinks he has got rid of his dead mother"—along with all her equally ungratifying replacements—but, unbeknownst to him, she has won a great victory: "He becomes his own mother, but remains prisoner to her economy of survival." She "only leaves him in peace in the measure that she herself is left in peace"—that is, only inasmuch as she does not feel assailed by rivals, and the mirror on the wall still declares her to be the fairest in the land. Adopting the dead mother's chilling perspective, Green writes: "As long as there is no candidate to the succession, she can well let her child survive, certain to be the only one to possess this inaccessible love" (p. 184).

Nancy Mitford's resonant title *Love in a Cold Climate* (1949) comes to mind, as Green's wintry metaphors continue to proliferate. But, he declares, "These are barely metaphors." In the frigid psychic grip of the dead mother, patients complain at times of feeling physically cold, even in warm weather. As Green tells us, "This cold core burns like ice, and numbs like it as well, but as long as it is felt to be cold, love remains unavailable." Like unfed vampires or the zombie undead, these patients "are cold below the surface of the skin, in their bones; they feel chilled by a funereal shiver, wrapped in their shroud". Still, the surface of life can seem unperturbed and undisturbed for a while; ordinary development appears to proceed without much incident or mishap.

Many such people start well, "have a more or less successful professional life; they marry and have children". This, however, is a situation that cannot last, and failure gradually overtakes these "two essential sectors of life, love and work"; disappointments and disturbances begin to abound in both arenas. There is an ominous sense that there must never be too much of anything good. Even when there are children to raise and the ostensibly selfless function of parenthood is "hyperinvested", it is often spoiled and undermined, "infiltrated by narcissism: children are loved on condition that they fulfil the narcissistic objectives which the parents have not succeeded in accomplishing themselves" (pp. 184–185).

Green now explores the direct effect of these dynamics on the nature of the Oedipus complex—when development manages to get that far—and becomes a bit more even-handed where gender is concerned, having seemed heretofore to be speaking primarily of male subjects. He tells us that girls who are fixated to the dead mother either cannot become attached to the father for fear of betraying her or end up transferring onto him qualities belonging to her. The confusing phenomenon of the "phallic mother" (which Green has addressed elsewhere) can arise instead, or as a corollary. While this may occur in both genders, a more specific consequence for the boy is that the homosexual bond with his father does not strengthen his internal structure, because the father seems "insignificant or tired, depressed, and overwhelmed by this phallic mother" (p. 185).

There are, of course, retrograde consequences here, and it appears that sufferers from the dead mother complex will struggle to work through the Oedipus complex to any comprehensive or sustainable extent. Green regards "a regression to anality" as inevitable in every case, a backwards move that leaves the subject in fear of dropping back further into the perhaps wished for, but also even more disturbing, oral merger with the mother. One is reminded of Karl Abraham's account of how regression becomes a kind of inexorable slide down a slippery slope, where it is difficult to get a grip or arrest one's descent.

As Green puts it, "the dead mother complex and the metaphoric loss of the breast reverberate each other", and he now describes the subject's desperate defensive scrabbling for a foothold in the real world in an attempt to avoid the blurring and potential disappearance of certain vital distinctions: "When fantasy and reality are telescoped together, intense anxiety appears. Subjective and objective are confused, which gives the subject the impression of the threat of psychosis." Order can only be restored by means of "a structuring anal reference", and a hyperbolic form of splitting ensues, leading to an extreme "negation of psychic reality" that "keeps the subject away from what he has learned of his unconscious". Psychoanalysis then comes to seem much more useful for the understanding of others (and is made use of accordingly, presumably in over-intellectual and projective ways). Though it may continue to be valued and "strongly cathected" by the patient, there is "inevitable disappointment with the results of the analysis" (pp. 185–186).

In an oddly heartfelt and hyperbolic paragraph, Green appears suddenly to speak out vehemently on behalf of the very hatred and aggression that he has assiduously attempted to relegate to a secondary or derivative place. As the analyst, he understandably feels frustrated and aggrieved that "The dead mother refuses to die a second death." As if taking up, from behind the couch, the narrative position of a third-person centre of consciousness—and thus adopting a view that not only supports, but is completely in line with, the thwarted subject's perspective—Green dramatically voices his own grievances and wishes: "'This time it's done, the old woman is really dead, he (or she) will finally be able to live and I shall be able to breathe a little'" (p. 186).

But of course, this is not at all what happens: when even "a small traumatism appears in the transference or in life", this "maternal imago" returns with full force and with "renewed vitality". Here Green seems momentarily to give way to his own venom, to indulge in the vicious mythopoetic "mother-bashing" imagery that now emerges from his mind and pen: "It is because she is a thousand-headed hydra whom one believes one has beheaded with each blow; whereas, in fact, only one of its heads has been struck off. Where then is the beast's neck" (p. 186)?

It is a literary critical rule of thumb that we attempt to avoid conflating the views of the narrator with those of the protagonist. Despite the powerful magnetic pull of countertransferential identification, the same could be said to apply in psychoanalysis between the perspective of the analyst and that of the analysand. Such cautions notwithstanding, the murderous zeal of Green's language here seems to be his way of expressing, empathizing with, and even participating in the plight of these entrapped, embattled patients. He goes on to rescue both himself and them by claiming that there is no need to do this, to descend "to the deepest level: to the primordial breast"—that is, to the primitive oral depths of both merger and rage.

With an eye again on the logic of the *après coup*, he reminds us that it is still the oedipal constellation that holds the key:

> For just as the relation with the second object in the Oedipus situation retroactively reveals the complex which affects the primary object, the mother, it is not by attacking the oral relation face on that one can extirpate the core of the complex. The solution is to be found in the prototype of the Oedipus complex, in the symbolic matrix which allows for its construction. Then the dead mother complex delivers its secret: it is the fantasy of the primal scene. [p. 186]

Green is reverting briefly to a more theoretical perspective, suggesting that we must not become too invested in specifying the real-time phenomenology of the psychosexual phases and stages of development or take them too literally. He believes that "contemporary psychoanalysis" has finally come to understand "that if the Oedipus complex remains the indispensable structural reference, the determining conditions for it are not to be sought in its oral, anal or phallic forerunners, seen from the angle of realistic references". They will also not be found in "a generalized fantasizing of their structure, à la Klein, but in the isomorphic fantasy of the Oedipus complex: that of the primal scene" (p. 186).

Here again we have Green in provocative guise. This is not only a description, but a challenge and urge to his contemporaries to keep paying the right kind of psychoanalytic attention to the patterning of the psyche, and not to get too "hung up" on sequential, evidential, empiricist, or scientistic pursuits. Even Freud is taken to task for betraying his own inclination to regard the primal scene as a structural fantasy when, in the Wolf Man case, he goes searching instead "for proof of its reality". Green insists that "what counts in the primal scene is not that one has witnessed it but precisely the contrary; namely, that it has taken place in the absence of the subject" (pp. 186). As Green had previously suggested, it is a preceding scene such as this, one that necessarily occurs "without" the subject—that is, both outside of it and *sans* its participation—that ordinarily brings forth the germinal entity that will eventually become the subject, or self, itself.

However, Green insists, it is particularly in the dead mother cases that he is investigating in this paper that "the fantasy of the primal scene is of capital importance". Sounding not a little like Bion (when he speaks, in structural-symbolic terms, of a preconception meeting a conception) and other post-Kleinian analysts (like Ron Britton who treats the oedipal "third" and the primal scene in conceptual or structural ways), Green explains that "it is on the occasion of an encounter between a conjuncture and a structure, which brings *two* objects into play, that the subject will be confronted with memory traces in relation to the dead mother".

The original decathexis has, until this moment, kept these traces under repression, where they have remained vague and inchoate, "in abeyance within the subject". The primal scene fantasy will not only restore these "vestiges" or fragments, "but will confer to them, through a new cathexis, new effects which constitute a real *conflagration*, setting fire to the structure which gives the complex of the dead mother retrospective significance" (pp. 186–187).

There is, it appears, a sudden move from the freezer to the furnace when this fantasy is reactivated: "Every resurgence of this fantasy constitutes a *projective actualization*, the projection aiming to assuage the narcissistic wound" of the original loss. This is not just projection as a defensive action, a means of getting rid of "inner tensions" by emptying them into the object. Projection here also appears to carry its cinematic meaning, whereby the subject effectively re-screens the primal scene, reproduces it as a virtual re-enactment that takes place before his eyes: it is "a *revivescence* and not a *reminiscence*, an *actual* traumatic and dramatic repetition" (p. 187).

Notwithstanding the fiery indignation that can consume the subject at such moments, the exclusion from the primal scene brings home "the insuperable distance that separates him from the mother" and leaves him, ultimately, with nothing but "impotent rage". He is put in touch with his own tragic hopelessness and helplessness and the realization that while he may be "incapable of awakening this dead mother, of animating her, or giving life back to her", there is someone else who has had—and may still have—the wherewithal to accomplish such a task.

Recalling the composite figure mentioned earlier in the paper, Green says that whereas this third-position rival–other was previously "the object who had captivated the dead mother in her experience of bereavement, he becomes on the contrary the third party who shows himself apt, against all expectation, to return her to life and to give her the pleasure of orgasm". The child is forced to face squarely the shaming fact that he simply has not got the goods, so to speak; it is thus no wonder that a deep and unendurable depression sets in. Green again reveals his identification with and sympathy for the subject here: this is a frankly "revolting" state of affairs that "reactivates the loss of narcissistic omnipotence and awakens the feeling of an incommensurable libidinal infirmity" (pp. 186–187).

In fact, Green now specifies not just one, but a listed and numbered "series of consequences", six in all. Defensive in nature, they may show themselves, he says, "singly or in groups". First, there is the sense of hating or being persecuted by the (parental) couple, formed "to the detriment of the subject". Second, the primal scene is imagined as a violent, sadistic encounter into which the mother is coerced by the father and where her pleasure is either absent or enforced. The third consequence is a "variation" of the second, whereby the mother does experience orgasm, but it renders her "cruel, hypocritical . . . a sort of lewd monster"—she is no longer the mother but the Sphinx of the Oedipus story. In the fourth response there are "alternating identifications with the two imagos": with the dead mother as either "unaltered" or perversely excited, and with the father as either her "aggressor" or her sexual healer. Hyper-intellectualization and "de-libidinization of the primal scene" characterize the fifth situation, where the purpose is to restore "wounded narcissistic omnipotence" via the construction of meaning through a theoretical or artistic "fantasy of auto-satisfaction" (pp. 187–188).

The sixth consequence is rather complex and requires a far more extensive explication. Its headline reads, "The negation, 'en bloc', of the whole fantasy", implying a total wiping out of "everything pertaining to sexual relations" and making "the emptiness of the dead mother and the obliteration of the primal scene coincide for the subject". But with the primal scene fantasy now predominating as "the central axis of the subject's life", there are psychic developments "in two directions: forwards and backwards". There is a prospective pre-emption or anticipation of the Oedipus complex in a defensive manner, and what are—for Green—the "three anti-erotic factors, namely hatred, homosexuality and narcissism" will combine forces to cause the complex to be "adversely structured" (p. 188).

One might now rightly expect dispute and voices raised in protest regarding the role of the second of these factors. Green's rather off-hand, throw-away homophobia is unbecoming and hopefully belongs to a by-gone psychoanalytic era. While I cannot go any further into such matters here, I can point the reader to a collection of papers on gender and sexuality by Hertzmann and Newbigin (2020) that deals with them judiciously and admirably.

The second, retrospective effect of the negation is that "the relation to the breast is the object of a radical reinterpretation". On the surface, "blank mourning" for this mother can lead to the breast being "laden with destructive projections", but Green thinks that it holds something far more devastating in store for the subject, simultaneously more subtle and more all-consuming than overt enmity or aggression:

> In fact it is less a question of a bad breast, which is ungiving, than a breast which, even when it does give, is an absent breast (and not lost), absorbed with nostalgia for a relation that is grieved for; a breast that can neither be full nor filling. The consequence of this is that the recathexis of the happy relation to the breast that existed prior to the occurrence of the dead mother complex, is this time affected with the fleeting signal of a catastrophic threat, and, if I dare say so, it is a *false* breast, carried within a *false* self, nourishing a *false* baby. [p. 188]

Appearing somewhat self-conscious about his own daring here, Green boldly echoes Winnicott (1960b) to the effect that a false breast may be worse than a bad one, and that a false mother feeding a false baby represents a very precarious relationship indeed.

When he reverts to his own terms, moreover, we recognize that absence is not the same as loss, that their difference is crucial. Something that is genuinely lost can potentially be re-found or recovered (from). By contrast, this kind of blank absence—which became Green's hallmark and special area of expertise—might provoke grievance and nostalgia (for what never was), but it does not invoke or allow true, mutative grief. Under its shadow, there is no prospect of better times nor, even, a sense that any such times had really existed before. This is made yet more explicit: from now on, the dead mother subject treats happiness as a "decoy" and claims never to have been loved, a claim that he even "strives to confirm in his subsequent love-life" (p. 188). This sounds like quite a typical melancholic trait, recalling Freud's comment that such a person regards himself always to have been the worst kind of sinner and to be fully deserving of his unloved, miserable, depressed state.

Green also corroborates that one is here "faced with a situation of mourning that is impossible, and that the metaphoric loss of the breast cannot be worked through for this reason". However, he also tries to distinguish the dead mother situation from other forms of depression in what he regards as a precise way. Unlike "what happens in melancholia", he says, these patients do not regress to the oral cannibalistic phase as such. Instead,

> What one witnesses above all is an identification with the dead mother on the level of the oral relation and with the defences that arise from it, the subject fearing to the utmost either the ultimate loss of the object or the invasion of emptiness. [pp. 188–189]

This might be an important caveat for Green, as he brings this sixth consequence to a conclusion. Perhaps the difference here between oral regression and oral identification might be worth exploring further.

However, as I mentioned near the beginning of this chapter, though Green has singled out a specific form or source of depression or melancholia, his thoughts provide a powerful and encompassing theoretical understanding of many similar pathological conditions—indeed, of the illnesses of loss at large. For the purposes of my book, at least, it is this more general achievement that is most valuable, and perhaps, therefore, Green's finer distinctions may be of slightly less relevance in this context.

Green ends this section with an introduction to the next, where the focus will be on transference. Sounding briefly quite hopeful and optimistic, he provides a kind of recipe for positive outcomes with these patients: if one analyses the transference "by means of these three positions"—and I assume he means "the breast, the Oedipus complex, the primal scene" named in the title of this section—it "will lead to the rediscovery of the early happiness that existed prior to the appearance of the dead mother complex".

He acknowledges, of course, that this will take much time and working-through, but he does not deem impossible the prospect of "marking a victory" over "blank mourning and its resonance with castration anxiety" that might "allow one to reach a transferential repetition of a happy relationship with a mother who is alive at last and desirous of the father". With this result, the analyst might justly assume that "one has passed through the analysis of the narcissistic wound, which consumed the child in his mother's bereavement" (p.189).

Picking up the relevant word from Green here and adopting the parlance of my own organizing metaphor, the result of such a hoped-for outcome would be the conversion of the patient from being passively subjected to consumption *by* the dead mother and her losses, into a subject actively ready to resume once again the capacity to consume, digest, and metabolize.

"The Characteristics of the Transference"

It is a little surprising—given the title of this section—to read Green's opening sentence, where he says that he "cannot dwell on the technical implications which arise in those cases where one may identify the dead mother complex in the transference". This is accurate insofar as his account is not strictly technical—that is, not preoccupied with analytic technique as such. This is in keeping perhaps with the fact that there is only minimal presentation and discussion of specific clinical work in the paper at large.

Green nevertheless speaks right away of the "remarkable features" of this dead-mother version of the transference, the first characteristic of which is the strong attachment of the patient to "the analysis more than the analyst". He then adds that though the patient may "present the whole scale of the libidinal spectrum", it is all deeply rooted "in a tonality of a narcissistic nature". Green sees the reason for this in the "secret disaffection" felt towards the analytic object. He again gives us, in the first person, a surmised unconscious thought addressed to the analyst by the analysand: "'I know the transference is but a lure, and that, in fact, everything is quite impossible with you in the name of reality: so what's the use of it'" (p. 189)?

The cynicism implied here does not necessarily preclude the patient's "idealisation of the analyst's image", whether for its own sake or for the purpose "of being seductive to attract his interest and his admiration". The legacies of the dead mother conundrum—namely, the need for narcissistic replenishment, as well as the "search for lost meaning"—induce the patient to take this attempted seduction of the analyst onto the intellectual plain. The patient tries to impress, bringing "precious gifts" of rich material and clever, adept "self-interpretation", but this strongly "contrasts with its meagre effect on the patient's life, which is only slightly modified, especially in the affective sphere" (p. 189).

Drawing attention to an earlier chapter in his book, Green comments on the rhetorical or narrative function of the patient's efforts directed at the inattentive mother, via the analyst:

> Its role is to move the analyst, to implicate him, to call him to witness in the reciting of conflicts which are encountered outside; like a child telling his mother of his day at school and the thousand small dramas which he has experienced, to attract her interest and make her participate in what he has been through during her absence. [pp. 189–190]

There is something poignant about Green's implicit juxtaposition of the ordinary enthusiasm with which a well-mothered child might come home and make a spontaneous story of his or her school day, and the desperate, deliberate expertise to which the dead mother's child must resort to gain a mere modicum of attention from either the original or the transferential object.

Continuing his rhetorical critique, Green notes that the "style is relatively unassociative", but should there be any associations at all, they would contribute towards "a movement of discrete withdrawal ... as though it were the analysis of someone else not present at the session". The analyst is led away from the personal dimension of the communication: these subjects prefer detachment and disconnection, "so as not to be overcome by revivifying emotion" and not to risk the revelation and exposure of their "naked despair" (pp. 189–190).

Green now brings two characteristics of the dead mother transference to our attention: first, what he terms "the non-domestication of the drives", meaning the failure to relinquish incestuous wishes and thus the refusal to mourn and metabolize this primary object. Again, one is tempted to generalize this, to note its truth in so many instances of melancholia or depression. It is curiously paradoxical, perhaps, that Green refers here to "non-domestication", when surely what such patients suffer from is a kind of over-domestication: an inability to leave home, and hence their struggle—and this is his point—to make a new home in the analysis. The second "and more remarkable feature", Green says, is that "the analysis induces emptiness". Going on to connect the two, Green effectively admits that even if the new home appears to provide shelter and comfort, it may still feel too strange and unfamiliar; that is, even where the analyst as substitute or adoptive object is doing a good job, he may nevertheless be experienced as somehow just wrong. In Green's own words, "when the analyst succeeds in touching an important element of the nuclear complex of the dead mother, for a brief instant, the subject feels himself to be empty, blank, as though he were deprived of a stop-gap object, and a guard against madness" (p. 190).

Having acknowledged their influence earlier, Green again sounds remarkably like his compatriots, Abraham and Torok, as he tells us that "behind the dead mother complex, behind the blank mourning for the mother, one catches a glimpse of the mad passion of which she is, and remains, the object, that renders mourning for her an impossible experience". One might quibble and say that, on the contrary, Abraham and Torok place their focus on the passion *of* the parental object *for* the child-subject: the latter becomes convinced that the former is, in fact, "mad about" or in thrall to him- or herself, and that is the reason for their seduction. In fact, Green does, himself, entertain a similar idea of reversal later in his text; however, to quote Abraham and Torok's oft-used phrase, this "hardly matters", because ultimately the fantasy is about a mutual, completely symmetrical infatuation or love affair.

However, as all three of these French analysts recognize, there are at least two obstacles to this union: one is incest, and the other is death. Abraham and Torok say that the subject's melancholic solution to these problems lies in secret entombment or encryption. Green's version is similar:

> The subject's entire structure aims at a fundamental fantasy: to nourish the dead mother, to maintain her perpetually embalmed. This is what the analysand does to the analyst: he feeds him with the analysis, not to help himself live outside the analysis, but to prolong it into an interminable process. For the subject wants to be the mother's polar star, the ideal child, who takes the place of an ideal dead object, who is necessarily invincible, because not living, which is to be imperfect, limited, finite. [p. 190]

There is a fundamental tension in this transference relation: between whether the analyst represents the dead mother or is regarded as her dangerous enemy. Far from being nurtured by either analyst or mother, the patient reverses the roles and puts both on a diet of pacifying pabulum or a sedating drip, to maintain both objects in a state of undeath.

The alternative is to treat the analyst as the mother's actual or purported undertaker who wishes to bury her and thus must be fended off at any cost. In a difficult theoretical-poetic sentence in which Green may be trying to capture these complexities, the transference is seen as a "geometric space" where a triumvirate of elements—"the primal scene, the Oedipus complex and the oral relation"—condense and displace each other and are "constituted by a double inscription: on the one hand, peripheral and luring and, on the other, central and veracious, around the blank mourning for the dead mother". It is not clear whether Green's idea of doubling here coincides precisely with the tension I have tried to outline, but the next sentence seems to corroborate this view of the transference: "What is essentially lost here is contact with the mother, who is secretly maintained in the depths of the psyche, concerning whom all attempts of replacement by substitute objects are destined to fail" (p. 190).

In what is really the only attempt in his paper to broach specifically "technical attitudes", Green suggests that the dead mother complex presents the analyst with a choice. If she or he opts for "the classical solution", this "attitude of silence" may register in the analysand's mind as a repetition of the mother's silence or absence. There is then a danger that "the analysis may sink into funereal boredom", bringing despair and a harsh form of disillusionment in its wake. Wearing his Winnicottian colours proudly, Green declares his preference for the other option, "which, by using the setting as a transitional space, makes an ever-living object of the analyst, who is interested, awakened by his analysand, giving proof of his vitality by the associative links he communicates to him, without ever leaving his neutrality" (pp. 190–191).

The analyst, in other words, also attempts a reversal of the usual situation and must do so in subtle fashion, to avoid impinging or being invasive. If the analyst is not to become either the mother's clone or her all-too-obvious nemesis, the liveliness that counteracts her deadliness must come to reside in sustained analytic curiosity about the patient. This serves to demonstrate and provide a type of attentive engagement probably not experienced since the dead mother's death, so to speak, and which the patient is incapable of finding in his or her own contemporary life.

A more gradual disillusionment will ensue if "the analysand feels himself to be narcissistically invested by the analyst", and this will occur only "if the latter remains constantly awake to what the patient is saying, without falling into intrusive interpretation". Adding some nuance, Green claims that there are ways of manifesting this interest by working with preconscious links supporting the "tertiary processes" and without the intrusiveness of "going directly to the unconscious fantasy". Again, Green is indicating his preference for British Independent over Kleinian technique and seems to think that even a patient who might easily feel intruded upon by intimate closeness to the analyst can be brought to recognize "without being excessively traumatizing, the defensive role of this feeling against a pleasure which provokes anxiety" (p. 191).

One may imagine that there are many psychoanalysts of other persuasions who would take issue with these claims. Though Green seems prepared to dip in and out of them, he does not wade around for long enough in these contentious close-clinical waters to entertain objections and criticisms: his primary penchant, as always, is for the more abstract or conceptual perspective. He now says that "it is passivity that is at the heart of the conflict here: passivity or *passivation* as primary femininity, femininity common to the mother and the infant" and speaks of blank mourning as a kind of sharing of "the common body of their deceased loves" (p. 191).

What Green appears to be returning to here is an exploration of the precise nature of the identification between the dead mother and her child—featuring merger, interchangeability, and "a strange reversal"— which comes into view once the analysis succeeds "in rendering life, at least partially, to the aspect of the child which is identified with the dead mother". Thus, even when a modicum of vitality is recovered via the analytic work, it "remains the prey of a captive identification", and the consequences are, we are told, "not easily interpretable". There is an inversion of the child's earlier dependency upon the mother, a circumstance that is described by means of a useful metaphor: "From now on, the relation between the child and the dead mother is turned inside-out like the fingers of a glove." The child cannot simply accept, embrace— or, indeed, grasp—his own healing, because it is gained at the expense of "the incomplete reparation of the mother who remains ill", and this, says Green, is "translated by the fact that it is then the mother who depends on the child" (p. 191).

Lest anyone should think of this child as demonstrating a benign version of "reparation" in Klein's sense and thus manifesting depressive-position capacity, Green is quick to qualify his use of the term: "It has less to do with positive acts, which are the expression of remorse, than simply a sacrifice of this vitality on the altar of the mother, by renouncing the use of these new potentialities of the ego, to obtain possible pleasures." Clearly, this quite familiar and typical trait of depression performs a kind of parody of true reparation (akin, perhaps to manic or obsessional reparation in Kleinian terms), reducing it to a form of masochistic self-martyrdom. Venturing another rare clinical recommendation, Green suggests a transference interpretation that might be needed to point out to the patient that his actions are "aimed at furnishing the analysis with an occasion to interpret, less for himself than for the analyst, as though it were the analyst who needed the analysand", and not vice versa. I believe that many an analyst has had experiences with depressed patients which necessitate interpretations of this kind, triggered by the disturbing realization that he or she might be deriving far more benefit from the analysis than the patient!

Nearing the end of this section, Green abandons the transference to focus directly and exclusively on the child's relation with the dead mother. How, he asks, have the tables been turned so diametrically? With hints at many a horror film trope, he describes "an inverted vampire-like fantasy" beneath the manifest surface, in which the patient's life is spent "nourishing his dead, as though he alone has charge of it". Extrapolating from the image, we might conclude that the child opens a vein, as it were, proffering his or her own lifeblood to feed this mother-as-vampire, with the aim of keeping her both alive and dead.

Gender differences notwithstanding, it will immediately be apparent that much said here about the dead mother and her child would apply equally well to the dead father and his daughter in "A Rose for Emily", although there the macabre tasks are carried out yet more literally and concretely, and upon a substitute or transference object. Continuing to outline the bereaved child's dedicated role, Green writes:

> Keeper of the tomb, sole possessor of the key of the vault, he fulfils his function of foster-parent in secret. He keeps the dead mother prisoner, and she remains his personal property. The mother has become the infant of the child. It is for him to repair her narcissistic wound. [p. 191]

We note, again, that this is very much the territory also traversed by Abraham and Torok.

In the section's final paragraph, Green reminds us of certain possible consequences of the dead mother's literal and/or figurative presence, via a paradox: "if the mother is in mourning, dead, she is lost to the subject, but at least, however afflicted she might be, she is there. Dead and present, but present nonetheless." This circumstance permits and perpetuates the continued ministrations of the priestly child towards his deity-like mother. Though the words "depressed" or "melancholic" would seem to apply aptly to both parties in this arrangement, one feels that Green is intent on eschewing them. But what if the mother—who is not actually dead, after all—should be resurrected, return from her death-in-life, recover from her mourning or melancholia? The child is then placed in a terrible bind:

> But in return, if cured, she awakens, is animate and lives, the subject loses her again, for she abandons him to go about her own affairs, and to become attached to other objects—with the result that the subject is caught between two losses: presence in death, or absence in life. Hence the extreme ambivalence concerning the desire to bring the dead mother back to life. [p. 192]

Whether she is "cured" by her child—which Green has earlier indicated is unlikely, because he would lack the wherewithal—or by someone else (there may be nothing preventing her from getting some therapy or analysis, after all), there is the terrible danger that the mother will then be lost once again, albeit to a less toxic form of loss: "absence in life" rather than "presence in death", as Green puts it.

Is there also a suggestion here that the route to the cure of the child would also finally lie in this disillusioning direction? Perhaps this would require his acceptance of the ordinary misery that Freud says is about the only thing psychoanalysis has to offer. But then one might not be surprised if, after everything he has gone through, such a patient might turn around and ask: "Is that all there is?", or "If this is cure, who needs it?"

"Metapsychological Hypotheses: The Effacement of the Primary Object and the Framing Structure"

Green returns to his real forte in this long paper's penultimate section. As its title might suggest, the structural and theoretical implications sketched out earlier are now going to be pursued with considerable vigour and rigour, requiring a renewed engagement with the contributions of his psychoanalytic predecessors and contemporaries. Green does now say that, among all other attempts at "defining more precisely the characteristics of the most primitive maternal imago", Melanie Klein stands out as having "accomplished a mutation in theory". However, because of her analytic work with children and significantly disturbed adults, she was "mainly concerned with the internal object": thus, the role of the external mother "in the constitution of her imago" was neglected or underestimated, and this opened the way for Winnicott's work, "born of this neglect" (p. 192).

Green clearly recognizes that Klein's followers, with Bion at the helm, were able to make the necessary adjustments to take her powerful legacy forward. It is nevertheless ironic for Green that, for all her foregrounding of the mother, Klein's own dogged focus on the innate death and life instincts and their relative strengths within the infant should lead to "the maternal variable hardly entering into the question". For her, therefore, the actual external mother is developmentally less significant and influential than are the child's own instinctual endowments. Perhaps adding insult to injury, Green says that in taking this approach "she was following Freud's lead."

Putting it succinctly, Green says that "Kleinian contributions concentrated on projections relative to the bad object". He sees this as a reaction to Freud's original reluctance to countenance and contemplate the bad mother because of "his immovable faith in the quasi-paradisical bond uniting the mother to her infant". It became the job of Klein and her school to "touch up" this only "partial picture of the mother–infant relationship" (p. 192).

Green now presents a rather tidy—if also slightly wry—summary of Klein's fundamental ideas. He describes her penchant for patients with "maniaco-depressive or psychotic structure" who make excessive defensive use of projection. There are her fulsome accounts of the "omnipresent internal breast which threatens the infant with annihilation, with fragmentation and infernal cruelty of all kinds". She conveys the process whereby "the schizo-paranoid phase starts to give way to the depressive position", leading to "the unification of the object and the ego" and "the progressive cessation of projective activity". The Kleinian infant is said to attain "a growing capacity to assume his own aggressive drives" and "becomes 'responsible' for them". The child is now minded "to take care of the maternal object, to worry about her, to fear losing her, by reflecting his aggressivity against himself owing to archaic guilt, and with a view to making reparation". The account culminates as follows: "This is why, more than ever, there is no question here of incriminating the mother" (pp. 192–193).

Whether one regards Green as having produced an accurate or a reductively skewed précis of Klein's work here, he does present it as the most complex, comprehensive, and compelling theory of the early mother–child drama that psychoanalysis had yet put forward. And he is doing so by way of a prelude and foil to the presentation of his own theoretico-structural account of these primary dynamics, which will deal, in turn, with both healthy and pathological versions of these developments.

First, he reiterates the claim that even "where vestiges of the bad object may persist, as a source of hatred" in the dead mother "configuration", these "hostile characteristics are secondary to a primary imago of the mother where she has found herself devitalized by a mirror reaction of the child who was affected by her bereavement". This mention of the mirror serves to hint at other psychoanalytic theories in which mirrors play an important part: it simultaneously re-introduces Winnicott (1967b), alludes to Kohut (who was mentioned earlier), and puts a more Lacanian spin on the proceedings. Though he does not spell this out, one glimpses the substance of Green's own view of the failure of mutual reflection in the dead mother complex: she has suffered a real loss, an unexpected but actual bereavement, with significant consequences at the narcissistic level for both mother and child. This creates an extra dimension of disturbance in the already complex mutual, imaginary, self-actualizing or self-compromising reflections that are in any case passing back and forth within the dyad.

Prefaced by the phrase, "When conditions are favourable", there is a long passage in the text detailing André Green's version of what optimal early development looks like in metapsychological terms. If the "inevitable separation between the mother and the child" occurs as it should, we are told, "a decisive mutation arises in the depths of the ego". The mother, as "primary object of fusion, fades away, making way for the ego's own cathexes which are the source of his personal narcissism". Thenceforward, as the mother steps back or away, the subject can begin to do his own cathecting, more separately and with less participation from the "primitive object". However, "this effacing of the mother" (a resonant phrase that repeats a key word from the section's title) does not amount to the simple or complete disappearance of this primitive object. The latter now recedes into the background, and, as such, "becomes a 'framing structure' for the ego, sheltering the negative hallucination of the mother" (p. 193).

If I understand Green correctly, all future representations—which, of course, continue to be produced—are screened upon or "projected inside this framing structure onto the backdrop of the negative hallucination". That is, unlike the originating "*frame-representations*" (those "that fuse what comes from the mother with what comes from the child"), the newer images are no longer quite as necessary for the ego's very constitution and survival. Following the logic of these painterly or filmic metaphors, once the encompassing frame or screen has been properly set up in the first instance, it serves as container, context, or backdrop for those later, less formative, and less structurally crucial representations; the latter, says Green, are no longer such that their "corresponding affects express a vital character, which is indispensable for the baby's existence" (p. 193).

Again, these are difficult formulations but, like good poetry, they deserve and can bear interpretive scrutiny; the more one persists with them, the more they yield and ramify. We witness the very architecture of Green's structuralist psychoanalysis being laid out and exemplified here, and detect in it deep-structural similarities with Loewald's version of the internal world, as well as with Freud's original and more inchoate account of such matters in *The Ego and the Id*. An explicit connection is made with Freudian ideas—later to be elaborated by Winnicott—concerning the baby's earliest capacity to imagine or hallucinate the absent breast.

The original and originating entities, Green says, "hardly deserve the name of representations" at all, because they are in a sense prior to representation proper:

> They are the compounds of barely outlined representations, probably of a hallucinatory nature rather than representative, and loaded affects which one could almost call affective hallucinations. This is just as true in the hopeful state anticipating satisfaction as in states of want. When these are prolonged, they give rise to the emotions of anger, rage, and then catastrophic despair. [p. 193]

As Winnicott (1967a) tells us, timing is all in such primary situations: an inevitable delay in satisfaction of x duration is fine, and $x + y$ is still tolerable, but $x + y + z$ is unbearable, and perhaps unsurvivable.

In Green's schema, this also depends fatefully on whether "the effacing of the maternal object that has been transformed into a framing structure comes about when love for the object is sufficiently sure to play this role of a container of representative space" (p. 193). Bearing in mind that Green sees the mother, midst her other roles, as also the guardian of meaning and meaning-making and thus of language and representation, the status of this space is contingent in the extreme: when the love that ensures it does suffice, Green says, it "is no longer threatened with cracking".

Here, then, is a different metaphor: the shell of the "eggo" (that is, of the ego as egg) can be rendered robust enough to withstand "waiting and even temporary depression, the child feeling supported by the maternal object even when it is not there". Perhaps Green has the ideas of his colleague Didier Anzieu (1985) in mind as he seems now to be envisaging not only two-dimensional frames or screens but enclosed, enveloping, three-dimensional regions, bounded by shells, skins, or other integuments. A good vessel like this (as Bion has told and shown us most clearly) "offers the guarantee of the maternal presence in her absence, and can be filled with fantasy of all kinds, to the point of, and including, aggressive violent fantasies which will not imperil the container" (pp. 193–194).

At this stage, we are still being given Green's account of a good or good-enough situation. As we saw previously, in the fifth chapter on Loewald, albeit expressed there in very different terms, it seems clear that emptiness, absence, separation, and loss are not always negative phenomena. These can be transitionally enabling areas, positively inviting vacuums that summon normal development by providing the right spaces for its accomplishment:

> The space which is thus framed constitutes the receptacle of the ego; it surrounds an empty field, so to speak, which will be occupied by

erotic and aggressive cathexes, in the form of object representations. This emptiness is never perceived by the subject, because the libido has cathected the psychical space. Thus it plays the role of primordial matrix of the cathexes to come. [p. 194]

This, then, is how the set-up *should* look, so that the ego may be primed—with the requisite maternal help—for the introduction of the drives and object relations proper, as opposed to having these overwhelm an insufficiently prepared ego system. Might one suggest another relevant metaphor: that this system be conceived of as a digestive or metabolic one, with its psychic enzymes at the ready, its processing and absorbing capacities fully functional, for pending encounters with the nourishing forces and experiences of life—no less than the impoverishing depletions of death and loss.

But such preparedness is not always possible or available. As Green goes on to say, "if a traumatism such as blank mourning occurs before the infant has been able to establish this framework solidly enough, there is no psychical space available within the ego". By contrast with the elaborations above, this is where he adumbrates the circumstances in which a fundamental or early form of depression can take hold. A framing structure of sorts may have been established, but it is not properly in place to promote freedom and positive prospects: it can only provide "a conflictual space which strives to hold the mother's image captive, struggling against its disappearance, and alternately noting the revival of the memory traces of lost love, with nostalgia, which is expressed by the impression of painful vacuity" (p. 194).

Under these conditions, ambivalence is rife, absence and loss are too painful, and there can be no progressive or non-incestuous development. Green closes his much shorter paragraph about such failed outcomes with an important sentence:

These alternations reproduce the ancient conflict of unsuccessful primary repression, in the measure that effacing the primordial object will not have been an acceptable experience, nor mutually accepted by the two parties of the former mother–infant symbiosis. [p. 194]

Sylvia Plath, "Morning Song" (1961)

Yet again, it is a single word in Green's text that has ensnared me, set off my literary associations, and put the theoretical discourse on pause by bringing another poem to mind, again by Sylvia Plath. As I hope to make clear, its aptness for the occasion is almost impossible to ignore. Like the troubling "Daddy" discussed in chapter six, "Morning Song" (1961, p. 11) is also from Plath's renowned posthumous collection *Ariel* (1965).

In this poem, too, she addresses a close family member, this time her new-born daughter, the elder of her two children with Ted Hughes. Its first line reads:

Love set you going like a fat gold watch.

Plath situates "Morning Song" as the opening poem of her volume, thus launching the latter in—or at least with—the name of love. But what kind of love is this? Striking though the line may be, does it signify a rather feelingless, mechanical beginning for the poem, the book, and the life that it heralds, regarding love as perhaps nothing other than a kind of primary impetus or first cause? It immediately evokes scepticism and concern: can this type of love be sustained, and is it likely to be containing enough for the future good of the addressee of the poem and her internal world?

Having taught this poem many times, I became aware over time of one of its quite predictable effects: namely, the extent to which it divides its readers. This is achieved, I believe, by Plath creating a work almost perfectly poised in its ambivalence, balanced in its ambiguity. Is this opening line—spoken by a first-time mother to her first-born daughter—unconventionally charming and witty, or just distant and cold? Yes, the child's chubby value is acknowledged, but perhaps not very tenderly. And is there already the suggestion that, having kicked things off, love will have no further part to play in the proceedings? Oedipally speaking, the love that sets things going may be a restricted, limited form of sexual love between the procreating couple that is not necessarily transformed and transferred to the product of their union.

Little if any warmth is added to this picture in the lines that follow. They contain a slightly violent image of the baby's feet being slapped (again, to get things going, as it were) and her reduction to a synecdochic and synaesthetic hairless voice assuming its place in the universe—as if she has been ordered militarily to fall in, to join the rank-and-file of humanity. The images in the second stanza, and its clipped sentences, reinforce the frigid atmosphere, reminding me of Green's earlier characterization of the dead mother syndrome in terms of "frozen love". The baby's entrance may be an important, even monumental event—it must be magnified, and a formal fuss made of it—but while the adults enunciate and annunciate the arrival with clarion call, their voices echo emptily. This is hardly an enthusiastic welcome to the naked newcomer: she is treated as just another stiff and static exhibit in the gallery of existence.

Of course, what may be intended here is not necessarily a sense of indifference to the new creature so much as genuine terror and helplessness before her advent. Perhaps what is palpable in these early lines is Plath's need to numb the panic instilled in her by the birth of this first child. The infant's very nakedness and vulnerability, and the demanding duties and responsibilities that she will call forth, seem to cast a melancholic shadow over the parents, who are only apparently safe and secure within their adult attire.

Will such anxious parents be capable of (per)forming the framing role, providing the reliable structure for their child's later development? The sentence with which the second stanza ends—"We stand round blankly as walls"—immediately puts us in mind of Green's "blank mourning", the potential emptiness and depression that lurks in these primary moments, for mother (and father?) no less than for child. Whether Plath's well-documented depressive episodes took a particular postpartum form after the birth of this child (it is known to have done so later, after her son was born) is neither here nor there: Plath's proneness to periods of profound melancholia—as well as brilliantly creative, manic elations—had already been in place since her own childhood.

But now we come to the crucial, and pivotal, third stanza, consisting of this psychologically resonant if somewhat opaque sentence and metaphor:

> I'm no more your mother
> Than the cloud that distils a mirror to reflect its own slow
> Effacement at the wind's hand.

If we pause after the first line—as the line break bids us do—there is an apparent denial of motherhood that maintains the low emotional temperature and prolongs the chilly and chilling absence of feeling. Having extruded her offspring quite matter-of-factly and mechanically, is Plath now simply reneging on her maternal role? But we continue, following the trajectory and sense of the sentence, plunging into the deeper waters of the image. Is there another disturbing, disowning, self-distancing implication here: that she contributes no more to the child's molecular-chemical make-up than any cloud or bit of the natural atmosphere might do?

But the poem's own syntactical clouds eventually part, revealing at least the gist of what Plath's image means. The fate of a mother, it seems, is like that of a cloud: it rains down its burden of moisture to form a pool or puddle below, reflected in which it can then only watch and witness its own gradual demise.

For many a reader, the impact of this imagery is shocking: having done the biological job of birthing a child, does the mother see—reflected in the child itself—nothing other than her own decline? Does she observe herself merely blowing off on the breeze, her life's substance ebbing away?

The key word hinted at earlier is, of course, "effacement". As the first word of the ninth line of this 18-line poem, it is well-nigh as central to Plath's poem as it can be, both literally and figuratively, and to its structure as well as its meaning. This centrality reinforces the word's undeniable, if negative, importance here, just as it governs Green's deliberations in the section of his paper that we are now interrupting. Where Green is exploring the vicissitudes of maternal effacement in theoretical psychoanalytic terms, Plath is doing so "up close and personal", via her existential proximity to the actual experience of motherhood, something that no man can ever have or know.

We remember that both love and effacement are words that feature in Green's account of how the developmentally optimal version of the mother's withdrawal and change of role works: "the effacing of the maternal object that has been transformed into a framing structure comes about when love for the object is sufficiently sure to play this role of a container of representative space" (p. 193). The positive connotations of effacement in Green's text clearly draw on Winnicott's ideas, suggesting that—if all is well and love is "sufficiently sure" or good enough—the maternal function mutates gradually from one of intense, concentrated initial engagement to a protective and encompassing guardianship of separate development. However, in the context of Plath's poem, and at least from *this* mother's perspective, the solidly frame-forming or structure-building function attributed to maternal effacement may not apply or come about. Some mothers may experience nothing more than the simple disappearance or creeping irrelevance enshrined in Plath's metaphor.

At this point, it is difficult to ignore the *medical* meaning of the term "effacement", which refers to the thinning of the mother's cervix at the latter end of a pregnancy as it readies itself for the imminent birth. Incidentally, this is heralded by the loosening of a mucus plug that has sealed the uterus to protect the foetus, referred to in its passing out of the body as a "bloody show"—a phrase that is brutally poetic, almost too down-to-earth, and thus somehow evocative of and congruent with Plath's distinctive style. She is surely too knowing a poet to have chosen the word "effacement" without being aware of its physiological significance in this context. And, having evoked this meaning, the point remains the same: that in the process of giving rise to a child, a mother's own physical—and mental—substance does indeed thin or give way. She plays, at best, the part of temporary receptacle or vehicle, consecrated to the advent of a new other; she is a living proscenium arch, a mere backdrop, for the emergence onto the stage of a new act. What a performance, what a bloody show, indeed!

As Freud had suggested in "Mourning and Melancholia", someone with self-effacing sentiments or convictions like these—no matter how existentially right or just they may sound—must nevertheless be considered ill, depressed. As many people have suggested, however, this is a poem of two halves: after the dourness of the first three stanzas, it is in the final three that it begins to warm up and find its compassionate, responsive voice.

With echoes of Shakespeare's *Winter's Tale*, both daughter and mother—once lost and now found—begin to thaw, wake from sleep, and come to life by degrees. It is charming—not to mention a relief—when the mother appears progressively to recover her love and her lyricism as her sleeping daughter begins to wake, stir, and utilize her own vocal capacities. In both senses of the word, she is no longer still, is not a stillbirth.

The first faint evidence of this coming to life is in the fourth stanza, when it is just the sound of the child's faint breathing that can be heard emerging from the two-dimensional flatness—not just of the bedsheets, but of the emotional fabric of the poem thus far. Though as the poetic mother, Plath seems herself to have been in something of a defensively unconscious coma thus far, we recognize that, as the real mother, she has nevertheless been semi-consciously vigilant throughout the night, attuned to her baby's breathing as well as to oceanic signals and frequencies deep inside herself. When her infant cries out, her briny "*la mère*-hood" registers fully on her consciousness at last.

The new sound makes immediate contact and, like a reflex or an electric shock, galvanizes the mother into motion: summoned to her maternal tasks, she is both encumbered and encouraged by her swollen breasts, which, after all, need emptying no less than her infant needs filling. The more tuned-in maternal responsiveness (or preoccupation) is nicely captured by the mutuality of the patterned flowers on both the daughter's and the mother's bedclothes. One may, of course, also read some lingering resentment or negativity into these images, as if Plath might also feel that having this child has ruined her body, reduced it—by expanding it—to heavy, sexless functionality. But clearly, the overall movement is now away from such feelings, not least because her diva-daughter is beginning to exercise her voice, to run through her scales—something, we assume, that is bound to please and impress her poet–mother.

There is much in this poem—as well as in in Green's deliberations on effacement—that is reminiscent of Wallace Stevens's late impressions of the mother in "The Auroras of Autumn", explored in chapter five: her fading and transparent, but nonetheless framing and containing image. As in Stevens's poem, the changing atmosphere of the latter half of "Morning Song" is filled with rich images, full of sound and motion. It is populated by the lively presence of animals—moths, cows, cats—and its closing themes all seem to converge on a kind of openness, transparency, and clarity.

Plath seems to invest and express all these qualities in the wonderful simile of the baby's mouth opening "clean as a cat's". We are familiar with these wide feline yawns that simultaneously bespeak the kind of relaxation and indolence of which only cats are capable, while affording an undistorted view of their dangerous dentition. In this context, however, the main connotation is that of a clearly defined aperture or cavity—albeit toothless for the moment—that is readying itself not only for the breast that will soon be brought to it, but for the sounds that it is about to emit.

In emulation of the baby's open mouth (preparing for a feed, but also for the "communion of empty mouths", in Abraham and Torok's resonant phrase), the window "swallows its dull stars" and thereby lets in the light of day. Hearing her baby exercising her musical and proto-verbal skills, Plath brings the poem to a close with a delightfully childish, life-affirming image reminding us of the time of day and the title of the poem:

The clear vowels rise like balloons.
[161, p.11]

Notwithstanding this new dawn, however, with its soaring voices and rising emotional temperatures, we cannot afford to forget or ignore the wintry, dirge-like tones of the first three stanzas. As I have always thought, the maternal ambiguities and ambivalences—the strains, no less than the joys, of motherhood, especially for a mother dogged and haunted by the shadow of melancholia—surely require us to see and hear the first part of this lyric as a *mourning* song, even if it does eventually become a *morning* song.

* * *

Re-opening Green's text at the bookmarked place where the poetic digression began, one finds him trying to address the issue of narcissism directly and explicitly, to bring it into his metapsychological equation, as we saw that Loewald and Abraham and Torok were also moved to do in their respective ways.

In his typically well-informed fashion—and surely with the work of Michael Balint (1952, 1968) in mind—Green simultaneously introduces and tries to dispel the psychoanalytic debate over "the antagonism between primary narcissism and primary object-love", playfully claiming that it is "without object"—that is to say, somewhat irrelevant and beside the point. Seeming, again, to have thoroughly digested Winnicott's (1960b) insights concerning the parent–infant relationship, he defuses the argument by saying that it really depends on who is looking and from where: "That primary object-love can be observed straightaway by a third party, an onlooker, can hardly be disputed. On the other hand, that this love should be narcissistic from the child's point of view could hardly be otherwise" (p. 194).

Elaborating further, Green astutely recognizes that these disagreements are based on metapsychological presumptions and, therefore, on what precisely one might intend by the designation "primary narcissism". If the term is used to mean "a primitive form of relation" where the child is seen as a needy initiator of an interpersonal connection from the onset of life, "then, there is certainly a characteristic primary narcissistic structure of inaugural forms of cathexis". But if it means "the accomplishment of a feeling of unity which is established only after a phase dominated by fragmentation, then one must conceive primary narcissism and object-love as two modes of cathexis centred around opposite and distinct polarities". I am not sure I understand this difference fully or correctly, but Green seems to want to reconcile and bring together views as ostensibly divergent (and overlapping) on these matters as those of Balint, Kohut, Klein, and Winnicott.

For his part, Green seems to think he can have it both ways, one *after* the other, so to speak. As the last of his theoretical contributions—in a paper that is packed with them—he offers a complex metapsychological position on narcissism, based on "two successive moments of our mythical construction of the psychical apparatus". Paradoxically treating the concept as if there can be two forms of it, his belief is that "earliest primary narcissism encompasses *all* cathexes in a confused way"—including primary versions of both object-love and object-hatred—and is predicated upon and characterized by an "early lack of subject–object distinction".

However, when greater subsequent separation is achieved, "later primary narcissism"—effectively the cathexis of one's own ego—can be differentiated and seen as "distinct from object cathexis". While I find myself wondering why this later moment cannot be designated as one type of secondary narcissism, Green pushes on and adds a distinction between *"positive"* and *"negative"* forms of primary narcissism, linking these, respectively, to Eros ("tending towards unity and identity") and the death instinct ("connected with the destructive instincts"). While this appears to bring his views into proximity with those of Herbert Rosenfeld's (1971) distinction between libidinal and destructive forms of narcissism, Green's negative form is "not manifested by hatred towards the object". Instead, it is viewed as a self-directed internal "withdrawal" or coming apart, marked clinically by empty feelings; there is, in other words, a "tendency of the ego to undo its unity and to proceed towards zero" (pp. 194–195).

Making yet another foray into the implications of his dead mother complex, this time from the angle of Margaret Mahler's (1975) theory of "individuating separation", Green endeavours to explain "cases where the evolution is unfavourable" and a narcissistic predicament ensues. After what is only ostensible separation in such cases, the young ego, instead of constituting the receptacle for future cathexes, relentlessly endeavours to retain the primary object and thus relives its loss repetitively:

> At the level of the primary ego (which is fused with the object) this gives rise to the feeling of narcissistic depletion, expressed phenomenologically by the sentiment of emptiness, so characteristic of depression, which is always the result of a narcissistic wound experienced on the level of the ego. [p. 195]

These sentiments serve to link Green's ideas with those explored in the previous two chapters of this book. Loewald, Abraham, and Torok also explore such entrapping circumstances where the ego is not at liberty to leave, because it is in thrall to a strength-sapping object that either will not let go or cannot be relinquished—which amounts to the same thing.

Such an ego is left, in effect, neither separate nor free. To recall Miss Emily's fate in Faulkner's story yet again: she must hold fast to the very object that had deprived her. The object—in her case a father, but usually a mother—both clings and is clung to, can neither release nor be released. For the subject or ego, there is unfinished business with this object because it has not been able either to provide enough initial psychic sustenance or, therefore, to exercise and complete its subsequent emancipating task. The outcome, as Green says, is the relentless re-living of loss, enmeshment with the object, narcissistic wounding and depletion, a sense of emptiness—in a word: depression.

Returning to the fundamental predicament—that of having a mother who is not psychically alive but not actually dead—Green depicts the magnetic pull of this object, which "draws the ego towards a deathly, deserted universe. The mother's blank mourning induces blank mourning in the infant, burying part of the ego in the maternal necropolis". The roles of nourisher and nourished are reversed, as it becomes the child's job to feed this mother, which "amounts, then, to maintaining the earliest love for the primordial object under the seal of secrecy, enshrouded by the primary repression of an ill-accomplished separation of the two partners of primitive fusion" (p. 195).

At this juncture, Green explicitly pays tribute—in a note—to the contributions of Abraham and Torok and acknowledges the convergence between his ideas and theirs, while also distinguishing their respective approaches to these matters:

> One might summarise these differences by stating that narcissism constitutes the axis of my theoretical reflection, whereas N. Abraham and M. Torok are essentially concerned with the relation between incorporation and introjection, with the crypt-like effect to which they give rise. [note 10, p. 241]

This heralds Green's wish to address the general and widely recognizable psychoanalytic relevance of his ideas, alongside their more specific application. Aware that he may have rather "schematised the structure of this dead mother complex", he admits the possibility "that it may be found in more rudimentary forms" (p. 195).

Wishing now to both loosen up and expand his structure, Green grants that both the timing and the severity of this complex may vary, leading sometimes to potentially less dire consequences: "more partial, more moderate depression, which was easier to overcome". He also acknowledges that his emphasis here on externally caused "maternal traumatism" may seem somewhat out of synch with his own psychoanalytic era, when—perhaps especially under the influence of Kleinian thinking—"one tends to insist a great deal more on the vicissitudes of intra-psychical organization" and to be "prudent" about attributing psychic effects to actual events. Though he reiterates that the depressive position is now a widely recognized "fact", he bemoans the lack of proper articulation of "any general accord . . . between the importance of the trauma and the observed depressive manifestations", despite the clinically well-documented and much-described "depressing effects of early separations between mother and infant" (pp. 195–196).

In concluding this metapsychological section, Green returns to the specificity of his dead mother theory, saying that it "cannot be reduced to the level of the common depressive position, nor likened to the serious traumatisms of real separations". That there is no actual absence or "effective break in the continuity of the mother–infant relationship" might even be regarded as part of the problem. The continued physical presence and proximity of the mother turns into "an important maternal contribution" that disturbs ordinary depressive-position developments, in the form of "the reality of maternal decathexis which is sufficiently noticeable to the infant to wound his narcissism". In other words, the mother—though "there"—loses interest, disappears psychically, and becomes otherwise engaged, at least temporarily.

Suddenly, in the last sentence of the section, Green soars up to rather heady and extraordinarily perspectival heights, away from these particularities, but for the purpose of linking them structurally with the origins of psychoanalysis—namely, "Freud's views on the aetiology of the neuroses". Perhaps this is Green's attempt to herald his own version of a Lacan-like "return to Freud" in the final section of the paper. It seems not quite to come off, however, as the section ends on a bathetic, almost banal note, with the implication that even the dead mother complex, for all its particularity, conforms to a quite fundamental and familiar psychoanalytic formula, "where the child's psychical make-up is formed by the combination of his personal inherited dispositions and the events of his earliest infancy" (p. 196).

"Freud and the Dead Mother"

In the last part of the paper, Green is quick to point out that though he sees his work in terms of "contemporary clinical experience which has arisen from Freud's writings", he has not adopted the usual approach of beginning with Freud, opting instead to end with him. He also makes it seem as if this was not a consciously planned move but, rather, a belated consequence of the fact "that repression in me has lifted, and that I have remembered retrospectively something in Freud that can be related to my subject". This "something" turns out to be as much personal as it is metapsychological. Green emphasizes that its textual link is not to "Mourning and Melancholia" but to *The Interpretation of Dreams*, the final dream adduced and discussed by Freud in the final chapter of that work: "It is the dream of the 'beloved mother', and the only childhood dream he recounted" (p. 196).

Green reminds us of the manifest content of Freud's dream: his mother is carried into a room by two or three people with bird beaks and laid on a bed; she seems peacefully asleep. Freud had woken up from this dream screaming and tearful, thus waking his parents, too. What Green seizes on here is the fact that this is a nightmare, an incomplete anxiety-dream, something to which he thinks insufficient attention has been paid by other commentators. He proposes that the traumatic question—the answer to which the dreamer cannot bear to await by staying asleep—is: which of these beaked figures "will join the mother in her sleep?" Instead, Green quips, the boy Freud awoke and "interrupted, killing two birds with one stone, the dream and the parents' sleep".

Freud's own analysis of the dream centres around twin themes—"that of the dead mother and that of sexual intercourse"—and later commentators and biographers have followed suit. Despite having said earlier that he "cannot go into all the details of this dream or the multiple commentaries to which it gives rise", Green does mention a few of the latter, singling out what he calls Didier Anzieu's (1974) "remarkable analysis". Thus, he seems already to have gathered ample corroboration of his own "hypothesis concerning the relation between the dead mother, the primal scene and the Oedipus complex" (pp. 196–197). And yet he is clearly not content to leave the implications of this general connection resonating; in fact, he goes on to draw quite extensively on the history of commentary on this dream to support an explicit, elaborate biographical sleuthing exercise of his own into Freud's life and times.

Strangely, perhaps, this is the one place in Green's text where I do not experience the usual, perhaps obsessional, urge to follow him closely and explicate all his moves. It suffices to summarize these as concisely as possible: the dream imagery is linked to a certain illustration from the famous Phillipson Bible that Freud had received from his father, leading to several strands of association. The illustration consists of "two pharaonic personages" and several birds on the columns of a bier, a depiction of King David attending the funeral of Abner, his right-hand man, after the latter's murder. As Green says, the Biblical saga of which this moment is an episode "abounds with themes of incest, parricide and, I should like to stress, fratricide". He agrees with Anzieu that the two figures represent Freud's much older father, Jacob, and his half-brother, Phillip, who was "suspiciously" close in age to Freud's mother, Amalie.

What we realize is that Green is in search of a moment in Amalie's life when a dead mother situation might have pertained and affected her son. There are two possibilities, the first being the death of her own father when Sigmund was already 9½—something Freud himself had referenced in relation to the dream. Green is of the view that the far likelier (because earlier) object of her bereavement was Julius, the younger brother, who was born when Freud was less than 18 months old and died before he turned two.

I will not try to reproduce the heady, Freud-emulating, interpretive-associative frenzy that now ensues, focusing on paternal–oedipal paranoia and recurrent names and time frames. It includes references or allusions to Freud's Moses and his obsession with Rome, his grandson of *"fort–da"* fame (18 months old when Freud observed him, but dead at 2 years), the death of his favourite daughter, Sophie, and the primal scene in the Wolf Man case. Citing Anzieu yet again, Green forges a link between Freud and Bion "who, besides love and hatred, gave a specific place to knowledge as a primordial reference within the psychical apparatus: the quest for meaning" (pp. 197–198). Perhaps this is important not least because Green's own search for meaning, linking, and knowledge (or "K") is being so assiduously enacted before our eyes here.

One may have some inkling of the general direction in which Green is headed, but his precise destination is not yet clear. The last "hypothesis pending" in this foraging exercise through Freud's life and works concerns what he calls "the oral relationship". He now cites "the dream of the 'Three Fates'" (1900a, pp. 204–205), in which Freud's mother is cooking dumplings; though "little Sigmund is waiting to eat them she intimates that he should wait until she is ready". Green seems tacitly to challenge the tendency to focus primarily on the sexual-incestuous aspects of the wishes depicted here. His focus on Freud's comments reveals associations not only to the mother's death, but also to hunger and the longing for the breast; thus, the entire gamut of loss is being invoked. Green sees the need to "question this triple image of a woman in Freud's thinking, which is examined again in the 'Theme of the Three Caskets': the mother, the wife (or beloved), and death." In Green's view, if there is a neglected or repressed theme among these relations and dynamics, it is "the censure of the dead mother: the mother of silence as heavy as lead" (p. 199).

In the next and penultimate paragraph—one that might well have sufficed as fitting last words for this powerful paper—Green returns to the threefold theoretical structure, which, he feels, he has fleshed-out sufficiently and satisfactorily at last. Here he speaks clearly and definitively on behalf of the mother's ultimate task: that of liberating her child (and herself) from the entrapping bonds of merger and incest. As a timely bequest, she graciously withdraws from her vitally necessary position of primacy and centrality, nourishing even as she gradually disappears and fades from view; in the process, she enables and promotes the flourishing of love and extra-familial relationships:

> Now our trilogy is complete. Once again we are led to think of the metaphoric loss of the breast, interrelating with the Oedipus complex,

or the primal scene fantasy, and that of the dead mother. The lesson of the dead mother is that she too must die one day so that another may be loved. But this death must be slow and gentle so that the memory of her love does not perish, but may nourish the love that she will generously offer to whoever takes her place. [p. 199]

Of course, this is precisely what does not and cannot happen easily or at all, should a dead mother situation—indeed, any major depressive or melancholic predicament—be too prevalent or remain untreated.

I trust that such ideas resonate not only with the loss-work of other analysts explored in this book, but also with some of the poetry perused too, not least Plath's "Morning Song" in this chapter. As I suggested, Green's account of the optimally "slow and gentle" fading of the mother into the background will also remind readers of Wallace Stevens's moving lines from "The Auroras of Autumn" in which he bids farewell to (the idea of) the maternal object. By contrast with Plath's poem, the situation there is seen from the children's point of view: though they are losing their mother, they in a sense still have her, even where there can be no doubt about the finality of her demise.

What this auroral mother has accomplished, in the interim, is the requisitely slow disappearing act that Green is talking about, while not neglecting to leave behind what is essential. While Klein and her followers might regard these lines as a poetic account of how a good internal version of the mother is established and retained, Green (and Loewald) would probably see them as exemplifying the mother stepping back from personal prominence to provide a frame or structure inside which further development can occur. Either way, the children remain behind and alive as separate entities or personae, but they have also gained a psychic legacy, an ancestor, someone to be going on with.

Green himself, however, has not quite finished; there is one final paragraph to go, where he finds himself quite struck by the way that he seems to have "come full circle". He has been acquainted for a long time with Freud's dreams and their various interpretations—they "were printed in my mind as significant memory traces"—but only now does their significance emerge. They "have been re-cathected by the discourse of certain analysands" and he is finally able to attend to them. Which way around is it, he asks: "Is it this discourse that permitted me to rediscover Freud's written word, or is it the cryptomnesia of this reading that made me permeable to my analysands' words?" Green's question is reminiscent of the typical concern of the literary scholar about whether an idea is genuinely one's own or unconsciously plagiarized from somewhere or someone else—though, how could it not be? For Green, a "rectilinear conception of time" would reinforce the second option in his question, whereas "Freud's concept of *Nachträglichkeit*" (deferred action or *après coup*) would support the first.

However, for Green, answering this question—to resort again to a phrase that seems to have cropped up often enough in this book—hardly matters, is beside the point. He wants, in any case, to emphasize and marvel at the very existence, beauty, and mystery of the *après coup*, perhaps what we might call its facticity in the human mind:

> Be that as it may, in the concept of *Nachträglichkeit*, nothing is more mysterious than this preliminary statute of a registered meaning which remains in abeyance in the psyche while awaiting its revelation. For it is a question of "meaning", otherwise it would not have been able to be recorded in the psyche. But this meaning-in-waiting is only truly significant when it is reawakened by a re-cathexis which takes place in an absolutely different context. [pp. 199–200]

Following Green's exposition, one could say that the logic of deferred action is, in fact, the logic of metaphor: when meaning crops up in a newer, fresher moment or location, its aptness is renewed, revived, takes one by surprise.

There are further questions among Green's very last sentences: "What meaning is this? A lost meaning, re-found?" Here he seems to renege slightly on his claims on behalf of the *après coup*, as if not wishing to overstate them. His question seems to be: how much meaning can we consider as having always already been there, present in the first place, as it were? Is this to "give too much credit to this presignificative structure" and to ignore that "its rediscovery is much more in the order of a discovery"?

Green's final, evocative demi-sentence resonates fatefully, uncannily, with the aims of this book, as if it has itself been put there specifically—as a "meaning-in-waiting"—to provide me with a moment of magical coalescence: "Perhaps potential meaning which only lacks the analytic—or poetic?—experience to acquire real meaning" (p. 200).

As my own close-reading endeavours have tried to suggest, the finding and drawing out of the significance that inheres or lies dormant, inchoately stored-up within texts, is a craft that can be practiced on "poetic" and "analytic" language alike. The phrase "potential meaning" resonates with potential space, re-invoking Green's devotion to Winnicottian thinking; and the earlier "meaning-in-waiting" might well invite association with a "*lady*-in-waiting". Let us not forget that the analytic voices of Klein, Winnicott, Abraham & Torok, and Green himself have already spoken in their respective ways of the mother—whether she still lives or has already died—as the guardian, guarantor, and repository of all meaning, of everything worthwhile. The poetic voice of Stevens seems to concur, so perhaps I can do no better than to bring this chapter to a close by reiterating his famous lines from "Sunday Morning" about finality and satisfaction, forging links between fore and aft:

> Death is the mother of beauty; hence from her,
> Alone, shall come fulfilment to our dreams
> And our desires.
>
> [Stevens, 1915, pp. 68–69]

Conclusion: meaning, mourning, and mortality in Freud and Auden

Connecting existentially as well as intellectually with loss as a literary subject occurred gradually over the course of my previous career as an academic in literary studies, critical theory, and related fields. The acting out of personal psychological unsettledness and vocational indecisiveness had by then already resulted in an itinerant succession of prolonged but ultimately impermanent sojourns in cities on three different continents.

After completing a first degree (in philosophy and psychology) in my African birthplace of Cape Town, I embarked on an extended period of postgraduate study (in English literature) in the Asian city of Jerusalem, later fetching up in Boston, North America, where I taught at several universities and colleges in the vicinity. It was there that I had my first, much-needed analysis, and where the texts and theories of psychoanalysis began to feature more prominently among my interests; I also had a stint as an affiliate scholar on a psychoanalytic training programme. In due course, I made the decision to change careers and was therefore induced to move again—to a fourth continent and city, the European metropolis of London—to begin a second analysis and my training as an analyst.

London is where I still reside and work and have now lived for longer than anywhere else. Ironically, it was only after making my new start here that I belatedly discovered Freud's wonderful little essay, "On Transience" (1916a). Its title resonating so personally with my own peripatetic restlessness, I felt as ashamed of my earlier ignorance of it as I was delighted to have finally made its acquaintance. It has since assumed all manner of retrospective prominence and significance. I came to regard it—with some help from the temporal distortions of hindsight—as my transatlantic theme tune, companion text of my most recent relocation, marking my transition from one field or world of endeavour to another. I therefore revisit it often, in my thoughts, teaching, and writing. Of course, as the essay title suggests and as this book attests, no transition is ever complete or once and for all: such worlds and fields do not themselves stay put but are carried with us internally and therefore tend to infuse, interpenetrate, and pervade one another.

"On Transience" was written by Freud during the same period as "Mourning and Melancholia" and very much shares its concerns. No more than a three-page vignette, it is also one of the most lyrical pieces of writing that he ever produced: it provides, as Strachey puts it in his Introduction, "excellent evidence of his literary powers" (1957d, p. 304). Freud wrote it as a response to the outbreak of the First World War and under its cloud, for a collection of essays entitled *Goethe's Land*, which featured contributions by some of the foremost German writers of the time. Because of its brevity and subject matter, one is tempted to regard it as a kind of prose poem in its own right; it is therefore eminently suited to the close-reading method that I have been employing throughout this book. The themes of "On Transience" resonate with those of literary elegy and will thus provide me with a further opportunity to introduce more poetry into these deliberations.

As far as physical or geographical transience and its attendant losses are concerned, Freud had an early experience of these as a young child, when his family uprooted itself from small-town Moravia and relocated to the city of Vienna. Spared any further trials of migration and transition until almost the end of his life, the Nazi *Anschluss* forced Freud to abandon his home and flee to London, where he lived out in exile the brief months still left to him; he died just three weeks after another world war had been declared.

It seems fitting that the final poem I consider closely—the one I wish to link and juxtapose with "On Transience"—is an elegy to Freud by an important English poet. W. H. Auden wrote "In Memory of Sigmund Freud" (1939a) late in the year of the latter's death; crucially, 1939 had already featured a migratory sea change for Auden himself. The combination of a romantic choice, the threat of war in Europe, and a crisis of belief and creativity propelled him away from England, conveying him to America, where he would remain for several decades.

Auden in fact produced several remarkable poems during that fateful year, including two more elegies for exiles: for W. B. Yeats, the great Irish modernist poet who died in France at the beginning of that year; and for the radical German playwright Ernst Toller, who, like Auden, sought sanctuary in New York but committed suicide there on hearing that his family members had been sent to concentration camps by the Nazis. (This was also to be the fate of Freud's sisters, who remained behind in Austria.) Auden's poetic, political, and personal development was significantly influenced by these three figures, and one assumes that the coincidence of their deaths in that same year must have been of special and ominous significance to him.

Indeed, one of Auden's best-known poems bears the title "September 1, 1939" (1939c) and begins with the poet sitting in a bar in Manhattan on the very day that war is declared, feeling bewildered and terrified as awful events begin to unfold. These poems of 1939 are all suffused with the language of loss; together, they constitute a kind of farewell, not merely to an old world that Auden clearly felt betrayed by and was abandoning in turn, but also to his earlier politics and poetics. His own struggles with transience, transition, and the dynamics of mourning are clearly represented there. However, after his geographical emigration, Auden felt the rather apocalyptic and perhaps regressive need for a complete ideological make-over as a person and a poet: he ended up reverting to his Anglican faith and turning, rather savagely, on his former self and poetic style.

Though 1939 was the year that Freud's own existential story came to an end, my initial focus in this final chapter is on the little essay that he wrote in the shadow of that earlier world war, a quarter of a century before. I then return to what Auden had to say in his elegiac tribute to Freud himself. This temporal movement back and forth between those two catastrophic wars is perhaps timely, as significant anniversaries of both have recently been commemorated and as fears surface of another prolonged era dominated by hyper-nationalistic, fascistic leadership, and the breakdown and fragmentation of hard-won international alliances established in the aftermath of those wars. Uncannily, we are not only feeling assailed by a figurative cultural malaise reminiscent of that explored in Auden's poetry and by Freud in *Civilization and Its Discontents* (1930a), but being plagued by a literal and deadly viral disease on a scale that has not been seen for almost precisely a hundred years, since the influenza epidemic that ran amok in the wake of the First World War, killing many more people (including Freud's daughter) than the war itself. More ominously yet, recent months have seen the actual return of war to the continent of Europe.

Sigmund Freud, "On Transience"

There are some striking features that exemplify the very literariness of "On Transience". Though it belongs firmly within the genre of the literary essay, it might be seen to allude to and have the characteristics of other genres, too. To start with, it is presented in a quite dramatic, play-like manner: Freud begins with a scene-setting sentence for a particular occasion, listing the *dramatis personae* and sketching the theatrical unities of place and time: "Not long ago I went on a summer walk through a smiling countryside in the company of a taciturn friend and of a young but already famous poet" (1916a, p. 305).

So, three characters are identified, including Freud himself, and this suggests the triangularity on which psychoanalysis places such emphasis; it also stimulates literary–historical associations to Sophocles—author of the play that gave Freud the name and theme of the Oedipus complex—who is also credited with having introduced the third character into the structure of ancient Greek drama. We may further note that, in addition to giving us access to his own thoughts, Freud—or, more correctly, "Freud", who is both first-person narrator and participating fictional character—sets up and engages in an impassioned debate with the interlocutors at the scene. What we might call Freud's Socratic dialogue is primarily with the "famous poet" rather than the "taciturn friend", who appears to serve as a mostly silent, albeit chorus-like, witness.

In a book entitled *Freud's Requiem: Mourning, Memory and the Invisible History of a Summer Walk,* Matthew von Unwerth (2005) has used "On Transience" as the primary text of a delightfully meandering, lyrical meditation on themes not dissimilar to my own here. The author strongly supports the contention that Freud's companions on the summer walk in question were in fact Rainer Maria Rilke and the latter's then lover, Lou Andreas-Salomé.

Rilke, arguably the most important German-language poet of the twentieth century, is famed for his powerful, affecting, mystical, elegiac—indeed, melancholic—poetry. Like Auden, he struggled personally and psychically with matters of faith and morality and was thus much admired, and even emulated, by him. Andreas-Salomé was a brilliant and fascinating woman, a genuinely free spirit who became intensely involved, both intellectually and emotionally, with some of the major creative and cultural figures of her time, including Friedrich Nietzsche. She was drawn to and shared a special closeness with Freud and his science as it was coming of age (also becoming a great friend of his daughter, Anna); they exchanged letters and confidences and he regarded her very highly. She became one of the first female psychoanalysts, breaking into a domain that was, at the time, overwhelmingly, almost exclusively, male. Though there have been biographical challenges and some controversy surrounding these identities, suffice it to say that if von Unwerth were right, it would serve my purposes admirably that Freud's interlocutors in the essay were figures of such substantial literary and cultural eminence.

From the very outset of this brief text, Freud draws attention to the despair and depression of the young poet whom he has just introduced. We are told that while he "admired the beauty of the scene" they were traversing, he "felt no joy in it". He seems quite unable to savour or to be a fully present participant in the experience, being too acutely aware of its transitory or ephemeral nature, "that it would vanish when winter came", that all its beauty was "fated to extinction". This poet finds all transience—the temporary nature of everything—intolerable, insufferable, his responses and feelings applying no less to human creations than to natural ones: "All that he would otherwise have loved or admired seemed to him shorn of its worth by the transience which was its doom" (p. 305).

To Freud, this view is overly freighted with and distorted by the heavy weight of destruction and oblivion. Though he faithfully represents the poet's potently negative point of view, Freud will soon cast doubt on whether it amounts to an argument at all: it seems to him to depict a tormented state of mind or malaise rather than an intellectual position or stance.

The poet's sentiments—and perhaps that word better captures their status—sets all manner of poetic echoes resonating, at least in this reader's mind. I am reminded particularly of Samuel Taylor Coleridge's "Dejection: An Ode", written in 1802, especially its early lines, where the poet's depressed and melancholic mood is powerfully conveyed:

> A grief without a pang, void, dark, and drear,
> A stifled, drowsy, unimpassioned grief,
> Which finds no natural outlet, no relief,
> In word, or sigh, or tear.

Though Coleridge also describes evocatively the features of a lovely evening sky, his appreciation of the scene is severely compromised by his mental state:

> I see them all so excellently fair,
> I see, not feel, how beautiful they are
> [1802, p. 362]

Clearly, Coleridge and Rilke are seeing and feeling their respective landscapes in remarkably similarly manner.

In the second paragraph of his essay, Freud extrapolates and speaks in more general terms of the "proneness to decay of all that is beautiful", saying that this can give rise to at least two kinds of negative reaction: either to the "aching despondency" of the poet, or to a more rebellious refusal to even believe that "all this loveliness of Nature and Art, of the world of our sensations and of the world outside", is in fact destined to perish without trace. The person thus afflicted will plead the impossibility of the inevitable demise and decay of such lovely things and insist that it would be "too senseless and too presumptuous" to believe in or accede to this fate: somehow it must be possible for the beauty to persist, resist, and "escape all the powers of destruction" (p. 305).

Applying his brand of straight talking familiar from his case studies, Freud quickly debunks any such stance as a myth: "what is painful may none the less be true." He would treat these points of view—whether the poet's or anyone else's—not as a debatable argument, but as a fervent "demand for immortality", an attitude that reduces to little more than a wish. He himself appears, at this moment in the essay, to have no trouble accepting the transience and eventual destruction of all things. He cannot see why, how, or in what sense beautiful phenomena could be regarded as exempt from or an exception to this common and universal outcome.

Moreover, and perhaps more significantly, for Freud it is "incomprehensible" that the transience of beauty should detract from its worth. "On the contrary, an increase!" he exclaims, as he begins the fourth paragraph; the limited scope and duration of beauty only enhances its worth, rendering it that much more precious. "Transience value is scarcity value in time" (p. 305), runs his pithy maxim—a view we have already come across elsewhere.

Freud's line surely echoes Wallace Stevens's credo, "Death is the mother of beauty", discussed in earlier chapters. However, in the poem "Sunday Morning", where this line appears twice, Stevens also gives voice to the fact that it is not easy to resist the temptations of everlastingness, to surrender the promise of heaven. It is thus perhaps not all that surprising that Freud himself should, despite himself, begin to sneak in or succumb to a version of the immortality argument—indeed, in this very paragraph. As we shall see, he does so again right at the end of the essay, where his resolve in the face of destruction flags and his own resistance to transience makes itself felt even more forcefully.

This first occasion takes the form of a suggestion that seasonal cyclicality, the fact that we get to see the year turning again and again, is tantamount to a kind of continual resurrection and therefore a kind of immortality sufficient to the purpose: "in relation to the length of our lives it can in fact be regarded as eternal". In the very next sentence, however, he tries to recover the more hard-line, clear-sighted perspective but, again, not without trying to offer us another bit of comfort or compensation: "The beauty of the human form and face vanish forever in the course of our own lives, but their evanescence only lends them a fresh charm" (pp. 305–306).

In psychoanalytic terms, this might be seen as an incipient expression of the *après coup*, Freud's own challenge to temporal linearity as evidenced in his clinical work with the Wolf Man (Freud, 1918b) who had, in fact, only just ended his treatment with Freud at the time of writing. For me, the echoes here are with W. B. Yeats, subject of one of Auden's elegies and a poet who also attempted to wrest for himself a kind of ambivalent or ambiguous solace from the passage of time.

Yeats was preoccupied—indeed, obsessed—with the unattainable Maude Gonne, a formidable woman with whom he was in love for many years but whom he never won: her thwarting presence thoroughly suffuses his poetry. In two poems written in the same year, 1902, Yeats expresses feelings of frustration, despondency, and regret about this situation. Both poems have some interesting structural similarities with "On Transience", each featuring a three-way debate between a first-person speaker and two interlocutors.

We might first compare Freud's sentiments about the ephemerality of physical beauty with Yeats's sonnet, "The Folly of Being Comforted" (1902b). The more external of the two voices in the poem, a kindly friend, tries to console the lovelorn poet by cautioning patience ("Time can but make it easier to be wise") and reminding him that his "well-beloved" is ageing and will soon be losing her looks. But the second, more internal, persecutory voice, one that might represent a melancholic inability or unwillingness to mourn, retorts defiantly:

> Heart cries, "No,
> I have not a crumb of comfort, not a grain.
> Time can but make her beauty over again:
> Because of that great nobleness of hers
> The fire that stirs about her when she stirs,
> Burns but more clearly. O she had not these ways
> When all the wild summer was in her gaze."
> [1902b, p. 21]

One might take these lines as an explication of what Freud calls "evanescence": a kind of "nobleness" of being that—in the face of death, as it were—not only increases and deepens worth but even exceeds and trumps the beauty of youth. For Freud, these evanescent qualities seem only to lend "fresh charm" and offer a kind of compensation, whereas for Yeats (and Rilke?) this special, virtually timeless "beauty of the human form and face" comes to represent life itself and thus "burns", becoming a further source of acute torment for both the spurned lover and the one destined to die and lose everything.

In the other Yeats poem, called "Adam's Curse" (1902a), we glean, from the title as well as the conversation, that not only poets, but also other devotees of beauty and pleasure—not least women who work hard to make and keep themselves beautiful and alluring—shoulder the serious and onerous burden of presenting a bulwark against our mortal state and fate. Also set "at one summer's end", this dialogue bears many similarities to Freud's essay: it, too, asks whether we can psychically survive the ordinary but inevitable threats posed by physical deterioration and decay and, in this instance, the loss of love.

Can life remain meaningful and not descend into depression under these conditions? After all, the curse of Adam, as well as Eve, is twofold: in our postlapsarian state, we are not only obliged to toil for our living, we are also destined to age and die and to experience loss, time and again. Yeats's sense of futility, like that of Rilke in Freud's essay, is profound: as the poem concludes, a wasted, washed-out integument of a moon—the now tired and well-worn symbol of high romance and passion—rises in an empty evening sky.

Though Yeats has spent most of the poem in dialogue with her (also beautiful) sister, he addresses his final lines to Maude Gonne, who, like Andreas-Salomé in the essay, has kept her counsel, a silent but potent presence in the poem:

> I had a thought for no one's but your ears:
> That you were beautiful, and that I strove
> To love you in the old high way of love;
> That had all seemed happy, and yet we'd grown
> As weary-hearted as that hollow moon.
> [1902a, p. 23]

Is it too much of a stretch to speculate that Freud, though not as hopelessly smitten as was Yeats by his love-object, might have been quite taken with the "taciturn friend" accompanying him on his summer walk (as we assume Rilke, her lover, certainly was)? Or, to put it differently, is it at least part of the purpose of Andreas-Salomé's role, as the third player in that scene, to represent in person—indeed, to embody—for the two male interlocutors a here-and-now object of admiration, attraction, desire, or love? Might she have possessed more than enough of the "beauty of the human form or face" as well as "evanescence" to occasion and add spice to their (competitive) debate about transience?

In any case, whether as a source of comfort or of torment, Yeats's poems reinforce Freud's awareness that human time moves not only inexorably forward but is also retrospective and retroactive. It cannot always be treated as a linear vector, and therefore the pain it hosts cannot always be dealt with by its mere passage or by simply "waiting it out". Indeed, when it comes to being in love—as Yeats's unrequited feelings for Maude Gonne repeatedly attested—one can find oneself ensnared not merely by an unmoved, immovable, and immutable image or object, but also by a living, breathing, aging woman, simultaneously both beautiful and terrible. This is surely a fate not dissimilar to—perhaps it is even an instance of—being in the relentless grip of a melancholic object. Was it not Freud (1914c), after all, who warned us of the narcissistic dangers of being too much in love, too in thrall to an object?

Returning to the essay at hand, one realizes that Freud may himself be in quite an ambivalent state, struggling to sustain the tough, more mature argument for the rational truths of transience in the face of his own wishes and desires. These are powerful states of mind the motive force of which, after all, no one has better attested to than Freud himself. He again tries to take hold of the strong position on transience by reiterating his primary point in relation to human creativity: "Nor can I understand any better why the beauty and perfection of a work of art or an intellectual achievement should lose its worth because of its temporal limitation." What then follows is a long sentence beginning with the acknowledgement that "A time may indeed come when the pictures and statues which we admire today will crumble to dust, or a race of men will follow us who no longer understand the works of our poets and thinkers" (p. 306).

Again, English poetry offers us famous lines that pre-empt and reinforce Freud's perspective. As in chapter seven, on Green, I am again reminded of Shelley's sonnet "Ozymandias", written in 1817: his "immortal" image of an over-confident and long-since felled despot, whose arrogant words ring ironically through the ages, with sobering lessons to impart. Shelley's description is attributed to "a traveller from an antique land": the scene is a desert-scape featuring nothing but the legs of a toppled statue and the half-buried, "shattered visage" of a ruler who had once presided over a vast domain.

The sculptor has had the talent to capture, in at least relatively durable stone, his long-dead subject's attitudes, his "expressions", in two senses of this word, because they are depicted verbally as well as sculpturally. On the statue's face, the

> frown,
> And wrinkled lip, and sneer of cold command

are still discernible. The sonnet's concluding sestet, moreover, reads as follows:

> And on the pedestal these words appear:
> "My name is Ozymandias, king of kings:
> Look on my works, ye Mighty, and despair!"
> Nothing beside remains. Round the decay
> Of that colossal wreck, boundless and bare,
> The lone and level sands stretch far away.
> [1817, p. 100]

Shelley, like Freud, is under no illusions about the fact that artistic expressions also disintegrate and disappear in the end, and this piece of sculpture is itself in bits and close to oblivion. Though it is the latter that triumphs in the end, we nevertheless register, on the sculptor's behalf, an albeit temporary victory for art and irony over dictatorship and tyranny, one in which the poet himself may also claim a share.

It was Shelley who famously declared—in concluding his 1821 essay, *A Defence of Poetry*—that "poets are the unacknowledged legislators of the world" (p. 90). This enables me to reiterate that the very point of sculpture, poetry, essay writing, or any other artistic or intellectual endeavour is what we might call metabolic: losses are not only *captured* in stone or clay or *rendered* in words (including words about words): they are also *processed or digested* in and by these forms. Even though artistic and linguistic quests are themselves ultimately futile and subject to the same predations of time, they represent and embody ways of actively laying claim to or taking internal possession of objects that are outwardly mortal, on the way to inevitable extinction, going and soon to be gone.

Picking up Freud's essay again—mid-sentence, as it were—we find him extending his vision to an apocalyptic, end-of-days situation, though one scarcely requiring much imagination to envisage from the vantage point of our own ecologically precarious historical moment: "a geological epoch may even arrive when all animate life upon the earth ceases". He then makes a striking claim, one that provokes questioning: "but since the value of all this beauty and perfection is determined only by its significance for our own emotional lives, it has no need to survive us and is therefore independent of absolute duration" (p. 306).

Can we really accept this statement, even in the face of the threat of eventual (or imminent) global demise? Perhaps this would depend on who or what is included by the words "our" and "us". And does it not significantly underestimate at least the longing for some form of immortality, contradicting other comments that Freud posits earlier in this same paragraph? Given what we know about his personal and professional ambitions, can we really believe that he was ever so ready to dispense with textual immortality, the desire and hope that his works might be read forever—or at least by all the generations still to come? Perhaps most pertinently, is it not vital for him that psychoanalysis, fruit of his own loins, should achieve a modicum of permanence, precisely for the sake of these future generations? In other words, need such desires be regarded as merely selfish and self-serving, significant only "for our own emotional lives"?

This moment is the mid-point of the essay; Freud is now four paragraphs into his eight-paragraph text. It also marks his return to the more uncompromising roles of clinician and scientist of the mind—and perhaps to a "one-person" psychology, at that. He appears abruptly to hone and reduce his focus, suddenly seeming interested only in what the creative products of a civilization might offer to any given individual, in the narrow remit of his or her own selfish needs. How is this position compatible with our image of an expansive, humanistic Freud who is situated among and keeps company with writers and poets? It is nevertheless apt that he then goes on to outline—in explicit, if not quite diagnostic, terms—what he sees as the key psychological issue here.

As he tells us, neither of his interlocutors was impressed by *his* arguments; both resisted his recommendation that they accept, and even embrace, transience. But this "failure" to prevail in the debate leads him "to infer that some powerful emotional factor was at work which was disturbing their judgement", and he claims to have found out—albeit "later", with hindsight—what it was. Freud surmises that the unassailable facts of transience had led to a "painful" spoiling of the beauty and hedonistic enjoyment of the natural landscape for "these two sensitive minds"; they were experiencing "a foretaste of mourning over its decease", to which—because one "instinctively recoils from anything that is painful"—they reacted with "a revolt in their minds against mourning" (p. 306).

We will subsequently see, in the final two paragraphs, what "later" means, when Freud reveals where he is at the time of writing and what has occurred in the world at large since that summer walk had taken place. However, we are now reminded that this discovery about his companions' mental "revolt" must be closely linked with his thought processes in "Mourning and Melancholia", where the dynamics of loss are more thoroughly gone into and investigated than is possible in the current context.

Accordingly, in the next (sixth) paragraph, he rehearses only some of the arguments from that paper, written at virtually the same time but only published three years later. Here, as there, he insists that mourning is not itself a pathological phenomenon, making the case that grieving over our losses is normal and ordinary, something "so natural to the layman that he regards it as self-evident". The psychologists, by contrast, find that "mourning is a great riddle", inexplicable in itself but somehow fundamental for the understanding of "other obscurities"—among which one imagines that melancholia and depression are implicit, though they go unmentioned here.

What Freud now adumbrates is a simplified account of what one might call the egocentric and economic machinations of the libido, derived from his recently conceived theory of narcissism (Freud, 1914c). We each begin, he says, with "a certain amount of capacity for love . . . directed towards our own ego"—what we might call a store of loving capital that we initially keep all to ourselves. We then gradually become capable of turning some of this precious libido outwards. This seems to mean, however, that "libido is diverted from the ego on to objects, which are thus in a sense taken into our ego" (p. 306).

One is aware that Freud is leaving out many steps and cutting to the chase here, given the need for keeping his deliberations succinct for the purposes of this brief essay. His focus is on the fact that to love (and lose) other people means somehow to absorb, assimilate—I would add to digest and metabolize—them and to make them part of ourselves, by way of a primary, possessive form of internalizing identification. It is interesting that Freud seems quickly and accurately to adopt the Ferenczian meaning of introjection here, even when not actually using this technical term.

Freud appears to appreciate its implicit *modus operandi* in relation to reality, how the ego constitutes and strengthens itself by reaching out and connecting to external objects, by taking them in. We would have to wait until *Group Psychology* and the genesis of both ego and superego in *The Ego and the Id* before we hear him speaking in similar vein again. And even there he does not really manage, according to Abraham and Torok, to recapture his colleague's, and their Hungarian predecessor's, proper meaning.

However, Freud is not apparently concerned with—or has no room here to explore—the distinctions between mourning and melancholia that preoccupy him in the text that bears that name. What he does say is that "If the objects are destroyed or if they are lost to us", the other-directed loving energy is eventually redeemed and released—"liberated", as Freud says here, or "emancipated", as Loewald might have said. After a period of mourning the reclaimed libido becomes available again—at least in theory—either for keeping within the ego or redistribution to other objects.

Echoing a similar moment in "Mourning and Melancholia"—and as Klein particularly remarked and drew to our attention—Freud is nevertheless profoundly puzzled by the fact that we do not easily detach ourselves from a lost object: "But why it is that this detachment of libido from its objects should be such a painful process is a mystery to us and we have not hitherto been able to frame any hypothesis to account for it." This seems to suggest that we humans are not quite as self-serving and self-protective as Freud had previously considered us to be—or even, perhaps, as he thinks we ought to be! Indeed, it seems that once attached, we cling resolutely, desperately, and foolishly to what is gone—"even when a substitute lies ready to hand". Somewhat disappointed with the state of his knowledge, Freud ends the paragraph on a note of resigned bathos, sounding frankly rather melancholic when he says, "Such then is mourning" (pp. 306–307).

It is worth pointing out that certain formal literary features can be seen to characterize not just the beginning but also the ending of Freud's essay. We now arrive at a typographical gap in the text, its emptiness signifying a temporal hiatus. The essay will conclude with the convention of presenting a kind of aftermath, transporting the reader to a more recent moment. This is a familiar and even traditional manner of bringing novels to a close, although in this instance the purpose is not to narrate the fate of the individual characters.

With the gap again representing something like a large intake of breath, Freud offers the final two paragraphs as a portrait of a far more troubled and turbulent present, contrasting starkly with the earlier idyllic summer setting. This way of ending will also serve to round off the text's themes, reinforcing the elegiac shift of mood, as well as season, that characterizes the whole. The essay, one might say, not only discusses thematically—or "tells"—the topics of mourning and/or melancholia, but also formally demonstrates—or "shows"—them, too.

Freud brings his focus to bear on how the external world has been devastated, altered on a massive scale, by the unprecedented destructiveness of a world war. The private event that Freud had been describing and analysing, his "conversation with the poet", had happened a year earlier, "in the summer before the war": it now seems to have receded into the mists

CONCLUSION 381

of the past. In the interim, the early impact of the conflict had already been enormous and profound, bringing catastrophe and death, opening terrible chasms—indeed, hellish trenches—into which so many people's lives had already been plunged, rendering that typographical gap even more apt. In this penultimate paragraph, Freud leaves theoretical puzzlement and perplexity behind and returns to a more lyrical style, gazing with clear-seeing eyes at the utter wanton destruction wrought by the war he is living through. It is worth recalling that, amidst the general impact and misery, Freud would have to bear the personal anguish of having two of his own sons sent to the front.

Freud describes not only the physical carnage, the massive damage to the natural environment, but also the predatory effects perpetrated on all human endeavours, be they artistic, cultural, philosophical, political, scientific, spiritual, or educational: "robbed", "destroyed", "shattered", "tarnished", and "robbed" again, are his verbs here. Even when hampered by having to keep things very brief, Freud manages paradoxically to give voice to how the war dashed hopes of "a final triumph" over the narcissistic differences of nationalism while simultaneously lamenting that it brought low a centuries-old empire and "made our country small again".

Freud takes no smug solace from the clear corroboration here of psychoanalytic insights about the overwhelming power of primitive drives. The pulling down of "the lofty impartiality of our science" and the faltering of "centuries of continuous education by the noblest minds", he says, are failures that not only lay bare "our instincts in all their nakedness", but "let loose the evil spirits within us which we thought had been tamed forever", sending rationality itself regressively back into the embrace of superstition. No doubt aware of how this apocalypse might be used to confirm retroactively the despair and despondency—as well as the prescience—of his poet–interlocutor during their now poignant summer's walk, Freud uses the paragraph's last sentence to reinforce his primary position. He does so adamantly but without a hint of triumph: such events had merely confirmed the truths of transience "and showed how ephemeral were many things that we had regarded as changeless" (p. 307).

Freud begins his final paragraph by claiming to be unsurprised that under these circumstances "our libido, thus bereft of so many of its objects"—that is, when so many tangible external phenomena have been lost—should cling more strongly to more abstract possessions, like patriotic, parochial, and familial connections. And yet he again insists that even the concrete loss of things that "have proved so perishable and so unresistant" need not occasion the abandonment of their worth.

Although melancholia or depression are not mentioned by name, Freud might well have described his two interlocutors as reacting in a melancholic way or exhibiting a fundamental failure to mourn. Instead, he now resorts to an interesting alternative phrase to denote reactions like theirs, saying that people in such states of mind "seem ready to make a permanent renunciation". But what is being renounced, one may ask: life itself, perhaps?

It is precisely because successful mourners do the work of acknowledging the finality of loss—by both giving up the external object and metabolizing the internal one—that they do not have to exist either in thrall to the object or in "permanent renunciation" of their prospects. As Freud has already said, the libidinal investment of the mourner can eventually be reclaimed or recouped. Ironically, it is the melancholic, with his or her refusal to mourn, who can end up with a life not just voided by permanent renunciation, but burdened by an unwelcome permanent acquisition, in the form—as Abraham and Torok would have it—of an indigestible object encrypted within.

What Freud now reiterates is that people who renounce and reject in this way what is transient "are simply in a state of mourning for what is lost". One ought to take immediate issue with that "simply", for it is clear from all our theoretical forays into the machinations of mourning that there is nothing simple about it! He does now appear to want to render it simple—for his lay audience, perhaps—by claiming that, with the mere passage of time, our tenacious grip on what is lost can finally be relinquished, if only via an angry repudiation of its value.

Though painful, we are told, mourning "comes to a spontaneous end", liberating us to love again and to value new objects:

> When it has renounced everything that has been lost, then it has consumed itself, and our libido is once more free (in so far as we are still young and active) to replace the lost objects by fresh ones equally or still more precious. [p. 307]

This hopeful but simplistic insistence rather flies in the face of Freud's theoretical bafflement of a couple of paragraphs earlier, where he seems to acknowledge that such outcomes may be a long time coming and may, in some instances, never come.

We are also reminded of his struggles near the end of "Mourning and Melancholia", where he debates whether these two states are in fact quite similar or substantively different from one another—and where he tends to err on the side of their resemblance. As was also the case in that text, his use of the word "consumed" recalls the oral-alimentary aspect of these processes. At this time, however, Freud had perhaps not yet established firmly or clearly enough the important difference between the digestive consumption and metabolization *of* an object on the part of the ego in mourning and the impression that it is the other way around in melancholia, where the ego is consumed *by* an intractable object eating away at it from within.

As he brings this short essay to a close, we understand that Freud may not have had the luxury of sufficient textual leeway for such fine or subtle distinctions. Indeed, it might not have been only the requirement of brevity that prevented him from properly exploring the differences between mourning and melancholia in this context. For all we know, the editor of *Goethe's Land* may have insisted on a more positive tone from the contributors—perhaps for the sake of morale and the war effort? Either way, we might have wanted less certainty and more circumspection from Freud, rather than his confident declaration that mourning comes to a natural or inevitable end. The insistently optimistic tone of these penultimate sentences strikes a stridently false note:

> It is to be hoped that the same will be true of the losses caused by this war. When once the mourning is over, it will be found that our high opinion of the riches of our civilization has lost nothing from our discovery of their fragility. [p. 307]

Really? At the denouement of his essay, it is now Freud who appears to resort to what he had previously identified as wishful thinking on the part of his peripatetic companions: he seems to have changed places with his interlocutors, at least where naivety as opposed to worldliness is concerned, sounding almost foolish or childish in venturing such a bold prediction.

Later, in *Civilization and Its Discontents* (1930a), as another war approaches, he will express significant reservations about, and testify vehemently against, the so-called advantages of civilization. While the latter may be a necessary force that seeks to alleviate human suffering and malaise, it can also end up exacting too high a price and exacerbating these difficulties. Ironically enough, his final statement in "On Transience" reads rather less like the conclusion of a well-established argument than a rhetorical flourish or heartfelt plea: "We shall build up again what the war has destroyed, and perhaps on firmer ground and more lastingly than before".

The essay itself might be said to have a somewhat bipolar structure, shifting as it does from Freud's initial exploration of the depressive feelings of his interlocutor, to his own need for a perhaps more manically reparative, overly optimistic ending. Perhaps Freud is touchingly allowing his own naked and even desperate wishes to express themselves, though we may have wished and expected him to acknowledge these more self-consciously and to manifest greater emotional self-awareness than his last words bespeak.

We are left, finally, with the unsurprising impression that Freud had his own difficulties with transience; it is his own (in)ability to mourn that is at stake here. Significantly, within a few years he will be confronted with such awful personal realities—and undeniable occasions for mourning—as the deaths of a child and a grandchild and the onset of a disfiguring and debilitating illness. His theoretical or metapsychological response will be to resort to and develop perhaps that most controversial of psychoanalytic concepts, the death drive. The conclusion of "On Transience" is hardly his last word on the subject, and all of Freud's attempts to reflect on how we deal with our losses remain pertinent and germane. They, like all the other psychoanalytic and literary works considered in this book, are creative, fertile responses to the state of primary—or at least perennial—mourning that might be said to characterize the human condition.

W. H. Auden, "In Memory of Sigmund Freud"

Extrapolating from something that Freud suggested in *Beyond the Pleasure Principle* (1920g), one might wish to regard timely or even untimely deaths as the coping mechanisms of great minds that are sufficiently prescient or self-aware to recognize the bounds of their endurance and creativity. In the face of ultimate destruction—or the death drive in full force—they seem to know just when to quit and thus to "die in their own fashion".

Freud had in fact made pre-emptive arrangements to do just this with his personal physician, Max Schur, who had for many years been treating and keeping an eye on his cancer of the jaw. Freud secured Schur's promise that he would act when things became unbearable. His physical condition having deteriorated significantly in London, Freud finally made his request, and Schur duly and dutifully administered a fatal dose of morphine. Freud died in the early hours of 23 September 1939. As Mark Edmundson (2007, p. 225) reminds us, that year the date coincided with the fast of Yom Kippur, the Day of Atonement, holiest day in the Jewish calendar.

Auden's poems of that year mark the temporal coincidence of the outbreak of a second great war with the deaths of certain significant individuals, as if he is thereby attesting to their knowledge that worse, or the worst, was yet to come. Auden was, in other words, commemorating individuals who inspired, assisted, and consoled him in relation to trauma and loss but were also somehow aware of their limitations in the face of these forces. He, of course, survived the war and went on to have a long career as poet, playwright, essayist, reviewer, librettist, and venerable man of letters. However, at this juncture—perhaps as we witnessed at the end of "On Transience", when Freud's resolutely realistic relationship with impermanence seemed to give way to wishful naivety and a hankering for immortal verities and certainties—Auden opted to turn back to religion and to reject his secular, leftist-Freudian former self.

In keeping with this change of heart, Auden became notorious for trying to revise his earlier poems (including the elegy to Yeats) and even to suppress some of them altogether (including "September 1, 1939"). However, these poems have survived in their original form and stand insistently for Auden's earlier self, perhaps as its last hurrah. They mark various endings: of the world as he had known it, assailed by another terrible war; the deaths of Freud, Yeats, and Toller, whose work meant so much to him; and his disillusionment with the more youthful phase of his own life and work. It is the sound of this earlier voice that I wish to preserve and commemorate here. It is the voice that speaks up for freedom and justice, celebrates and echoes the wisdom of psychoanalysis, and makes a valuable contribution to the poetics of mourning and internalization.

If, before proceeding to the Freud elegy itself, we glance again at "September 1, 1939", we note the critical power and reach of Auden's politico-historical acumen and his undimmed psychological insight, still very much in evidence. He writes scathingly of the development of Germanic intolerance, beginning with Luther and culminating in the advent of Hitler, who, though not named, is alluded to as a perverse, insane deity. He articulates a fundamental psychic truth—namely, that any person who experiences abuse is more than likely to become its perpetrator—while adding that this is something that even children know well enough. He recalls that ancient thinkers like Thucydides (another exile) already understood these dynamics many centuries ago, but this seems not to stop us going round yet again, repeating the same errors of judgement, committing the same incompetent and irresponsible acts, suffering the same misery and distress.

Though he had himself sought safety in the United States, Auden is quite aware of America's isolationist reluctance to countenance and take seriously the events transpiring in Europe. He criticizes the Babel-like false optimism of its grandiose tall buildings and its avoidant ways of clinging stubbornly to private hearths and material comforts. As if anticipating

Edward Hopper's melancholic paintings of several decades in the future, he conveys how lone, solitary people cleave mindlessly to quotidian practices that are only nominally public or social,

> Lest we should see where we are,
> Lost in a haunted wood,
> Children afraid of the night
> Who have never been happy or good.
> [Auden, 1939c, p. 87]

He couches his insights into human folly and selfishness in boldly psychoanalytic terms, specifying our essentially selfish drives and impossible incestuous hankerings. He enters the minds of the strangers on the subway, who make their silent but futile vows to stay committed to the verities of love and work when faith in these pillars of sanity has already been shattered.

So, to whom does one turn, Auden asks, to gainsay such egoistic wilfulness, to help such people—and thus ourselves—to listen more carefully or speak more authentically? The poet has already implicitly turned to Freud and will do so more explicitly in the elegy to come. Assessing his own meagre powers in the penultimate stanza of this poem, he undertakes to keep at it, to continue exposing the mendacity of the ordinary citizen as well as the untruths of the state. And then he makes the (in)famous, desperate proclamation for which this poem is perhaps best known (and which he himself wished later to recant): "We must love one another or die" (p. 88).

Despite the dark carnage being unleashed in Europe, the poem concludes on a tentatively hopeful note: Auden tunes into the flickering, intermittent, ironic signals already passing back and forth among the fractured, scattered upholders of justice: they remain clandestinely, if only barely, in contact with one another. The poem closes with what one might call a poetico-psychoanalytic prayer:

> May I, composed like them
> Of Eros and of dust,
> Beleaguered by the same
> Negation and despair,
> Show an affirming flame.
> [p. 89]

Here again is a state of mind that bears comparison and contrast with that of Freud at the end of "On Transience". As we saw, that essay was written near the start of the First World War where, in spite of despair being close at hand and notwithstanding his brand new and complex theory of mourning, Freud concludes, with tenacious if unconvincing insistence: "We shall build up again all that war has destroyed, and perhaps on firmer ground and more lastingly than before" (p. 307).

Auden is distinctly less naive at the end of his poem and the start of this Second World War. A quarter of a century on, and despite his own need for hope, he would certainly not have been convinced by Freud's claim that "When once the mourning is over, it will be found that our high opinion of the riches of civilization has lost nothing from our discovery of their fragility." At the very least, this second war has come too soon for any potential benefits from mourning the first to be evident or to have taken effect. Civilization is still very fragile indeed—still in the grip of economic as well as psychological depression, suffering from a collective melancholia, one might say—and this poet is beset with far more doubt and anxiety about a future that Freud himself would not live to see.

Auden's fealty, no doubt, would have been to the later Freud of *Civilization and Its Discontents*, with its far more solemn and circumspect conclusion. By then Freud had thoroughly anatomized human destructiveness and aggression, anticipated a new battle between the forces of Eros and the death drive, and predicted only tentatively (if incorrectly) that the former might now reassert itself and make a comeback. His last words there were appropriately far more tentative: "But who can foresee with what success and with what result" (1930a, p. 145)?

By the time we get to Auden's elegy for Freud, it is late in 1939; another winter is looming, bleaker than the last, when he had suffered and written about the loss of Yeats. The war is underway and, by resorting immediately to funereal language in his opening lines, Auden shows his awareness that there will be a great deal more of death to be suffered henceforth, much more mourning and grieving still to do. He again seeks to single out—from among all the useful or usable humans who are now dying at such an alarming rate—a single persona who might make a lively, life-enhancing contribution, do a good-enough job of ameliorating, if not redeeming, these dreadful, anxious, helpless times.

And he chooses to speak of a certain physician—the recently deceased Freud. Auden's familiarity with both the man and his ideas is impressive: the poem is packed with Freudian tropes, addressing—albeit poetically—such themes as conscience, anxiety, the unconscious, family, jealousy, childhood, wishes, neurosis, repression, denial, memory, and others besides. He also tries to provide a more personal and ordinary portrait of Freud himself, resorting to several apparently deflating and unflattering judgements, though one recognizes this as Auden's manner of highlighting, by way of contrast, what he regards as more praiseworthy attributes.

With a nod to the elegiac convention of describing the dead subject as having been cut down in their prime—Auden indicates in the early stanzas that, even in his eighties, Freud had by no means completed his psychic work: he had died with plenty left undone. He would have continued to speak for psychic (and civil) disobedience, says Auden, but his desire to continue was not granted. Aggrieved that the doctor was no longer receiving, there were still many complexes and symptoms lining up, expecting to be cured. These are portrayed as patients in a waiting room or poor relations, gathered in grief and in hope of a hand-out, a belated inheritance. To the very last, Auden suggests, Freud was surrounded by these ailing, ghost-like objects of his endeavour who still clamoured for the light of his attention. But these still-suffering patients or unrequited children must finally turn away and take their dissatisfaction with them.

In turn, Freud himself is reluctantly and finally forced

> To go back to the earth in London,
> An important Jew who died in exile.
> [1939a, p. 92]

Auden, with his fondness for the allegorical personification of concepts or emotions, then portrays "Hate" as Freud's professional competitor, who may now see the field clear to employ dubious therapeutic methods of his own, proffering a quicker fix than psychoanalysis.

The clients of such a therapist might be encouraged to

> think they can be cured by killing
> And covering the gardens with ashes.
> [p. 92]

There is a chilling prescience here of the Holocaust, of the systematic and efficient fate that would befall millions of other Jews at the hands of the Nazis in the following years, including several of Freud's family members. However, though these ominous figures with their evil intent live on, they must now dwell in a cultural and psychosocial environment utterly altered by this one man.

Auden's deep respect for Freud's ideas also extends to the psychoanalytic method, which, however, he seems at times to want to simplify, reduce, and distil—either naively or deliberately. We are told that Freud made his profound impression, altered our awareness, by merely changing the perspective and bidding us yield to our memories: to be as curious and frank about them as a child might be. This notion of Freud's legacy having changed everything will return later in the poem and give us occasion to consider how Auden writes about processes associated with the internalizing and metabolizing of cultural and poetic objects.

Even as he praises Freud here, Auden seems determined to use a light touch and will not resort to the hyperbole of orthodox elegy: on the contrary—and one balks and reacts with protest when reading that Freud "wasn't clever at all" (p. 92)! However, besides knowing (as we do via the views of Winnicott, for example) that it is not cleverness that is paramount in the psychoanalytic vocation, it would also appear that Auden is manifesting what we might call a projection. He not only admires but wishes to identify with the analytic process and to connect it with his own endeavours and vocation: he describes evocatively, though again with typical bathos and quasi-allegorical intent, how Freud simply induced

> The unhappy Present to recite the Past
> Like a poetry lesson . . .
> [p. 92]

But how do things proceed once this recitation of the past by the present has begun? What follows in the poem gives the lie to any suggestion that Auden's view of psychoanalysis is banalizing or reductive.

In a series of difficult, syntactically obscure lines, one gleans a sophisticated description of the process, as well as a sense that something intensely personal being revealed—perhaps the product of Auden's own foray into analysis or psychotherapy. There is even an account of how the transference works, certainly as Freud conceived it: the patient's reciting—or free associating—may well proceed easily enough for a while, but only until such time as it runs into the obstacle of a difficult historical moment or significant past relationship finding representation in the here and now in the physician's disturbing presence in the present. Such faltering at this juncture inevitably brings superegoic judgements into play, but it will eventually also enable the perspective from which the patient might appreciate retrospectively what had been both valuable and trivial about those past moments and reap the psychic rewards of forgiveness and humility.

These gratifying therapeutic results seem both to echo Loewald's positive orientation towards the future and to offer relief at being able to drop Winnicottian false-self disguises. The patient is now

> Able to approach the Future as a friend
> Without a wardrobe of excuses, without

> A set mask of rectitude or an
> Embarrassing over-familiar gesture.
> [p. 92]

In the next stanza, Freud's analytic methodology is beautifully named as "his technique of unsettlement" (p. 93), incidentally capturing the connection between exile or immigration and the arduous, destabilizing journey undergone in an analysis.

Maintaining the often-ignored analogy or family resemblance between individual and socio-political defensiveness, Auden's potent critique of establishment power now comes to the fore. Traditional autocratic religions, political regimes, and profiteering enterprises, he suggests, are right to be suspicious of Freud's method of disconcerting the subject: in it they might see their own demise foretold. The prospect of Freud's success would trouble any corrupt establishment precisely because his interrogations challenge and expose the ploys of institutionalized privilege. Those who would replace genuine provision and respect for the individual citizen with the mass appeal of trinkets, sops, and circuses; those who would shore up their authority by stirring up populist resentment and aggression, not for the righting of social wrongs but for wholly self-serving ends—all these have much to fear from Freud's ideas and praxis.

Auden then contrasts the sanctimonious, on-high, *pro forma* appeals to religion of such authoritarian politicians with Freud's braver readiness to descend, as Dante did, into the realms of the psychopathological unconscious, where the deformed, malodorous, unattractive aspects of life can be found and abound. He seems to appreciate that Freud does so by turning away from punitive or persecutory denouncements and towards a less judgemental consideration of internal states of mind in which repression and disavowal hold sway and imprison the subject.

However, in continuing to take Freudian aim at both psychological abusers and political perpetrators, Auden refers to the "concupiscence of the oppressor", and his use of this rich theological term—attributed to St. Augustine and denoting sexual lust—reinforces the impression that Auden may well be doing battle here with the reproaches of his own superego: there is a hint of his own sinfulness and that his version of psychoanalysis may indeed be quite a faith-inflected one.

Acutely aware, therefore, of how discomfiting and threatening psychoanalysis must be for the status quo, Auden alludes to Freud's personal detractors and professional adversaries and appreciates how much guile, subtlety, and even self-distortion Freud may have had to employ to fend them off. In Auden's view, the prevailing image of Freud—that of the no-nonsense, strict-seeming, Old Testament father who would brook no opposition—was itself a ploy, an almost parodic disguise necessary

> For one who lived among enemies so long.
> [p. 93]

It is immediately after this moment, and by contrast with it, that we find Auden musing on the assimilation—or digestion and metabolization—of the Freudian ethos, as it unconsciously enters the *zeitgeist*.

Putting forth ideas that are uncannily congruent with my own preoccupations here, Auden's elegiac concerns seem to gravitate to the question of what happens to lost objects—human as well as textual—when they enter the minds of those who succeed and survive them. Perhaps also on his own behalf and in relation to the legacy that he might leave, Auden is clearly interested in this relationship between creative artists and thinkers and the products of their vocations, as these live on beyond personal death.

There is such a moment in one of Auden's other elegies from 1939, the commemoration of his great poetic precursor, "In Memory of W. B. Yeats" (1939b). In the first canto of that poem, Auden asks: what will become of Yeats and his poetry after his passing? Another of Auden's best-known poems from the same period, "Musée des Beaux Arts" (1938), comments on depictions in some of the works of the Dutch painter Bruegel, which suggest that events of huge cultural significance, like the birth of Jesus or the death of Icarus, may go completely unnoticed by people going about their business, preoccupied with their workaday activities. Having begun his elegy for Yeats with the announcement that in death the poet had slipped away under cover of the season's frozen wintry gloom, Auden expects his demise to pass similarly unremarked, at least by the natural world: the wolves and rivers, he says, would run on regardless.

However, after making the rather odd suggestion that Yeats's own personified poems might be cut off from knowing about his death (suggesting, perhaps, that the relative durability of the poems themselves might render them indifferent to their creator's mortality), Auden arrives at a less gloomy view of what happens immediately after the poet draws his last breath. Though aware that only a few people would consciously register the day's significance, he nevertheless imagines or conjures a crucially transformative or even revelatory moment: at the very instant that Yeats's own sentience and consciousness disappear and his existential being empties itself out, he is thereby immediately spread abroad and transmuted into all those other beings who continue to read his poetry and appreciate his craft.

Thus, the separation or severing by death of the poems from their author has, for Auden, an instantaneous and an almost literally momentous consequence. As he adds, resorting to a satisfyingly blunt alimentary and metabolic image,

> The words of a dead man
> Are modified in the guts of the living.
> [Auden, 1939b, p. 81]

This dispersing of Yeats's poetic being contrasts with that ominous moment earlier in the Freud elegy when Auden imagines how malevolent figures and forces might spread ashes over a garden with the intention to stifle and suffocate, to perpetrate a murderous cover-up.

These opening stanzas of the Yeats elegy, however, convey a more hopeful and positive perspective on such acts of distribution: the metaphorical scattering, and subsequent internalization, of Yeats's poetic self—his seeds, no less than his ashes—might lead, as a joint consequence of both germination and fertilization, to the flourishing of other minds. These are the possible consequences not only of a death *per se*, but of any occasion upon which—to alter the metaphor—poets or writers risk sending their creative doves out into the world in the hope of having them taken up or in by others.

Of course, Auden's forthright, even brutal, digestive metaphor appeals because what he suggests is that, insofar as each person's style or method of psychic processing is singular or *sui generis*, what anyone may make of a given text (and, implicitly, of any lost or past event, relationship, or experience) will be particular to that receiver. As close readers know, this occurs to some extent regardless of what the original sender or author may have wished or intended—a lesson, ironically, that Auden himself failed to heed when he later sought to modify or suppress his earlier poetry and control its reception.

Returning now to the point at which we interrupted the Freud elegy, we find Auden saying similar things about *his* legacy. Once more introducing a statement of profound praise with a bit of faint damnation, Auden writes:

> If often he was wrong and at times absurd,
> To us he is no more a person
> Now but a whole climate of opinion
> Under whom we conduct our differing lives.
> [1939a, p. 93]

Having quoted these famous, frequently cited lines, we might ask a fundamental question: is it the case that we take in, digest, and metabolize

Freud, or does he take us in, under the encompassing wing of his ideas and theories?

Auden's lines seem to confirm that the appropriation or absorption of a legacy like this is experienced, simultaneously, in both ways: as something to be assimilated into one's personal internal space and structure *and* as an ambient element or environment within which to operate. It is precisely because Freud's influence has indeed atomized, gone viral, become a virtual atmosphere, and is therefore (in) the very air that we breathe, that we do not always pay conscious attention to it and therefore take it mostly for granted. The internal consequence of having it is nevertheless profound, and the effect is, as it were, meteorological; as Auden puts it,

> He quietly surrounds all our habits of growth.
> [p. 93]

That is, for better or worse, and whether we know or like it, or not, we all live in the age of Freud and dwell under his aegis.

Having referred earlier in this book to Maurice Sendak's *Where the Wild Things Are* (1963), I want to invoke, by way of illustration and corroboration here, his no less brilliant *In the Night Kitchen* (1970), which deals with an earlier stage of development. Sendak would, in fact, complete a trilogy of such stages in 1981 with his third book in the series, entitled *Outside Over There*, this time featuring an older female child and the ominous kidnapping of a baby. Though Sendak wrote some gloriously uplifting tales for children, he is also a writer who was very much in touch with dread and, indeed, death; all his stories and illustrations tread a very fine line between mourning and melancholia. In a beautifully written book entitled *The Violet Hour*, Katie Roiphe (2016) chooses to explore how six modern authors fathomed and faced their own demise; it is only too fitting for my purposes that two of those writers were Freud and Sendak.

Where Max of *Wild Things* is perhaps 6 or 7 years old, the protagonist of *Night Kitchen* is a younger but no less disgruntled boy called Mickey, who also finds himself descending—quite literally—into a dream world. He is awakened angrily by things going bump in the night and then suddenly begins to drop through space. Passing his sleeping parents and losing his pyjamas along the way, he arrives in the kitchen of the title. There he discovers three plump bakers in a crisis: they cannot bake the morning cake because they have run out of that all-important ingredient, milk. One suspects that milk may also be the very thing that our hero is lacking, but the pale, naked, vulnerable boy is first mistaken *for* the milk, as the bakers stir him into the dough and put him in the oven.

Thwarting death by baking, Mickey pops out just in time, encased in batter, and says indignantly that he is *not* the milk, nor is the milk he. He precociously undertakes to go and *fetch* some of that precious liquid by flying off in an aeroplane that he fashions out of the dough, up into the night sky, towards and over the Milky Way. We then watch, frame by frame, as he first hovers above a giant milk bottle and then plunges into its depths, naked again, having shed all his defensive batter cladding in the process. He will soon come back up to the surface to pour some cake-saving milk into the bakers' bowl below, but not before he sings out from the bottom of the bottle that he now *is* in the milk and the milk is also in *him*.

Speaking psychoanalytically, one might say that his song is now coming from the depths of a regressive dream/fantasy of having re-merged with a benignly containing maternal environment, which, at least for the moment, he no longer needs to fear or resist. As a result, the day has been saved by his resourcefulness, enabling the bakers to finish their task, and the book can end with Mickey sliding down the milk bottle and back into bed, reclaimed and enveloped by the snug embrace of untroubled sleep.

We might have entered a good psychoanalytic debate here about developmental stages and the merits and demerits of regression, but leaving this for another day, suffice it here to say that Auden's lines and Sendak's story exemplify similar viewpoints. In fact, they both testify to the logic of Michael Balint's (1952, 1968) thinking, where he explicitly states that the optimal or necessary psychic situation in the primary love relation between mother and infant in earliest development—and perhaps also at crucial later moments in life—is the provision of an ambient, immersive, harmonious interpenetrative environment, which, like amniotic fluid or air, is experienced pervasively, both without and within. Though it may be too late to explore this thoroughly, I would also suggest that the radical coining and defining of introjection made by Balint's analyst and mentor, Ferenczi, lie somewhere at the root of these extrapolations.

We re-join Auden's as he acknowledges that some people are bound to feel hindered and thwarted by Freud's legacy. Others, however, feel enormously helped by and thrive within it: as he puts it, they

> Have felt the change in their bones and are cheered
> [1939a, p. 94]

At this moment in his career and this dreadful historical juncture, Auden himself is still feeling cheered by and at home in this Freudian environment and climate—like Mickey in the milk, he seems to revel in it—and he goes on to specify some its qualities and advantages more particularly.

The special legacies that Freud's passing leaves to posterity are the attaining of a certain mood of calm and the prospect of freedom from *toxic* environments. Psychoanalysis is said to provide solace, to be a boon for the troubled, oppressed, anxious, and thus enslaved child who is subject to traumatic life circumstances. Even as Auden goes on to parse the Freudian gaze, he also seems to anticipate Winnicott's veneration of playfulness and transitional space. He speaks movingly of lost or cast-off activities, gestures, and playthings (we think, perhaps, of "Rosebud", the precious sled in the Orson Welles film *Citizen Kane*). These literal or material belongings—along with the accompanying quirks or characteristics of our psychic selves that we were forced to abandon in childhood—are recovered and cherished again under the benign, attentive gaze that the psychoanalytic perspective can shed upon them.

But Freud, says Auden, would bequeath us even more than that. In similar restorative vein, psychoanalysis is seen as an attempt to replenish other precious commodities: not only to give us back our freedom, often experienced only in solitude, but to heal our splits and reunite our splintered fragments. The sundering is the consequence in the first place of desperate, moralistic, paranoid-schizoid quests to grab and clutch at what is right and good, thus alienating these too categorically from what is wrong and bad.

Another of these divisions is between the intellect and the emotions, and Auden sees Freud as offering minds used solely for the purpose of dry debate, the chance of recovering contact with the affective dimension of life. Maintaining the connection with the grieving inner child who lives on in the mind of every adult, both Freud and Auden

> ... would give back to
> The son the mother's richness of feeling.
> [p. 94]

Nearing the end of his elegy, the poet seems to have reserved the most significant of Freud's teachings and legacies for last.

We are urged by the Freudian legacy, he suggests,

> To be enthusiastic over the night
> Not only for the sense of wonder
> It alone has to offer, but also
> Because it needs our love.
> [p. 94]

It is not immediately clear what meanings Auden is assigning to the night here, but he goes on to invoke its denizens: importunate, sad-eyed, dog-like creatures who look to us for leadership or guidance. These, we imagine, are strays from the nocturnal unconscious (beings from the dreamscapes of Sendak's children and Loewald's unlaid ghosts are surely also of their ilk). Auden calls them "exiles who long for the future" (p. 94).

He seems here to adopt the first-person-plural pronoun as a way of joining forces with Freud, pooling the strengths of their respective endeavours. There is the suggestion that, between them, the analyst and the poet might have the orphic potency to save and restore these lost souls by bringing them up from the underworld of unknowing, into the light of conscious knowledge. In so doing, they might also acquire a popular following, gain other adherents willing to dedicate themselves to, and, if need be, even suffer insult and abuse for the cause.

Having celebrated at some length Freud's contributions to what we might call psychic climate change and his enduring legacies, the poem's final stanza cuts abruptly to the moment after the dark night of actual death has claimed the man himself. As if having arrived late for Freud's funeral, we suddenly find ourselves at the graveside, just as Auden is intoning the names of the chief mourners gathered there. He does so allegorically, formally, ceremonially, and with some pomp:

> One rational voice is dumb: over a grave
> The household of Impulse mourns one dearly loved.
> Sad is Eros, builder of cities,
> And weeping anarchic Aphrodite.
> [p. 95]

It is surely apt that the grieving couple identified here is the mother–son pair Aphrodite, goddess of love, beauty, pleasure, and procreation, and Eros, child-god of sexual attraction and passion and later consort of Psyche.

Given their well-nigh incestuous bond, they stand for powerful irrational drives and feelings: to welcome and embrace them, as Freud did—albeit in the rational voice now rendered dumb by his death—is to risk the ego- and civilization-threatening dangers of anarchy and chaos. But Eros is also a builder, a unifier, and—as Freud frequently warned—we dare not abjure this libidinally bonded and bond-creating couple or eschew the love and the life-drive that they represent. To do that would be to leave the way clear for the victory of deadly opposing urges, which strive to break free for the purpose of wreaking complete, uncompromising destruction and with which, therefore, the more positive drives must strive to remain alloyed or fused, as Freud was at pains to tell us.

Perhaps some of the negativity of the poetic personae, presences, or voices in the texts examined here—not least those nay-saying aspects of Auden himself—can be seen to mirror Freud's own prevailing mood in later life (for example, in *Civilization and Its Discontents* and "Analysis Terminable and Interminable"), by which time he had become much more familiar with the most dire consequences of the death drive that he had named more than a decade earlier. In stark contrast to the note of desperate optimism on which "On Transience" ends, Freud came to see more clearly, if belatedly, that there exist in us undeniable and seemingly unquenchable urges of destructiveness and aggression. The consequence of this discovery was that Freud would fight, until the very end of his life, an ongoing rear-guard action against his own disappointment, pessimism, and despair.

In summary, I would suggest that Freud and Auden are trying to assess—each in his own way, on different scales, and in different registers—the human capacity to withstand, particularly by creative means, the human difficulties variously captured by such words and phrases as transience, the passage of time, the loss of love, decay, mortality, and death itself, but also the violent, destructive, and aggressive drives that constitute the specific and direct opposition to the life-force in the human emotional repertoire.

Both poetry and psychoanalysis might be thought of, indeed, as responses to war. This is literally and concretely so in the texts examined here, in that Auden and Freud were writing in response to actual apocalyptic wars that threatened to do away completely with all that was creative and beautiful and civilized. However, their texts must also be read as part of an internal war of attrition that we cannot help but wage against separations, losses, and endings of all kinds. Aptly enough, the very last of Freud's "Thoughts for the Times on War and Death"—written at virtually the same moment as "On Transience"—was the transposition of the famous injunction, "If you want to preserve peace, arm for war", to: "If you want to endure life, prepare yourself for death" (1915b, p. 300).

* * *

I wish to bring the book to an end by closing the circle opened in my Introduction with the mention of two instances of Freud's textual self-doubt regarding the viability of the topics he was about to discuss at those moments. Here I want to draw attention to another significant two-fold Freudian textual repetition. It is perhaps apt that on *this* pair of occasions he resorts to citing the same brief but particularly resonant bit of poetry. The first citation occurs near the end of his psycho-genetic fable of origins, *Totem and Taboo* (the very text with which my own Freud readings began). The other comes at the very end of one of his very last works, the unfinished *An Outline of Psycho-Analysis*. It is also quite unsurprising that this twice-adduced poetic sentence should be from Goethe's *Faust*, given how often Freud mined that text in the course of his works; it reads as follows: "What thou hast inherited from thy fathers, acquire it to make it thine."

On both occasions, Freud seems moved to quote this when trying to grapple with and speak to the translation of phylogenetic characteristics or traits into their individual, ontogenetic appearance within a given human life. In *Totem and Taboo*, the Goethe quote succeeds the following questions: "how much can we attribute to psychical continuity in the sequence of generations? and what are the ways and means employed by one generation in order to hand on its mental states to the next one" (1912–13, p. 158)? In the *Outline*, it comes after Freud makes the claim that "not a few of the child's new experiences will be intensified because they are repetitions of some primaeval phylogenetic experience" (1940a, p. 207).

We are reminded that these profound questions and considerations would be subject to some vexed criticism and earn for Freud a rather contentious reputation: anthropologists and theorists of evolution have roundly criticized him for falling foul of the so-called Lamarckian fallacy when indulging in speculations of this kind. Interestingly, this matter is by no means as scientifically settled as it once seemed. Counterarguments have recently been mounted supporting of some of Freud's more intuitive-sounding or far-fetched theories. However, as I said earlier, these problems lie outside the remit of my concerns, and I am not about to broach them at this late moment, either.

The sentence from Goethe—and Freud's wish to quote it—can in any case be considered in quite a different light, outside the evolutionary contexts of ontogeny, phylogeny, or the so-called recapitulation theory. Might we not regard Freud as inquiring—in a more ordinary, if heartfelt and even desperate way—into the processes or mechanisms whereby significant personal (as well as cultural) internal possessions, abstract mental contents, or psychic qualities come to be passed down the generations, handed on from mothers and fathers to daughters and sons?

The questions asked in *Totem and Taboo*—and answered by way of the Goethe line—reverberate into the future. When Freud is moved to quote the line for a second time, a quarter of a century later and not long before his death (indeed, in the final sentences of an unfinished work's brief last chapter entitled "The internal world"), we recognize that they must have been of real and personal concern to him, not least in relation to the inheritance of psychoanalysis. As I surmised above, in the reading of "On Transience", it must surely have mattered very deeply to Freud whether, for how long, and in what form his science would continue after his own death. Auden, too, was not only concerned with the same general questions in relation to poetry and literature, but also seemed deeply invested in the survival of psychoanalysis.

My own interest in these lines is not dissimilar and linked intimately to the central question of this book: by what metapsychological means do we mourn and work through our losses, and, indeed, how do we glean or gain something internally valuable from that assimilatory process? There are wise and subtle implications in Goethe's injunction: an inheritance may be left, given, or bequeathed to you, but it is not yours until you make or render it your own. Clinically and psychically, we know that not everyone can manage the negotiations, transitions, and transformations that such acquisition requires. As in the case of the loss of an actual person, if one fails to acquire or absorb an inheritance, one can end up being guiltily burdened or unbearably lumbered with it.

To put it differently, both the human objects that are lost in the course of life and the other kinds of objects—be they material, intellectual, personal, or cultural—that these forebears may leave behind must be properly taken in, digested, and metabolized by their heirs if they are not to go to waste or lie neglected, if they are not to leave in their wake the melancholic discomforts of unfinished business, the bad taste of psychic indigestion. As I hope I have demonstrated, the texts of psychoanalysis (and literature) teach us that there is a vast variety of ways to take in what has been lost and to make or constitute from it something serviceable within the psyche.

Freud wrestled with these issues and gradually brought an internal world into being and focus, perhaps at first via the concrete zonal incorporations of the oral psycho-sexual stage and later through his attempts to understand and utilize the concept of identification while building his structural model of the mind.

Ferenczi added the invaluable but much-misunderstood notion of introjection, connoting a less literal or superficial and more metaphoric or metabolic process and constituting the very method whereby an ego or subject encounters the outside world and its objects.

Karl Abraham, given a wealth of experience with manic-depressed patients, brought richness of detail to his clinical accounts and his elaboration of the psycho-sexual stages, attributing special prominence to anal-evacuative as well as oral-incorporative aspects of the melancholic psyche.

Klein inherited legacies from Freud as well as her two analysts, and she bequeathed to future generations a new temporal order for the mind as successively dominated by positions rather than stages. She created a complex inner world populated by phantasy representations of external objects and saw the goal of mourning and the Sisyphean task of the depressive position as the continual re-establishing and repairing of the good internal object.

Loewald adopted a different legacy from Freud, seeing the homuncular entities occupying the psychic inner world as unlaid ghosts, buried too shallowly and mourned insufficiently. For the sake of emancipation, for the ghosts to be turned into ancestors, the agency-building processes of metabolic internalization must prevail over the entrapments of both repression and identification.

Torok and her partner, Nicolas Abraham, revived and promoted a more fully digested incarnation of Ferenczi's introjection and pointedly contrasted it with incorporation: if mourning meant a thoroughgoing metaphorical ingestion and metabolization of the lost object, melancholia implied the concrete, encrypted immurement of an indigestible object within the psyche.

Green's metapsychological endeavour to put mothers on a par with fathers in the symbolic-structural schema of psychoanalytic theory is predicated upon absence and the negative. After providing a vivid account of the melancholic mother who can neither live nor die in the mind of her bereft child, he also describes the optimal alternative whereby the initial intensity of maternal engagement recedes to form a framework for the holding and unfolding of psycho-libidinal development.

It is, of course, in my interests to believe that this book also exemplifies its own themes, by being the product of a slow digestive and metabolic process, bearing the marks of my personal, vocational, and intellectual development. It represents an internal aggregation and assimilation of the transitions that led me from an academic career in literature and philosophy to becoming a psychoanalyst and psychotherapist. This process has latterly included the reclaiming and reframing of older intellectual and textual interests and their embedding in a new context. A long maturation within this newer field eventually brought me to the point of feeling that perhaps I had something more extensive and comprehensive to say about psychoanalysis.

Of course, I wish the book to be a contribution to the metabolic processes of my readers, too. As the initial epigraph from Freud suggests, an effective analogy does not only *bring* something home, in an intellectual sense: it might also allow one to *feel* at home, by providing a more direct and immediate apprehension and thus a more vivid familiarity with—in this instance—the themes of loss and the internal world. Resorting to metaphor once more, I hope that those who have dined here will have found this many-coursed meal sufficiently palatable, sustaining, and nutritious.

REFERENCES

Abraham, K. (1911). Notes on the psycho-analytical investigation and treatment of manic-depressive insanity and allied conditions. In: *Selected Papers on Psychoanalysis*, trans. D. Bryan & A. Strachey (pp. 137–156). London: Hogarth Press, 1942.

Abraham, K. (1924). A short study of the development of the libido, viewed in the light of mental disorders. In: *Selected Papers on Psychoanalysis*, trans. D. Bryan & A. Strachey (pp. 418–501). London: Hogarth Press, 1942.

Abraham, N., & Torok, M. (1972). Mourning *or* melancholia: introjection *versus* incorporation. In: N. Abraham & M. Torok, *The Shell and the Kernel: Renewals of Psychoanalysis, Vol. 1* (pp. 125–138), trans. & ed. N. Rand. Chicago, IL: University of Chicago Press, 1994.

Abraham, N., & Torok, M. (1986). *The Wolf Man's Magic Word: A Cryptonomy*, trans. N. Rand. Minneapolis, MN: University of Minnesota Press.

Abraham, N., & Torok, M. (1994). *The Shell and the Kernel: Renewals of Psychoanalysis, Vol. 1*, trans. & ed. N. Rand. Chicago, IL: University of Chicago Press, 1994.

Alexander, F., Eisenstein, S., & Grotjahn, M. (1966). *Psychoanalytic Pioneers*. New York: Basic Books.

Anzieu, D. (1974). *Freud's Self-Analysis*. London: Hogarth Press, 1986.

Anzieu, D. (1985). *The Skin Ego: A Psychoanalytic Approach to the Self*, trans. C. Turner. New Haven, CT: Yale University Press, 1989.

Auden, W. H. (1938). Musée des Beaux Arts. In: *Selected Poems* (pp. 79–80), ed. E. Mendelson. London: Faber & Faber, 1979.

Auden, W. H. (1939a). In memory of Sigmund Freud. In: *Selected Poems* (pp. 91–95), ed. E. Mendelson. London: Faber & Faber, 1979.

Auden, W. H. (1939b). In memory of W. B. Yeats. In: *Selected Poems* (pp. 80–83), ed. E. Mendelson. London: Faber & Faber, 1979.

Auden, W. H. (1939c). September 1, 1939. In: *Selected Poems* (pp. 86–89), ed. E. Mendelson. London: Faber & Faber, 1979.

Balint, M. (1952). *Primary Love and Psycho-Analytic Technique*. London: Hogarth Press.

Balint, M. (1959). *Thrills and Regressions*. London: Hogarth Press.

Balint, M. (1968). *The Basic Fault: Therapeutic Aspects of Regression*. London: Tavistock Publications.

Barthes, R. (1957). *Mythologies*, trans. A. Lavers. London: Jonathan Cape, 1972.

Bion, W. R. (1962). *Learning from Experience*. London: Karnac, 1984.

Botella, C., & Botella, S. (2004). *The Work of Psychic Figurability: Mental States without Representation*, trans. A. Weller. Hove: Brunner-Routledge.

Britton, R. (1998). *Belief and Imagination: Explorations in Psychoanalysis*. London: Routledge.

Carter, A. (1979). *The Bloody Chamber*. London: Victor Gollancz.

Cavell, S. (1990). *Conditions Handsome and Unhandsome: The Constitution of Emersonian Perfectionism*. Chicago, IL: University of Chicago Press.

Cavell, S. (1992). *The Senses of Walden: An Expanded Edition*. Chicago, IL: University of Chicago Press.

Coleridge, S. T. (1802). Dejection: An ode. In: *The Complete Poetical Works, Vol. 1: Poems* (pp. 362–365), ed. E. A. Coleridge. Oxford: Clarendon Press, 1912.

Dickens, C. (1860). *Great Expectations*. London: Penguin Classics, 1965.

Edmundson, M. (2007). *The Death of Sigmund Freud: Fascism, Psychoanalysis and the Rise of Fundamentalism*. London: Bloomsbury.

Fairbairn, W. R. D. (1952). *Psychoanalytic Studies of the Personality*. London: Tavistock Publications.

Faulkner, W. (1930). A rose for Emily. In: *Collected Stories of William Faulkner* (pp. 119–130). New York: Vintage, 1977.

Faulkner, W. (1977). *Collected Stories of William Faulkner*. New York: Vintage.

Ferenczi, S. (1909). On introjection and transference. In: *First Contributions to Psychoanalysis* (pp. 35–93). London: Hogarth Press, 1955.

Ferenczi, S. (1912). On the definition of introjection. In: *Final Contributions to the Problems and Methods of Psychoanalysis* (pp. 316–318). London: Hogarth Press, 1955.

Ferenczi, S. (1933). Confusion of tongues between adults and the child: the language of tenderness and passion. In: *Final Contributions to the Problems and Methods of Psychoanalysis* (pp. 156–167). London: Hogarth Press, 1955.
Flaubert, G. (1856). *Madame Bovary: A Story of Provincial Life*, trans. G. Wall. London: Penguin Classics, 2003.
Freud, A. (1965). *Normality and Pathology in Childhood: Assessments of Development*. London: Hogarth Press.
Freud, S. (1895d) (with Breuer, J.). *Studies on Hysteria. Standard Edition 2*.
Freud, S. (1900a). *The Interpretation of Dreams. Standard Edition, 4–5*.
Freud, S. (1905d). *Three Essays on the Theory of Sexuality. Standard Edition, 7*.
Freud, S. (1905e). Fragment of an analysis of a case of hysteria. *Standard Edition, 7*: 1–122.
Freud, S. (1909b). Analysis of a phobia in a five-year-old boy. *Standard Edition, 10*: 1–149.
Freud, S. (1909d). Notes upon a case of obsessional neurosis. *Standard Edition, 10*: 151–318.
Freud, S. (1910c). *Leonardo da Vinci and a Memory of His Childhood. Standard Edition, 11*.
Freud, S. (1911b). Formulations on the two principles of mental functioning. *Standard Edition, 12*: 213–226.
Freud, S. (1911c). Psycho-analytic notes on an autobiographical account of a case of paranoia (Dementia paranoides). *Standard Edition, 12*: 1–82.
Freud, S. (1912–13). *Totem and Taboo. Standard Edition, 13*.
Freud, S. (1913f). The theme of the three caskets. *Standard Edition, 12*: 289–301.
Freud, S. (1914c). On narcissism: An introduction. *Standard Edition, 14*: 67–102.
Freud, S. (1915b). Thoughts for the times on war and death. *Standard Edition, 14*.
Freud, S. (1915c). Instincts and their vicissitudes. *Standard Edition, 14*: 109–140.
Freud, S. (1915e). The unconscious. *Standard Edition, 14*: 159–215.
Freud, S. (1916a). On transience. *Standard Edition, 14*: 303–307.
Freud, S. (1917d). A metapsychological supplement to the theory of dreams. *Standard Edition, 14*: 217–235.
Freud, S. (1917e). Mourning and melancholia. *Standard Edition, 14*: 239–258.
Freud, S. (1918b). From the history of an infantile neurosis. *Standard Edition 17*: 1–122.
Freud, S. (1920g). *Beyond the Pleasure Principle. Standard Edition, 18*.
Freud, S. (1921c). *Group Psychology and the Analysis of the Ego. Standard Edition, 18*.
Freud, S. (1923b). *The Ego and the Id. Standard Edition, 19*.
Freud, S. (1924b). Neurosis and psychosis. *Standard Edition, 19*: 147–153.
Freud, S. (1924d). The dissolution of the Oedipus complex. *Standard Edition, 19*: 171–179.

Freud, S. (1924e). The loss of reality in neurosis and psychosis. *Standard Edition, 19*: 181–187.
Freud, S. (1925h). Negation. *Standard Edition, 19*: 233–239.
Freud. S. (1926d). *Inhibitions, Symptoms and Anxiety. Standard Edition, 20.*
Freud, S. (1930a). *Civilization and Its Discontents. Standard Edition, 21.*
Freud, S. (1933a). *New Introductory Lectures on Psycho-Analysis. Standard Edition, 22.*
Freud, S. (1937c). Analysis terminable and interminable. *Standard Edition, 23*: 209–253.
Freud, S. (1937d). Constructions in analysis. *Standard Edition, 23*: 255–269.
Freud, S. (1939a). *Moses and Monotheism. Standard Edition, 23.*
Freud, S. (1940a). *An Outline of Psycho-Analysis. Standard Edition, 23.*
Freud, S. (1940e). Splitting of the ego in the process of defence. *Standard Edition, 23*: 271–278.
Freud, S. (1950 [1892–1899]). Extracts from the Fliess papers. *Standard Edition, 1.*
Freud, S., & Abraham, K. (1966). *A Psycho-Analytic Dialogue: The Letters of Sigmund Freud and Karl Abraham, 1907–1926.* New York: Basic Books.
Fuss, D. (1995). *Identification Papers.* New York: Routledge.
Gay, P. (1988). *Freud: A Life for Our Times.* New York: Anchor Books.
Green, A. (1977). The borderline concept: A conceptual framework for the understanding of borderline patients. In: *On Private Madness* (pp. 60–83). London: Routledge, 2018.
Green, A. (1980). The dead mother. In: *Life Narcissism, Death Narcissism* (pp. 170–200), trans. A. Weller. London: Free Association Books, 2001.
Green, A. (1983). *Narcissisme de vie, narcissisme de mort.* Paris: Éditions de Minuit. [*Life Narcissism, Death Narcissism*, trans. A. Weller. London: Free Association Books, 2001.]
Green, A. (1986). *On Private Madness.* London: Routledge, 2018.
Groddeck, G. (1923). *The Book of the It.* New York: International Universities Press, 1976.
Grosskurth, P. (1986). *Melanie Klein: Her World and Her Work.* New York: Alfred A. Knopf.
Grosskurth, P. (1991). *The Secret Ring: Freud's Inner Circle and the Politics of Psychoanalysis.* Reading, MA: Addison-Wesley.
Hartmann, H. (1939). *Ego Psychology and the Problem of Adaptation.* New York: International Universities Press.
Heimann, P. (1942). A contribution to the problem of sublimation and its relation to processes of internalization. *International Journal of Psychoanalysis, 23*: 8–16.
Hertzmann, L., & Newbigin, J. (2020). *Sexuality and Gender Now: Moving Beyond Heteronormativity.* London: Routledge.

Holland, N. (1975). *5 Readers Reading*. New Haven, CT: Yale University Press.
Isaacs, S. (1948). The nature and function of phantasy. *International Journal of Psychoanalysis, 29*: 73–97.
James, H. (1921). Preface. In: *The Tragic Muse*. London: Macmillan & Co.
Keats, J. (1816). On first looking into Chapman's Homer. In: *The Complete Poetical Works and Letters* (p. 9). Boston and New York: Houghton, Mifflin & Co., 1899.
Keats, J. (1819). Ode on a Grecian urn. In: *The Complete Poetical Works and Letters* (pp. 134–135). Boston and New York: Houghton, Mifflin & Co., 1899.
Klein, M. (1935). A contribution to the psychogenesis of manic-depressive states. *International Journal of Psychoanalysis, 16*: 145–174.
Klein, M. (1940). Mourning and its relation to manic-depressive states. *International Journal of Psychoanalysis, 21*: 125–153.
Klein, M. (1946). Notes on some schizoid mechanisms. In: *Envy and Gratitude and Other Works 1946–1963* (pp. 1–24). London: Hogarth Press, 1975.
Klein, M. (1955). On identification. In: *Envy and Gratitude and Other Works 1946–1963* (pp. 141–175). London: Hogarth Press, 1975.
Kohon, G. (Ed.) (1999). *The Dead Mother: The Work of André Green*. London: Routledge.
Kohut, H. (1971). *The Analysis of the Self: A Systematic Approach to the Psychoanalytic Treatment of Narcissistic Personality Disorders*. New York: International Universities Press.
Kohut, H. (1977). *The Restoration of the Self*. New York: International Universities Press.
Kristeva, J. (2000). *Melanie Klein*, trans. R. Guberman. New York: Columbia University Press.
Lacan, J. (1949). The mirror stage as formative of the function of the I as revealed in psychoanalytic experience. In: *Ecrit: A Selection* (pp. 1–7), trans. A. Sheridan. London: Tavistock Publications, 1977.
Laplanche, J. (1970). *Life and Death in Psychoanalysis*, trans J. Mehlman. Baltimore, MD: Johns Hopkins University Press, 1976.
Laplanche, J. (1977). *Seduction, Translation and the Drives*, ed. J. Fletcher & M. Stanton. London: ICA.
Lear, J. (2003). *Therapeutic Action: An Earnest Plea for Irony*. London: Karnac.
Likierman, M. (2001). *Melanie Klein: Her Work in Context*. London: Continuum.
Loewald, H. (1960). On the therapeutic action of psycho-analysis. In: *Papers on Psychoanalysis* (pp. 221–256). New Haven, CT: Yale University Press, 1980.
Loewald, H. (1962). Internalization, separation, mourning, and the superego. In: *Papers on Psychoanalysis* (pp. 257–276). New Haven, CT: Yale University Press, 1980.

Loewald, H. (1973). On internalization. In: *Papers on Psychoanalysis* (pp. 69–86). New Haven, CT: Yale University Press, 1980.

Loewald, H. (1978a). Primary process, secondary process and language. In: *Papers on Psychoanalysis* (pp. 178–206). New Haven, CT: Yale University Press, 1980.

Loewald, H. (1978b). *Psychoanalysis and the History of the Individual*. New Haven, CT: Yale University Press.

Mahler, M. (1975). *The Psychological Birth of the Human Infant*. New York: Basic Books, 2008.

Malcolm, J. (1981). *Psychoanalysis: The Impossible Profession*. New York: Alfred A. Knopf.

Malcolm, J. (1984). *In the Freud Archives*. New York: Alfred A. Knopf.

Malcolm, J. (1994). *The Silent Woman: Sylvia Plath and Ted Hughes*. New York: Alfred A. Knopf.

Marvell, A. (1681). *Miscellaneous Poems*. London: Robert Boulter.

Meyerowitz, R. (1995). *Transferring to America: Jewish Interpretations of American Dreams*. New York: SUNY Press.

Meyerowitz, R. (2018). "A quandary of borders": theoretical and clinical thoughts on the borderline predicament. In: R. Meyerowitz & D. Bell, eds. *Turning the Tide: The Psychoanalytic Approach of the Fitzjohn's Unit to Patients with Complex Needs* (pp. 131–147). London: Karnac, 2018.

Meyerowitz, R., & Bell, D. (Eds.) (2018). *Turning the Tide: The Psychoanalytic Approach of the Fitzjohn's Unit to Patients with Complex Needs*. London: Karnac.

Mitchell, S. A., & Black, M. (1995). *Freud and Beyond: A History of Modern Psychoanalytic Thought*. New York: Basic Books.

Mitford, N. (1949). *Love in a Cold Climate*. London: Penguin, 1954.

Ogden, T. (2002). *Conversations at the Frontier of Dreaming*. London: Karnac.

Ogden, T. (2012). *Creative Readings: Essays on Seminal Analytic Works*. London: Routledge.

Parsons, M. (2000). *The Dove that Returns, The Dove that Vanishes: Paradox and Creativity in Psychoanalysis*. London: Routledge.

Plath, S. (1961). Morning song. In: *Ariel* (p. 11). London: Faber & Faber, 1965.

Plath, S. (1962). Daddy. In: *Ariel* (pp. 54–56). London: Faber & Faber, 1965.

Plath, S. (1965). *Ariel*. London: Faber & Faber.

Poe, E. A. (1847). Ulalume. *The American Review, 36*: 39.

Ramazani, J. (1994). *Poetry of Mourning: The Modern Elegy from Hardy to Heaney*. Chicago, IL: University of Chicago Press.

Rank, O. (1924). *The Trauma of Birth*. New York: Dover, 1993.

Riviere, J. (1936). A contribution to the analysis of negative therapeutic reaction. *International Journal of Psychoanalysis, 17*: 304–320.

Roiphe, K. (2016). *The Violet Hour: Great Writers at the End*. London: Virago.
Rosenfeld, H. (1971). A clinical approach to the psychoanalytic theory of the death and life instincts: An investigation into the aggressive aspects of narcissism. *International Journal of Psychoanalysis, 52*: 169–178.
Sacks, P. M. (1985). *The English Elegy: Studies in the Genre from Spenser to Yeats*. Baltimore, MD: Johns Hopkins University Press.
Sandler, J. (1993). Fantasy, defence, and the representational world. *Bulletin of the Anna Freud Centre, 16* (4): 337–347.
Sandler, J., & Rosenblatt, B. (1962). The concept of the representational world. *Psychoanalytic Study of the Child, 17*: 128–145.
Sandler, J., Sandler, A., & Davies, R. (2000). *Clinical and Observational Psychoanalytic Research: Roots of a Controversy—André Green & Daniel Stern*. London: Karnac.
Schmideberg, M. (1930). The role of psychotic mechanisms in cultural development. *International Journal of Psychoanalysis, 11*: 387–418.
Segal, H. (1954). Notes on symbol formation. In: E. Bott Spillius (Ed.), *Melanie Klein Today: Developments in Theory and Practice, Vol. 1: Mainly Theory* (pp. 160–177). London: Routledge, 1988.
Sendak, M. (1963). *Where the Wild Things Are*. London: Red Fox, 2000.
Sendak, M. (1970). *In the Night Kitchen*. London: Red Fox, 2001.
Sendak, M. (1981). *Outside Over There*. London: Red Fox, 2002.
Shelley, P. B. (1817). Ozymandias. In: *Miscellaneous and Posthumous Poems* (p. 100). London: W. Benbow, 1826.
Shelley, P. B. (1821). *A Defence of Poetry*. Indianapolis, IN: Bobbs-Merrill, 1904.
Shengold, L. (1989). *Soul Murder: The Effects of Childhood Abuse and Neglect*. New Haven, CT: Yale University Press.
Sodré, I. (2004). Who's who: Notes on pathological identification. In: E. Spillius & E. O'Shaughnessy (Eds.), *Projective Identification: The Fate of a Concept* (pp. 132–146). London: Routledge, 2012.
Stamelman, R. (1990). *Lost Beyond Telling: Representations of Death and Absence in Modern French Poetry*. Ithaca, NY: Cornell University Press.
Steiner, J. (1993). *Psychic Retreats: Pathological Organizations in Psychotic, Neurotic and Borderline Patients*. London: Routledge.
Stern, J. (1999). Psychoanalytical psychotherapy in a medical setting. *Psychoanalytic Psychotherapy, 13* (1): 51–68.
Stern, J. (2003). Thirty years of abdominal pain. *Psychoanalytic Psychotherapy, 17* (4): 300–311.
Stern, J. (2010). The relevance of applied psychoanalytic practice and thinking to the treatment of medically symptomatic patients. In: A. Lemma & M. Patrick (Eds.), *Off the Couch: Contemporary Psychoanalytic Applications* (pp. 130–142). London: Routledge.
Stern, J. (2013). "No entry", an invitation to intrude, or both? Reflections on a group of anorexic patients. *International Journal of Psychoanalysis, 94* (4): 689–713.

Stevens, W. (1915). Sunday morning. In: *The Collected Poems of Wallace Stevens* (pp. 66–70). New York: Alfred A. Knopf, 1955.

Stevens, W. (1939). The woman that had more babies than that. In: *Opus Posthumous: Poems, Plays, Prose* (pp. 81–83). New York: Alfred A. Knopf.

Stevens, W. (1947). The auroras of autumn. In: *The Collected Poems of Wallace Stevens* (pp. 411–421). New York: Alfred A. Knopf, 1955.

Strachey, J. (1955). Editor's note to *Group Psychology and the Analysis of the Ego*. In: S. Freud, *Standard Edition*, Vol. 18 (pp. 67–68). London: Hogarth Press.

Strachey, J. (1957a). Editor's introduction to *Papers on Metapsychology*. In: S. Freud, *Standard Edition*, Vol. 14 (pp. 105–107). London: Hogarth Press.

Strachey, J. (1957b). Editor's note to "Mourning and Melancholia". In: S. Freud, *Standard Edition*, Vol. 14 (pp. 239–242). London: Hogarth Press.

Strachey, J. (1957c). Editor's note to "On Narcissism". In: S. Freud, *Standard Edition*, Vol. 14 (pp. 69–71). London: Hogarth Press.

Strachey, J. (1957d). Editor's note to "On Transience". In: S. Freud, *Standard Edition*, Vol. 14 (p. 304). London: Hogarth Press.

Strachey, J. (1959). Editor's introduction to *Inhibitions, Symptoms and Anxiety*. In: S. Freud, *Standard Edition*, Vol. 20 (pp. 77–86). London: Hogarth Press.

Tolstoy, L. (1877). *Anna Karenina*, trans. R. Pevear & L. Volokhonsky. London: Penguin Classics, 2000.

Torok, M. (1968). The illness of mourning and the fantasy of the exquisite corpse. In: N. Abraham & M. Torok, *The Shell and the Kernel: Renewals of Psychoanalysis*, Vol. 1 (pp. 107–124), trans. & ed. N. Rand. Chicago, IL: University of Chicago Press, 1994.

von Unwerth, M. (2005). *Freud's Requiem: Mourning, Memory and the Invisible History of a Summer Walk*. New York: Riverhead.

Whitman, W. (1855). Song of myself. In: *Leaves of Grass*. New York: Rome Brothers.

Winnicott, D. W. (1945). Primitive emotional development. In: *Through Paediatrics to Psychoanalysis: Collected Papers* (pp. 145–156). London: Karnac, 1984.

Winnicott, D. W. (1949). Hate in the countertransference. In: *Through Paediatrics to Psychoanalysis: Collected Papers* (pp. 194–203). London: Karnac, 1984.

Winnicott, D. W. (1951). Transitional objects and transitional phenomena. In: *Playing and Reality* (pp. 1–25). London: Tavistock Publications, 1971.

Winnicott, D. W. (1954). The depressive position in normal emotional development. In: *Through Paediatrics to Psychoanalysis: Collected Papers* (pp. 262–277). London: Karnac, 1984.

Winnicott, D. W. (1956). Primary maternal preoccupation. In: *Through Paediatrics to Psychoanalysis: Collected Papers* (pp. 300–305). London: Karnac, 1984.

Winnicott, D. W. (1958a). The capacity to be alone. In: *The Maturational Processes and the Facilitating Environment* (pp. 29–36). London: Hogarth Press, 1965.
Winnicott, D. W. (1958b). Psychoanalysis and the sense of guilt. In: *The Maturational Processes and the Facilitating Environment* (pp. 15–28). London: Hogarth Press, 1965.
Winnicott, D. W. (1960a). Ego distortion in terms of true and false self. In: *The Maturational Processes and the Facilitating Environment* (pp. 140–152). London: Hogarth Press, 1965.
Winnicott, D. W. (1960b). The theory of the parent-infant relationship. In: *The Maturational Processes and the Facilitating Environment* (pp. 37–55). London: Hogarth Press, 1965.
Winnicott, D. W. (1967a). The location of cultural experience. In: *Playing and Reality* (pp. 95–103). London: Tavistock Publications, 1971.
Winnicott, D. W. (1967b). Mirror-role of mother and family in child development. In: *Playing and Reality* (pp. 111–119). London: Tavistock Publications, 1971.
Winnicott, D. W. (1969). The use of an object and relating through identifications. In: *Playing and Reality* (pp. 86–94). London: Tavistock Publications, 1971.
Winnicott, D. W. (1971). *Playing and Reality*. London: Tavistock Publications.
Winnicott, D. W. (1974). Fear of breakdown. *International Review of Psycho-Analysis, 1*: 103–107.
Wordsworth, W. (1807). Ode: Intimations of immortality from recollections of early childhood. In: *The Poetical Works: Volume VIII* (pp. 190–198), ed. W. Knight. New York: Macmillan & Co., 1896.
Wordsworth, W. (1812). Surprised by joy. In: *The Poetical Works: Volume VI* (p. 72), ed. W. Knight. New York: Macmillan & Co., 1896.
Wright, N. (1988). *Mrs Klein*. London: Samuel French.
Yeats, W. B. (1902a). Adam's curse. In: *In the Seven Woods: Being Poems Chiefly of the Irish Heroic Age* (pp. 24–25). London: Macmillan & Co., 1903.
Yeats, W. B. (1902b). The folly of being comforted. In: *In the Seven Woods: Being Poems Chiefly of the Irish Heroic Age* (p. 21). London: Macmillan & Co., 1903.

INDEX

Abraham, K. (*passim*):
  bipolar illness, study of, 114
  criticism of, and oedipal strugglewith Freud, 123
  on depressive states, 114
  and Freud:
    oedipal competition between, 261
    relationship between, 97–98
  on introjection, 96–151
  on mania, 142–147
  on manic-depressive illness, 114–151
  "Notes on the Psycho-Analytical Investigation and Treatment of Manic-Depressive Insanity and Allied Conditions", 22, 114–118
  "A Short Study of the Development of the Libido, Viewed in the Light of Mental Disorders", 22, 118–151
  "Stages of Libidinal Organization", 120
  "Stages of Object-Love", 120–121
Abraham, N. (*passim*):
  introjection versus incorporation, 288–311
  "Mourning or Melancholia: Introjection versus Incorporation", 25, 260, 288–311

The Shell and the Kernel, 258–259, 289–290
The Wolf Man's Magic Word, 258, 279
abstract expressionism, 246
Adler, A., 29, 35, 96–97
affective hallucination(s), 352
  of dead mother, 334
aggression, primary, 229, 329
aggressor, identification with, 228
Alexander, F., 98
alimentary conceit or trope, 6
alimentary perspectives on internal world, 5
alpha-elements, 205
alpha-function, maternal, 207
  Bion's concept of, 205
ambient environments versus discrete objects, 7
American Transcendentalist literature, 232
anal-sadistic phase, 122, 134, 136–137
analysis, end phase of, 216, 230
analyst, image of, idealization of, 343
analytic rule of silence, 334
ancestors, turning of ghosts into, 254
Andreas-Salomé, L., 371, 375
Anna O [Freud's case], 28, 100–101
anorexia, 144, 287, 295

and melancholia, connection
between, 44
in melancholia, 53
anthropological ur-myths, 31
anticathexis, 47
antidepressant medication, 94
antimetaphor, 301
anxiety(ies):
blank, 320
castration, see castration anxiety
first theory of, Freud's, 104
hysteria, 28
and loss, 85–95
persecutory: see persecutory anxiety
primary, 152
psychotic: see psychotic anxiety(ies)
signal: see signal anxiety
theory of, 21, 86, 104
traumatic: see traumatic anxiety
anxiety-neurosis, 114
Anzieu, D., 352, 363–364
Aphrodite, 396
après coup/Nachträglichkeit/deferred
action, 321, 338, 366, 374
art, non-objective forms of, 246
Auden, W. H., 14
"In Memory of Ernst Toller", 370, 385
"In Memory of W. B. Yeats", 385, 391
"In Memory of Sigmund Freud", 27,
369, 384–397
meaning, mourning, and mortality,
368–401
"Musée des Beaux Arts", 391
"September 1, 1939", 370, 385
aurora borealis/Northern Lights, 223
auto-erotic excitation, 330
auto-satisfaction, fantasy of, 340

baby, no such thing as [Winnicott], 251
Balint, M., 112, 136, 292, 359, 394
Ferenczi's influence on, 106
Barthes, R., 16, 274
Baudelaire, C., 16
beauty, transience of, 373
Bell, D., 8
Berlin, I., 254
Bernheim, H., 101
beta-elements, 205
Bion's concept of, 204
biological metabolic processes, analogy
of, 245

Bion, W. R., 4, 24, 292, 339, 349, 352, 364
alpha-elements, 205
beta-elements, 205
container and contained, 231
theory of, 205
containment, theory of, 23, 204
digestion, analogy of, 6
Klein's heir, 204–208
Learning from Experience, 201, 205
maternal reverie, 207
psychoanalytic containment, concept
of, 103
bipolar affective disorder, 8, 46
bipolar illness, 22, 71, 144
Abraham's study of, 114
birth, "loss" of, 187
bisexuality, constitutional, 77–78
Black, M., 210, 319
Blanchot, M., 16
blank anxiety, 320
blank mourning, 320, 334, 341–342, 345,
347, 353, 355, 361
blank psychosis, 320
Bonaparte, M., 97, 317
borderline personality disorder, 8, 235,
247, 314–315, 323
Borges, J. L., 14
Botella, C., 3
Botella, S., 3
breast:
false, in false self, 341
loss of, 319, 321–322, 330, 332, 337,
342, 364
patched, 330
primordial, 338
Breuer, J., 39, 96, 100–101
British Independent technique, 106, 346
Britton, R., 4, 321, 339
Bruegel, P., the Elder, 391
bulimia, 295
Burghölzli Clinic, 97

cannibalism, 76, 135, 174, 297
cannibalistic impulses, 135, 137, 156
cannibalistic phase, 53, 135, 342
carnivals, value of, 71
Carroll, L., *Alice in Wonderland*, 224
Carter, A., 277–278
Caruth, C., 19
castration, 317
arch-fantasy of, 290

castration anxiety, 87–89, 91, 227, 304, 318, 342
Cavell, S., 232
Charcot, J.-M., 101
Christianity, 219
Coleridge, S. T., "Dejection: An Ode", 372
compensatory mirroring, 232
confusion of tongues:
Ferenczi's term, 1, 266
in psychoanalysis, 1, 266
conscience, 36, 41, 43–44, 49, 66, 72, 81–82, 139, 165, 236
bullying, moralistic, superego as, 53
voice of, as mouthpiece of superego, 237
constancy principle, 242, 249
container and contained, 231
theory of, 205
containment:
psychoanalytic, Bion's concept of, 103
theory of, 23, 204
conversion hysteria, 28
coprolalia, 301
countertransference, importance of, 13
Crohn's disease, 144
cryptophoria, 299, 301, 303

Dante, 390
Darstellung vs *Vorstellung*, 3
Davies, R., 322
dead father, 189, 235, 308, 348
concept of, 317
dead mother:
affective hallucination of, 334
animating of, 340
child's relation with, 348
death of, 346
identification with, 327, 329, 342, 347
and primal scene and Oedipus complex, relation between, 363
reanimating, 334
dead mother complex, 26, 316, 324, 329, 335–338, 341–346, 350, 354, 360–362
dead mother transference, 344
death:
life after, belief in, 221
as mother of beauty, 221
death instinct/drive, 48, 60, 62, 79, 82, 115, 137, 162, 225, 249, 328–329, 360, 384, 387, 397
and life instinct, fusion of, 335

versus Eros, 7
introduction of, 20, 58
and life instinct, fusion of, 335
decathexis, maternal, 362
defence(s), manic, 134, 172, 183
deferred action/*après coup*/*Nachträglichkeit*, 321, 338, 366, 374
dementia praecox, 104
demetaphorization, 291, 302
de Montaigne, M., 16
de M'Uzan, M., 288
denial, defence of, 155
depression:
and mania, relation and contrast between, 46
maternal, 324
melancholic, 135–136
versus mourning, 7
depressive functioning and paranoid-schizoid functioning, distinctions between, 106, 122, 127
depressive illness, aetiological factors in, 138–139
depressive position, 85, 152, 157–160, 166–172, 176–183, 186–188, 193, 198, 220, 254, 299, 316, 350, 361, 400
concept of, 201
early, 182, 188, 194, 200
infantile, 179, 182, 186, 193, 198, 200
overcoming, 182, 204
and paranoid-schizoid position, spiralling alternations between, 230
depressive psychosis, 116
depressive sadism, 45
depressive states, 38, 142, 155, 170, 177
Abraham on, 114
Derrida, J., 19, 258
desexualization, 77, 214, 248
Dickens, C., *Great Expectations*, 40, 325
digestion:
analogy of, and workings of psychic inner world, 6
mental/psychological, analogy of, 50–57
and metabolization, 149, 194, 202, 234
and mourning, analogy between, 5, 20, 145, 186, 201, 253, 259, 391
psychic, 186, 213, 311

disillusionment, premature, 326
dream interpretations, 8
drive-discharging versus object-seeking, 7
drive/instinct theory, 58, 79, 207

early psychotic anxieties, 190
eating disorders, 295
Edmundson, M., 384
effacement, 349, 358
  maternal, 356
ego:
  as first and foremost a bodily ego, 6, 73
  and id and superego, 72–84
    dynamic mental intercourse among, 212
  ruthlessness of, 159
  secondary autonomy of, concept of, 229
  shadow of object falling upon, 20, 42, 44, 53, 66, 143, 229
  splitting of, 299, 305
ego ideal, 33, 36, 41, 66–67, 70–72, 79, 139, 173, 219, 232–236, 268, 300, 303, 323
  and ideal ego, distinction between, 232
  triumph of ego over, 71
ego identity, 255
ego libido, 34–35, 42
ego-nuclei, oral and anal, 157
ego psychology, 211–212, 220, 227, 240–241
Eisenstein, S., 98
Eitingon, M., 97
emancipation, and internalization, 209–257
Emerson, R. W., 232
environment mother, 225
Erikson, E., 255
Eros, 58, 79, 160, 249, 265, 360, 386–387, 396
  versus death drive, 7
erotic transference, 100
evacuation, forms of in psychic life, 54
exquisite corpse, 277, 288
  fantasy of, 260

Fairbairn, W. R. D., 4, 90, 112, 236, 238, 292
false self, false breast in, 341
father:
  dead: *see* dead father
  primal, 31–32, 147

Faulkner, W., 278, 296
  "A Rose for Emily", 39–40, 46, 64, 69, 124–135, 189–191, 196, 228, 235, 248, 270–272, 276, 280, 282, 290–291, 306–308, 328, 348, 360
    story, summary of, 9–14
  "The Village", 196
Ferenczi, S. (*passim*):
  "Confusion of Tongues between Adults and the Child", 266
  "On the Definition of Introjection", 20–21, 31–32, 108–113, 266, 268, 398
  and Freud:
    Clark University lectures, 99
    relationship between, 97–98
  introjection, concept of, 68, 99–114
  "On Introjection and Transference", 21, 68, 76, 99–108, 114, 266
  oral-alimentary behaviours, 102
  sphincter morality, 234
  transference, concept of, 99
fetishism, 305
Few Good Men, A, 59
figurative language, annulment of, 301
film, horror, and dynamics of melancholia, 52
First World War, 20, 26, 27, 29, 57, 190, 225, 369–370, 386
Fitzjohn's Unit, Tavistock, 8
Flack, R., 13
Flaubert, G., *Madame Bovary*, 325
Fliess, W., 28, 96
Fox, C., *Killing Me Softly*, 13
framing structure, effacement of, 349–353
Frankenstein's monster, 298
fratricide, 363
free association, 389
Freud, A., 97, 121, 363, 371
Freud, J., 363
Freud, P., 363
Freud, S. (*passim*):
  "Analysis of a Phobia in a Five-Year-Old Boy", Little Hans, 28, 87, 141
  "Analysis Terminable and Interminable", 99, 304, 397
  anxiety:
    and loss, 85–95
    theory of, 21, 86, 104
  Beyond the Pleasure Principle, 20, 58–61, 72, 79, 83, 88, 384

Civilization and Its Discontents, 1, 136, 245, 251, 370, 383, 387, 397
Clark University lectures, 99
"Constructions in Analysis", 245, 321
Darstellung vs *Vorstellung*, 3
dead mother, 362–367
death drive, introduction of, 20, 58
"The Dissolution of the Oedipus Complex", 194, 244
dream interpretations, 8, 365
drive/instinct theory, 58, 79, 207
dynamic model, 2
ego, first and foremost a bodily ego, 6, 73
The Ego and the Id, 6, 21, 36, 61, 66, 70, 72–84, 108, 126, 139, 142, 165, 195, 213, 244, 267, 351, 379
and Ferenczi, relationship between, 97–98
Fliess, correspondence with, 28
"Formulations on the Two Principles of Mental Functioning", 29
"Fragment of an Analysis of a Case of Hysteria", Dora, 28, 64, 100–101
on group functioning, 60–72
Group Psychology and the Analysis of the Ego, 21, 60–61, 67–77, 142, 195, 261, 267, 379
"From the History of an Infantile Neurosis", Wolf Man, 29, 87, 302–303, 339, 364, 374
id, first named, 73
identification, theory of, 17
incorporation, 76
Inhibitions, Symptoms and Anxiety, 21, 85–86, 88, 93, 318
"Instincts and Their Vicissitudes", 42, 264
The Interpretation of Dreams, 29, 209, 362
internal world, psycho-active, concept of, 28
and Karl Abraham:
    criticism of and oedipal struggle with, 123, 261
    relationship between, 97–98
Leonardo da Vinci and a Memory of His Childhood, 20, 29, 65
"The Loss of Reality in Neurosis and Psychosis", 84
on mania, 45–50
meaning, mourning, and mortality, 368–401

on melancholia, analysis of, 36–40
mind:
    agencies of, construction of, 72–84
    later models of, 58–95
    mapping, 28–57
    structural model of, 3, 21, 72–84, 87, 212, 233, 237–238, 243, 269, 399
mourning, in *Totem and Taboo*, 31–33
"Mourning and Melancholia" (*passim*)
Nachträglichkeit, concept of, 366
on narcissism, 33–36
"On Narcissism", 20, 29–30, 33–36, 73, 109, 232, 291, 376, 379
on narcissistic structure and functioning, 33–36
"Negation", 84, 322
"Neurosis and Psychosis", 84, 155
"Notes upon a Case of Obsessional Neurosis", Rat Man, 28
An Outline of Psycho-Analysis, 237, 322, 398
"Papers on Technique", 29
paternalism of, 18
"Psycho-Analytic Notes on an Autobiographical Account of a Case of Paranoia (Dementia Paranoides)", Schreber, 28, 327
self-other relations, concept of, 17
self-protection, need for, 58–60
"Splitting of the Ego in the Process of Defence", 1
Studies on Hysteria, Anna O, 28, 100–101
superego, introduction of, 73, 77
systemic model, 2
"The Theme of the Three Caskets", 222
theories of unconsciousness, 3
"Thoughts for the Times on War and Death", 397
Three Essays on the Theory of Sexuality, 5, 29, 86–87, 120, 180, 274
topographical model, 2–3, 269, 289, 304
Totem and Taboo, 20, 31–32, 33, 62, 76, 135, 147, 317, 397–398
"On Transience", 26–27, 57, 190, 221–222, 368–369, 371–386, 397, 399
transference, concept of, 100

"The Unconscious", 48
Wednesday Psychological Society, 96
word- and thing-representations, 3
Frost, R., 14
fulfilments, hallucinatory, 271
Fuss, D., 17–18, 19
  Identification Papers, 16, 63

Gay, P., 97
ghosts:
  turning of, into ancestors, 209–257,
    298, 400
  of the unconscious, 210, 218, 298
Gimbel, N., *Killing Me Softly*, 13
Glover, J., 157, 170
Goethe, J. W. von, 369, 383, 399
  Faust, 398
Golem, 298
Gonne, M., 374–376
Greek tragic drama, 32
Green, A. (*passim*):
  "The Borderline Concept", 314
  and Daniel Stern, public debate and
    confrontation, 322
  "The Dead Father and the Dead
    Mother", 317–323
  "The Dead Mother", 26, 293,
    312–316, 323
  dead mother complex, 323–335
  frozen love, vicissitudes of, 335–343
  homophobia of, 341
  on infant observation, 322
  Life Narcissism, Death Narcissism, 314
  mother, lost and restored, 312–367
  negative, work of, 26
  On Private Madness, 314
  structuralist psychoanalysis of, 351
Green, J., 202
Groddeck, G., 73, 127–128
Grosskurth, P., 154
  The Secret Ring, 97
Grotjahn, M., 98
group functioning, Freud's study of,
  60–72

hallucinations, affective, 352
hallucinatory wish-fulfilment, 271, 303
Hamlet, as mythical prototype of patient,
  314
Hartmann, H., 211, 229, 241, 250
hatred, secondary, releasing of, 330

Heaney, S., 14
Heidegger, M., 211
Heimann, P., 199, 203
Hertzmann, L., 341
historical truth vs material truth, 321
Hitchcock, A., *Psycho*, 291
Hitler, A., 68, 385
holding, concept of, 333
Holland, N., 12
Holocaust, 19, 280, 388
Homer:
  Iliad, 152
  Odyssey, 209
homophobia, 341
homosexuality, 65, 341
  male, and identification with
    mother, 65
Hopper, E., 386
horror in film and literature, and
  dynamics of melancholia, 52
Hughes, T., 279, 282–283, 354
hypnosis, 101, 106
hysterical contagion, 65
hysterical identification, 330

id, 72
  and ego and superego, 3, 72–84, 87,
    233, 238, 243
  dynamic mental intercourse
    among, 212
  first named, 73
ideal ego, 72, 166, 232–233
  and ego ideal, distinction between, 232
idealization and sublimation, distinction
  between, 36
identification (*passim*):
  with aggressor, 228
  concept of, 17, 35, 42, 108, 399
  and group functioning, 60–72
  hysterical, 330
  incorporative, 328
  melancholic, 129
  narcissistic, 43, 140
  nature of, 31
  negative, 334
  oedipal, 229
  oral, 342
    primitive, 54
  with parental figures, 21
  positive, 334
  primary, 78, 214–215, 334

symptomatic, 64
  theory of, 17
  transferential act of, 17
id psychology, 239
imagine, compulsion to, 330
imago, 276–278, 284–285, 313, 350
  maternal, 325, 338
    primitive, 349
incest, 276, 301, 306, 310, 345, 363–364
  prohibition, 321
inclusion topography, 305
incorporation (*passim*):
  fantasy of, 273, 284, 290, 295, 297, 299, 305
  Freud's term, 76
  hypothesis of, 305
  imaginary, 303
  and introjection, relation between, 55, 69, 111, 160, 178, 195, 272, 284, 292, 361
  of penis, fantasy of, 292
incorporative identification, 328
Independent tradition in Britain, 136
individuating separation, 360
individuation, duality or polarity of, and primary narcissistic identity with environment, 238
infantile depression, 324
infantile depressive position, 179, 182, 186, 193, 198, 200
infantile neurosis, 182, 186
infantile psychotic anxiety, 155
infant observation, 322
ingestion, fantasy of, 272
insanity, circular, hypothesis of, 46
insomnia, 327
  depressive symptom of, 45
instinct theory, Freud's, final, 249
internality, 17, 241, 249
  uncovering, 2
internalization (*passim*):
  concept of, Loewald's definition of, 241
  and emancipation, Loewald on, 209–257
  Kleinian concept of, 242
  limits of, 94
  metabolic, 235, 400
  processes of, Loewald's elaboration of, 213
  as re-structuring, 220
internal object(s) (*passim*):

assimilation of, concept of, 202–203
  concept of, 22–23
  good, 160, 168, 170, 172, 188, 191, 202, 206
    establishing of, 220
  Kleinian concept of, 242
  paranoid-schizoid, 280
internal world:
  concept of, 1
  psycho-active, concept of, 28
intersubjectivity, 227
intrapsychic crypt, 299
intrapsychic immurement, 302
introjection (*passim*):
  concept of, 21, 99, 106, 113, 259, 266, 399
  and digestion, psychic, 205
  Ferenczi's concept of, 66, 68, 100–114, 267
  and incorporation:
    differences and similarities between, 55, 69, 111, 160, 178, 195, 272, 284, 292, 361
    relationship between, 111, 178, 195, 272, 284, 292, 361
  mechanism of, 153
  phallic and genital, 278
  primary, 187
  and projection, differences between, 112
  temporary, 125–128, 235
intrusive interpretation, 346
Isaacs, S., 4, 289

Jabès, E., 16
James, H., 3, 86
Jesus, 391
Jones, E., 97
Jung, C. G., 29, 31, 96–97, 99, 106

Kant, I., 205
Keats, J., 222, 266
  "On First Looking into Chapman's Homer", 266
  "Ode on a Grecian Urn", 222
Klein, M. (*passim*):
  "A Contribution to the Psychogenesis of Manic-Depressive States", 22, 152–178
  depressive position, 85, 152, 157–160, 166–172, 176–179, 182–183, 186, 188, 193–194, 198, 200–201, 204, 220, 254, 299, 316, 350, 361, 400

Ferenczi's influence on, 106
"On Identification", 201
on internal world, 152–208
"Mourning and Its Relation to Manic-Depressive States", 22, 178–201
Mrs A, 188, 191–193
"Notes on Some Schizoid Mechanisms", 201–202, 234
patient D, 191, 197–198
Kleinian technique, 335, 346
kleptomania, 298
Kohon, G., *The Dead Mother: The Work of André Green*, 312
Kohut, H., 185, 211, 232–233, 315, 323, 350, 359
Kris, E., 211
Kristeva, J., 15, 154

Lacan, J., 15, 16, 26, 180, 205, 232, 269, 273, 312, 317–318
Lacanian theory, 275, 293, 317–319, 350
lack, concept of, in, 318
Laforgue, R., 155
Lamarckian fallacy, 398
Laplanche, J., 6, 300
Laub, D., 19
Law of the Father, 293
Lear, J., 210
Leonardo da Vinci, 20, 29, 65
liberty, positive and negative forms of, 254
libidinal liberation, 269, 275
libidinal phase, oral or cannibalistic, 43
libidinal wishes/drives and self-preservative needs, distinction between, 7, 91
libido, quantities of, 35
life instinct, 60
and death instinct, fusion of, 335
Likierman, M., 154
literature, horror, and dynamics of melancholia, 52
Loewald, H. (*passim*):
ghosts:
of patient's unconscious, 103
turning of, into ancestors, 209–257
"On Internalization", 24, 238–257
internalization and emancipation, 209–257
"Internalization, Separation, Mourning, and the Superego", 24, 213–220, 226–237, 250

Psychoanalysis and the History of the Individual, 212
"On the Therapeutic Action of Psycho-Analysis", 209
transference, workings of, 209–211
Loewenstein, R., 211, 241
loss:
immutability or permanence of, 16
manic-melancholic way of dealing with, 56
mourning of, versus depression, 7
necessity and relentlessness of, 16
lost object, pining for, 183
love, frozen by decathexis, 335–343
love-object, incorporation of, concept of, 260
Luther, M., 385

Maeder, A., 108, 113
Mahler, M., 360
Malcolm, J., 279
mania (*passim*):
and depression, relation and contrast between, 46
gobbling, 143, 172
machinations of, 45–50
normal, 275
triumphant nature of, 47
manic defence(s), 134, 172, 183
manic-depressive circularity, 48
manic-depressive dynamic, 45
manic-depressive illness, 44, 46, 55, 114, 117, 120, 143, 197–198
manic-depressive psychosis, 304
manic-depressive states, 47, 71, 152, 154, 156, 179, 183, 190, 200–203, 284
and mourning, distinction between, 200
manic omnipotence, 184, 186
manic reparation, 303
manic triumph, 140, 173, 184, 190
Marvell, A., 257
"The Garden", 256
Marvin, L., *I Was Born Under a Wandrin' Star*, 216
material truth vs historical truth, 321
maternal decathexis, 362
maternal depression, 324
maternal effacement, 356
maternal imago, 325, 338
primitive, 349
maternal object, decathexis of, 327

maternal preoccupation, primary, 325
  concept of, 251
maternal primary object, decathexis
  of, 320
maternal reverie, 207
meaning, loss of, 326, 329
megalomania, negative, 329
melancholia (*passim*):
  ambivalence in, 48
  and anorexia, connection between,
    44, 53
  dynamics of, 40, 44–45, 52, 146
  Freud's study of, 36–45
  and mourning:
    distinction between, 38, 69, 133,
      186, 383
    as ways of dealing with loss, 38
  mysteries of, 36–45
  and obsessional states, object-
    relational differences between,
    119–120
  oral and anal dimensions of, 301
  and paranoia, genetic connection
    between, 161
  preconditions of, 50
  regression in, 122
  and transference neuroses, distinctions
    between, 44
  work of, 48–49
melancholic depression, 135–136
melancholic ego, ambivalence of, 48
melancholic identification, 129
melancholic narcissism, 126
mental functioning, conscious and
  unconscious aspects of, Freud's
  ideas about, 72
metabolic internalization, 235, 400
metabolization:
  and digestion, analogy with
    mourning, 5, 20, 145, 186, 201,
    253, 259, 391
  psychic, 186, 213, 311
metaphor(s) (*passim*):
  body-based, 6
  capacity for, loss of, 301
  and identification, connection
    between, 17
  as privileged domain in language of
    psychoanalysis, 6
  use of, 141
metaphora, 17

mind:
  agencies of:
    construction of, 72–84
    id, ego, superego, 3, 72, 81, 212, 233,
      238, 243
  structural model of, 3, 21, 72–73, 79,
    87, 212, 237, 243, 399
mirroring, compensatory, 232
mirror stage, 232
Mitchell, S. A., 210
Mitford, N., *Love in a Cold Climate*, 336
mixed metaphor system, psychoanalysis
  as, 17
monotheistic faiths versus pagan beliefs, 32
mother:
  dead: *see* dead mother
  loss of, 86, 91
  negative hallucination of, 351
  oral merger with, 337
  phallic, 337
mother-as-vampire, 348
mother–infant relationship, 350
  break in continuity of, 362
mourning:
  blank, 320, 334, 341–342, 345, 347, 353,
    355, 361
  centrality of, in psychoanalysis, 1
  versus depression, 7
  and digestion and metabolization,
    analogy between, 5, 20, 145, 186,
    201, 253, 259, 391
  illness of, 115, 260, 262, 275–278,
    286–288
  internal dynamics of, 234
  loss versus depression, 7
  and manic-depressive states,
    distinction between, 200
  and melancholia:
    differences between, 38, 69, 133,
      186, 383
    as ways of dealing with loss, 38
  metabolic theory of, 59
  normal, 47, 55, 118, 124, 126, 179, 186,
    190–196, 260
  primary, 78, 213–214
  reluctant, 296
  in *Totem and Taboo*, 31–33
  work of, 23, 40, 49, 53, 55, 125, 145,
    188, 191, 197–198, 237, 246, 253,
    267, 284, 298, 311
Mrs A, Klein's patient, 188, 191–193

Nachträglichkeit/deferred action/*après coup*, 321, 338, 374
  concept of, 366
narcissism (*passim*):
  concept of, psychoanalytic, 30, 34
  libidinal and destructive, 360
  melancholic, 126
  metapsychological position on, 359
  negative, 138
  positive, 138
  primary: *see* primary narcissism
  secondary, 360
  theory of, Freud's, 43, 379
narcissistic cathexis, 214
narcissistic neurosis, 304
  and obsessional neurosis, distinction between, 122
narcissistic omnipotence, 340
narcissistic patients, 34
narcissistic psychoneuroses, 84, 115
narcissistic structure and functioning, Freud's explorations of, 33–36
narcissistic union, primary, 228
Nazi *Anschluss*, 369
Nazism, 17, 97, 211, 280–281, 369–370, 388
necrophagia, 135, 297
negative, work of, 26, 320
negative hallucination, 320, 351
negative identification, 334
negative megalomania, 329
negative narcissism, 138
negative therapeutic reaction, 80, 116
neurosis:
  infantile, 182, 186
  narcissistic, 122, 304
  and paranoia, distinction between, 105, 111
neurotic functioning and psychotic functioning, distinction between, 104, 111
neutralization, 248
Newbigin, J., 341
Nietzsche, F., 181, 241, 371
Nirvana principle, constancy of, 243
nocturnal terrors, 327
non-objective art, 292
Northern Lights/aurora borealis, 223

object:
  loss of, 43, 47–48, 50, 55, 89, 120, 268, 300, 342
  shadow of, falling upon ego, 20, 42, 44, 53, 66, 143, 229
objectalization, 302
object choice, "anaclitic" or narcissistic, 35
objectification, 302
objectivation, 291
object libido, 34
object love, 18, 35, 64, 108–111, 121–122, 147–149, 178
  primary, 359
object-relational school, 119, 122, 142, 148, 151, 169, 206–207, 212, 235, 250, 293, 313
object relations:
  external, and structure of self, intra-subjective change in, 212
  internalization of, 253
  role of, 250
object-relations theories, 123
objects, discrete, versus ambient environments, 7
object-seeking, versus drive-discharging, 7
obsessional neurosis, 28, 81–82, 104, 116, 121, 172
  and narcissistic neurosis, distinction between, 122
obsessional states, and melancholic states, object-relational differences between, 119–120
oceanic feeling, concept of, 136
ocnophils versus philobats, 106
oedipal identifications, 229
oedipal phase, 214–215
oedipal "third", 339
Oedipus, as mythical prototype of patient, 314
Oedipus complex, 21, 63, 67, 73, 79, 81, 138–139, 165, 220, 233, 245–246, 253, 255, 268, 304, 317, 321, 337–342, 345, 363–364, 371
  axiomatic triangulation of, 320
  destruction of, 244
  dissolution of, 231, 248
    or repression of, 244
  fantasy of, isomorphic, 339
  libidinal-aggressive object cathexes of, 246
  precocious, 329

and primal scene and dead mother, relationship between, 363
resolution of, 139, 231, 253
superego as heir of, 233
triangularity of, 321
Oedipus myth, Sphinx in, 340
Oedipus situation, 180, 188, 250, 338
triangular character of, 77
Ogden, T., 4, 14, 37, 40, 56–57, 189
Conversations at the Frontier of Dreaming, 14
Creative Readings, 4
omnipotence, narcissistic, 340
oppressor, concupiscence of, 390
oral-alimentary behaviours, Ferenczi on, 102
oral cannibalistic phase, 342
oral identification, 342
primitive, 54
oral phase, 43–44, 62, 74, 76, 136
cannibalistic, 53, 137

pagan beliefs versus monotheistic faiths, 32
Paint Your Wagon, 216
paranoia:
and melancholia, genetic connection between, 161
and neurosis, distinction between, 105, 111
paranoid persecutory anxiety, 188
paranoid position, primary, 182
paranoid projection, 113
paranoid-schizoid, 23, 85, 106, 152, 157, 174, 176, 191–192, 198, 201, 230, 395
paranoid-schizoid functioning and depressive functioning, distinctions between, 106, 127
paranoid-schizoid position and depressive position, spiralling alternations between, 230
paranoid-schizoid states of mind, 25
parathymia, primal, 142
parental figures, identification with, 21
parricide, 33, 363
Parsons, M., 4
patient D, Klein's patient, 197–198
patient's unconscious, ghosts of, Loewald on, 103
persecutory anxiety, 202

phallic mother, 337
phallic phase, 171
phantasy, 22, 34, 101, 135, 158, 160–162, 172, 174, 176, 187, 192, 196, 289, 400
concept of, Kleinian, 289
unconscious, 101, 246
philobats versus ocnophils, 106
Plath, S., 14, 279, 280–283, 353–358, 365
"Daddy", 279–283, 354
"Morning Song", 353–358, 365
pleasure-ego, 85
pleasure principle, 51, 216, 249, 271
pleasure-unpleasure principle, 249
Poe, E. A., 278, 288
"Ulalume", 277
positive identification, 334
positive narcissism, 138
potential meaning, 366
potential space, 366
premature disillusionment, 326
primal father, 31–32, 147
primal parathymia, 142
primal scene, 29, 335, 338–342, 345
arch-fantasy of, 290
de-libidinization of, 340
exclusion from, 340
fantasy, 339, 341, 365
fantasy of, 321, 338–339
and Oedipus complex and dead mother, relation between, 363
primary aggression, 229, 329
primary anxieties, 152
primary ego autonomy, concept of, 250
primary introjection, 187
primary love, 292, 394
Balint's theories on, 106
primary love relation, mother–infant, 394
primary maternal preoccupation, 325
concept of, 251
primary mourning, 78, 213–214
primary narcissism, 35, 136, 229, 232, 252
later, 359
positive and negative forms of, 360
primary narcissistic union, 228
primary object:
effacement of, 349–353
maternal, decathexis of, 320
primary object-love, 359
primary paranoid position, 182

primary repression, 320, 335, 353
primitive maternal imago, 349
primordial breast, 338
primordial envy, 33
projection, 6, 23, 68, 73, 85, 104–106,
    111–113, 155, 158, 162, 196, 205,
    226, 232, 339, 389
  defensive use of, 350
  and introjection, differences
      between, 112
  mechanism of, 42, 104, 153
  paranoid, 113
  term and concept of, Freud's use of, 112
projective identification, 112–113,
    201–206
  concept of, 68, 112, 206
  term, difficulties with, 112
projective mechanisms, 54
Proust, M., 16
psychic emancipation, 254, 275
psychic inner world, workings of, and
    analogy of digestion, 6
psychic metabolization, 186, 213, 311
psychic reality, 160–161, 171, 181, 185,
    302, 316
  denial of, 155
  negation of, 337
psychic relativity, Loewald's theory of, 242
psychic structure, point of view of, 240
psychoanalysis, maternal dimension of, 317
psychoanalytic containment, Bion's
    concept of, 103
psychoanalytic psychology, richness and
    imprecision of, 240
psychoneuroses, 29
  narcissistic, 84, 115
psychosexual metabolism, 144
psychosexual phase, 161
psychosis(es), 28, 84, 337
  blank, 320
  blankness of, 34
  depressive, 116
  hallucinatory wish-fulfilment, 38–39
  manic-depressive, 304
psychotic anxiety(ies):
  early, 190
  infantile, 155
psychotic functioning, 33, 201
  and neurotic functioning, distinction
      between, 111

psychotic mechanisms, and neurotic
    mechanisms, distinction
    between, 104
Putin, V., 68

Ramazani, J., *Poetry of Mourning*, 14–15
Rand, N., 258–259, 289
Rank, O., 89, 97
  The Trauma of Birth, 86
Rapaport, D. A., 241
Rat Man [Freud's case], 28
reality-ego, 85
reality testing, 20, 38, 44, 85, 156, 179, 181,
    188, 192, 283
recapitulation theory, 398
regression, in melancholia, 122
relational analysis, 227
reluctant mourning, 296
reorganization, process of, 291
representational world, self- and other-
    representations within, 3
repressed, return of, 243
repression, primary, 320, 335, 353
reverie, 207
Rilke, R. M., 371–372, 375
Riviere, J., 116
Róheim, G., 135, 145
Roiphe, K., *The Violet Hour*, 393
Rolland, R., 251
  oceanic feeling, concept of, 136
Rolling Stones, *You Can't Always Get
    What You Want*, 95
Rosenblatt, B., 3
Rosenfeld, H., 360
Rosolato, G., 315
rule of silence, analytic, 334
Russian Revolution, 61

Sachs, H., 97
Sacks, P. M., *The English Elegy*, 14–15
sadism, depressive, 45
sadistic anal phase, 137
sadomasochism, 46
  internal, 66
Sandler, A.-M., 322
Sandler, J., 3, 241, 322
Saturnalia, Roman, 71
Schafer, R., 241
schizo-paranoid phase, 350
schizophrenia, 28, 306

Schmideberg, M., 178, 203
Schreber, D., psychosis or schizophrenia [Freud's case], 28, 327
Schur, M., 241, 384
scotomization, 155
Searles, H., 4
secondary narcissism, 360
Second World War, 27, 258, 380–381, 384, 387
seduction, arch-fantasy of, 290
Segal, H., 294
  symbolic equation, 25
self-other relations, Freud's concept of, 17
self-preservation, instinct of, 34
self-preservative needs/instincts and libidinal desires, distinction between, 7, 91
self-protection, need for, 58–60
self-psychology, 185, 211, 227
Sendak, M., 396
  In the Night Kitchen, 393–394
  Outside Over There, 393
  Where the Wild Things Are, 146–147, 210, 393
separation, significance of, 226
setting, as transitional space, 346
shadow of object falling upon ego, 20, 42, 44, 53, 66, 143, 229
Shakespeare, W.:
  Hamlet, 40–41
  Macbeth, 326
  Richard III, 116
  The Tempest, 257
  The Winter's Tale, 357
Shelley, P. B., 14
  A Defence of Poetry, 377
  "Ozymandias", 325, 376–377
Shengold, L., *Soul Murder: The Effects of Childhood Abuse and Neglect*, 327
signal anxiety, 90, 94
silence, analytic rule of, 334
Simon, P., *Slip Slidin' Away*, 123
Sodré, I., 205
Sophocles, *Oedipus Rex*, 371
sphincter control, 234
sphincter morality, 234
splitting, 23, 85, 158, 166, 183, 202, 203
  of ego, 299, 305
Stamelman, R., *Lost Beyond Telling*, 15–16
St. Augustine, 390

Steiner, J., 164
Stekel, W., 96–97
Stern, D., and Green, A., and infant observation, public debate and confrontation over, 322
Stern, J., 144–145, 322
Stevens, W., 13–14, 220–257, 358, 365, 367
  "The Auroras of Autumn", 223–226, 358, 365
  "Sunday Morning", 220–223, 225, 373
  "Waving Adieu, Adieu, Adieu", 225
  "The Woman That Had More Babies Than That", 256
Strachey, J., 3, 28, 30, 31, 36, 51, 61, 65, 76, 86, 369
structuralist psychoanalysis, 351
structural model of mind, 269
sublimation, 77, 204, 219, 224, 248, 317
  and idealization, distinction between, 36
suicide, 40, 44–45, 154, 170, 282–283, 306, 309–313, 370
superego (*passim*):
  as bullying, moralistic conscience, 53
  conscience, voice of, as mouthpiece of, 237
  and ego and id, dynamic mental intercourse among, 212
  Freud's creation of, 77
  genesis of, 53, 72, 108, 317
  as heir of Oedipus complex, 233
  and id and ego, 72–84
  introduction of, 73, 213
symbolic equation, 25, 294
symbolic order, 293
symbolization, theory of, 294

teeth, 286–287
  preoccupation with, 135
Thanatos, 249
think, compulsion to, 330
Thoreau, H. D., 232
Thucydides, 385
Toller, E., 370, 385
Tolstoy, L., *Anna Karenina*, 325
topographical model, 269, 304
Torok, M. (*passim*):
  exquisite corpse, fantasy of, 260
  "The Illness of Mourning and the Fantasy of the Exquisite Corpse", 25, 260
  introjection vs incorporation, 288–311

on mourning, illness of, 260–288
"Mourning or Melancholia: Introjection versus Incorporation", 25, 260, 288–311
The Shell and the Kernel, 258–259, 288–289
The Wolf Man's Magic Word, 258, 279
totem meals, 31, 76
transference(s):
  characteristics of, 343–349
  concept of, 99–100
  dead mother, 344
  erotic, 100
  Freud's concept of, 100
  neurotic passion for, 104
  repetition in, 7
  twinship, 232
transference depression, 324
transference neurosis(es), 28, 95, 98, 100, 209, 220, 324
  analytic, 219
  and melancholia, distinctions between, 44
  resolution of, 219
transition, neurosis of, 263
transitional object(s), concept of, Winnicottian, 330
transitional space(s), 164, 251, 395
  setting as, 346
traumatic anxiety, 88, 90
  and signal anxiety, distinction between, 94
triangular situation, early, 329
triumph, manic, 140, 173, 184, 190
triumphalism, 54, 190
Trump, D., 68
twinship transferences, 232

unconscious, ghosts of, 210, 218, 298
ur-myths, anthropological, 31

Viennese Psychoanalytic Society, 97
von Unwerth, M., *Freud's Requiem*, 371–372

war, poetry and psychoanalysis as responses to, 397
Wednesday Psychological Society, 96
Welles, O., *Citizen Kane*, 395
Whitman, W., "Song of Myself", 144
Winnicott, D. W. (*passim*):
  baby, no such thing as, 251
  ego, ruthlessness of, 159
  influence of, on Green, 315
  libidinal desires and self-preservative needs, distinction between, 91
  Playing and Reality, 289
  potential space, 366
  primary maternal preoccupation, 251, 325
  transitional object(s), 330
  transitional space(s), 164, 251, 346, 395
Wolf Man [Freud's case], 29, 87, 302–303, 339, 364, 374
word- and thing-representations, 3
Wordsworth, C., 264–266
Wordsworth, W., 14, 137
  "Surprised by Joy", 263–265, 277
Wright, N., *Mrs Klein*, 199

Yeats, W. B., 14, 370, 376, 385, 387, 391–392
  "Adam's Curse", 375
  "The Folly of Being Comforted", 374
Yom Kippur, 384

zombies, 25, 52, 175